MW01138407

THE GRACE OF OUR LORD JESUS CHRIST BE WITH YOU ALL AMEN
IN THE BEGINNING GOD CREATED THE HEAVEN AND THE EARTH
777

First Edition, 2022 (Revised)

Word counts verified with *King James Pure Bible Search* software (KJPBS).
purebiblesearch.com

Companion search files (.kjs) for KJPBS can be downloaded at:
sealedbytheking.com

Word Counts:

KJB = King James Bible, Cambridge Text
KJB1611 = 1611 King James Bible, Original Text
NKJV = New King James Version, © 1982. by Thomas Nelson
ESV = English Standard Version, © 2016. by Crossway Bibles
NASB1971 = New American Standard Bible, © 1971. by The Lockman Foundation
NASB2020 = New American Standard Bible, © 2020. by The Lockman Foundation
NIV = New International Version, © 2011. by Biblica, Inc

All scripture is quoted from the Authorized King James Bible (KJB) unless otherwise stated.

SEALED BY THE KING

Intricate Patterns and Details Pointing to God's Inspiration over the 1611 Holy Bible in English

BRANDON PETERSON

Acknowledgments

Laura Peterson
My other half. My wife and best friend. Thank you for your wisdom, opinions, and never-ending support. Thank you for loving me always.

Mom & Dad
The parental squadron. Thank you for always praying for me. For loving me unconditionally. Thank you for fixing the book formatting.

Leo Tavares
The man whose research in Hebrew / Greek Bible numerics inspired me to seek these wondrous things from the law of the Lord. Thank you for your great diligence and exaltation of the Lord Jesus Christ.

Donna W.
The mad scientist who invented King James Pure Bible Search. Thank you for all the countless hours you have poured into KJPBS, and for all the advanced technological support & resources that you have gifted me over the past year. You are truly a blessing to the church in these last hours.

Kevin M., Lowin D., Jason P., Joshua H., Randall H.
Fellowlabourers in Bible numeric studies. Thank you for all your encouragement. Several notes detailed in this book are direct results of studying your own notes and discoveries. To Christ be the glory!

Christopher Yetzer
A man filled with knowledge on the history of Bible printing and translation. Thank you for all your assistance with Appendix 1- researching when these miracles first appeared (approximately) in the King James Bible.

Mark Henderson
A meek and lowly spirit whose heart is ever toward the Lord. Thank you for proofreading, editing, and contributing toward the miracles detailed in these notes.

Matt Barylski
A brother of sincerity and truth, with sharpness of mind and purity of heart. Thank you for the long hours and late nights that you dedicated to this book, editing with much wisdom and deep thought that greatly improved the overall body of work. May the Father bless you and your family for all that you have done for the praise and glory of our Lord Jesus Christ.

...he that holdeth the seven stars in his right hand, who walketh in the midst of the seven golden candlesticks;

Revelation 2:1

...the first and the last, which was dead, and is alive;

Revelation 2:8

...he which hath the sharp sword with two edges;

Revelation 2:12

...the Son of God, who hath his eyes like unto a flame of fire, and his feet are like fine brass;

Revelation 2:18

...he that hath the seven Spirits of God, and the seven stars;

Revelation 3:1

...he that is holy, he that is true, he that hath the key of David, he that openeth, and no man shutteth; and shutteth, and no man openeth;

Revelation 3:7

...the Amen, the faithful and true witness, the beginning of the creation of God;

Revelation 3:14

Dedicated to

The Lord Jesus Christ

Foreword

The wonder of wonders.
The monarch of all books.
The King James Holy Bible.

God is infinite. He never changes, He is constant.

No matter how far you run, you can never run out of God.

Numbers are a TYPE of God.
Numbers never change.
Numbers are constant.
Numbers are infinite.
You can never run out of numbers;
so numbers are a type of God.

So God has used numbers to seal and authenticate his one true word of God: the KJB.

There are too many "coincidences" in the chapter and verse numbering system to doubt that God Himself is its Author.

There are too many "coincidences" in the placement of words and phrases, and the numbers/counts associated with them, to not take a very serious look at how God put this book together and handed it to us with bloody hands, through prison bars.

The King James Holy Bible is supernatural. It is inerrant. It is God's perfect revelation to mankind in the last universal language prior to the second advent of the Lord Jesus Christ, the **KING OF KINGS AND LORD OF LORDS**.

Study it. Love it. Press the boundaries and behold its numerical magnificence. And always remember that God has placed his word above all His name. (Psalm 138:2)

In this marvelous revelation of God given to men, we have a first-class miracle open before our faces.

I say, *Bless His holy name.*

Bro. Kevin Mann
Preacher, Teacher, Reacher

Preface

Five years ago, I did not own a single copy of the King James Bible.

I was saved in May of 2014 without any doubt in my mind. I will never forget that moment. But I didn't have any serious hunger to read the Bible thereafter. I would cling to the words of pastors and teachers, who didn't emphasize Bible reading very much themselves. If I did read, it was usually the NIV, NASB or ESV on my phone. I owned a physical copy of the NIV, but I didn't open it very much. That went on for 5 years. And in that time, I had no idea there were any big differences between Bible versions.

I was like most Laodicean Christians: Biblically illiterate. Reading the Bible felt like a chore to me, and I didn't really understand how important the Bible is. I looked to pastors for truth, instead of the source in which those pastors based all of their teachings. The last thing on my mind was the King James Bible. This book did not exist in my mind or in my world.

But now, my bookshelves are overflowing with them…

Big ones. Small ones. Old ones. New ones.
Red ones. Blue ones. Never-used ones.

When I first got ahold of a King James Bible, everything in my walk with Christ changed. The battle of flesh vs the Spirit (Galatians 5:17) took a complete 180° turn in my life as the Holy Ghost changed me from the inside out. My perpetual backsliding turned to diligence in seeking the Lord- day and night- with joy and delight in my soul. As I read more and more each day, I drew closer and closer to the Lord. And He drew closer and closer to me. Things of the world were no longer appealing. My soul was being fed with something so much greater. Something I've never had before. The words of eternal life (John 6:68). And all I could do was read and marvel over this Book that seemed to know every thought in my head before I opened it.

I want everyone to know that I did not start off looking for concealed numeric patterns in the KJB for any esoteric or weird new age reasons. I started off with a Bible that forever changed my life. And after I was reading the KJB, I started to believe all of the words within were purposely placed by God. Meanwhile, I learned about patterns that existed in Hebrew and Greek- specifically Genesis 1:1 and John 1:1, as detailed in Leo Tavares' website *Mathematical Monotheism*. Sometime after I learned of his discoveries, I began to wonder about the KJB. The thoughts started falling into place: *If there are numeric patterns that verify God's inspiration of the original tongues, what if there are patterns in this Bible that is speaking to me and sanctifying me.*

If true, how marvellous would that be? Proof that God not only inspired the original writings, but preserved them all the way through history into one complete book that is available to us today.

So I asked. I seeked. I knocked. (Matthew 7:7). And I diligently sought after the Lord with faith (Hebrews 11:6), praying for wisdom from God (James 1:5-6) to see whether these things are so (Acts 17:11).

And it wasn't long until an unimaginable treasure was found. Glorious pearls, of perfection, and without price.

This great treasure is what you'll find in the notes of this book. And whether you choose to take hold of it, or trample it under foot, I pray you seek God over it- first and foremost. Ask Him with a humble heart, *Did You do this?*

Nothing in the world is comparable to the Bible. If you haven't read it, you're not just missing out on the most important thing in life, you're missing out on life itself.

If you're looking for answers to any of life's questions, whether it's *"What happens after I die?"* Or *"Why are there 7 days in a week?,"* the Bible has the answers.

The year of our calendar is not based on an arbitrary date in antiquity. It is counting forward from a particular Person who lived on this earth 2000 years ago. A Man who changed history forever. That Man's story is found in the Bible.

When you see automobiles racing down the freeway, you are looking at something that was prophesied over 2,600 years ago.

> **...the chariots shall be with flaming torches in the day of his preparation... The chariots shall rage in the streets, they shall justle one against another in the broad ways: they shall seem like torches, they shall run like the lightnings.**
>
> Nahum 2:3-4 KJB

When you see Jerusalem and Israel in the news, you are witnessing something unheard of amongst any other tribe or nation. A place that didn't belong to the Hebrew people for the great majority of the last 2,000 years. A place God promised to one day restore.

> **Hear the word of the LORD, O ye nations, and declare it in the isles afar off, and say, He that scattered Israel will gather him, and keep him, as a shepherd doth his flock.**
>
> Jeremiah 31:10 KJB

And now they are gathered back together in their land, so that together they will see the Son of man returning in the clouds, just as the Bible declares.

> **Behold, he cometh with clouds; and every eye shall see him, and they also which pierced him: and all kindreds of the earth shall wail because of him. Even so, Amen.**
>
> Revelation 1:7 KJB

This is what sets the Bible apart from any other book.

It's not just a collection of ancient writings. It's the living word of God.

The most High God <u>who knows and declares the end from the beginning.</u> (Isaiah 46:10)

I've put together this book of notes in hopes to demonstrate just how true that statement is. I am grateful that God has blessed me in so many different ways to be able to study His word in great detail.

Everything in this book is factual and research-oriented, and I've spent many countless hours putting it all together. But it doesn't require a technical mind or a special intellect to understand the things within.

I highly recommend you read the Introductory chapters. The second introductory chapter is more-so for those who are already familiarized with the KJB-only vs Originals-only debate. But the first and last introductory chapters (Introduction & Laying the Foundation) make some important notes to bear in mind for the rest of the book.

After the introductory chapters, you'll find the meat and potatoes. The numeric notes are divided into two parts.

Part I includes the great majority of content and is all about the miracles / patterns marked by God's perfect number: 7.

The rest of the notes in Part II are more "miscellaneous"–but by no means less interesting. It is here where you will find notes on the 153 fishes, the number of the beast (666), and others.

The beauty of it all is that you can fact check anything you see. Although you can use any Bible Software, I recommend King James Pure Bible Search for various reasons that are explained further in the last introductory chapter; *Laying the Foundation*. It's free, easy to learn, and, by far, the most reliable.

You can also download the entire collection of (.kjs) Pure Bible Search "search files" for free from sealedbytheking.com. These files will let you quickly load any of the searches presented in the notes of this book. They are especially convenient when you can't quite figure out how to get the same results as the counts shown.

And finally, after the notes, the Appendices at the end provide great amounts of detail and insight. I poured just as much time into them as the notes themselves. Appendix 1 involved a lot of laborious research- where I searched through antique King James Bibles in pursuit of knowing when these miracles first appeared in the text *(No, they were not all present in 1611- nor 1769!)*.

Appendices 4, 5 and 6 are useful resources for examining some of the corruptions in modern Bibles.

If you have any thoughts or questions about any of the things in this book, I would love to hear from you. My email is peterson6x@gmail.com.

If you are not saved, I pray this book will clear any doubts that hinder you from trusting Jesus Christ. Take the time to read through the gospel of John and the book of Romans. Reach out to me with any questions you have. There is nothing worse for a man than to unexpectedly die in his sins without his name written in heaven. (See John 8:28, Romans 3:23, Luke 10:20, Revelation 20:15). If you want to be saved and have your name written in the Lamb's book of life, see page 578.

If you are saved, I pray this book will strengthen your faith in the Lord, and bring you to a greater realization of how infinite and perfect His mind truly is. I pray it will lead you to deeper Bible study and time with the

Lord. I have personally found a much more profound understanding of God's word when I stopped questioning the authenticity of the words and started believing every word as it stands.

Thank you for taking the time to read this book, and may God alone receive the glory.

Thine, O LORD, is the greatness, and the power, and the glory, and the victory, and the majesty: for all that is in the heaven and in the earth is thine; thine is the kingdom, O LORD, and thou art exalted as head above all.

Both riches and honour come of thee, and thou reignest over all; and in thine hand is power and might; and in thine hand it is to make great, and to give strength unto all.

Now therefore, our God, we thank thee, and praise thy glorious name.

1 Chronicles 29:11-13

Amen

Table of Contents

Part II

All scripture quotations and word counts unless otherwise noted:
KJB = King James Bible, Concord Cambridge Text

According to direct correspondence with Cambridge University, the Concord edition is their standard "base" text. Not to be confused with the "Standard Text Edition" (a.k.a Emerald) which can be easily detected by its lowercase "spirit of God" in Genesis 1:2. The Emerald edition is based on an old hot metal image (printed like a facsimile) inherited from the King's Printer, Eyre and Spottiswoode, when it was acquired by Cambridge, and thus, cannot be aligned with Cambridge's style.

Recommended Bible software:
King James Pure Bible Search
purebiblesearch.com

Other versions, used to compare word counts:
NKJV = New King James Version, © 1982. by Thomas Nelson
ESV = English Standard Version, © 2016. by Crossway Bibles
NASB1971 = New American Standard Bible, © 1971. by The Lockman Foundation
NASB2020 = New American Standard Bible, © 2020. by The Lockman Foundation
NIV = New International Version, © 2011. by Biblica, Inc

Disclaimer:
Word counts for modern versions are not easy to get. I did my best with the resources at my disposal. Some counts may be slightly off, and I estimate 90-95% accuracy for modern versions (meaning the word counts should be correct about 9 out of 10 times). Results for the KJB should have 100% accuracy. If you have questions about any of the word counts, please email the author at peterson6x@gmail.com.

UPDATES

This revised edition of *SEALED BY THE KING* includes the following updates:

- New details added throughout
- Note replaced on p. 62 with a more significant and relevant one.
- Removal of notes on John the Baptist (Counts for John the Baptist were recounted by both Kevin Mann & the author and found to be incorrect on pp. 208-209 of the FIRST EDITION) The true count is **92x** for all mentions of **John** when referring to John the Baptist, **37x** for all mentions of **John** the Apostle, **3x** for all mentions of **John** Mark, and **1x** for the unknown **John** in Acts 4:6.
- New note added (to replace John the Baptist notes) on pp. 209-210
- Corrections to spelling, grammar, etc
- Other small tweaks that do not affect anything of importance

I have shewed thee new things from
this time, even hidden things, and thou
didst not know them. They are created
now, and not from the beginning; even
before the day when thou heardest
them not; lest thou shouldest say,
Behold, I knew them.

Isaiah 48:6-7

Introduction

The most important thing that could enter the door of your mind is the gospel of Jesus Christ. If you do not know Him, I pray that through this book, God opens your eyes and reveals in your heart the glorious light and truth of our Saviour. His gospel can be found in 1 Corinthians 15:1-4.

He is the **I AM**. His word is **faithful and true**. And I pray you receive the fear and wisdom you need to believe on the literal death, burial, and resurrection of Jesus Christ, and to fall down before Him in repentance, receiving new life and forgiveness of sins by His grace.

Do you know He who bought you with the blood of God? Do you know the Prince of life who is seated on the right hand of the Father, holding the keys of hell and of death? Does He know you? Nothing else matters.

> **That if thou shalt confess with thy mouth the Lord Jesus, and shalt believe in thine heart that God hath raised him from the dead, thou shalt be saved.**
>
> Romans 10:9 KJB

If you're not sure if you're saved, hide Romans 10:9 in your heart as you journey through the things in this book. Jesus said He is the only way to the Father. Never forget that He gave his life willingly in your place, so that all of your sins would enter His perfect, sinless body, nailed to that cross at Calvary. All of life's hardest questions are answered at the cross, the empty tomb, and the throne of God.

So what is the point of this book if nothing else matters?

That's quite simple:

> **But the word of the Lord endureth for ever. And this is the word which by the gospel is preached unto you.**
>
> 1 Peter 1:25 KJB

The gospel is preached unto you by the word of God.

The Bible is the foundation of the gospel.

Without the word of God, there would be no testimony to share, no sermon to preach, no books to write, no hymns to sing, no name to pray in, and worst of all: no knowledge of the gospel by which we are saved. Everything in the Christian faith depends solely on the Bible.

If the testimony of the Bible is false, then Christianity is a vain religion, and we can turn our attention elsewhere.

But if the Bible is truly the word of God, then everything in our bones should tremble at the knowledge it contains. Heaven is real. Hell is real. You were made in the image of Jehovah, in a universe that was made by Him and for Him. His angels of light, and Satan with his angels of rebellion, exist in a world that is directly connected to our own.

This book of notes will show you that not only is the Bible a trustworthy historical document once inspired in the ancient past, the Bible has been supernaturally guided and preserved over time by God himself.

You will see for yourself that we do not hold a mere translation of God's once-inspired words. We hold in our hands the absolute supreme truth revealed to all mankind by our omnipotent Creator exactly as he intended to reveal it. Every word of it. Yea, every jot and tittle.

When we read the Bible, specifically the King James Bible in the English language, we are not interacting with something that is earthly and perishable. We are interacting with something from above: the most powerful thing on this earth, the source of all life and material in existence, the true and living word of God.

> **Being born again, not of corruptible seed, but of incorruptible, by the word of God, which liveth and abideth for ever.**
>
> 1 Peter 1:23 KJB

So how exactly could somebody go about proving the King James Bible, or any Bible for that matter, is truly God's infallible word from heaven?

Good question.

Let me start by answering that question with a similar question: *How would you prove that Jesus Christ is sinless?*

Short answer: You can't.

You would have to know every thought of his heart at every moment of his life along with every deed that he has ever done. Besides those, you would have to know the true intent behind each thought and deed. Was it out of love for God and His neighbor? Or was it out of selfish ambition? Furthermore, you would have to know every single commandment given by God, and every correct nuanced interpretation of every word of every sentence of every commandment. Then you would have to filter all of his thoughts, deeds and heart-intentions through the filter of God's perfect law… circumstance by circumstance.

Even if you had the heavenly record of every detail of the life and mind of Jesus Christ, could you imagine such a task? In the wise words of Jethro, "**this thing is too heavy for thee…**"

To perfectly judge perfection, we ourselves would need to be omniscient (knowing all things) in order to understand *what perfection is.*

We would have to be God. However; if we have even the slightest amount of sanity, we can determine that we are not God.

Our mind is not his mind. His ways are higher than our ways, and his thoughts are higher than our thoughts. No man on this earth can perfectly judge perfection. Quite the contrary is true: He who is perfect in heaven, knowing all things past, present and future, can perfectly judge and determine that which is perfect.

> **The Pharisees therefore said unto him, Thou bearest record of thyself; thy record is not true.**
> **Jesus answered and said unto them, Though I bear record of myself, yet my record is true: for I know whence I came, and whither I go; but ye cannot tell whence I come, and whither I go.**
> John 8:13-14 KJB

The same pattern of thought can be applied to the Bible.

How can we know the Bible is perfect? How can we prove it has no errors and reads exactly how God intended it to read?

Short answer: *We cannot!*

In order to have a 100% perfect Bible translated from different languages, we would need to know, first of all, if God even desired for a perfect Bible to be produced in that language. If we knew with 100% certainty that this was in his sovereign will, then we would need the wisdom to know which manuscripts are flawed and not to be used as well as which ones to keep, and which readings within those accurate manuscripts are truly inspired, since nearly all of them have slight variations in their readings. There are no original manuscripts available that can be compared to, so everything must be extracted from what's available.

Once we (somehow) know all of the faithful and true readings from those manuscripts, we must deal with "word-for-word" vs "thought-for-thought" translations and the idioms that cannot be gracefully carried from one language into another. This in itself is almost universally regarded as an impossible task. Thus we hear it said, "*The original meaning is lost in translation…*"

So let's face reality.

In order to perfectly translate a non-translatable idiom, and translate every word and thought exactly as God wills–from the correct words that God originally inspired, the Holy Ghost would need to directly intervene throughout the entire process. There is no other way of getting around it. If a translation is perfect by God's standard, then His own hand would have needed to guide the minds of the translators and editors to make perfect every word of the Bible.

The task of perfectly producing an infallible Bible is impossible… unless God is directing it.

And even if he did orchestrate it, how could we judge it to be perfect or imperfect, as if our minds are equal to God's?

> **…he hath set the world in their heart, so that no man can find out the work that God maketh from the beginning to the end.**
>
> Ecclesiastes 3:11 KJB

Statistically, according to a quick Google search, humans forget around 50-80% of things they learn after a period of 24 hours. I can't even remember what I ate last night for dinner.

If we, as mortal men, can only retain 50% of the information we learn each day, how could we know the Bible in our hands is perfect according to the measure of God?! *We cannot!* Not with absolute certainty. We are as dumb as sheep.

But that's okay, because, like sheep, we don't need to know everything. We can have faith. We can trust the good shepherd, who calls us all by name, knows exactly what He's doing. We can believe Him.

We can believe that God's words are **perfect** (Psalm 19:7 KJB).
We can believe that God's words are **preserved** (Psalm 12:6-7 KJB).
We can believe that God's words are **pure** (Proverbs 30:5 KJB).

We can believe that God's word is **truth** (John 17:17 KJB).
We can believe that God's word is **living** (Hebrews 4:12 KJB).
We can believe that God's word is **incorruptible** (1 Peter 1:23 KJB).
We can believe that God's word is **inspired** (2 Timothy 3:16 KJB).

We, as the flock of His pasture, can believe there is a perfect Bible because the good shepherd has told us these things.

He didn't have to give us a perfect Bible, just like He didn't have to give us a perfect atonement. But His word says otherwise, which is why He did.

But how then shall the scriptures be fulfilled, that thus it must be? Matthew 26:54

In the last days, the Bible says there will be a book that can be sought after and read. And that book is called **the book of the LORD.**

Isaiah 34 is entirely about end time prophecy. The end of the chapter commands us to **read** from **the book of the LORD**.

Seek ye out of the book of the LORD, and read: no one of these shall fail... Isaiah 34:16 KJB

According to the Bible, men will be able to look at the world, and look at **the book of the LORD** and verify, *"Nothing failed..."* All of it came to pass exactly as God said it would.

Consider this carefully. Even if we are not in the last days, the vast majority of the church around the world believes the 66-book volume known as the Holy Bible to be the completed written word of God.

The canon is closed. Nothing can be added to it. Nothing can be taken from it. And that in itself is proof that God has delivered His **book** into our hands today.

Nobody is going to alter the books or chapters of the Bible.

So how do we identify the King James Bible specifically as **the book of the LORD**?

Of all Bibles, the King James Bible should demand our attention first and foremost. No other Bible *(or any book at all)* has been printed more often in human history. Do you know how many copies have been printed since 1611?

Not tens of millions.
Not hundreds of millions.
Billions.

One cannot imagine how many that is. The amount of paper required for such an amount would come out to roughly 50 million trees- with each tree producing 10,000 pieces of paper. If you could look at one Bible and say, "*This is the Bible that God used to reach the most souls*," it would be, without second thought, the KJB.

Besides its colossal reach, millions of people around the world today actually believe the King James Bible is perfect. No other Bible that I know of can make such a claim with such magnitude. I have directly received testimonies of fellow believers in Zambia, Nigeria, Brazil, Indonesia, Philippines, Netherlands, India, Ukraine, New Zealand, etc who believe the King James Bible in English is the infallible word of God. Most, if not all, view the KJB with higher regard than their own native language. Different cultures, churches, and languages, with the same conclusion: the English KJB is a perfect Bible.

What other Bible has online forums (stretching back to the days when the internet first went mainstream) and thick volumes of books dedicated to the debate of its infallibility? Only the KJB.

There are no books, movements, or denominations (that I'm aware of) proposing positions such as NASB-only or NIV-only. There is no Geneva-only or Tyndale-only debate. Sure, there are many who are Geneva-preferred or ESV-preferred, but they do not believe their favored version is infallible. The debate is *(and has always been)* over the King James Bible. Why? Because it's the only Bible so highly regarded by so many people in so many places.

All secular and Christian historians agree with a near-absolute unanimous voice: the King James Bible is the most influential book in the history of the world.

In his book "*The Bible in English*" David Daniell (not to be confused with David W. Daniels) writes,

> *"On a historical scale, the sheer longevity of this version is a phenomenon, without parallel. English translations come and go, some with strong effect: but 'King James' is still the bestselling book in the world. Geographically, its spread has been global for hundreds of years: wherever in the world there are English readers, there are copies. In the story of the earth we live on, its influence cannot be calculated. Its words have been found to have a unique quality, of being able both to lift up a dedicated soul higher than had been thought, and to reach even below the lowest depths of human experience."* [1]

It must be noted that this author (David Daniell) does not hold a KJB-only position. He believes there are translation errors in the KJB. And yet, that does not prevent him from acknowledging the great and sincere reality of the matter. There is nothing else on this earth that can be compared to the King James Bible. Its power is seen and felt. It is loved by the multitudes.

Jesus had multitudes following Him as well.

What gave the apostles such certainty that this man was the Christ?

What did God *use* to show the world that Jesus Christ was His only begotten Son? Yes, Jesus said He was the I AM (John 8:58), but what made people believe His words?

What set Him apart from everyone else?

The answer is quite simple.

Miracles.

Giving sight to the blind.
Walking on the sea.
Turning water to wine.
Casting out devils.
Transfiguring.
Healing the sick.
Calming the storm.
Cursing a tree.
Raising the dead.

Every miracle performed by Jesus was a sign and witness from God to all mankind- this man, Jesus Christ, is exactly who He says He is. His words are truth- even the words of eternal life (John 6:68). And His miracles verify His words.

> **But I have greater witness than that of John: for the works which the Father hath given me to finish, the same works that I do, bear witness of me, that the Father hath sent me.**
>
> John 5:36 KJB

Miracles reveal and confirm to us that God is at work. Even throughout the Old Testament, God performs miracles to give us certainty that it is truly His words being spoken.

And that brings us to the heart of the matter of this book.

What if we found signs and wonders, even miracles, in the King James Bible that point to God as its author? Miracles that defy all natural circumstances, witnessing to the perfect source from which it came.

Richard Dawkins, one of the most notorious atheists of our time, has suggested, "*I suppose it's possible that you might find evidence for that [an intelligent civilization seeding the earth] if you look at the details of biochemistry/molecular biology, you might find a signature of some sort of designer.*" [2]

Well, Sir Richard, and all who agree with him, I have a question for you.

What if God has verified and "signed" His own book to prove that He is the Author of *it?* Such a thing would be 100,000 times more beneficial than a signature in your DNA, wouldn't it? Not only would you know who God is, but you would know what He thinks, what He has done, and where you're going after your heart stops beating.

What if the Holy Bible, and more specifically- the most influential version in history, is signed and sealed by God Himself?

What you're about to see is a series of precisely coordinated strikes, movements of the hand of God, in the most specific locations of scripture, with clear purpose and wisdom. What you're about to see is an act of Almighty God that no man could have ever conceived.

You will not be confronted with obscure references that could be repeated in any large body of text. You will not see lots of "iffy" somewhat-sensical patterns.

You will see complete, whole, patterns that are found in the most remarkable places of God's word. Exactness in the first and last verses of the Bible. Perfection in the first and last words of the Bible. Flawless, jaw-dropping patterns surrounding the name of Jesus from over 25 different angles. And perhaps most convincing of all, miracles surrounding the Father, the Word, and the Holy Ghost.

You will see all of these things perfectly arranged in a language that didn't exist until thousands of years after the scriptures were first written.

Remember the former things of old: for I am God, and there is none else; I am God, and there is none like me,
Declaring the end from the beginning, and from ancient times the things that are not yet done, saying, My counsel shall stand, and I will do all my pleasure:

Isaiah 46:9-10 KJB

What you're about to see is God bearing witness of Himself that He knew the end from the beginning.

What you're about to see is that God- is truly a God of numbers. The God who made us, has glorified His name through His own Book.

For it is written, I will destroy the wisdom of the wise, and will bring to nothing the understanding of the prudent. Where is the wise? where is the scribe? where is the disputer of this world? hath not God made foolish the wisdom of this world?

1 Corinthians 1:19-20

---

1. David Daniell, *The Bible in English, Its History and Influence* (Yale University Press, 2003), 427

2. *Expelled: No Intelligence Allowed*, Directed by Nathan Frankowski, featuring Ben Stein, Premise Media Corporation, Rampant Film, 2008.

If the Bible is miraculously sealed by God...

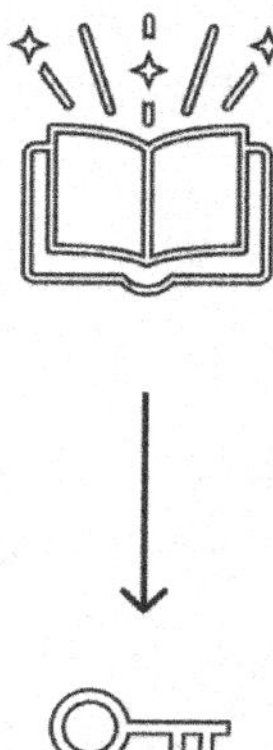

It would provide verification to us that...

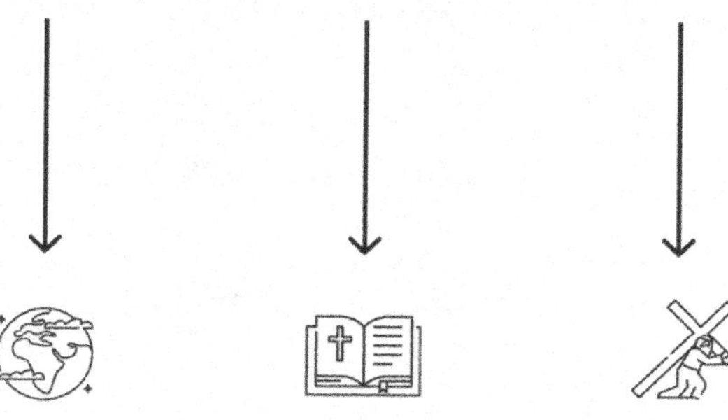

God knew the end from the very beginning	The Bible is God's word, pure and preserved	Without Jesus Christ, we are dead in our sins

"Originals-only" vs The Bible

But the natural man receiveth not the things of the Spirit of God: for they are foolishness unto him: neither can he know them, because they are spiritually discerned. 1 Corinthians 2:14

Before diving into these notes, I believe it's very important to address this issue, since many will assume that I am not aware the Bible was written in Hebrew, Aramaic and Greek. Trust me, I am fully aware the Bible was originally written in those languages. I've studied Bible numerics in those languages. But I hope to share some wisdom with you that will hopefully shed some light on my position and stance on the languages of the Holy Bible, before we go on thinking all of the things in this book are done out of ignorance. Yes I am ignorant of a lot of things. But I am not at all ignorant of the Originals-only Bible position. I am aware the King James Bible was first printed in 1611 and went through many editions until it was finalized into the version we have today.

What I believe about the King James Bible in English is probably a lot different than most Christians today- even different in comparison to what the King James translators believed themselves. And that's okay. The King James translators have no authority to decide whether or not the Holy Bible is infallible. They were men- just like us, working on what they felt God was calling them to do. They were far smarter than me, and probably a lot smarter than you as well. One of the translators, John Bois, read through the entire Bible in Hebrew when he was 5 years old, and could write elegantly in Hebrew by the age of 6. And he wasn't even the cream of the crop. Nevertheless, there is only one authority who can truly tell us if the Bible is infallible: Almighty God.

The original-only belief is held by most Christians today. Most church doctrinal statements and biblical institutions are agreed on this principle: *The scriptures were only inspired in the original writings.*

This is the short and easy explanation as to why there are so many different Bible versions today. And, well, they might mean well when they say such a thing, but *are they right*?

Of course they are right in one degree- in the sense that the Bible was inspired in the original languages. But their statement, as a whole, is missing the mark.

"Original-only" philosophy assumes God's words were once supernaturally inspired: prophets once moved by the Holy Ghost, but thereafter preserved by mankind. *Supernaturally inspired by God but naturally preserved by man.*

There is a massive problem with this philosophy.

If you believe the Bible is truly God's word... may I ask you to do something?

Search the scriptures. Be a Berean. And prove "original-onlyism" from the Bible. Search for yourself to see if this "originals-only" philosophy is derived from the living word of God, or if, perhaps, it originates from the feeble wisdom of men?

If you do, you will come to the same conclusion as millions of KJB-believers around the world have come to: the Bible doesn't say anything about "only the original scriptures" being inspired.

In fact, it says the opposite.

It describes the scriptures as **LIVING**, **ABIDING**, **PURE**, **PERFECT**, and **PRESENT**. In Paul's second letter to Timothy, he says **all scripture is given** (present tense) **by inspiration of God** (2 Timothy 3:16).

And Paul is not referring to the "*original writings*" unless Timothy had ALL the originals as a child- **from a child thou hast known the holy scriptures** (2 Timothy 3:15). If Timothy, as a child, had possession of ALL the ORIGINAL HOLY SCRIPTURES, he would have owned animal skins that are 1500 years old, taken straight out of the side of the ark of the covenant. Combined with all the writings of Joshua, Samuel, David, Solomon, Isaiah, Jeremiah, Ezekiel, Daniel, Ezra, Zechariah, Malachi and all the rest of them. Quite a collection! If only they found the ruins of Timothy's house, we would unearth all the original writings... right?!

Medieval man holds up sign to the audience, "*Laugh out loud.*"

Here is something I've learned: the natural man doesn't understand that God's words are spiritual.

The natural mind cannot comprehend why there are different readings amongst the English translations, nor can it understand the different readings amongst the Hebrew and Greek manuscripts, so it heedlessly proclaims, "*Corruption upon the text! Corruption upon the text!*"

On the contrary, Almighty God proclaims HIS WORD to be **incorruptible** (1 Peter 1:23). Not once does that natural man ever think *"Perhaps God has moved on from Hebrew and Greek, since we have a Bible today that has been printed millions and millions and millions and millions and millions more times than all Hebrew and Greek texts combined."*

The natural minded Christian believes God is omnipotent and omniscient, sovereign over all things. He believes the Bible is the incorruptible word of God. And yet he also believes all Bibles in existence are full of error, and God would never do such a thing as *inspire the Bible in a language that didn't exist a thousand years ago. How could God overcome such a difficult obstacle?!*

For a thousand years in thy sight are but as yesterday when it is past, and as a watch in the night. Psalm 90:4

Medieval man's sign: "*Nervous laughter.*"

Can we all agree the words of holy scriptures are not of the vain **thoughts of man** (Psalm 94:11), but rather, of the everlasting God- the very **thoughts of his heart** (Psalm 33:11)?

The words of God are quite literally **spirit** and **life** (John 6:63).

And God, quite literally, **cannot lie** (Titus 1:2) when He says His **words shall not pass away** (Mark 13:31) and **abideth for ever** (1 Peter 1:23).

Here is the biggest "issue" in the mind of a natural man, which includes many Christians in this day and age: A translation of the original languages can be greater than the original languages themselves. The natural mind is not capable of understanding this. It just shuts off. Even if that language of translation is universally spoken and used by the entire world today.

Does the natural mind read and believe the Bible where it says **with God nothing shall be impossible** (Luke 1:37) and where it says He declares **the end from the beginning** (Isaiah 46:10)?

It may think it believes. But how shallow it wades!

The natural mind's desire to bring God's words down to his own level (man's words), is the cause for which this type of thought will never click into place: *God reveals Himself over time, and He, who wills all men to be saved, knew His word would be translated into a worldwide spoken language long before it was ever written.*

O natural mind, will you consider this: *If God was limited to original languages, why was the New Testament penned in Greek and not Hebrew?*

The answer is simple. Very simple! God's plan of salvation was ready to be revealed to the world. And thus, God's word was revealed in the language of the world: Greek.

Here we are today. And the world language around us is no longer Greek. It's English.

As we look for that blessed hope, the glorious appearing of our Lord Jesus Christ, the entire world speaks English.

And the most influential book in human history is an English Bible.

Just by these two facts alone, our spiritual antennas should be twirling around, wondering if God has done something profound in this worldwide spoken tongue. Has He collated both Hebrew/Aramaic and Greek into one language for all mankind to have His finished book?

Well, perhaps He did.

But the carnal mind continues in its downward spiral of humanism, insisting that the problem is "translation" and "loss of original meaning."

But let's cut to the chase.

This entire debate boils down to one question. And that question is: *Can an English translation of the Bible triumph over the original languages?*

The answer is simply, Yes. If God ordains it, a translation of the original languages can be greater than the original languages themselves.

The natural mind is not capable of understanding this.

Now, everybody including myself must admit that translating a book written by a human author would certainly involve a natural process, of losing the author's original meaning, and failing to bring the complete idea over from the original language into the new.

...But that's dealing with a human author.

Translating a book authored by man is a natural matter.
Translating a book inspired by God is a spiritual matter.

We are not dealing with a human author when it comes to the holy scriptures.

We are dealing with the words of Almighty God. Who are we to say that God didn't want/will/plan to translate His words into another language?

Languages that we speak today (such as English) might be relatively "new" to us, but not to God, who inhabits eternity. The Author of the Bible can speak light into existence, form people out of dust, flood the earth, part the sea, stop the sun, heal the leper, bring the dead back to life, create new languages in an instant, declare things that have not yet come to pass, and get this... give us His words through imperfect men.

Why listen to what Bible scholars and pastors say about the Bible, when you could instead just listen to what God says in the Bible itself?

Take for example, Bob. Bob cannot look at God in the face and counsel Him. Bob can't even look at His face and live. And yet, when Bob makes up something out of the clear blue sky about God, such as: "*God's word was only inspired in the originals*" ...why do you accept Bob's wisdom as supreme truth... when nothing in God's word supports it?

Stop believing Bob. Bob only has opinions about God's word. But what saith the scriptures? Start believing God's written truth. God's truth reveals the truth about His word. It was enough for Jesus to defeat Satan in the wilderness; and therefore, it's enough for us too.

It is written...

God's words are spirit and life. Pure. Incorruptible. For ever settled in heaven. Enduring to all generations. Given with certainty. Above all His name. Faithful and true.

God's word does not submit to natural processes. But rather, natural processes are formed and upheld by the word of God.

Through faith we understand that the worlds were framed by the word of God, so that things which are seen were not made of things which do appear. Hebrews 11:3

By the word of the LORD were the heavens made; and all the host of them by the breath of his mouth. Psalm 33:6

...upholding all things by the word of his power...
Hebrews 1:3

The words of the LORD are pure words: as silver tried in a furnace of earth, purified seven times. Thou shalt keep them, O LORD, thou shalt preserve them from this generation for ever. Psalm 12:6-7

Thy righteousness is an everlasting righteousness, and thy law is the truth. Psalm 119:142

Thy word is true from the beginning: and every one of thy righteous judgments endureth for ever. Psalm 119:160

For the LORD is good; his mercy is everlasting; and his truth endureth to all generations. Psalm 100:5

All the words of my mouth are in righteousness; there is nothing froward or perverse in them. Proverbs 8:8

Have not I written to thee excellent things in counsels and knowledge, That I might make thee know the certainty of the words of truth; that thou mightest answer the words of truth to them that send unto thee? Proverbs 22:21

Sanctify them through thy truth: thy word is truth.
John 17:17

Laying the Foundation

Before diving into the notes, let's establish some groundwork.

The Bible is a massive book, and I have not walked through every gate, secret entrance and passageway of God's infinite word. Nobody has. And I do not believe this book of notes comes anywhere close to reaching the great unknown depths of God's wisdom. God's mind is infinite. His thoughts are very deep. And I will never master His word.

His word will always teach, reprove and master me.

How can we determine if these "miracles" are truly from God and not the vain imaginations of men?

When it comes to an actual miracle performed by God, I believe the results should be four-fold:

- It should be in absolute agreement with the scriptures. Truth is found in the written text of the Bible. Miracles do not bring forth new truth, but rather verify what (and who) the truth already is.
- It should be clear to believers with joy, wonder, and even fear that, *"this is truly a work of God,"* not possible by human means nor remotely probable by random chance.
- It should fit in with a larger body of evidence. It is nearly guaranteed to find pseudo-miracles here and there throughout so many Bible versions. That is- things that appear to be perfect, but are in fact, isolated instances that do not build up into anything significant. For example, Genesis 1 has 797 words in the King James Bible. There are undoubtedly several versions out there that contain 777 words in Genesis 1 just because of the sheer number of versions. True wisdom requires looking at a larger body of evidence. As you go through this book of notes, you will see that body of evidence pile up to the heavens pretty quickly.
- It should harden the hearts of the proud, arrogant, and self-righteous men of high authority/degree. It will make self-proclaimed Bible-gurus angry and upset because it goes against their own man-made doctrines and commandments.

When we see true miracles in the text of the Bible, we should expect them to be part of micro and macro patterns working individually and in parallel, as several paths of God's inspired thoughts intersect to exercise His full counsel toward us. They don't necessarily have to be performed exactly the same way. Sometimes Jesus healed with His hands, other times He spoke the word only. Sometimes He was present, other times He was not.

But every miracle was for the glory of Jesus Christ, as a sign to the world that He is truly sent from God. And the same applies with these miracles. All of these miracles verify to the world that the KJB is **the book of the LORD**, signed and sent by God before the days where Babylon's habitation becomes **a cage of every unclean and hateful bird** (Revelation 18:2, Isaiah 34:11-17, Leviticus 11:13-17).

Did all of these miracles exist in the 1611 King James Bible, or are they only in the KJB we have today?

That's a good question. And the answer is perhaps one of the most intriguing things of all. I have dedicated a great deal of research into this, which is documented in Appendix 1, showing when these major miracles first appeared in the KJB. A lot of them appeared in the original 1611 print. But a lot of them also fell into place over time. It almost seems like the Holy Ghost was purposely arranging these things into a specific order. There was not an immediate perfection, but rather a process of refinement, just as the Bible describes itself. **As for God, his way is perfect; the word of the LORD is tried...** (2 Samuel 22:31). **The words of the LORD are pure words: as silver tried in a furnace of earth, purified seven times.** (Psalm 12:6).

The reason why that's so important is because the glory of these miracles cannot be ascribed to the King James translators- nor to any of the editors of the KJB over the years (most of whom were anonymous).

The glory for all of these miracles can only be attributed to one entity: the Lord God Almighty, who was, and is, and is to come.

I know that, whatsoever God doeth, it shall be for ever: nothing can be put to it, nor any thing taken from it: and God doeth it, that men should fear before him. Ecclesiastes 3:14

Which edition of the KJB can these miracles be found in?

Nearly every single miracle in this book can be found in any version of the KJB that is printed today- whether Oxford or Cambridge or Pure Cambridge. I always recommend Cambridge, who are the principal custodians of the text. 100% of the miracles in this book can be found in a Cambridge Concord Bible (the standard text of Cambridge University).

Why did God wait thousands of years to put all these miracles into His book?

I'm not God, so I cannot answer on His behalf. If I were to guess: Maybe it would have been pointless in an age without computers. Maybe He wanted to show His power over all flesh, and bear witness to His truth in a way that no man could deny in his right mind. A witness in these last days, before His return, to open the eyes of many unto the realization that He is sovereign over all things, *especially* His own book.

But I don't know for sure. All I can do is believe. I believe His words **shall not pass away**… and will always remain **faithful and true**… **purified seven times**… **from this generation for ever.**

And that brings us to the final point.

What specific number would pass as God's seal of inspiration?

The number of numbers. God's number of perfection. The number closest to God's heart- repeated over and over again in scriptures. If you're not familiar with the Bible, you will still recognize the importance of this number, as it's seen just about everywhere in society, from lottery machines to people's usernames online. *JohnDoe777*

7

Seven in the Bible is the number of rest, ending, completion, and perfection. 7, 7×7, 70, 70×7…. It shows up all throughout the scriptures, from beginning to end.

God created all things in 7 days. And He rested on the 7th day and sanctified it. And the world today still goes by God's original blueprint. In fact, it's now a global standard. 6 days of work and 1 day of rest, without any scientific or astronomical justification.

Creation was ended in seven days.

Lamech, was the last man born before the flood who would not pass over into the new world, dying at 777 years old. He typified God the Father when he prophesied that his son, Noah, would give comfort to them from the curse that was on all mankind (Gen 5:29, 3:17-19). But that's not all. God gave a 7-day warning before the flood came. God commanded clean animals to enter the ark by 7's. The ark landed on the mountains in the 7th month. Noah sent out the dove in 7-day periods.

The pre-flood world ended with sevens across the board.

In Revelation, the last book of the Bible, we read about 7 churches, 7 Spirits, 7 candlesticks, 7 stars, 7 lamps, 7 seals, 7 horns, 7 eyes, 7 angels, 7 trumpets, 7 thunders, 7 crowns, 7 plagues, 7 vials, 7 mountains, 7 kings, 7 thousand men slain, and 7 heads of the beast.

The world we live in will end in sevens upon sevens upon sevens.

God's number of completion, all the way through His word, is 7. And that's the number you'll see throughout these notes. That's the number I can say for certain, is what God used to seal His book.

You should also know that you don't need a Hebrew or Greek scholar to verify these miracles. You can check them all yourself, firsthand. With all the manipulation and click-baits that exist in the world today, I feel that's very important. All those of a meek heart, seeking after the truth, can find out whether these things truly exist together in one Bible. They do. And anybody who says otherwise has no ground to stand on, no matter how professionally trained they may be.

The Bible software that I recommend is King James Pure Bible Search from purebiblesearch.com (Available 100% free for Windows, Mac, and Linux). This software, from my experience, is by far the gold standard when it comes to counting word mentions and appearances. You can use other programs as well to verify the results, but they will not give you the exactness required to check a lot of these notes. Sometimes they will not give you the number of Mentions, but rather *Appearances* (The difference between a Mention and an Appearance is explained in Appendix 10 on p. 529). Sometimes other software will count Psalms' headings and Epistles' colophons as verses (but they are not verses). So you can use other software if you wish, but be forewarned of the varying inaccuracies, limitations and differences they might have because they are not built specifically for exact word counts.

If you have Pure Bible Search downloaded, you can also go to sealedbytheking.com to download every single search file that is associated with each note, when applicable. Loading the file is quite easy. Just click the Load Search File icon and select the (.kjs) Search File that you want to load.

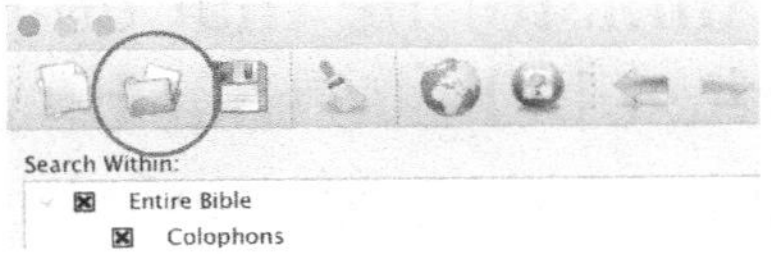

Or you can verify manually, which I encourage you to do. The choice is yours. I've made it as easy as I could for anybody to confirm for themselves that these notes are true and trustworthy. Believe me when I say this: you will not believe some of them are true when you first see them. You will want to verify them yourself. God has revealed magnificent things, and may He alone be praised.

The foundation is laid. The King James Bible will never change. The words are tried and purified seven times. The world speaks English. And all these miracles, concealed in the most printed book of all time, are now available to be seen plainly by whosoever will.

May the Lord Jesus Christ receive all the praise and glory. May the Holy Ghost bless you richly with wisdom from above.

But without faith it is impossible to please him: for he that cometh to God must believe that he is, and that he is a rewarder of them that diligently seek him.

Hebrews 11:6

Background notes on the King James Bible

The proposition to translate a new complete English Bible was first suggested to King James in 1604 at the Hampton Court Conference by John Rainolds (7th President of Corpus Christi College). Surprisingly, the King approved and authorized the translation. Without John Rainolds, the KJB would literally not exist.

<u>First 7 Presidents of Corpus Christi College</u>

1.	John Claymond	1517 - 1537
2.	Robert Morwent	1537 - 1558
3.	William Chedsey	1558 - 1559
4.	William Butcher	1559 - 1561
5.	Thomas Greenway	1562 - 1568
6.	William Cole	1568 - 1598
7.	**John Rainolds**	**1598 - 1607**

The KJB was the 7th English translation in succession of those which influenced its text. (A few other English Bibles existed but had no major influence.)

<u>First 7 Protestant English Bibles of Successive Influence</u>

1.	The Tyndale Bible	1525
2.	The Coverdale Bible	1535
3.	The Matthew's Bible	1537
4.	The Great Bible	1539
5.	The Geneva Bible	1560
6.	The Bishop's Bible	1568
7.	**The King James Bible**	**1611**

The KJB took **7 years** to complete.

1604 - 1611

The temple of God was also built in 7 years from the 4th to the 11th year.

In the fourth year was the foundation of the house of the LORD laid... And in the eleventh year... was the house finished throughout all the parts thereof, and according to all the fashion of it. So was he seven years in building it. (1 Kings 6:37-38)

King James (VI of Scotland) & (I of England) (VI+I = **7**) became King of England in 1603... 77 years after Tyndale's Bible was first printed.

William Tyndale was burned at the stake for illegally translating the Bible into English, with his last words famously engraved into history, "*Oh Lord, open the King of England's eyes…*"

Where the word of a king is, there is power: and who may say unto him, What doest thou? Ecclesiastes 8:4

There were 47 translators who worked on the King James Bible, and the #1611 word of James is the exact #47 mention of **sinners** in the KJB. Detailed further on page 388

The Lord gave the word: great was the company of those that published it. Psalm 68:11

The #**1611** mention of **Lord** is in Deuteronomy **16:11**. Detailed on p. 61

For hundreds of years, it was simply called **The Holy Bible**. It is now known as the KJB / KJV / AV / AV1611. (AV = Authorized Version)

I call it the King James Bible, because I do not see it merely as a "version" of God's word. I perceive it as the Bible itself, and thus, the KJB, standing alone and distinct from all other modern versions that flood the market today.

The counsel of the LORD standeth for ever, the thoughts of his heart to all generations.

Psalm 33:11

Part I

The secret things belong unto the
LORD our God: but those things
which are revealed belong unto us
and to our children for ever, that we
may do all the words of this law.

Deuteronomy 29:29

The Words of God 7×7×7 / 7×7, First Chapters

And God said... Genesis 1:3

When you add up all the words spoken directly by God in both Genesis 1 and Matthew 1 (the first chapters of both testaments), the sums are perfectly factorized by God's perfect number: **7**.

Words spoken directly by God	
Genesis 1	**Matthew 1**
Let there be light: Let there be a firmament in the midst of the waters, and let it divide the waters from the waters Let the waters under the heaven be gathered together unto one place, and let the dry land appear Let the earth bring forth grass, the herb yielding seed, and the fruit tree yielding fruit after his kind, whose seed is in itself, upon the earth Let there be lights in the firmament of the heaven to divide the day from the night; and let them be for signs, and for seasons, and for days, and years: And let them be for lights in the firmament of the heaven to give light upon the earth: Let the waters bring forth abundantly the moving creature that hath life, and fowl that may fly above the earth in the open firmament of heaven Be fruitful, and multiply, and fill the waters in the seas, and let fowl multiply in the earth. Let the earth bring forth the living creature after his kind, cattle, and creeping thing, and beast of the earth after his kind Let us make man in our image, after our likeness: and let them have dominion over the fish of the sea, and over the fowl of the air, and over the cattle, and over all the earth, and over every creeping thing that creepeth upon the earth. Be fruitful, and multiply, and replenish the earth, and subdue it: and have dominion over the fish of the sea, and over the fowl of the air, and over every living thing that moveth upon the earth. Behold, I have given you every herb bearing seed, which is upon the face of all the earth, and every tree, in the which is the fruit of a tree yielding seed; to you it shall be for meat. And to every beast of the earth, and to every fowl of the air, and to every thing that creepeth upon the earth, wherein there is life, I have given every green herb for meat:	Joseph, thou son of David, fear not to take unto thee Mary thy wife: for that which is conceived in her is of the Holy Ghost. And she shall bring forth a son, and thou shalt call his name JESUS: for he shall save his people from their sins. ——— Note: The words are spoken by the angel of the LORD, but are still the direct words of God. See example... Genesis 22:15-16 **And the angel of the LORD called unto Abraham out of heaven the second time, And said, By myself have I sworn, saith the LORD, for because thou hast done this thing, and hast not withheld thy son, thine only son...**
Total Words = 343	**Total Words = 49**
= 7×7×7 words	**= 7×7 words**
KJB1611 = 344, NKJV = 336, ESV = 333, NASB1971 = 325, NASB2020 = 326 , NIV = 321	KJB1611 = 49, NKJV = 50, ESV = 46, NASB1971 = 52, NASB2020 = 50 , NIV = 51

Words spoken directly by God (by verse)

Genesis 1 — *Spoken words of God*							
	KJB	KJB1611	NKJV	ESV 2016	NASB 1971	NASB 2020	NIV 2011
Gen 1:3	**4**	4	4	4	4	4	4
Gen 1:6	**20**	20	20	20	20	20	13
Gen 1:9	**18**	18	18	18	17	17	16
Gen 1:11	**27**	28	30	26	23	24	24
Gen 1:14-15	**49**	49	48	48	49	49	48
Gen 1:20	**26**	26	26	22	23	23	20
Gen 1:22	**18**	18	18	18	18	18	21
Gen 1:24	**23**	23	26	24	22	23	28
Gen 1:26	**47**	47	45	47	47	47	45
Gen 1:28	**37**	37	34	37	36	36	35
Gen 1:29-30	**74**	74	67	69	66	65	67
Genesis 1 Total Sum	**343 =7×7×7**	344*	336	333	325	326	321

*The KJB1611 included two words that later conjoined into one, circa 1762. See Appendix 1

In the KJB: Starting on verse 14, God directly speaks a perfect **7×7 words**, which separates the rest of his words by **13×13 words** in the **first 13 verses**, and **15×15 words** in the **last 15 verses**

Matthew 1 — *Spoken words of God*							
	KJB	KJB1611	NKJV	ESV 2016	NASB 1971	NASB 2020	NIV 2011
Mat 1:20-21	**49**	49	50	46	52	50	51
Matthew 1 Total Sum	**49 = 7×7**	49 = 7×7	50	46	52	50	51

Jesus 7/7, First and Last Mentions

Matthew 1:1 **The book of the generation of Jesus Christ, the son of David, the son of Abraham.**

Revelation 22:21 **The grace of our Lord Jesus Christ be with you all. Amen.**

The first and the last mentions of Jesus are the 7th words from the beginning and ending of the New Testament.

I am Alpha and Omega, the beginning and the end, the first and the last. Revelation 22:13

Beginning and Ending of New Testament	
Counting from the beginning (Matthew 1:1)	Counting from the end (Revelation 22:21)
1. The 2. book 3. of 4. the 5. generation 6. of **7. Jesus** 8. Christ, 9. the 10. son 11. of 12. David	1. Amen. 2. all. 3. you 4. with 5. be 6. Christ **7. Jesus** 8. Lord 9. our 10. of 11. grace 12. The

Notice how the first and last mention of "Christ" is word #8 and word #6. Which also perfectly averages to 7.

This pattern does not exist in the Greek.

Iησου [Jesus] = word #3 from the beginning of the Greek T.R. N.T.	**Iησου** [Jesus] = word #6 from the end of the Greek T.R. N.T.

Except for the NKJV (which mimics the KJB in many important places, but subtly distorts the KJB in many discreet places- see Appendix 4), most modern Bibles will not repeat this simple pattern.

Bible	**Jesus**, word # from the beginning of N.T. in Matthew 1:1	**Jesus**, word # from the end of N.T. in Revelation 22:21
KJB	**7**	**7**
KJB1611	7	7
NKJV	7	7
ESV	7	5
NASB1971	7	5
NASB2020	7	5
NIV	6	6

First Mention of Jesus 77%, the 77th from God

Matthew 1:1 **The book of the generation of Jesus Christ, the son of David, the son of Abraham.**

Jesus (word # 610,288 out of 790,849) is first mentioned 77% of the way through the words of God's book. 610,288 / 790,849 = ~0.77

Matthew 1:1 The book of the generation of Jesus Christ, the son of David, the son of Abraham.

```
[7] "Jesus" is Word/Phrase:
    610288 of 790849 of Bible
    7 of 180568 of New Testament
    7 of 23684 of Matthew
```

Jesus is the 77th generation from **God** in Luke 3:23-38

1 God	12 Sem	23 Isaac	34 Jesse	45 Levi	56 Salathiel	67 Naum
2 Adam	13 Arphaxad	24 Jacob	35 David	46 Matthat	57 Zorobabel	68 Amos
3 Seth	14 Cainan	25 Juda	36 Nathan	47 Jorim	58 Rhesa	69 Mattathias
4 Enos	15 Sala	26 Phares	37 Mattatha	48 Eliezer	59 Joanna	70 Joseph
5 Cainan	16 Heber	27 Esrom	38 Menan	49 Jose	60 Juda	71 Janna
6 Maleleel	17 Phalec	28 Aram	39 Melea	50 Er	61 Joseph	72 Melchi
7 Jared	18 Ragau	29 Aminadab	40 Eliakim	51 Elmodam	62 Semei	73 Levi
8 Enoch	19 Saruch	30 Naasson	41 Jonan	52 Cosam	63 Mattathias	74 Matthat
9 Mathusala	20 Nachor	31 Salmon	42 Joseph	53 Addi	64 Maath	75 Heli
10 Lamech	21 Thara	32 Booz	43 Juda	54 Melchi	65 Nagge	76 Joseph *(as was supposed)*
11 Noe	22 Abraham	33 Obed	44 Simeon	55 Neri	66 Esli	**77 Jesus**

Extra note: ***Jesus*** *is 42 generations from* ***David****, and (42 =* ***7 × 6****). The number of perfection / rest / completion (7) × the number of man (6). See pp. 52-53 where it is noted that the combined sum of mentions of:* ***Jesus*** *+* ***David*** *=* ***7×7×7 × 6*** *mentions in the entire Bible.*

Jesus the **77th** from God first appears **77%** of the way through his **book**			
Bible	**First mention of Jesus (word count)**	**Total words in the scriptures**	**Percent of the way through the scriptures**
KJB	610,288	790,849	**77%**
KJB1611 = 77%, NKJV = 77%, ESV = 77%, NASB1971 = 77%, NASB2020 = 77% , NIV = 76%			

Jesus, the 77th from God, appears 77% of the way through the **book**, and according to Matthew's genealogy in Matthew 1:17, is (7+7)+(7+7) generations from **David** and another (7+7) generations from **Abraham**.

Matthew 1:1 **The book of the generation of Jesus Christ, the son of David, the son of Abraham.**

The word **"book"** in Matthew 1:1 is mention #147 of **book** in the KJB.
KJB1611 = 147 NKJV = 145 ESV = 131 NASB1971 = 129 NASB2020 and NIV do not use "book" in Mat 1:1

147 has a very strong relationship with the number 7.

- 147 = 77+70
- 147 = 7 × (7+7+7)
- 147 = (7×7)+(7×7)+(7×7)

Exactly 147 chapters contain both **Jesus + Christ** (Excluding antimentions).

The word "**book**" is mentioned 188 times in the Bible.
David + Abraham combined are mentioned 188 × 7 times.

Matthew 1:1 **The book of the generation of Jesus Christ, the son of David, the son of Abraham.**

book	David + Abraham
188 mentions in the KJB	**188 × 7** mentions in the KJB

Matthew 1:1 contains the #147 mention of **book**.
Exactly 147 chapters contain both **Jesus** and **Christ.**
147 = 49+49+49 **= (7×7)+(7×7)+(7×7)**

All chapters that contain both
Jesus and **Christ**

1. Matthew 1
2. Matthew 2
3. Matthew 11
4. Matthew 16
5. Matthew 22
6. Matthew 23
7. Matthew 24
8. Matthew 26
9. Matthew 27
10. Mark 1
11. Mark 8
12. Mark 9
13. Mark 12
14. Mark 13
15. Mark 14
16. Mark 15
17. Luke 2
18. Luke 3
19. Luke 4
20. Luke 9
21. Luke 20
22. Luke 22
23. Luke 23
24. Luke 24
25. John 1
26. John 3
27. John 4
28. John 6
29. John 7
30. John 9
31. John 10
32. John 11
33. John 12
34. John 17
35. John 20
36. Acts 2
37. Acts 3
38. Acts 4
39. Acts 5
40. Acts 8
41. Acts 9
42. Acts 10
43. Acts 11
44. Acts 15
45. Acts 16
46. Acts 17
47. Acts 18
48. Acts 19
49. Acts 20
50. Acts 26
51. Acts 28
52. Romans 1
53. Romans 2
54. Romans 3
55. Romans 5
56. Romans 6
57. Romans 7
58. Romans 8
59. Romans 10
60. Romans 13
61. Romans 14
62. Romans 15
63. Romans 16
64. 1 Corinthians 1
65. 1 Corinthians 2
66. 1 Corinthians 3
67. 1 Corinthians 4
68. 1 Corinthians 5
69. 1 Corinthians 6
70. 1 Corinthians 8
71. 1 Corinthians 9
72. 1 Corinthians 11
73. 1 Corinthians 12
74. 1 Corinthians 15
75. 1 Corinthians 16
76. 2 Corinthians 1
77. 2 Corinthians 4
78. 2 Corinthians 5
79. 2 Corinthians 8
80. 2 Corinthians 11
81. 2 Corinthians 13
82. Galatians 1
83. Galatians 2
84. Galatians 3
85. Galatians 4
86. Galatians 5
87. Galatians 6
88. Ephesians 1
89. Ephesians 2
90. Ephesians 3
91. Ephesians 4
92. Ephesians 5
93. Ephesians 6
94. Philippians 1
95. Philippians 2
96. Philippians 3
97. Philippians 4
98. Colossians 1
99. Colossians 2
100. Colossians 3
101. 1 Thessalonians 1
102. 1 Thessalonians 2
103. 1 Thessalonians 3
104. 1 Thessalonians 4
105. 1 Thessalonians 5
106. 2 Thessalonians 1
107. 2 Thessalonians 2
108. 2 Thessalonians 3
109. 1 Timothy 1
110. 1 Timothy 2
111. 1 Timothy 3
112. 1 Timothy 4
113. 1 Timothy 5
114. 1 Timothy 6
115. 2 Timothy 1
116. 2 Timothy 2
117. 2 Timothy 3
118. 2 Timothy 4
119. Titus 1
120. Titus 2
121. Titus 3
122. Philemon 1
123. Hebrews 3
124. Hebrews 6
125. Hebrews 10
126. Hebrews 13
127. James 1
128. James 2
129. 1 Peter 1
130. 1 Peter 2
131. 1 Peter 3
132. 1 Peter 4
133. 1 Peter 5
134. 2 Peter 1
135. 2 Peter 2
136. 2 Peter 3
137. 1 John 1
138. 1 John 2
139. 1 John 3
140. 1 John 4
141. 1 John 5
142. 2 John 1
143. Jude 1
144. Revelation 1
145. Revelation 12
146. Revelation 20
147. Revelation 22

Total Chapters = 147 = (49 + 49 + 49) =

(7 × 7) + (7 × 7) + (7 × 7)

Excluding antimentions of **Jesus** and **Christ** (Joshua / Justus / Christs - see appendix 7)

The 777 Code of Matthew 1:1

The book of the generation of Jesus Christ, the son of David, the son of Abraham. Matthew 1:1

In the 4 gospels, the first verse of Matthew 1:1 and the identity of our Lord Jesus Christ is sevened and sealed by the word of God. The **generation** of **Jesus Christ** is, without dispute, of **David** and **Abraham**.

Search Filters: **Matthew, Mark, Luke, John**		Case Sens	Mentions
Search Phrase 1	**generation**	-	32
Search Phrase 2	**Jesus**	-	617
Search Phrase 3	**Christ**	-	60
Search Phrase 4	**David**	-	38
Search Phrase 5	**Abraham**	-	30
Total Mentions	**generation + Jesus + Christ + David + Abraham** *(in the Gospels)*		**777**
KJB1611 = 786 NKJV = 744 ESV = 731 NASB2020 = 719 NASB1971 = 686 NIV = 1025 Modern Bibles use "**genealogy**" instead of "**generation**" in Mat 1:1, and some use "**Messiah**" instead of "**Christ**". The above counts for modern Bibles include the substituted words used in their own specific reading of Mat 1:1. Using KJB words instead of modern words for counts (which is illogical) also does not produce any sum of 777.			

Concerning his Son Jesus Christ our Lord, which was made of the seed of David according to the flesh; Romans 1:3

Total Mentions of each name (standard, non-possessive) in the Bible		
Jesus = 7 × 139 mentions	**David** = 7 × 155 mentions	**Abraham** = 7 × 33 mentions

The number of perfection is **7**. The number of man is **6**.

Jesus (7 × 139) + **David** (7 × 155) = 2058

= 7 × 7 × 7 × 6

Total mentions in the KJB. (Also, **Jesus** is **7 × 6** generations from **David** in Luke. See p. 49)

I am the root and the offspring of David... Revelation 22:16

In the Gospels, **generation + Jesus + Christ + David + Abraham** = **777** mentions (Perfectly coinciding with Matthew 1:1)

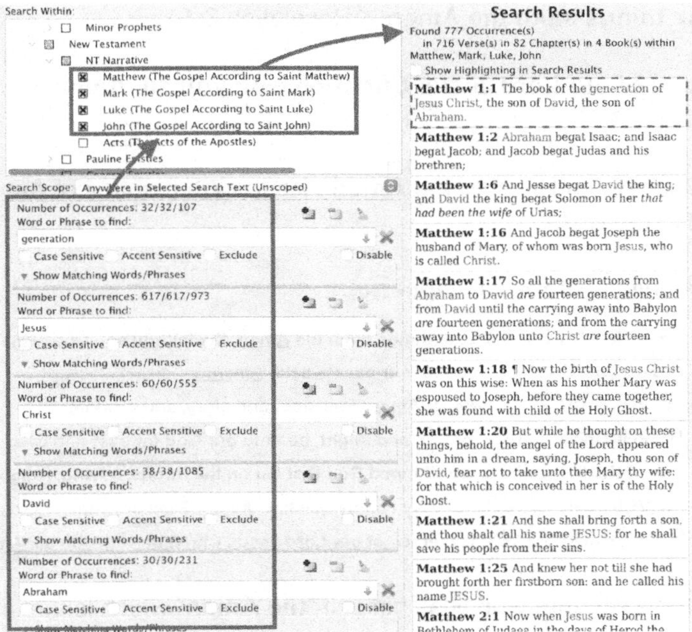

An expanded version of this note (featuring all 7 keywords of Mat 1:1; **book, generation, Jesus, Christ, son, David, Abraham**) can be found on p. 384.

In the Bible, **Jesus + David** = **7×7×7×6** mentions

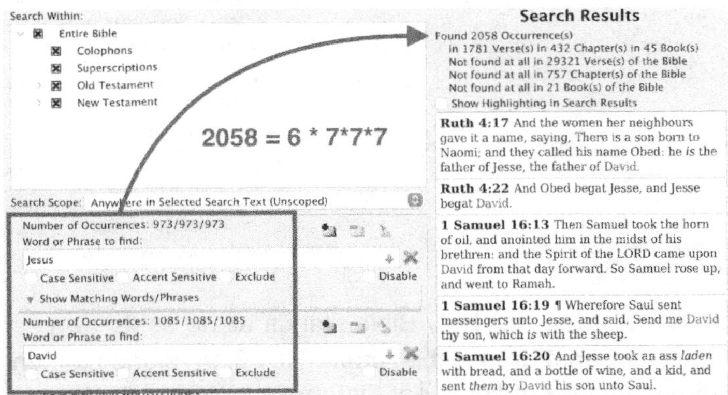

Jesus is exactly **7 × 6** generations away from **David** in Luke's genealogy (see p. 49), and there are **7 × 6** generations reported in Matthew's genealogy (see Mat 1:17).

Amen 77, The Last Word of the Bible

...**These things saith the Amen...** Revelation 3:14

The grace of our Lord Jesus Christ be with you all. Amen.
Revelation 22:21

When Jesus titles Himself "**the Amen**", it's the 7th mention of **Amen** from the end of the Bible.

Last 7 mentions of **Amen** (Capitalized)

71. Revelation 3:14 **These things saith the Amen, the faithful and true witness...**
72. Revelation 5:14 **And the four beasts said, Amen...**
73. Revelation 7:12 **Saying, Amen: Blessing, and glory, and wisdom...**
74. Revelation 7:12 **...power, and might, be unto our God for ever and ever. Amen.**
75. Revelation 19:4 **...worshipped God that sat on the throne, saying, Amen;**
76. Revelation 22:20 **...Surely I come quickly. Amen. Even so, come, Lord Jesus.**
77. Revelation 22:21 **The grace of our Lord Jesus Christ be with you all. Amen.**

Jesus, the 77th from God titles himself "**the Amen**" which is the last word of the Bible. **Amen**, capitalized, is mentioned exactly 77 times.

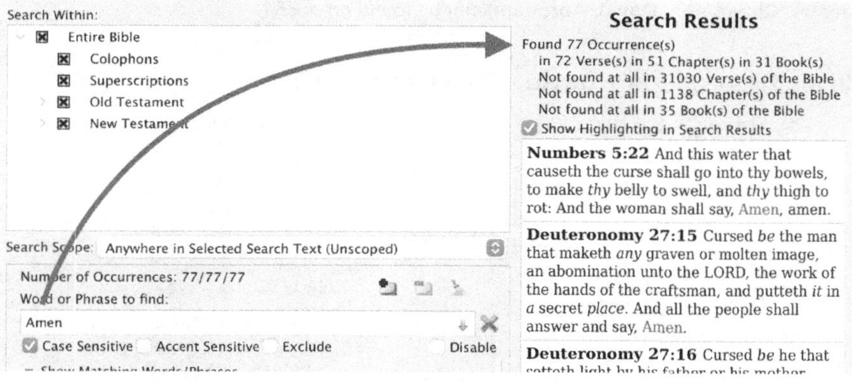

The very last word in the Holy Bible stands alone as its own sentence. Our Lord Jesus Christ, who is the **Amen** (Rev 3:14) signed the end of the book with his name. But He is not just the last. **Jesus Christ** is **the first and the last**... Let's go deeper.

First and Last Words of God's Word 777

The first word of the Bible: **In...** (Genesis 1:1)
The last word of the Bible: **...Amen** (Revelation 22:21)

These two words **(In + Amen)** combined are mentioned exactly 777 times in the first and last books, Genesis and Revelation.

Search Filters: **Genesis, Revelation**		Case Sens	Mentions
Search Phrase 1	**In**	-	767
Search Phrase 2	**Amen**	-	10
Total Mentions	**In + Amen**		**777**

Do you think this is just a coincidence? Try pointing to any word in Genesis and any word in Revelation, and let's see how long it takes you to get two words with the sum of 777 mentions.

Genesis + any other book never produces a sum of 777 for **In + Amen**
Revelation + any other book never produces 777 for **In + Amen**

I am Alpha and Omega, the beginning and the end, the first and the last. (Revelation 22:13)

The First and the Last Words - Bible Version Comparison:

Total mentions of: **In + Amen** *(in Genesis and Revelation)*				
KJB 777	NKJV 758	ESV 719	NASB2020 707	NIV 676
KJB1611 781			NASB1971 740	
KJB1611 had 4 extra mentions of "**in**" because "**instead**" was "**in ftead**" (Gen 2:21,4:25,44:33) and "**indeed**" was "**in deede**" (Gen 17:19). Standardized circa 1728. This miracle has been in King James Bibles for nearly 300 years.				

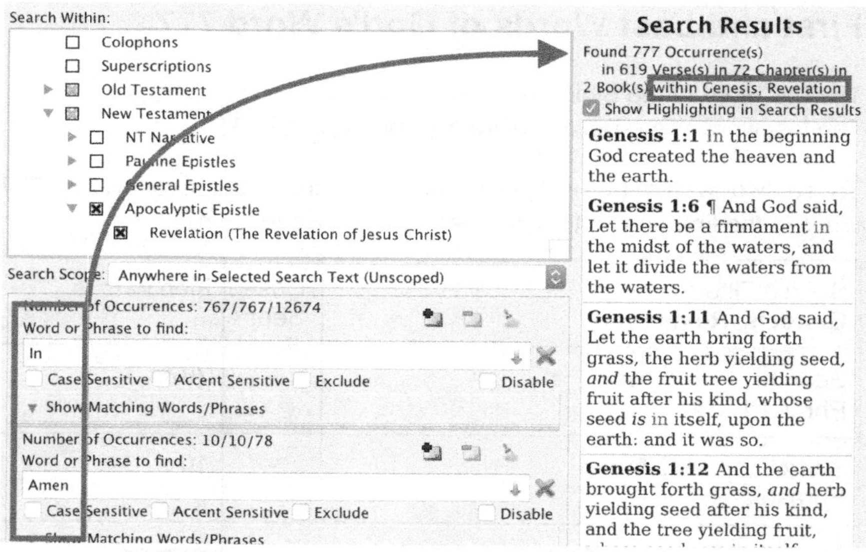

In + **Amen** doesn't occur 777 times in any other combination of books besides (Genesis + Revelation). The last word of the Bible is a mighty demonstration of the Holy Ghost sealing God's word with perfection.

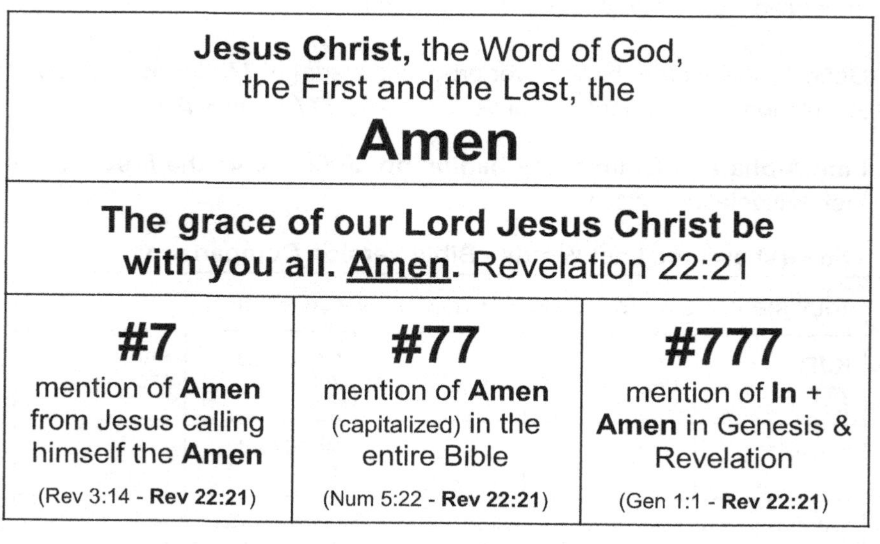

Jesus Christ, the Word of God,
the First and the Last, the
Amen
The grace of our Lord Jesus Christ be with you all. Amen. Revelation 22:21
#7
mention of **Amen** from Jesus calling himself the **Amen**
(Rev 3:14 - **Rev 22:21**)
#77
mention of **Amen** (capitalized) in the entire Bible
(Num 5:22 - **Rev 22:21**)
#777
mention of **In** + **Amen** in Genesis & Revelation
(Gen 1:1 - **Rev 22:21**)

#7 Words from the Beginning and the End

The #7 word from the beginning of the Bible **...heaven...** (Genesis 1:1)
The #7 word from the end of the Bible **...Jesus...** (Revelation 22:21)

When you take the sum of all mentions of "**heaven**" and all mentions of "**Jesus**" in the Bible (excluding "Justus" in Colossians 4:11, *see appendix* 7), you will end up with 1554 total mentions. 1554 = 777+777 mentions.

Search Filters: **Entire Bible**		Case Sens	Mentions
Search Phrase 1	**heaven** *The #7 word from the beginning*	-	582
Search Phrase 2	**Jesus** *The #7 word from the end*	-	973
Exclude	*Exclude Jesus, which is called Justus (Col 4:11) See appendix 7*	-	-1
Total Mentions	**heaven + Jesus**		1554 **=777+777**

If Joshua was not translated as **Jesus** in the New Testament (Acts 7:45, Hebrews 4:8), this pattern simply wouldn't be possible. Modern bibles do not translate Joshua as Jesus, even though they are both exactly the same in Greek. (Joshua / Jesus = ιησου).

Total mentions of: **heaven + Jesus** *(excluding Justus in Colossians 4:11)*				
KJB 1554 =777+777	NKJV 1501	ESV 1451	NASB2020 1430	NIV 1679
KJB1611 1564			NASB1971 1365	
The KJB1611 actually had 777+777 as well, but it was masked, as there were not any apostrophes on possessive **Jesus'** - thus boosting the count by +10. See Appendix 8				

When "**heaven**" and "**Jesus**" are mentioned together in the same verse, there are exactly 7×7 combined mentions of **heaven** + **Jesus**.

All verses where **heaven** and **Jesus** are mentioned together	
Matt 4:17	[**heaven** = 1x, **Jesus** = 1x]
Matt 11:25	[**heaven** = 1x, **Jesus** = 1x]
Matt 16:17	[**heaven** = 1x, **Jesus** = 1x]
Matt 18:1	[**heaven** = 1x, **Jesus** = 1x]
Matt 19:14	[**heaven** = 1x, **Jesus** = 1x]
Matt 19:21	[**heaven** = 1x, **Jesus** = 1x]
Matt 19:23	[**heaven** = 1x, **Jesus** = 1x]
Matt 26:64	[**heaven** = 1x, **Jesus** = 1x]
Matt 28:18	[**heaven** = 1x, **Jesus** = 1x]
Mark 10:21	[**heaven** = 1x, **Jesus** = 1x]
Mark 14:62	[**heaven** = 1x, **Jesus** = 1x]
Luke 3:21	[**heaven** = 1x, **Jesus** = 1x]
Luke 10:21	[**heaven** = 1x, **Jesus** = 1x]
Luke 18:22	[**heaven** = 1x, **Jesus** = 1x]
John 6:32	[**heaven** = 2x, **Jesus** = 1x]
John 6:42	[**heaven** = 1x, **Jesus** = 1x]
John 17:1	[**heaven** = 1x, **Jesus** = 1x]
Acts 1:11	[**heaven** = 3x, **Jesus** = 1x]
Acts 7:55	[**heaven** = 1x, **Jesus** = 1x]
Phil 2:10	[**heaven** = 1x, **Jesus** = 1x]
Phil 3:20	[**heaven** = 1x, **Jesus** = 1x]
1Thess 1:10	[**heaven** = 1x, **Jesus** = 1x]
2Thess 1:7	[**heaven** = 1x, **Jesus** = 1x]
[**heaven** 26x] + [**Jesus** 23x] Total = 49 **= 7×7 mentions**	

And to top it off, there are only two words in Gen 1:1 / Rev 22:21 that were standardized from the 1611 KJB to the King James Bible we read today. Which ones?

From the KJB1611 to the KJB we have today, the **#7 word** from the beginning "Heauen" was standardized to "heaven"; and the **#7 word** from the end "Iesus" was standardized to "Jesus."

No other words were standardized in the first and last verses.

	KJB1611	**KJB**
Genesis 1:1 *The only standardized word is* **Word #7** *from the beginning:* **Heauen → heaven**	In the beginning God created the **Heauen**, and the Earth.	In the beginning God created the **heaven** and the earth.
Revelation 22:21 *The only standardized word is* **Word #7** *from the end:* **Iesus → Jesus**	The grace of our Lord **Iesus** Christ be with you all. Amen.	The grace of our Lord **Jesus** Christ be with you all. Amen.
Standardization occurred circa 1637		

Screenshot proof from the first table of this note. (**heaven** + **Jesus** = 777+777)

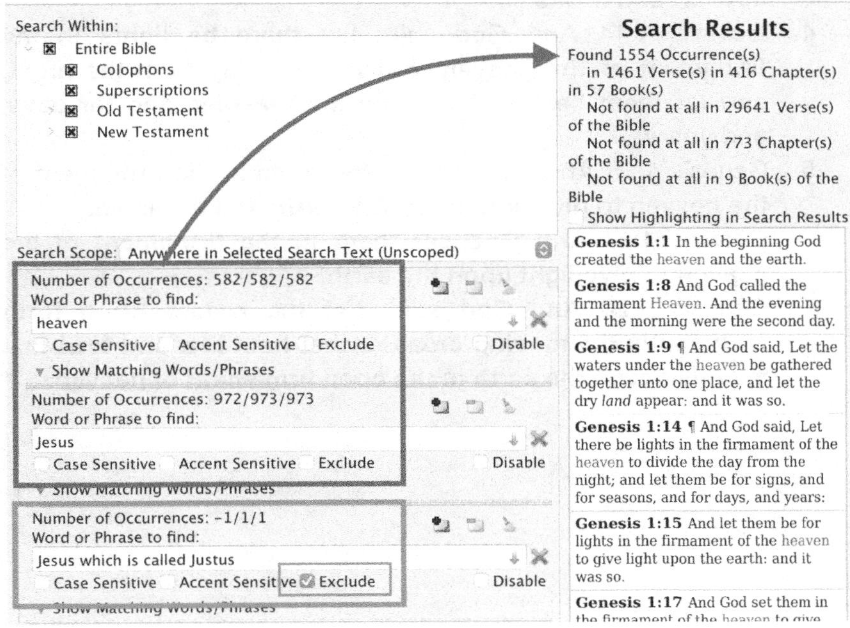

And one final note, though it may seem insignificant at this point, count it not against me, dear reader. **For who hath despised the day of small things?** (Zech 4:10)

"**heaven**" is only mentioned 7 times in one chapter of the Bible...

Which chapter?
Genesis 1.

The #7 word of the Bible appears 7 times in the first chapter of the Bible, and no other chapter of the Bible repeats this anomaly (out of 291 additional chapters where **heaven** is mentioned).

1. Genesis 1:1 **In the beginning God created the heaven and the earth.**
2. Genesis 1:8 **And God called the firmament Heaven. And the evening and the morning were the second day.**
3. Genesis 1:9 **And God said, Let the waters under the heaven be gathered together unto one place, and let the dry land appear: and it was so.**
4. Genesis 1:14 **And God said, Let there be lights in the firmament of the heaven to divide the day from the night; and let them be for signs, and for seasons, and for days, and years:**
5. Genesis 1:15 **And let them be for lights in the firmament of the heaven to give light upon the earth: and it was so.**
6. Genesis 1:17 **And God set them in the firmament of the heaven to give light upon the earth,**
7. Genesis 1:20 **And God said, Let the waters bring forth abundantly the moving creature that hath life, and fowl that may fly above the earth in the open firmament of heaven.**

LORD 1611, His Name 7×7

Do you rejoice in the **place** where God puts **his name**? What if I told you the **#1611** mention of **LORD** in the KJB is located in Deuteronomy **16:11**? Deuteronomy **16:11** also houses the #49 mention of "**his name.**"

LORD is mentioned perfectly in this verse, twice: word #7 and word #49.

<table>
<tr><td colspan="2">Deuteronomy 16:11</td></tr>
<tr><td colspan="2">And thou shalt rejoice before the <u>LORD</u> thy God, thou, and thy son, and thy daughter, and thy manservant, and thy maidservant, and the Levite that is within thy gates, and the stranger, and the fatherless, and the widow, that are among you, in the place which the LORD thy God hath chosen to place <u>his name</u> there.</td></tr>
<tr><td>LORD
(#1 of 2)
word #7
of Deuteronomy 16:11</td><td>LORD
(#2 of 2)
word #(7×7)
of Deuteronomy 16:11</td></tr>
<tr><td colspan="2">#(7×7) mention of
"his name"</td></tr>
<tr><td colspan="2">#1611 mention of LORD
(Not case-sensitive) in the KJB, (word #7 of Deuteronomy 16:11)</td></tr>
<tr><td colspan="2">Throughout the history of the KJB, there have been several switches between LORD and Lord in a few places- (E.g. In Gen 18:30, the original KJB1611 had Lord (Capitalized), but in Blayney's 1769, the Gen 18:30 reading is LORD (UPPERCASE). I also have a 1795 KJB in my possession that reads LORD (UPPERCASE). I have 3 KJBs in my possession from the 19th century (1855, ~1871, ~1883), and all of them read Lord (Capitalized). Most KJBs printed in modernity read Lord (Capitalized)). But the interesting thing to note is that–until this day, the #1611 mention of Lord/LORD is, and always has been located in Deuteronomy 16:11 –since the KJB was first printed in 1611. Most of the miracles detailed in this book appeared post-1611, but this one was always present, without any recognition until 400+ years after its appearance. See Appendix 1 for full timeline.</td></tr>
</table>

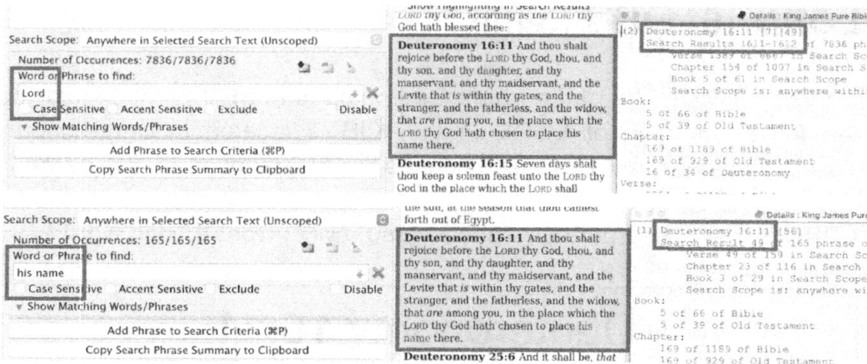

The Bible is not just sealed by the **LORD**, it is sealed by the **KING**. And not just any king. The final mention of **"king"** in the New Testament is found in Revelation 19:16: ...**<u>KING</u> OF KINGS AND LORD OF LORDS**.

This final mention of "**king**" gives us a total of 86 in the New Testament. And that gives us a total N.T. sum of...

King = 86 mentions
Jesus = 970 mentions (excl. Joshua/Justus)
Christ = 555 mentions

Search Filters: **New Testament**		Case Sens	Mentions
Search Phrase 1	**King**	-	86
Search Phrase 2	**Jesus**	-	973
Search Phrase 3	**Christ**	-	555
Exclude	*Exclude all others named **Jesus**, specifically Joshua (Act 7:45, Heb 4:8) and Justus (1x) (Col 4:11)*		-3
Total Mentions	**King + Jesus + Christ**		**1611**
KJB1611 = 1621 NKJV = 1610 ESV = 1577 NASB2020 = 1591 NIV = 1855			

And the last verse of the Bible calls this KING.... **our Lord**.

...our Lord Jesus Christ... Revelation 22:21

our Lord = 86 mentions (capitalized Lord)
Jesus = 970 mentions (excl. Joshua/Justus)
Christ = 555 mentions

Search Filters: **Entire Bible**		Case Sens	Mentions
Search Phrase 1	**our Lord**	Y	86
Search Phrase 2	**Jesus**	Y	973
Search Phrase 3	**Christ**	Y	555
Exclude	*Exclude all others named* ***Jesus****, specifically Joshua (Act 7:45, Heb 4:8) and Justus (1x) (Col 4:11)*		-3
Total Mentions	**"our Lord" + Jesus + Christ**		**1611**
If using Pure Bible Search (case sensitive), you must include **Jesus** and **JESUS**			
KJB1611 = 1619 NKJV = 1610 ESV = 1563 NASB2020 = 1576 NASB1971 = 1510 NIV = 1792			
The KJB1611 count includes possessive **Iesus** (+10 mentions, see appendix 8). That total would have been (1611 + 10) = 1621 mentions, but the missing 2 mentions occur where "**our Lord**" was misprinted as "**the Lord**" in 2 Thess 2:14 and 2 Pet 3:15. (Both updated circa 1638)			

Great is our Lord, and of great power: his understanding is infinite.
Psalm 147:5

There are 6 mentions of "our Lord" in the Old Testament, which makes the #7 mention in this search the first mention of the New Testament.

1. Nehemiah 8:10 **...for this day is holy unto our Lord...**
2. Nehemiah 10:29 **...commandments of the LORD our Lord...**
3. Psalm 8:1 **O LORD our Lord, how excellent is thy name...**
4. Psalm 8:9 **O LORD our Lord, how excellent is thy name...**
5. Psalm 135:5 **...and that our Lord is above all gods.**
6. Psalm 147:5 **Great is our Lord, and of great power...**
7. Matthew 1:1 **The book of the generation of Jesus Christ...**

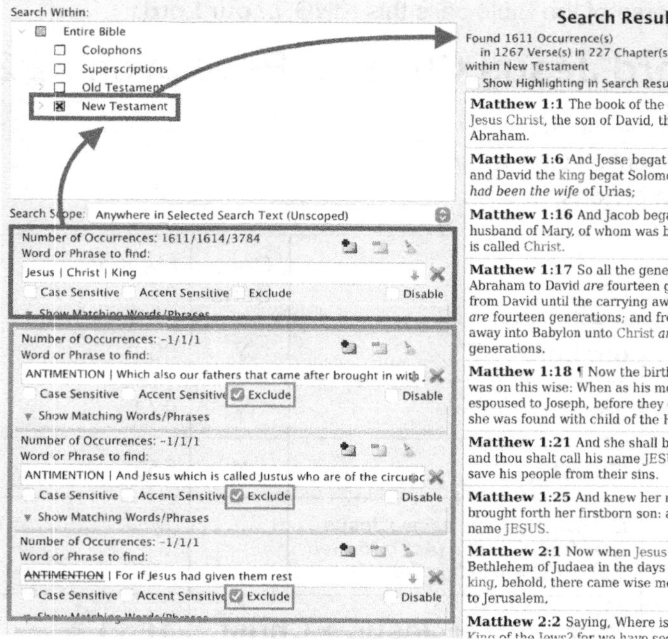
Search Within:
Entire Bible
Colophons
Superscriptions
Old Testament
New Testament
Search Scope: Anywhere in Selected Search Text (Unscoped)
Number of Occurrences: 1611/1614/3784
Word or Phrase to find:
Jesus | Christ | King
Case Sensitive Accent Sensitive Exclude Disable
Number of Occurrences: -1/1/1
Word or Phrase to find:
ANTIMENTION | Which also our fathers that came after brought in with
Case Sensitive Accent Sensitive Exclude Disable
Show Matching Words/Phrases
Number of Occurrences: -1/1/1
Word or Phrase to find:
ANTIMENTION | And Jesus which is called Justus who are of the circumc
Case Sensitive Accent Sensitive Exclude Disable
Show Matching Words/Phrases
Number of Occurrences: -1/1/1
Word or Phrase to find:
ANTIMENTION | For if Jesus had given them rest
Case Sensitive Accent Sensitive Exclude Disable
Search Results
Found 1611 Occurrence(s)
in 1267 Verse(s) in 227 Chapter(s) in 26 Book(s)
within New Testament
Show Highlighting in Search Results
Matthew 1:1 The book of the generation of Jesus Christ, the son of David, the son of Abraham.
Matthew 1:6 And Jesse begat David the king; and David the king begat Solomon of her *that had been the wife* of Urias;
Matthew 1:16 And Jacob begat Joseph the husband of Mary, of whom was born Jesus, who is called Christ.
Matthew 1:17 So all the generations from Abraham to David *are* fourteen generations; and from David until the carrying away into Babylon *are* fourteen generations; and from the carrying away into Babylon unto Christ *are* fourteen generations.
Matthew 1:18 ¶ Now the birth of Jesus Christ was on this wise: When as his mother Mary was espoused to Joseph, before they came together, she was found with child of the Holy Ghost.
Matthew 1:21 And she shall bring forth a son, and thou shalt call his name JESUS: for he shall save his people from their sins.
Matthew 1:25 And knew her not till she had brought forth her firstborn son: and he called his name JESUS.
Matthew 2:1 Now when Jesus was born in Bethlehem of Judaea in the days of Herod the king, behold, there came wise men from the east to Jerusalem,
Matthew 2:2 Saying, Where is he that is born

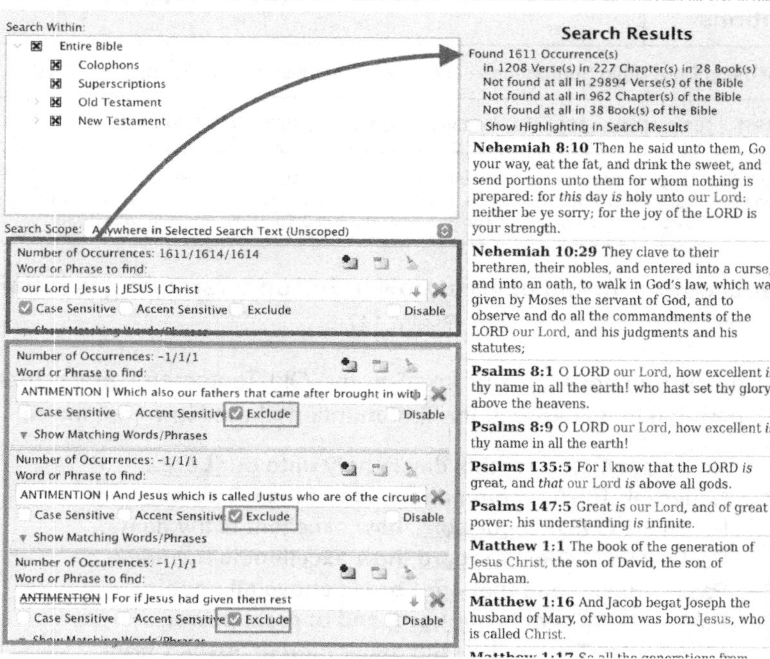
Search Within:
Entire Bible
Colophons
Superscriptions
Old Testament
New Testament
Search Scope: Anywhere in Selected Search Text (Unscoped)
Number of Occurrences: 1611/1614/1614
Word or Phrase to find:
our Lord | Jesus | JESUS | Christ
Case Sensitive Accent Sensitive Exclude Disable
Number of Occurrences: -1/1/1
Word or Phrase to find:
ANTIMENTION | Which also our fathers that came after brought in with
Case Sensitive Accent Sensitive Exclude Disable
Show Matching Words/Phrases
Number of Occurrences: -1/1/1
Word or Phrase to find:
ANTIMENTION | And Jesus which is called Justus who are of the circumc
Case Sensitive Accent Sensitive Exclude Disable
Show Matching Words/Phrases
Number of Occurrences: -1/1/1
Word or Phrase to find:
ANTIMENTION | For if Jesus had given them rest
Case Sensitive Accent Sensitive Exclude Disable
Search Results
Found 1611 Occurrence(s)
in 1208 Verse(s) in 227 Chapter(s) in 28 Book(s)
Not found at all in 29894 Verse(s) of the Bible
Not found at all in 962 Chapter(s) of the Bible
Not found at all in 38 Book(s) of the Bible
Show Highlighting in Search Results
Nehemiah 8:10 Then he said unto them, Go your way, eat the fat, and drink the sweet, and send portions unto them for whom nothing is prepared: for *this* day *is* holy unto our Lord: neither be ye sorry; for the joy of the LORD is your strength.
Nehemiah 10:29 They clave to their brethren, their nobles, and entered into a curse, and into an oath, to walk in God's law, which was given by Moses the servant of God, and to observe and do all the commandments of the LORD our Lord, and his judgments and his statutes;
Psalms 8:1 O LORD our Lord, how excellent *is* thy name in all the earth! who hast set thy glory above the heavens.
Psalms 8:9 O LORD our Lord, how excellent *is* thy name in all the earth!
Psalms 135:5 For I know that the LORD *is* great, and *that* our Lord *is* above all gods.
Psalms 147:5 Great *is* our Lord, and of great power: his understanding *is* infinite.
Matthew 1:1 The book of the generation of Jesus Christ, the son of David, the son of Abraham.
Matthew 1:16 And Jacob begat Joseph the husband of Mary, of whom was born Jesus, who is called Christ.

The 1611 Holy Bible is literally sealed with the name of our King.

#1611 mention of **LORD** *(Not case-sens)* **In the Bible**	**#1611** mention of **King + Jesus + Christ** **In the N.T.**	**#1611** mention of **our Lord + Jesus + Christ** **In the Bible**
And thou shalt rejoice before the LORD thy God... in the place which the LORD thy God hath chosen to place his name there. Deuteronomy **16:11**	**The grace of our Lord Jesus Christ be with you all. Amen.** Revelation 22:21 *The Last Verse of the Bible*	

And while we're touching on 1611, I feel compelled to add one more note concerning the other 2 persons of the Godhead.

Perhaps it's a coincidence, or perhaps it's not...

In the New Testament:

God (Capitalized) = 1349 mentions
Father (Capitalized, God) = 258 mentions
Holy Spirit = 4 mentions

(Father- excluding Father Abraham in Luke 16:24)
(Holy Spirit- is not case sensitive, but always refers to the Holy Ghost- the Spirit of God)

God + Father + Holy Spirit
= **1611** mentions in the N.T.

KJB1611 = 1560 NKJV = 1676 ESV = 1614 NASB2020 = 1640 NASB1971 = 1637 NIV = 1582

Jesus + Christ 777+777

Philippians 2:11 **And that every tongue should confess that Jesus Christ is Lord, to the glory of God the Father.**

The difference between a "mention" and an "**appearance**" is simple to grasp: A mention is a mention. An "**appearance**" is very similar, but could also be seen within another word. (E.g. "seven" **appears** in "sevenfold") "**Christ**" **appears** in "**Christ**ian" - and of course, a Christian is one who believes in Christ Jesus our Lord. A "Christian" would count as an **appearance** of Christ but not a mention. *Explained fully in Appendix 10.*

Appearances of **Jesus**			Appearances of **Christ**	
Jesus(')	983		**Christ('s)**	571
Exclude **other people named Jesus**, specifically **Joshua** (2x) (Acts 7:45, Hebrews 4:8) and **Justus** (1x) (Colossians 4:11)	-3		**Christ**ian(s)	3
Do not include "**Bar-jesus**"	0		Do not include "**antichrist(s)**" or "**false Christs**"	0
Appearances of **Jesus**	**980 = 7 × 140**		Appearances of **Christ**	**574 = 7 × 82**
980		**+**	**574**	
980 + 574 = 1554 **(777 + 777)** Total Appearances of **Jesus + Christ** in the KJB *Excluding Joshua / Justus. See Appendix 7*				
KJB1611 = 1554 NKJV = 1551 ESV = 1504 NASB2020 = 1522 NASB1971 = 1452 NIV = 1782				
KJB1611 = Iesus + Iesvs + Christ* (excl. false Christs & christal *[old spelling for crystal]*)				

There are no other *appearances* of Jesus or Christ in the entire Bible. And since 2 words are being used, both **Jesus** and **Christ** average out to 777 appearances each.

Average appearances: (**Jesus** (980) + **Christ** (574)) / 2 = 777

Even if you disregard direct appearances, and only look at **mentions**, you can simply take the name of **Jesus(')** and His title **Christ('s)** in both standard/possessive forms to find the exact same sum.

Search Filters: **Entire Bible**		Case Sens	Mentions
Search Phrase 1	**Jesus | Jesus'**	-	983
Search Phrase 2	**Christ | Christ's**	-	571
Total Mentions	**Jesus + Jesus' + Christ + Christ's**		**1554 = 777+777**
KJB1611 = 1554 NKJV = 1549 ESV = 1502 NASB2020 = 1520 NASB1971 = 1450 NIV = 1780			
KJB1611 = Iesus + Iesvs + Christ + Christs + Christes (excl. false Christs)			

This pattern doesn't omit Joshua nor Justus (who are named Jesus in Acts 7:45, Colossians 4,8 & Hebrews 4:8), but due to its simplicity, it stands with just as much authority on its own. After all, the name of Jesus is STILL the name above all names, and always points you to Jesus Christ (no matter who wears it as their name tag). It is yet another witness to establish the matter. No other modern versions have the same amount of Appearances vs Mentions in the last two charts. KJB Only.

The Name Above Every Name (in the King James Bible)	
Jesus* + Christ* *(by person / title)*	**777 + 777** appearances
Jesus(') + Christ('s) *(by name / title)*	**777 + 777** mentions

Jesus* + **Christ*** (by person / title) = **777 + 777** appearances

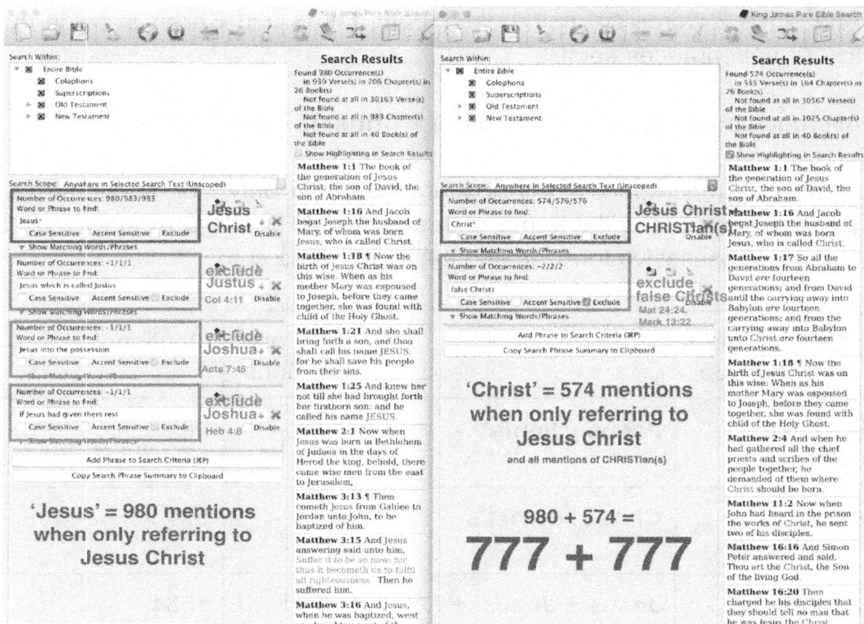
Search Results
Jesus
Christ
exclude
Justus
Col 4:11
exclude
Joshua
Acts 7:45
exclude
Joshua
Heb 4:8
'Jesus' = 980 mentions
when only referring to
Jesus Christ
Jesus Christ
CHRISTian(s)
exclude
false Christs
Mat 24:24
Mark 13:22
'Christ' = 574 mentions
when only referring to
Jesus Christ
and all mentions of CHRISTian(s)
980 + 574 =
777 + 777

Jesus(') + **Christ**('**s**) (by name / title) = **777 + 777** mentions

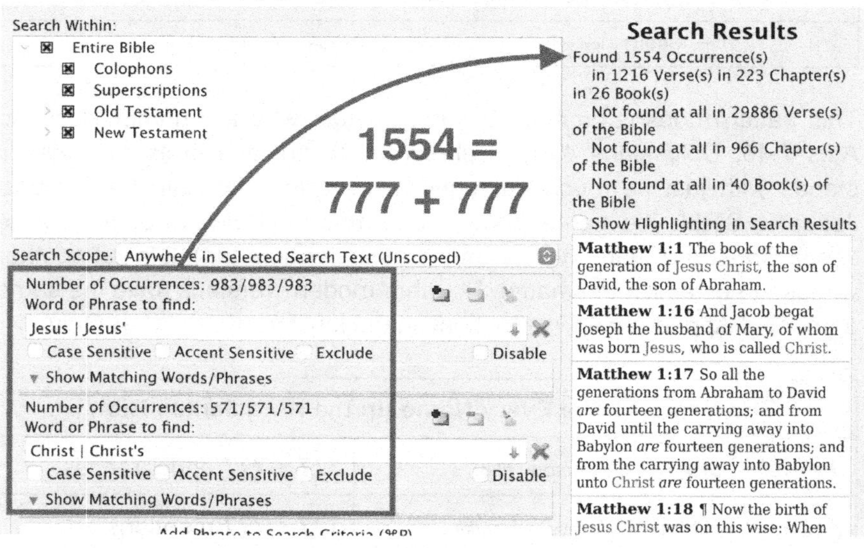
Search Within:
Entire Bible
Colophons
Superscriptions
Old Testament
New Testament
1554 =
777 + 777
Search Results
Found 1554 Occurrence(s)
in 1216 Verse(s) in 223 Chapter(s)
in 26 Book(s)
Not found at all in 29886 Verse(s)
of the Bible
Not found at all in 966 Chapter(s)
of the Bible
Not found at all in 40 Book(s) of
the Bible
Show Highlighting in Search Results
Search Scope: Anywhere in Selected Search Text (Unscoped)
Number of Occurrences: 983/983/983
Word or Phrase to find:
Jesus | Jesus'
Case Sensitive Accent Sensitive Exclude Disable
Show Matching Words/Phrases
Number of Occurrences: 571/571/571
Word or Phrase to find:
Christ | Christ's
Case Sensitive Accent Sensitive Exclude Disable
Show Matching Words/Phrases
Matthew 1:1 The book of the generation of Jesus Christ, the son of David, the son of Abraham.
Matthew 1:16 And Jacob begat Joseph the husband of Mary, of whom was born Jesus, who is called Christ.
Matthew 1:17 So all the generations from Abraham to David are fourteen generations; and from David until the carrying away into Babylon are fourteen generations; and from the carrying away into Babylon unto Christ are fourteen generations.
Matthew 1:18 ¶ Now the birth of Jesus Christ was on this wise: When

Moses + Jesus + Christ 7×7×7×7

The phrase "**man of God**" is mentioned **77** times in the verse text (excluding superscriptions) of the KJB.

The #1 of 77 mentions of "**man of God**" is referring to **Moses**, who is mentioned **77** times in the New Testament. (The first mention of **Moses** in the N.T. is the **#77** word of the chapter.)

<table>
<tr><td>First of 77 mentions
of "man of God"
is Moses</td><td rowspan="2">Moses = 77 mentions in the N.T.

The (#1 of 77) mention of Moses in the N.T. is the #77 word of the chapter (in Matthew 8)

Besides the 77 N.T. mentions, there are 770 appearances of Moses(') in the rest of the verse text (O.T.+N.T.)</td></tr>
<tr><td>And this is the blessing, wherewith Moses the <u>man of God</u> blessed the children of Israel before his death.
Deuteronomy 33:1</td></tr>
</table>

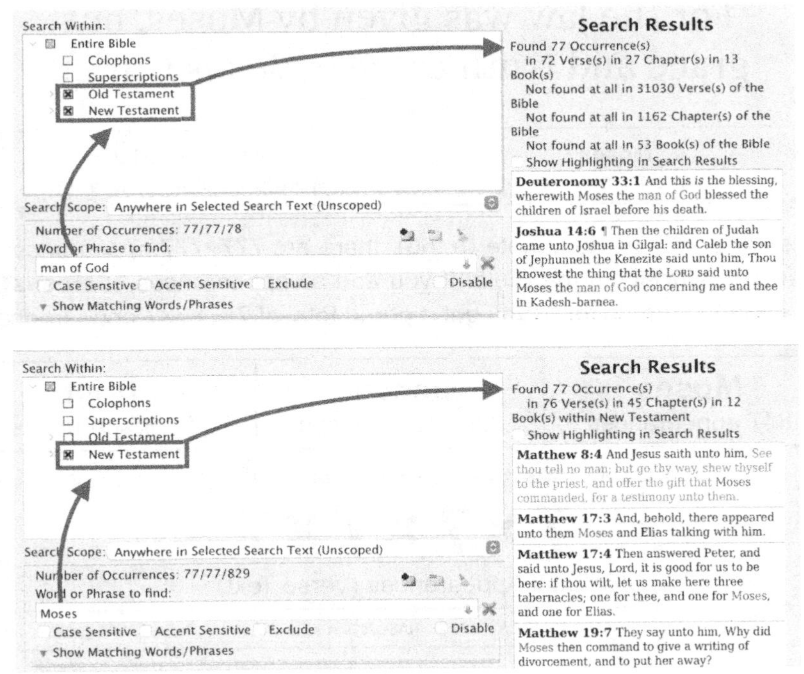

The last (#**77**) mention of "**man of God**" is about the "**perfect**" (#**7** is the number of perfection/completion) **man of God** whose life is fully revolved around the scriptures:

#**77** mention (last) of "**man of God**"
All scripture is given by inspiration of God, and is profitable for doctrine, for reproof, for correction, for instruction in righteousness: That the <u>man of God</u> may be perfect, throughly furnished unto all good works. 2 Timothy 3:16-17

The #**777** mention of **Moses** the **man of God,** is in John 1:17, which gives us the 30,000-foot view of all the scriptures.

#**777** mention of **Moses** The 30,000-foot view of all the scriptures	
For the law was given by Moses, but grace and truth came by Jesus Christ. John 1:17	
Moses word #7 of verse	**Jesus Christ** word/phrase #7+7 of verse

As seen in the previous note (p. 66), there are **777+777** appearances of **Jesus*** + **Christ*** in the Bible. If you add all appearances of **Moses*** to the equation (verse text), you get a grand total of 7×7×7×7 appearances.

Moses 847 appearances	**Jesus** 980 appearances	**Christ** 574 appearances
Moses + **Jesus** + **Christ** = 2401 = **7×7×7×7** Total Appearances (Verse Text)		
KJB1611 = 2401 NKJV = 2401 ESV = 2355 NASB2020 = 2375 NASB1971 = 2302 NIV = 2628		

And on top of all that, **<u>Moses</u>** <u>in John 1:17</u> is not only the **#777** mention of **Moses**, it is also the exact <u>middle</u> appearance (#1201 out of 2401) of the total search: **Moses + Jesus + Christ** in the entire Bible.

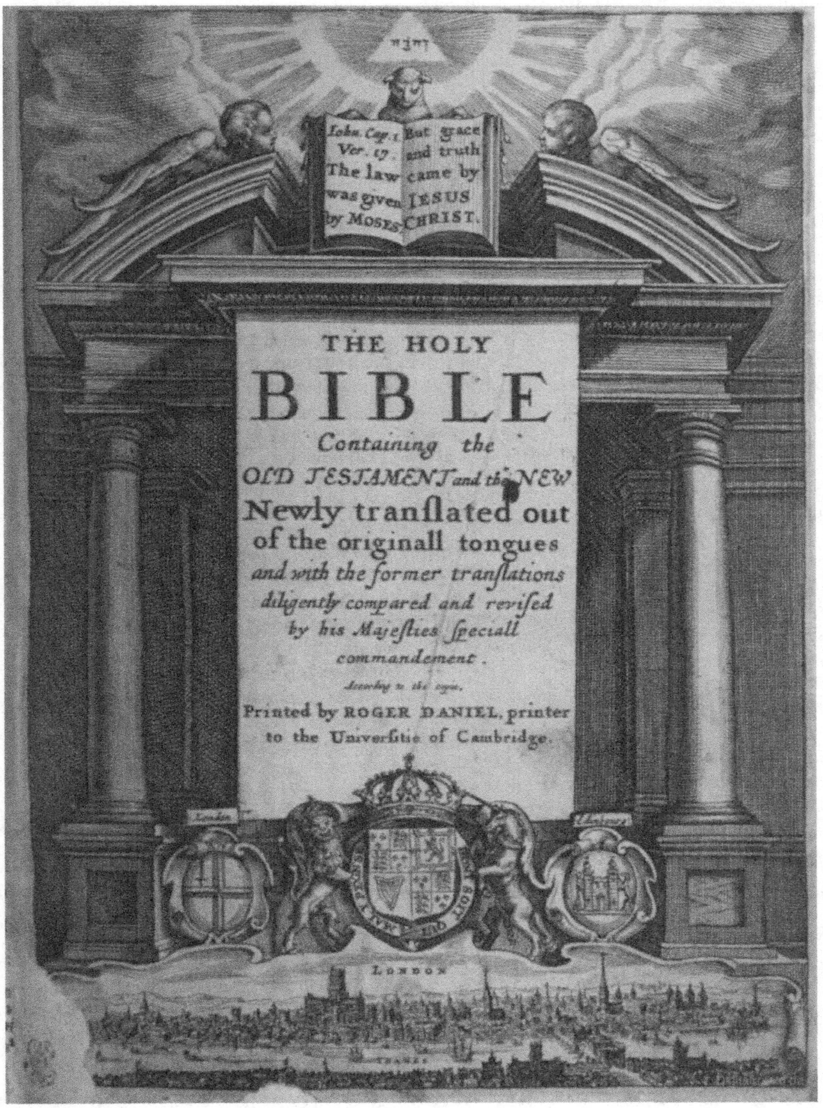

John. Cap. 1. Ver. 17. The law was given by Moses. But grace and truth came by IESUS CHRIST.

THE HOLY BIBLE

Containing the OLD TESTAMENT and the NEW

Newly tranſlated out of the originall tongues and with the former tranſlations diligently compared and reviſed by his Majeſties ſpeciall commandement.

Printed by ROGER DANIEL, printer to the Univerſitie of Cambridge.

LONDON

The title page of a 1645 King James Bible printed at Cambridge with John 1:17 featured at the top of the illustration, representing the entire Bible.

The Word was Made Flesh (70+70)×7

With 777+777 appearances of **Jesus** and **Christ** (see previous note), it would seem absurd to think there would also be a perfectly sevened count of the name of **Jesus(')** by itself. *Absurd by random chance at least.* But we are not dealing with the words of men.

In the King James Bible, **Jesus(')** is mentioned 980 times. This was seen in the last note as well, but let's take a deeper look at this number.

980 = 7 × 140
= 7 × (70 +70)

980 = 14 × 70
= (7+7) × 70

980 = 490 × 2
= (70 × 7) + (70 × 7)

Note: "Bar-jesus" in Acts 13:6 is excluded by default in Pure Bible Search.

"Case Sensitive" looks at letter capitalization. You could also simply type in **Jesus*** with the asterisk (without Case-Sensitive). The asterisk counts both Jesus and Jesus'

"Exclude" removes the specific "Jesus" found in that phrase from the total count

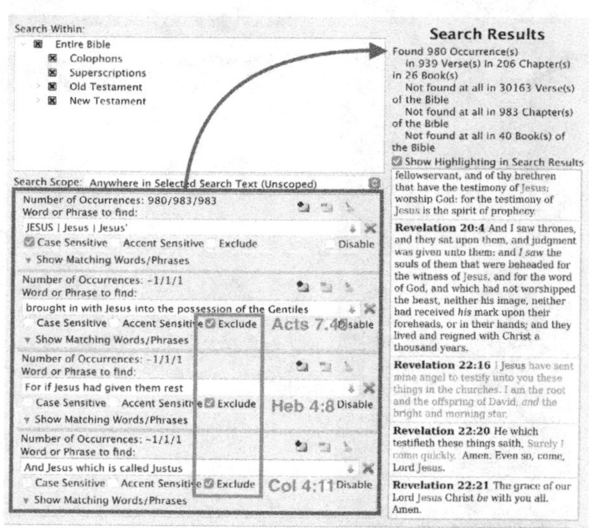

But one of the most amazing things of all is the exact number of words in Genesis 1 and Malachi 4, the first and the last chapters of the Old Testament. Remember, Jesus entered the world as the Word, to abolish <u>in his flesh</u> the law of commandments contained in ordinances.

And the Word was made flesh, and dwelt among us... John 1:14

Having abolished in his flesh the enmity, even the law of commandments contained in ordinances... Ephesians 2:15

...Fear not; I am the first and the last: Revelation 1:17

You could literally write the name of **Jesus** over top of every word in the first and last chapters of the Old Testament, and perfectly fulfill every appearance of **Jesus** in the Bible.

Genesis 1 contains: 31 Verse(s) 797 Word(s)	Malachi 4 contains: 6 Verse(s) 183 Word(s)

KJB	Total Words
Genesis 1 (the first chapter of the O.T.)	797
Malachi 4 (the last chapter of the O.T.)	183
First + Last Chapters of the **Old Testament**	980 = 490+490 **= (70+70) × 7**
KJB1611 = 980 NKJV = 968 ESV = 965 NASB2020 = 958 NASB1971 = 958 NIV = 923	

KJB	Total Mentions
Jesus	973
Jesus'	10
Subtract other people named Jesus, specifically Joshua (2x) (Acts 7:45, Hebrews 4:8) and Justus (1x) (Colossians 4:11)	-3
Total Mentions of **Jesus(')**	980 = 490+490 **= (70+70) × 7**
KJB1611 = 980 NKJV = 979 ESV = 967 NASB2020 = 995 NASB1971 = 917 NIV = 1298	

Note for the KJB1611: **Jesus** is spelled as **Iesus** or **Iesvs**

Jesus saith unto him, I say not unto thee, Until seven times: but, Until seventy times seven.

Matthew 18:22

Jesus 70×7 in Even and Odd Books

A just weight and balance are the LORD'S: all the weights of the bag are his work. Proverbs 16:11

Mentions of <u>Jesus(')</u> in the Bible *Only referring to Jesus Christ- Excluding all antimentions. See appendix 7.*			
ODD books of the New Testament		**EVEN** books of the New Testament	
Book	Mentions of **Jesus(')**	Book	Mentions of **Jesus(')**
Matthew	172	**Mark**	97
Luke	100	**John**	256
Acts	66	**Romans**	38
1 Corinthians	27	**2 Corinthians**	20
Galatians	17	**Ephesians**	21
Philippians	22	**Colossians**	7
1 Thessalonians	17	**2 Thessalonians**	12
1 Timothy	14	**2 Timothy**	14
Titus	4	**Philemon**	7
Hebrews	14	**James**	2
1 Peter	11	**2 Peter**	9
1 John	12	**2 John**	2
3 John	0	**Jude**	5
Revelation	14		
Total mentions of **Jesus(')** = 490 **= 70 × 7** **in ODD N.T. books**		Total mentions of **Jesus(')** = 490 **= 70 × 7** **in EVEN N.T. books**	
Total mentions of **Jesus(')=(70 + 70) × 7**			

Exactly 7 books mention **Jesus(')** in multiples of 7, starting with Ephesians (Book #7×7 of the Bible)

1) Ephesians 2) Colossians 3) 1 Timothy 4) 2 Timothy 5) Philemon 6) Hebrews 7) Revelation

Jesus(') in the ODD books of the N.T. = 70×7 mentions
Jesus(') in the EVEN books of the N.T. = 70×7 mentions
Jesus(') in the New Testament (and Entire Bible) = (70+70)×7 mentions

How does such a thing happen?

Let's put this into better perspective to see how unlikely this is:

	ODD books of the N.T.	**EVEN** books of the N.T.	Difference / Spread
Total Chapters	166	94	-72
Total Verses	5098	2859	-2239
Total Words	117,753	62,629	-55,124
Total Mentions of **Jesus(')**	**70×7**	**70×7**	—

Despite the fact that ODD books of the New Testament outnumber EVEN books by 55,124 words, the total word count of **Jesus** remains perfectly divided into **seventy times seven**, which of course is the exact mathematical equation that Jesus Himself spoke in Matthew 18:22.

This is unprecedented. If you make a list of all the words in the New Testament, sorted by number of mentions, this EVEN/ODD balance doesn't occur with any other largely mentioned word in the New Testament. And I'm not talking about a perfectly "sevened" balance of 70×7 (or similar). What I'm saying is... there isn't any balance at all. No other heavily mentioned word (280+ unique words) is balanced between EVEN and ODD books. In fact, the threshold is **Moses** (mentioned 77 times in the N.T.). After **Moses**, the word "**can**" is mentioned 38 times in both ODD and EVEN books (total of 76 mentions). No other word from

Moses (77 mentions) and upward, does this miracle occur except for the name of **Jesus**. Is this all just a random accident? You be the judge.

Then came Peter to him, and said, Lord, how oft shall my brother sin against me, and I forgive him? till seven times?
Jesus saith unto him, I say not unto thee, Until seven times: but, Until seventy times seven.
Matthew 18:21-22

Here are all the most-mentioned words in the New Testament, to get a better idea of how unlikely all of this is.

Word mentions in ODD and EVEN Books of the New Testament (KJB)

Word	Mentions (ODD Books)	Mentions (EVEN Books)	Total N.T. Mentions
the	7349	3650	10999
and	7522	3206	10728
of	4064	2044	6108
that	2292	1470	3762
to	2267	1097	3364
he	1960	1111	3071
in	1813	1087	2900
him	1495	972	2467
unto	1562	889	2451
for	1436	845	2281
I	1272	913	2185
is	1328	842	2170
not	1202	861	2063
they	1325	640	1965
a	1363	548	1911
be	1114	603	1717
them	1141	558	1699
but	1012	658	1670
ye	931	628	1559
which	1081	473	1554

Word	Mentions (ODD Books)	Mentions (EVEN Books)	Total N.T. Mentions
his	941	496	1437
shall	941	474	1415
with	908	461	1369
was	958	400	1358
God	860	494	1354
it	839	440	1279
you	719	522	1241
all	779	351	1130
have	662	422	1084
said	676	385	1061
as	685	355	1040
Jesus(')	490 **= 70 × 7**	490 **= 70 × 7**	980 **= (70+70) × 7**
when	692	281	973
are	621	342	963
we	514	355	869
man	535	334	869
thou	526	331	857
me	444	399	843
by	491	327	818
this	527	290	817
were	587	197	784
from	487	259	746
things	477	251	728
Lord	452	259	711
into	437	207	644
had	441	202	643
my	337	282	619
one	395	212	607
if	362	240	602
also	352	247	599

Word	Mentions (ODD Books)	Mentions (EVEN Books)	Total N.T. Mentions
then	369	219	588
come	385	202	587
on	388	186	574
there	388	179	567
hath	332	225	557
Christ	291	264	555
will	354	201	555
out	357	151	508
came	369	137	506
us	311	176	487
their	345	141	486
thee	332	151	483
no	285	185	470
your	258	197	455
saying	357	98	455
say	278	150	428
son	300	122	422
do	244	172	416
thy	297	119	416
up	276	133	409
what	236	172	408
now	225	182	407
these	267	125	392
at	268	123	391
men	295	91	386
who	223	155	378
so	243	132	375
our	208	158	366
should	218	148	366
therefore	194	162	356
father	159	193	352
let	241	101	342
went	232	106	338

Word	Mentions (ODD Books)	Mentions (EVEN Books)	Total N.T. Mentions
or	219	105	324
day	209	107	316
an	228	86	314
saith	119	188	307
whom	173	133	306
her	216	88	304
because	175	126	301
know	169	130	299
after	199	97	296
before	212	82	294
made	177	109	286
many	177	109	286
may	148	136	284
any	173	111	284
every	196	84	280
even	161	114	275
am	136	127	263
upon	196	66	262
spirit	156	105	261
heaven	203	52	255
great	201	53	254
go	170	82	252
good	170	78	248
heard	171	77	248
faith	147	98	245
disciples	132	110	242
world	116	125	241
might	116	123	239
down	168	65	233
brethren	168	63	231
people	176	55	231

Word	Mentions (ODD Books)	Mentions (EVEN Books)	Total N.T. Mentions
called	170	59	229
again	120	107	227
how	142	85	227
more	142	84	226
law	118	105	223
behold	172	50	222
saw	159	62	221
neither	162	58	220
another	140	74	214
away	128	83	211
against	146	64	210
see	139	69	208
own	125	81	206
word	134	72	206
house	157	49	206
among	126	79	205
himself	122	82	204
answered	96	107	203
give	134	65	199
sent	112	85	197
yet	105	90	195
earth	158	34	192
did	110	81	191
being	116	74	190
dead	109	78	187
life	99	87	186
forth	122	62	184
would	120	62	182
holy	134	47	181
through	94	85	179
love	94	85	179
she	115	64	179
glory	92	85	177

Word	Mentions (ODD Books)	Mentions (EVEN Books)	Total N.T. Mentions
same	108	66	174
name	124	49	173
time	115	56	171
Jews	95	74	169
first	117	50	167
cast	119	48	167
days	132	34	166
took	119	45	164
given	91	72	163
speak	99	62	161
take	103	58	161
about	106	55	161
Peter	106	52	158
hand	114	44	158
kingdom	123	35	158
put	96	61	157
children	110	47	157
Paul	141	16	157
having	98	57	155
city	134	20	154
power	97	55	152
those	107	44	151
other	98	52	150
flesh	69	80	149
some	93	55	148
written	87	59	146
make	94	52	146
without	85	60	145
hear	104	41	145
Jerusalem	116	28	144
hast	91	52	143

Word	Mentions (ODD Books)	Mentions (EVEN Books)	Total N.T. Mentions
done	100	41	141
than	98	41	139
two	105	34	139
death	82	56	138
where	76	61	137
way	84	53	137
together	94	43	137
spake	92	44	136
certain	118	18	136
body	83	52	135
eat	86	49	135
gave	92	42	134
nor	96	38	134
brought	107	27	134
art	83	50	133
evil	77	55	132
grace	56	75	131
John	86	45	131
much	81	49	130
receive	73	55	128
received	90	38	128
according	61	66	127
believe	46	78	124
verily	56	68	124
cometh	55	68	123
over	86	36	122
thing	71	48	119
voice	95	24	119
truth	46	72	118
pass	99	19	118
works	66	51	117
temple	87	30	117
found	91	26	117

Word	Mentions (ODD Books)	Mentions (EVEN Books)	Total N.T. Mentions
brother	69	46	115
nothing	71	44	115
sin	42	70	112
been	71	41	112
peace	60	51	111
chief	83	28	111
whosoever	77	33	110
hands	72	35	107
both	76	31	107
shalt	78	29	107
woman	74	32	106
heart	64	41	105
place	65	40	105
themselves	51	53	104
wherefore	71	33	104
why	61	41	102
gospel	61	40	101
blood	84	17	101
seen	63	36	99
Gentiles	63	36	99
while	67	32	99
only	55	43	98
sea	64	34	98
ghost	77	21	98
righteousness	36	61	97
words	59	38	97
angel	94	3	97
sat	68	28	96
light	54	41	95
believed	49	45	94
like	75	19	94

Word	Mentions (ODD Books)	Mentions (EVEN Books)	Total N.T. Mentions
such	54	39	93
whole	58	35	93
spoken	57	34	91
stood	65	26	91
seven	81	10	91
known	46	44	90
lest	55	35	90
hour	59	30	89
multitude	67	22	89
prophets	71	18	89
ever	61	27	88
under	66	21	87
mother	54	32	86
Pharisees	54	32	86
king	58	28	86
sins	58	28	86
laid	59	26	85
blessed	66	19	85
departed	71	14	85
though	47	37	84
bring	56	28	84
high	56	28	84
tell	57	27	84
servant	60	24	84
set	62	22	84
fear	65	19	84
wife	67	17	84
fell	69	15	84
little	55	28	83
priests	57	26	83
fire	60	23	83
must	60	23	83
yourselves	53	28	81

Word	Mentions (ODD Books)	Mentions (EVEN Books)	Total N.T. Mentions
angels	68	13	81
bread	43	37	80
church	58	22	80
whose	53	25	78
feet	56	22	78
thine	57	21	78
Moses	**48**	**29**	**77**
can	38	38	76

Notice how **Moses** (77 mentions) is the threshold by which the anomaly happens again. **For the law was given by Moses, but grace and truth came by Jesus Christ.** John 1:17

This miraculous division of 70×7 mentions in both ODD/EVEN books only happens in the King James Bible.

70×7 Mentions in ODD/EVEN Books - Bible Version Comparison:

Total mentions of **Jesus(')** *(in Odd and Even books)* *Excluding Joshua (if named Jesus in Acts 7:45/Heb 4:8) and Justus (in Col 4:11)*				
KJB **ODD: 490** **= 70×7** **EVEN: 490** **= 70×7**	NKJV ODD: 491 EVEN: 488	ESV ODD: 482 EVEN: 485	NASB2020 ODD: 512 EVEN: 483	NIV ODD: 683 EVEN: 615
KJB1611 ODD: 490 EVEN: 490			NASB1971 ODD: 458 EVEN: 459	

Modern versions don't produce this miracle. But even if they did, most versions do not mention 70×7 in Matthew 18:22, unless you count footnotes as God's word…

Matthew 18:22				
KJB **70×7**				
...Until seventy times seven. Mat 18:22 KJB				
NKJV 70×7	ESV 77	NASB1971 70×7	NASB2020 77	NIV 77
...up to seventy times seven. Mat 18:22 NKJV	**...but seventy-seven times.** Mat 18:22 ESV	**...up to seventy times seven.** Mat 18:22 NASB1971	**...up to seventy-seven times.** Mat 18:22 NAB2020	**...but seventy-seven times.** Mat 18:22 NIV

Most Christians do not realize how different modern versions really are from the KJB. For an in-depth comparison, see Appendices 4, 5 and 6.

Since I have a lot of extra space left on this page, here is a small sample of Appendix 4, which can be found on p. 479.

KJB	Modern	*Corrupted in*	Notes
1 Samuel 13:1 KJB **Saul reigned one year; and when he had reigned two years over Israel,**	1 Samuel 13:1 ESV **Saul lived for one year and then became king, and when he had reigned for two years over Israel,** 1 Samuel 13:1 NASB2020 **Saul was thirty years old when he began to reign, and he reigned for forty-two years over Israel.** 1 Samuel 13:1 NRSV **Saul was ... years old when he began to reign, and he reigned ... and two years over Israel.** 1 Samuel 13:1 GNT *Omitted*	ESV NASB1995 NASB2020 NIV NLT CSB HCSB AMP NET NRSV MEV CEB GNT ISV	The ESV makes a pretty stunning claim- that Saul was a 1 year old baby when he became king over Israel. Can you imagine a 1 year old who **from his shoulders and upward he was higher than any of the people**...? (1 Sam 9:2 KJB) The NASB and many other modern translations have way different numbers and meanings. The NRSV literally has dots instead of words/numbers. The GNT completely omits the verse.
Matthew 7:14 KJB **Because strait is the gate, and narrow is the way, which leadeth unto life, and few there be that find it.**	Matthew 7:14 NKJV **Because narrow is the gate and difficult is the way which leads to life, and there are few who find it.**	NKJV ESV NLT CSB HCSB AMP NET NRSV CEB GNT	The way is not difficult. The way is Jesus Christ. **I am the way, the truth, and the life: no man cometh unto the Father, but by me.** John 14:6

Father & Son 7×7×7, in the Gospels

Then answered Jesus and said unto them, Verily, verily, I say unto you, The Son can do nothing of himself, but what he seeth the Father do: for what things soever he doeth, these also doeth the Son likewise. John 5:19

In the 4 gospels, a general search of **Father + Son** (both capitalized) will yield a result of 77 chapters.

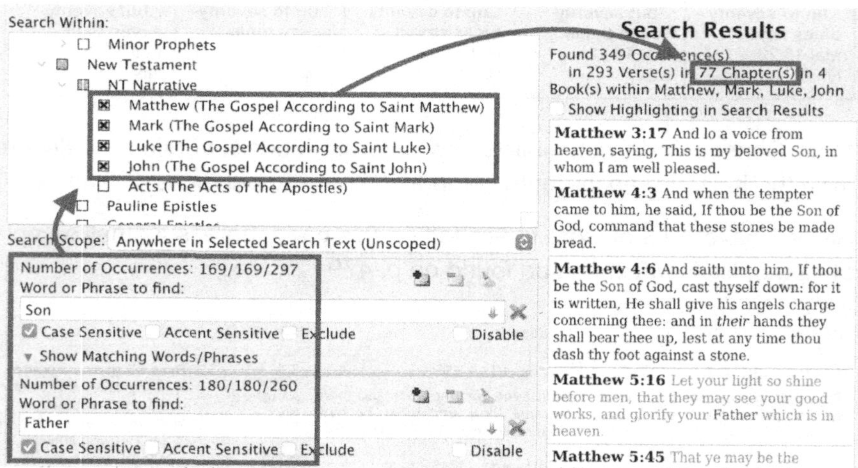

But thou shalt see greater things than these.

The more carefully you look, the more perfection you will see.

Ask, and it shall be given you; seek, and ye shall find; knock, and it shall be opened unto you; Matthew 7:7

The careful student realizes that not all mentions of **Son** and **Father** in the gospels are referring to Jesus Christ or God the Father. So what does this student do? He goes and finds them, and removes them from the count.

Here are all the capitalized mentions of **Father** and **Son** that are <u>not</u> referring to God or Jesus:

<u>Not</u> God the Father	**<u>Not</u>** Jesus the Son
And he cried and said, <u>Father</u> Abraham, have mercy on me, and send Lazarus, that he may dip the tip of his finger in water, and cool my tongue; for I am tormented in this flame. Luke 16:24	**... Jesus seeing their faith said unto the sick of the palsy; <u>Son</u>, be of good cheer...** Matthew 9:2
A total of 1 antimention of **<u>Father</u>** in the gospels (**<u>not</u>** referring to God the Father) Total antimentions = 1	**...A certain man had two sons; and he came to the first, and said, <u>Son</u>, go work to day in my vineyard. He answered and said, I will not...** Matthew 21:28-29
	When Jesus saw their faith, he said unto the sick of the palsy, <u>Son</u>, thy sins be forgiven thee. Mark 2:5
	And he said unto him, <u>Son</u>, thou art ever with me, and all that I have is thine. It was meet that we should make merry, and be glad: for this thy brother was dead, and is alive again; and was lost, and is found. Luke 15:31-32
	But Abraham said, <u>Son</u>, remember that thou in thy lifetime receivedst thy good things, and likewise Lazarus evil things: but now he is comforted, and thou art tormented. Luke 16:25
	A total of 5 antimentions of **<u>Son</u>** in the gospels (**<u>not</u>** referring to Jesus Christ) Total antimentions = 5
Mentions that are NOT referring to God / Jesus Total mentions to exclude = 6	

There are 6 "antimentions" of **Father** and **Son** (not referring to God / Jesus Christ). Let's <u>exclude</u> them from the search, and see what happens...

Father (180-1=**179**) + **Son** (169-5=**164**) in the gospels = **7×7×7** mentions

Search Filters: **Matthew, Mark, Luke, John**		Case Sens	Mentions
Search Phrase 1	**Father**	Y	180
Search Phrase 2	**Son**	Y	169
Exclude	*Exclude all antimentions (those that do not refer to God / Jesus.)*	-	-6
Total Mentions	**Father + Son** (Capitalized, in the 4 gospels, only referring to God the Father and his Son Jesus Christ)		343 **=7×7×7**

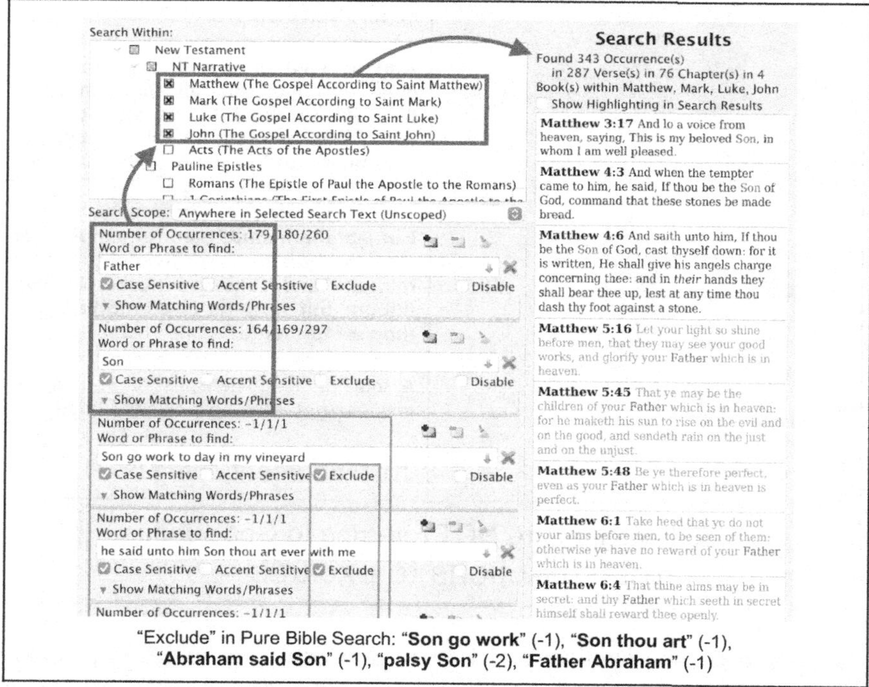

"Exclude" in Pure Bible Search: "**Son go work**" (-1), "**Son thou art**" (-1), "**Abraham said Son**" (-1), "**palsy Son**" (-2), "**Father Abraham**" (-1)

This pattern very well could be the final seal of God on the settled text of the KJB. **Son of David** was lowercase (**son of David)** in Mat 21:9,15, 22:42 from 1611 until ~1873. Today, all King James Bibles (Cambridge / Oxford / PCE) capitalize **Son** in these verses.

Father + Son in the Gospels - **Bible Version Comparison:**

Total mentions of: **Father + Son** *(Capitalized, in the 4 gospels, excluding antimentions, that is, only referring to God the Father and his Son Jesus Christ)*				
KJB 343 = **7×7×7**	NKJV 354	ESV 337	NASB2020 342	NIV 317
KJB1611 230 †			NASB1971 342	
† Capitalization was not standardized in the KJB1611, which throws off case-sensitive counts by a lot				

After excluding the 5 mentions of **Son** that are not Jesus Christ, the original total of 169 becomes 164 mentions of **Son** in the gospels.

Son (capitalized) = **164** mentions in the gospels, when referring to Jesus
Salvation = **164** mentions in the entire Bible

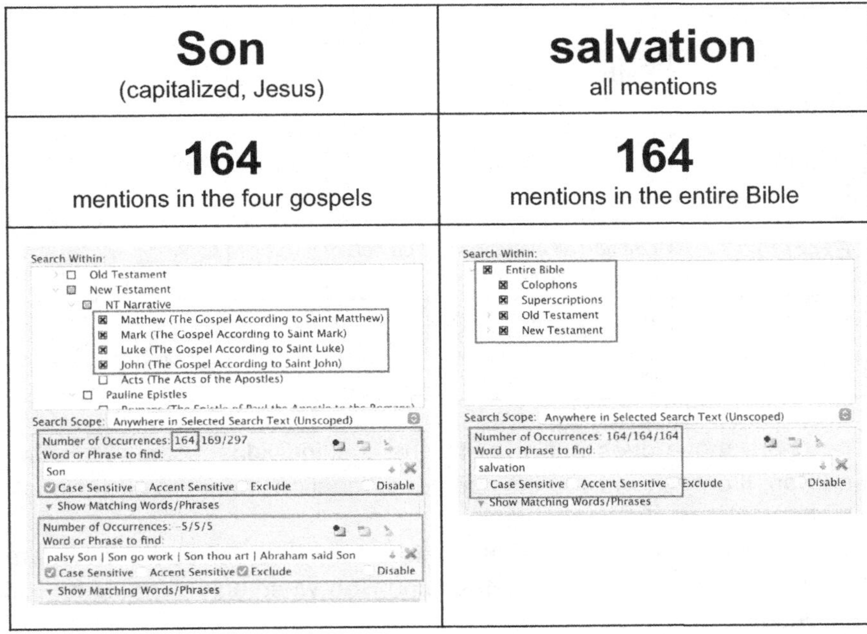

Son (capitalized, Jesus)	**salvation** all mentions
164 mentions in the four gospels	**164** mentions in the entire Bible

Father & Son 70×7, in the Entire Bible

And we have seen and do testify that the Father sent the Son to be the Saviour of the world. 1 John 4:14

If you haven't read the previous note, you may want to go back and do so now (*7×7×7 Father & Son, in the Gospels*).

Here is the recap: In the four gospels, **Father** and **Son** (both capitalized) combined are mentioned exactly **7×7×7** times. That is only possible by omitting the mentions of *Father* and *Son* that are not directly referring to **God the Father** and his only begotten **Son, Jesus Christ**. (Located in Matthew 9:2, 21:28, Mark 2:5, Luke 15:31, 16:24,25)

If we apply this exact same search scope to the entire Bible, we get exactly **70×7** mentions of **Father** and **Son.**

Search Filters: **Entire Bible**		Case Sens	Mentions
Search Phrase 1	**Father**	Y	260
Search Phrase 2	**Son**	Y	297
Exclude	*Exclude all mentions that do not refer to God / Jesus.*	-	-67
Total Mentions	**Father + Son** (Capitalized, only referring to God the Father and his Son Jesus Christ)		490 **=70×7**

The chart above does not give you the final individual counts of Father and Son. It only shows you the number of mentions after the exclusions.

But the individual counts are also miraculous in themselves. What are the final individual counts of **Father** and **Son** when only referring to God and Jesus?

Final Counts of **Father** and **Son** in the Bible *Excluding antimentions (Not-God, Not-Jesus)*		
Father	**Son**	Total
260 mentions (-1) antimention	297 mentions (-66) antimentions	557 mentions (-67) antimentions
259= **7×37** mentions of **Father** (God) in the KJB	231= **7×33** mentions of **Son** (Jesus) in the KJB	490= **70×7** mentions
= 777÷3	**= 77+77+77**	

Jesus saith unto him, I say not unto thee, Until seven times: but, Until seventy times seven. Matthew 18:22

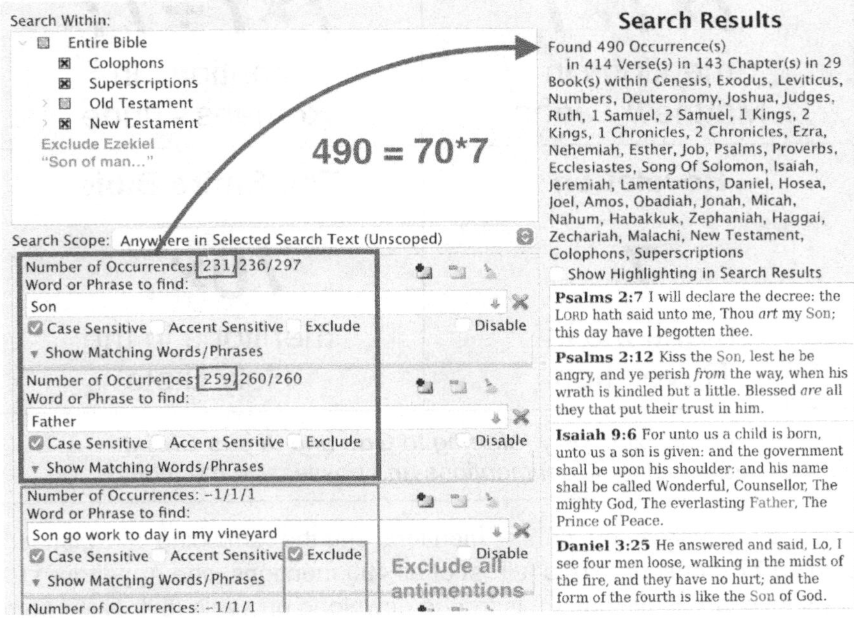

All antimentions outside of the gospels are located in the book of Ezekiel, where "**Son of man...**" (referring to Ezekiel) is mentioned 61 times.

If you exclude Ezekiel from the search filters, and also exclude all 6 of the antimentions in the gospels (found in Matthew 9:2, 21:28, Mark 2:5, Luke 15:31, 16:24,25), you will be left with all of the proper, Capitalized, non-possessive mentions of **Father** (God) and **Son** (Jesus).

Father and **Son**, combined, are mentioned a total of **70×7** times in the Bible and **7×7×7** times in the Gospels. In the first 7 Epistles (Rom-Col), **Father** + **Son** = 7×7 mentions, and in the remaining 14 Epistles (1Thess-Jude), 77 mentions. In Revelation, **Father** + **Son** = 7 mentions.

Father + Son in the King James Bible	
The Gospels	**The Epistles**
7×7×7 mentions in Matthew - John	**7×7+77** mentions in Romans - Jude
Revelation	**The Entire Bible**
7 mentions in Revelation	**70×7** mentions in the Holy Bible
*Capitalized, only referring to **God** and **Jesus Christ**.* *(Excluding all antimentions and possessive mentions)*	

The first 7 Epistles contain 7×7 mentions and the remaining 14 Epistles contain 77 mentions. For a full list of all 490 mentions, see Appendix 11. A visual chart of this pattern is free to download on sealedbytheking.com.

The perfect fine-tuning of the KJB! See Hebrews 3:6 where " **son** " (talking about Jesus) is *not capitalized!* In fact, **son** (in Heb 3:6) *was* capitalized in the KJB up until circa 1769, when it went lowercase.

For with God nothing shall be impossible.

Luke 1:37

Jesus Christ T7×7

Jesus saith unto them, Did ye never read in the scriptures, The stone which the builders rejected, the same is become the head of the corner: this is the Lord's doing, and it is marvellous in our eyes? Matthew 21:42

The **head of the corner.**

There are **196** mentions of "**Jesus Christ**" in the Holy Bible.

196 = 7 + 14 + 21 + 28 + 35 + 42 + 49

7

7 + 7

7 + 7 + 7

7 + 7 + 7 + 7

7 + 7 + 7 + 7 + 7

7 + 7 + 7 + 7 + 7 + 7

7 + 7 + 7 + 7 + 7 + 7 + 7

T7 of 7s. 7 Rows, 7-Base Total sum of 7's **= 196**
Jesus Christ Total mentions **= 196 = T7×7**
KJB1611 = 197 NKJV = 184 ESV = 139 NASB2020 = 130 NASB1971 = 137 NIV = 132

196 has a strong connection to the number 7 in just about every way you look at it..

196 = 49 + 49 + 49 + 49
196 = 14 × 14
196 = 7 × 28

If you're using software other than King James Pure Bible Search, a count of 198 may appear. That's because there are two mentions of Jesus Christ's (possessive). There are patterns associated with the possessive form as well. See p. 190.

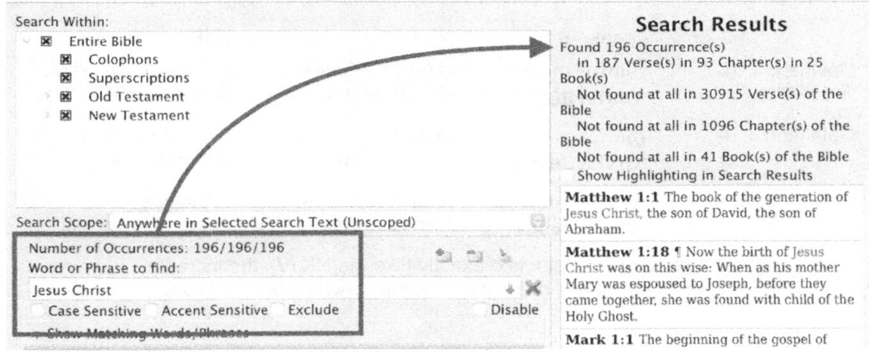

The KJB1611 had 1 extra mention of **Jesus Christ** in Romans 3:24, which would be changed to **Christ Jesus** circa 1769.

When translating from the Greek, the King James translators were moved to switch around **Christ Jesus** and **Jesus Christ** multiple times- where it read "**Christ Jesus**" in Greek, but they translated it as **Jesus Christ** in English.

Galatians 2:16 - **Christ Jesus** Greek > **Jesus Christ** English *(2nd mention in verse)*
Galatians 3:14 - **Christ Jesus** Greek > **Jesus Christ** English
Galatians 5:6 - **Christ Jesus** Greek > **Jesus Christ** English

The instance in Romans 3:24 was eventually reversed back to the way it stands in the Greek, while the flipped instances in Galatians were kept as they are.

It just so happened to settle with a perfect count of 196.

Scholarship demands consistency, and without a doubt, the King James translators were among the finest scholars in the history of Bible translation. But what thing is this? What intention did they have? And why was just one of these bizarre instances updated in 1769 to match the Greek, while the others stayed put - such as those in Galatians?

This is why these miracles we find so abundantly in the KJB cannot be attributed to scholarship or **the understanding of the prudent**. They cannot be traced to any particular scribes, nor are they grounded in human logic. The **wisdom of the wise** is found in the NKJV, which translates **Christ Jesus** in the order of which it reads in Greek.

	Greek	NKJV	**KJB**
Galatians 2:16 *(2nd instance)*	χριστον ιησουν **"Christ Jesus"**	*(Matches Greek)* **Christ Jesus**	*(Deviates from Greek)* **Jesus Christ**
Galatians 3:14	χριστω ιησου **"Christ Jesus"**	*(Matches Greek)* **Christ Jesus**	*(Deviates from Greek)* **Jesus Christ**
Galatians 5:6	χριστω ιησου **"Christ Jesus"**	*(Matches Greek)* **Christ Jesus**	*(Deviates from Greek)* **Jesus Christ**
If the KJB followed the Greek text exactly (like the NKJV), the incredible numeric miracle of T7×7 mentions of **Jesus Christ** would not exist.			

There is no textual reasoning to explain what happens in the KJB- with the most important name in the entire Bible. Nor is it understood what happened in the minds of the translators and editors of the KJB when they decided to keep it this way over the centuries. But surely, there was a stir inside their soul that decided to keep the reading as "**Jesus Christ**" when the Greek plainly reads "*Christ Jesus*". Perhaps they simply felt moved to preserve beauty and flow in the text.

That inspiration came from somewhere. Was it from their hearts, or was it from the Holy Ghost?

Who hath directed the Spirit of the LORD, or being his counsellor hath taught him?

Isaiah 40:13

Jesus' First and Last Words in the Gospels 7×7

And he said unto them, How is it that ye sought me? wist ye not that I must be about my Father's business? Luke 2:49

I find it nothing short of amazing that the first and only verse that Jesus speaks in as a youth is the #49 verse of the chapter (Luke 2:49).

In the final chapter of Luke, Jesus speaks a total of (70+70+70) words, and the last verse Jesus speaks in is Luke 24:49. Both the first and last verses in Luke where Jesus speaks are (7×7) verses.

But the most remarkable fact about this is that these are not only the first and the last words spoken by **Jesus** in Luke, they are chronologically the first and last words spoken by **Jesus** in *all of the gospels*, Matthew, Mark, Luke, and John.

Chronological first and last sentences that **Jesus** speaks in the four gospels	
First spoken words (12 years old)	**Last spoken words** (Right before His ascension)
Luke 2:49 **= 7×7 verse**	Luke 24:49 **= 7×7 verse**
First sentence: **= 7 words** **7+7+7 letters**	Last sentence: **= 7+7+7+7 words** **(7×7)+(7×7)+7 letters**
Total words spoken by Jesus in the last chapter of Luke *(post-resurrection)* **= 70+70+70 words**	

The first sentence that **Jesus** chronologically speaks in the scriptures is a 7-word question made up of (7+7+7) letters.

First sentence spoken by Jesus in the gospels *(Chronologically, when 12 years old)*		
...How is it that ye sought me?... Luke 2:49		
7 words	**7+7+7 letters**	**7×7 verse**

If you look at the complete statement starting at "**he**" (Jesus), there are exactly 77 letters to the end of the verse.

...**he said unto them, How is it that ye sought me? wist ye not that I must be about my Father's business?** = 77 letters

The last sentence that **Jesus** chronologically speaks in the gospels is a (7×4) word question made up of (7×15) letters.

Last sentence spoken by Jesus in the gospels *(Chronologically, right before His ascension)*		
And, behold, I send the promise of my Father upon you: but tarry ye in the city of Jerusalem, until ye be endued with power from on high. Luke 24:49		
7×4 words	**7×15 letters**	**7×7 verse**

In Luke, "**Father***" (capitalized) appears (7+7+7) times, all spoken by Jesus. Luke 2:49 and Luke 24:49 are, of course, the first and last.

The first letter of "**Father**" in Luke 24:49 is the #77 letter from the end of the sentence. Back in Luke 2:49, His #(7×7) letter was "**Father's**"

The letter "F" in **Father** is the **#(7×7) letter** from the beginning of **Jesus'** first spoken words	The letter "F" in **Father** is the **#77 letter** from the end of **Jesus'** last spoken words
How is it that ye sought me? wist ye not that I must be about my Father's... Luke 2:49	**...Father upon you: but tarry ye in the city of Jerusalem, until ye be endued with power from on high.** Luke 24:49

Concealed in the text:

Read Luke 2:40-50. Jesus is 12 years old in Jerusalem at the feast of Passover. He would be crucified at age 33, which means He is exactly **7+7+7** years away from His death on the cross when He first speaks chronologically in the Bible.

He also goes MISSING for 3 days until He is found by His sorrowing parents who certainly feared that He was dead (like any normal parent would after a single hour). It is all quite clearly foreshadowing His death and appearance at the resurrection!

...How is it that ye sought me? wist ye not that I must be about my Father's business? Luke 2:49

...Woman, why weepest thou? whom seekest thou?... John 20:15

Bible Comparison - First chronological sentence of Jesus

Luke 2:49	KJB	KJB1611	NKJV	ESV	NASB1971	NASB2020	NIV
Verse # of chapter	**7×7**	7×7	7×7	7×7	7×7	7×7	7×7
Words in his first sentence	**7**	7	5	6	9	9	6
Letters in his first sentence	**7×3**	7×3	15	22	30	30	24
Letter position of **Father's** in first words of **Jesus**	**7×7**	51	47	51	60	60	7×7

Bible Comparison - Last chronological sentence of Jesus

Luke 24:49	KJB	KJB1611	NKJV	ESV	NASB1971	NASB2020	NIV
Verse # of chapter	**7×7**	7×7	7×7	7×7	7×7	7×7	7×7
Words in last sentence	**7×4**	7×4	26	26	30	29	26
Letters in last sentence	**7×15**	108	102	99	7×16	107	7×14
Letter position of **Father** from the end of last words of **Jesus**	**77**	80	77	66	74	74	75

Last words of Jesus 777

The last words that Jesus Christ speaks in the Bible:

Surely I come quickly... Revelation 22:20

The first and last words are adverbs. They are beautiful. But it's the middle words of this promise that make our hearts skip a beat.

...I come...

This is His last promise. These are the two words that give meaning, hope, and dread to the millions of souls who read the words of this prophecy.

Jesus Christ is coming. And every eye shall see Him.

"I" is the #(7+7+7) word from the end of the Bible, and those dreadful two words **(I + come)** combined are mentioned exactly 777 times in the first and last books, Genesis and Revelation.

Search Filters: **Genesis, Revelation**		Case Sens	Mentions
Search Phrase 1	**I**	-	651
Search Phrase 2	**come**	-	126
Total Mentions	**I + come**		**777**
KJB1611 = **777**, NKJV = 713, ESV = 720, NASB1971 = 714, NASB2020 = 705, NIV = 718			

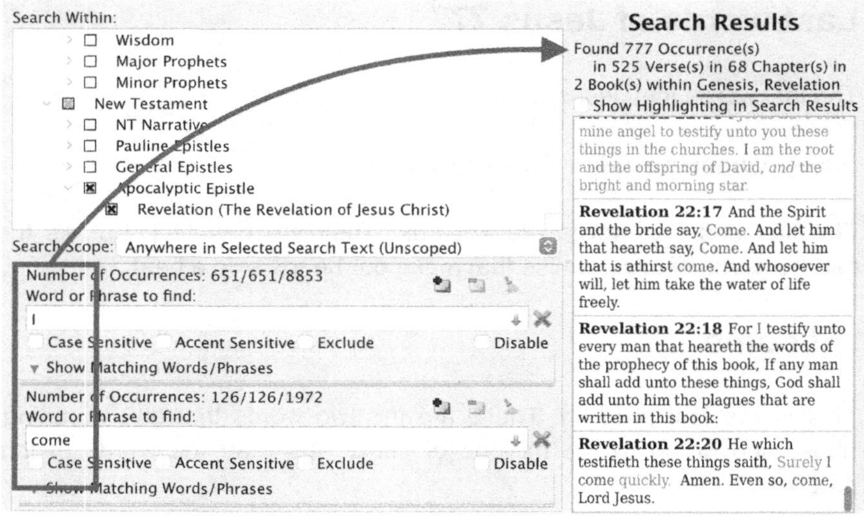

"**I come**" is mentioned 7 times in Malachi / Revelation (The last books).
1) Mal 4:6 2) Rev 2:25 3) Rev 3:11 4) Rev 16:15 5) Rev 22:7 6) Rev 22:12 7) Rev 22:20

Surely = (7+7+7) mentions in Genesis, Revelation
I + **come** = 777 mentions in Genesis, Revelation
quickly = 7 mentions in Revelation

Extra note: The last sentence spoken by Jesus in the Bible has the exact same Ordinal value forward as reverse. (See appendix 9 if unfamiliar with alphanumerics.)

English Ordinal (A=1, B=2, C=3 ... Z=26)
Surely I come quickly = 243 = 3×3×3×3×3

English Reverse Ordinal (A=26, B=25, C=24 ... Z=1)
Surely I come quickly = 243 = 3×3×3×3×3

This is a very rare thing to see. While it's unknown how many phrases this occurs in, only 2 out of 31,102 verses in the Bible have an equal forward/reverse value (2 Corinthians 4:5, 1 Thessalonians 5:20).

First mentions of LORD (UPPERCASE)

The LORD said unto my Lord, Sit thou on my right hand, till I make thine enemies thy footstool? - Matthew 22:44

This is the first time that **LORD** (UPPERCASE) is mentioned in the New Testament. It's the #777 word of Matthew 22. And it matches with the first mention of **LORD** in the Old Testament. (Genesis 2:4 → Matthew 22:44)

These are the generations of the heavens and of the earth when they were created, in the day that the LORD God made the earth and the heavens, - Genesis 2:4

LORD + GOD (Both UPPERCASE) First mentions in **Old Testament** and **New Testament**	
Genesis **2:4** **...the day that the LORD...**	Matthew **22:44** **The LORD said unto my Lord...**
word #88 = **(22×4)** = **(2×44)** **= (22+22+22+22) = (44+44)** of its chapter, Gen 2	word **#777** of its chapter, Mat 22
#1 mention in the Bible	**#6777** mention in the Bible
Total mentions of **LORD + GOD** (UPPERCASE) in the O.T. = 6776 **= 7×22×44**	
First mention of "**father**" in O.T. = Gen **2:24**	First mention of "**father**" in N.T. = Mat **2:22**
Father('s) (Capitalized, God) = **242** verses in the KJB *Excluding antimentions: "Father Abraham" (Luke 16:24) and "Fathers" (Col 3:21)	

[2] "LORD" is Word/Phrase:
627634 of 790849 of Bible
17353 of 180568 of New Testament
17353 of 23684 of Matthew
777 of 828 of Matthew 22
2 of 19 of Matthew 22:44 [2]
6468 of 6472 of Search Phrase "LORD" Results in Ent

Malachi 4:5 ¶ Behold, I will send you Elijah the prophet before the coming of the great and dreadful day of the LORD:

Matthew 22:44 The LORD said unto my Lord, Sit thou on my right hand, till I make thine enemies thy footstool?

Mark 12:36 For David himself said by the Holy

Counting all mentions of **LORD** (UPPERCASE) + **GOD** (UPPERCASE), which both are directly translated from יהוה (Jehovah) in Hebrew will yield Matthew 22:44 as the #6777 mention of uppercased **LORD** / **GOD** in the Bible.

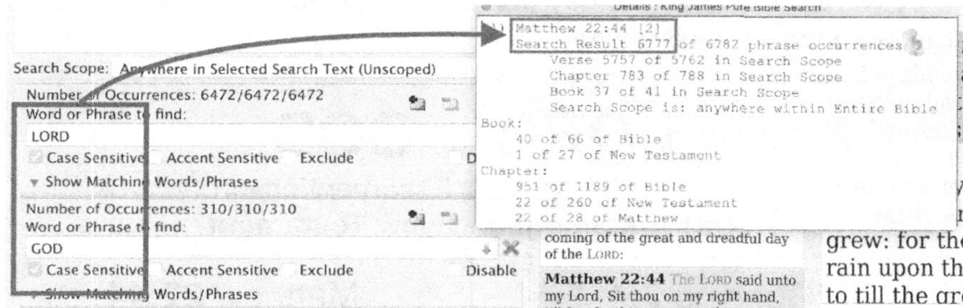

Since this is the #6777 overall mention of **LORD / GOD** (UPPERCASE), that means there are 6776 mentions in the Old Testament.

6776 O.T. mentions of **LORD / GOD** (UPPERCASE) = 7 × 22 × 44

First mention of **LORD / GOD** (UPPERCASE) in OT = Gen 2:4
First mention of **LORD / GOD** (UPPERCASE) in NT = Mat 22:44

Gen 2:4 + 22×44×7 mentions of **LORD** / **GOD** (UPPERCASE) = Mat 22:44

If you simply look up all mentions of **LORD** (UPPERCASE), you will find that this same mention of **LORD** in Mat 22:44 *(word #777 of the chapter, mention #6777 of **LORD/GOD**)* is the #**6468** overall mention of **LORD** in the KJB. That is incredibly significant because 6468 = **77×7×12**. It could also be expressed as **77×(77+7)**. 6468 is quite the number to represent the first mention of **LORD** in the N.T., since it is divisible by all of the following: 7, 7×7, (7×7+7×7), (7×7+7×7+7×7), T7, T7×7, 77, 77×7, (77+7), (77+77), (77+77+77). Mat 22:44 is also the #**5488** verse to mention **LORD** (UPPERCASE) which is equal to **T7×T7×7** (or 28×28×7).

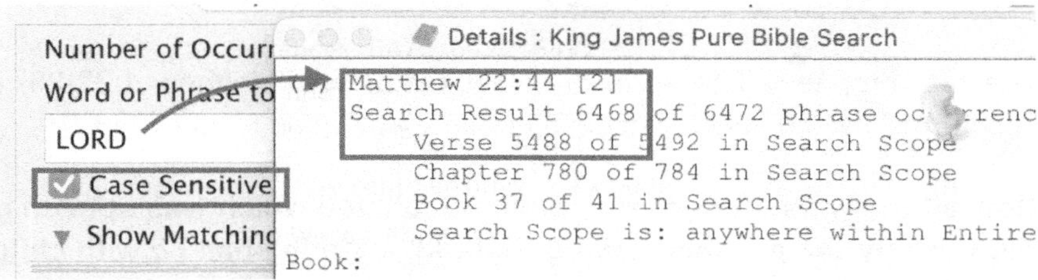

Extra notes on 2 & 4:

First mentions of **Father** (not case-sensitive):

- First mention of "**father**" in O.T. = Gen 2:24
  First mention of "**father**" in N.T. = Mat 2:22
- #2 mention of "**father**" in O.T. = Gen 4:20
- #4 mention of "**father**" in N.T. = Gen 4:22
- All mentions of **Father*** (capitalized, referring to God) in the KJB = 242 verses

*All capitalized mentions of Father('s) excluding "Father Abraham" (Luke 16:24) and "Fathers" (Col 3:21)

God concludes His book with Revelation, which has 22 chapters / 404 verses, and Revelation 4 (with God's throne detailed, surrounded by 4 beasts and 24 elders) is the #242 chapter of the New Testament. The first temple was built in the 4th year and 2nd month of Solomon's reign, 240+240 years after Israel left Egypt (as recorded in 1 Kings 6:1). The 24th book of the Bible contains the #777 chapter, where the phrase "**Lord GOD**" (Jeremiah 32:25) begins on the #777 word of the chapter. Shortly after this amazing anomaly, God says:

Behold, I am the LORD, the God of all flesh: is there any thing too hard for me? Jeremiah 32:27

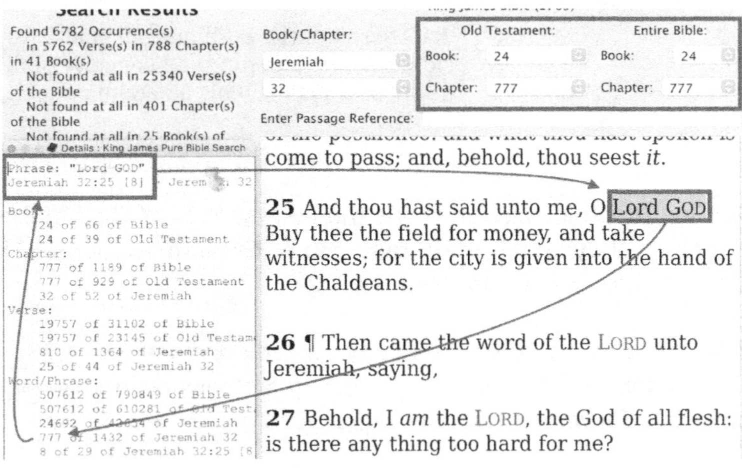

Isaiah 7:(7+7), the First Prophecy Fulfilled

The first prophecy fulfilled in the New Testament (Matthew 1:22-23) is Isaiah 7:14, which could also be accurately written as Isaiah 7:(7+7).

Now all this was done, that it might be fulfilled which was spoken of the Lord by the prophet, saying, <u>Behold, a virgin shall be with child, and shall bring forth a son, and they shall call his name Emmanuel,</u> which being interpreted is, God with us. Matthew 1:22-23

Therefore the Lord himself shall give you a sign; <u>Behold, a virgin shall conceive, and bear a son, and shall call his name Immanuel.</u> Isaiah 7:14

Isaiah 7:(7+7) begins on word #343 of Isaiah 7.

343 = **7×7×7**

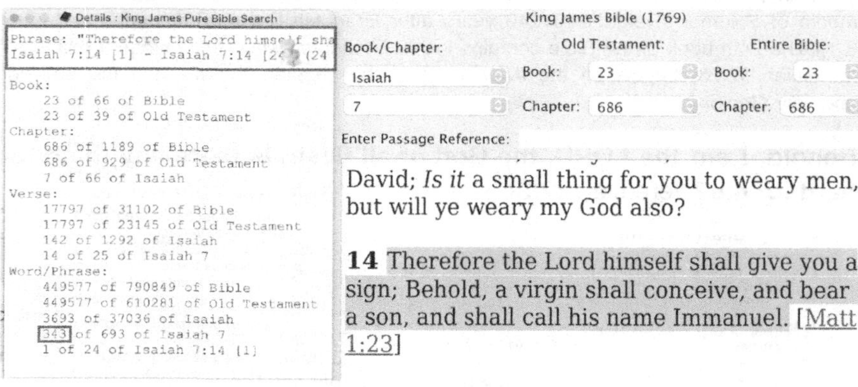

This fulfilled prophecy also contains the first mention of **God** in the New Testament. ...**they shall call his name Emmanuel, which being interpreted is, <u>God</u> with us.** Matthew 1:23.

The first mention of **God** in the New Testament (Matthew 1:23) is the #3091 mention of **God** in the Bible. At first glance this may seem meaningless. But when I first saw it, I rejoiced greatly! Here's why...

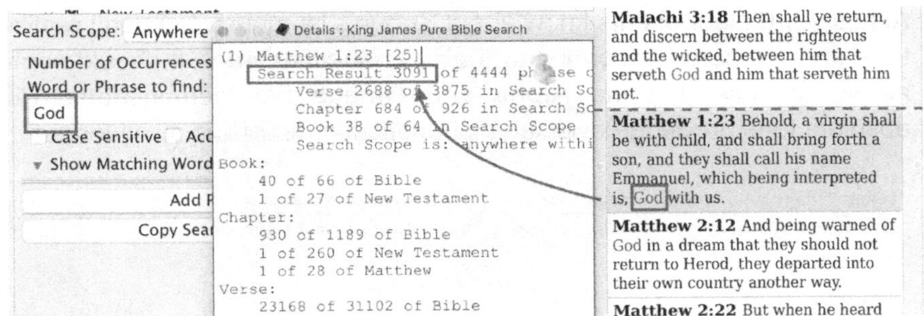

The first 777 words of scripture are made up of exactly 3091 letters.

Order	Verse [#word]	Word	Letters in word	Running sum
1	Gen 1:1 [1]	**In**	2	2
2	Gen 1:1 [2]	**the**	3	5
3	Gen 1:1 [3]	**beginning**	9	14
4	Gen 1:1 [4]	**God**	3	17
...	...	...	...	...
774	Gen 1:31 [2]	**God**	3	3078
775	Gen 1:31 [3]	**saw**	3	3081
776	Gen 1:31 [4]	**every**	5	3086
777	**Gen 1:31 [5]**	**thing**	**5**	**3091**

Side note- it's kind of interesting that "**thing**" is the #777 word of the Bible. **It is the glory of God to conceal a <u>thing</u>: but the honour of kings is to search out a matter.** Proverbs 25:2

...**therefore also that holy <u>thing</u> which shall be born of thee shall be called the Son of God.** Luke 1:35 = the #447 mention of "**thing**" ... and "**blood**" = 447 mentions in the KJB.

But tha'ts not all. If you alphabetize all the words of the Hebrew Bible, sorting them from Aleph to Tau, the #<u>3091</u> alphabetically sorted word is [יהושע] "**Joshua**" which is literally the name of **Jesus** in Hebrew.

Almost all Bible students know about Strong's Numbers, but don't realize they are numbered according to their alphabetical order. It should come as no surprise that the **Alpha and Omega** has demonstrated His absolute foreknowledge over the alphabetical order of His own words.

Lexicon :: Strong's H3091 - *yᵊhôšûa* Aa

יְהוֹשׁוּעַ

Transliteration	Pronunciation
yᵊhôšûaʿ	yeh-ho-shoo'-ah

Part of Speech	Root Word (Etymology)
proper masculine noun	From יְהֹוָה (H3068) and יָשַׁע (H3467)

Variant Spellings

Variant spellings for this word: יהושוע (Strongs and Gesenius) יהושע (Strongs and Gesenius)

KJV Translation Count — Total: 218x

The KJV translates Strong's H3091 in the following manner: Joshua (218x).

Source: blueletterbible.org/lexicon/h3091/kjv/wlc/0-1/

יהושע = H3091, **Joshua,** which is **Jesus** (Jehovah is Salvation)

Mention #3091 of **God** in the Bible *(mention #1 in the N.T.)*, is literally about the prophetic name of Jesus **"Emmanuel"** in its interpretation: **God with us.**

Behold, a virgin shall be with child, and shall bring forth a son, and they shall call his name Emmanuel, which being interpreted is, God with us. Matthew 1:22-23

Amazingly, Jesus' Hebrew numeric value also contains the exact whole number digits of 3091. In Hebrew, **[יהושע] Jesus** = 391.

Value of [יהושע] **Jesus / Joshua** in Hebrew				
ע	ש	ו	ה	י
Ain **70**	Schin **300**	Vau **6**	He **5**	Jod **10**
Total Value (10+5+6+300+70) **= 391**				

This is further verified by the word “**salvation**” in the Old Testament.

Remember, Jesus/Joshua’s name means “Jehovah is **salvation**”

The first mention of “**salvation**” (pronounced “*Yesh-oo'-aw*” in Hebrew) in the King James Bible is the #**391** word of the #(7×7) chapter.

First mention of “**salvation**” in the KJB	
I have waited for thy salvation, O LORD. Genesis 49:18	**word #391 of chapter #(7×7)** In the only other #(7×7) chapter where salvation is mentioned, (Isaiah 49), **salvation** is word #27772 of Isaiah. (in Isaiah 49:8)
Salvation is mentioned in 77 chapters of the Old Testament	

The number for **Jehovah’s salvation** is **391.**
The number of man is **6.**

God(‘s) + Jesus(‘)
in the New Testament = 2346 mentions
= 391 × 6

Search Filters: **New Testament**		Case Sens	Mentions
Search Phrase 1	**GOD, God, God's**	Y	1366
Search Phrase 2	**JESUS, Jesus, Jesus'**	Y	983
Exclude	*Subtract other people named Jesus, specifically Joshua (2x) (Acts 7:45, Hebrews 4:8) and Justus (1x) (Colossians 4:11)*	-	-3
Total Mentions	**God('s) + Jesus(')**		2346 **=391×6** **Jehovah's Salvation × man**
KJB1611 = 2350 NKJV = 2321 ESV = 2304 NASB1971 = 2238 NASB2020 = 2319 NIV = 2732			

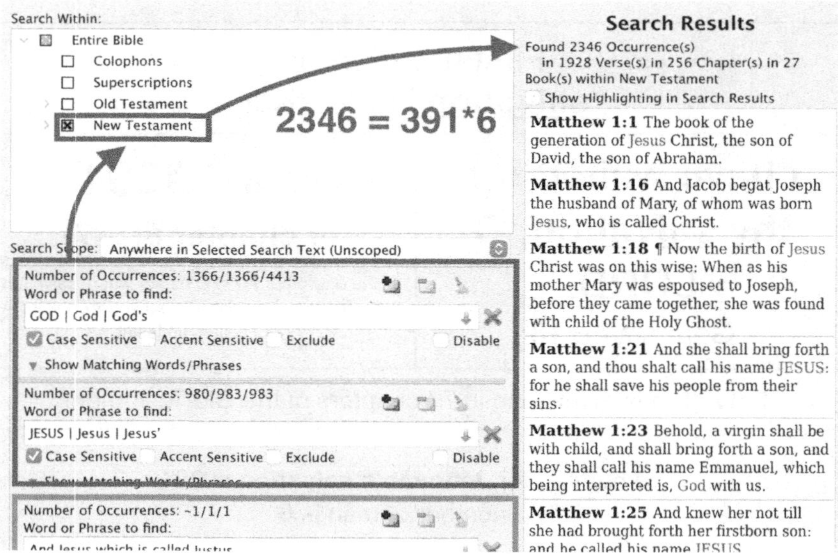
Search Within:
Entire Bible
Colophons
Superscriptions
Old Testament
New Testament
2346 = 391*6
Search Results
Found 2346 Occurrence(s) in 1928 Verse(s) in 256 Chapter(s) in 27 Book(s) within New Testament
Show Highlighting in Search Results
Matthew 1:1 The book of the generation of Jesus Christ, the son of David, the son of Abraham.
Matthew 1:16 And Jacob begat Joseph the husband of Mary, of whom was born Jesus, who is called Christ.
Matthew 1:18 ¶ Now the birth of Jesus Christ was on this wise: When as his mother Mary was espoused to Joseph, before they came together, she was found with child of the Holy Ghost.
Matthew 1:21 And she shall bring forth a son, and thou shalt call his name JESUS: for he shall save his people from their sins.
Matthew 1:23 Behold, a virgin shall be with child, and shall bring forth a son, and they shall call his name Emmanuel, which being interpreted is, God with us.
Matthew 1:25 And knew her not till she had brought forth her firstborn son:
Search Scope: Anywhere in Selected Search Text (Unscoped)
Number of Occurrences: 1366/1366/4413
Word or Phrase to find:
GOD | God | God's
Case Sensitive Accent Sensitive Exclude Disable
Show Matching Words/Phrases
Number of Occurrences: 980/983/983
Word or Phrase to find:
JESUS | Jesus | Jesus'
Case Sensitive Accent Sensitive Exclude Disable
Number of Occurrences: -1/1/1
Word or Phrase to find:

Salvation in the O.T. is mentioned 119 times, (119 = 7 × Prime #7)
The #77 mention of **salvation** is in Psalm 119.
Lord Jesus *[Jehovah is salvation]* is mentioned 119 times in the N.T.

The #77 mention of **salvation** produces a profound miracle that seems nearly impossible to designate to random chance. It is one of the strongest verifications of alphanumerics in the entire Bible.

I have longed for thy salvation, O LORD; and thy law is my delight. Psalm 119:174

<table>
<tr><td colspan="2">#77 mention of <u>salvation</u>
in the KJB
[יְשׁוּעָה] pronounced yesh-oo'-aw in Hebrew</td></tr>
<tr><td colspan="2">I have longed for thy <u>salvation</u>, O LORD; and thy law is my delight. Psalm 119:174</td></tr>
<tr><td colspan="2">salvation (#77) is word #38110 of Psalms
= 74 × 515</td></tr>
<tr><td>JESUS = 74
English Ordinal
J=10 E=5 S=19 U=21 S=19</td><td>JESUS = 515
English Standard
J=10 E=5 S=100 U=300 S=100</td></tr>
<tr><td colspan="2">If unfamiliar with alphanumerics, see appendix 9</td></tr>
</table>

Therefore I will look unto the LORD; I will wait for the God of my <u>salvation</u>: my God will hear me. Micah 7:7

Micah 7:7 … is 7 mentions of "**salvation**" from … Luke 1:77

To give knowledge of <u>salvation</u> unto his people by the remission of their sins, Luke 1:77

Last but not least, my final note on Isaiah 7:14 being the first prophecy fulfilled in the New Testament is that **Jesus(‘)** is mentioned 7×140 times in the Bible, matching Isaiah 7:14, which is specifically talking about His name.

The First Fulfilled Prophecy *in the New Testament*	
First N.T. prophecy fulfilled (Matthew 1:23) specifically about **the name of Jesus**	**Total mentions of Jesus(‘)** in the Bible excluding Joshua and Justus (See appendix 7)
Isaiah **7:14**	All Mentions of **Jesus(’)** **7×140**
...and bear a son, and shall call <u>his name</u> Immanuel. Isaiah 7:14	
Isaiah 7:(7+7) begins on word #7×7×7 of Isaiah 7	

Revelation 22, The Last Chapter Sevened

And he saith unto me, Seal not the sayings of the prophecy of this book: for the time is at hand. Revelation 22:10

Revelation has 404 verses.
The #404 Prime is 2777.

It would be interesting if Jesus returns 2000 years after His ascension (See Acts 1:6-11). 2000 (years) + 777 = Prime #404 (Revelation)

If you look at all the chapters of the Bible that contain 21 verses (7+7+7), you'll count exactly 49 of them (7×7).

This, of course, means Revelation 22, the last chapter of the Bible, is the #(7×7) chapter of the Bible to contain (7+7+7) verses.

Jesus first speaks in verse #7.

Behold, I come quickly: blessed is he that keepeth the sayings of the prophecy of this book. Revelation 22:7

"**I come**" is mentioned 7 times in Malachi / Revelation (Last books).
"**I**" + "**come**" are mentioned 777 times in Genesis / Revelation.

In Rev 22:20 the last verse where Jesus speaks in the Bible, He starts on the #7 word of the verse. The last word Jesus speaks in the Bible is "**quickly**" which is the #7 and last mention of **quickly** in Revelation.

"**He which testifieth these things saith, Surely I come quickly. Amen. Even so, come, Lord Jesus**" Revelation 22:20

The #(7×7) word of Rev 22 is the final mention of **twelve** in the Bible. And not only is this the last mention of "**twelve**" in the Bible, this is the last mention of any number at all. 12, of course, is God's final number of perfection in New Jerusalem (Rev 21:12).

All appearances of [**Jesus** + **Christ** + **seven***] = 7 × 12 mentions in the book of Revelation.

And he shewed me a pure river of water of life, clear as crystal, proceeding out of the throne of God and of the Lamb.
Revelation 22:1

The #7 word of Rev 22 is **river**, which is literally a **river** of **life,** which waters the tree of **life**.

river + **life** = 7 mentions in Revelation 22.
river + **life** = (7+7+7) mentions in the book of Revelation.

The word **life** appears 7 times in the first and last chapters of the Bible.

The 7 mentions of **life** in the first and last chapters of the Bible:

1. Genesis 1:20 ...**the moving creature that hath life...**
2. Genesis 1:30 **...wherein there is life...**
3. Revelation 22:1 **...a pure river of water of life...**
4. Revelation 22:2 **...was there the tree of life...**
5. Revelation 22:14 **...have right to the tree of life...**
6. Revelation 22:17 **...let him take the water of life...**
7. Revelation 22:19 **...out of the book of life...**

And in Genesis and Revelation, **life** is mentioned a total of 7x7 times.

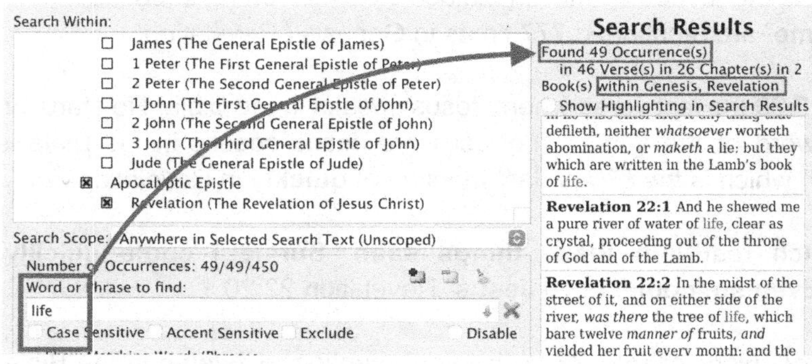

There are 7 things "...**of life**" in Genesis / Revelation.

The first thing "**...of life**" in Genesis is in Gen 2:7
The first thing "**...of life**" in Revelation is in Rev 2:7.

7 things "of life" in Genesis / Revelation			
1	**breath of life**	Genesis 2:7, 6:17, 7:15, 7:22	-
2	**tree of life**	Genesis 2:9, 3:22, 3:24	Revelation 2:7, 22:2, 22:14
3	**time of life**	Genesis 18:10, 18:14	-
4	**crown of life**	-	Revelation 2:10
5	**Spirit of life**	-	Revelation 11:11
6	**book of life**	-	Revelation 3:5, 13:8, 17:8, 20:12, 20:15, 21:27, 22:19
7	**water of life**	-	Revelation 21:6, 22:1, 22:17

The #(7+7+7) word of Revelation 22 is **God**. **God** is mentioned 7 times in Revelation 22. **Lord** + **Jesus** combined are mentioned 7 times. **Even so, come, Lord Jesus.** Revelation 22:20

Revelation 22	
7 mentions of **God**	7 mentions of **Lord + Jesus**
1. Revelation 22:1 - **God** 2. Revelation 22:3 - **God** 3. Revelation 22:5 - **God** 4. Revelation 22:6 - **God** 5. Revelation 22:9 - **God** 6. Revelation 22:18 - **God** 7. Revelation 22:19 - **God**	1. Revelation 22:5 - **Lord** 2. Revelation 22:6 - **Lord** 3. Revelation 22:16 - **Jesus** 4. Revelation 22:20 - **Lord** 5. Revelation 22:20 - **Jesus** 6. Revelation 22:21 - **Lord** 7. Revelation 22:21 - **Jesus**

The first mention of **God** in Revelation 22 (word #7+7+7) begins precisely on the #77 letter of the chapter. This is the **#7 mention** of **God** from the end of the Bible.

The first mention of **Lord** in Revelation 22 begins precisely on the #490 letter of the chapter. 490 = 70 × 7. This is also the **#7 mention** of **Lord / Jesus** from the end of the Bible.

First mention of **God** in Revelation 22	First mention of **Lord** in Revelation 22
Starts on **#77 letter** of the chapter	Starts on #(**70×7**) **letter** of the chapter

Here are all the words mentioned exactly 7 times in Revelation 22. Most of which carry incredible significance– even the small words that we would normally think of as trivial.

God / In / Which / For / Things / Come / This / Let

Detailed table:

Words mentioned 7 times in Revelation 22			
Word	Mentions in Rev 22	Verse Mentions	Significance
God	7	22:1 [1x] 22:3 [1x] 22:5 [1x] 22:6 [1x] 22:9 [1x] 22:18 [1x] 22:19 [1x]	The Creator. Word #7 of Revelation. **The Revelation of Jesus Christ, which <u>God</u> gave unto him...** (Rev 1:1)
In	7	22:2 [1x] 22:3 [1x] 22:4 [1x] 22:14 [1x] 22:16 [1x] 22:18 [1x] 22:19 [1x]	The first word of the Bible. **<u>In</u> the beginning God...** (Gen 1:1) In Genesis & Revelation only, **In** + **Amen** (the first and last words of the Bible) are mentioned a combined 777 times.
Which	7	22:2 [1x] 22:6 [1x] 22:8 [1x] (22:9 [1x] 22:11 [1x] 22:19 [1x] 22:20 [1x]	Its first mention in Revelation connects God to the title of the book. **The Revelation of Jesus Christ, <u>which</u> God gave unto him...** (Rev 1:1)

For	7	22:2 [1x] 22:5 [2x] 22:9 [1x] 22:10 [1x] 22:15 [1x] 22:18 [1x]	The 7th word spoken directly by Jesus. **Suffer it to be so now: <u>for</u>...** (Mat 3:15)
Things	7	22:6 [1x] 22:8 [2x] 22:16 [1x] 22:18 [1x] 22:19 [1x] 22:20 [1x]	In context of Revelation 22, this word is always in reference to the **things** written/described in Revelation. "**thing**" is the #777 word of the Bible
Come	7	22:7 [1x] 22:12 [1x] 22:17 [3x] 22:20 [2x]	The cry of the Spirit and the bride, and the final promise of Jesus, answering that cry. **And the Spirit and the bride say, <u>Come.</u>** ... **Surely I <u>come</u> quickly.** (Rev 22:17,20)
This	7	22:7 [1x] 22:9 [1x] 22:10 [1x] 22:18 [2x] 22:19 [2x]	Always refers to "**this book**" or "**this prophecy**". **Behold, I come quickly: blessed is he that keepeth the sayings of the prophecy of <u>this book.</u>** (Rev 22:7)
Let	7	22:11 [4x] 22:17 [3x]	First word God speaks directly. **And God said, <u>Let</u> there be light...**(Gen 1:3)

When Jesus says "**I am...**" in verse 13, the first and last words of His declaration are triple sevened: **I am <u>Alpha</u> and Omega, the beginning and the end, the first and the <u>last</u>.** Revelation 22:13

"**Alpha**" is word #(7×7×7) of Revelation 22.
"**last**" is word #11,777 of Revelation.

Alpha **I am <u>Alpha</u> and Omega...**	**last** **...the first and the <u>last</u>.**
First word of "**I am**" declaration	Last word of "**I am**" declaration
Word #(7×7×7) of Revelation 22	Word #11,777 of Revelation

Why the 11 in front of 11,777? I'm not sure, but the first time that "**last**" is mentioned in Revelation is word #11 of Revelation 1:11

Saying, I am Alpha and Omega, the first and the <u>last</u>: and, What thou seest, write in a book... Revelation 1:11

Revelation 22:13 is the #7 and final verse in the Holy Bible where the Lord declares Himself as **the first** and **the last.** Unless you're an NIV, ESV, NASB, etc. Most modern versions put Revelation 22:19 in their back pocket and **take away from the words of** Revelation 1:11, thereby desolating the pattern from 7 to 6.

God declares Himself **the first** and **the last** in...

1. Isaiah 41:4 **I the LORD, the first, and with the last; I am he**
2. Isaiah 44:6 **I am the first, and I am the last**
3. Isaiah 48:12 **I am he; I am the first, I also am the last**
4. Revelation 1:11 **I am Alpha and Omega, the first and the last**
5. Revelation 1:17 **Fear not; I am the first and the last**
6. Revelation 2:8 **These things saith the first and the last**
7. Revelation 22:13 **I am... the first and the last**

This is also the 7th and final mention of "**last**" in the book of Revelation.

Besides "**last**", There are a lot of significant phrases and words that are mentioned 7 times in the book of Revelation. Here is a partial list:

blessed, book of life, church, Jesus Christ, last, light, names, patience, prophecy, quickly, repent, rest, right hand, sharp, the saints, the word, tree, worthy, bottomless pit, brimstone, earthquake, horses, make war, Satan, sound, sounded, vial, wine, woe, world

The following page contains a complete list of words which are mentioned 7 times in Revelation *AND* have their final mention in the last chapter, Revelation 22.

<table>
<tr><th colspan="3">Words/Phrases mentioned 7 times in Revelation,
with last mention in Revelation 22</th></tr>
<tr><td>Word / Phrase</td><td colspan="2">Mentions in Revelation / [Word # of verse]
Final Chapter Mentions in Bold</td></tr>
<tr><td>light</td><td>7</td><td>1. Revelation 7:16 [14]
2. Revelation 18:23 [3]
3. Revelation 21:11 [8]
4. Revelation 21:23 [31]
5. Revelation 21:24 [13]
6. Revelation 22:5 [14]
7. Revelation 22:5 [24]</td></tr>
<tr><td>last</td><td>7</td><td>1. Revelation 1:11 [11]
2. Revelation 1:17 [32]
3. Revelation 2:8 [18]
4. Revelation 2:19 [19]
5. Revelation 15:1 [16]
6. Revelation 21:9 [20]
7. Revelation 22:13 [15]</td></tr>
<tr><td>blessed</td><td>7</td><td>1. Revelation 1:3 [1]
2. Revelation 14:13 [12]
3. Revelation 16:15 [7]
4. Revelation 19:9 [7]
5. Revelation 20:6 [1]
6. Revelation 22:7 [5]
7. Revelation 22:14 [1]</td></tr>
<tr><td>tree</td><td>7</td><td>1. Revelation 2:7 [27]
2. Revelation 6:13 [14]
3. Revelation 7:1 [40]
4. Revelation 9:4 [22]
5. Revelation 22:2 [19]
6. Revelation 22:2 [39]
7. Revelation 22:14 [15]</td></tr>
<tr><td>any man</td><td>7</td><td>1. Revelation 3:20 [10]
2. Revelation 11:5 [3]
3. Revelation 11:5 [20]
4. Revelation 13:9 [2]
5. Revelation 14:9 [13]
6. Revelation 22:18 [18]
7. Revelation 22:19 [3]</td></tr>
<tr><td>prophecy</td><td>7</td><td>1. Revelation 1:3 [14]
2. Revelation 11:6 [16]
3. Revelation 19:10 [45]
4. Revelation 22:7 [14]
5. Revelation 22:10 [12]
6. Revelation 22:18 [13]
7. Revelation 22:19 [16]</td></tr>
</table>

Words/Phrases mentioned **7 times** in **Revelation,** *with* ***last*** *mention in Revelation 22 (continued)*		
book of life	7	1. Revelation 3:5 [23] 2. Revelation 13:8 [18] 3. Revelation 17:8 [38] 4. Revelation 20:12 [25] 5. Revelation 20:15 [9] 6. Revelation 21:27 [30] **7. Revelation 22:19 [26]**
quickly *The last word spoken by Jesus in the Bible*	7	1. Revelation 2:5 [22] 2. Revelation 2:16 [9] 3. Revelation 3:11 [4] 4. Revelation 11:14 [12] **5. Revelation 22:7 [4]** **6. Revelation 22:12 [5]** **7. Revelation 22:20 [10]**
Jesus Christ	7	1. Revelation 1:1 [4] 2. Revelation 1:2 [14] 3. Revelation 1:5 [3] 4. Revelation 1:9 [19] 5. Revelation 1:9 [39] 6. Revelation 12:17 [31] **7. Revelation 22:21 [6]**

Other noteworthy words that appear for their final time in Revelation 22 in multiples of 7 are:

- **name** in Rev 22:4 is the #(7+7+7+7) mention in Revelation
- **city** in Rev 22:19 is the #(7+7+7+7) mention in Revelation (which is also the #777 verse mentioning "**city**" in the Bible)
- **Jesus** in Rev 22:21 is the #(7+7) mention in Revelation

The last word of the Bible to have 777 in its word count is "**book**" the last word of Revelation 22:18, which is word #790,777 of the KJB.

For I testify unto every man that heareth the words of the prophecy of this book, If any man shall add unto these things, God shall add unto him the plagues that are written in this <u>book</u>: Revelation 22:18

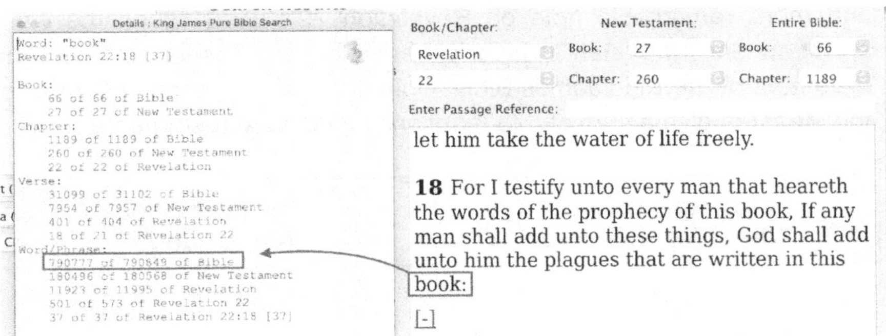

Random note (unrelated to Revelation 22)… "**book**" is the 7th word of a verse in exactly 7 verses of the KJB. (Numbers 21:14, Jeremiah 36:2, Luke 3:4, Luke 20:42, Acts 1:20, Revelation 5:7, Revelation 5:8)

The last word of the chapter, "**Amen**" (capitalized), is mentioned 77 times in the Bible. Revelation 22 contains 573 words, which of course means **Amen** is word #573. This is noteworthy because the seventh appearance of **seven*** in the Bible is also the #573 word of its chapter.

Significance	Word	Appearance #	Chapter	Word # of chapter
Final word of Bible	**Amen**	**77**	Rev 22	**573**
God's number of completion	**seven***	**7**	Gen 4	**573**
seven* = Any word with "**seven**" inside of it (E.g. **seven** / **seventh** / **sevenfold** / **seventy** / etc.)				

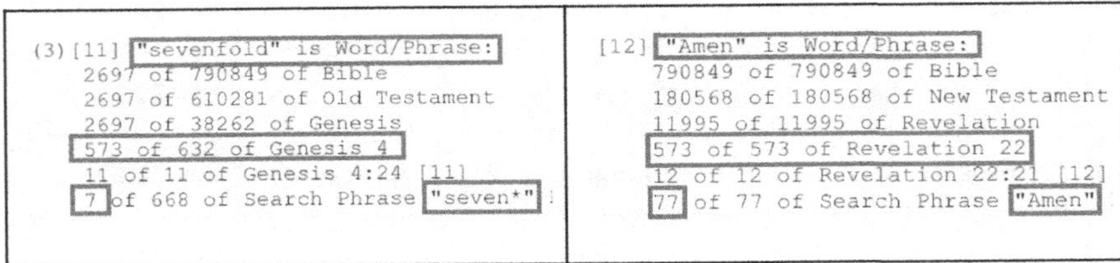

A note on the Holy Ghost's fine-tuning of the KJB: if the KJB was consistent (by scholar's standards), the word **Amen** (capitalized) would appear either 76 or 78 times, not 77. Compare Numbers 5:22 (**Amen, amen**) with Nehemiah 8:6 (**Amen, Amen**). Why isn't the second "**amen**" capitalized in Numbers 5:22? If it was, the pattern would break.

One more remarkable note on Revelation 22's word count: the word **Christ** means "**Messiah**" which is translated as **Messias** in the New Testament of the King James Bible. Combined, all mentions of **Christ('s)** and **Messias** give a sum of 573 mentions in the New Testament.

Total mentions of **Christ('s) + Messias**	Total words in **Revelation 22**
573	**573**

The letter "**D**" in "**Lord**" in the last verse of the Bible concludes an ELS-code (Equidistant Letter Sequence) of 389 letters that spell out **L-O-R-D**.

- 389 is the middle of 777.
- The #777 Prime is the #389 Additive Prime.
- 389 is the #77 Prime

Revelation 22:10-21

L ...77-Prime letters... **O** ...77-Prime letters... **R** ...77-Prime letters... **D**

Another point of particular interest is where this ELS starts: the letter "**L**" in... "**Seal not the sayings of the prophecy of this book**..."
In fact, all of the passages surrounding **L-O-R-D** are full of glory.

The book. The tree of life. The water of life. Our Lord Jesus Christ.

L	SEAL NOT THE SAYINGS OF THE PROPHECY OF THIS BOOK	Rev 22:10
O	THAT THEY MAY HAVE RIGHT TO THE TREE OF LIFE	Rev 22:14
R	WHOSOEVER WILL, LET HIM TAKE THE WATER OF LIFE FREELY	Rev 22:17
D	THE GRACE OF OUR LORD JESUS CHRIST BE WITH YOU ALL.	Rev 22:21

"L-O-R-D" #77 Prime (389) ELS

389 is the #77 Prime, the middle of 777, and #389 Additive Prime is the #777 Prime

Revelation 22:10-21

```
..........ANDHESAITHUNTOMESEA[L]NOTTHESAYINGSOFTHEPROPHECYOFTHISB
OOKFORTHETIMEISATHANDHETHATISUNJUSTLETHIMBEUNJUSTSTILLANDHEWHICHI
SFILTHYLETHIMBEFILTHYSTILLANDHETHATISRIGHTEOUSLETHIMBERIGHTEOUSST
ILLANDHETHATISHOLYLETHIMBEHOLYSTILLANDBEHOLDICOMEQUICKLYANDMYREWA
RDISWITHMETOGIVEEVERYMANACCORDINGASHISWORKSHALLBEIAMALPHAANDOMEGA
THEBEGINNINGANDTHEENDTHEFIRSTANDTHELASTBLESSEDARETHEYTHATDOHISCOM
MANDMENTSTHATTHEYMAYHAVERIGHTT[O]THETREEOFLIFEANDMAYENTERINTHROUG
HTHEGATESINTOTHECITYFORWITHOUTAREDOGSANDSORCERERSANDWHOREMONGERSA
NDMURDERERSANDIDOLATERSANDWHOSOEVERLOVETHANDMAKETHALIEIJESUSHAVES
ENTMINEANGELTOTESTIFYUNTOYOUTHESETHINGSINTHECHURCHESIAMTHEROOTAND
THEOFFSPRINGOFDAVIDANDTHEBRIGHTANDMORNINGSTARANDTHESPIRITANDTHEBR
IDESAYCOMEANDLETHIMTHATHEARETHSAYCOMEANDLETHIMTHATISATHIRSTCOMEAN
DWHOSOEVERWILLLETHIMTAKETHEWATE[R]OFLIFEFREELYFORITESTIFYUNTOEVER
YMANTHATHEARETHTHEWORDSOFTHEPROPHECYOFTHISBOOKIFANYMANSHALLADDUNT
OTHESETHINGSGODSHALLADDUNTOHIMTHEPLAGUESTHATAREWRITTENINTHISBOOKA
NDIFANYMANSHALLTAKEAWAYFROMTHEWORDSOFTHEBOOKOFTHISPROPHECYGODSHAL
LTAKEAWAYHISPARTOUTOFTHEBOOKOFLIFEANDOUTOFTHEHOLYCITYANDFROMTHETH
INGSWHICHAREWRITTENINTHISBOOKHEWHICHTESTIFIETHTHESETHINGSSAITHSUR
ELYICOMEQUICKLYAMENEVENSOCOMELOR[D]JESUSTHEGRACEOFOURLORDJESUSCHR
ISTBEWITHYOUALLAMEN..............................................
```

77 letters before "**Lord**" in Rev 22:20 is the #389 (and final) appearance of **write*** + **written** in the KJB (Rev 22:19).

The grace of
our Lord Jesus Christ
be with you all.
Amen.

Revelation 22:21

The phrase "**our Lord Jesus Christ**" is the concluding title of Jesus in the Bible. This is the only mention in Revelation, but throughout the Bible, from its very first mention, **our Lord Jesus Christ** (mentioned 55 times) is packed with *sevened* anomalies. In fact, there are 7 major ones.

"our Lord Jesus Christ" 7 anomalies of sevens in the King James Bible		
1	**Men that have hazarded their lives for the name of our Lord Jesus Christ.** Acts 15:26	First mention. **our Lord Jesus Christ** begins on word/phrase #96,777 of the New Testament.
2	**Grace be to you and peace from God the Father, and from our Lord Jesus Christ,** Galatians 1:3	**our Lord Jesus Christ** begins on word #(7×7) of Galatians
3	**Blessed be the God and Father of our Lord Jesus Christ, who hath blessed us with all spiritual blessings in heavenly places in Christ:** Ephesians 1:3	**our Lord Jesus Christ** begins on word #(7×7) of Ephesians (which is the 7×7 book of the Bible)
4	**Blessed be the God and Father of our Lord Jesus Christ, who hath blessed us with all spiritual blessings in heavenly places in Christ:** Colossians 1:3	**Jesus** is word # 751,777 of the Bible
5	**Now we command you, brethren, in the name of our Lord Jesus Christ, that ye withdraw yourselves from every brother that walketh disorderly, and not after the tradition which he received of us.** 2 Thessalonians 3:6	**our Lord Jesus Christ** begins on word #777 of 2 Thessalonians
6	**Keep yourselves in the love of God, looking for the mercy of our Lord Jesus Christ unto eternal life.** Jude 1:21	Next-to-last mention. **our Lord Jesus Christ** begins on word/phrase #778,777 of the Bible
7	**The grace of our Lord Jesus Christ be with you all. Amen.** Revelation 22:21	The King's seal on the King James Bible (See next pages)

Known unto God are all his works from the beginning of the world.

Acts 15:18

...for the writing which is written in the king's name, and sealed with the king's ring, may no man reverse.

Esther 8:8

The Last Mention of Jesus Christ. The King's Seal on the KJB...

The Last mention *of* our Lord Jesus Christ *in* Revelation 22:21

Word	Within	Mention / Appearance #
our	Genesis, Revelation	**77**
our	Revelation	**7+7**
Lord	Matthew, Revelation	**7×7+7×7**
Lord *Case-sensitive*	Genesis, Matthew–Acts, Revelation *(7 books total)*	**7×7×7**
Lord *Case-sensitive*	Matthew, Revelation	**77**
Lord *Case-sensitive*	Revelation	**7+7+7**
Jesus	Revelation	**7+7**
Jesus Christ	Revelation	**7**
Christ	Matthew, Revelation	**T7** *1+2+3+4+5+6+7* = T7
God, Jesus *Total mentions combined*	Genesis, Revelation	**7×7×7**
Jesus, David *Total mentions combined*	Entire Bible	**7×7×7×6**
Jesus(') *Excluding Justus & Joshua named Jesus. See appendix 7*	Entire Bible	**70×7+70×7**
Lord, Jesus	Revelation 22	**7**
Lord Jesus	Entire Bible	**7×7th Prime** *17* = **#7 Prime**
our Lord Jesus	Entire Bible	**7×7+7**
Jesus Christ	Entire Bible	**T7×7** *See p. 96*
Lord Jesus Christ	Entire Bible	**77+7**
our, Lord, Jesus, Christ *Case-sensitive.* *Total mentions combined*	New Testament	**7×7×52** *52 weeks (Sevens) in a year*
heaven, Jesus *(The #7 words from beginning and end)* *Total mentions combined, excluding Justus. See appendix 7*	Entire Bible	**777+777**
Jesus('), Christ('s) *Total mentions combined*	Entire Bible	**777+777**
Jesus*, Christ* *Total appearances combined, excluding Justus & Joshua named Jesus & false Christs (Mat 24:24, Mark 13:22)*	Entire Bible	**777+777**
Moses*, Jesus*, Christ* *Total appearances combined, excluding antimentions, excluding Superscriptions*	Entire Bible	**7×7×7×7**
LORD, Jesus *Case-sensitive*	Genesis, Revelation	**16×11**
King, Jesus, Christ *excluding Justus & Joshua. See appendix 7*	New Testament	**1611**
our Lord, Jesus, Christ *Case-sensitive, excluding Justus & Joshua. See appendix 7*	Entire Bible	**1611**

Godhead 777 - Part 1, Entire Bible

For there are three that bear record in heaven, the Father, the Word, and the Holy Ghost: and these three are one. 1 John 5:7

Search Filters: **Entire Bible**		Case Sens	Mentions
Search Phrase 1	**The Father**	-	218
Search Phrase 2	**The Word**	-	469
Search Phrase 3	**Holy Ghost**	-	90
Total Mentions	**"The Father" + "The Word" + "Holy Ghost"**		**777**

Notice how it says in the end of the verse, "**...and these three are one.**" Three in the Godhead. Three perfect sevens. Amen.

The Godhead in 1 John 5:7 - Bible Version Comparison:

Total mentions of: **"The Father" + "The Word" + "Holy Ghost"**				
KJB 218 + 469 + 90 = **777**	NKJV 205 + 483 + 96 = 784	ESV 258 + 459 + 94 = 811	NASB2020 201 + 463 + 93 = 757	NIV 364 + 359 + 94 = 817
KJB1611 218 + 468 + 90 = 776			NASB1971 351 + 464 + 93 = 908	
*This miracle has existed in the KJB for over 250 years. See Appendix 1 for how this happened. (Related to the #7 verse mentioning "**the word**" in the N.T.). Counts for modern versions were completed by substituting "Holy Spirit" for "Holy Ghost" (even though they mutilate 1 John 5:7).*				

It must be noted that 1 John 5:7 is by far the most controversial verse in the King James Bible. Many "study" Bibles have footnotes or marginal notes claiming this is a spurious verse that does not belong in scriptures.

Besides the many ancient witnesses in both manuscripts and church history, we now realize there is an even greater witness: the Bible itself. God doesn't need anything other than the Bible to prove that He Himself is its Author.

If we believe this is God's doing, we must also accept the following statement as true: Every word of the King James Bible is placed by inspiration of God, including *the italics.* For example, ***The Father*** is *italicized* 3 times in the KJB (Acts 7:16, Colossians 1:19, 1 John 2:23), and ***Holy*** Ghost is *italicized* in (Matthew 12:31); and without those mentions, we would not reach 777 mentions in the overall count.

In their vain thoughts and imaginations, many will say, *"That's double inspiration if you think that inspired words could be added later to the text that were not there in previous manuscripts."*

No, that's just how God works. He reveals Himself over time. Just as our Saviour did not arrive for thousands of years, so did His perfect, pure Bible take thousands of years to be revealed. Besides this characteristic of God, we read in Jeremiah 36:

Jeremiah 36:32 **Then took Jeremiah another roll, and gave it to Baruch the scribe, the son of Neriah; who wrote therein from the mouth of Jeremiah all the words of the book which Jehoiakim king of Judah had burned in the fire: <u>and there were added besides unto them many like words</u>.**

Did you catch that last part? "...**and there were added besides unto them many like words."** Jeremiah wrote a book, it got burned, and he wrote the same book again with ADDED words. So, yeah. God can "double inspire His word" (if that's what you want to call it), and even add new words to the text if He chooses to do so.

An interesting way that I believe verifies the 777-count is when you make the counts case-sensitive.

Notice how "**the Father**" (Not case-sensitive) is mentioned 218 times in the Bible.

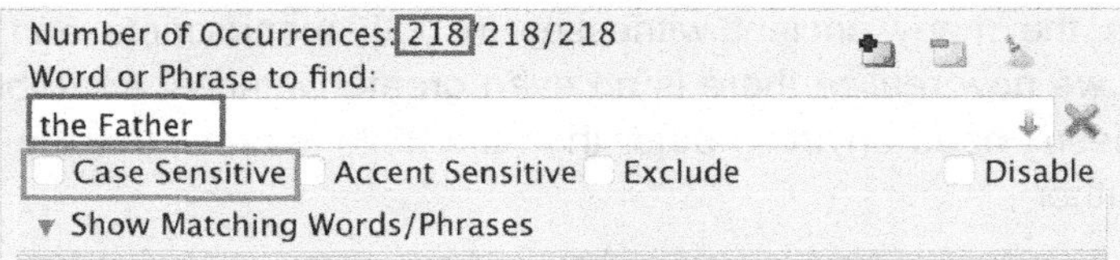

The only time 218 is mentioned in the text of the Bible itself is Ezra 8:9.

The only mention of "218" in the Bible	The name meaning of **Joab** **"God is the Father"**
Of the sons of Joab; Obadiah the son of Jehiel, and with him <u>two hundred and eighteen</u> males. Ezra 8:9	

"the Father" + "the Word" + "Holy Ghost" = 218 mentions (Case-sens)

Search Filters: **Entire Bible**		Case Sens	Mentions
Search Phrase 1	**the Father**	Y	122
Search Phrase 2	**the Word**	Y	6
Search Phrase 3	**Holy Ghost**	Y	90
Total Mentions	**"the Father" + "the Word" + "Holy Ghost"**		**218**

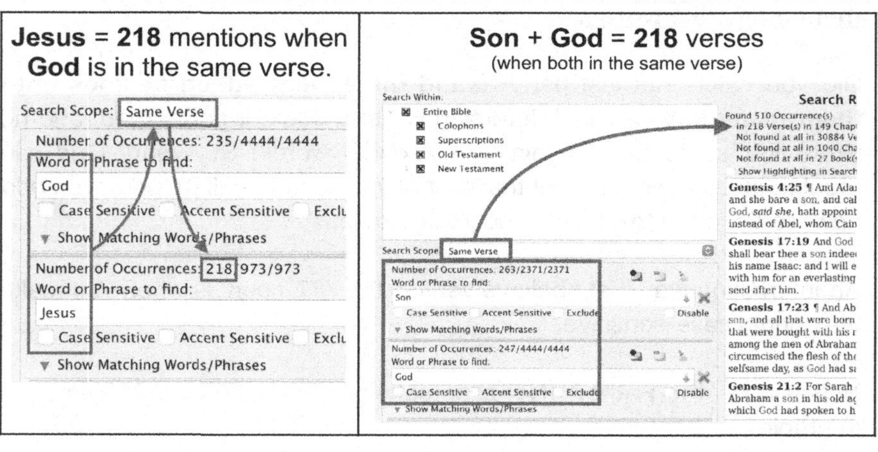

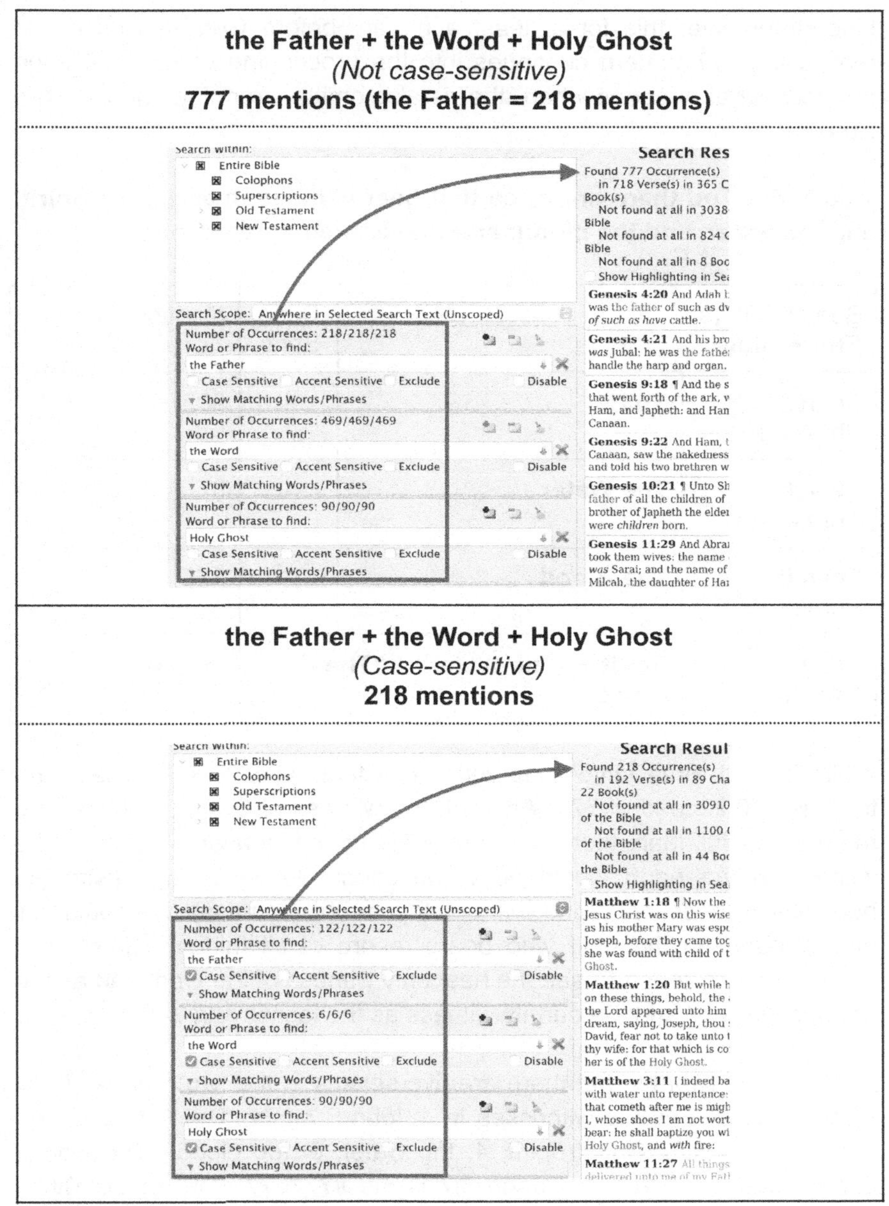

Now, one thing I wondered over, is why "**the**" is not included in the count for "**~~the~~ Holy Ghost**" ("the Holy Ghost" = 89 mentions and "**Holy Ghost**" = 90 mentions).

I pondered over this for at least a month, before God allowed me to realize the 777 pattern continues into the proceeding verse. In, 1 John 5:8, look what happens when “the” is also omitted from the count of “**~~the~~ Spirit**”.

1 John 5:8 **And there are three that bear witness in earth, the Spirit, and the water, and the blood: and these three agree in one.**

Search Filters: **Entire Bible**		Case Sens	Mentions
Search Phrase 1	**Spirit**	-	505
Search Phrase 2	**The Water**	-	87
Search Phrase 3	**The Blood**	-	178
Total Mentions	**Spirit + “The Water” + “The Blood”**		**770**

While it’s not three sevens as verse 7, it feels very “right” to have the total as 770 instead of 777. After all, the witness of God in heaven is far more powerful than that on earth. Without the heavenly witness, the witness in the earth would be of no effect. But vice versa (with the heavenly witness only, and without the earthly witness), we could still fully depend on the God who bears record of all things. Therefore it makes a lot of sense to see the heavenly witness of the Godhead as the greater with 777 and the earthly witness as the lesser with 770.

It is also noteworthy that there are five sevens in the two groups (777 / 770) to match the five witnesses in 1 John 5:7-8 (1. The Father, 2. the Word, 3. the Holy Ghost/Spirit, 4. the water, 5. the blood). The word / phrase “**bear record**” in 1 John 5:7 is the #777277 word of the Bible, literally- 5 sevens separated into 2 groups.

Group 1 = 3 sevens (777)
Group 2 = 2 sevens (770)

"**bear record...**" in 1 John 5:7

```
Word/Phrase:
    777277 of 790849 of Bible
```

The record in heaven: **777** mentions, **The Father, The Word, Holy Ghost**

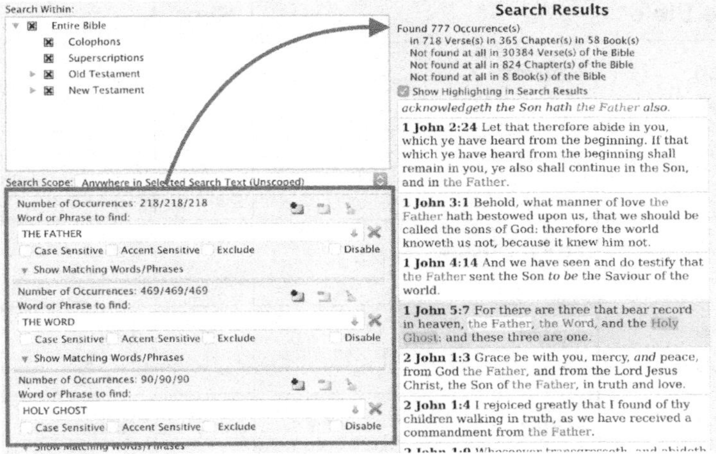

The witness in earth: **770** mentions, **Spirit, The Water, The Blood**

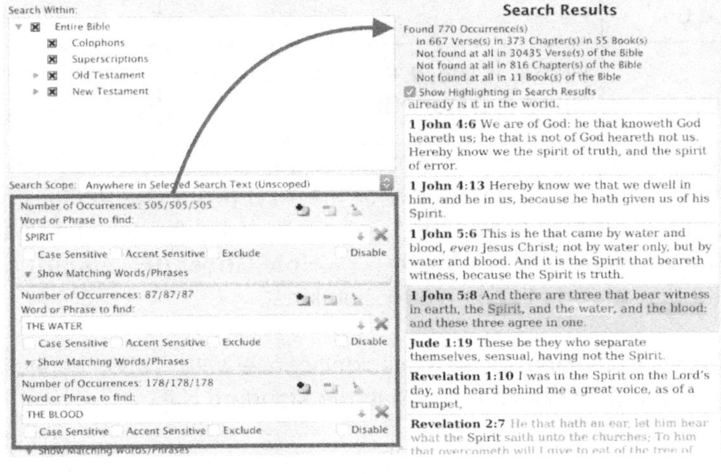

And if that were not enough, there is also a triple-7 pattern in the same two verses:

Here are the "cAsE SeNsiTiVe" counts for 1 John 5:7-8

"Father" + **"Word"** + **"Holy Ghost"** + **"Spirit"** + **"water"** + **"blood"** = 1372
The Prime factorization of 1372 = 2×2×7×7×7

Search Filters: **Entire Bible***		Case Sens	Mentions
Search Phrase 1	**Father**	Y	260
Search Phrase 2	**Word**	Y	7
Search Phrase 3	**Holy Ghost**	Y	90
Search Phrase 4	**Spirit**	Y	172
Search Phrase 5	**water**	Y	396
Search Phrase 6	**blood**	Y	447
Total Mentions	**Father + Word + "Holy Ghost" + Spirit + water + blood**		**1372** = **7×7×7× 4**

*Important note- the PCE version of the KJB (Pure Cambridge Edition) lowercases "**Spirit**" to "**spirit**" in 1 John 5:8, giving the total count for the KJB-PCE of (**Father** (260) + **Word** (7) + **Holy Ghost** (90) + **spirit** (336) + **water** (396) + **blood** (447)) = 1536 mentions.

I cannot find anything of special significance with 1536, especially in comparison to (7×7×7×4) as found in the standard KJB.

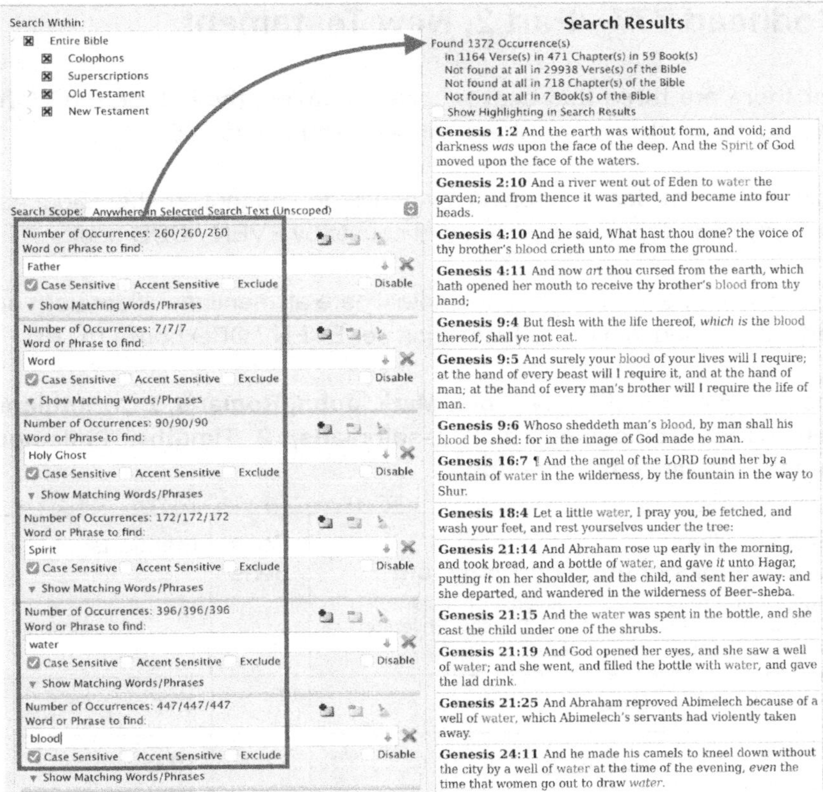

1372 = 343 × 4
1372 = 7×7×7 × 4
1372 = (7×7×7) + (7×7×7) + (7×7×7) + (7×7×7)

The Godhead, each member with the definite article "**the**" is made of exactly 7 words and 28 letters, which is T7.
1 + 2 + 3 + 4 + 5 + 6 + 7 = T7

the Father + the Word + the Holy Ghost	
7 words	**T7 letters**

Godhead 777 - Part 2, New Testament

For there are three that bear record in heaven, the Father, the Word, and the Holy Ghost: and these three are one. 1 John 5:7

This note provides supporting evidence to the notion that God has perfectly and purposely divided word counts by EVEN / ODD books.

If you haven't already, check the note where all mentions of **Jesus(')** are perfectly divided into (70×7) mentions per EVEN / ODD books (p. 75).

The EVEN books of the N.T. are: **Mark, John, Romans, 2 Corinthians, Ephesians, Colossians, 2 Thessalonians, 2 Timothy, Philemon, James, 2 Peter, 2 John, or Jude.**

Search Filters: **EVEN Books of the New Testament** Mark, John, Romans, 2 Corinthians, Ephesians, Colossians, 2 Thessalonians, 2 Timothy, Philemon, James, 2 Peter, 2 John, Jude		Case Sens	Mentions
Search Phrase 1	**God**	-	494
Search Phrase 2	**Father**	-	193
Search Phrase 3	**Word**	-	72
Search Phrase 4	**Holy Ghost**	-	18
Total Mentions	**God + Father + Word + Holy Ghost**		**777**

KJB 494 + 193 + 72 + 18 = **777**	NKJV 480 + 193 + 83 + 20 = 776	ESV 462 + 185 + 73 + 20 = 740	NASB2020 468 + 190 + 80 + 19 = 757	NIV 438 + 184 + 55 + 19 = 696
KJB1611 494 + 193 + 72 + 18 = 777 (including "**worde**")			NASB1971 470 + 189 + 79 + 19 = 757	
Counts for modern versions were completed (even though they mutilate 1 John 5:7) by substituting "Holy Spirit" for "Holy Ghost"				

The Godhead in the New Testament, and in ODD / EVEN books.

<table>
<tr><td colspan="3">God + Father + Word + Holy Ghost
in the New Testament</td></tr>
<tr><td>ALL books
Divisible by 77</td><td>ODD books
Divisible by 7×7</td><td>EVEN books
Exactly 777</td></tr>
<tr><td>2002 =
77 × 26
total mentions</td><td>1225 =
7×7 × 25
total mentions</td><td>777
total mentions</td></tr>
</table>

The number 26 is the infamous Hebrew numeric value of **JEHOVAH** [יהוה] and bears weighty significance in many other respects to God and His word (in both Hebrew and English). For more notes on 26, see *Thy Word Be Verified* on YouTube.

Holy Ghost or Holy Spirit?

Not only are there 777 mentions of "**The Father**" + "**The Word**" + "**Holy Ghost**", but there is also a 7-7-7 pattern of the Godhead discovered by a search for **Jehovah**, **Word** (capitalized), and **Holy Spirit**.

Search Filters **Entire Bible**		Case Sens	Appearances
Search Phrase 1	**Jehovah***	-	**7**
Search Phrase 2	**Word**	Y	**7**
Search Phrase 3	**Holy Spirit**	-	**7**
Jehovah* includes **Jehovah–jireh** (Gen 22:14), **Jehovah–nissi** (Ex 17:15), & **Jehovah–shalom** (Jdg 6:24)			

It's amazing that all of these phenomena only occur in the King James Bible. What's even more amazing is that "**Holy Ghost**" and "**Holy Spirit**" are not different whatsoever in the Greek N.T. They are the exact same.

ἅγιος πνεῦμα (Strong's G40, G4151) = **<u>Holy Ghost</u>** (90 mentions in N.T.)
ἅγιος πνεῦμα (Strong's G40, G4151) = **<u>Holy Spirit</u>** (4 mentions in N.T.)

Which means... if **Holy Ghost** were translated as **Holy Spirit** just 1 more time, the 777-miracle in 1 John 5:7 would be broken (with an updated count of 776) and Holy Spirit would be changed to 8 mentions instead of the perfect 7.

But the plot thickens, because **God** + **Spirit** = 4949 mentions in the KJB.

4949 = 7×707

So if any of the 4 mentions of **Holy Spirit** in the N.T. were changed to **Holy Ghost** for the sake of scholarship / consistency (or vice versa), this perfect sevened "anomaly" would be gone too!

Search Filters: **Entire Bible***		Case Sens	Mentions
Search Phrase 1	**God**	-	4444
Search Phrase 2	**spirit**	-	505
Total Mentions	**God + spirit**		**4949** = **7×707**

When Jesus makes the famous declaration "**God is a Spirit**" (in John 4:24) – He says it in the **777th** chapter where either **'God'** or **'Spirit'** is mentioned.

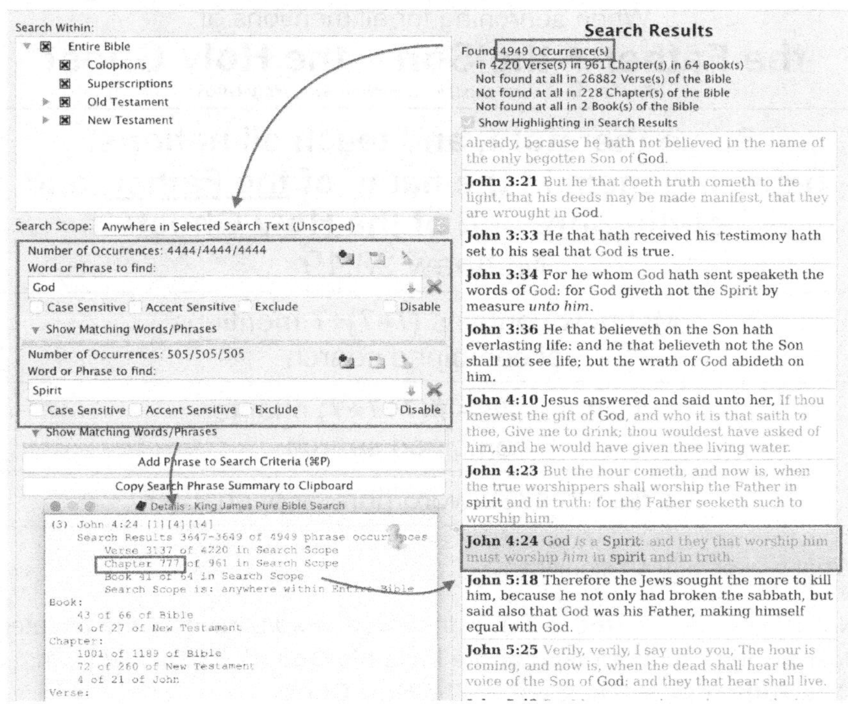

The Father, the Son, the Holy Ghost Mid-777

Go ye therefore, and teach all nations, baptizing them in the name of the Father, and of the Son, and of the Holy Ghost: Matthew 28:19

Matthew 28:19 is the only verse of the Bible to mention the Godhead's names all together in the following manner:

- **the Father**
- **the Son**
- **the Holy Ghost**

In a combined search, (looking up all 3 of them at once), the book of Matthew contains (7×7)+7 combined mentions, and Matthew 28 is the #(7+7+7) chapter in the search results.

When searching for all mentions of **the Father + the Son + the Holy Ghost** *"The" or "the" - and capitalized **Father, Son, Holy Ghost***
Go ye therefore, and teach all nations, baptizing them in the name of <u>the Father</u>, and of <u>the Son</u>, and of <u>the Holy Ghost</u>: Matthew 28:19
Matthew contains **(7×7)+7** mentions of combined search
Matthew 28 = **#(7+7+7)** chapter of combined search
the Son = #389 word/phrase of chapter

What makes 389 so significant?

Notice how Jesus (**the Son**) is the #389 word/phrase of the chapter. Jesus is the express **image of the invisible God** (Col 1:15), Jehovah.
"The Father('s)" + **"The Son"** + **"The Holy Ghost"**
(capitalized "**F**", "**S**" and "**H/G**")
= 389 mentions, **the exact middle of 777**

Note: There are no mentions of "The Son's" or "The Holy Ghost's"

Search Filters: **Entire Bible**		Case Sens	Mentions
Search Phrase 1	**The Father*** **the Father***	Y	125
Search Phrase 2	**The Son*** **the Son***	Y	175
Search Phrase 3	**The Holy Ghost*** **the Holy Ghost***	Y	89
Total Mentions	**"the Father('s)" + "the Son" + "the Holy Ghost"** (capitalized "**F**", "**S**" and "**H/G**")		389 **= #77 Prime** **= Mid-777**
The simplest way to search for this on Pure Bible Search: add 3 search phrases exactly like this (Case-sensitive checked): **?he Father* | ?he Son* | ?he Holy Ghost***			

The deep connection between **389**, **77**, and **777**…

	The relationship of **389** and **777**
389 is the **#77** Prime number	
389 is **Mid-777** (the middle number of **777**)	
389×**777** = **T777** (T777 = 1+2+3+4+5…up to 777)	
The #389 Additive Prime* (5903) is the **#777** Prime (5903)	
3889 is the **#77×7** Prime number	
3889 is **Mid-7777**	
3889×**7777** = **T7777** (T777 = 1+2+3+4+5…up to 7777)	
*An Additive Prime Number is a prime number in which the sum of digits also produces a prime number. The #777 Prime is 5903. 5+9+0+3 = 17 and 17 is a prime number. Therefore, 5903 is an Additive Prime.	

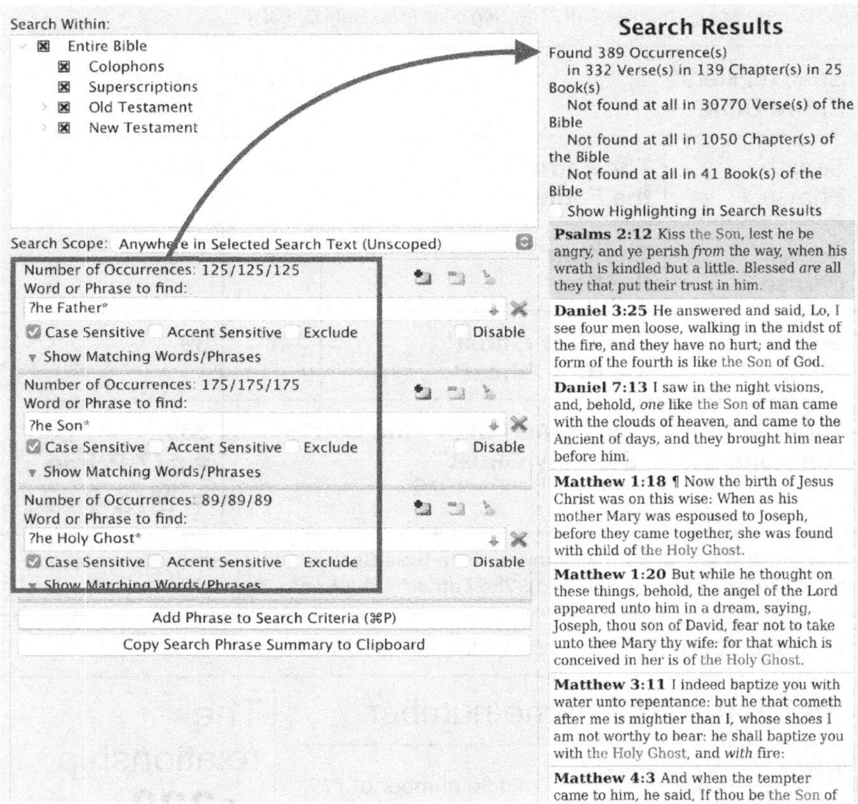

The Godhead in Matthew 28:19 - Bible Version Comparison:

Total appearances of: **The Father* + The Son* + The Holy Ghost*** *Not case-sensitive for "**The**" and Capitalized **Father**, **Son**, **Holy Ghost***				
KJB 125 + 175 + 89 = **389** **#77 Prime** **Mid-777**	NKJV 123 + 180 + 91 = 394	ESV 132 + 161 + 88 = 381	NASB2020 134 + 162 + 88 = 384	NIV 117 + 161 + 87 = 365
KJB1611 111 + 121 + 89 = 321			NASB1971 132 + 166 + 88 = 386	
*Counts for modern versions were completed by substituting "Holy Spirit" for "Holy Ghost" and all extra antimentions such as "~~**the Son**~~ **of Hinnom**" were excluded*				

The English Ordinal sum of 1 John 5:7 + Matthew 28:19 =
389 + 389 + 389 + 389 + 389
= #77 Prime + #77 Prime + #77 Prime + #77 Prime + #77 Prime
= Mid777 + Mid777 + Mid777 + Mid777 + Mid777

<table>
<tr><td colspan="2">The Godhead verses
English Ordinal</td></tr>
<tr><td>1 John 5:7</td><td>Matthew 28:19</td></tr>
<tr><td>For there are three that bear record in heaven, the Father, the Word, and the Holy Ghost: and these three are one.</td><td>Go ye therefore, and teach all nations, baptizing them in the name of the Father, and of the Son, and of the Holy Ghost:</td></tr>
<tr><td>English Ordinal
= 946</td><td>English Ordinal
= 999</td></tr>
<tr><td colspan="2">Total Sum
946 + 999 = 1945

= 389 + 389 + 389 + 389 + 389

= Mid777 + Mid777 + Mid777 + Mid777 + Mid777

= 777 + 777 + 391

• In Hebrew Numerics, יהושע [Joshua/Jesus] = 391
• Jesus' name means Jehovah is salvation and the first mention of salvation in the Bible is the #391 word of chapter #(7×7) (Gen 49:18)
• LORD + GOD (BOTH UPPERCASE) = 3391 + 3391 mentions
• All appearances of Father* capitalized = 3×91 mentions in the N.T.
• The first 777 words of the Bible contain 3091 letters
• The #3091 mention of God is the #1 mention of God in the N.T., which defines Jesus' prophetic name (Mat 1:23)
• The #3091 alphabetically sorted word of the Hebrew Bible = Joshua/Jesus [יהושע] which means (Jehovah is salvation)</td></tr>
</table>

Holy One + Father + Son + Spirit 777

...and these three are <u>one</u>. 1 John 5:7

...The Lord our God is <u>one</u> Lord: Mark 12:29

To whom then will ye liken me, or shall I be equal? saith the <u>Holy One</u>. Isaiah 40:25

Who is the **Holy One**? He is **God**. The **Godhead**.

Father* + Son* + Spirit* (All Capitalized) (Concealed appearances: "Son" in "Song")
= 777 appearances

Holy + Father* + Son* + Spirit* + Godhead (All Capitalized)
(No concealed appearances)
= 777 verses

Holy One + Father + Son + Spirit (All Capitalized)
= 777 mentions

Search Filters: **Entire Bible**		Case Sens	Mentions
Search Phrase 1	**Holy One**	Y	48
Search Phrase 2	**Father**	Y	260
Search Phrase 3	**Son**	Y	297
Search Phrase 4	**Spirit**	Y	172
Total Mentions	**Holy One + Father + Son + Spirit** (All Capitalized)		**777**
KJB-PCE = 774 KJB1611 = 363 NKJV = 991 ESV = 930 NASB2020 = 916 NASB1971 = 926 NIV = 944			

Holy (capitalized) is mentioned 144 times. The #144 mention of the search (**Holy One + Father + Son + Spirit**) (Capitalized) is at Jesus' baptism where all 3 are clearly listed: the **Son** being baptized, the **Spirit** descending on him like a dove, and the **Father** speaking from heaven.

Holy (Capitalized) 144 mentions in the entire Bible	**Holy One +** **Father + Son + Spirit** (All Capitalized) #144 out of 777 mentions is **<u>Son</u>** in Matthew 3:17

And Jesus, when he was baptized, went up straightway out of the water: and, lo, the heavens were opened unto him, and he saw the Spirit of God descending like a dove, and lighting upon him: And lo a voice from heaven, saying, This is my beloved <u>Son</u>, in whom I am well pleased.

Matthew 3:16-17

The #144 mention *(of the combined search)* is…

The **<u>Son</u>** with the **Spirit** lighting upon him and the **Father** speaking to him…

They are all together in the same passage.

The **Holy One.**

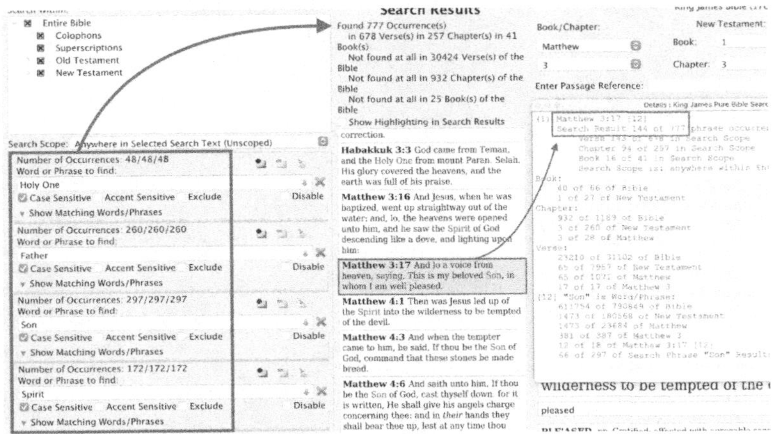

For in him dwelleth all the fulness of
the Godhead bodily.

Colossians 2:9

Jesus Christ, the Godhead bodily 777 - Part 1

For in him dwelleth all the fulness of the Godhead bodily.
Colossians 2:9

Jesus + Christ + the Father + the Word + the Holy Ghost
= 777 mentions in the four gospels (case sensitive, including **JESUS**)

Search Filters: **Matthew, Mark, Luke, John**		Case Sens	Mentions
Search Phrase 1	**Jesus**	Y	617
Search Phrase 2	**Christ**	Y	60
Search Phrase 3	**the Father**	Y	72
Search Phrase 4	**the Word**	Y	4
Search Phrase 5	**the Holy Ghost**	Y	24
Total Mentions	**Jesus + Christ + "the Father" + "the Word" + "the Holy Ghost"** *Case sensitive, in the gospels*		**777**
If using Pure Bible Search, you must include (case sensitive) **Jesus** and **JESUS**			
KJB1611 = 773 NKJV = 775 ESV = 771 NASB2020 = 796 NASB1971 = 727 NIV = 1008			

God, who at sundry times and in divers manners spake in time past unto the fathers by the prophets, Hath in these last days spoken unto us by his Son, whom he hath appointed heir of all things, by whom also he made the worlds; Who being the brightness of his glory, and <u>the express image of his person</u>, and upholding all things by the word of his power, when he had by himself purged our sins, sat down on the right hand of the Majesty on high; Being made so much better than the angels, as he hath by inheritance obtained a more excellent name than they. Hebrews 1:1-4

There are few words to describe how incredible this is, knowing that God was manifest in the flesh, wherein the fulness of the Godhead dwells.

And it doesn't just happen once… Nor twice… Nor three times…
God did *not* want us to miss this:

The Godhead Bodily in the Four Gospels (*All searches are case-sensitive within **Matthew, Mark, Luke, John***)			
Search Combination A	Search Combination B	Search Combination C	Search Combination D
Jesus / JESUS **Christ** **the Father** **the Word** **the Holy Ghost**	**Jesus** **Christ / Messias** **?he Father*** **?he Word*** **?he Holy Ghost***	**the Father*** **Jesus*** **Christ** **the Holy Ghost***	**?he Father** **Jesus*** **Christ** **?he Holy Ghost**
777 **mentions in the gospels (KJB)**	**777** **mentions in the gospels (KJB)**	**777** **mentions in the gospels (KJB)**	**777** **mentions in the gospels (KJB)**
KJB1611 = 773 NKJV = 775 ESV = 773 NASB2020 = 799 NASB1971 = 728 NIV = 1008	KJB1611 = 777 NKJV = 775 ESV = 782 NASB2020 = 806 NASB1971 = 734 NIV = 1066	KJB1611 = 769 NKJV = 773 ESV = 780 NASB2020 = 799 NASB1971 = 731 NIV = 1038	KJB1611 = 769 NKJV = 775 ESV = 777 NASB2020 = 799 NASB1971 = 729 NIV = 1035
Asterisk (*) means all possessive mentions are included. (**?he**) means both capitalized "**The**" and lowercase "**the**" are included *Holy Spirit was included for modern versions instead of **Holy Ghost**, as well as Messiah instead of **Messias**.*			

Even though modern Bible counts are included here, there really is no business adding them at all (for combination A & B), since they (except the NKJV) completely take out the Godhead from 1 John 5:7. To modern scholars, this verse with **the Father, the Word, and the Holy Ghost** is "spurious" and therefore you have little to no purpose in searching for these three words in conjunction with Jesus Christ in the gospels.

For there are three that bear record in heaven, the Father, the Word, and the Holy Ghost: and these three are one. 1 John 5:7

Combination A

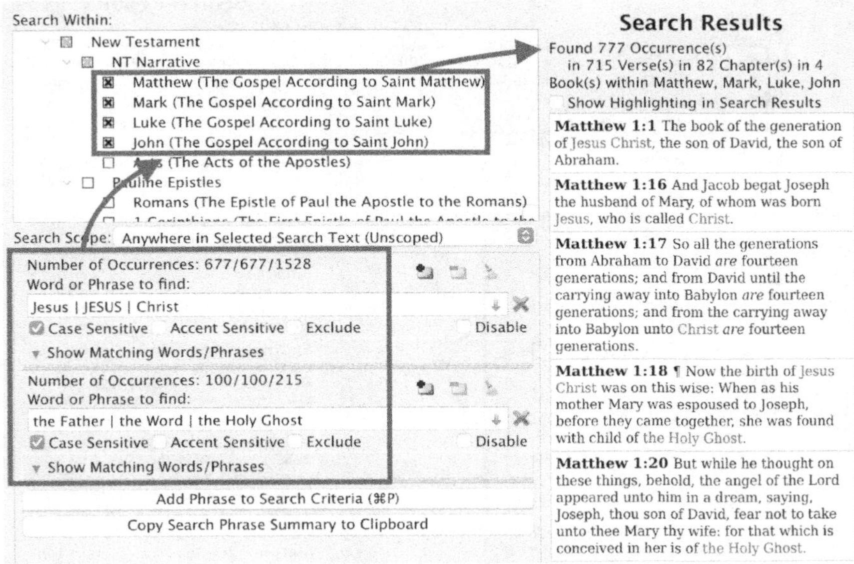

Combination B

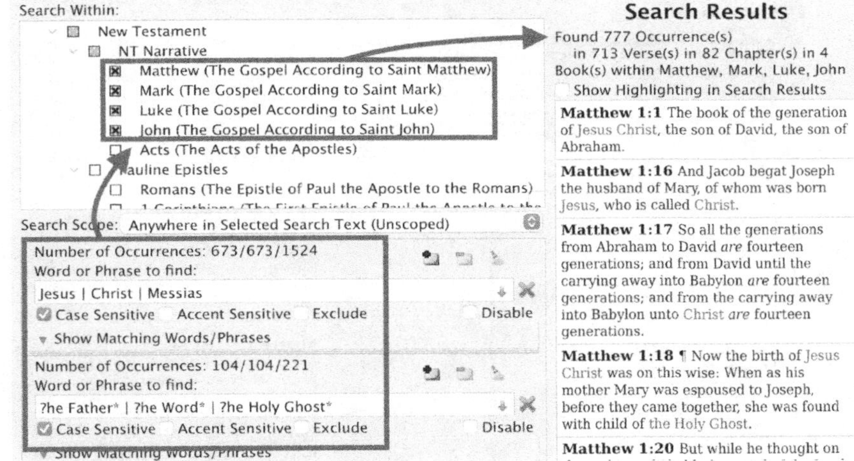

Combination C

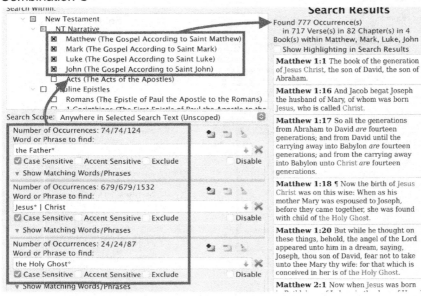

Combination D

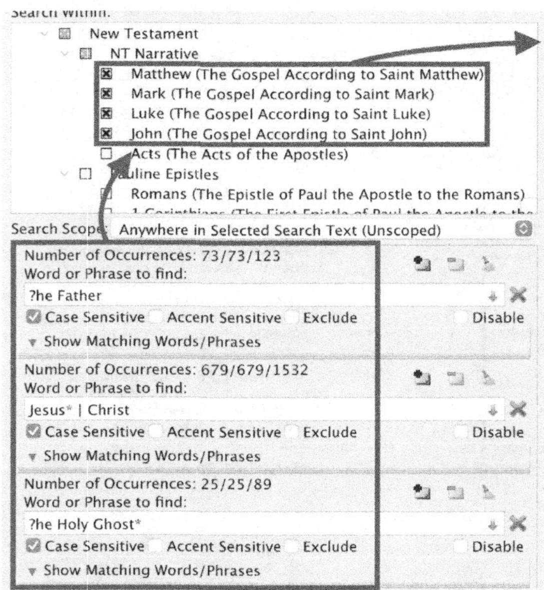

Jesus Christ, the Godhead bodily 777 - Part 2

In the King James Bible, **Holy Spirit** is mentioned 7 times. Although we've already covered this on p. 140, the interesting thing is that only 1 of those mentions is fully capitalized. Why did **Holy Ghost** get fully capitalized every single time, but not **Holy Spirit**? If God perfectly inspired this book, there is obviously a reason for this.

Here are all seven mentions of **Holy Spirit** in the KJB, with only the middle-mention in Luke 11:13 being fully capitalized:

All 7 mentions of **Holy Spirit** in the KJB	
holy spirit	Psalms 51:11 **Cast me not away from thy presence; and take not thy holy spirit from me.**
holy Spirit	Isaiah 63:10 **But they rebelled, and vexed his holy Spirit: therefore he was turned to be their enemy, and he fought against them.**
holy Spirit	Isaiah 63:11 **Then he remembered the days of old, Moses, and his people, saying, Where is he that brought them up out of the sea with the shepherd of his flock? where is he that put his holy Spirit within him?**
Holy Spirit	Luke 11:13 **If ye then, being evil, know how to give good gifts unto your children: how much more shall your heavenly Father give the Holy Spirit to them that ask him?**
holy Spirit	Ephesians 1:13 **In whom ye also trusted, after that ye heard the word of truth, the gospel of your salvation: in whom also after that ye believed, ye were sealed with that holy Spirit of promise,**
holy Spirit	Ephesians 4:30 **And grieve not the holy Spirit of God, whereby ye are sealed unto the day of redemption.**
holy Spirit	1 Thessalonians 4:8 **He therefore that despiseth, despiseth not man, but God, who hath also given unto us his holy Spirit.**

I believe without question that this is God's way of **sevening** both **Holy Spirit** and **Holy Ghost**. What do I mean? Since **Holy Ghost** is always capitalized, the only mention of **Holy Spirit** that matches it by case-sensitivity is the one in Luke 11:13. **Holy Spirit** is directly related to **Holy Ghost** in this one instance. Which means, combined, **Holy Ghost** (90 mentions) + **Holy Spirit** (1 mention) = 91 = 7 × 13 mentions.

In case you haven't been keeping track, let's take a look at the Godhead by each person in the King James Bible.

Father	Son	Holy Ghost / Holy Spirit
259 = **7 × 37** mentions (capitalized / God)	231 = **7 × 33** mentions (capitalized / Jesus)	91 = **7 × 13** mentions (fully capitalized)

The Godhead, three in one, is perfectly sevened across the board when you exclude all of the antimentions (the mentions which are not actually referring to God the Father or His Son, Jesus).

And here is what happens when you add His name, **Jesus Christ**.

Jesus Christ = 196 = **7 × 28** mentions

The total sum in the entire Bible...

Father + Son + Holy Ghost/Holy Spirit + Jesus Christ (All Fully Capitalized, excluding antimentions)
= 777 mentions in the Holy Bible
KJB1611 = 408 NKJV = 803 ESV = 707 NASB2020 = 712 NASB1971 = 723 NIV = 707
The KJB1611 was much lower because "**Holy Ghost**" was spelled "**holy Ghost**" (not fully capitalized) - See details in Appendix 1

Father (capitalized, God) = 259 = 7 × 37 mentions
Son (capitalized, Jesus) = 231 = 7 × 33 mentions
Holy Ghost / Holy Spirit (capitalized) = 91 = 7 × 13 mentions
Jesus Christ = 196 = 7 × 28 mentions

259 + 231 + 91 + 196 =

777 mentions

Father, Son, Holy Ghost/Holy Spirit, Jesus Christ

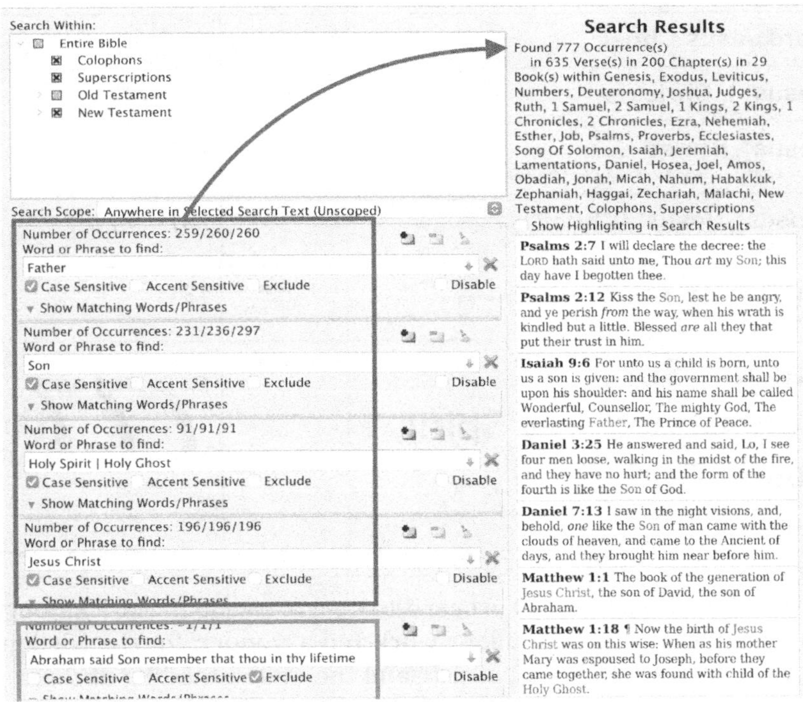

"Exclude" in Pure Bible Search: " **Son go work** " (-1), " **Son thou art** " (-1), " **Abraham said Son** " (-1), " **palsy Son** " (-2), " **Father Abraham** " (-1), " **Son of man** " in Ezekiel (-61) *[Shortcut: just deselect "Ezekiel" in filters]*

This means we have an item to add to the King's seal: the last mention of **our Lord Jesus Christ** in the Holy Bible. For sake of space, let's only look at instances within the Entire Bible. *(The full chart is on p. 583)*

The Last mention *of* our Lord Jesus Christ in Revelation 22:21		
Word	Within	Mention / Appearance #
Jesus(') *Excluding Justus & Joshua named Jesus. See appendix 7*	Entire Bible	**70×7+70×7**
Jesus, David	Entire Bible	**7×7×7×6**
Lord Jesus	Entire Bible	**7×7th Prime**
our Lord Jesus	Entire Bible	**7×7+7**
Jesus Christ	Entire Bible	**T7×7**
Lord Jesus Christ	Entire Bible	**77+7**
Jesus('), Christ('s) *Total mentions combined*	Entire Bible	**777+777**
Jesus*, Christ* *Total appearances combined, excluding Justus & Joshua named Jesus & false Christs (Mat 24:24, Mark 13:22)*	Entire Bible	**777+777**
Moses*, Jesus*, Christ* *Total appearances combined, excluding antimentions, excluding superscriptions*	Entire Bible	**7×7×7×7**
our Lord, Jesus, Christ *Case-sensitive, excluding Justus & Joshua. See appendix 7*	Entire Bible	**1611**
Father, Son, Holy Ghost/Holy Spirit, Jesus Christ *Total mentions combined, Case-sensitive, excluding antimentions (Only referring to God the Father, and Jesus the Son)*	Entire Bible	**777**

Therefore, behold, I will proceed to do a marvellous work among this people, even a marvellous work and a wonder: for the wisdom of their wise men shall perish, and the understanding of their prudent men shall be hid.

Isaiah 29:14

God + Jesus + Holy Spirit in the N.T. 777×3

For there are three that bear record in heaven, the Father, the Word, and the Holy Ghost: and these three are one. 1 John 5:7

The Father + The Word + Holy Ghost = 777 mentions (see p. 130)

Alternate names (most commonly used by all Christians)

The Father = **God**

The Word = **Jesus**

Holy Ghost = **Holy Spirit**

Following the same pattern as the 777-Godhead pattern of 1 John 5:7, all you have to do is search for these words in the New Testament, without any fancy exclusions or case-sensitivity settings.

In the New Testament		
God	**Jesus**	**Holy Spirit**
1354 mentions	973 mentions	4 mentions
Total Mentions: 2331 = **777 + 777 + 777**		
KJB1611 = 2340 NKJV = 2394 ESV = 2330 NASB2020 = 2378 NASB1971 = 2296 NIV = 2604		

The word count of the name of **Jesus** (973) is in the text of the Bible itself (Neh 7:39), directly beside Jesus' name in Hebrew. See p. 382.

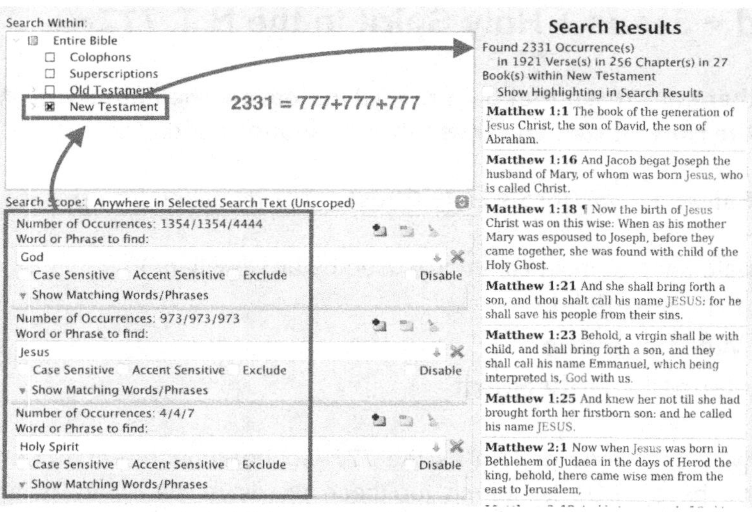

<table>
<tr><th colspan="4">The Godhead</th></tr>
<tr><td>The Father</td><td rowspan="3">777
Total mentions in the Bible</td><td>God</td><td rowspan="3">777+
777+
777
Total mentions in the N.T.</td></tr>
<tr><td>The Word</td><td>Jesus</td></tr>
<tr><td>Holy Ghost</td><td>Holy Spirit</td></tr>
<tr><td colspan="4">Come ye near unto me, hear ye this; I have not spoken in secret from the beginning; from the time that it was, there am I: and now the Lord GOD, and his Spirit, hath sent me.

Isaiah 48:16</td></tr>
<tr><td colspan="4">Then said they unto him, Who art thou? And Jesus saith unto them, Even the same that I said unto you from the beginning. I have many things to say and to judge of you: but he that sent me is true; and I speak to the world those things which I have heard of him.

John 8:25-26</td></tr>
</table>

The Godhead, These Three Are One 777

Before the mountains were brought forth, or ever thou hadst formed the earth and the world, even from everlasting to everlasting, thou art God. Psalm 90:2

God knew all of His words would be gathered and translated into a completed book in these last days. Do you believe that?

The Godhead *in* the Holy Bible		
Words	Within	Mention / Appearance #
the Father, the Word, Holy Ghost *See p. 130*	Entire Bible	**777**
God, Father, Word, Holy Ghost *See p. 138*	N.T. EVEN books	**777**
The Father, The Son, The Holy Ghost *("The" or "the," capitalized "F", "S" and "H/G") See p. 143*	Entire Bible	**Mid-777 (#77 Prime)**
Father*, Son*, Spirit* *(all capitalized) See p. 146*	Entire Bible	**777**
Holy One, Father, Son, Spirit *(all capitalized) See p. 146*	Entire Bible	**777**
the Father, the Word, the Holy Ghost, Jesus, Christ *(case sensitive) See p. 149*	Gospels	**777**
The Father*, The Word*, The Holy Ghost* Jesus, Christ, Messias *(case sensitive except for The/the, *includes possessive) See p. 150*	Gospels	**777**
the Father*, Jesus*, Christ, the Holy Ghost* *(case sensitive, *includes possessive) See p. 150*	Gospels	**777**
the Father, Jesus*, Christ, the Holy Ghost *(case sensitive except for The/the, *includes possessive) See p. 150*	Gospels	**777**
God, Jesus, Holy Spirit *See p. 157*	New Testament	**777+ 777+ 777**
Father, Son, Holy Ghost / Holy Spirit, Jesus Christ *Total mentions combined, Case-sensitive, excluding antimentions (Only referring to God the Father, and Jesus the Son). See p. 154*	Entire Bible	**777**

The Lord + Jesus + Christ 777 in the Gospels

Acts 16:31 **...Believe on the Lord Jesus Christ, and thou shalt be saved...**

Maybe it's just me, but I feel that the most complete name/title of our Saviour in the Bible is "the Lord Jesus Christ." There is a certain weight and power behind it that permeates my soul whenever I hear it proclaimed from the preacher's lips. When we look at the four gospels, which of course are completely unique books of the Bible that detail the life and ministry of Jesus, this is what we find...

Search Filters: **Matthew, Mark, Luke, John**		Case Sens	Mentions
Search Phrase 1	**the Lord**	Y	90
Search Phrase 2	**Jesus | Jesus'**	-	625
Search Phrase 3	**Christ | Messias**	-	62
Total Mentions	**"the Lord" + Jesus + Jesus' + Christ + Messias**		**777**
Notes: There are not any possessive mentions of **Christ's** in the gospels. **Christ** and **Messias** are synonymous (John 1:41).			
KJB1611 = 784 NKJV1982 = 750 ESV = 753 NASB2020 = 757 NASB1971 = 712 NIV = 1069			

Now I openly admit, this pattern feels a bit cherry-picked compared to the other discoveries I typically publish. **Jesus** includes possessive **Jesus'**, while **the Lord** does not. Nevertheless, it's worth publishing, as the chances are still incredibly slim that one could so easily put these words together to produce such a sum. Plus, there seems to be validation in two or three other ways. Take, for example, the mentions of "possessive" **the Lord's** in the gospels and elsewhere in the Bible, and notice what happens:

(Case sensitive for all counts)
the Lord (in the Bible) = 765 mentions
the Lord's (in the Bible, *except the 4 gospels*) = 12 mentions
Total mentions (765 + 12) = 777 mentions (Excluding **the Lord's** in the Gospels)

It feels like a very strong witness to exclude possessive **the Lord's** from the gospels count.

There is yet another witness that does include **the Lord's**...

When you include all forms of **the Lord** in the gospels (where Lord is capitalized), including double capitalized **The Lord** and possessive **the Lord's**, the 777-pattern emerges again without struggle (simply flipping it around to count standard, non-possessive **Jesus** and **Christ/Messias**)

Search Filters: **Matthew, Mark, Luke, John**		Case Sens	Mentions
Search Phrase 1	**The Lord | the Lord | the Lord's**	Y	98
Search Phrase 2	**Jesus**	-	617
Search Phrase 3	**Christ | Messias**	-	62
Total Mentions	**"The Lord" + "the Lord" + "the Lord's" + Jesus + Christ + Messias**		**777**
Note: There are not any possessive mentions of **The Lord's** (capitalized T) in the gospels.			
KJB1611 = 796 NKJV = 756 ESV = 761 NASB2020 = 762 NASB1971 = 719 NIV = 1059			

And it was revealed unto him by the Holy Ghost, that he should not see death, before he had seen the Lord's Christ.

Luke 2:26

...for that thy name is near thy wondrous works declare.

Psalm 75:1

UPPERCASE Names/Titles of GOD + Jesus 7777

This is perhaps the most mind-boggling "coincidence" in the entire Bible. It is found by taking the sum of **ALL** UPPERCASE standard (non-possessive) names/titles of God (**JEHOVAH, I AM, JAH, LORD, GOD**) plus **ALL** UPPERCASE names/titles of Jesus (**JESUS, BRANCH, KING**) together with the sum of **ALL** remaining mentions of **Jesus(')**.

Search Filters: **Entire Bible**		Case Sens	Mentions
Search Phrase 1	**LORD**	Y	6472
Search Phrase 2	**GOD**	Y	310
Search Phrase 3	**JEHOVAH**	Y	4
Search Phrase 4	**I AM**	Y	3
Search Phrase 5	**JAH**	Y	1
Search Phrase 6	**BRANCH**	Y	2
Search Phrase 7	**KING**	Y	5
Search Phrase 8	**JESUS**	Y	6
Search Phrase 9	**Jesus(')**	Y	977
Exclude	*Exclude all others named* **Jesus**, *specifically Joshua (Act 7:45, Heb 4:8) and Justus (1x) (Col 4:11)*		-3
Total Mentions	**LORD + GOD + JEHOVAH + I AM + JAH + BRANCH + KING + JESUS + Jesus + Jesus'**		**7777**
KJB1611 = ? NKJV = 7830 ESV = 7762 NASB2020 = 7921 NASB1971 = ? NIV = 7848			
The KJB1611 and NASB1971 databases I have do not contain LORD in uppercase.			

What makes this incredible is that there are no other UPPERCASED names or titles for God / Jesus in the entire Bible. What you see in the table are ALL the possibilities. It really makes you wonder, was it God or random chances that determined certain names/titles to be fully uppercased? For example, compare the following verses.

Example 1 **BRANCH** Zechariah 6:12	**...Thus speaketh the LORD of hosts, saying, Behold the man whose name is The BRANCH; and he shall grow up out of his place, and he shall build the temple of the LORD:**
Example 2 **Jealous** Exodus 34:14	**For thou shalt worship no other god: for the LORD, whose name is Jealous, is a jealous God:**
Example 3 **Holy** Isaiah 57:15	**For thus saith the high and lofty One that inhabiteth eternity, whose name is Holy; I dwell in the high and holy place...**

Why is **BRANCH** fully uppercased but not **Jealous** nor **Holy**?

Or take, for example, **LORD** in the New Testament.

The LORD said unto my Lord, Sit thou on my right hand, till I make thine enemies thy footstool? Matthew 22:44

Jesus said unto him, It is written again, Thou shalt not tempt the Lord thy God. Matthew 4:7

Why is **LORD** fully uppercased in Matthew 22:44 but not in Matthew 4:7 or most other places where the LORD (Jehovah) is mentioned in the NT?

Without these anomalies that most people would consider as "inconsistent," the KJB would not be able to produce the incredible sum of **7777** mentions of **UPPERCASE NAMES/TITLES of God + Jesus.**

Furthermore, the combination of God's UPPERCASE names (**LORD, GOD, I AM, JEHOVAH, JAH**) produce a sum of 7 × 970 mentions.

Jesus (non-posssessive, excluding antimentions) = 970 mentions in the KJB. See Appendix 7.

Who ascribes this to random chance?!

The “**GOD-MIRACLE**” of the King James Bible
(UPPERCASE) **LORD, GOD, I AM, JEHOVAH, JAH** **7 × 970 mentions**
(UPPERCASE) **BRANCH, KING** **7 mentions**
All mentions of Jesus, *excluding Joshua/Justus*: **JESUS, Jesus(‘)** **7 × 140 mentions**
Total Mentions in the KJB = **7777**
There are no other UPPERCASE names/titles of God or Jesus in the Bible. These are all of them.

The God-miracle of the King James Bible, screenshot proof:

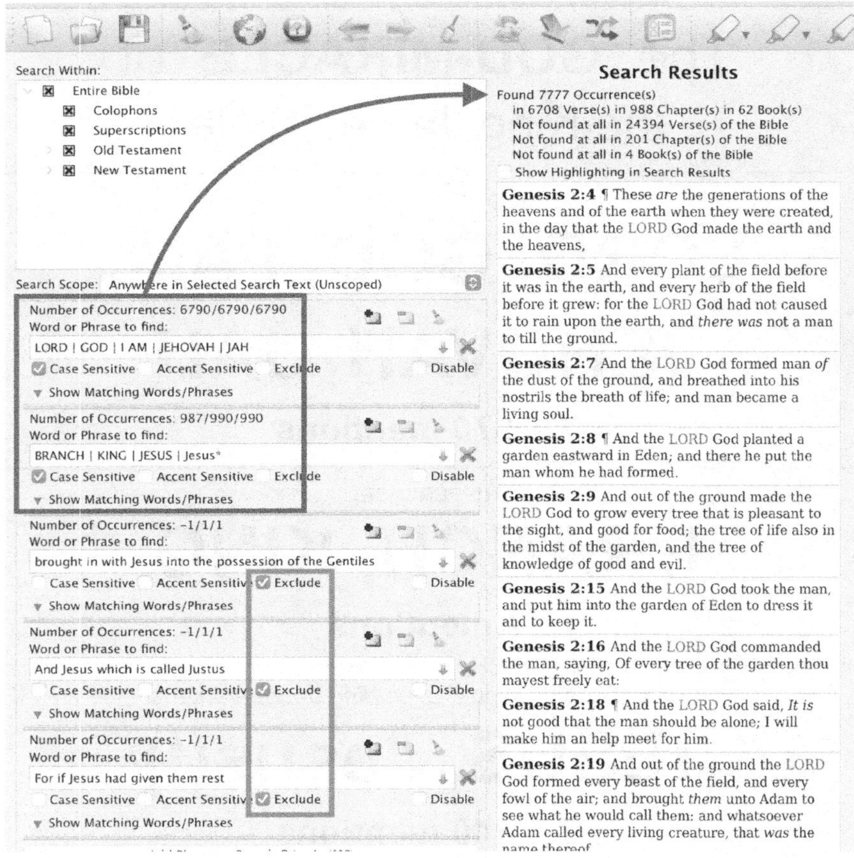

Unto thee it was shewed, that thou mightest know that the LORD he is God; there is none else beside him.

Deuteronomy 4:35

JESUS (UPPERCASE) 77+77

The sum of verse numbers at Jesus' birth/circumcision where His name is fully UPPERCASE, **JESUS** = **7×7 + 7×7**.

All **birth / circumcision** mentions of **JESUS** (UPPERCASE)		
All mentions of **JESUS**	Book, Chapter	Verse
And she shall bring forth a son, and thou shalt call his name JESUS: for he shall save his people from their sins.	Matthew 1	21 **(7+7+7)**
And knew her not till she had brought forth her firstborn son: and he called his name JESUS.	Matthew 1	25
And, behold, thou shalt conceive in thy womb, and bring forth a son, and shalt call his name JESUS.	Luke 1	31
And when eight days were accomplished for the circumcising of the child, his name was called JESUS, which was so named of the angel before he was conceived in the womb.	Luke 2	21 **(7+7+7)**
Sum of Verse Numbers		98 = **7×7+7×7**

The only other mentions of **JESUS** (UPPERCASE) in the actual text of the Bible are at His crucifixion. In total, there are 6 mentions *(the number of man)* of **JESUS** (UPPERCASE) in the Bible, perfectly representing His humanity- since all mentions are directly tied to His birth / circumcision and His death *(the beginning and end of man)*.

All **death / crucifixion** mentions of **JESUS** (UPPERCASE)		
All mentions of **JESUS**	Book, Chapter	Verse
And set up over his head his accusation written, THIS IS JESUS THE KING OF THE JEWS.	Matthew 27	37
And Pilate wrote a title, and put it on the cross. And the writing was, JESUS OF NAZARETH THE KING OF THE JEWS.	John 19	19
	Sum of Verse Numbers	56 = **7×7+7**

Total Sum of Verse Numbers mentioning

JESUS (UPPERCASE) = 154

Birth/Circumcision **(7×7+7×7)** + Death/Crucifixion **(7×7+7)**

= 77+77

There is also a concealed 7th mention of **JESUS** *(not found in the actual text) but printed in the text of most King James Bibles- pointing to His deity. See the table in Appendix 7.*

Son + God 777 O.T. chapters

Search the scriptures; for in them ye think ye have eternal life: and they are they which testify of me. John 5:39

In the Old Testament, **Son** + **God** are mentioned in **777** chapters.

In the Old Testament
Son + God
777
chapters
KJB1611 = 777 NKJV = 776 ESV = 775 NASB2020 = 770 NASB1971 = 770 NIV = 766

For had ye believed Moses, ye would have believed me: for he wrote of me. But if ye believe not his writings, how shall ye believe my words? John 5:46-47

For verily I say unto you, That many prophets and righteous men have desired to see those things which ye see, and have not seen them; and to hear those things which ye hear, and have not heard them. Matthew 13:17

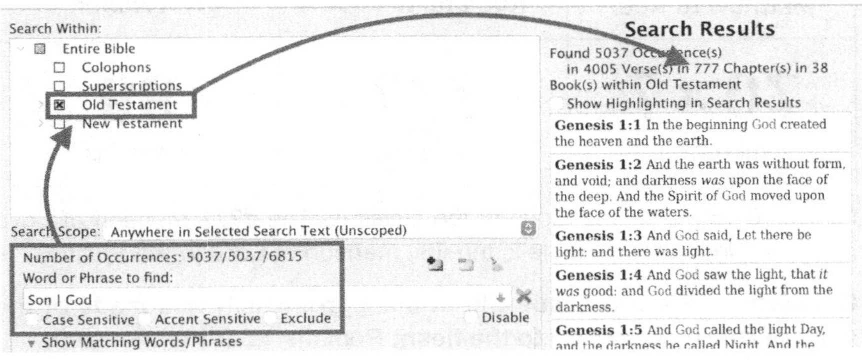

God in the New Testament 70×7, 777, 99

In the New Testament, there are a total of 1366 mentions of God('s) when capitalized / uppercase.

God (Capitalized) = 1349 mentions
GOD (UPPERCASE) = 1 mention
God's (Capitalized) = 16 mentions

On the surface, nothing of significance appears. That's exactly how God is perceived by those with a hardened heart. All they see is the surface. They never press in. They never go to their closet on their knees before their Creator. They never humble their hearts before the King of glory. So they mock and cast God's words behind them.

But God reveals himself to those who are humble- who fear Him. **The secret of the LORD is with them that fear him; and he will shew them his covenant.** Psalm 25:14

Do you fear **God**? Take those 1366 mentions and watch how they are revealed in the New Testament.

God (Capitalized, **God**, **GOD**, **God's**) in the New Testament		
Historical **Matthew to Acts**	Epistles **Romans to Jude**	Apocalypse **Revelation**
70×7 mentions	**777** mentions	**99** mentions

Notice, **God** = **777** mentions in the *Epistles*. The **#777** mention of **Lord** (Case-sens) in the entire Bible is the first mention of **Lord** in the *Epistles*.

Concerning his Son Jesus Christ our <u>Lord</u>, which was made of the seed of David according to the flesh; Romans 1:3 (#777 mention)

God('s) in the Historical books (Gospels + Acts): 490 = 70 × 7 mentions

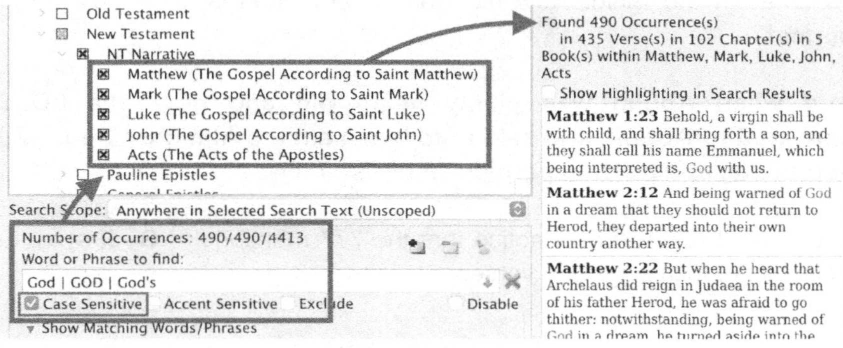

God('s) in the Epistles (Romans to Jude): 777 mentions

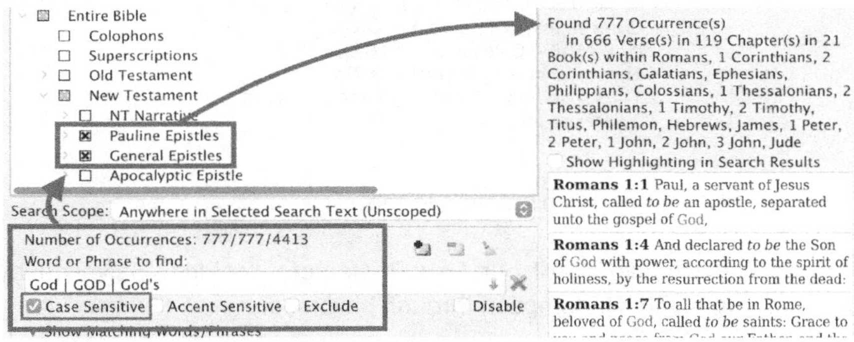

God('s) in the Apocalypse (Revelation): 99 mentions

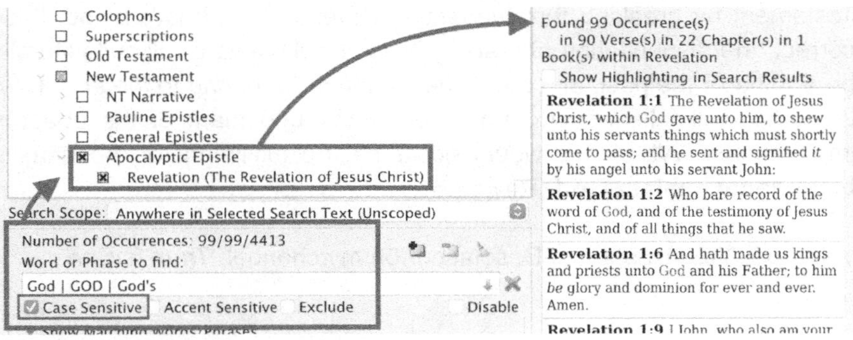

Why 99 mentions of **God** in Revelation? The word "**perfect**" is mentioned 99 times in the Bible. How old was Abram when **God** told him to be **perfect**?

And when Abram was ninety years old and nine, the LORD appeared to Abram, and said unto him, I am the Almighty God; walk before me, and be thou perfect. Genesis 17:1

The careful eye will also notice that the 777 mentions of **God('s)** in the Epistles are located in 666 verses.

Search Results

Found 777 Occurrence(s)
in 666 Verse(s) in 119 Chapter(s) in 21 Book(s) within Romans, 1 Corinthians, 2 Corinthians, Galatians, Ephesians, Philippians, Colossians, 1 Thessalonians, 2 Thessalonians, 1 Timothy, 2 Timothy, Titus, Philemon, Hebrews, James, 1 Peter, 2 Peter, 1 John, 2 John, 3 John, Jude

There might be an eerie connection to that.

The Epistles contain all of our New Testament doctrine. Salvation by grace through faith. Redemption through his blood.

I have a 3.5 hour long Bible study / theory on YouTube that explores the disturbing possibility of the antichrist completely voiding the New Testament by breaking the everlasting covenant of Christ's blood. If it's correct, the dispensation of grace given to Paul us-ward will quite literally be a thing of the past, and the dispensation of "*enduring to the end*" (Mat 24:13-31) will take effect… right before the 666 mark of the beast is implemented. All of this would occur as the fulfillment of the beast's **blasphemy against God** (Rev 13:6).

YouTube: "Abomination of Desolation" on my channel: *Truth is Christ*.

Father 7×7

At that time Jesus answered and said, I thank thee, O Father, Lord of heaven and earth, because thou hast hid these things from the wise and prudent, and hast revealed them unto babes.
Matthew 11:25

In Matthew and Revelation only (the first and last books of the New Testament), there are **7×7** mentions of **Father('s)** (Capitalized).

Search Filters: **Matthew, Revelation**		Case Sens	Mentions
Search Phrase 1	**Father**	Y	47
Search Phrase 2	**Father's**	Y	2
Total Mentions	**Father*** *(capitalized)*		49 **=7×7**
KJB1611 = 18 NKJV = 49 ESV = 49 NASB1971 = 49 NASB2020 = 49 NIV = 49			

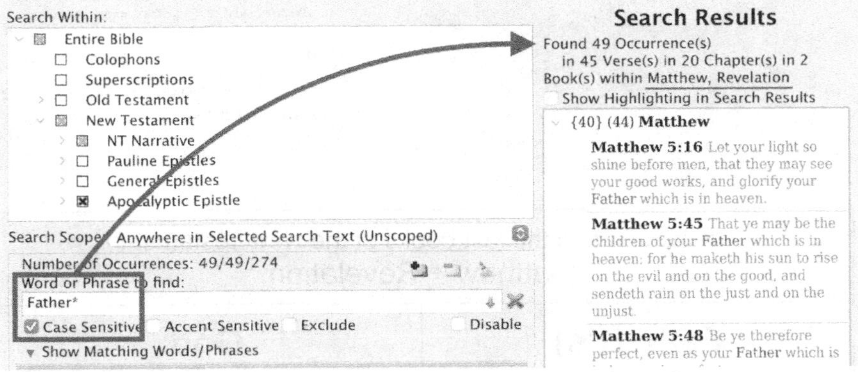

Also in Matthew & Revelation, there are a total of 154 mentions of **God**.
154 = **77+77**

Search Filters: **Matthew, Revelation**		Case Sens	Mentions
Search Phrase 1	**God**	Y	154
Total Mentions	**God**		154 **=77+77**
KJB1611 = 154 NKJV = 154 ESV = 145 NASB1971 = 146 NASB2020 = 134 NIV = 136			

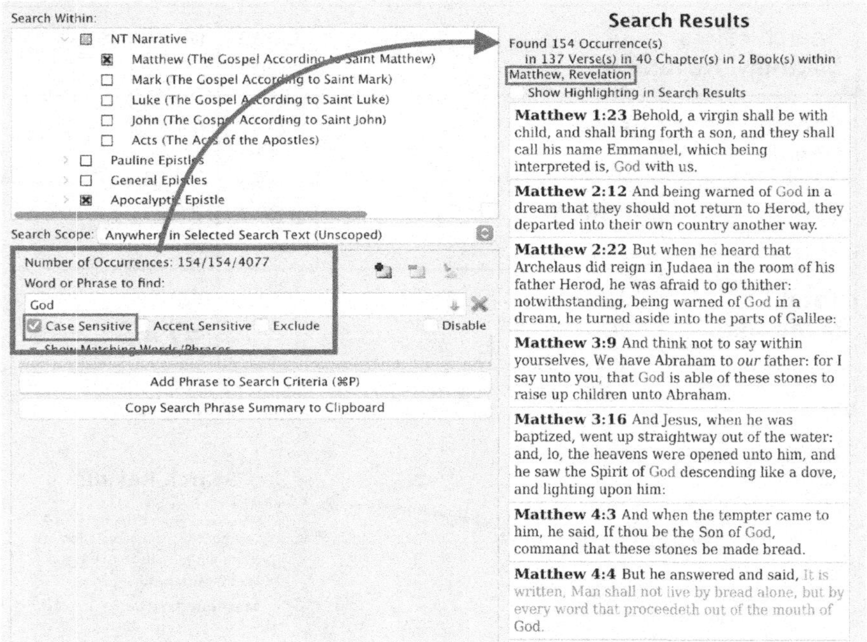

Search Within:
NT Narrative
Matthew (The Gospel According to Saint Matthew)
Mark (The Gospel According to Saint Mark)
Luke (The Gospel According to Saint Luke)
John (The Gospel According to Saint John)
Acts (The Acts of the Apostles)
Pauline Epistles
General Epistles
Apocalyptic Epistle

Search Scope: Anywhere in Selected Search Text (Unscoped)
Number of Occurrences: 154/154/4077
Word or Phrase to find:
God
Case Sensitive Accent Sensitive Exclude Disable
Add Phrase to Search Criteria (⌘P)
Copy Search Phrase Summary to Clipboard

Search Results
Found 154 Occurrence(s)
in 137 Verse(s) in 40 Chapter(s) in 2 Book(s) within
Matthew, Revelation
Show Highlighting in Search Results

Matthew 1:23 Behold, a virgin shall be with child, and shall bring forth a son, and they shall call his name Emmanuel, which being interpreted is, God with us.

Matthew 2:12 And being warned of God in a dream that they should not return to Herod, they departed into their own country another way.

Matthew 2:22 But when he heard that Archelaus did reign in Judaea in the room of his father Herod, he was afraid to go thither: notwithstanding, being warned of God in a dream, he turned aside into the parts of Galilee:

Matthew 3:9 And think not to say within yourselves, We have Abraham to *our* father: for I say unto you, that God is able of these stones to raise up children unto Abraham.

Matthew 3:16 And Jesus, when he was baptized, went up straightway out of the water: and, lo, the heavens were opened unto him, and he saw the Spirit of God descending like a dove, and lighting upon him:

Matthew 4:3 And when the tempter came to him, he said, If thou be the Son of God, command that these stones be made bread.

Matthew 4:4 But he answered and said, It is written, Man shall not live by bread alone, but by every word that proceedeth out of the mouth of God.

In the first and the last books of the New Testament Matthew + Revelation	
Father(‘s) **7×7** mentions	**God** **77+77** mentions

Although it's apparent God has sealed His book with countless "firsts and lasts", it's also worth noting that **Father('s)** (Capitalized, God) is sevened in various ways across the entire Bible.

Father('s) (capitalized, God) in the Bible	
First and Last of N.T. **Matthew, Revelation**	**Father* = 7 × 7** appearances
Gospels **Matthew to John**	**Father = 77+77** verses
Historical (Gospels + Acts) **Matthew to Acts**	**Father = 7 × 26** mentions **Father* = 7 × 24** verses **Father* = 7 × 7** chapters
Rest of New Testament **Romans to Revelation**	**Father* = 77** mentions **Father* = 7 × 7** chapters **Father* = 7+7+7** books
Entire Bible **Old & New Testament**	**Father = 7 × 37** mentions Ask anybody who has studied Bible numerics, especially in Hebrew and Greek, and they will immediately know the profound significance of the number 37. It is heavily connected with Genesis 1:1 and the name of Jesus Christ. See "Thy Word Be Verified" on YouTube.
Excludes the 2 mentions of **Father*** (Capitalized) that are not referring to God in Luke 16:24; "Father Abraham", and Colossians 3:21; "Fathers")	

If you include the antimention of Father Abraham:

Father (Capitalized) = 260 mentions in 231 verses (**77 + 77 + 77**)

#7 N.T. mention of "Father"

The #1 and only O.T. mention of **Father**	Both **#7** mentions of **Father** (entire Bible & N.T.)
For unto us a child is born, unto us a son is given: and the government shall be upon his shoulder: and his name shall be called Wonderful, Counsellor, The mighty God, The everlasting Father, The Prince of Peace. Isaiah 9:6	**But thou, when thou prayest, enter into thy closet, and when thou hast shut thy door, pray to thy Father which is in secret; and thy Father which seeth in secret shall reward thee openly.** Matthew 6:6

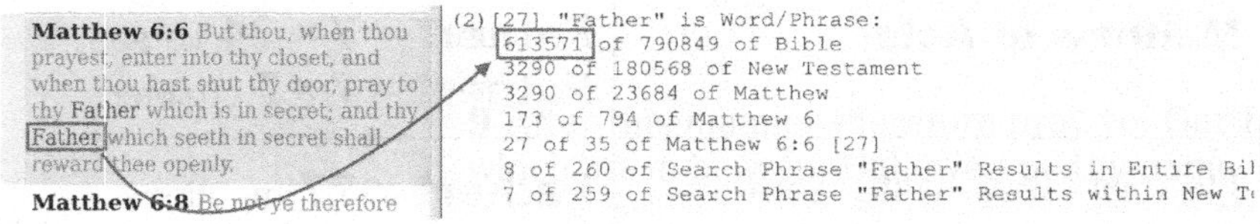

Matthew 6:6 But thou, when thou prayest, enter into thy closet, and when thou hast shut thy door, pray to thy Father which is in secret; and thy Father which seeth in secret shall reward thee openly.

Matthew 6:8 Be not ye therefore

```
(2) [27] "Father" is Word/Phrase:
    613571 of 790849 of Bible
    3290 of 180568 of New Testament
    3290 of 23684 of Matthew
    173 of 794 of Matthew 6
    27 of 35 of Matthew 6:6 [27]
    8 of 260 of Search Phrase "Father" Results in Entire Bi
    7 of 259 of Search Phrase "Father" Results within New T
```

The second mention of **Father** in Mat 6:6 is word #613,571 of the KJB

#7 N.T. mention of **Father**

word #613,571 of the KJB

= (7 × 37) × 2369

(Total mentions of **Father**) × (**God** in Isaiah 9:6)

Father	**...The mighty God, The everlasting Father...**
*Capitalized, **God** (excl. "Father Abraham")*	Isaiah 9:6
7 × 37	**#2369**
total mentions in the KJB	mention of **God** in the KJB (First mention of **Father**)

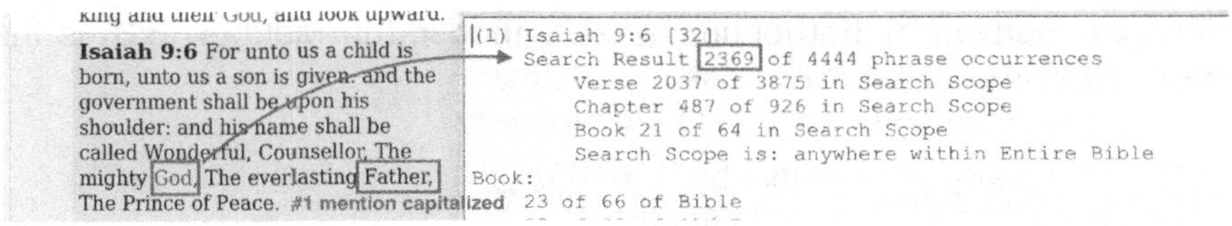

king and their God, and look upward.

Isaiah 9:6 For unto us a child is born, unto us a son is given: and the government shall be upon his shoulder: and his name shall be called Wonderful, Counsellor, The mighty God, The everlasting Father, The Prince of Peace. *#1 mention capitalized*

```
(1) Isaiah 9:6 [32]
Search Result 2369 of 4444 phrase occurrences
    Verse 2037 of 3875 in Search Scope
    Chapter 487 of 926 in Search Scope
    Book 21 of 64 in Search Scope
    Search Scope is: anywhere within Entire Bible
Book:
23 of 66 of Bible
```

In case it was difficult to understand the previous table, here is a step-by-step explanation:

Father (capitalized, **God**) = 259 mentions in the KJB
259 mentions = **7 × 37**

The #7 verse to mention **Father** (Matthew 6:6) contains both the #7 mention of **Father** in the KJB as well as the #7 mention of **Father** in the New Testament.

First 7 verses that mention **Father** (capitalized)

1. Isaiah 9:6 **For unto us a child is born, unto us a son is given: and the government shall be upon his shoulder: and his name shall be called Wonderful, Counsellor, The mighty God, The everlasting <u>Father</u>, The Prince of Peace.**

----- *New Testament* -----

2. Matthew 5:16 **Let your light so shine before men, that they may see your good works, and glorify your <u>Father</u> which is in heaven.**
3. Matthew 5:45 **That ye may be the children of your <u>Father</u> which is in heaven: for he maketh his sun to rise on the evil and on the good, and sendeth rain on the just and on the unjust.**
4. Matthew 5:48 **Be ye therefore perfect, even as your <u>Father</u> which is in heaven is perfect.**
5. Matthew 6:1 **Take heed that ye do not your alms before men, to be seen of them: otherwise ye have no reward of your <u>Father</u> which is in heaven.**
6. Matthew 6:4 **That thine alms may be in secret: and thy <u>Father</u> which seeth in secret himself shall reward thee openly.**
7. Matthew 6:6 **But thou, when thou prayest, enter into thy closet, and when thou hast shut thy door, pray to thy <u>Father</u> which is in secret; and thy <u>Father</u> which seeth in secret shall reward thee openly.**

Interesting sidenote: Genesis 6:6 is the #144 verse of the O.T. and Matthew 6:6 is the #144 verse of the N.T. 144 is associated with holiness / heavenly perfection.

The #7 mention of **Father** in the N.T. (housed in Matthew 6:6) is the #613,571 word of the KJB.

613,571 is perfectly divisible by (7 × 37).
Father is mentioned (7 × 37) times.

And not only is it perfectly divisible by all mentions of **Father**, its third factor (2369) has heavy significance.

The complete equation: 613,571 = **(7 × 37) × 2369**

The first mention of **Father** (in Isaiah 9:6) is directly accompanied by the **#2369** mention of **God**.

And of course, **God** is the **Father**.

#2369 mention of **God**, #1 mention of **Father**

For unto us a child is born, unto us a son is given: and the government shall be upon his shoulder: and his name shall be called Wonderful, Counsellor, The mighty God, The everlasting Father, The Prince of Peace. Isaiah 9:6

This is not a random Bible character we are talking about. This is the **eternal, immortal, invisible, Father of lights** and **of spirits.** This is the **Holy One of Israel, The LORD, The LORD God, merciful and gracious, that inhabiteth eternity**, who knows every thought and deed done in secret, and is **no respecter of persons**. Who sits in heaven on His throne between the cherubims, and looks upon your heart as you read about Him right now.

The source of life, knowledge, and everything good: **God the Father.**

Do you trust Him? Are any of His words lost in time or translation? Was the English language outside of His infinite understanding? Was a perfect Bible too hard for the omnipotent author of everlasting truth?

God/Almighty 7×7×7 in the First and Last Books

And the four beasts had each of them six wings about him; and they were full of eyes within: and they rest not day and night, saying, Holy, holy, holy, Lord God Almighty, which was, and is, and is to come. Revelation 4:8

In Genesis and Revelation only, there are 343 mentions of **God** + **Almighty**.

Search Filters: **Genesis, Revelation**		Case Sens	Mentions
Search Phrase 1	**God**	-	329
Search Phrase 2	**Almighty**	-	14
Total Mentions	**God Almighty**		343 **=7×7×7**
KJB1611 = 343, NKJV = 341, ESV = 336, NASB1971 = 336, NASB2020 = 336 , NIV = 326			

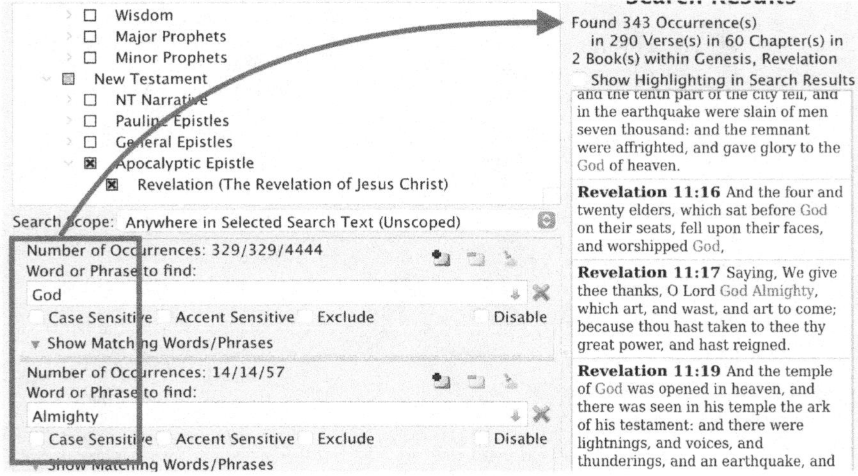

Jesus/God 7×7×7 in the First and Last Books

...I am the first, and I am the last; and beside me there is no God.
Isaiah 44:6

In Genesis and Revelation only, there are 343 mentions of **Jesus** + **God**.

Search Filters: **Genesis, Revelation**		Case Sens	Mentions
Search Phrase 1	**Jesus**	-	14
Search Phrase 2	**God**	-	329
Total Mentions	**Jesus + God**		343 **=7×7×7**
KJB1611 = 343, NKJV = 341, ESV = 335, NASB1971 = 335, NASB2020 = 335 , NIV = 325			

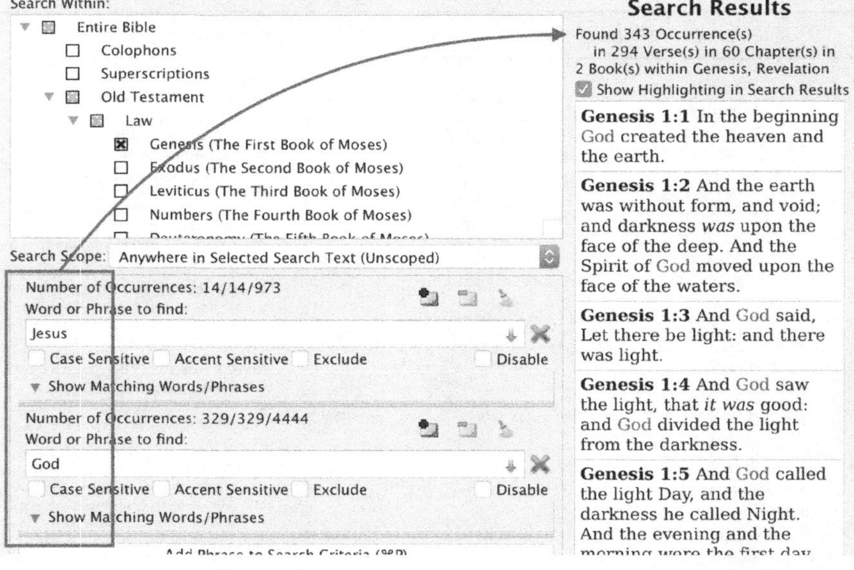

Jesus and God in Revelation 7 / 7 / 7

The Revelation of Jesus Christ, which God... Revelation 1:1

...Jesus Christ be with you all. Amen. Revelation 22:21

- **God** is the #7 word from the beginning of Revelation. (Rev 1:1)
- **Jesus** is the #7 word from the end of Revelation. (Rev 22:21)

- Exactly 7 chapters in Revelation contain both **Jesus** and **God** when they are both in the same chapter.
- Exactly 7 verses in Revelation contain both **Jesus** and **God** when they are both in the same verse.

When **Jesus** and **God** are both in the same...	
Chapter	**Verse**
Revelation 1 Revelation 12 Revelation 14 Revelation 17 Revelation 19 Revelation 20 Revelation 22	Revelation 1:1 Revelation 1:2 Revelation 1:9 Revelation 12:17 Revelation 14:12 Revelation 19:10 Revelation 20:4
Total = **7 Chapters** *No other chapter in Revelation mentions both **Jesus** and **God***	Total = **7 Verses** *No other verse in Revelation mentions both **Jesus** and **God***

Thy throne, O God 7×7×7

But unto the Son he saith, Thy throne, O God, is for ever and ever: a sceptre of righteousness is the sceptre of thy kingdom. Hebrews 1:8

Hebrews 1:8 is the only place in the Bible where we read God the Father explicitly calling His Son **God**. It's a reference back to Psalm 45.

Hebrews 1:8-9	Psalm 45:6-7
But unto the Son he saith, **Thy throne, O God, is for ever and ever: a sceptre of righteousness is the sceptre of thy kingdom.**	**Thy throne, O God, is for ever and ever: the sceptre of thy kingdom is a right sceptre.**
Thou hast loved righteousness, and hated iniquity; therefore God, even thy God, hath anointed thee with the oil of gladness above thy fellows.	**Thou lovest righteousness, and hatest wickedness: therefore God, thy God, hath anointed thee with the oil of gladness above thy fellows.**

When you read through Psalm 45, you realize that **God, *the Father*,** is talking to **God, *the Son*** throughout the entire Psalm.

Psalm 45

God the Father talking to God the Son

(Every word including the heading) = 343 words

= 7×7×7 words

```
Psalms 45 contains:
    17 Verse(s)
    343 Word(s)
```

And it is one of the most hair-raising chapters in the Bible, especially when you read the last verse (7+7+7 words)...

I *[the Father]* **will make thy name** *[Jesus]* **to be remembered in all generations: therefore shall the people praise thee for ever and ever.** Psalm 45:17

7 appearances of Jehovah

That men may know that thou, whose name alone is JEHOVAH, art the most high over all the earth. Psalm 83:18

Jehovah, the name of God, appears 7 times in the Bible. 4 times fully uppercase (**JEHOVAH**), and 3 times standard (**Jehovah**).

All appearances of Jehovah

1. Genesis 22:14 **...the name of that place Jehovah–jireh...**
2. Exodus 6:3 **...by my name JEHOVAH was I not known...**
3. Exodus 17:15 **...called the name of it Jehovah–nissi:**
4. Judges 6:24 **...and called it Jehovah–shalom...**
5. Psalm 83:18 **...whose name alone is JEHOVAH...**
6. Isaiah 12:2 **...for the LORD JEHOVAH is my strength...**
7. Isaiah 26:4 **...in the LORD JEHOVAH is everlasting strength:**

When you break those mentions down by order of book...

Books mentioning Jehovah		
Mention # of **Jehovah**	Book	Book Order in Bible
#1 - Jehovah-jireh	Genesis	1
#2 - JEHOVAH	Exodus	2
#3 - Jehovah-nissi	Exodus	2
#4 - Jehovah-shalom	Judges	7
#5 - JEHOVAH	Psalms	19
#6 - JEHOVAH	Isaiah	23
#7 - JEHOVAH	Isaiah	23
Total Sum of Books		**77**

Godhead 77

The word "**Godhead**" is mentioned exactly 3 times in the KJB.

If you add up all the words of the verses where it's mentioned, the total sum is 77 words.

All Mentions of "**Godhead**" in the KJB		
Acts 17:29	Romans 1:20	Colossians 2:9
Forasmuch then as we are the offspring of God, we ought not to think that the Godhead is like unto gold, or silver, or stone, graven by art and man's device.	**For the invisible things of him from the creation of the world are clearly seen, being understood by the things that are made, even his eternal power and Godhead; so that they are without excuse:**	**For in him dwelleth all the fulness of the Godhead bodily.**
Godhead = word #17 Words after **Godhead** = 14 Total Verse 31 words	**Godhead** = word #29 Words after **Godhead** = 6 Total Verse 35 words	**Godhead** = word #10 Words after **Godhead** = 1 Total Verse 11 words
Sum of **Godhead** word #s (17+29+10) = **7×7+7**	Sum of words after **Godhead** (14+6+1) = **7+7+7**	Total Words in Verses (31+35+11) = **77**

"The Godhead" = **77** English Ordinal (A=1, B=2, C=3… Z=26)

The Mighty God 7 mentions, from 7×7 to 777

Ah Lord GOD! behold, thou hast made the heaven and the earth by thy great power and stretched out arm, and there is nothing too hard for thee: Thou shewest lovingkindness unto thousands, and recompensest the iniquity of the fathers into the bosom of their children after them: the Great, the Mighty God, the LORD of hosts, is his name, Jeremiah 32:17-18

Starting in the #(7×7) chapter of the Bible (Genesis 49), and ending in the #777 chapter (Jeremiah 32), you can find all 7 mentions of **the mighty God**. Adding up all the verse numbers produces a sum of 77.

All 7 mentions of "the mighty God"		
Mention # of **"the mighty God"**	Book, Chapter	Verse
#1 - the mighty *God* Only unique name of God in Genesis 49 This is the #7 mention of **mighty** Gen 6:4, 10:8, 10:9 [2x], 18:18, 23:6, 49:24	Genesis 49 **#(7×7)** chapter of the Bible	24
#2 - The mighty God	Psalm 50	1
#3 - the mighty *God*	Psalm 132	2
#4 - the mighty *God*	Psalm 132	5
#5 - The mighty God	Isaiah 9	6
#6 - the mighty God	Isaiah 10	21
#7 - the Mighty God	Jeremiah 32 **#777** chapter of the Bible	18
Sum of Verse Numbers		**77**

3 + 4 = 7... Mention #3 + Mention #4 = Sum of 7 verse numbers
2 + 5 = 7... Mention #2 + Mention #5 = Sum of 7 verse numbers

And of course, Isaiah 9:6 makes it absolutely clear that "**the mighty God**" is the name of our Lord and Saviour.

For unto us a child is born, unto us a son is given: and the government shall be upon his shoulder: and his name shall be called Wonderful, Counsellor, The mighty God, The everlasting Father, The Prince of Peace. Isaiah 9:6

All names of our Lord in Isaiah 9:6	
Wonderful	(7+7+7) mentions in the Bible (Isaiah 9:6 = #7 mention from the end)
Counsellor	(7+7) mentions in the Bible (Isaiah 9:6 = #7 mention)
The mighty God	7 mentions in the Bible
The everlasting Father	Only mention in the Bible
The Prince of Peace	Only mention in the Bible

The phrase "**mighty one**" is also mentioned 7 times, including the #(7×7) chapter of Isaiah. The #7 and last mention of **mighty one** is in the #777 verse of Ezekiel.

1) Gen 10:8 2) Is 1:24 3) Is 10:34 4) Is 30:29 5) Is 49:26 6) Is 60:16 7) Ezek 31:11

O LORD, thou art my God; I will exalt thee, I will praise thy name; for thou hast done wonderful things; thy counsels of old are faithfulness and truth.

Isaiah 25:1

Jesus #777 / Holy Ghost #77

The #777 mention of **Jesus** is in a verse with all three members of the Godhead listed out, including the #77 mention of **Holy Ghost.** This occurs in the very last verse of the book of 2 Corinthians.

<table>
<tr><td colspan="2">2 Corinthians 13:14</td></tr>
<tr><td colspan="2">The grace of the Lord <u>Jesus</u> Christ, and the love of God, and the communion of the <u>Holy Ghost</u>, be with you all. Amen.</td></tr>
<tr><td>#777 Mention of <u>Jesus</u>

2 Corinthians 13:14 The grace of the Lord Jesus Christ, and the love of God, and the communion of the Holy Ghost, be with you all. Amen.
Details : King Jame
(1) 2 Corinthians 13:14 [6]
Search Result 777 of 980 phr
Verse 749 of 939 in Sear
Chapter 133 of 206 in Se
Book 8 of 26 in Search S</td><td>#77 Mention of <u>Holy Ghost</u>

2 Corinthians 13:14 The grace of the Lord Jesus Christ, and the love of God, and the communion of the Holy Ghost, be with you all. Amen.
Details : King Jam
(1) 2 Corinthians 13:14 [18]
Search Result 77 of 90 phra
Verse 76 of 89 in Search
Chapter 43 of 55 in Sea
Book 8 of 16 in Search</td></tr>
</table>

Note: This is looking at all mentions of the person of **Jesus** (980), excluding Joshua / Justus. See appendix 7.

Jesus #77 / Christ #77 / Jesus Christ #77

The #77 mention of **Jesus** in the KJB rests consecutively after the #7 mention of **Christ,** with 7 words in-between. And in context, it's about **Jesus** being revealed as **the Christ, the Son of the living God.**

Matthew 16:14-17	
And they said, Some say that thou art John the Baptist: some, Elias; and others, Jeremias, or one of the prophets. He saith unto them, But whom say ye that I am? And Simon Peter answered and said, Thou art the Christ, the Son of the living God. And Jesus answered and said unto him, Blessed art thou, Simon Bar–jona: for flesh and blood hath not revealed it unto thee, but my Father which is in heaven.	
#7 Mention of Christ	**#77 Mention of Jesus**
[10] "Christ" is Word/Phrase: 622401 of 790849 of Bible 12120 of 180568 of New Testament 12120 of 23684 of Matthew 345 of 688 of Matthew 16 10 of 16 of Matthew 16:16 [10] 7 of 555 of Search Phrase "Christ"	[2] "Jesus" is Word/Phrase: 622409 of 790849 of Bible 12128 of 180568 of New Testament 12128 of 23684 of Matthew 353 of 688 of Matthew 16 2 of 29 of Matthew 16:17 [2] 77 of 973 of Search Phrase "Jesus"

This is a clear example of a pattern that wouldn't exist if it wasn't for the apostrophe of the English language. Why? This pattern is only looking at **Jesus** / **Christ** (excluding **Jesus'** / **Christ's**).

And it is easier for heaven and earth to pass, than one tittle of the law to fail. Luke 16:17

And it doesn't stop there.

Notice how the #77 mention of Jesus is when He is revealed by the Father as the Christ, the Messiah of the Jews.

If you look at the #77 mention of **Christ**, and the #77 mention of "**Jesus Christ**", each instance contains an advanced revelation.

Advanced Revelation *in each* **#77 mention**		
#77 mention of Jesus	**#77 mention of Christ**	**#77 mention of "Jesus Christ"**
Matthew 16:15-17	Acts 10:34-36	Galatians 1:11-12
He saith unto them, But whom say ye that I am? **And Simon Peter answered and said, Thou art the Christ, the Son of the living God.** **And Jesus answered and said unto him, Blessed art thou, Simon Bar–jona: for flesh and blood hath not revealed it unto thee, but my Father which is in heaven.**	**Then Peter opened his mouth, and said, Of a truth I perceive that God is no respecter of persons:** **But in every nation he that feareth him, and worketh righteousness, is accepted with him.** **The word which God sent unto the children of Israel, preaching peace by Jesus Christ: (he is Lord of all:)**	**But I certify you, brethren, that the gospel which was preached of me is not after man.** **For I neither received it of man, neither was I taught it, but by the revelation of Jesus Christ.**
Revealed by: **The Father**	Revealed by: **The Holy Ghost**	Revealed by: **Jesus Christ**
Revealed to: **Peter**	Revealed to: **Peter**	Revealed to: **Paul**
Revelation: **Jesus is the Christ, the Son of God**	Revelation: **Jesus Christ is Lord of all**	Revelation: **The gospel of grace by which we are saved**

Jesus Christ + Christ Jesus 77, First 7 Books

Take a moment to consider how sometimes the Lord's name/title are worded forward (**Jesus Christ**), and sometimes reverse (**Christ Jesus**). If it were only one or the other, than we wouldn't have miracles like:

Jesus Christ = T7 mentions (see p. 96)

Christ Jesus is mentioned exactly 7 times in Ephesians, the 49th book of the Bible (49 = 7×7). **Christ Jesus** is not mentioned 7 times in any other book. **Jesus Christ** is also mentioned 7 times in just one book: Revelation.

When we search for all appearances of **Jesus Christ*** and **Christ Jesus*,** the **#77** appearance marks the exact end of the first 7 books of the New Testament- in the last verse of the 7th book (1 Corinthians).

The very end of the **7th** book of the New Testament
1 Corinthians 16:24
My love be with you all in Christ Jesus. Amen.
The **#77** appearance of **Jesus Christ* / Christ Jesus***
The **(70×7)+(70×7)** appearance/mention of **Jesus* / Christ**
The **(7+7)** N.T. mention of **Amen**

The last words of the **#7** N.T. book…

“**in Christ**” is mentioned **77 times** in the Bible.

Amen (capitalized) is mentioned **77 times** in the Bible.
(This is the #**(7+7)** mention of **Amen** in the N.T.)

This is the **#77** appearance of **Jesus Christ(‘s) + Christ Jesus.** Note: Christ Jesus’ does not appear in the KJB.

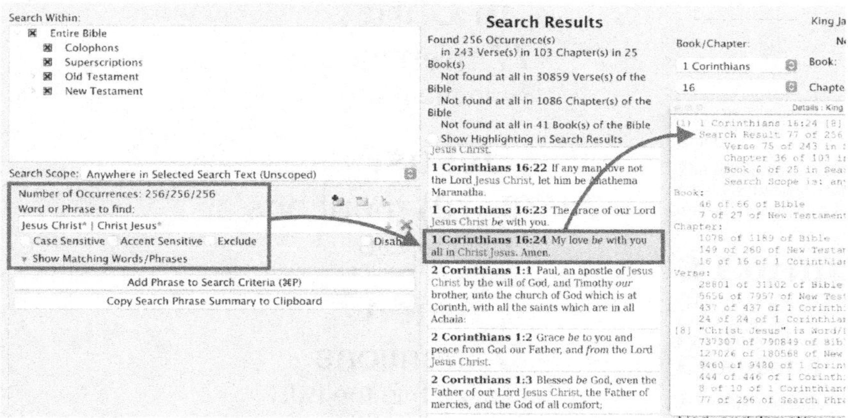

This is the **#980 = (70×7)+(70×7)** appearance / mention of **Jesus* + Christ.**

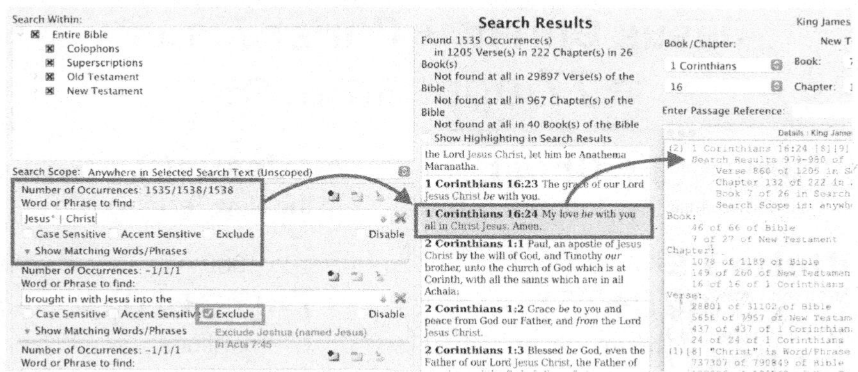

<table>
<tr><td colspan="2">The last words of the
#7 N.T. book:
...<u>in Christ</u> <u>Jesus</u>. <u>Amen</u>.
1 Corinthians 16:24</td></tr>
<tr><td colspan="2">**“in Christ”**
77 mentions
in the KJB

Jesus(‘)
7×(70+70) mentions
in the KJB

Amen
77 mentions
(Capitalized) in the KJB</td></tr>
<tr><td colspan="2">In the first **7** N.T. books
Matthew, Mark, Luke, John, Acts, Romans, 1 Corinthians
Jesus Christ* + Christ Jesus*
= 77 appearances</td></tr>
<tr><td>**Jesus(‘) + Christ**
in the first 7 N.T. books</td><td>**Jesus(‘)**
in the New Testament</td></tr>
<tr><td>980 =
7×(70+70)
appearances/mentions</td><td>980 =
7×(70+70)
mentions</td></tr>
</table>

Jesus + Christ verse 70, the 70×7 N.T. verse

The #**70** verse to mention either **Jesus** or **Christ** is Matthew 15:1, which is the #**490** verse of the New Testament.

The #490 = #**(70×7)** verse of the N.T.
Then came to Jesus scribes and Pharisees, which were of Jerusalem, saying, Matthew 15:1

First **70 verses** that contain **Jesus** or **Christ**		
1. Matthew 1:1	25. Matthew 8:13	49. Matthew 11:7
2. Matthew 1:16	26. Matthew 8:14	50. Matthew 11:25
3. Matthew 1:17	27. Matthew 8:18	51. Matthew 12:1
4. Matthew 1:18	28. Matthew 8:20	52. Matthew 12:15
5. Matthew 1:21	29. Matthew 8:22	53. Matthew 12:25
6. Matthew 1:25	30. Matthew 8:29	54. Matthew 13:1
7. Matthew 2:1	31. Matthew 8:34	55. Matthew 13:34
8. Matthew 2:4	32. Matthew 9:2	56. Matthew 13:36
9. Matthew 3:13	33. Matthew 9:4	57. Matthew 13:51
10. Matthew 3:15	34. Matthew 9:9	58. Matthew 13:53
11. Matthew 3:16	35. Matthew 9:10	59. Matthew 13:57
12. Matthew 4:1	36. Matthew 9:12	60. Matthew 14:1
13. Matthew 4:7	37. Matthew 9:15	61. Matthew 14:12
14. Matthew 4:10	38. Matthew 9:19	62. Matthew 14:13
15. Matthew 4:12	39. Matthew 9:22	63. Matthew 14:14
16. Matthew 4:17	40. Matthew 9:23	64. Matthew 14:16
17. Matthew 4:18	41. Matthew 9:27	65. Matthew 14:22
18. Matthew 4:23	42. Matthew 9:28	66. Matthew 14:25
19. Matthew 7:28	43. Matthew 9:30	67. Matthew 14:27
20. Matthew 8:3	44. Matthew 9:35	68. Matthew 14:29
21. Matthew 8:4	45. Matthew 10:5	69. Matthew 14:31
22. Matthew 8:5	46. Matthew 11:1	**70. Matthew 15:1**
23. Matthew 8:7	47. Matthew 11:2	**Verse #70×7 of the New Testament**
24. Matthew 8:10	48. Matthew 11:4	

Let's compile this with the previous note: In the first 7 books of the Bible, **Jesus(')** & **Christ** are mentioned 70×7 + 70×7 times. And the #70 verse of that same search (**Jesus*** + **Christ**) is the #70×7 verse of the N.T.

Perhaps Matthew 15:1 would never stand out by itself, but in light of the whole counsel of God, there is power, purpose and perfection in every last detail where the Holy Ghost places the name of Jesus. The name above all names.

(Also going along with Matthew ***15:1*** *- "****Jesus Christ****" =* ***151*** *English Ordinal., see Appx. 9)*

Chapters where Jesus is mentioned 7 times

10 chapters mention **Jesus** exactly 7 times, and 7 chapters mention **Jesus** in exactly 7 verses. Here are the sums of those chapter numbers:

	10 × 7	
	The **10 Chapters** where **Jesus** is mentioned **7 times**	
1	Matthew	4
2	Matthew	16
3	Matthew	19
4	Luke	4
5	Acts	4
6	Acts	19
7	Ephesians	1
8	1 Timothy	1
9	Philemon	1
10	2 Peter	1
	Sum of Chapters	**70**
	Total = 10 × 7	

	7 × 7	
	The **7 Chapters** where **Jesus** is mentioned in **7 verses**	
1	Matthew	4
2	Matthew	16
3	Matthew	19
4	Luke	4
5	Acts	4
6	Philippians	1
7	Philemon	1
	Sum of Chapters	**49**
	Total = 7 × 7	

These are not cherry picked. There are no other chapters in the Bible where Jesus is mentioned 7 times / in 7 verses.

There is no logical reason for the sum of the chapter numbers to be correlated with the numbers of chapters where Jesus is mentioned exactly 7 times (or in 7 verses).

Ephesians, Book 7×7

Most of the facts in this note are scattered throughout previous pages, but it is nice to see them all put together.

The 49th book **(7×7)** of the Bible is Ephesians.

There are **7** mentions of **Jesus** in the first chapter of Ephesians. (Ephesians 1:1 (2x), 1:2, 1:3, 1:5, 1:15, 1:17)

Ephesians 1 is the **#7** chapter in the Bible to mention **Jesus 7** times.

1. Matthew 4
2. Matthew 16
3. Matthew 19
4. Luke 4
5. Acts 4
6. Acts 19
7. **Ephesians 1**

There are **7+7+7** total mentions of **Jesus** in Ephesians. No other book has **7+7+7** total mentions of **Jesus.**

Ephesians is the first of 7 books to mention **Jesus** in multiples of **7**.

1. Ephesians **(7+7+7)**
2. Colossians **(7)**
3. 1 Timothy **(7+7)**
4. 2 Timothy **(7+7)**
5. Philemon **(7)**
6. Hebrews **(7+7)**
7. Revelation **(7+7)**

There are **7** mentions of **Christ Jesus** in Ephesians. No other book mentions **Christ Jesus** 7 times.

The final title of Jesus in the Bible (Rev 22:21) "**our Lord Jesus Christ**" begins on word #49 of Ephesians **(7×7)**.

Believest thou not that I am in the Father, and the Father in me? the words that I speak unto you I speak not of myself: but the Father that dwelleth in me, he doeth the works.

John 14:10

Sent 7×7

And the Father himself, which hath sent me, hath borne witness of me. Ye have neither heard his voice at any time, nor seen his shape. And ye have not his word abiding in you: for whom he hath sent, him ye believe not. Search the scriptures; for in them ye think ye have eternal life: and they are they which testify of me. John 5:37-39

God's witness of his Son to us today is the Bible. And all we need is the Bible to prove that **Jesus Christ** was sent by the **Father**.

The word "**sent**" is mentioned in 7×7 chapters in the gospels (the first four books of the New Testament detailing the events and person of **Jesus Christ**).

In the gospels, Jesus describes himself as "**sent**" by God exactly 7×7 times.

Here are all 7×7 verses where **Jesus** declares Himself as "**sent**" by God.

And exactly 7 of the verse numbers are divisible by 7
John: 7:28, 8:42, 11:42, 12:49, 15:21, 17:21, 20:21

"**sent**" 7×7 times

Jesus refers to himself as "**sent**" (by God) 49 times in the Gospels

1. Matthew 10:40 **He that receiveth you receiveth me, and he that receiveth me receiveth him that sent me.**
2. Matthew 15:24 **But he answered and said, I am not sent but unto the lost sheep of the house of Israel.**
3. *[Parable]* Matthew 21:37 **But last of all he sent unto them his son, saying, They will reverence my son.**
4. Mark 9:37 **Whosoever shall receive one of such children in my name, receiveth me: and whosoever shall receive me, receiveth not me, but him that sent me.**

Jesus refers to himself as "**sent**" by **God 7×7** times in the gospels *(cont.)*

5. *[Parable]* Mark 12:6 **Having yet therefore one son, his wellbeloved, he sent him also last unto them, saying, They will reverence my son.**
6. Luke 4:18 **The Spirit of the Lord is upon me, because he hath anointed me to preach the gospel to the poor; he hath sent me to heal the brokenhearted, to preach deliverance to the captives, and recovering of sight to the blind, to set at liberty them that are bruised,**
7. Luke 4:43 **And he said unto them, I must preach the kingdom of God to other cities also: for therefore am I sent.**
8. Luke 9:48 **And said unto them, Whosoever shall receive this child in my name receiveth me: and whosoever shall receive me receiveth him that sent me: for he that is least among you all, the same shall be great.**
9. Luke 10:16 **He that heareth you heareth me; and he that despiseth you despiseth me; and he that despiseth me despiseth him that sent me.**
10. John 3:17 **For God sent not his Son into the world to condemn the world; but that the world through him might be saved.**
11. John 4:34 **Jesus saith unto them, My meat is to do the will of him that sent me, and to finish his work.**
12. John 5:23 **That all men should honour the Son, even as they honour the Father. He that honoureth not the Son honoureth not the Father which hath sent him.**
13. John 5:24 **Verily, verily, I say unto you, He that heareth my word, and believeth on him that sent me, hath everlasting life, and shall not come into condemnation; but is passed from death unto life.**
14. John 5:30 **I can of mine own self do nothing: as I hear, I judge: and my judgment is just; because I seek not mine own will, but the will of the Father which hath sent me.**
15. John 5:36 **But I have greater witness than that of John: for the works which the Father hath given me to finish, the same works that I do, bear witness of me, that the Father hath sent me.**
16. John 5:37 **And the Father himself, which hath sent me, hath borne witness of me. Ye have neither heard his voice at any time, nor seen his shape.**
17. John 5:38 **And ye have not his word abiding in you: for whom he hath sent, him ye believe not.**
18. John 6:29 **Jesus answered and said unto them, This is the work of God, that ye believe on him whom he hath sent.**

Jesus refers to himself as "**sent**" by **God 7×7** times in the gospels *(cont.)*

19. John 6:38 **For I came down from heaven, not to do mine own will, but the will of him that sent me.**
20. John 6:39 **And this is the Father's will which hath sent me, that of all which he hath given me I should lose nothing, but should raise it up again at the last day.**
21. John 6:40 **And this is the will of him that sent me, that every one which seeth the Son, and believeth on him, may have everlasting life: and I will raise him up at the last day.**
22. John 6:44 **No man can come to me, except the Father which hath sent me draw him: and I will raise him up at the last day.**
23. John 6:57 **As the living Father hath sent me, and I live by the Father: so he that eateth me, even he shall live by me.**
24. John 7:16 **Jesus answered them, and said, My doctrine is not mine, but his that sent me.**
25. John 7:18 **He that speaketh of himself seeketh his own glory: but he that seeketh his glory that sent him, the same is true, and no unrighteousness is in him.**
26. John 7:28 **Then cried Jesus in the temple as he taught, saying, Ye both know me, and ye know whence I am: and I am not come of myself, but he that sent me is true, whom ye know not.**
27. John 7:29 **But I know him: for I am from him, and he hath sent me.**
28. John 7:33 **Then said Jesus unto them, Yet a little while am I with you, and then I go unto him that sent me.**
29. John 8:16 **And yet if I judge, my judgment is true: for I am not alone, but I and the Father that sent me.**
30. John 8:18 **I am one that bear witness of myself, and the Father that sent me beareth witness of me.**
31. John 8:26 **I have many things to say and to judge of you: but he that sent me is true; and I speak to the world those things which I have heard of him.**
32. John 8:29 **And he that sent me is with me: the Father hath not left me alone; for I do always those things that please him.**
33. John 8:42 **Jesus said unto them, If God were your Father, ye would love me: for I proceeded forth and came from God; neither came I of myself, but he sent me.**
34. John 9:4 **I must work the works of him that sent me, while it is day: the night cometh, when no man can work.**
35. John 10:36 **Say ye of him, whom the Father hath sanctified, and sent into the world, Thou blasphemest; because I said, I am the Son of God?**

Jesus refers to himself as "**sent**" by **God 7×7** times in the gospels *(cont.)*

36. John 11:42 **And I knew that thou hearest me always: but because of the people which stand by I said it, that they may believe that thou hast sent me.**
37. John 12:44 **Jesus cried and said, He that believeth on me, believeth not on me, but on him that sent me.**
38. John 12:45 **And he that seeth me seeth him that sent me.**
39. John 12:49 **For I have not spoken of myself; but the Father which sent me, he gave me a commandment, what I should say, and what I should speak.**
40. John 13:20 **Verily, verily, I say unto you, He that receiveth whomsoever I send receiveth me; and he that receiveth me receiveth him that sent me.**
41. John 14:24 **He that loveth me not keepeth not my sayings: and the word which ye hear is not mine, but the Father's which sent me.**
42. John 15:21 **But all these things will they do unto you for my name's sake, because they know not him that sent me.**
43. John 16:5 **But now I go my way to him that sent me; and none of you asketh me, Whither goest thou?**
44. John 17:3 **And this is life eternal, that they might know thee the only true God, and Jesus Christ, whom thou hast sent.**
45. John 17:18 **As thou hast sent me into the world, even so have I also sent them into the world.**
46. John 17:21 **That they all may be one; as thou, Father, art in me, and I in thee, that they also may be one in us: that the world may believe that thou hast sent me.**
47. John 17:23 **I in them, and thou in me, that they may be made perfect in one; and that the world may know that thou hast sent me, and hast loved them, as thou hast loved me.**
48. John 17:25 **O righteous Father, the world hath not known thee: but I have known thee, and these have known that thou hast sent me.**
49. John 20:21 **Then said Jesus to them again, Peace be unto you: as my Father hath sent me, even so send I you.**

One more instance, but is spoken by John the Baptist instead of Jesus: John 3:34 **For he whom God hath sent speaketh the words of God: for God giveth not the Spirit by measure unto him.**

Notice the fine-tuning: the gospel of Luke contains the same parable as Matthew and Mark regarding the beloved son who is sent to the vineyard, however, the word "**send**" is used instead of "**sent**" for the beloved son in Luke 20:13. Even though "**sent**" was used to describe the other servants 5 times in the previous 3 verses (Luke 20:10-12). If "**sent**" were used for the beloved son, the overall 49-count would have been thwarted.

But what's most incredible of all? How can a man see this and not believe in God! In the New Testament, "**sent**" is mentioned 196 times... the exact same amount of mentions as **Jesus Christ**.

Jesus Christ = **196** mentions
sent (N.T.) = **196** mentions

7 + 14 + 21 + 28 + 35 + 42 + 49 = **196**

7
7 + 7
7 + 7 + 7
7 + 7 + 7 + 7
7 + 7 + 7 + 7 + 7
7 + 7 + 7 + 7 + 7 + 7
7 + 7 + 7 + 7 + 7 + 7 + 7

196 = **T7×7**

In the New Testament	
Jesus Christ **T7×7** mentions	**sent** **T7×7** mentions
Jesus Christ + sent **77+77** chapters in the N.T.	

Out of those 7×7 mentions where Jesus describes Himself **sent** from God, ~80% of them are located in the gospel of John. The entire gospel of John is themed around **Jesus** being **sent** from **God the Father**.

In the Gospel of John

God + **Father**
(Capitalized)
T7×7 mentions

The T7×7 Verse of John (Verse #196) contains the #7+7 instance of Jesus mentioning "**sent**" in John 5:30, **I can of mine own self do nothing: as I hear, I judge: and my judgment is just; because I seek not mine own will, but the will of the Father which hath sent me.**

And yet the pattern goes further: "**sent**" in the Old Testament (including Psalm headings) is mentioned 490 times, which equals 70 × 7.

"sent" in the **Old Testament** *(including Psalm superscriptions)* †	**"sent"** in the **New Testament** *(Verse text. excluding colophons)*
490 = **70 × 7** mentions	196 = **T7×7** mentions
† Are superscriptions inspired? Absolutely. Compare 2 Samuel 22:1 with Psalm 18's superscription.	

And there is yet a greater verification. That same number, 196, is perfectly divisible by the total mentions of **sent** + **Jesus**(') in the N.T. *(without His Messianic title, **Christ**)*

There are 1176 total mentions of **sent** + **Jesus(')** in the New Testament
1176 = **196** × 6

T7×7 (196) is the number of mentions of **sent / Jesus Christ**
6 is the number of man
Jesus is the **SENT** MAN from God.

In the New Testament	
Jesus(') **196** × 5 mentions	**sent** **196** mentions
Total: **Jesus(')** + **sent** = **196** × 6 mentions (**Jesus Christ / sent**) × number of man **SENT** × MAN	

Bible Comparison - "sent"

	KJB	KJB1611	NKJV	ESV	NASB1971	NASB2020	NIV
Chapters containing **sent** in the 4 gospels	49 = **7×7**	49 = **7×7**	50	49 = **7×7**	50	51	50
Verses in the gospels where Jesus declares himself as "**sent**" (from God the Father)	49 = **7×7**	49 = **7×7**	48	47	43	47	47
Mentions of **sent** in the N.T. *(excl. Colophons)*	196 = **T7×7**	196 = **T7×7**	199	188	190	196 = **T7×7**	194
Mentions of **Jesus Christ**	196 = **T7×7**	197 †	184	139	137	130	132
Mentions of **God + Father** in John *(Capitalized)*	196 = **T7×7**	180	197	196 = **T7×7**	194	194	186
N.T. Chapters containing **sent** or **Jesus Christ**	154 = **77+77**	154 = **77+77**	152	140	139	139	139
Mentions of **sent** in the O.T. *(incl. Psalm headings)*	490 = **70×7**	493	489	480	491	483	457
Mentions of **Jesus(')** *(excl. Joshua / Justus, see appendix 7)*	980 = **70×7+ 70×7**	980 = **70×7+ 70×7**	979	967	917	995	1284
Mentions of **sent + Jesus(')** in the N.T.	1176 = 196×6 **SENT×MAN** **= (7+7+7) × (7×7+7)**	1177	1178	1155	1107	1191	1486
N.T. Chapters containing **sent** or **Jesus(')**	217 = **77+70 +70**	217 = **77+70+ 70**	215	216	213	217 = **77+70+ 70**	222

† In the KJB1611, Romans 3:24 has "**Iesus Christ**" - which was later standardized to "**Christ Jesus**" - see Appendix 1

sent **T7×7** (196) N.T. mentions	T7×7 Verse of the Bible (Verse #196)
	And he stayed yet other <u>seven</u> days; and <u>sent</u> forth the dove; which returned not again unto him any more. Genesis 8:12

"The Lord" in the Gospels

The phrase "**the Lord**" (excluding all lowercase mentions of "lord") in the Gospels is mentioned 49 + 49 = (7×7) + (7×7) times.

Search Filters: **Matthew, Mark, Luke, John**		Case Sens	Mentions
Search Phrase 1	**The Lord**	Y	5
Search Phrase 2	**the Lord**	Y	90
Search Phrase 3	**The LORD**	Y	3
Search Phrase 4	**the LORD**	Y	0
Total Mentions	**The Lord + the Lord + The LORD** *Capitalized / UPPERCASE, in the gospels*		98 =49+49 **=7×7+7×7**
KJB1611 = 109 NKJV = 100 ESV = 99 NASB2020 = 72 NASB1971 = 101 NIV = 96			

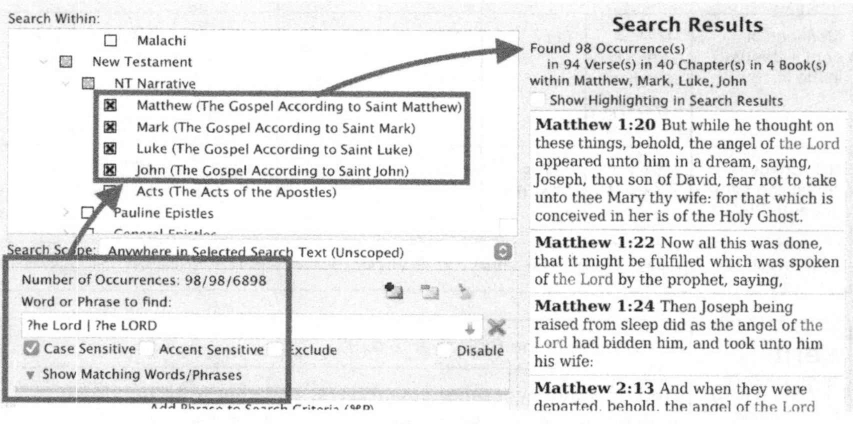

The Father and the Holy Ghost in the Gospels

The same sum of 49+49 mentions is equal to all mentions of "**the Father**" and "**the Holy Ghost**" in the Gospels.

Search Filters: **Matthew, Mark, Luke, John**		Case Sens	Mentions
Search Phrase 1	**The Father**	Y	1
Search Phrase 2	**the Father**	Y	72
Search Phrase 3	**The Holy Ghost**	Y	1
Search Phrase 4	**the Holy Ghost**	Y	24
Total Mentions	**The Father + the Father + The Holy Ghost + the Holy Ghost** *Capitalized, in the Gospels*		98 =49+49 **=7×7+7×7**
KJB1611 = 85 NKJV = 105 ESV = 111 NASB2020 = 110 NASB1971 = 109 NIV = 99			

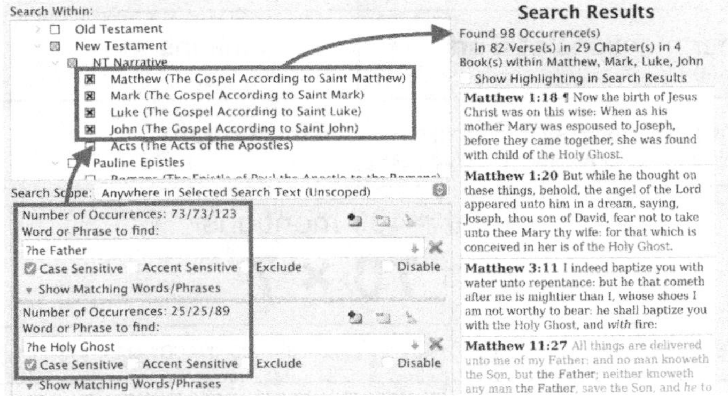

Another interesting pattern in the gospels:
The Holy Ghost = 25 appearances, **Jesus** = 25×25 appearances

God the Father 70×7, in the Gospels

In the 4 gospels, there is only one mention of "**God the Father**." Many other references make it clear that **God** is the **Father**, but only time is "**God the Father**" conjoined.

The only mention of **"God the Father"** in the 4 gospels	**Labour not for the meat which perisheth, but for that meat which endureth unto everlasting life, which the Son of man shall give unto you: for him hath God the Father sealed.** John 6:27

Because this is the only mention of **God the Father**, it seems pretty convincing that God has purposely left this pattern:

In the Gospels, **God** + **Father** = 491 mentions
(Father, when only referring to God the Father)

If you conjoin the lone mention of **God the Father** into one mention, the total mentions of **God** + **Father** = 490 **= 70 × 7** mentions

God the Father in the four Gospels	
"God the Father"	1 mention (John 6:27)
All other mentions of **God** (Capitalized)	311 mentions
All other mentions of **Father** (God, Excluding Father Abraham in Luke 16:24)	178 mentions
Total = 490 mentions **= 70 × 7**	
KJB1611 = 437 NKJV = 493 ESV = 484 NASB2020 = 483 NASB1971 = 483 NIV = 464	

Moses and Elijah, The two witnesses

And it came to pass about an eight days after these sayings, he took Peter and John and James, and went up into a mountain to pray. And as he prayed, the fashion of his countenance was altered, and his raiment was white and glistering. And, behold, there talked with him two men, which were Moses and Elias: Who appeared in glory, and spake of his decease which he should accomplish at Jerusalem. Luke 9:28-31

The transfiguration of **Jesus** is accompanied by **Moses** and **Elijah**. The Law and the Prophets. The two witnesses. The two men who encountered God, with 40-day-patterns, on His holy mount Sinai.

So what about these men, **Moses** and **Elijah**, do we discover in the numerics of the KJB?

To begin, as you might expect, they are sevened. It is concealed to those who quickly search their names without careful attention, since the name **Elijah** is also the name of a man in Ezra 10:21, who is not **Elijah** the holy prophet. When you exclude the Ezra 10:21-antimention of **Elijah**, you get the following search results in the verse text of holy scriptures:

Moses*	Elijah / Elias†
847 = 77 × 11 **=777+70** **appearances in the Bible**	98 = 49 + 49 **=7×7+7×7** **appearances in the Bible**

* Excludes 1 mention of **Moses** in the Psalm 90 superscription (outside of verse text). Includes standard & possessive; **Moses** and **Moses'**

† Excludes 1 antimention of Elijah (Ezra 10:21). There are no possessive mentions of *Elijah's* or *Elias'* in the KJB.

Moses (standard- not possessive) is mentioned 77 times in the New Testament and the first mention is the #77 word of the chapter.

One last note of interest: most people don't realize this, but God conceals the number 7 in the Biblical text itself, without ever mentioning it (...which is similar to what we are finding with all these numbers). In order to find out the account, we must do some math. The transfiguration of Jesus with **Moses** and **Elijah** occurs __ days after Jesus says "**...there be some standing here, which shall not taste of death, till they see the kingdom of God.**" (Luke 9:27)

Notice how it's worded in each of the gospels:

Matthew 17:1	Mark 9:2	Luke 9:28
And after six days Jesus taketh Peter, James, and John his brother, and bringeth them up into an high mountain apart,	**And after six days Jesus taketh with him Peter, and James, and John, and leadeth them up into an high mountain apart by themselves: and he was transfigured before them.**	**And it came to pass about an eight days after these sayings, he took Peter and John and James, and went up into a mountain to pray.**
"...after six days"	**"...after six days"**	**"...about an eight days"**
What is **after** 6 and **about** an 8?		

The transfiguration occurs on the **7th** day, God's number of perfection. But God doesn't record it as such. He leaves you with one option if you want to find out the account: read and consider His whole counsel, and do some simple math. This happens elsewhere in scripture as well. God separated Israel from exactly 7 plagues on Egypt. Jesus performed 7 recorded miracles on the sabbath (the seventh day). He spoke 7 times on the cross, with the last being, **It is finished**: (John 19:30). Is God a God of numbers or is He not? ***Who hath believed our report?***

Behold, this have I found, saith the preacher, counting one by one, to find out the account:

Ecclesiastes 7:27

Jesus, Christ, Italics 7

Are *words in italics* inspired in the King James Bible?

For those who are not aware, *italicized* words are words that cannot be found in the original languages, but are rather added to make the text more perfectly understood in English. What if, we could prove the KJB's italicized words are inspired by God, using only the name of our Lord...

In the KJB, there are a total of 5 *italicized* mentions of ***Jesus.***

- Mark 5:24 **And *Jesus* went with him...**
- Mark 16:9 **Now when *Jesus* was risen early...**
- Luke 7:37 **...when she knew that *Jesus* sat at meat...**
- Luke 19:1 **And *Jesus* entered and passed through...**
- John 9:1 **And as *Jesus* passed by, he saw...**

Take note of the middle mention in Luke 7:37.

And there are 2 italicized mentions of Christ.

- Mark 13:6 **...in my name, saying, I am *Christ*...**
- Luke 21:8 **...in my name, saying, I am *Christ*...**

Italicized mentions of ***Jesus*** + ***Christ***		
1	Mark 5:24 - ***Jesus***	**Total = 7** *italicized* mentions Note: They are 100% symmetrical. The middle mention remains in Luke 7:37.
2	Mark 13:6 - ***Christ***	
3	Mark 16:9 - ***Jesus***	
4	Luke 7:37 - ***Jesus***	
5	Luke 19:1 - ***Jesus***	
6	Luke 21:8 - ***Christ***	
7	John 9:1 - ***Jesus***	

In Luke 7, **Jesus** is mentioned 8 times. The 7th is *italicized.*

1. Luke 7:3 - **Jesus**
2. Luke 7:4 - **Jesus**
3. Luke 7:6 - **Jesus**
4. Luke 7:9 - **Jesus**
5. Luke 7:19 - **Jesus**
6. Luke 7:22 - **Jesus**
7. Luke 7:37 - ***Jesus***
8. Luke 7:40 - **Jesus**

And in Luke 7, there are 3 anomalies related to one another dealing with the numbers 7 and 8, with the middle anomaly being the italicized.

- **Jesus** = Word #**7087** of Luke (Luke 7:9)
- ***Jesus*** = Word #**7778** of Luke (Luke 7:37) *(italicized!)*
- **Jesus** = Word #**7870** of Luke (Luke 7:40)

Italicized mentions of ***Jesus*** + ***Christ*** are only found in Mark, Luke, and John. Not Matthew or any other book of the N.T. There is a very interesting pattern between these three books:

- **Jesus** = Word #**7778** of Mark (Mark 9:27)
- ***Jesus*** = Word #**7778** of Luke (Luke 7:37) *(italicized!)*
- **Jesus** = Word #**7778** of John (John 8:42)

Again, the middle anomaly is Luke 7:37. Is this proof that *italics* are inspired?

It should be noted that 7×37 is the exact number of times that **Father** (singular, not possessive) occurs in the KJB, when referring to God. 37 is also the number of mentions of the word **Saviour** in the KJB. It should be noted as well that Luke is the #3 book of the New Testament, so the reference Luke 7:37 could be seen as: 3:7:37 … **3×7×37 = 777**

Luke 7:37 is about the woman who would break the alabaster box to anoint Jesus for his burial. 8 is the number for New beginnings. In Mark, Luke, and John, **Jesus** is word #**7778** in each book. But in the entire New Testament, **Jesus** is word #**87770**. This occurs in the book of Acts, post-resurrection (in Acts 5:30).

- The new beginning (8) is ahead of the 777 before the resurrection. (word #7778)
- The new beginning (8) is behind the 777 after the resurrection. (word #87770)

Acts 5:30 - **The God of our fathers raised up Jesus, whom ye slew and hanged on a tree.** (Jesus = word #87770 of the N.T.)

Book 7, Chapter 7, Word/Phrase 777

And the three companies blew the trumpets, and brake the pitchers, and held the lamps in their left hands, and the trumpets in their right hands to blow withal: and they cried, The sword of the LORD, and of Gideon Judges 7:20

Judges is the 7th book, which means Judges 7 is the 7th chapter of the 7th book of God's word. And the #777 word/phrase of this chapter is "**the LORD**" in the phrase "**The sword of the LORD**" of Judges 7:20

This verse mentioning "**The sword of the LORD**" is the #1769 verse in the Bible where the phrase "**the Lord**" is mentioned.

#1769 verse in KJB to mention **"the Lord"**	Word/phrase **#777** of the **#7 chapter** of the **#7 book**	**And the three companies blew the trumpets, and brake the pitchers, and held the lamps in their left hands, and the trumpets in their right hands to blow withal: and they cried, The sword of the LORD, and of Gideon** Judges 7:20

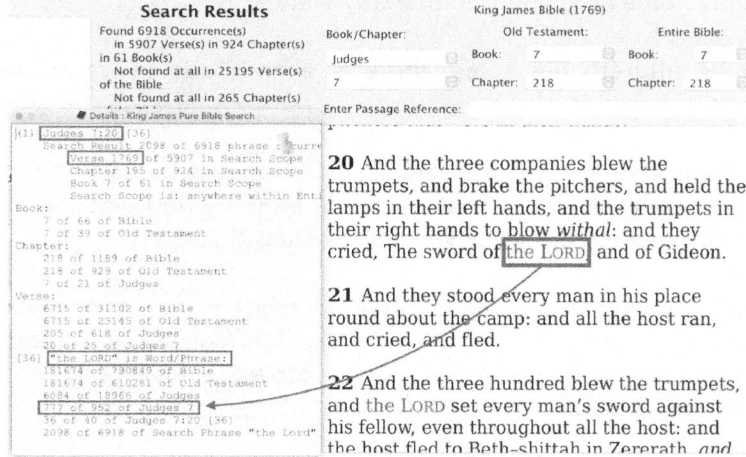

The year 1769 is the most widely recognized year of standardization for the KJB. Some patterns appeared later, but that does not take away from the monumental title and reputation that the year 1769 holds. See appendix 1.

Verse #7 of the Bible

And God made the firmament, and divided the waters which were under the firmament from the waters which were above the firmament: and it was so. Genesis 1:7

God divides "**the waters**".

Water is a type of God's word in many different places of scripture.

The voice of the LORD is upon the waters... Psalm 29:3

For as the rain cometh down, and the snow from heaven, and returneth not thither, but watereth the earth, and maketh it bring forth and bud, that it may give seed to the sower, and bread to the eater: So shall my word be that goeth forth out of my mouth: it shall not return unto me void, but it shall accomplish that which I please, and it shall prosper in the thing whereto I sent it. Isaiah 55:10-11

And, behold, the glory of the God of Israel came from the way of the east: and his voice was like a noise of many waters... Ezekiel 43:2

...and his voice as the sound of many waters. Revelation 1:15

When he uttereth his voice, there is a multitude of waters in the heavens... Jeremiah 10:13

Husbands, love your wives, even as Christ also loved the church, and gave himself for it; That he might sanctify and cleanse it with the washing of water by the word, Ephesians 5:25-26

The 7th word of the 7th verse is "**divided**" which is mentioned in exactly 66 verses of the Bible. (The words "**King**" (capitalized) and "**read**" are also mentioned in 66 verses. The word "**crown**" is mentioned 66 times and "**throne**" is mentioned 16×11 times.)

The **King** James Bible we **read** is **divided** into 66 books.

Verse #77 of the Bible

Unto Adam also and to his wife did the LORD God make coats of skins, and clothed them. Genesis 3:21

Here we have the first sacrifice in the Bible. While it doesn't say it directly in the text, there is, without question, a sacrifice performed by God as He makes two "**coats of skins**" to clothe Adam and Eve's nakedness.

"**coats**" is mentioned 7+7 times in the KJB
"**skin**" is mentioned 77 times in the KJB
"**skin(s)**" is mentioned in 77+7 verses in the KJB

The first sacrifice in the Bible (as it seems) occurs in the #77 verse. **Jesus Christ**, the Lamb of God, appears 77% of the way through the Bible, as the 77th generation from God. The #77 mention of "**sacrifice**" is in Numbers 7:77.

Verse #77 implies the first sacrifice performed in the Bible. Made by God for Adam and Eve. Covers their nakedness and shame with skins of sacrificed animals.	**The #77** from God, **Jesus Christ** (see p. 49 or Luke 3:23-38) becomes the sacrifice for our sins, for all of Adam (mankind). Covers our sins and shame with the righteousness of the Lamb.

Genesis 3:21 (Verse #77) = 707 English Ordinal

"Unto Adam also and to his wife did the LORD God make coats of skins, and clothed them." = **707** (English Ordinal)

U n t o 70 A d a m 19 a l s o 47 a n d 19 t o 35 h i s 36 w i f e 43
21 14 20 15 | 1 4 1 13 | 1 12 19 15 | 1 14 4 | 20 15 | 8 9 19 | 23 9 6 5

d i d 17 t h e 33 L O R D 49 G o d 26 m a k e 30 c o a t s 58 o f 21
4 9 4 | 20 8 5 | 12 15 18 4 | 7 15 4 | 13 1 11 5 | 3 15 1 20 19 | 15 6

s k i n s 72 a n d 19 c l o t h e d 67 t h e m 46 **707**
19 11 9 14 19 | 1 14 4 | 3 12 15 20 8 5 4 | 20 8 5 13

Verse #777 of the Bible

And God Almighty bless thee, and make thee fruitful, and multiply thee, that thou mayest be a multitude of people; Genesis 28:3

Genesis 28:3 is the 777th verse of the Bible, and it just so happens to be the verse where Jacob (Israel) receives the Abrahamic blessing, a **SWORN** promise from God. That's very important to know because **swearing** is equivalent to "**sevening**" in the Bible.

The 777th verse of the Bible is God's **SEVENED** Abrahamic promise being given to Jacob, who would later be named Israel. And of course, the rest of the Bible exists because of this promise, in both the Old Testament and the New.

Genesis 22:15-17	Genesis 28:1,3-4	Hebrews 6:14
And the angel of the LORD called unto Abraham out of heaven the second time, And said, By myself have I sworn, saith the LORD, for because thou hast done this thing, and hast not withheld thy son, thine only son: That in blessing I will bless thee, and in multiplying I will multiply thy seed as the stars of the heaven, and as the sand which is upon the sea shore; and thy seed shall possess the gate of his enemies;	**And Isaac called Jacob, and blessed him, and charged him, and said unto him, Thou shalt not take a wife of the daughters of Canaan... And God Almighty bless thee, and make thee fruitful, and multiply thee, that thou mayest be a multitude of people; And give thee the blessing of Abraham, to thee, and to thy seed with thee; that thou mayest inherit the land wherein thou art a stranger, which God gave unto Abraham**	**For when God made promise to Abraham, because he could swear by no greater, he sware by himself, Saying, Surely blessing I will bless thee, and multiplying I will multiply thee.**

The following side-by-side comparison shows how "**swear**" and "**seven**" are nearly identical twins in the Hebrew language.

Hebrew for **swear / oath**	Hebrew for **seven**
שָׁבַע	שֶׁבַע

And while I do not look up to concordances for absolute truth, the lexiconic definitions of **swear** and **seven** are very helpful in understanding the relationship between these two words. Here are the Strong's definitions for **swear** (H7650) and **seven** (H7651). They are numbered together because they are alphabetically back to back in the Hebrew language.

Strong's H7650 - šāḇaʿ	**Strong's H7651 - šeḇaʿ**
שָׁבַע	שֶׁבַע
shâbaʻ, shaw-bah'; a primitive root; properly to be complete, but used only as a denominative from H7651; to seven oneself, i.e. swear (as if by repeating a declaration seven times):—adjure, charge (by an oath, with an oath), feed to the full (by mistake for H7646), take an oath, × straitly, (cause to, make to) swear.	shebaʻ, sheh'-bah; or (masculine) (שִׁבְעָה shibʻâh); from H7650; a primitive cardinal number; seven (as the sacred full one); also (adverbially) seven times; by implication, a week; by extension, an indefinite number:—(+ by) seven(-fold),-s, (-teen, -teenth), -th, times).

It's quite clear these words share meaning and purpose. In the Bible itself, the first person who **swears** is Abraham in Genesis 21, which is proceeded by Abraham giving **seven** ewe lambs to Abimelech as a token/proof of their sworn covenant. (See Genesis 21:23-32). Also, notice how the first time **swearing** happens in the Bible is in the 21st chapter. 21= (7+7+7).

Genesis 21:23-32		
And it came to pass at that time, that Abimelech and Phichol the chief captain of his host spake unto Abraham, saying, God is with thee in all that thou doest: Now therefore <u>swear</u> unto me here by God that thou wilt not deal falsely with me, nor with my son, nor with my son's son: but according to the kindness that I have done unto thee, thou shalt do unto me, and to the land wherein thou hast sojourned.	**And Abraham said, I will <u>swear</u>. And Abraham reproved Abimelech because of a well of water, which Abimelech's servants had violently taken away. And Abimelech said, I wot not who hath done this thing: neither didst thou tell me, neither yet heard I of it, but to day. And Abraham took sheep and oxen, and gave them unto Abimelech; and both of them made a <u>covenant</u>. And Abraham took sheep and oxen, and gave them unto Abimelech;**	**and both of them made a <u>covenant</u>. And Abraham set <u>seven</u> ewe lambs of the flock by themselves. And Abimelech said unto Abraham, What mean these <u>seven</u> ewe lambs which thou hast set by themselves? And he said, For these <u>seven</u> ewe lambs shalt thou take of my hand, that they may be a witness unto me, that I have digged this well.**

Now that you understand the deep connection between **swearing** and **seven**, let's go back to the beginning of this trail and look at the most important part of all.

Verse #777, God's **Sevened** Promise passed to Jacob (Israel)	Old Testament significance	New Testament significance
And God Almighty bless thee, and make thee fruitful, and multiply thee, that thou mayest be a multitude of people; Genesis 28:3	The entire rest of the O.T. is about the people of Israel, where the promised Messiah will come from. Which all traces back to this promise.	Jesus Christ is the direct fulfillment of this promise. And all who are Christ's are also heirs of the promise.

Without this sevened promise of God being passed to Israel, which occurs in the 777th verse of the Bible, the Old and New Testaments would be gutted of all virtue and substance. This is the promise of the seed of Abraham that would turn out to be none other than Jesus Christ, the promised Messiah.

Verse #777, God's **Sevened** Promise	The seed of promise is Jesus Christ	The seed of promise are all Christians
Genesis 28:3-4	Galatians 3:16	Galatians 3:29
And God Almighty bless thee, and make thee fruitful, and multiply thee, that thou mayest be a multitude of people; And give thee the blessing of Abraham, to thee, and to thy seed with thee;	**Now to Abraham and his seed were the promises made. He saith not, And to seeds, as of many; but as of one, And to thy seed, which is Christ.** *Also see Hebrews 2:16*	**And if ye be Christ's, then are ye Abraham's seed, and heirs according to the promise.**

What an amazing feeling it is to know I am Christ's and an heir of the Abrahamic blessing of verse #777. I am not worthy. But by faith I am in Him who is worthy. Thank you, Lord.

But that's not all…

The #777 verse is specially about Isaac passing the promise to Jacob, the promise that God originally swore to Abraham.

- God **swears** to **Abraham** (Gen 22:16-18)
- Abraham's son **Isaac** passes the promise to **Jacob** (Verse #777)

A combined search for:
Swear + Abraham + Isaac + Jacob = 777 mentions in the KJB

For when God made promise to Abraham, because he could swear by no greater, he sware by himself

Hebrews 6:13

Abraham + Isaac + Jacob + swear = 777 mentions in the KJB

Search Filters: **Entire Bible**		Case Sens	Mentions
Search Phrase 1	**Abraham**	-	231
Search Phrase 2	**Isaac**	-	128
Search Phrase 3	**Jacob**	-	358
Search Phrase 4	**swear**	-	60
Total Mentions	**Abraham + Isaac + Jacob + swear**		**777**
KJB1611 = 778 NKJV = 771 ESV = 811 NASB2020 = 779 NASB1971 = 776 NIV = 783			

The #77 mention of the combined search is God providing the substitute, right before He gives the promise *(in v. 16)...*

And <u>Abraham</u> lifted up his eyes, and looked, and behold behind him a ram caught in a thicket by his horns: and Abraham went and took the ram, and offered him up for a burnt offering in the stead of his son. Genesis 22:13

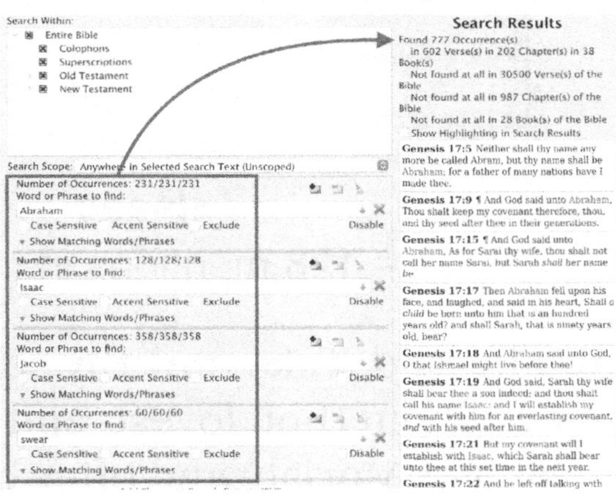

And I will bring you in unto the land, concerning the which I did **<u>swear</u>** to give it to **<u>Abraham</u>**, to **<u>Isaac</u>**, and to **<u>Jacob</u>**; and I will give it you for an heritage: I am the LORD.

Exodus 6:8

The same combination in the New Testament

Abraham + Isaac + Jacob + swear
= **128** N.T. mentions

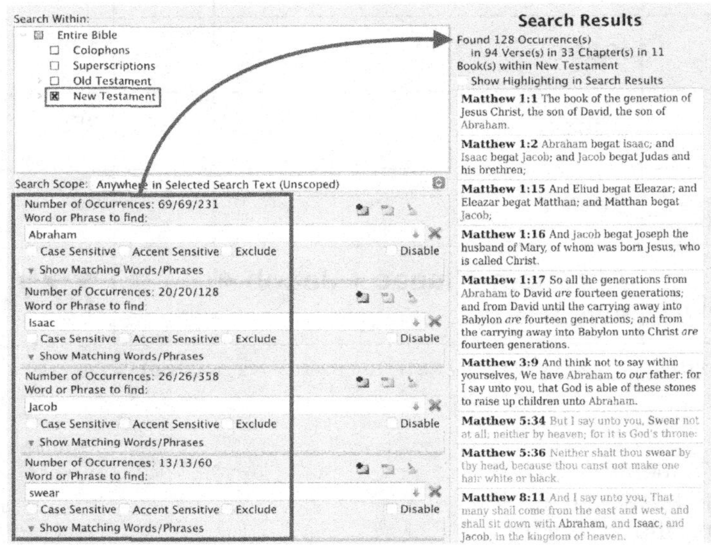

Isaac
= **128** mentions in the KJB

And he said, Take now thy son, thine only son Isaac, whom thou lovest, and get thee into the land of Moriah; and offer him there for a burnt offering upon one of the mountains which I will tell thee of.

Genesis 22:2

Verse #7777 of the Bible

And the priest answered David, and said, There is no common bread under mine hand, but there is hallowed bread; if the young men have kept themselves at least from women. 1 Samuel 21:4

1 Samuel 21:4 (verse #7777 of the Bible) and its surrounding passage is the first thing that Jesus talks about when the **sabbath** is first mentioned in the N.T. (which is the #77 mention of "**sabbath**" in the KJB, *excluding Psalm headings*).

These passages also have the exact same digits in their numeric references: (1, 2, 1, 4)
1 Samuel 21:4 >>> Matthew 12:1,4

#77 mention of sabbath *(First mention in the New Testament)*	**#7777 verse of Bible**
Matthew 12:1-4 1 **At that time Jesus went on the sabbath day through the corn; and his disciples were an hungred, and began to pluck the ears of corn, and to eat.** 2 **But when the Pharisees saw it, they said unto him, Behold, thy disciples do that which is not lawful to do upon the sabbath day.** 3 **But he said unto them, Have ye not read what David did, when he was an hungred, and they that were with him;** 4 **How he entered into the house of God, and did eat the shewbread, which was not lawful for him to eat, neither for them which were with him, but only for the priests?**	1 Samuel 21:4 4 **And the priest answered David, and said, There is no common bread under mine hand, but there is hallowed bread; if the young men have kept themselves at least from women.**

The #7777 word of the New Testament is "**do**" in Mat 12:2, in direct reference to what the disciples are "doing" (eating the corn) - which is what Jesus compares with verse #7777 of the Bible. **But I say unto you, That in this place is one greater than the temple... For the Son of man is Lord even of the sabbath day.** Matthew 12:6,8. Amen, Amen!

It's also interesting how verse #7777 uses the phrase "**hallowed bread**" instead of "**shewbread**". The word "**hallowed**", which means *holy* or *sanctified*, is <u>first</u> mentioned in reference to the **sabbath** in Exodus 20:11, spoken by God Himself in fire from Mount Sinai.

For in six days the LORD made heaven and earth, the sea, and all that in them is, and rested the seventh day: wherefore the LORD blessed the sabbath day, and <u>hallowed</u> it. Exodus 20:11

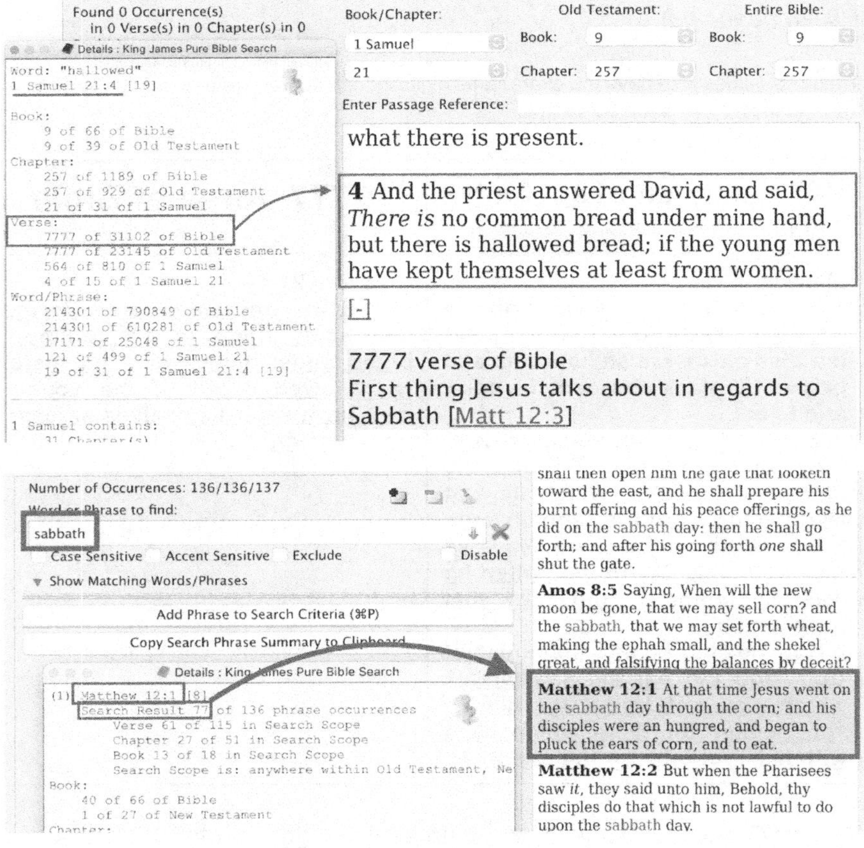

Note: to get this same result in King James Pure Bible Search, be sure to disable "Superscriptions" in the filters. Only "Old Testament" / "New Testament" should be selected.

For more detailed notes on the word count of **sabbath**, see p. 294.

Seven, 77 verses in First and Last Books

The first time "**seven**" refers to an actual quantity/order of 7 (not apart of a larger number such as 807 "*eight hundred and <u>seven</u>*") is in the #7 chapter of the Bible, Genesis 7...

...which is also the #7 verse where **seven*** <u>appears</u>, (when referring to an actual 7).

Appearances of <u>seven</u>* when directly referring to cardinal number 7

1. Genesis 2:2 **And on the <u>seven</u>th day... he rested on the <u>seven</u>th day...**
2. Genesis 2:3 **And God blessed the <u>seven</u>th day, and sanctified it...**
3. Genesis 4:15...**vengeance shall be taken on him <u>seven</u>fold...**
4. Genesis 4:24 **If Cain shall be avenged <u>seven</u>fold, truly Lamech...**
5. Genesis 7:2 **Of every clean beast thou shalt take to thee by <u>seven</u>s...**
6. Genesis 7:3 **Of fowls also of the air by <u>seven</u>s, the male and the female...**
7. Genesis 7:4 **For yet <u>seven</u> days, and I will cause it to rain...**

Notice how the #7 verse is the first time **<u>seven</u>** stands alone without any "**-th**", "**-fold**", "**-s**". This is the difference between an appearance and a mention. The #7 verse where the actual number 7 <u>appears</u> is also the first <u>mention</u> of "**<u>seven</u>**" in the Bible (when not part of a larger number).

If you disregard actual-7 and simply look at every time the word **seven** is mentioned, there are exactly 77 verses containing the word "**seven**" in Genesis and Revelation, the first and last books of the Bible.

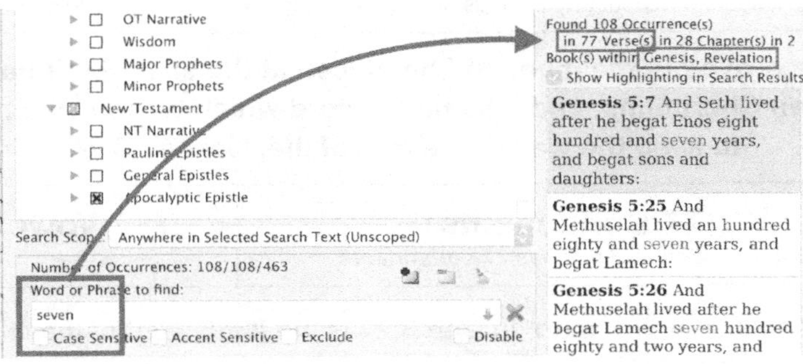

77-letter Verses

And Seth lived after he begat Enos eight hundred and seven years, and begat sons and daughters: Genesis 5:7

Genesis 5:7 contains the first mention of the word "**seven**" in the KJB when it stands alone without a suffix such as seventh / sevenfold.

Genesis 5:7 also *just so happens* to be the first verse of the Bible made up of exactly 77 letters.

First verse of exactly **77 letters** is also the **First verse** mentioning "**seven**" As it stands, without any endings such as seventh (-th), sevenfold (-fold), etc		
And Seth lived after he begat Enos eight hundred and seven years, and begat sons and daughters: Genesis 5:7		
77 Letters *First verse in KJB made of exactly **77 letters***	**7×7 Consonants**	**T7 Vowels** T7 = 1+2+3+4+5+6+7 = 7×4

The first verse of the Bible to contain 77 consonants has exactly 7×7 vowels, when God seals off Eden from mankind. (Genesis 3:24)

First verse with **77 consonants** has **7×7 Vowels** As it stands, without any endings such as seventh (-th), sevenfold (-fold), etc	
So he drove out the man; and he placed at the east of the garden of Eden Cherubims, and a flaming sword which turned every way, to keep the way of the tree of life. Genesis 3:24	
77 Consonants *First verse in KJB that has **77 consonants***	**7×7 Vowels**

Interesting side-note: "**man**" in Gen 3:24 is the #666 word of the chapter. See Revelation 13:18.

Other significant notes on verses with 77 letters:

The **#77 verse** in the KJB that is made of **77 letters**	
2 Kings 5:9 **So Naaman came with his horses and with his chariot, and stood at the door of the house of Elisha.**	Significance
77 letters (#77 of 295 verses)	Naaman was told by Elisha to dip seven times to be healed of his leprosy. The very next verse describes it: **And Elisha sent a messenger unto him, saying, Go and wash in Jordan seven times, and thy flesh shall come again to thee, and thou shalt be clean.** 2 Kings 5:10

7, the number of completion, is not always a good thing. If you're on the wrong side of God's will, completion for you will result in plagues, captivity, destruction, death and damnation. This is clearly demonstrated in the only 77-letter verse to have an English Ordinal value of 777.

The only **777** English Ordinal verse that is made of **77 letters**	
2 Kings 24:19 **And he did that which was evil in the sight of the LORD, according to all that Jehoiakim had done.**	Significance
77 letters **777 English Ordinal** (A=1, B=2, C=3 … Z=26)	This passage is describing the last king of Judah, Zedekiah, who began to reign when he was (7+7+7) years old (2 Kings 24:18). The following verse (2 Kings 24:20) describes the sad and brutal end of the kingdom of Judah, before Jerusalem was destroyed (2 Kings 25) and the LORD'S chosen people were taken to Babylon for 70 years of captivity. **For through the anger of the LORD it came to pass in Jerusalem and Judah, until he had cast them out from his presence, that Zedekiah rebelled against the king of Babylon.** 2 Kings 24:20

What are letters? Letters are the things, usually representing sounds, that join together to form words.

In the beginning was the Word... John 1:1.

The first chapter of John has two verses with exactly 77 letters:

<table>
<tr><td colspan="2"><u>Only</u> verses with 77 letters in John 1
In the beginning was the Word...</td></tr>
<tr><td>Verse #7</td><td>Verse #7×7</td></tr>
<tr><td>John 1:7</td><td>John 1:49</td></tr>
<tr><td>The same came for a witness, to bear witness of the Light, that all men through him might believe.</td><td>Nathanael answered and saith unto him, Rabbi, thou art the Son of God; thou art the King of Israel.</td></tr>
<tr><td>77 Letters</td><td>77 Letters</td></tr>
</table>

God's words are pure. Perhaps the most memorized and quoted verse in the Bible about God's pure words is Psalm 12:6

<table>
<tr><td colspan="2">Psalm 12:6, God's words are
Purified 7 times</td></tr>
<tr><td>The words of the LORD are pure words: as silver tried in a furnace of earth, purified <u>seven times</u>.</td><td>77 Letters</td></tr>
<tr><td>Psalm 12:6</td><td>Psalm 12 is the #(70×7) chapter of the Bible</td></tr>
</table>

The name of Jesus(') is mentioned 980 times in the King James Bible when directly referring to Jesus Christ (See appendix 7). When I searched to see if there were any 77-letter verses with a value of 980, there was 1 that appeared.

That verse is Psalm 140:13

<table>
<tr><th colspan="2">The only 980 English Ordinal verse
that is made of 77 letters</th></tr>
<tr><td>Psalm 140:13

Surely the righteous shall give thanks unto <u>thy name</u>: the upright shall dwell in thy presence.</td><td>Significance</td></tr>
<tr><td>77 letters

980 English Ordinal
(A=1, B=2, C=3 … Z=26)</td><td>The <u>name</u> of Jesus(') is mentioned 980 times in the King James Bible when directly referring to Jesus Christ (See appendix 7).

Psalm 140:13 mentions "thy name" and is the only 77-letter verse with an English Ordinal value of 980.</td></tr>
</table>

How likely is it that all these things of significance occur in 77-letter verses? It reminds me a lot of Judges 7:7. God only needs a few, and because of that, a heavy application of Matthew 7:7 may be required to see these things. **Give unto the LORD the glory due unto his name.**

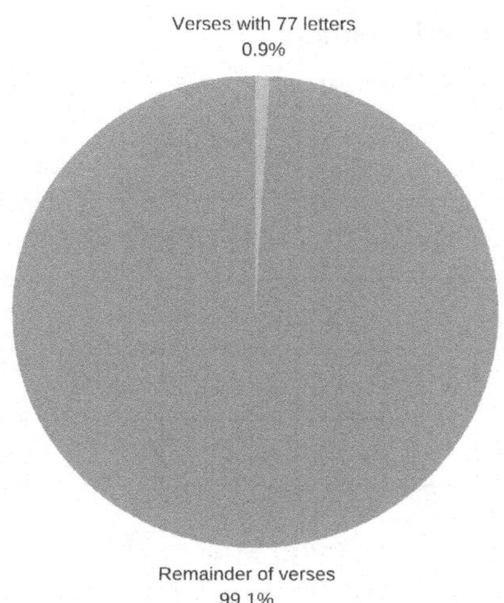

"G-O-D" 7 & 777 Letter Gaps in First Books

I would seek unto God, and unto God would I commit my cause: Which doeth great things and unsearchable; marvellous things without number: Job 5:8-9

Most people who have heard of ELS (Equidistant-Letter-Sequence) codes, have heard or seen that there are strong cases for them in the Hebrew language.

Because English has vowels built directly into its alphabet, it's not as simple as Hebrew to find these types of patterns in English. Or at least, in theory, it should be much more difficult.

But... is there anything significant in modern-day Anglo-Saxon? Did God really foreordain His words to be translated into the language of barbarians? Amazingly, it appears so.

First chapter of the Old Testament

Genesis 1:1 - **G** ...7-letter gap... **O** ...7-letter gap... **D**

Begins after the first 7 letters of the O.T.

First chapter of the New Testament

Matthew 1:2-21 - **G** ...777-letter gap... **O** ...777-letter gap... **D**

Ends in the # (7+7+7) verse of the N.T.

"G-O-D" 7-LETTER GAP																							
Genesis 1:1																							
I	N	T	H	E	B	E	**G**	I	N	N	I	N	G	G	**O**	D	C	R	E	A	T	E	**D**
1	2	3	4	5	6	7		1	2	3	4	5	6	7		1	2	3	4	5	6	7	

In Matthew 1, for the sake of page space, I'm unable to put it into a nice table like the one above. However, I will use a monospaced font (letters are the same width) to help see the pattern better within a big blob of text.

"G-O-D" 777-LETTER GAP

Matthew 1:2-21

```
............ABRAHAMBEGATISAACBE[G]ATJACOBANDJACOBBEGATJUDASANDHISB
RETHRENANDJUDASBEGATPHARESANDZARAOFTHAMARANDPHARESBEGATESROMANDES
ROMBEGATARAMANDARAMBEGATAMINADABANDAMINADABBEGATNAASSONANDNAASSON
BEGATSALMONANDSALMONBEGATBOOZOFRACHABANDBOOZBEGATOBEDOFRUTHANDOBE
DBEGATJESSEANDJESSEBEGATDAVIDTHEKINGANDDAVIDTHEKINGBEGATSOLOMONOF
HERTHATHADBEENTHEWIFEOFURIASANDSOLOMONBEGATROBOAMANDROBOAMBEGATAB
IAANDABIABEGATASAANDASABEGATJOSAPHATANDJOSAPHATBEGATJORAMANDJORAM
BEGATOZIASANDOZIASBEGATJOATHAMANDJOATHAMBEGATACHAZANDACHAZBEGATEZ
EKIASANDEZEKIASBEGATMANASSESANDMANASSESBEGATAMONANDAMONBEGATJOSIA
SANDJOSIASBEGATJECHONIASANDHISBRETHRENABOUTTHETIMETHEYWERECARRIED
AWAYTOBABYLONANDAFTERTHEYWEREBROUGHTTOBABYLONJECHONIASBEGATSALATH
IELANDSALATHIELBEGATZOROBABELANDZOROBABELBEGATABIUDANDABIUDBEGATE
LIAKIMANDELIAKIMBEGATAZORANDAZ[O]RBEGATSADOCANDSADOCBEGATACHIMAND
ACHIMBEGATELIUDANDELIUDBEGATELEAZARANDELEAZARBEGATMATTHANANDMATTH
ANBEGATJACOBANDJACOBBEGATJOSEPHTHEHUSBANDOFMARYOFWHOMWASBORNJESUS
WHOISCALLEDCHRISTSOALLTHEGENERATIONSFROMABRAHAMTODAVIDAREFOURTEEN
GENERATIONSANDFROMDAVIDUNTILTHECARRYINGAWAYINTOBABYLONAREFOURTEEN
GENERATIONSANDFROMTHECARRYINGAWAYINTOBABYLONUNTOCHRISTAREFOURTEEN
GENERATIONSNOWTHEBIRTHOFJESUSCHRISTWASONTHISWISEWHENASHIŞMOTHERMA
RYWASESPOUSEDTOJOSEPHBEFORETHEYCAMETOGETHERSHEWASFOUNDWITHCHILDOF
THEHOLYGHOSTTHENJOSEPHHERHUSBANDBEINGAJUSTMANANDNOTWILLINGTOMAKEH
ERAPUBLICKEXAMPLEWASMINDEDTOPUTHERAWAYPRIVILYBUTWHILEHETHOUGHTONT
HESETHINGSBEHOLDTHEANGELOFTHELORDAPPEAREDUNTOHIMINADREAMSAYINGJOS
EPHTHOUSONOFDAVIDFEARNOTTOTAKEUNTOTHEEMARYTHYWIFEFORTHATWHICHISCO
NCEIVEDINHERISOFTHEHOLYGHOSTAN[D]SHESHALLBRINGFORTHASONANDTHOUSHA
LTCALLHISNAMEJESUSFORHESHALLSAVEHISPEOPLEFROMTHEIRSINS...........
```

A critic will be quick to point out that "God" is a very easy ELS code to occur by random chance. Yeah, that's true. But in these exact locations, in the first chapters of each testament, with 7 / 777 letter gaps?

In the first chapter of Genesis, "S-E-V-E-N" is spelled by skipping every 77 letters <u>as God makes man in His own image.</u>

This type of thing seems very bizarre to occur by random chance, especially knowing God's only begotten Son arrives as the express image of God (Hebrews 1:3) in the 77th generation from God, 77% of the way through scriptures.

Genesis 1:25-28

S ...77-letters... **E** ...77-letters... **V** ...77-letters... **E** ...77-letters... **N**

"S-E-V-E-N" 77-LETTER ELS
Genesis 1:25-28
..WA**[S]**GOODANDGODSAIDLETUSMAKEMANINOURIMAGEAFTEROURLIKENESSANDLET THEMHAVEDOMINIONOV**[E]**RTHEFISHOFTHESEAANDOVERTHEFOWLOFTHEAIRANDOVE RTHECATTLEANDOVERALLTHEEARTHANDO**[V]**EREVERYCREEPINGTHINGTHATCREEPE THUPONTHEEARTHSOGODCREATEDMANINHISOWNIMAGEINTH**[E]**IMAGEOFGODCREATE DHEHIMMALEANDFEMALECREATEDHETHEMANDGODBLESSEDTHEMANDGODSAIDU**[N]**TO THEMBEFRUITFULANDMULTIPLYANDREPLENISHTHEEARTHANDSUBDUEIT.........

This is <u>the *only* possible way</u> to spell out "S-E-V-E-N" by skipping letters in Genesis 1.

In Genesis 2, <u>the *only* possible way</u> to spell out "S-E-V-E-N" is by skipping every 70 letters, starting in the first verse of the Bible that mentions **LORD** (right after the 7 days of creation are finished).

Genesis 2:4-6

S ...70-letters... **E** ...70-letters... **V** ...70-letters... **E** ...70-letters... **N**

"S-E-V-E-N" 70-LETTER ELS
Genesis 2:4-6
...THEGENERATION**[S]**OFTHEHEAVENSANDOFTHEEARTHWHENTHEYWERECREATEDIN THEDAYTHATTHELORDGODMAD**[E]**THEEARTHANDTHEHEAVENSANDEVERYPLANTOFTHE FIELDBEFOREITWASINTHEEARTHANDE**[V]**ERYHERBOFTHEFIELDBEFOREITGREWFOR THELORDGODHADNOTCAUSEDITTORAINUPONTHE**[E]**ARTHANDTHEREWASNOTAMANTOT ILLTHEGROUNDBUTTHEREWENTUPAMISTFROMTHEEARTHA**[N]**DWATEREDTHEWHOLE..

Genesis 1: "S-E-V-E-N" = 77-letter ELS, *man made in God's image*
Genesis 2: "S-E-V-E-N" = 70-letter ELS, end of *day 7, mention #1 of **LORD***

Bible Comparison of 77 / 70 ELS anomaly in Genesis 1 & 2 KJB

KJB **Genesis 1 "S-E-V-E-N" = 1 ELS code (77-letters)** **Genesis 2 "S-E-V-E-N" = 1 ELS code (70-letters)**
KJB1611 *"**seven**" was spelled as "**seuen**" in the KJB1611* Genesis 1 "S-E-U-E-N" = 2 ELS codes (329-letters, 223-letters) Genesis 2 "S-E-U-E-N" = 1 ELS code (195-letters)
NKJV Genesis 1 "S-E-V-E-N" = 1 ELS code (45 letters) Genesis 2 "S-E-V-E-N" = 0 ELS codes
ESV Genesis 1 "S-E-V-E-N" = 0 ELS codes Genesis 2 "S-E-V-E-N" = 1 ELS code (325-letters)
NASB1971 Genesis 1 "S-E-V-E-N" = 1 ELS code (95-letters) Genesis 2 "S-E-V-E-N" = 1 ELS code (372-letters)
NASB 2020 Genesis 1 "S-E-V-E-N" = 2 ELS codes (441-letters, 464-letters) Genesis 2 "S-E-V-E-N" = 0 ELS codes
NIV Genesis 1 "S-E-V-E-N" = 2 ELS codes (175-letters, 159-letters) Genesis 2 "S-E-V-E-N" = 0 ELS codes

Consider the "fine-tuning" of the KJB. All these other translations show the randomness you would expect. Just one extra letter in Genesis 1:25-28, 2:4-6 KJB would pulverize this "coincidence" entirely out of existence.

When God Sevens (Swears by) Himself

...By myself have I sworn, saith the LORD, for because thou hast done this thing, and hast not withheld thy son, thine only son: That in blessing I will bless thee, and in multiplying I will multiply thy seed as the stars of the heaven, and as the sand which is upon the sea shore; and thy seed shall possess the gate of his enemies; Genesis 22:16-17

I have sworn by myself, the word is gone out of my mouth in righteousness, and shall not return, That unto me every knee shall bow, every tongue shall swear. Isaiah 45:23

God swears many times in the Bible. But in some instances, such as the ones above in Genesis 22:16 and Isaiah 45:23, God doesn't just swear. He swears *BY HIMSELF*.

It's important to know that "SWEARING" is equivalent to "SEVENING" in the Bible. When God swears by Himself, He sevens Himself.

Hebrew for **swear / oath**	Hebrew for **seven**
שָׁבַע	שֶׁבַע

(See pp. 214-216 for a more detailed comparison.)

Genesis 22:16, the Abrahamic blessing which passes onto Israel in the 777th verse of the Bible, is the first out of seven times in the Bible where God swears by Himself / His name. Here are the other places just in case you are curious:

All instances where God Swears By Himself (שָׁבַע) (Sevens Himself)		
1	Genesis 22:16	**And said, <u>By myself have I sworn</u>, saith the LORD, for because thou hast done this thing, and hast not withheld thy son, thine only son:**
2	Isaiah 45:23	**<u>I have sworn by myself</u>, the word is gone out of my mouth in righteousness, and shall not return, That unto me every knee shall bow, every tongue shall swear.**
3	Jeremiah 22:5	**But if ye will not hear these words, <u>I swear by myself</u>, saith the LORD, that this house shall become a desolation.**
4	Jeremiah 44:26	**Therefore hear ye the word of the LORD, all Judah that dwell in the land of Egypt; Behold, <u>I have sworn by my great name</u>, saith the LORD, that my name shall no more be named in the mouth of any man of Judah in all the land of Egypt, saying, The Lord GOD liveth.**
5	Jeremiah 49:13	**For <u>I have sworn by myself</u>, saith the LORD, that Bozrah shall become a desolation, a reproach, a waste, and a curse; and all the cities thereof shall be perpetual wastes.**
6	Jeremiah 51:14	**<u>The LORD of hosts hath sworn by himself</u>, saying, Surely I will fill thee with men, as with caterpillers; and they shall lift up a shout against thee.**
7	Amos 6:8	**<u>The Lord GOD hath sworn by himself</u>, saith the LORD the God of hosts, I abhor the excellency of Jacob, and hate his palaces: therefore will I deliver up the city with all that is therein.**

Another interesting fact is how the Lord starts off the sentence with the word "**By**"...

By myself have I sworn [sevened]...

"**By**" (capitalized) is mentioned 77+7 times in the Bible. And, if you skip ahead 7 mentions of "**By**" (capitalized) from this verse (Gen 22:16), your destination will be Book 7, Chapter 7, Verse 7, Word 7.

By myself have I sworn [sevened]... + 7 mentions of "**By**" = The #7 word of the #7 verse of the #7 chapter of the #7 book.

And the LORD said unto Gideon, By the three hundred men that lapped will I save you... Judges 7:7 - A verse where God shows us His salvation is dependent on Him alone, and the predetermined mathematical equation to get it done (**By the three hundred men...**) is chosen by Him as well. Amen.

But there's something even more peculiar about the first time He "**sevens**" Himself. The word "**sworn**" in Genesis 22:16 is the first time God Himself speaks this word, and it is the 13,627th word of the King James Bible.

13,627. Seems a bit random at first glance. 13,627? What's noteworthy about it?

Let's start with the fact that it's a Prime number. Prime numbers are numbers that have no factors besides one and itself (E.g. 7 is a prime number because only (1 × 7) gives you 7. No other numbers can produce 7 when multiplied together).

Thus, as a Prime number, there are no two numbers you can multiply together to get 13,627 besides (1 × 13627) = 13,627.

Still nothing noteworthy. There are many prime numbers, and nothing about 13,627 feels significant.

But wait... The interesting thing about 13,627 is discovered when you look at the **order** of all Prime numbers.

Prime Numbers in Order		
#1 Prime is 2 #2 Prime is 3 #3 Prime is 5 #4 Prime is 7 #5 Prime is 11	#6 Prime is 13 #7 Prime is 17 #8 Prime is 19 #9 Prime is 23 #10 Prime is 29	#11 Prime is 31 #12 Prime is 37 #13 Prime is 41 #14 Prime is 43 etc…

There are many deep patterns in the Bible that go back to Prime Index / Order.

If you list out all the Primes, what # Prime is 13,627?
The answer: #1611

The 1611th Prime number is 13,627

1611 of course is the year that the King James Bible was first printed.

And that's not all.

The digit sum of 13627 is 1+3+6+2+7 = 19
…19 is a Prime Number…

…which means 13627 is an "Additive Prime."

Additive Primes are primes where the sum of digits is also prime. I am not making this up by the way. You can search for *"additive primes"* online and verify it for yourself.

Additive Prime Numbers in Order		
#1 Additive Prime is 2 #2 Additive Prime is 3 #3 Additive Prime is 5 #4 Additive Prime is 7 #5 Additive Prime is 11	#6 Additive Prime is 23 #7 Additive Prime is 29 #8 Additive Prime is 41 #9 Additive Prime is 43 #10 Additive Prime is 47	#11 Additive Prime is 61 #12 Additive Prime is 67 #13 Additive Prime is 83 #14 Additive Prime is 89 etc…

As seen earlier on p. 143, the #777 Prime Number is the #389 Additive Prime, and 389 is the #77 Prime Number. According to mathematicians, there are absolutely zero patterns that exist in the order of Prime Numbers. But there does appear to be some sort of divine hand over the order of these numbers. 777 × Prime #77 = T777 (Sum of all numbers from 1 to 777)

So what # Additive Prime is 13,627?
Answer: #777

The 777th Additive Prime is 13,627, *which is also the 1611th Prime.*

That's incredible in itself. 1611 and 777 are directly woven together in the very fibers of mathematics, just as 777 and 77.

But to have God's first mention of "**sworn**" (שָׁבַע) as the exact ***#1611-Prime & #777-Additive-Prime*** word of the Bible is... beyond fathomable.

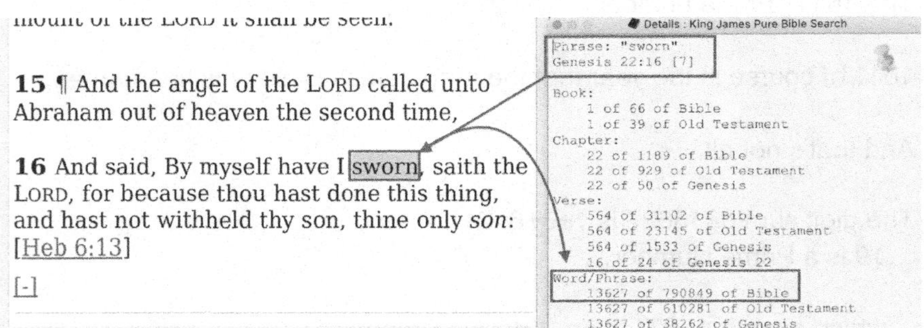

One more note on "**sworn**" (שָׁבַע)...

English Ordinal, as seen elsewhere in these notes (and detailed in Appendix 9) is a system where each letter is equivalent to a number.

English Ordinal						
A = 1	E = 5	I = 9	M = 13	Q = 17	U = 21	Y = 25
B = 2	F = 6	J = 10	N = 15	R = 18	V = 22	Z = 26
C = 3	G = 7	K = 11	O = 15	S = 19	W = 23	
D = 4	H = 8	L = 12	P = 16	T = 20	X = 24	

In Psalm 119, the longest chapter of the Bible (which is entirely about the word of God), the word "**sworn**" is only mentioned one time.

I have <u>sworn</u>, and I will perform it, that I will keep thy righteous judgments. Psalm 119:106

This is the <u>only</u> verse out of 176 verses in Psalm 119 that contains the word "**sworn**" – which, as we already know, means "**sevened**".

And this verse has a total English Ordinal value of 777.

Psalm 119:106 KJB

Reverse Ordinal

I h a v e s w o r n , a n d I
9 8 1 22 5 19 23 15 18 14 1 14 4 9

w i l l p e r f o r m i t , t h a t
23 9 12 12 16 5 18 6 15 18 13 9 20 20 8 1 20

I w i l l k e e p t h y
9 23 9 12 12 11 5 5 16 20 8 25

r i g h t e o u s j u d g m e n t s .
18 9 7 8 20 5 15 21 19 10 21 4 7 13 5 14 20 19

I (9) + **have** (36) + **sworn,** (89) + **and** (19) + **I** (9) +
will (56) + **perform** (91) + **it,** (29) + **that** (49) +
I (9) + **will** (56) + **keep** (37) + **thy** (53) +
righteous (122) + **judgments.** (113)

Total Sum = **777**

KJB1611 = 795 NKJV = 705 ESV = 676 NASB1971 = 753 NASB2020 = 790 NIV = 743

For more notes on Psalm 119, see pp. 310-315.

777 Genesis 1:1 Reverse Ordinal

In the beginning God created the heaven and the earth. Genesis 1:1

English Reverse Ordinal						
A = 26	E = 22	I = 18	M = 14	Q = 10	U = 6	Y = 2
B = 25	F = 21	J = 17	N = 13	R = 9	V = 5	Z = 1
C = 24	G = 20	K = 16	O = 12	S = 8	W = 4	
D = 23	H = 19	L = 15	P = 11	T = 7	X = 3	

We're not dealing with the words of a man. We're dealing with God, who knows the end from the beginning... Is this really a coincidence?

Genesis 1:1 KJB

Reverse Ordinal

I n t h e b e g i n n i n g G o d
18 13 7 19 22 25 22 20 18 13 13 18 13 20 20 12 23

c r e a t e d t h e h e a v e n
24 9 22 26 7 22 23 7 19 22 19 22 26 5 22 13

a n d t h e e a r t h .
26 13 23 7 19 22 22 26 9 7 19

In (31) + **the** (48) + **beginning** (162) + **God** (55) +
created (133) + **the** (48) + **heaven** (107) +
and (62) + **the** (48) + **earth**. (83)

Total Sum = 777

KJB1611 = 778, NKJV = 785, ESV = 785, NASB1971 = 785, NASB2020 = 785 , NIV = 785

See Appendix 9 for more info on alphanumerics.

I am Alpha and Omega, the beginning and the ending, saith the Lord, which is, and which was, and which is to come, the Almighty.

Revelation 1:8

Alpha and Omega 7777, First and Last Books

And he said unto me, It is done. I am Alpha and Omega, the beginning and the end. I will give unto him that is athirst of the fountain of the water of life freely. Revelation 21:6

Alpha [A] is the first letter of the Greek alphabet.
Omega [Ω] is the last letter of the Greek alphabet.

A is the first letter of the English alphabet.
Z is the last letter of the English alphabet.

Positionally, **Alpha** = **A**, **Omega** = **Z**

If you look at Genesis and Revelation only, the first and the last books, there is an amazing coincidence that occurs when you search for words with these letters. The letter A is pretty common. Words starting with A can be found on every page of the Bible. But the letter Z is rare. It's difficult to quickly find a word with the letter Z in it. But if you list out all the words that start with the letter A in Genesis/Revelation, and separately make a list with all words that contain a letter Z in Genesis/Revelation, you will end up with the following sum:

Search Filters: **Genesis, Revelation**		Case Sens	Words
Search Phrase 1	**A*** *All words starting with A*	-	7674
Search Phrase 2	***Z*** *All words containing a Z*	-	103
Total Mentions	**A* + *Z***		**7777**
KJB1611 = 7777, NKJV = 6299, ESV = 6140, NASB1971 = 7115, NASB2020 = 6419 , NIV = 5597			

a* + ***z*** = 7777 words in Genesis | Revelation
a* + ***z*** = 677×7 words in Matthew | Revelation
a* + ***z*** = 77×76 words in Genesis

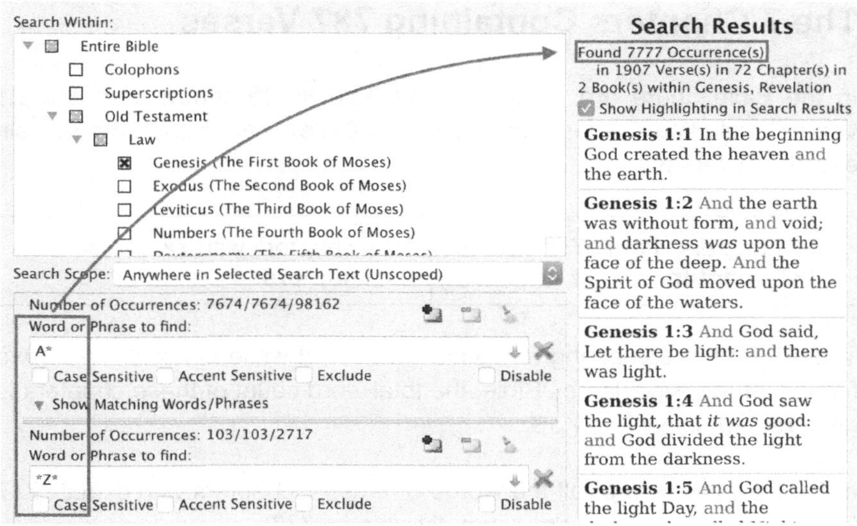

Genesis & Revelation		
A *First letter of the alphabet* 7674 words start with letter "a"	**Z** *First letter of the alphabet* 103 words contain letter "z"	**7777** total word sum
In *First word of the BIble* 767 mentions	**Amen** *Last word of the Bible* 10 mentions	**777** total mentions

And Ezra blessed the LORD, the great God. And all the people answered, Amen, Amen, with lifting up their hands: and they bowed their heads, and worshipped the LORD with their faces to the ground. Ezra 8:6

*For details on **In + Amen = 777 mentions**, see p. 55.*

The 7 Chapters Containing 7×7 Verses

In the Bible, there are 1189 chapters. Exactly 49 chapters contain 21 verses (including the last chapter of the Bible), and 7 chapters contain exactly 49 verses.

Total chapters with 7+7+7 verses **= 7×7 chapters**	Total chapters with 7×7 verses **= 7 chapters**

This in itself is something to wonder over. And while is not an exclusive feature of the King James Bible, the total word count of these chapters is quite remarkable in the KJB.

If you take the sum of all the words of these 7 chapters with exactly 7×7 verses, you get a total word count divisible by 777.

Search Filters: **All chapters with exactly 49 verses**		Verses	Words
#1	**Numbers 4**	7×7	1416
#2	**Deuteronomy 4**	7×7	1503
#3	**Ezekiel 20**	7×7	1601
#4	**Ezekiel 23**	7×7	1322
#5	**Ezekiel 40**	7×7	1530
#6	**Daniel 2**	7×7	1500
#7	**Luke 6**	7×7	1229
Total Sum		343 **= 7×7×7**	10101 **= 13 × 777**
KJB1611 = 10120 NKJV = 9646 ESV = 9652 NASB2020 = 9885 NASB1971 = 9855 NIV = 9098			

There is a 99.9% chance that a random 5-digit number will <u>NOT</u> be divisible by 777

The 777-seal of Chronicles

The fifteenth to Bilgah, the sixteenth to Immer, 1 Chronicles 24:14

The #777 verse of Chronicles.

What is it talking about? Bilgah and Immer?

These are 2 of the 24 men that are appointed as governors to the house of the LORD (His temple).

These 24 governors of the temple are types of the 24 crowned elders surrounding God's throne in the book of Revelation. Their name meanings seem to reveal something way deeper going on than simply an ancient record of names. A lot of their name meanings fit perfectly with the 24 elders surrounding God's throne. Everything in the Bible is **profitable for doctrine, for reproof, for correction, for instruction in righteousness.** It's also interesting that they are listed in the #24 chapter of Chronicles.

Name meanings of the **24 governors** appointed in 1 Chronicles **24** **(Typifying the 24 elders)**	
1. **Jehoiarib**, Jehovah contends / pleads	13. **Huppah**, Canopy for bridegroom/bride
2. **Jedaiah**, Jehovah has known	14. **Jeshebeab**, Seat of his father
3. **Harim**, Dedicated to God	15. **Bilgah**, Cheerfulness
4. **Seorim**, Barley	16. **Immer**, He hath said
5. **Malchijah**, Jehovah is my king	17. **Hezir**, Boar (perhaps Protected)
6. **Mijamin**, From the right hand	18. **Aphses**, To break
7. **Hakkoz**, A thorn, summer, the end	19. **Pethahiah**, Jehovah has opened
8. **Abijah**, Jehovah is my father	20. **Jehezekel**, God strengthens
9. **Jeshua**, Jehovah is salvation	21. **Jachin**, He will establish
10. **Shecaniah**, Dweller with Jehovah	22. **Gamul**, Recompensed
11. **Eliashib**, God restores	23. **Delaiah**, Jehovah has delivered
12. **Jakim**, He will raise	24. **Maaziah**, Consolation of Jehovah

But what is the big deal about the #777 verse of Chronicles, that giant book of names and genealogies that everybody wants to skip?

The fifteenth to Bilgah, the sixteenth to Immer, 1 Chronicles 24:14

The #777 verse of Chronicles is T777 words away from Matthew 1:1
T777 = (1 + 2 + 3 … + 775 + 776 + 777) **= 777 × #77-Prime**

T777 is the sum of all numbers from 1 to 777. 1+2+3...+775+776+777 **= 302,253**	**T777** (302,253) = **777 × 389** Both **777** and **389** are directly related to the **Godhead**	**389** is the **#77** Prime **389** is the middle of **777** Additive Prime **#389** is the **#777** Prime (5903)
"The Father" + **"The Word"** + **"Holy Ghost"** = **777** mentions **"The Father*"** + **"The Son"** + **"The Holy Ghost"** = **389** mentions See previous notes for exact details. (p. 130, 143)		

The first verse mentioning **Jesus Christ** is **T777**, (**777** × **#77**-Prime) words away from the #777 verse of Chronicles, *the infamous book of names.*

1 Chronicles 24:14 + T777 words = the beginning of the New Testament
1 Chronicles 24:14 - T777 words = the beginning of the post-flood world

T777 words ⟵	**Verse #777 of Chronicles**	**⟶ T777 words**
Genesis 8:13	1 Chronicles 24:14	Matthew 1:1
And it came to pass in the six hundredth and first year, <u>in the first month, the first day of the month</u>, the waters were dried up from off the earth: and Noah removed the covering of the ark, and looked, and, behold, the face of the ground was dry.	**The fifteenth to Bilgah, the sixteenth to Immer,** - *Name meanings:* **Bilgah**, Cheerfulness **Immer,** He hath said ***These things I have spoken unto you, that in me ye might have peace. In the world ye shall have tribulation: but be of good cheer; I have overcome the world.*** *John 16:33*	**The book of the generation of Jesus Christ, the son of David, the son of Abraham.** The first verse mentioning the blessed name of **Jesus Christ** is exactly T777 = (777 × 389) words away from verse #777 of Chronicles, the infamous book of names.

Note: This pattern works with verse text only. *Excludes Psalm headings.*

There are exactly (7+7+7) words between Verse #777 of Chronicles and the name of **Jeshua** (1 Chron 24:11) which is the same as **Jesus**.

Lamech 777 years

The only time in the Bible that the number 777 is mentioned, is the age of Lamech in Genesis 5:31.

And all the days of Lamech were seven hundred seventy and seven years: and he died. Genesis 5:31

A simple observation on **Lamech** is that he is the father of **Noah**. Which means he was the last of the "ancients" in the Biblical record- that is, the last man born on Adam's side of the flood. By these credentials alone, we see how his age was prophetic. A triple seven to close out the age of the ancients- just as there will be a triple seven at the close of the modern era before the Lord returns (7 seals, 7 trumpets, 7 vials).

And the only 2 "ancients" before Noah to prophesy in the Bible are Enoch (**the seventh from Adam** Jude 1:14) and Lamech (age of **777**).

The only "ancients" who prophesy in scripture (pre-Noah)	
Enoch (7th from Adam)	**Lamech** (lives exactly 777 years)
And Enoch also, the seventh from Adam, prophesied of these, saying, Behold, the Lord cometh with ten thousands of his saints, To execute judgment upon all, and to convince all that are ungodly among them of all their ungodly deeds which they have ungodly committed, and of all their hard speeches which ungodly sinners have spoken against him. Jude 1:14-15	**And Lamech lived an hundred eighty and two years, and begat a son: And he called his name Noah, saying, This same shall comfort us concerning our work and toil of our hands, because of the ground which the LORD hath cursed. And Lamech lived after he begat Noah five hundred ninety and five years, and begat sons and daughters: And all the days of Lamech were seven hundred seventy and seven years: and he died.** Genesis 5:28-31

At first glance, it appears Lamech is mentioned 12 times in the Bible. But, you have to remember that Cain's line also had a **Lamech** - who was also associated with the number 7…

If Cain shall be avenged sevenfold, truly Lamech seventy and sevenfold. Genesis 4:24

Something of particular interest is how this Lamech is also the lastly mentioned (and #7) of Cain's line.

1. Adam
2. Cain
3. Enoch
4. Irad
5. Mehujael
6. Methusael
7. Lamech

Cain's line disappears with sevens all over the board. In fact, if you skip ahead 777,777 words from Genesis 4:24, you wind up at the exact start of the 7 seals.

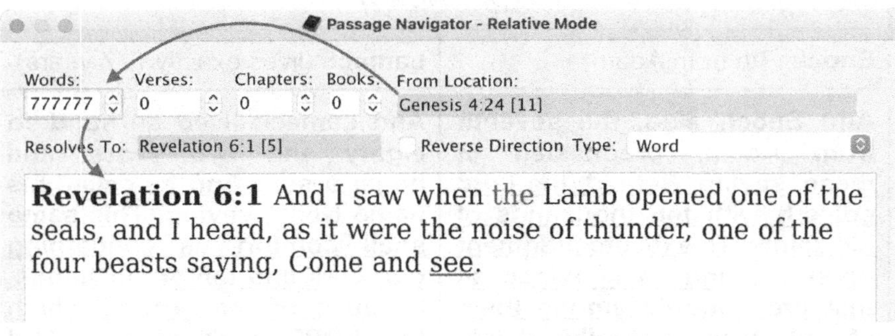

Lamech, of the line of Seth, is mentioned 7 times.

1. Genesis 5:25 **...and seven years, and begat Lamech:**
2. Genesis 5:26 **...lived after he begat Lamech seven hundred...**
3. Genesis 5:28 **And Lamech lived an hundred eighty and two...**
4. Genesis 5:30 **And Lamech lived after he begat Noah...**
5. Genesis 5:31 **...of Lamech were seven hundred seventy and seven...**
6. 1 Chronicles 1:3 **Henoch, Methuselah, Lamech,**
7. Luke 3:36 **...the son of Noe, which was the son of Lamech,**

From the verse mentioning Lamech's age of 777 years, a forward-skip of 777 words takes you to Noah and family entering the ark in Genesis 7:7 (because of God's 7-day warning a few verses prior).

And Noah went in, and his sons, and his wife, and his sons' wives with him, into the ark, because of the waters of the flood.
Genesis 7:7

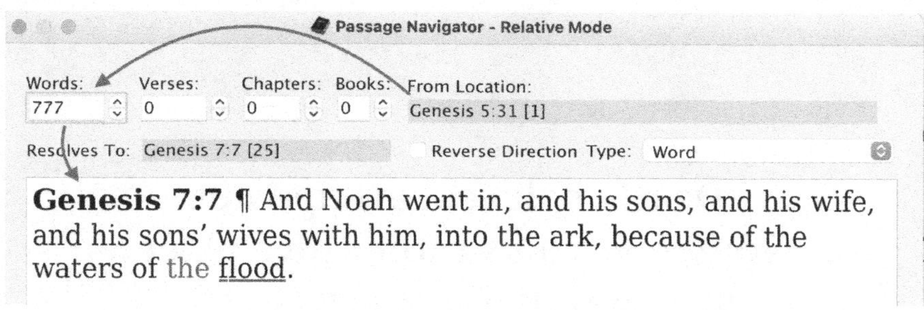

Dearly beloved, avenge not
yourselves, but rather give place
unto wrath: for it is written,
Vengeance is mine; I will repay,
saith the Lord.

Romans 12:19

#777 word directly spoken by God

And the LORD said unto him, Therefore whosoever slayeth Cain, vengeance shall be taken on him sevenfold. And the LORD set a mark upon Cain, lest any finding him should kill him. Genesis 4:15

If you count every word God directly speaks (beginning with "**Let there be light...**" Gen 1:3), the #777 word spoken by God in the Bible is "**vengeance**" in Genesis 4:15.

Genesis 4:15 begins on the #(7×7×7) word of the chapter.

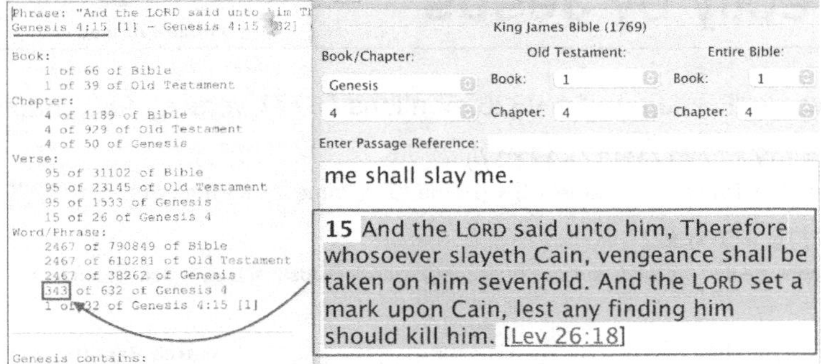

.... And "**vengeance**" is exactly 7 words away from the first time God speaks the word "seven" (to be exact "**sevenfold**") in the Bible.

Genesis 4:15

1. **...vengeance** (word #777 spoken by God)
2. **shall**
3. **be**
4. **taken**
5. **on**
6. **him**
7. **sevenfold** (describes word #777 - **sevenfold vengeance** ...and is exactly 7 words away)

The #49 verse of the Bible to contain either "**vengeance**" / "**avenge**" contains both: Romans 12:19 **Dearly beloved, avenge not yourselves, but rather give place unto wrath: for it is written, Vengeance is mine; I will repay, saith the Lord.**

#777 word spoken directly by Jesus

But I say unto you... Matthew 5:32

The word "**I**" in Matthew 5:32 is the #777 word spoken directly by Christ, which is Jesus referencing Himself. He is the 777. It's also the #7 mention / verse (out of 177 verses) to have the phrase "**I say**" in the New Testament. (Mat 3:9, 5:18,20,22,26,28,32)

#777 word spoken directly by **Jesus**	**"I"**

The words "**I**" + "**Jesus**" = 9826 mentions / 6777 verses / 980 chapters

9826 = (17×17×17)+(17×17×17)
= (Prime #7 × Prime #7 × Prime #7) + (Prime #7 × Prime #7 × Prime #7)

980 = (70 + 70) × 7
Exactly equivalent to the total mentions of **Jesus(')** excluding Joshua/Justus. See Appendix 7

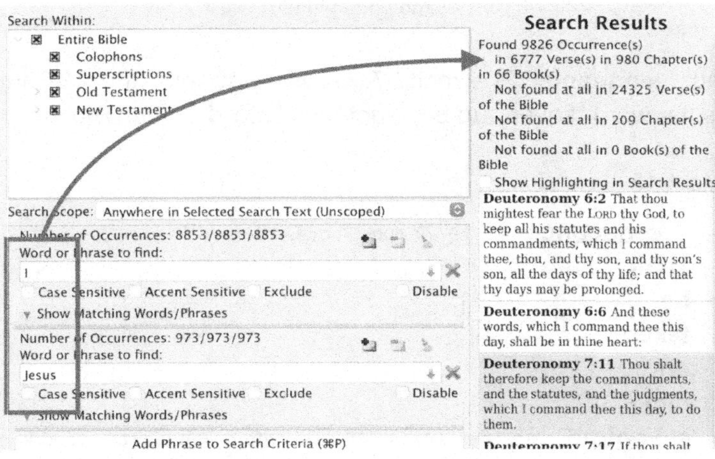

I + **Jesus** is concatenated one time in the Bible: Revelation 22:16 (the very last chapter). And it's one of the simplest and greatest proofs of the deity of Jesus Christ in the Bible.

I Jesus...

Revelation 22:16

Direct proof of Jesus' deity:
Whose angel was sent?

...the Lord God of the holy prophets sent his angel to shew unto his servants the things which must shortly be done. Revelation 22:6	**I Jesus have sent mine angel to testify unto you these things in the churches.** Revelation 22:16

Only mention of the phrase "**I Jesus**" in the Bible

#7 mention of **I** + **Jesus** (combined search)
from the end of the Bible (counting backward)

1. Rev 22:16 (1 of 2) **I** Jesus have sent mine angel...
2. Rev 22:16 (2 of 2) I **Jesus** have sent mine angel...
3. Rev 22:16 **I** am the root and the offspring of David...
4. Rev 22:18 For **I** testify unto every man...
5. Rev 22:20 Surely **I** come quickly.
6. Rev 22:20 come, Lord **Jesus**.
7. Rev 22:21 The grace of our Lord **Jesus** Christ be with you...

Total counts of **I** + **Jesus** in the KJB

Mentions: (Prime **#7** × Prime **#7** × Prime **#7**) + (Prime **#7** × Prime **#7** × Prime **#7**)

Verses: **6777**

Chapters: **(70 × 7) + (70 × 7)**

The **#777** word spoken by Jesus: "**I**"

7 verses, Signature words + Jesus

There is an overwhelming amount of signature words (e.g. **cross**, **faith**, **grace**, **name**, **the Lord**, etc) and signature combinations (e.g. **death/resurrection**, **God/Holy Ghost**, etc) that occur in exactly 7 verses (or multiples of 7 verses) when found in the same verse with **Jesus**. I call them "signature words" because they are of high importance to us as believers.

For example, there is a total of 7×2 verses that contain both words: "**crucified**" + "**Jesus**" *(Signature word = **crucified**)*

1. Matthew 27:22 **Pilate saith unto them, What shall I do then with Jesus which is called Christ? They all say unto him, Let him be crucified.**
2. Matthew 27:26 **Then released he Barabbas unto them: and when he had scourged Jesus, he delivered him to be crucified.**
3. Matthew 28:5 **And the angel answered and said unto the women, Fear not ye: for I know that ye seek Jesus, which was crucified.**
4. Mark 15:15 **And so Pilate, willing to content the people, released Barabbas unto them, and delivered Jesus, when he had scourged him, to be crucified.**
5. Mark 16:6 **And he saith unto them, Be not affrighted: Ye seek Jesus of Nazareth, which was crucified: he is risen; he is not here: behold the place where they laid him.**
6. John 19:16 **Then delivered he him therefore unto them to be crucified. And they took Jesus, and led him away.**
7. John 19:18 **Where they crucified him, and two other with him, on either side one, and Jesus in the midst.**
8. John 19:20 **This title then read many of the Jews: for the place where Jesus was crucified was nigh to the city: and it was written in Hebrew, and Greek, and Latin.**
9. John 19:23 **Then the soldiers, when they had crucified Jesus, took his garments, and made four parts, to every soldier a part; and also his coat: now the coat was without seam, woven from the top throughout.**
10. Acts 2:36 **Therefore let all the house of Israel know assuredly, that God hath made that same Jesus, whom ye have crucified, both Lord and Christ.**
11. Acts 4:10 **Be it known unto you all, and to all the people of Israel, that by the name of Jesus Christ of Nazareth, whom ye crucified, whom God raised from the dead, even by him doth this man stand here before you whole.**
12. 1 Corinthians 2:2 **For I determined not to know any thing among you, save Jesus Christ, and him crucified.**
13. Galatians 3:1 **O foolish Galatians, who hath bewitched you, that ye should not obey the truth, before whose eyes Jesus Christ hath been evidently set forth, crucified among you?**
14. Galatians 6:14 **But God forbid that I should glory, save in the cross of our Lord Jesus Christ, by whom the world is crucified unto me, and I unto the world.**

I don't have a complete list, because I'm not sure how to come up with one. But the ones I have found are detailed below in alphabetical order.

Verses in sevens
Signature words / phrases + Jesus

Signature word(s) + Jesus	Number of verses that mention both	List of Verses
alive | live* + Jesus *including **live**, **lived**, **lively**, **lives**, **living**, **liveth**	**7 × 2 verses**	1. Matthew 26:63 2. Luke 4:4 3. John 4:10 4. John 4:50 5. John 4:53 6. John 11:25 7. Acts 15:26 8. Acts 25:19 9. Romans 6:11 10. 2 Corinthians 4:11 11. 2 Timothy 3:12 12. 1 Peter 1:3 13. 1 Peter 2:5 14. Revelation 20:4
authority + Jesus	**7 verses**	1. Matthew 20:25 2. Matthew 21:24 3. Matthew 21:27 4. Mark 10:42 5. Mark 11:29 6. Mark 11:33 7. Luke 20:8
beginning + Jesus	**7 verses**	1. Mark 1:1 2. John 2:11 3. John 6:64 4. John 8:9 5. John 8:25 6. Ephesians 3:9 7. 2 Peter 2:20
believed + Jesus	**7 × 2 verses**	1. Matthew 8:13 2. John 2:11 3. John 2:22 4. John 4:50 5. John 4:53 6. John 6:64 7. John 8:31 8. John 10:25 9. John 11:45 10. John 12:11 11. John 20:29 12. Acts 8:12 13. Acts 11:17 14. Galatians 2:16
believeth + Jesus	**7 verses**	1. Mark 9:23 2. John 6:35 3. John 11:25 4. John 12:44 5. Romans 3:26 6. 1 John 5:1 7. 1 John 5:5

the blood + Jesus — **7 verses**

1. Ephesians 2:13
2. Hebrews 10:19
3. Hebrews 12:24
4. Hebrews 13:20
5. 1 Peter 1:2
6. 1 John 1:7
7. Revelation 17:6

body + Jesus — **7 × 2 verses**

1. Matthew 14:12
2. Matthew 26:26
3. Matthew 27:58
4. Mark 14:22
5. Mark 15:43
6. Luke 23:52
7. Luke 24:3
8. John 19:38
9. John 19:40
10. John 20:12
11. 2 Corinthians 4:10
12. Galatians 6:17
13. 1 Thessalonians 5:23
14. Hebrews 10:10

church* + Jesus — **7 verses**

*including **churches**

1. 1 Corinthians 1:2
2. 2 Corinthians 1:1
3. Ephesians 3:21
4. 1 Thessalonians 1:1
5. 1 Thessalonians 2:14
6. 2 Thessalonians 1:1
7. Revelation 22:16

confess* + Jesus — **7 verses**

*including **confesseth**, **confession**

1. Romans 10:9
2. Philippians 2:11
3. 1 Timothy 6:13
4. 1 John 4:2
5. 1 John 4:3
6. 1 John 4:15
7. 2 John 1:7

cross + Jesus — **7 verses**

1. Matthew 16:24
2. Mark 10:21
3. Luke 23:26
4. John 19:19
5. John 19:25
6. Galatians 6:14
7. Hebrews 12:2

crucified + Jesus — **7 × 2 verses**

1. Matthew 27:22
2. Matthew 27:26
3. Matthew 28:5
4. Mark 15:15
5. Mark 16:6
6. John 19:16
7. John 19:18
8. John 19:20
9. John 19:23
10. Acts 2:36
11. Acts 4:10
12. 1 Corinthians 2:2
13. Galatians 3:1
14. Galatians 6:14

death | resurrection + Jesus	**7 × 3 verses**	1. Matthew 26:59 2. Matthew 27:1 3. Mark 14:55 4. John 4:47 5. John 11:4 6. John 11:13 7. John 11:25 8. John 18:32 9. Acts 4:2 10. Acts 4:33 11. Acts 17:18 12. Romans 5:17 13. Romans 5:21 14. Romans 6:3 15. Romans 6:23 16. Romans 8:2 17. 2 Corinthians 4:11 18. 2 Timothy 1:10 19. Hebrews 2:9 20. 1 Peter 1:3 21. 1 Peter 3:21
disciple + Jesus	**7 verses**	1. John 18:15 2. John 19:26 3. John 19:38 4. John 20:2 5. John 21:7 6. John 21:20 7. John 21:23
eat + Jesus	**7 × 2 verses**	1. Matthew 12:1 2. Matthew 14:16 3. Matthew 15:32 4. Matthew 26:17 5. Matthew 26:26 6. Mark 8:1 7. Mark 11:14 8. Mark 14:18 9. Mark 14:22 10. John 6:5 11. John 6:26 12. John 6:53 13. John 18:28 14. 2 Thessalonians 3:12
faith + Jesus	**7 × 6 verses**	1. Matthew 8:10 2. Matthew 9:2 3. Matthew 9:22 4. Matthew 14:31 5. Matthew 15:28 6. Matthew 16:8 7. Matthew 17:20 8. Matthew 21:21 9. Mark 2:5 10. Mark 10:52 11. Mark 11:22 12. Luke 7:9 13. Luke 18:42 14. Acts 20:21 15. Romans 1:8 16. Romans 3:22 17. Romans 5:1 18. 2 Corinthians 13:5 19. Galatians 2:16 20. Galatians 3:14 21. Galatians 3:22

22. Galatians 3:26
23. Galatians 5:6
24. Ephesians 1:15
25. Ephesians 6:23
26. Colossians 1:4
27. 1 Thessalonians 1:3
28. 1 Timothy 1:2
29. 1 Timothy 1:14
30. 1 Timothy 3:13
31. 1 Timothy 4:6
32. 2 Timothy 1:13
33. 2 Timothy 3:15
34. Titus 1:1
35. Titus 1:4
36. Philemon 1:5
37. Philemon 1:6
38. Hebrews 12:2
39. James 2:1
40. 1 Peter 1:7
41. 2 Peter 1:1
42. Revelation 14:12

the Father + Jesus

7 × 4 verses

1. John 4:21
2. John 4:53
3. John 5:19
4. John 13:1
5. John 13:3
6. John 14:6
7. John 14:9
8. Romans 15:6
9. 1 Corinthians 8:6
10. 2 Corinthians 1:3
11. Galatians 1:1
12. Galatians 1:3
13. Ephesians 1:17
14. Ephesians 3:14
15. Ephesians 5:20
16. Ephesians 6:23
17. Philippians 2:11
18. Colossians 1:3
19. Colossians 3:17
20. 1 Thessalonians 1:1
21. 2 Timothy 1:2
22. Titus 1:4
23. 1 Peter 1:2
24. 1 John 1:3
25. 1 John 2:1
26. 1 John 2:22
27. 2 John 1:3
28. Jude 1:1

fear* + Jesus

*including **feared**

7 verses

1. Matthew 27:54
2. Matthew 28:5
3. Luke 5:10
4. Luke 8:50
5. John 19:38
6. John 20:19
7. Acts 19:17

first* + Jesus

*including **firstborn**

7 × 2 verses

1. Matthew 1:25
2. Matthew 17:11
3. Matthew 21:31
4. Matthew 26:17

		5. Mark 7:27 6. Mark 12:29 7. Mark 16:9 8. John 12:16 9. John 19:39 10. John 20:19 11. Acts 3:26 12. Romans 1:8 13. 1 Timothy 1:16 14. Revelation 1:5
for ever + Jesus	**7 verses**	1. Mark 11:14 2. Romans 16:27 3. Hebrews 6:20 4. Hebrews 13:8 5. Hebrews 13:21 6. 1 Peter 4:11 7. 2 Peter 3:18
God | Holy Ghost + Jesus (The Godhead)	**70 × 3 verses**	1. Matthew 1:18 2. Matthew 3:16 3. Matthew 4:7 4. Matthew 4:10 5. Matthew 8:29 6. Matthew 19:26 7. Matthew 21:12 8. Matthew 21:31 9. Matthew 22:29 10. Matthew 22:37 11. Matthew 26:63 12. Matthew 27:46 13. Matthew 27:54 14. Mark 1:1 15. Mark 1:14 16. Mark 1:24 17. Mark 5:7 18. Mark 10:14 19. Mark 10:18 20. Mark 10:23 21. Mark 10:24 22. Mark 10:27 23. Mark 11:22 24. Mark 12:17 25. Mark 12:24 26. Mark 12:29 27. Mark 12:34 28. Mark 15:34 29. Mark 15:43 30. Luke 2:52 31. Luke 4:1 32. Luke 4:4 33. Luke 4:8 34. Luke 4:12 35. Luke 4:34 36. Luke 8:28 37. Luke 8:39 38. Luke 9:43 39. Luke 9:60 40. Luke 9:62 41. Luke 18:16 42. Luke 18:19 43. Luke 18:24 44. Luke 24:19 45. John 1:29 46. John 1:36 47. John 3:2

48. John 3:3
49. John 3:5
50. John 4:10
51. John 6:29
52. John 7:39
53. John 8:42
54. John 8:54
55. John 9:3
56. John 9:35
57. John 11:4
58. John 11:40
59. John 13:3
60. John 13:31
61. John 17:3
62. John 20:17
63. John 20:31
64. Acts 1:16
65. Acts 2:22
66. Acts 2:32
67. Acts 2:36
68. Acts 2:38
69. Acts 3:13
70. Acts 3:26
71. Acts 4:10
72. Acts 5:30
73. Acts 7:45
74. Acts 7:55
75. Acts 7:59
76. Acts 8:12
77. Acts 8:37
78. Acts 9:17
79. Acts 10:36
80. Acts 10:38
81. Acts 11:17
82. Acts 13:23
83. Acts 13:33
84. Acts 20:21
85. Acts 20:24
86. Acts 28:23
87. Acts 28:31
88. Romans 1:1
89. Romans 1:7
90. Romans 1:8
91. Romans 2:16
92. Romans 3:22
93. Romans 5:1
94. Romans 5:11
95. Romans 5:15
96. Romans 6:11
97. Romans 6:23
98. Romans 7:25
99. Romans 8:39
100. Romans 10:9
101. Romans 15:5
102. Romans 15:6
103. Romans 15:8
104. Romans 15:16
105. Romans 15:17
106. Romans 15:30
107. Romans 16:20
108. Romans 16:27
109. 1 Corinthians 1:1

110. 1 Corinthians 1:2
111. 1 Corinthians 1:3
112. 1 Corinthians 1:4
113. 1 Corinthians 1:9
114. 1 Corinthians 1:30
115. 1 Corinthians 6:11
116. 1 Corinthians 8:6
117. 1 Corinthians 12:3
118. 1 Corinthians 15:57
119. 2 Corinthians 1:1
120. 2 Corinthians 1:2
121. 2 Corinthians 1:3
122. 2 Corinthians 1:19
123. 2 Corinthians 4:6
124. 2 Corinthians 5:18
125. 2 Corinthians 11:31
126. 2 Corinthians 13:14
127. Galatians 1:1
128. Galatians 1:3
129. Galatians 3:26
130. Galatians 4:14
131. Galatians 6:14
132. Ephesians 1:1
133. Ephesians 1:2
134. Ephesians 1:3
135. Ephesians 1:17
136. Ephesians 2:10
137. Ephesians 3:9
138. Ephesians 5:20
139. Ephesians 6:23
140. Philippians 1:2
141. Philippians 1:8
142. Philippians 1:11
143. Philippians 2:11
144. Philippians 3:3
145. Philippians 3:14
146. Philippians 4:7
147. Philippians 4:19
148. Colossians 1:1
149. Colossians 1:2
150. Colossians 1:3
151. Colossians 3:17
152. Colossians 4:11
153. 1 Thessalonians 1:1
154. 1 Thessalonians 1:3
155. 1 Thessalonians 2:14
156. 1 Thessalonians 2:15
157. 1 Thessalonians 3:11
158. 1 Thessalonians 3:13
159. 1 Thessalonians 4:1
160. 1 Thessalonians 4:14
161. 1 Thessalonians 5:9
162. 1 Thessalonians 5:18
163. 1 Thessalonians 5:23
164. 2 Thessalonians 1:1
165. 2 Thessalonians 1:2
166. 2 Thessalonians 1:8
167. 2 Thessalonians 1:12
168. 2 Thessalonians 2:16
169. 1 Timothy 1:1
170. 1 Timothy 1:2
171. 1 Timothy 2:5
172. 1 Timothy 5:21
173. 1 Timothy 6:13
174. 2 Timothy 1:1

175. 2 Timothy 1:2
176. 2 Timothy 4:1
177. Titus 1:1
178. Titus 1:4
179. Titus 2:13
180. Philemon 1:3
181. Hebrews 2:9
182. Hebrews 4:14
183. Hebrews 12:2
184. Hebrews 13:20
185. James 1:1
186. 1 Peter 1:2
187. 1 Peter 1:3
188. 1 Peter 2:5
189. 1 Peter 3:21
190. 1 Peter 4:11
191. 1 Peter 5:10
192. 2 Peter 1:1
193. 2 Peter 1:2
194. 1 John 4:2
195. 1 John 4:3
196. 1 John 4:15
197. 1 John 5:1
198. 1 John 5:5
199. 1 John 5:20
200. 2 John 1:3
201. Jude 1:1
202. Jude 1:4
203. Jude 1:21
204. Revelation 1:1
205. Revelation 1:2
206. Revelation 1:9
207. Revelation 12:17
208. Revelation 14:12
209. Revelation 19:10
210. Revelation 20:4

grace + Jesus

7 × 7 verses

1. John 1:17
2. Acts 4:33
3. Acts 15:11
4. Acts 20:24
5. Romans 1:7
6. Romans 3:24
7. Romans 5:15
8. Romans 5:17
9. Romans 5:21
10. Romans 16:20
11. Romans 16:24
12. 1 Corinthians 1:3
13. 1 Corinthians 1:4
14. 1 Corinthians 16:23
15. 2 Corinthians 1:2
16. 2 Corinthians 8:9
17. 2 Corinthians 13:14
18. Galatians 1:3
19. Galatians 6:18
20. Ephesians 1:2
21. Ephesians 2:7
22. Ephesians 6:24
23. Philippians 1:2
24. Philippians 4:23
25. Colossians 1:2

26. 1 Thessalonians 1:1
27. 1 Thessalonians 5:28
28. 2 Thessalonians 1:2
29. 2 Thessalonians 1:12
30. 2 Thessalonians 2:16
31. 2 Thessalonians 3:18
32. 1 Timothy 1:2
33. 1 Timothy 1:14
34. 2 Timothy 1:2
35. 2 Timothy 1:9
36. 2 Timothy 2:1
37. 2 Timothy 4:22
38. Titus 1:4
39. Philemon 1:3
40. Philemon 1:25
41. Hebrews 2:9
42. 1 Peter 1:2
43. 1 Peter 1:13
44. 1 Peter 5:10
45. 2 Peter 1:2
46. 2 Peter 3:18
47. 2 John 1:3
48. Jude 1:4
49. Revelation 22:21

hands + Jesus — **7 verses**

1. Matthew 17:22
2. Matthew 26:50
3. Luke 23:46
4. John 8:20
5. John 13:3
6. Acts 9:17
7. Revelation 20:4

heart + Jesus — **7 verses**

1. Matthew 22:37
2. Mark 8:17
3. Mark 10:5
4. Luke 9:47
5. Acts 8:37
6. Acts 21:13
7. Romans 10:9

hearts + Jesus — **7 verses**

1. Matthew 9:4
2. Mark 2:8
3. Luke 5:22
4. Romans 16:18
5. 2 Corinthians 4:6
6. Philippians 4:7
7. 1 Thessalonians 3:13

heaven* + Jesus — **7 × 4 verses**

*including **heavens**, **heavenly**

1. Matthew 3:16
2. Matthew 4:17
3. Matthew 11:25
4. Matthew 16:17
5. Matthew 18:1
6. Matthew 19:14
7. Matthew 19:21
8. Matthew 19:23
9. Matthew 26:64
10. Matthew 28:18
11. Mark 10:21
12. Mark 14:62
13. Luke 3:21
14. Luke 10:21
15. Luke 18:22
16. John 6:32
17. John 6:42

18. John 17:1
19. Acts 1:11
20. Acts 7:55
21. Ephesians 1:3
22. Ephesians 2:6
23. Philippians 2:10
24. Philippians 3:20
25. 1 Thessalonians 1:10
26. 2 Thessalonians 1:7
27. Hebrews 3:1
28. Hebrews 4:14

holy* + Jesus

*including **holiness, holiest**

7 × 3 verses

1. Matthew 1:18
2. Mark 1:24
3. Luke 4:1
4. Luke 4:34
5. John 7:39
6. Acts 1:16
7. Acts 2:38
8. Acts 4:27
9. Acts 4:30
10. Acts 7:55
11. Acts 9:17
12. Acts 10:38
13. Romans 15:16
14. 1 Corinthians 12:3
15. 2 Corinthians 13:14
16. 1 Thessalonians 3:13
17. 2 Timothy 1:9
18. 2 Timothy 3:15
19. Hebrews 3:1
20. Hebrews 10:19
21. 1 Peter 2:5

I am + Jesus

7 × 4 verses

1. Matthew 9:28
2. Matthew 20:22
3. Mark 8:27
4. Mark 10:38
5. Mark 10:39
6. Mark 14:62
7. Luke 7:6
8. John 6:35
9. John 7:28
10. John 8:12
11. John 8:28
12. John 8:58
13. John 9:39
14. John 10:7
15. John 11:25
16. John 14:6
17. John 18:5
18. John 18:8
19. John 18:37
20. John 20:17
21. Acts 9:5
22. Acts 21:13
23. Acts 22:8
24. Acts 26:15
25. Philippians 3:12
26. 1 Timothy 1:15
27. Revelation 19:10
28. Revelation 22:16

it is written + Jesus	**7 verses**	1. Matthew 4:7 2. Matthew 4:10 3. Matthew 26:31 4. Mark 14:27 5. Luke 4:4 6. Luke 4:8 7. John 12:14
Jews + Jesus	**7 × 4 verses**	1. Matthew 27:11 2. Matthew 27:37 3. Luke 7:3 4. John 5:1 5. John 5:15 6. John 5:16 7. John 7:1 8. John 8:31 9. John 11:33 10. John 11:45 11. John 11:54 12. John 12:11 13. John 18:12 14. John 18:20 15. John 18:33 16. John 18:36 17. John 19:19 18. John 19:20 19. John 19:38 20. John 19:40 21. John 20:19 22. Acts 18:5 23. Acts 18:28 24. Acts 19:10 25. Acts 19:13 26. Acts 19:17 27. Acts 20:21 28. 1 Thessalonians 2:14
Judaea + Jesus	**7 verses**	1. Matthew 2:1 2. Matthew 19:1 3. Mark 3:7 4. John 3:22 5. John 4:47 6. John 4:54 7. 1 Thessalonians 2:14
judgment + Jesus	**7 verses**	1. John 9:39 2. John 18:28 3. John 18:33 4. John 19:9 5. John 19:13 6. 1 Corinthians 1:10 7. Revelation 20:4
kingdom of heaven + kingdom of God + Jesus	**7 × 3 verses**	1. Matthew 4:17 2. Matthew 18:1 3. Matthew 19:14 4. Matthew 19:23 5. Matthew 21:31 6. Mark 1:14 7. Mark 10:14 8. Mark 10:23 9. Mark 10:24 10. Mark 12:34 11. Mark 15:43 12. Luke 9:60 13. Luke 9:62

14. Luke 18:16
15. Luke 18:24
16. John 3:3
17. John 3:5
18. Acts 8:12
19. Acts 28:23
20. Acts 28:31
21. Colossians 4:11

liberty | free* + Jesus

*including **freely**

7 verses

1. Matthew 17:26
2. Romans 3:24
3. Romans 5:15
4. Romans 8:2
5. 1 Corinthians 9:1
6. Galatians 2:4
7. Galatians 3:28

life + Jesus

7 × 3 verses

1. Luke 6:9
2. John 6:35
3. John 6:53
4. John 8:12
5. John 11:25
6. John 13:38
7. John 14:6
8. John 17:3
9. John 20:31
10. Acts 20:24
11. Romans 5:17
12. Romans 5:21
13. Romans 6:23
14. Romans 8:2
15. 2 Corinthians 4:10
16. 2 Corinthians 4:11
17. 1 Timothy 1:16
18. 2 Timothy 1:1
19. 2 Timothy 1:10
20. 1 John 5:20
21. Jude 1:21

light + Jesus

7 verses

1. John 8:12
2. John 11:9
3. John 12:35
4. John 12:36
5. 2 Corinthians 4:6
6. 2 Timothy 1:10
7. 1 John 1:7

the Lord + Jesus

77 verses

1. Matthew 4:7
2. Matthew 4:10
3. Matthew 22:37
4. Mark 5:19
5. Mark 12:29
6. Luke 4:8
7. Luke 4:12
8. Luke 24:3
9. John 4:1
10. John 20:2
11. John 21:7
12. John 21:12
13. Acts 1:21
14. Acts 4:33
15. Acts 8:16
16. Acts 9:5

17. Acts 9:17
18. Acts 9:27
19. Acts 9:29
20. Acts 11:17
21. Acts 11:20
22. Acts 15:11
23. Acts 16:31
24. Acts 19:5
25. Acts 19:10
26. Acts 19:13
27. Acts 19:17
28. Acts 20:24
29. Acts 20:35
30. Acts 21:13
31. Acts 28:31
32. Romans 1:7
33. Romans 10:9
34. Romans 13:14
35. Romans 14:14
36. Romans 15:30
37. 1 Corinthians 1:3
38. 1 Corinthians 5:5
39. 1 Corinthians 6:11
40. 1 Corinthians 9:1
41. 1 Corinthians 11:23
42. 1 Corinthians 12:3
43. 1 Corinthians 16:22
44. 2 Corinthians 1:2
45. 2 Corinthians 1:14
46. 2 Corinthians 4:5
47. 2 Corinthians 4:10
48. 2 Corinthians 4:14
49. 2 Corinthians 13:14
50. Galatians 6:17
51. Ephesians 1:2
52. Ephesians 1:15
53. Ephesians 6:23
54. Philippians 1:2
55. Philippians 2:19
56. Philippians 3:20
57. Colossians 1:2
58. Colossians 2:6
59. Colossians 3:17
60. 1 Thessalonians 1:1
61. 1 Thessalonians 2:15
62. 1 Thessalonians 4:1
63. 1 Thessalonians 4:2
64. 2 Thessalonians 1:1
65. 2 Thessalonians 1:2
66. 2 Thessalonians 1:7
67. 2 Thessalonians 1:12
68. 1 Timothy 5:21
69. 2 Timothy 4:1
70. 2 Timothy 4:22
71. Titus 1:4
72. Philemon 1:3
73. Philemon 1:5
74. James 1:1
75. James 2:1
76. 2 Peter 2:20
77. 2 John 1:3

love | compassion + Jesus

7 × 4 verses

1. Matthew 14:14
2. Matthew 15:32
3. Matthew 20:34

4. Matthew 22:37
5. Mark 1:41
6. Mark 5:19
7. Mark 6:34
8. John 8:42
9. John 14:23
10. John 21:15
11. John 21:17
12. Romans 8:39
13. Romans 15:30
14. 1 Corinthians 16:22
15. 1 Corinthians 16:24
16. 2 Corinthians 13:14
17. Galatians 5:6
18. Ephesians 1:15
19. Ephesians 6:23
20. Ephesians 6:24
21. Colossians 1:4
22. 1 Thessalonians 1:3
23. 1 Timothy 1:14
24. 2 Timothy 1:13
25. Philemon 1:5
26. 1 John 3:23
27. 2 John 1:3
28. Jude 1:21

mercy* + Jesus

*including **mercies**

7 × 2 verses

1. Matthew 9:27
2. Matthew 20:30
3. Mark 10:47
4. Luke 10:37
5. Luke 17:13
6. Luke 18:38
7. 2 Corinthians 1:3
8. 1 Timothy 1:2
9. 1 Timothy 1:16
10. 2 Timothy 1:2
11. Titus 1:4
12. 1 Peter 1:3
13. 2 John 1:3
14. Jude 1:21

name + Jesus

7 × 5 verses

1. Matthew 1:21
2. Matthew 1:25
3. Mark 9:39
4. Luke 1:31
5. Luke 2:21
6. Luke 8:30
7. John 10:25
8. John 20:31
9. Acts 2:38
10. Acts 3:6
11. Acts 4:10
12. Acts 4:18
13. Acts 4:30
14. Acts 5:40
15. Acts 8:12
16. Acts 8:16
17. Acts 9:27
18. Acts 9:29
19. Acts 15:26
20. Acts 16:18
21. Acts 19:5
22. Acts 19:13

23. Acts 19:17
24. Acts 21:13
25. Acts 26:9
26. 1 Corinthians 1:2
27. 1 Corinthians 1:10
28. 1 Corinthians 5:4
29. 1 Corinthians 6:11
30. Ephesians 5:20
31. Philippians 2:10
32. Colossians 3:17
33. 2 Thessalonians 1:12
34. 2 Thessalonians 3:6
35. 1 John 3:23

Nazareth + Jesus

7 × 3 verses

1. Matthew 21:11
2. Matthew 26:71
3. Mark 1:9
4. Mark 1:24
5. Mark 10:47
6. Mark 14:67
7. Mark 16:6
8. Luke 4:34
9. Luke 18:37
10. Luke 24:19
11. John 1:45
12. John 18:5
13. John 18:7
14. John 19:19
15. Acts 2:22
16. Acts 3:6
17. Acts 4:10
18. Acts 6:14
19. Acts 10:38
20. Acts 22:8
21. Acts 26:9

perfect* + Jesus

*including **perfected, perfectly**

7 verses

1. Matthew 19:21
2. Matthew 21:16
3. 1 Corinthians 1:10
4. Philippians 3:12
5. Colossians 1:28
6. Hebrews 13:21
7. 1 Peter 5:10

pray* + Jesus

*including **praying, prayer, prayers**

7 verses

1. Matthew 26:36
2. Luke 3:21
3. Acts 1:14
4. Romans 15:30
5. Philippians 1:19
6. Colossians 1:3
7. 1 Thessalonians 5:23

preach + Jesus

7 verses

1. Matthew 4:17
2. Matthew 11:1
3. Luke 9:60
4. Acts 5:42
5. Acts 17:3
6. 2 Corinthians 4:5
7. Colossians 1:28

prophet | prophecy + Jesus

7 verses

1. Matthew 13:57
2. Matthew 21:11
3. Mark 6:4
4. Luke 24:19
5. John 4:44
6. John 6:14
7. Revelation 19:10

sin + Jesus	**7 × 2 verses**	1. John 1:29 2. John 5:14 3. John 8:11 4. John 8:34 5. John 9:41 6. John 19:11 7. Romans 5:21 8. Romans 6:11 9. Romans 6:23 10. Romans 7:25 11. Romans 8:2 12. Galatians 3:22 13. 1 John 1:7 14. 1 John 2:1
Son + Jesus	**70 verses**	1. Matthew 1:1 2. Matthew 1:21 3. Matthew 1:25 4. Matthew 8:20 5. Matthew 8:29 6. Matthew 9:2 7. Matthew 9:27 8. Matthew 16:13 9. Matthew 17:9 10. Matthew 17:22 11. Matthew 19:28 12. Matthew 20:30 13. Matthew 26:63 14. Matthew 26:64 15. Matthew 27:54 16. Mark 1:1 17. Mark 2:5 18. Mark 5:7 19. Mark 10:47 20. Mark 12:35 21. Mark 14:62 22. Luke 1:31 23. Luke 3:23 24. Luke 8:28 25. Luke 9:41 26. Luke 9:58 27. Luke 18:38 28. Luke 19:9 29. Luke 22:48 30. John 1:42 31. John 1:45 32. John 4:46 33. John 4:47 34. John 4:50 35. John 4:53 36. John 5:19 37. John 6:42 38. John 6:53 39. John 8:28 40. John 9:35 41. John 11:4 42. John 12:23 43. John 13:26 44. John 13:31 45. John 17:1 46. John 19:26 47. John 20:31

48. John 21:15
49. John 21:17
50. Acts 3:13
51. Acts 3:26
52. Acts 8:37
53. Acts 13:33
54. Romans 1:3
55. 1 Corinthians 1:9
56. 2 Corinthians 1:19
57. 1 Thessalonians 1:10
58. 1 Timothy 1:2
59. 2 Timothy 1:2
60. 2 Timothy 2:1
61. Titus 1:4
62. Hebrews 4:14
63. 1 John 1:3
64. 1 John 1:7
65. 1 John 2:22
66. 1 John 3:23
67. 1 John 4:15
68. 1 John 5:5
69. 1 John 5:20
70. 2 John 1:3

the Son + Jesus **7 × 5 verses**

1. Matthew 1:1
2. Matthew 8:20
3. Matthew 16:13
4. Matthew 17:9
5. Matthew 17:22
6. Matthew 19:28
7. Matthew 26:63
8. Matthew 26:64
9. Matthew 27:54
10. Mark 1:1
11. Mark 12:35
12. Mark 14:62
13. Luke 3:23
14. Luke 9:58
15. Luke 22:48
16. John 1:42
17. John 1:45
18. John 5:19
19. John 6:42
20. John 6:53
21. John 8:28
22. John 9:35
23. John 11:4
24. John 12:23
25. John 13:26
26. John 13:31
27. John 20:31
28. Acts 8:37
29. 2 Corinthians 1:19
30. Hebrews 4:14
31. 1 John 2:22
32. 1 John 4:15
33. 1 John 5:5
34. 1 John 5:20
35. 2 John 1:3

Son of God + Jesus **7 × 2 verses**

1. Matthew 8:29
2. Matthew 26:63
3. Matthew 27:54
4. Mark 1:1
5. Luke 8:28
6. John 9:35

7. John 11:4
8. John 20:31
9. Acts 8:37
10. 2 Corinthians 1:19
11. Hebrews 4:14
12. 1 John 4:15
13. 1 John 5:5
14. 1 John 5:20

Son + God
(capitalized) in N.T.

77 verses

1. Matthew 4:3
2. Matthew 4:6
3. Matthew 8:29
4. Matthew 14:33
5. Matthew 16:16
6. Matthew 26:63
7. Matthew 27:40
8. Matthew 27:43
9. Matthew 27:54
10. Mark 1:1
11. Mark 3:11
12. Mark 5:7
13. Mark 15:39
14. Luke 1:32
15. Luke 1:35
16. Luke 4:3
17. Luke 4:9
18. Luke 4:41
19. Luke 8:28
20. Luke 12:8
21. Luke 22:69
22. Luke 22:70
23. John 1:18
24. John 1:34
25. John 1:49
26. John 1:51
27. John 3:16
28. John 3:17
29. John 3:18
30. John 3:36
31. John 5:25
32. John 6:27
33. John 6:69
34. John 9:35
35. John 10:36
36. John 11:4
37. John 11:27
38. John 13:31
39. John 19:7
40. John 20:31
41. Acts 3:13
42. Acts 3:26
43. Acts 7:56
44. Acts 8:37
45. Acts 9:20
46. Acts 13:33
47. Romans 1:4
48. Romans 1:9
49. Romans 5:10
50. Romans 8:3
51. 1 Corinthians 1:9
52. 1 Corinthians 15:28
53. 2 Corinthians 1:19

54. Galatians 2:20
55. Galatians 4:4
56. Galatians 4:6
57. Ephesians 4:13
58. Hebrews 1:8
59. Hebrews 4:14
60. Hebrews 6:6
61. Hebrews 7:3
62. Hebrews 10:29
63. 2 Peter 1:17
64. 1 John 3:8
65. 1 John 4:9
66. 1 John 4:10
67. 1 John 4:15
68. 1 John 5:5
69. 1 John 5:9
70. 1 John 5:10
71. 1 John 5:11
72. 1 John 5:12
73. 1 John 5:13
74. 1 John 5:20
75. 2 John 1:3
76. 2 John 1:9
77. Revelation 2:18

thank + Jesus	**7 verses**	1. Matthew 11:25 2. Luke 10:21 3. John 11:41 4. Romans 1:8 5. Romans 7:25 6. 1 Corinthians 1:4 7. 1 Timothy 1:12
word + Jesus	**7 × 2 verses**	1. Matthew 26:75 2. Mark 5:36 3. Mark 14:72 4. Luke 4:4 5. Luke 24:19 6. John 2:22 7. John 4:50 8. John 8:31 9. Acts 10:36 10. Acts 19:10 11. Colossians 3:17 12. Revelation 1:2 13. Revelation 1:9 14. Revelation 20:4

*Words with asterisks (*) include all forms of that word that are mentioned in verses together with **Jesus**. For example:*

holy* + Jesus
including **holiness, **holiest***

*The reason that other forms of **holy** (such as **holier** or **holily**) were not included is only because <u>they are not mentioned</u> together with **Jesus** in any verses. All forms of **holy*** were considered. No cherry-picking. The same applies to all other words with asterisks(*).*

The LORD in Numbers 7×7×7 Verses

The book of Numbers mentions **the LORD** in exactly 343 verses.

In the book of Numbers
The LORD
is mentioned in **7×7×7** verses
Including the first and last verses.

First verse of Numbers to mention **the LORD**	**7×7×7** verse of Numbers to mention **the LORD**
First verse of Numbers	*Last verse of Numbers*
Numbers 1:1 **And the LORD spake unto Moses in the wilderness of Sinai, in the tabernacle of the congregation, on the first day of the second month, in the second year after they were come out of the land of Egypt, saying,**	Numbers 36:13 **These are the commandments and the judgments, which the LORD commanded by the hand of Moses unto the children of Israel in the plains of Moab by Jordan near Jericho.**

Note: All mentions are "**the LORD**" (UPPERCASE, JEHOVAH). There are no mentions of "**the Lord**" (Capitalized, Adonai) in Numbers. There is 1 mention of **Lord** in the book of Numbers (Num 14:17), but it is "**my Lord**" and not "the Lord".

The LORD (standard, non-possessive) is mentioned in 343 verses **(7×7×7)** in Numbers.

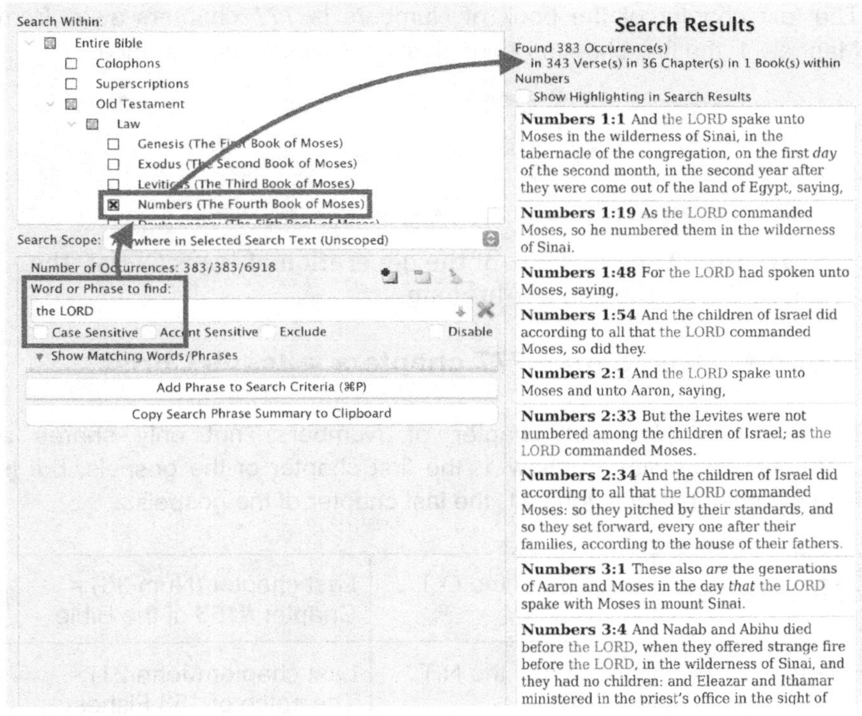

The LORD in Numbers - Bible Version Comparison:

Total verses mentioning: **the LORD** *(in Numbers)*				
KJB 343 **= 7×7×7**	NKJV 341	ESV 341	NASB2020 339	NIV 313
KJB1611 343 **= 7×7×7**			NASB1971 339	
The KJB vs. the NKJV Numbers 9:10,14 KJB: **the passover unto <u>the LORD</u>** NKJV: **the LORD<u>'S</u> passover**				

The Book of Numbers + 777 Chapters

The last chapter of the book of Numbers is 777 chapters away from Matthew 1, the first chapter of our blessed Saviour's appearance.

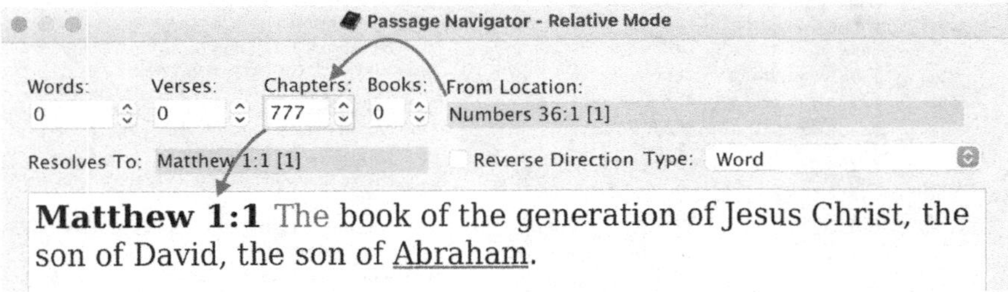

In short... Numbers + 777 chapters = Jesus Christ

Numbers 36 (the last chapter of Numbers) not only shares a 777-connection with Matthew 1, the first chapter of the gospels, but is also symmetrical with John 21, the last chapter of the gospels.

Numbers	Book #4 of the O.T.	Last chapter (Num 36) = Chapter #153 of the Bible
John	Book #4 of the N.T.	Last chapter (John 21) = The catch of 153 Fishes

For a full numeric study of the 153 fishes in John 21, see p. 353.

It's also worth noting that Numbers 7 is the longest unbroken chapter of the Bible with 89 verses and 1939 words. (Psalm 119 is longer but is divided into 22 groups of 8 verses).

That's worth repeating: God's perfect number is 7, and the **#7** chapter of **<u>Numbers</u>** is the longest unbroken chapter of the Bible, featuring the tabernacle (God's dwelling place) set up in the first verse (Numbers 1:1) and God speaking from between the cherubims from off the mercy seat of the ark of the covenant in the last verse (Numbers 7:89). It also contains the #77 mention of "**sacrifice**" in the KJB (in Numbers 7:77)

The next day John seeth Jesus coming unto him, and saith, Behold the Lamb of God, which taketh away the sin of the world.

John 1:29

Passover 77, lamb 77, Lamb T7

...For even Christ our passover is sacrificed for us:
1 Corinthians 5:7

In the KJB, **passover*** appears 77 times:
7×7 times in the Old Testament, and T7 times in the New Testament

lamb (lowercase) is mentioned 77 times.
Lamb (capitalized) is mentioned 7×4 times (which is T7).
Lamb + lamb together are mentioned 7×15 times in 7×14 verses.

passover* **77** appearances	**passover*** **7×7** O.T. appearances	**passover** **T7** (1+2+3+4+5+6+7) N.T. appearances
lamb (lowercase) **77** mentions		**Lamb** (Capitalized) **T7** (1+2+3+4+5+6+7) mentions
*Includes 1 mention of **passovers** (2 Chron 30:17), which is still referring to the **passover** lamb		

Lamb (Capitalized, total mentions) **× 7 = Jesus Christ** (Total mentions)

Lamb (Capitalized) in the Bible Total = 28 = **T7** mentions	**Jesus Christ** in the Bible Total = 196 = **T7×7** mentions
1 1 + 1 1 + 1 + 1 1 + 1 + 1 + 1 1 + 1 + 1 + 1 + 1 1 + 1 + 1 + 1 + 1 + 1 1 + 1 + 1 + 1 + 1 + 1 + 1 **1 + 2 + 3 + 4 + 5 + 6 + 7** = **Lamb** (Capitalized)	7 7 + 7 7 + 7 + 7 7 + 7 + 7 + 7 7 + 7 + 7 + 7 + 7 7 + 7 + 7 + 7 + 7 + 7 7 + 7 + 7 + 7 + 7 + 7 + 7 **7 + 14 + 21 + 28 + 35 + 42 + 49** **= Jesus Christ**

In the New Testament		
Lamb (Capitalized) **T7** mentions	**passover** **T7** mentions	**cross** **T7** mentions
T7 = 1+2+3+4+5+6+7 = 28 mentions		

Exodus 12:21 is the only verse of the Bible to mention both **passover** and **lamb** in the same verse. It is the #7 verse of the Bible to mention either **lamb** or **passover**.

1. Genesis 22:7 **And Isaac spake unto Abraham his father, and said, My father: and he said, Here am I, my son. And he said, Behold the fire and the wood: but where is the lamb for a burnt offering?**
2. Genesis 22:8 **And Abraham said, My son, God will provide himself a lamb for a burnt offering: so they went both of them together.**
3. Exodus 12:3 **Speak ye unto all the congregation of Israel, saying, In the tenth day of this month they shall take to them every man a lamb, according to the house of their fathers, a lamb for an house:**
4. Exodus 12:4 **And if the household be too little for the lamb, let him and his neighbour next unto his house take it according to the number of the souls; every man according to his eating shall make your count for the lamb.**
5. Exodus 12:5 **Your lamb shall be without blemish, a male of the first year: ye shall take it out from the sheep, or from the goats:**
6. Exodus 12:11 **And thus shall ye eat it; with your loins girded, your shoes on your feet, and your staff in your hand; and ye shall eat it in haste: it is the LORD'S passover.**
7. Exodus 12:21 **Then Moses called for all the elders of Israel, and said unto them, Draw out and take you a lamb according to your families, and kill the passover.**

The **#77** mention of **Lamb** or **lamb** is lowercase, and yet it is referring to **Jesus**.

#77 mention of **Lamb / lamb**
Acts 8:32 **The place of the scripture which he read was this, He was led as a sheep to the slaughter; and like a lamb dumb before his shearer, so opened he not his mouth:**

The #70 verse out of (7×7 + 7×7) verses in the Bible to mention **lamb** contains the first mention of **lamb** in the New Testament: **The next day John seeth Jesus coming unto him, and saith, Behold the Lamb of God, which taketh away the sin of the world.** John 1:29

Interestingly, the #70 verse to mention **atonement** is also the first (and only) mention of **atonement** in the New Testament.

lamb	**atonement**
#70 verse in Bible is the **first** mention in the New Testament	**#70** verse in Bible is the **first** (and last) mention in the New Testament
John 1:29 **The next day John seeth Jesus coming unto him, and saith, Behold the Lamb of God, which taketh away the sin of the world.**	Romans 5:11 **And not only so, but we also joy in God through our Lord Jesus Christ, by whom we have now received the atonement.**

...It is finished... John 19:30

Jesus Christ, our passover Lamb is revealed in 4 gospels. The passover lamb of the Old Testament was a shadow of the New Testament.

God does everything in patterns, foreshadowing what is to come.

Here are the counts for **passover** + **lamb** in the first 4 books of the O.T.; Genesis, Exodus, Leviticus, Numbers (shadowing the 4 gospels).

In Genesis + Exodus + Leviticus + Numbers *(First 4 O.T. books, shadowing the 4 Gospels)*
passover + lamb
77 mentions *in* **70 verses** *in* **7+7+7 chapters**

The shadow of the Gospels (First 4 books of the O.T.)

Passover + **lamb** = **77** mentions in **70** verses, **7+7+7** chapters

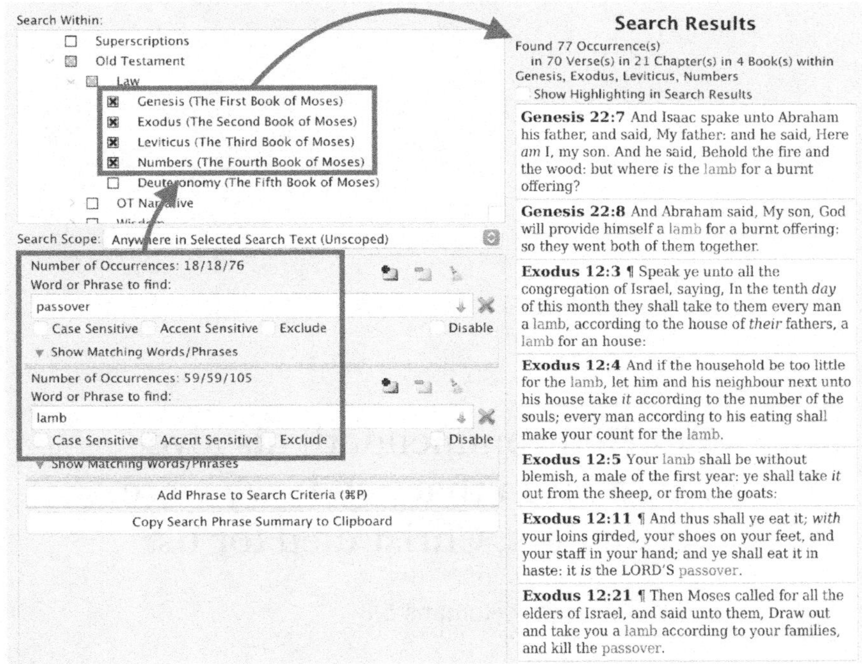

Bible Comparison: passover + lamb

	KJB	KJB1611	NKJV	ESV	NASB2020	NASB1971	NIV
passover* (Total)	**77**	**77**	78	79	81	79	**77**
passover* (O.T.)	**7×7**	**7×7**	**7×7**	50	50	50	47
passover* (N.T.)	**T7**	**T7**	29	29	31	29	30
lamb (lowercase)	**77**	74	74	82	70	72	70
Lamb (Capitalized)	**T7**	31	**T7**	30	32	29	33
passover + **lamb** (First 4 books)	**77** **(70v)**	**77** (69v)	72 (65v)	73 (66v)	71 (64v)	70 (64v)	66 (63v)

But God commendeth his love
toward us, in that, while we were
yet sinners, Christ died for us.

Romans 5:8

Love 777,777

...God is love. 1 John 4:8

GOD (UPPERCASE) is mentioned 310 times.
love is mentioned 310 times.

GOD really is the equivalent of **love** in the King James Bible.

The word **love** is sevened in many incredible ways.

The #777,777 word of the Bible is **love**.

And this is <u>love</u>, that we walk after his commandments. This is the commandment, That, as ye have heard from the beginning, ye should walk in it. 2 John 1:6

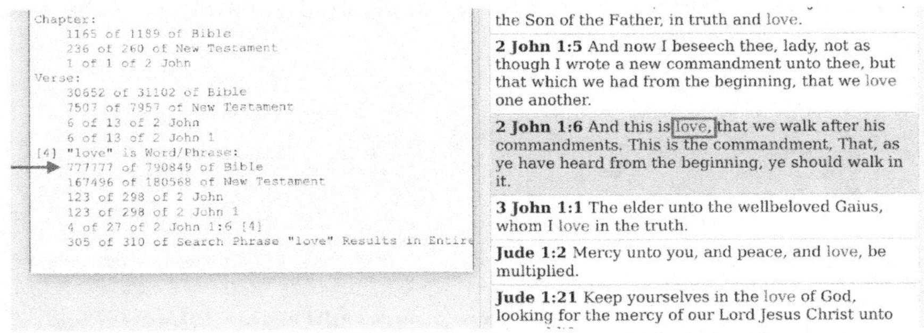

"**Love**" (capitalized) is mentioned 7 times.

1. Deuteronomy 10:19 **<u>Love</u> ye therefore the stranger...**
2. Proverbs 20:13 **<u>Love</u> not sleep, lest thou come to poverty...**
3. Matthew 5:44 **But I say unto you, <u>Love</u> your enemies...**
4. Luke 6:27 **...<u>Love</u> your enemies...**
5. Romans 13:10 **<u>Love</u> worketh no ill to his neighbour...**
6. 1 Peter 2:17 **Honour all men. <u>Love</u> the brotherhood. Fear God...**
7. 1 John 2:15 **<u>Love</u> not the world...**

"**love**" (lowercase) is mentioned 7x7 times in the gospels.

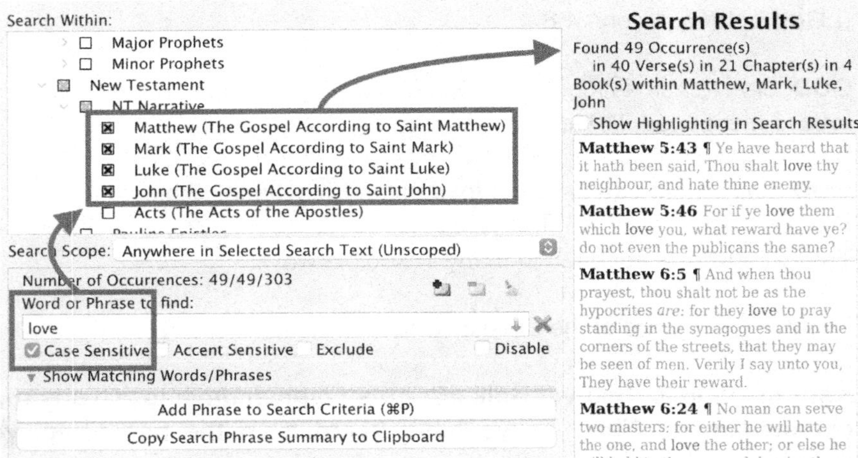

The two-word phrase "**his love**" is mentioned 7 times, with the first mention in Deuteronomy 7:7

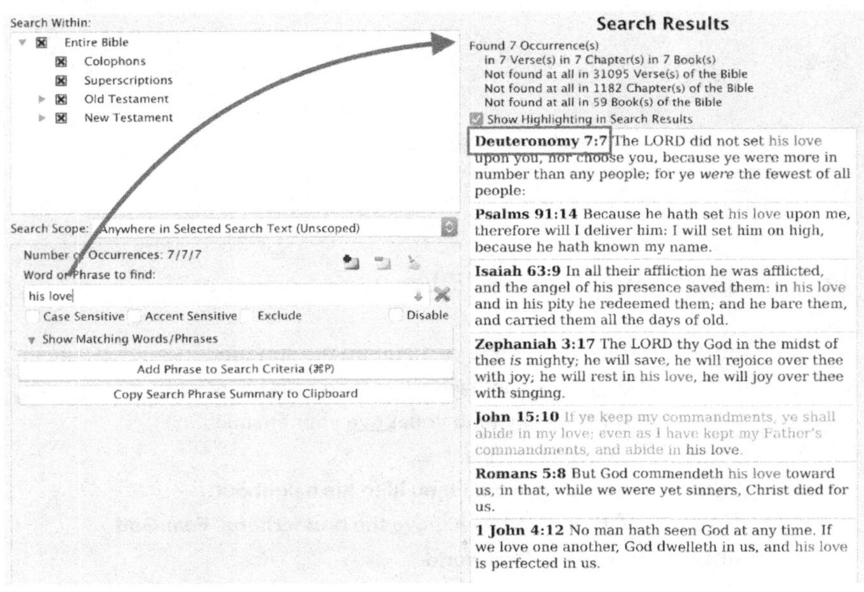

"**love**" and "**Christ**" combined show up in 777 verses. Praise the Lord!

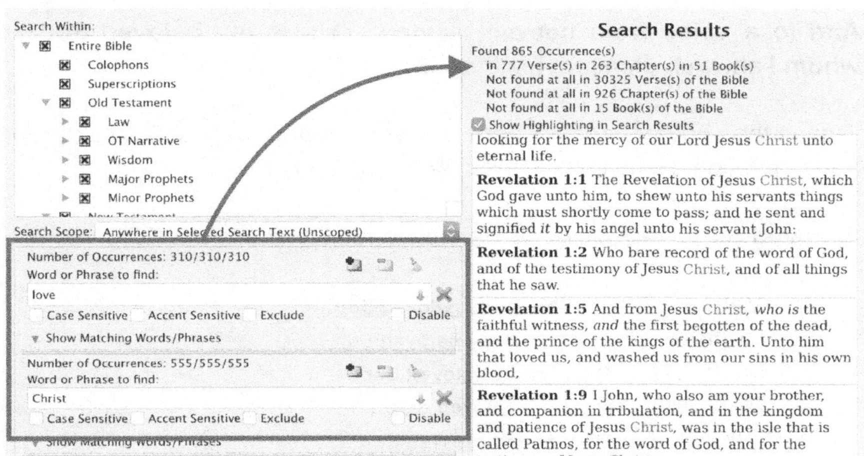

But God commendeth his love toward us, in that, while we were yet sinners, Christ died for us. Romans 5:8

If you look at all verses where "**love**" and "**Christ**" are both mentioned in the same verse, the #7 verse on the list is:

2 Corinthians 13:14 - **The grace of the Lord Jesus Christ, and the love of God, and the communion of the Holy Ghost, be with you all. Amen.**

As noted on p. 187, 2 Corinthians 13:14 contains both the #777 mention of **Jesus** and the #77 mention of **Holy Ghost**.

GOD (UPPERCASE) is mentioned 310 times in the KJB.
love is mentioned 310 times in the KJB.
...God is love. 1 John 4:8

Beloved Son 7

And lo a voice from heaven, saying, This is my beloved Son, in whom I am well pleased. Matthew 3:17

When the Father spoke from heaven during Jesus' baptism and transfiguration, He called Him His '**beloved Son**'

"**beloved Son**" (capitalized 'S') is mentioned 7 times in the KJB.

1. Matthew 3:17 …**This is my <u>beloved Son</u>…**
2. Matthew 17:5 …**This is my <u>beloved Son</u>…**
3. Mark 1:11 …**Thou art my <u>beloved Son</u>…**
4. Mark 9:7 …**This is my <u>beloved Son</u>…**
5. Luke 3:22 …**Thou art my <u>beloved Son</u>…**
6. Luke 9:35 …**This is my <u>beloved Son</u>…**
7. 2 Peter 1:17 …**This is my <u>beloved Son</u>…**

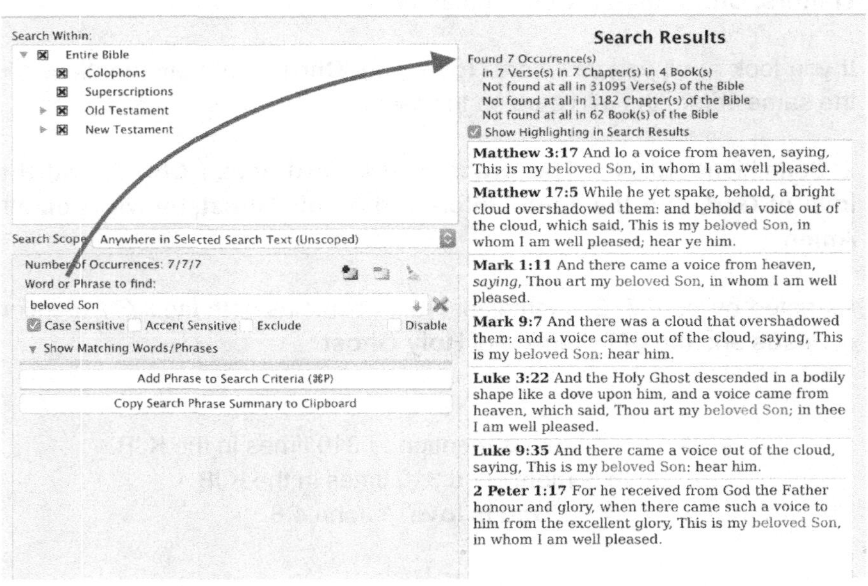

Begotten Son 7

In the New Testament, "**begotten**" + "**Son**" (capitalized S) do not always show up together as one phrase. However, when mentioned in the same verse (always referring to Jesus Christ), they are mentioned in 7 verses.

1. John 1:18 **...the only begotten Son, which is in the bosom of the Father...**
2. John 3:16 **...that he gave his only begotten Son...**
3. John 3:18 **...in the name of the only begotten Son of God.**
4. Acts 13:33 **...Thou art my Son, this day have I begotten thee.**
5. Hebrews 1:5 **...Thou art my Son, this day have I begotten thee...**
6. Hebrews 5:5 **...Thou art my Son, to day have I begotten thee.**
7. 1 John 4:9 **...God sent his only begotten Son into the world...**

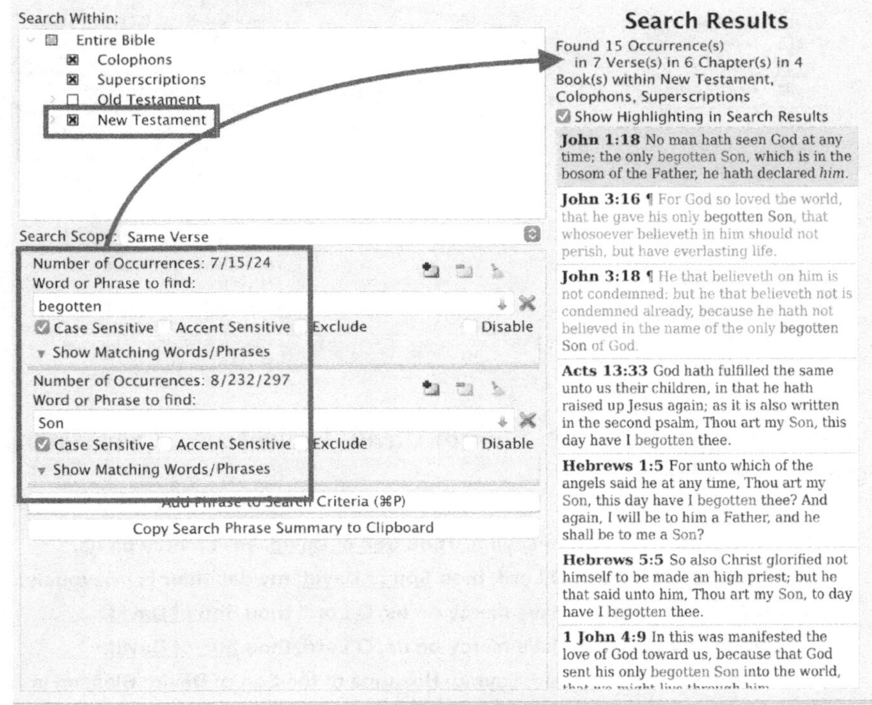

The Son of David 7, The Son of God 7

The first title given to Jesus Christ- "**the son of David**" is mentioned 7 times in the New Testament.

1. Matthew 1:1 **...book of the generation of Jesus Christ, the son of David...**
2. Matthew 12:23 **...were amazed, and said, Is not this the son of David?**
3. Matthew 21:9 **...cried, saying, Hosanna to the Son of David: Blessed is...**
4. Matthew 21:15 **...Hosanna to the Son of David; they were sore...**
5. Matthew 22:42 **...son is he? They say unto him, The Son of David.**
6. Mark 12:35 **...How say the scribes that Christ is the Son of David?**
7. Luke 3:31 **...the son of Nathan, which was the son of David,**

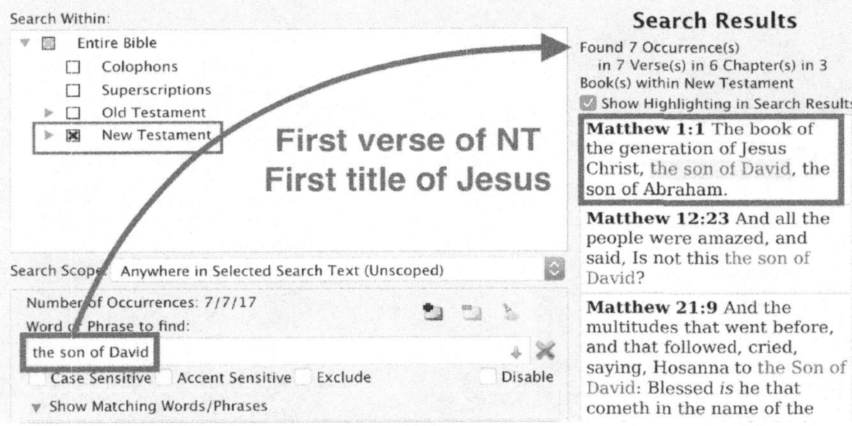

When "**Son**" is capitalized, "**Son of David**" is mentioned 7 times in the gospel of Matthew.

1. Matthew 9:27 **...and saying, Thou Son of David, have mercy on us.**
2. Matthew 15:22 **...O Lord, thou Son of David; my daughter is grievously...**
3. Matthew 20:30 **...Have mercy on us, O Lord, thou Son of David.**
4. Matthew 20:31 **...Have mercy on us, O Lord, thou Son of David.**
5. Matthew 21:9 **...cried, saying, Hosanna to the Son of David: Blessed is...**
6. Matthew 21:15 **...Hosanna to the Son of David; they were sore...**
7. Matthew 22:42 **...son is he? They say unto him, The Son of David.**

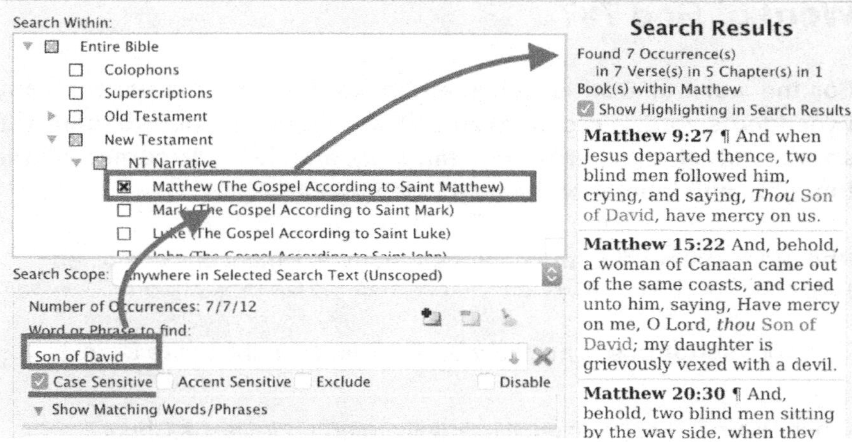

The phrase "**the Son of God**" is mentioned 7 times in Matthew.

1. Matthew 4:3 ...**If thou be <u>the Son of God</u>, command that these stones...**
2. Matthew 4:6 ...**If thou be <u>the Son of God</u>, cast thyself down...**
3. Matthew 14:33 ...**Of a truth thou art <u>the Son of God</u>.**
4. Matthew 26:63 ...**tell us whether thou be the Christ, <u>the Son of God</u>.**
5. Matthew 27:40 ...**If thou be <u>the Son of God</u>, come down from the cross.**
6. Matthew 27:43 ...**if he will have him: for he said, I am <u>the Son of God</u>.**
7. Matthew 27:54 ...**feared greatly, saying, Truly this was <u>the Son of God</u>.**

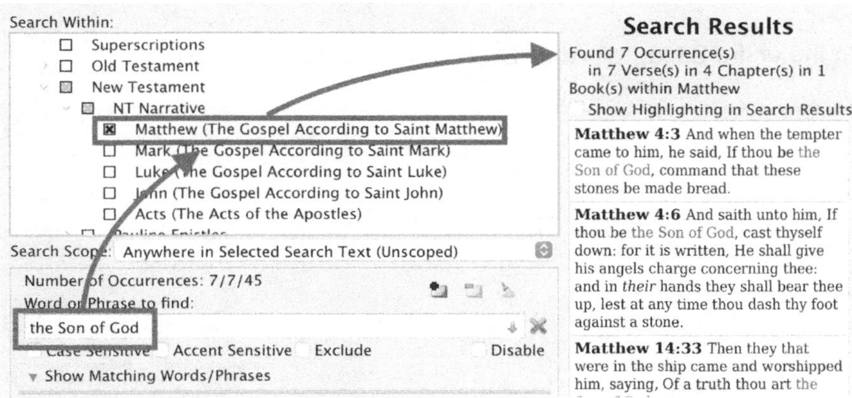

Word of God 7×7

For the word of God is quick, and powerful, and sharper than any twoedged sword, piercing even to the dividing asunder of soul and spirit, and of the joints and marrow, and is a discerner of the thoughts and intents of the heart. Hebrews 4:12

"the old testament" + **"the new testament"** = 7 mentions combined
1) Mat 26:28 2) Mark 14:24 3) Luke 22:20 4) 1 Cor 11:25 5) 2 Cor 3:6 6) 2 Cor 3:14 7) Heb 9:15

The word **scriptures** is mentioned 7+7+7 times in the entire Bible.

When "**Word**" is capitalized, it's directly referring to Jesus Christ.

Word (capitalized) = 7 mentions in the Bible
1, 2, 3) John 1:1 4) John 1:14 5) 1 John 1:1 6) 1 John 5:7 7) Rev 19:13

When "**word**" is lowercase, it refers to the written / spoken word.

word (lowercase) = 7 mentions in Genesis
1) Gen 15:1 2) Gen 15:4 3) Gen 30:34 4) Gen 37:14 5) Gen 41:40 6) Gen 44:2 7) Gen 44:18

word (lowercase) = 7 mentions in Revelation
1) Rev 1:2 2) Rev 1:9 3) Rev 3:8 4) Rev 3:10 5) Rev 6:9 6) Rev 12:11 7) Rev 20:4

In the entire Bible, "**word of God**" is mentioned 7×7 times.

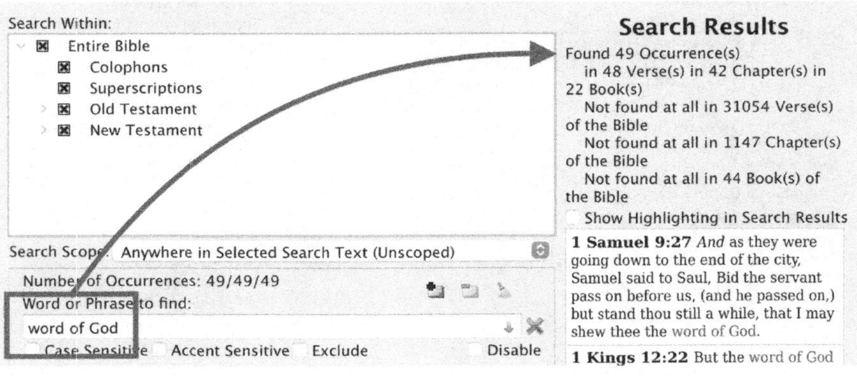

The #7 mention of "**word of God**" is found in Luke 4:4 - **And Jesus answered him, saying, It is written, That man shall not live by bread alone, but by every <u>word of God</u>.**

The phrase "**every word of God**" in Luke 4:4 begins on word #3777 of Luke (the #3 gospel).

In the entire Bible, "**the voice of the Lord**" is mentioned 7×7 times.

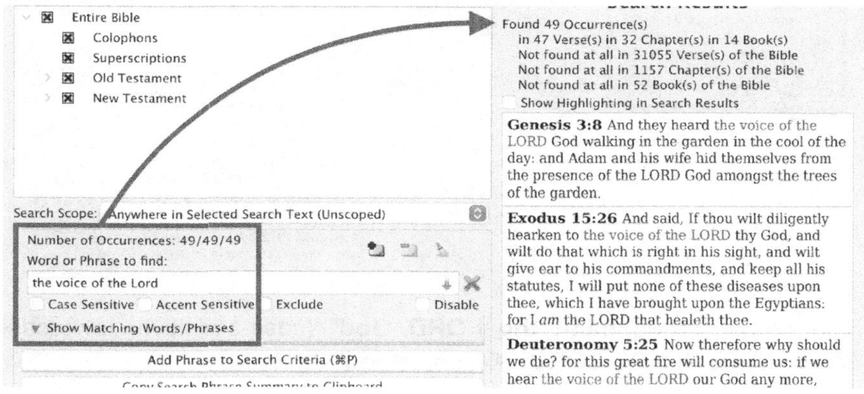

The phrase "**Thus saith the Lord GOD**" is first mentioned in Isaiah **7:7**.

When "**thus**" is lowercase, "**thus saith the Lord GOD**" (case-sensitive) is mentioned 7×7 times.

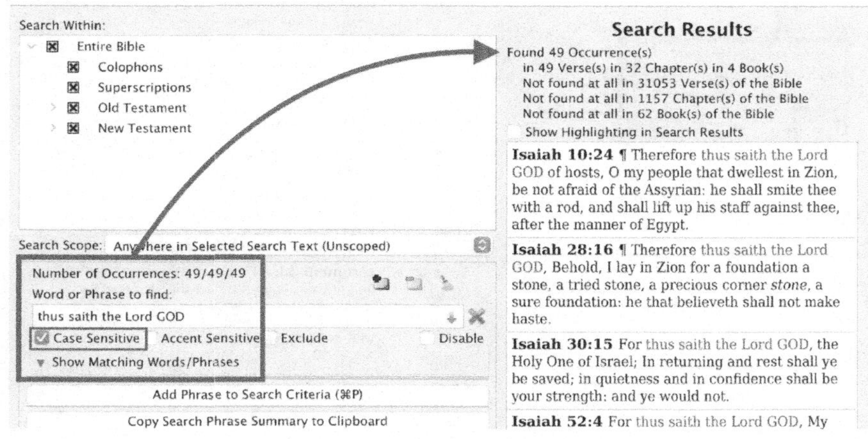

The phrase **"Thus saith the LORD God"** (case-sensitive, Capitalized **"Thus"**, UPPERCASE **LORD**) is mentioned 7+7+7 times.

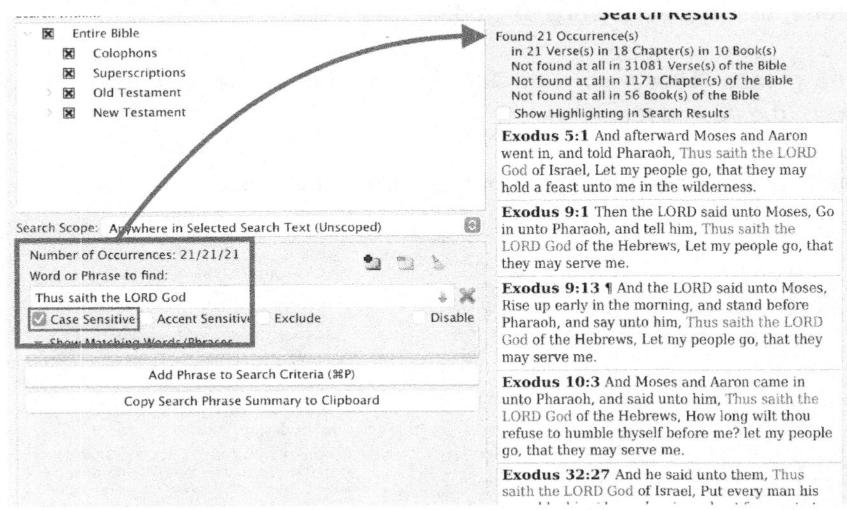

The phrase **"thus saith the LORD God"** (case-sensitive, lowercase **"thus"** UPPERCASE **LORD**) is mentioned 7 times.

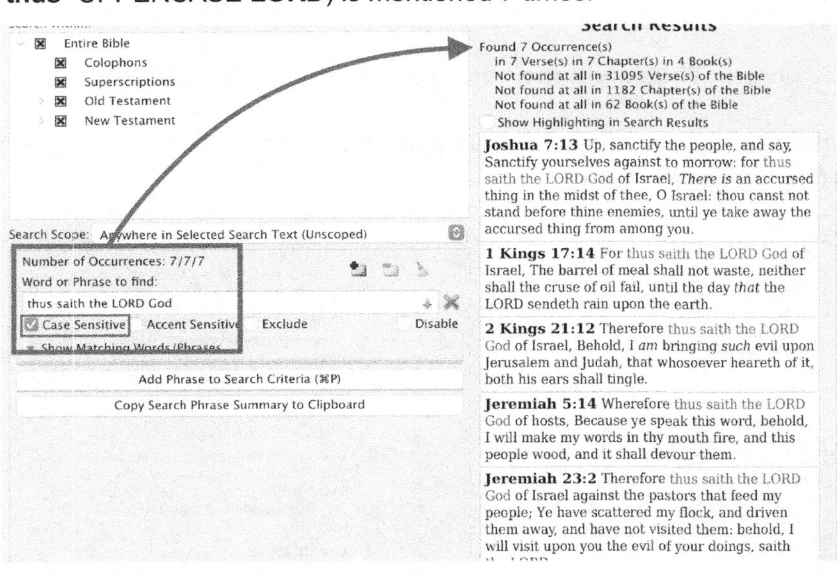

The phrase "**Thus saith the LORD**" (case-sensitive, Capitalized "**Thus**") is mentioned 196 = **7×T7** times (T7 = 1+2+3+4+5+6+7 = 28).

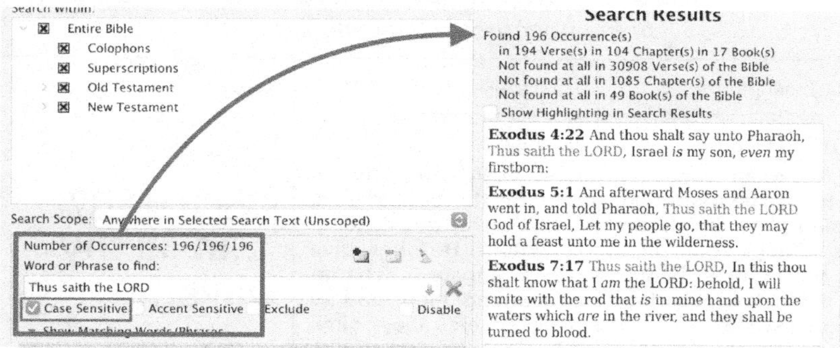

The phrase "**thus saith the LORD of hosts**" is mentioned 70 times.

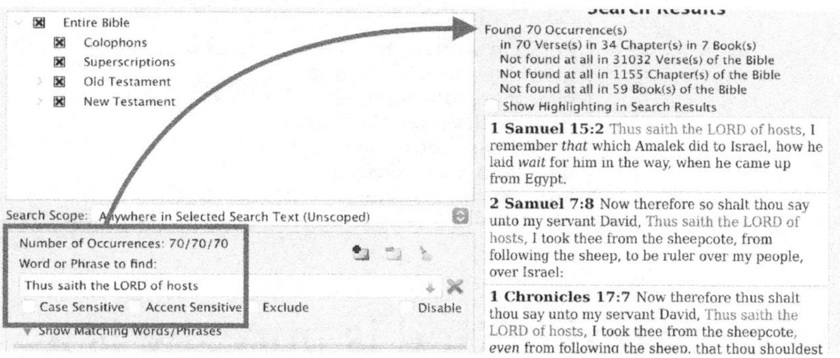

The phrase "**it is written**" is mentioned **77** times, excluding antimentions.

Antimentions:

- "***it is written in the book of Jasher***" (a Non-inspired, non-canonical book that cannot be searched in the scriptures)
- "***It is written He shall give his angels...***" (the two times where Satan misquotes scripture [Psalm 91:11-12]; Matthew 4:6, Luke 4:10-11)

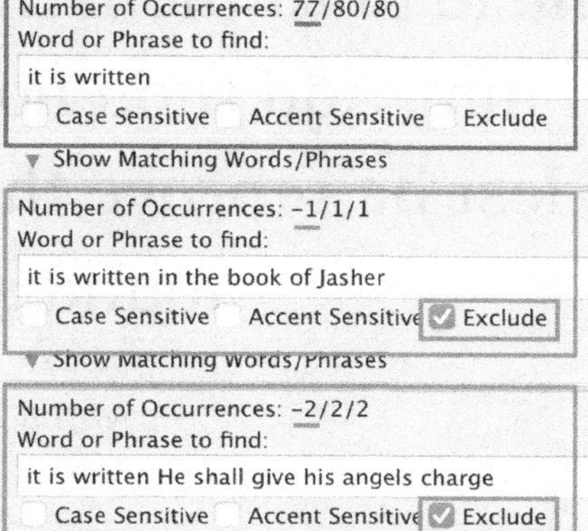

When Satan Misquotes the Scriptures *In the wilderness, tempting Jesus*		
The O.T. scriptures	The Devil's version	Notes
Psalm 91:11-12 **For he shall give his angels charge over thee, to keep thee in all thy ways. They shall bear thee up in their hands, lest thou dash thy foot against a stone.**	Matthew 4:6 **And saith unto him, If thou be the Son of God, cast thyself down: for it is written, He shall give his angels charge concerning thee: and in their hands they shall bear thee up, lest at any time thou dash thy foot against a stone.** Luke 4:10-11 **For it is written, He shall give his angels charge over thee, to keep thee: And in their hands they shall bear thee up, lest at any time thou dash thy foot against a stone.**	The devil takes away: "**...in all thy ways...**" ...and the devil adds: "**...at any time...**"

Every word of God is pure: he is a shield unto them that put their trust in him. Add thou not unto his words, lest he reprove thee, and thou be found a liar.

Proverbs 30:5-6

Holy, holy, holy 777

"**Holy, holy, holy**" – is cried out around God's throne by the seraphims in Isaiah 6:3, and the beasts in Revelation 4:8. Both of these verses have a 777 in their overall order. No other verses in the Bible have this phrase.

Only verses in Bible that say **Holy, holy, holy**	
Verse #17773 of the Bible	**Verse #30777 of the Bible**
Isaiah 6:3	Revelation 4:8
And one cried unto another, and said, Holy, holy, holy, is the LORD of hosts: the whole earth is full of his glory.	**And the four beasts had each of them six wings about him; and they were full of eyes within: and they rest not day and night, saying, Holy, holy, holy, Lord God Almighty, which was, and is, and is to come.**

Isaiah 6:3 and Revelation 4:8

Digit Sum = (6+3) + (4+8) **= 7+7+7**

Verse #17773 and Verse #30777

Digit Sum (1+7+7+7+3) + (3+0+7+7+7) **= 7×7**

Isaiah 6:3 Hebrew (7+7) words, (7×7) letters
וקרא זה אל זה ואמר קדוש קדוש קדוש יהוה צבאות מלא כל הארץ כבודו

Sabbath 77

The **sabbath** is the 7th day of the week, in which God rested from all his work. It is the first thing in the Bible that is "**sanctified**" or "made holy" by God.

The 7th mention of **holy** in the Bible is the **sabbath** commandment coming from God's own voice on Mount Sinai.

Remember the sabbath day, to keep it holy. Exodus 20:8

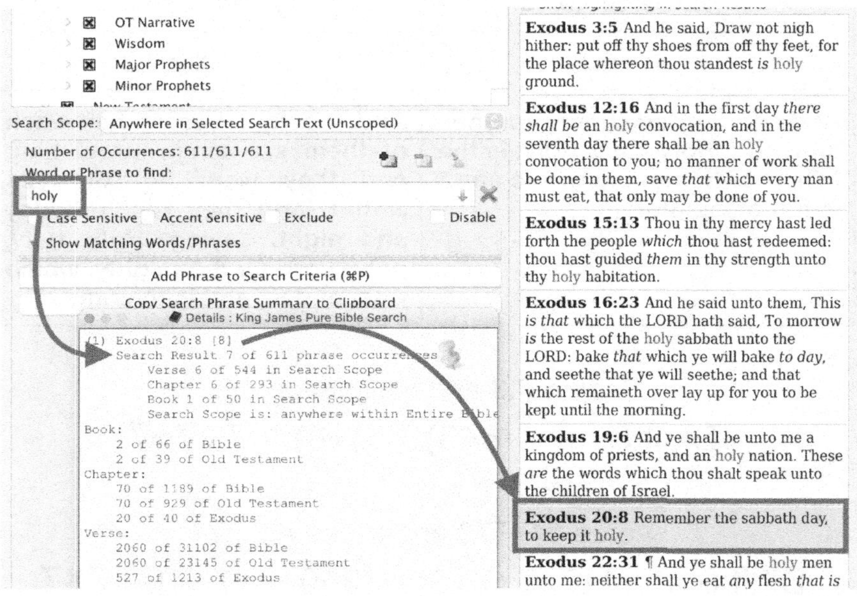

The word "**sabbath**" in the King James Bible has a unique word count because one of the times mentioned is in a Psalm superscription instead of a verse.

Psalms
Chapter 92

A Psalm or Song for the sabbath *day.*

1 *It is a* good *thing* to give thanks unto the LORD, and to sing praises unto thy name, O most High:

The #7 word of Psalm 92 is **sabbath**– the only mention of **sabbath** outside of the verse text.

1. **A**
2. **Psalm**
3. **or**
4. **Song**
5. **for**
6. **the**
7. **<u>sabbath</u>**

So, the question must be asked: what do you do with the word count of **sabbath**? Should we include the Psalm 92 heading's **sabbath** in the total word count for **sabbath**, or should we not since God did not place it in a verse?

I think God laid it out as such on purpose, because whether you skip it or count it, watch what happens…

If you skip the mention of **sabbath** in the Psalm 92 superscription, the #77 mention of **sabbath** is the first time it is mentioned in the N.T.

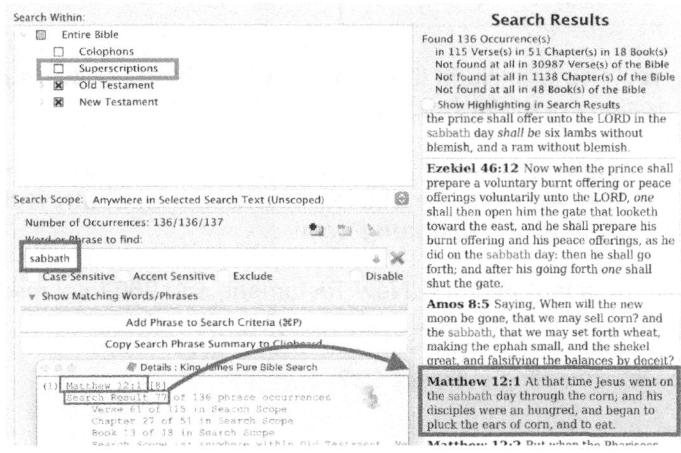

And if you include the Psalm 92 superscription *(instead of skipping it)*, the exact same mention (**sabbath** in the Psalm 92 superscription) is the #77 mention of **sabbath** from the end of the Bible.

If you include the Psalm 92 "**sabbath**" in the total count	If you exclude the Psalm 92 "**sabbath**" from the total count
It becomes the **#77** mention of **sabbath** from the end of the Bible (Starting in the New Testament and counting backward) It becomes the **#42** mention of **sabbath** (7 × 6) in the Bible *Those two numbers* ***77*** *&* ***42*** *bear significance because…* The first mention of **sabbath** in the New Testament is the **#7742** word of the N.T.	The #77 mention of **sabbath** in the Bible becomes the first mention of **sabbath** in the N.T.
The total number mentions of **sabbath** in the Old Testament becomes **77**. As a secondary witness, there are **77+77+77** mentions of the word "**rest**" in the O.T.	

Whether you skip or include this mention of **sabbath**, *it always points to the New Testament of our Lord Jesus Christ.*

Psalm 92 contains 266 words (which is divisible by 7) which means: if you count backward from the end of the chapter, **sabbath** is the #260 word from the end of the **sabbath** Psalm.

There are 260 chapters in the New Testament, and 260 total mentions of **Father** (Capitalized) in the Bible.

What else is interesting in Psalm 92?

First, let's play some Bible Trivia:

*Did God rest on the seventh day from all His "**work**" (singular) or all His "**works**" (plural)?*

If you guessed "**work** (singular)," you are correct:

And on the seventh day God ended his work which he had made; and he rested on the seventh day from all his work which he had made. Genesis 2:2

And if you guessed "**works** (plural)," you are also correct:

For he spake in a certain place of the seventh day on this wise, And God did rest the seventh day from all his works. Hebrews 4:4

Psalm 92, which is the "sabbath Psalm" contains both the #7 mention of '**thy work**' (singular) and the #7 mention of '**thy works**' (plural).

Psalm 92:4 **For thou, LORD, hast made me glad through thy work: I will triumph in the works of thy hands.**
Psalm 92:5 **O LORD, how great are thy works!** ***and*** **thy thoughts are very deep.**

...thy thoughts are very deep.

Psalm 92:5

#7 mention of **thy work** & **thy works** in "***the sabbath Psalm***" (Psalm 92)			
First 7 mentions of *singular* **"thy work"**		First 7 mentions of *plural* **"thy works"**	
1	Exodus 20:9 **Six days shalt thou labour, and do all thy work:**	1	Deuteronomy 3:24 **O Lord GOD, thou hast begun to shew thy servant thy greatness, and thy mighty hand: for what God is there in heaven or in earth, that can do according to thy works, and according to thy might?**
2	Exodus 23:12 **Six days thou shalt do thy work, and on the seventh day thou shalt rest: that thine ox and thine ass may rest, and the son of thy handmaid, and the stranger, may be refreshed.**	2	Deuteronomy 15:10 **Thou shalt surely give him, and thine heart shall not be grieved when thou givest unto him: because that for this thing the LORD thy God shall bless thee in all thy works, and in all that thou puttest thine hand unto.**
3	Deuteronomy 5:13 **Six days thou shalt labour, and do all thy work:**	3	2 Chronicles 20:37 **...Because thou hast joined thyself with Ahaziah, the LORD hath broken thy works. And the ships were broken, that they were not able to go to Tarshish.**
4	Ruth 2:12 **The LORD recompense thy work, and a full reward be given thee of the LORD God of Israel, under whose wings thou art come to trust.**	4	Psalms 66:3 **Say unto God, How terrible art thou in thy works! through the greatness of thy power shall thine enemies submit themselves unto thee.**
5	Psalms 77:12 **I will meditate also of all thy work, and talk of thy doings.**	5	Psalms 73:28 **But it is good for me to draw near to God: I have put my trust in the Lord GOD, that I may declare all thy works.**
6	Psalms 90:16 **Let thy work appear unto thy servants, and thy glory unto their children.**	6	Psalms 86:8 **Among the gods there is none like unto thee, O Lord; neither are there any works like unto thy works.**
7	Psalms 92:4 **For thou, LORD, hast made me glad through thy work: I will triumph in the works of thy hands.**	7	Psalms 92:5 **O LORD, how great are thy works! and thy thoughts are very deep.**

Ended 7+7+7

The first word used to describe the **sabbath** is... "**ended**."

Genesis 2:2 **And on the seventh day God ended his work...**

The word "**ended**" is mentioned (7+7) times in the O.T. and 7 times in the N.T., with both its first and last mentions related to 7 days.

The first and last mentions of **ended**:

First mention of **ended** #1	Last mention of **ended** #(7+7+7)
Genesis 2:2	Acts 21:27
And on the seventh day God ended his work...	**And when the seven days were almost ended...**
7+7 O.T. mentions	7 N.T. mentions

Seven is truly, biblically, the number of completion / ending / perfection. To my amazement, in just (7+7+7) mentions, there is a third mention of **ended** that is in direct connection with the number 7:

And the seven years of plenteousness, that was in the land of Egypt, were ended. Genesis 41:53

But one of the most interesting mentions of **ended** is in Luke 7, where Jesus says:

Now when he had ended all his sayings in the audience of the people... Luke 7:1

- Luke 7 is the #980 chapter of the Bible.
- Jesus is mentioned 980 times.
- 980 = (70 × 7) + (70 × 7)
- With N.T. chapters on a loop, the #1611 chapter is Luke 7.

And the first mention of **ended** in the N.T. is in the #7 chapter of Matthew.

And it came to pass, when Jesus had <u>ended</u> these sayings, the people were astonished at his doctrine: For he taught them as one having authority, and not as the scribes.

Matthew 7:28-29

Despite what all the critics and 21st-century scribes claim, this King James Bible has authority that no other book has. Modern versions do not carry the same weight of authority. They change so drastically, in so many verses, in such short spans of time (see Appendices 4, 5, and 6), that it's hard to believe any Christians take them seriously. I know that I didn't feel any "authority" when I read from modern versions in my first 5 years as a babe in Christ. Reading those bibles felt like reading dry, dead textbooks. The words of this King James Bible on the other hand, transcend time and space, and make me tremble in my soul. They overflow my cup with truth and righteousness. The word of the KJB has power and authority.

And I am forever thankful to the Lord for leading me to His perfect word.

...but to this man will I look, even to him that is poor and of a contrite spirit, and trembleth at my word. Isaiah 66:2

Rest 7×7×7

At the end comes **rest**. **Rest** is truly in perfect accord with the number 7 from God's perspective. This is demonstrated repeatedly in scriptures:

<table>
<tr><th colspan="2">7 is the number of rest in God's word</th></tr>
<tr><td rowspan="2">And on the seventh day God ended his work which he had made; and he rested on the seventh day from all his work which he had made. And God blessed the seventh day, and sanctified it: because that in it he had rested from all his work which God created and made.
Gen 2:2-3</td><td>And the ark rested in the seventh month...
Gen 8:4</td></tr>
<tr><td>And six years thou shalt sow thy land, and shalt gather in the fruits thereof:
But the seventh year thou shalt let it rest and lie still...
Ex 23:10-11</td></tr>
<tr><td>Six days thou shalt do thy work, and on the seventh day thou shalt rest: that thine ox and thine ass may rest, and the son of thy handmaid, and the stranger, may be refreshed.
Ex 23:12</td><td>Six days may work be done; but in the seventh is the sabbath of rest, holy to the LORD: whosoever doeth any work in the sabbath day, he shall surely be put to death.
Ex 31:15</td></tr>
<tr><td>So the people rested on the seventh day. Ex 16:30</td><td rowspan="2">Six days shall work be done: but the seventh day is the sabbath of rest, an holy convocation; ye shall do no work therein: it is the sabbath of the LORD in all your dwellings.
Lev 23:3</td></tr>
<tr><td>Six days thou shalt work, but on the seventh day thou shalt rest: in earing time and in harvest thou shalt rest.
Ex 34:21</td></tr>
<tr><td>Six days shall work be done, but on the seventh day there shall be to you an holy day, a sabbath of rest to the LORD: whosoever doeth work therein shall be put to death. Ex 35:2</td><td>But in the seventh year shall be a sabbath of rest unto the land, a sabbath for the LORD: thou shalt neither sow thy field, nor prune thy vineyard.
Lev 25:4</td></tr>
</table>

1 **Let us therefore fear, lest, a promise being left us of entering into his rest, any of you should seem to come short of it.** 2 **For unto us was the gospel preached, as well as unto them: but the word preached did not profit them, not being mixed with faith in them that heard it.** 3 **For we which have believed do enter into rest, as he said, As I have sworn in my wrath, if they shall enter into my rest: although the works were finished from the foundation of the world.** 4 **For he spake in a certain place of the seventh day on this wise, And God did rest the seventh day from all his works.** 5 **And in this place again, If they shall enter into my rest.** Hebrews 4:1-5

I don't believe any further comment is needed. It couldn't be more clear that the number 7 is very specifically associated with **rest** according to the Author of the Bible. It should bring no surprise that the book of Revelation contains **7** mentions of **rest**.

The word **rested** is mentioned **7+7+7** times in the entire Bible, with the first and last mentions being…

First mention of **rested** #1	Last mention of **rested** #(7+7+7)
Genesis 2:2	Luke 23:56
And on the seventh day God <u>ended</u> his work which he had made; and he rested on the seventh day from all his work which he had made.	**And they returned, and prepared spices and ointments; and rested the sabbath day according to the commandment.**
The #7 mention – **Wherefore the children of Israel shall keep the sabbath, to observe the sabbath throughout their generations, for a perpetual covenant. It is a sign between me and the children of Israel for ever: for in six days the LORD made heaven and earth, and on the seventh day he rested, and was refreshed.** Ex 31:16-17	

The words **rest** | **rested** | **resteth** | **resting** together are mentioned in 294 verses
= 49 + 49 + 49 + 49 + 49 + 49
= **7×7 + 7×7 + 7×7 + 7×7 + 7×7 + 7×7**

Here is the first mention of **rest** in the New Testament, in any form, wondrously appearing in the #343 verse of the N.T. (343 = **7×7×7**).

Verse **7×7×7**

of the New Testament

Come unto me, all ye that labour and are heavy laden, and I will give you rest.

Matthew 11:28

First mention of **rest** in the New Testament (in any form of the word); proceeding **77+77+77** mentions of "**rest**" in the Old Testament.

"**I will give you rest**" = 77+77+77 English Ordinal. See appendix 9

Of all the things I've ever noted, this one in particular speaks to me in a way that nothing else does. When I first saw it, I just sat there, seated in the same spot on our living room couch for hours, in pure satisfaction and peace as I meditated over this beloved truth. **Deep calleth unto deep at the noise of thy waterspouts: all thy waves and thy billows are gone over me.** Psalm 42:7

There is **rest** in His name. There is **rest** in His word. Don't move until you get ahold of this: There is **rest** in Him. Jesus Christ. Not a temporary rest of the mortal body, but an everlasting rest for the weary soul. There is **rest,** true **rest,** in Jesus like nothing else this world can ever offer.

The very next verse begins on the #7700 word of the New Testament.

Take my yoke upon you, and learn of me; for I am meek and lowly in heart: and ye shall find rest unto your souls. Matthew 11:29

Psalms, The Heart of God's word 777

Blessed are they that keep his testimonies, and that seek him with the whole heart. Psalm 119:2

Even though Psalms is the #19 book out of 66, it is the very heart and center of God's word. In Psalms, you are sure to find worship, wisdom, truth, hope, and prophecy unlike any other book in the scriptures. The book of Psalms was, is, and always will be an endless source of beauty and treasure. It teaches you how to pray. It teaches you how to praise and exalt God. It teaches you the mind of Christ. It's as deep as it is practical. It speaks to the soul of both the aged and the babe in Christ. It is the very heart of God's word. Not just spiritually, but physically:

- The middle chapter of the Bible is in Psalms. Psalm 117
- The middle verses of the Bible are in Psalms. Psalm 103:1-2
- The middle word of the Bible is in Psalms. (**Thou**) Psalm 59:5

No matter how you divide it- if you're in the middle of God's word- you're in the blessed book of Psalms. In the book of Psalms, **LORD / Lord** is mentioned exactly **777** times.

<table>
<tr><td colspan="2">In the book of Psalms
The Heart of God's Word</td></tr>
<tr><td>**LORD**
(UPPERCASE)
715 mentions</td><td>**Lord**
(Capitalized)
62 mentions</td></tr>
<tr><td colspan="2">**LORD / Lord**
(UPPERCASE / Capitalized)
777 mentions
(Verse text, excluding Superscriptions)</td></tr>
<tr><td colspan="2">KJB1611 = 777 NKJV = 777 ESV = 787 NASB2020 = 783 NASB1971 = 781 NIV = 782</td></tr>
<tr><td colspan="2">In Psalms & Proverbs (KJB), **LORD / Lord** = **777** verses
(This is actually true of all of Solomon's books- including Ecclesiastes & Song of Solomon since they do not mention **LORD** or **Lord**, the total verses remain at **777** for all 4)</td></tr>
</table>

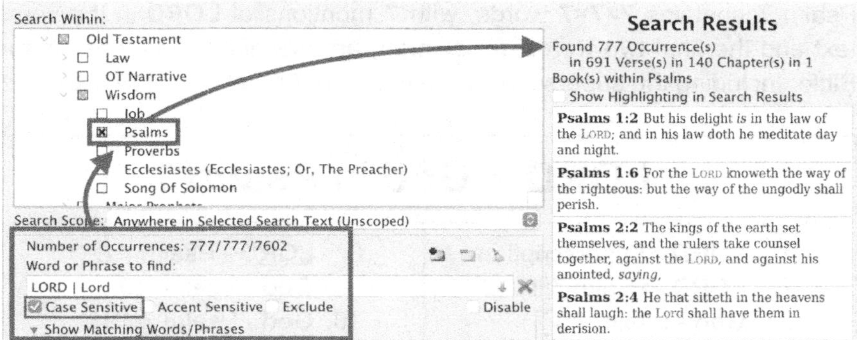

Something else noteworthy is that these 777 mentions are only found in the verse text-excluding superscriptions. This is significant because the Hebrew Bible combines superscriptions into the first verse. Thus, the pattern can only be found in verse divisions standardized in the English; another sign that the KJB is **the book of the LORD** (Is 34:16).

The first 3 verses of Psalms are perfectly parallel with the identity of Jesus Christ: **I am the way, the truth, and the life:** (John 14:6).

I am the way,	Psalm 1:1	**Blessed is the man that walketh not in the counsel of the ungodly, nor standeth in the way of sinners, nor sitteth in the seat of the scornful.**
the truth,	Psalm 1:2	**But his delight is in the law of the LORD; and in his law doth he meditate day and night.**
and the life:	Psalm 1:3	**And he shall be like a tree planted by the rivers of water, that bringeth forth his fruit in his season; his leaf also shall not wither; and whatsoever he doeth shall prosper.**
no man cometh unto the Father, but by me. John 14:6		

Psalm **7** contains **7×7×7** words, with **7** mentions of **LORD** in the verse text and the final two words, **most high,** are mentioned **7×7** times in the Bible. Including the superscription there are **7+7** mentions of **LORD/God**.

LORD + God in **Psalm 7**	
1. **LORD** - Superscription	8. **LORD** - Psalm 7:8
2. **LORD** - Psalm 7:1	9. **God** - Psalm 7:9
3. **God** - Psalm 7:1	10. **God** - Psalm 7:10
4. **LORD** - Psalm 7:3	11. **God** - Psalm 7:11
5. **God** - Psalm 7:3	12. **God** - Psalm 7:11
6. **LORD** - Psalm 7:6	13. **LORD** - Psalm 7:17
7. **LORD** - Psalm 7:8	14. **LORD** - Psalm 7:17
LORD and **God** are mentioned 7+7 times. **LORD** is mentioned 7 times in the 7 verses (excl. Superscription).	

The last two words of Psalm 7, "**most high**" = 7×7 mentions in the Bible.

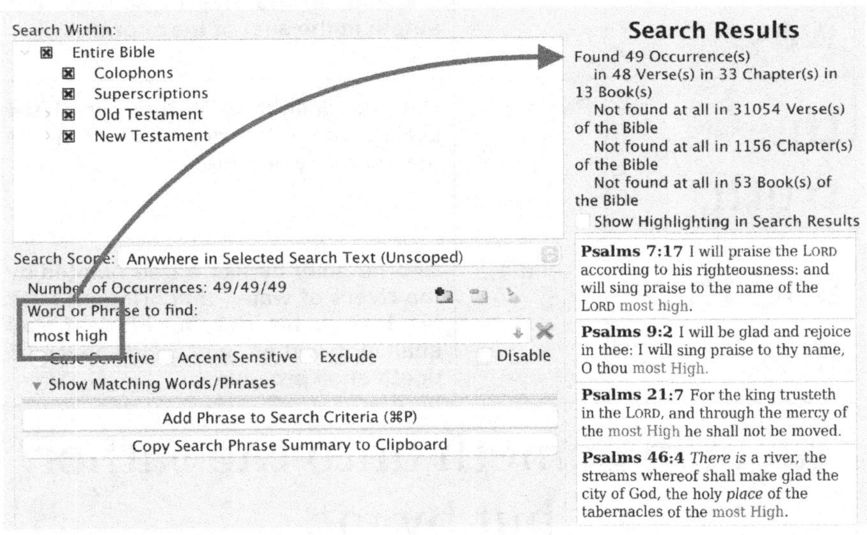

Psalm 7		Words
SS	***Shiggaion of David, which he sang unto the LORD, concerning the words of Cush the Benjamite.***	16
1	**O LORD my God, in thee do I put my trust: save me from all them that persecute me, and deliver me:**	22
2	**Lest he tear my soul like a lion, rending it in pieces, while there is none to deliver.**	18
3	**O LORD my God, if I have done this; if there be iniquity in my hands;**	16
4	**If I have rewarded evil unto him that was at peace with me; (yea, I have delivered him that without cause is mine enemy:)**	24
5	**Let the enemy persecute my soul, and take it; yea, let him tread down my life upon the earth, and lay mine honour in the dust. Selah.**	27
6	**Arise, O LORD, in thine anger, lift up thyself because of the rage of mine enemies: and awake for me to the judgment that thou hast commanded.**	27
7	**So shall the congregation of the people compass thee about: for their sakes therefore return thou on high.**	18
8	**The LORD shall judge the people: judge me, O LORD, according to my righteousness, and according to mine integrity that is in me.**	23
9	**Oh let the wickedness of the wicked come to an end; but establish the just: for the righteous God trieth the hearts and reins.**	24
10	**My defence is of God, which saveth the upright in heart.**	11
11	**God judgeth the righteous, and God is angry with the wicked every day.**	13
12	**If he turn not, he will whet his sword; he hath bent his bow, and made it ready.**	18
13	**He hath also prepared for him the instruments of death; he ordaineth his arrows against the persecutors.**	17
14	**Behold, he travaileth with iniquity, and hath conceived mischief, and brought forth falsehood.**	13
15	**He made a pit, and digged it, and is fallen into the ditch which he made.**	16
16	**His mischief shall return upon his own head, and his violent dealing shall come down upon his own pate.**	19
17	**I will praise the LORD according to his righteousness: and will sing praise to the name of the LORD most high.**	21
Total Words Psalm 7 contains 17 verses (Prime #7) and 7×7×7 words		343 **=7×7×7**

The **7 Psalms** containing exactly **7** mentions of **LORD / GOD**

Order	Chapter	(# Mentions) Verse [word position]
1	Psalm 19 *To the chief Musician, A Psalm of David.*	**LORD (7x)** (2x) Psalms 19:7 [5][15] (2x) Psalms 19:8 [5][15] (2x) Psalms 19:9 [5][15] (1x) Psalms 19:14 [19]
2	Psalm 84 *To the chief Musician upon Gittith, A Psalm for the sons of Korah.*	**LORD (7x)** (1x) Psalms 84:1 [7] (1x) Psalms 84:2 [12] (1x) Psalms 84:3 [25] (1x) Psalms 84:8 [2] (2x) Psalms 84:11 [3][11] (1x) Psalms 84:12 [2]
3	Psalm 92 *A Psalm or Song for the sabbath day.*	**LORD (7x)** (1x) Psalms 92:1 [11] (1x) Psalms 92:4 [3] (1x) Psalms 92:5 [2] (1x) Psalms 92:8 [3] (1x) Psalms 92:9 [6] (1x) Psalms 92:13 [10] (1x) Psalms 92:15 [5]
4	Psalm 99	**LORD (7x)** (1x) Psalms 99:1 [2] (1x) Psalms 99:2 [2] (1x) Psalms 99:5 [4] (1x) Psalms 99:6 [20] (1x) Psalms 99:8 [5] (2x) Psalms 99:9 [3][14]
5	Psalm 109 *To the chief Musician, A Psalm of David.*	**LORD (6x)** (1x) Psalms 109:14 [11] (1x) Psalms 109:15 [6] (1x) Psalms 109:20 [11] (1x) Psalms 109:26 [4] (1x) Psalms 109:27 [12] (1x) Psalms 109:30 [6] **GOD (1x)** (1x) Psalms 109:21 [7]
6	Psalm 140 *To the chief Musician, A Psalm of David.*	**LORD (6x)** (1x) Psalms 140:1 [4] (1x) Psalms 140:4 [4] (2x) Psalms 140:6 [5][17] (1x) Psalms 140:8 [4] (1x) Psalms 140:12 [5] **GOD (1x)** (1x) Psalms 140:7 [2]
7	Psalm 147	**LORD (7x)** (1x) Psalms 147:1 [4] (1x) Psalms 147:2 [2] (1x) Psalms 147:6 [2] (1x) Psalms 147:7 [4] (1x) Psalms 147:11 [2] (1x) Psalms 147:12 [3] (1x) Psalms 147:20 [22]
Psalm 7 also has 7 mentions of **LORD** if you only look at the verse text (exclude Superscription)		

Blessed be the LORD God, the God of Israel, who only doeth wondrous things. Psalm 72:18

The first word of Psalms, 7 letters, "**blessed**" is mentioned 7×7 times in the book of Psalms.

Blessed is the man that walketh not in the counsel of the ungodly, nor standeth in the way of sinners, nor sitteth in the seat of the scornful. Psalm 1:1

All mentions of "**blessed**" in the book of Psalms						
(1) Ps.1:1	(8) Ps.32:2	(15) Ps.41:2	(22) Ps.68:35	(29) Ps.84:12	(36) Ps.112:2	(43) Ps.119:12
(2) Ps.2:12	(9) Ps.33:12	(16) Ps.41:13	(23) Ps.72:17	(30) Ps.89:12	(37) Ps.113:2	(44) Ps.124:6
(3) Ps.18:46	(10) Ps.34:8	(17) Ps.45:2	(24) Ps.72:17	(31) Ps.89:52	(38) Ps.115:15	(45) Ps.128:1
(4) Ps.21:6	(11) Ps.37:22	(18) Ps.49:18	(25) Ps.72:18	(32) Ps.94:12	(39) Ps.118:26	(46) Ps.128:4
(5) Ps.28:6	(12) Ps.37:26	(19) Ps.65:4	(26) Ps.72:19	(33) Ps.106:3	(40) Ps.118:26	(47) Ps.135:21
(6) Ps.31:21	(13) Ps.40:4	(20) Ps.66:20	(27) Ps.84:4	(34) Ps.106:48	(41) Ps.119:1	(48) Ps.144:1
(7) Ps.32:1	(14) Ps.41:1	(21) Ps.68:19	(28) Ps.84:5	(35) Ps.112:1	(42) Ps.119:2	(49) Ps.147:13
Total = 49 mentions **= 7×7 mentions**						
Exactly **7 Psalms** (Psalm 1, 32, 41, 112, 119, 128, 144) are opened with the word "**Blessed**" in the first verse including the **#7** mention of **Blessed** in Psalms (32:1).						

Blessed is that man that maketh the LORD his trust, and respecteth not the proud, nor such as turn aside to lies. Psalm 40:4

"**Blessed**" (in Psalm 40:4) is the #77 word of Psalm 40, and...

Psalm 40:4 is the #7 verse of Psalms where "**Blessed**" is the first word of the verse.

1. Psalm 1:1 **Blessed is the man that walketh not in the counsel of the ungodly...**
2. Psalm 28:6 **Blessed be the LORD, because he hath heard the voice of my...**
3. Psalm 31:21 **Blessed be the LORD: for he hath shewed me his marvellous...**
4. Psalm 32:1 **Blessed is he whose transgression is forgiven, whose sin is covered.**
5. Psalm 32:2 **Blessed is the man unto whom the LORD imputeth not iniquity...**
6. Psalm 33:12 **Blessed is the nation whose God is the LORD, and the people...**
7. Psalm 40:4 **Blessed is that man that maketh the LORD his trust...**

The book of Psalms is quite literally the **heart** of God's word.

The #(**7×7×7**) mention of **heart** in the Bible is found in the #(**7×7**) chapter of Psalms. (Psalm 49:3)

My mouth shall speak of wisdom; and the meditation of my heart shall be of understanding. Psalm 49:3

And the very **heart** of God's word is Psalm 119.

Blessed (Capitalized) is mentioned in 119 verses in the KJB, including the first word of Psalms and the first word of Psalm 119, the longest chapter of the Bible.

The first word of **Psalm 119**

Blessed

Blessed (Capitalized) is found in exactly

119 verses of the Bible

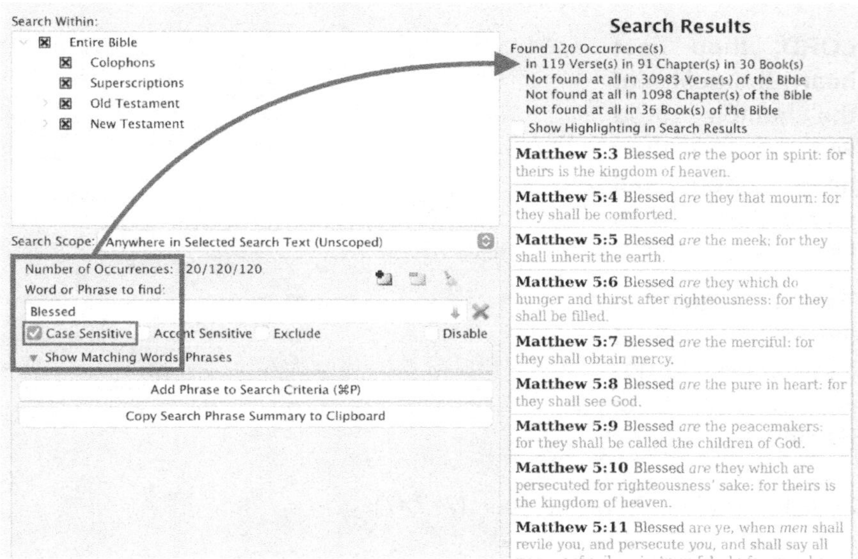

Let us journey into the heart of God's word…

The number 119 = 7 × 17
(17 is the #7 Prime)

Psalm 119 is the longest chapter in the Bible, and it's entirely about God's word. It is known as the **heart** of Psalms and the **heart** of the entire Bible by many teachers and students of God's word because of its contents. But it's also the heart of God's word because of its position. Since it's only 2 chapters away from Psalm 117, which is the middle chapter of the Bible, it's literally positioned like the heart of a man's body- *in the middle, but not dead centered*. The heart is located slightly on the right side (if you're facing the man) of the exact middle of the body. The same is true of Psalm 119. Whether you're looking at the middle chapter, verse or word (noted on p. 304), Psalm 119 is located slightly to the right.

The word "**heart**" is mentioned in 119 verses in the book of Psalms. This, of course, points to Psalm 119.

Psalm 119 is evenly divided into groups of 8 verses (with a total of 88+88 verses), and the #8 verse (out of 119) to mention **heart** in Psalms is the #119 verse of Psalms (Psalm 10:17).

LORD, thou hast heard the desire of the humble: thou wilt prepare their heart, thou wilt cause thine ear to hear: Psalms 10:17

That word "**heart**" in the #119 verse of Psalms (Ps. 10:17) is word #2309 of Psalms.

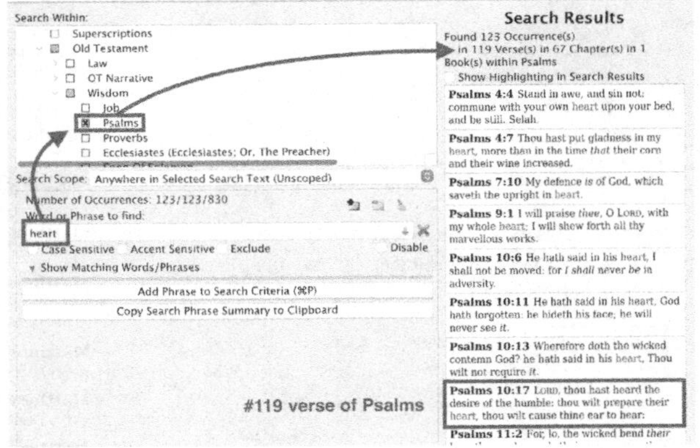

2309 is the #343 Prime Number. (7×7×7)

The #98 verse out of 119 containing "**heart**" in Psalms is the first mention in Psalm 119.

98 = 49 + 49 = (7×7)+(7×7)

The New Testament contains exactly 98 verses (7×7)+(7×7) that mention "**heart**"

The word **heart** is mentioned more often in Psalm 119 than any other chapter of the Bible.

The first mention of **heart** in Psalm 119 contains the #119 letter of Psalm 119… the exact middle letter "**a**" of **heart**.

Blessed are the undefiled in the way, who walk in the law of the LORD. Blessed are they that keep his testimonies, and that seek him with the whole heart. Psalm 119:1-2 (#119 letter of Psalm 119)

And the #119 word of Psalm 119 is… **"heart"** in Psalm 119:10

With my whole heart have I sought thee: O let me not wander from thy commandments. Psalm 119:10

<table>
<tr><td colspan="2">Psalm 119
The Heart of the Bible
119 = 7 × #7 Prime</td></tr>
<tr><td>Blessed
(Capitalized) is mentioned in
119 verses
of the Bible</td><td>Blessed
is the first word of
the first verse of
Psalm 119</td></tr>
<tr><td>heart
is mentioned in
119 verses of Psalms</td><td>heart
is mentioned in the
#119 verse of Psalms</td></tr>
<tr><td>Psalm 119
is positionally the
heart
of the Bible (slightly right of the middle verse / chapter)</td><td>heart
is mentioned more often in
Psalm 119
than any other chapter of the Bible</td></tr>
<tr><td>The letter "a" in
heart
is the
#119 letter of
Psalm 119</td><td>The word
heart
is the
#119 word of
Psalm 119</td></tr>
<tr><td colspan="2">The sum of the first (7+7) verse numbers that mention
heart in Psalm 119
2 + 7 + 10 + 11 + 32 + 34 + 36 + 58 + 69 + 70 + 80 + 111 + 112 + 145
= 777</td></tr>
</table>

The first (7+7) verses that mention "**heart**" in Psalm 119

1. Psalms 119:2 **Blessed are they that keep his testimonies, and that seek him with the whole heart.**
2. Psalms 119:7 **I will praise thee with uprightness of heart, when I shall have learned thy righteous judgments.**
3. Psalms 119:10 **With my whole heart have I sought thee: O let me not wander from thy commandments.**
4. Psalms 119:11 **Thy word have I hid in mine heart, that I might not sin against thee.**
5. Psalms 119:32 **I will run the way of thy commandments, when thou shalt enlarge my heart.**
6. Psalms 119:34 **Give me understanding, and I shall keep thy law; yea, I shall observe it with my whole heart.**
7. Psalms 119:36 **Incline my heart unto thy testimonies, and not to covetousness.**
8. Psalms 119:58 **I intreated thy favour with my whole heart: be merciful unto me according to thy word.**
9. Psalms 119:69 **The proud have forged a lie against me: but I will keep thy precepts with my whole heart.**
10. Psalms 119:70 **Their heart is as fat as grease; but I delight in thy law.**
11. Psalms 119:80 **Let my heart be sound in thy statutes; that I be not ashamed.**
12. Psalms 119:111 **Thy testimonies have I taken as an heritage for ever: for they are the rejoicing of my heart.**
13. Psalms 119:112 **I have inclined mine heart to perform thy statutes alway, even unto the end.**
14. Psalms 119:145 **I cried with my whole heart; hear me, O LORD: I will keep thy statutes.**

Sum of first (7+7) verse numbers to mention "heart" in Psalm 119

2 + 7 + 10 + 11 + 32 + 34 + 36 + 58 + 69 + 70 + 80 + 111 + 112 + 145

= 777

Who is the original author of Psalm 119? Many believe it's David, but nobody knows for certain which human hands penned it originally.

But I know one thing for sure: The one speaking through the writer is **Jesus Christ, the Word of God**, who even refers to Himself in first person (as He does in many other places in Psalms, for example, Psalm 16:10 → Acts 2:31, Psalm 22:1 → Matthew 27:46, Psalm 40:7 → Hebrews 10:7)

I believe without question that **Jesus** is speaking through Psalm 119 in many places:

They that fear thee <u>will be glad when they see me</u>; because I have hoped in thy word. Psalm 119:74

Let those that fear thee <u>turn unto me</u>, and those that have known thy testimonies. Psalm 119:79

And many other places. I encourage everybody reading this to read (or listen to) Psalm 119 often.

The only time 119 is mentioned in the text of the Bible (...**an hundred and nineteen...** Gen 11:25) is exactly 119 verses away from both Genesis 7:13 and Genesis 17:13.

Gen 11:25 (**an hundred and nineteen) + 119 verses** = Gen 17:13
Gen 11:25 (**an hundred and nineteen) - 119 verses** = Gen 7:13

That's interesting because the **#119 verse** mentioning **Jesus** is the #713 verse of the N.T.

The #119 verse mentioning **God** (Capitalized) is the #777 verse of the Bible (Genesis 28:3). For more on that verse, see p. 214.

The #119 word of the Bible is the #7 word of the #7 verse: **divided**.

The #119 letter of the Bible is the letter "i" in **Sp<u>i</u>rit of God** (Gen 1:2)

Notes on 1611 in Psalms

Psalm 119 contains 16×11 verses.

Psalm 103:1, the halfway verse of the Bible (#15551 out of 31102) is the #1611 verse of Psalms. See more on this on pp. 399-402.

```
Verse:
    15551 of 31102 of Bible
    15551 of 23145 of Old Testament
    1611 of 2461 of Psalms
    1 of 22 of Psalms 103
```

Psalm 77:7 is the #1161 verse of Psalms (Mirror of 1611).

```
Verse:
    15101 of 31102 of Bible
    15101 of 23145 of Old Testament
    1161 of 2461 of Psalms
    7 of 20 of Psalms 77
```

Psalm 16 contains 11 verses, with its first and last words being:
Preserve ... evermore Psalm 16:1,11

The greatest verse in the Bible about God's word (being above all His name) is in Psalm 138.

I will worship toward thy holy temple, and praise thy name for thy lovingkindness and for thy truth: <u>for thou hast magnified thy word above all thy name</u>. Psalm 138:2

Take note of verse 4, which is prophesying a future event from the time that David writes this Psalm.

All the kings of the earth shall praise thee, O LORD, <u>when they hear the words of thy mouth.</u> Psalm 138:4

Including the superscription, Psalm 138 contains 16×11 words.

The LORD will perfect that which concerneth me: thy mercy, O LORD, endureth for ever: forsake not the works of thine own hands.

Psalm 138:8

Church 77, in Christ 77

And hath put all things under his feet, and gave him to be the head over all things to the church, Which is his body, the fulness of him that filleth all in all. Ephesians 1:22-23

Not only Jesus Christ, but also His church, which is His body, is sevened in the King James Bible.

Excluding colophons (3 mentions), the word "**church**" (singular) is mentioned 77 times in the Bible (all in the New Testament).

But even more interesting is that "**church**" is broken down perfectly by sevens according to each of the 3 major divisions in the New Testament:

"**church**" in the 3 major divisions of the New Testament:

- 7+7+7 mentions in Historical Books (Gospels + Acts)
- 7×7 mentions in the Epistles
- 7 mentions in Revelation

	The word "church" in the 3 major divisions of the New Testament			
Division	Historical (Gospels + Acts)	Epistles	Apocalypse	Total
# Mentions	**7+7+7**	**7×7**	**7**	**77**

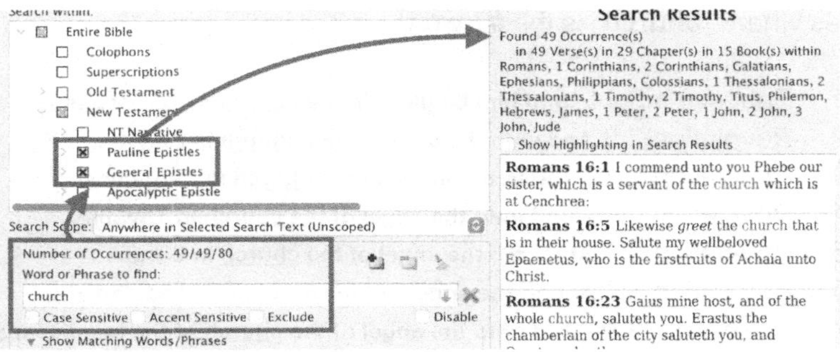

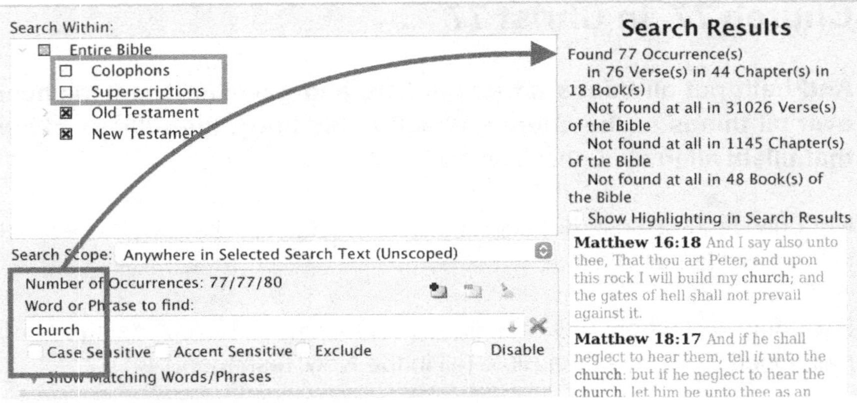

In Revelation, each mention of "**church**" is specifically assigned to one of the 7 churches of Revelation.

The seven mentions of "**church**" in Revelation:

1. Revelation 2:1 **Unto the angel of the church of Ephesus...**
2. Revelation 2:8 **And unto the angel of the church in Smyrna...**
3. Revelation 2:12 **And to the angel of the church in Pergamos...**
4. Revelation 2:18 **And unto the angel of the church in Thyatira...**
5. Revelation 3:1 **And unto the angel of the church in Sardis...**
6. Revelation 3:7 **And to the angel of the church in Philadelphia...**
7. Revelation 3:14 **And unto the angel of the church of the Laodiceans...**

And finally, there are exactly 7 verses where **church** is the #7 word of the verse.

Verses where "**church**" is the #7 word

1. Ephesians 3:21 **Unto him be glory in the church by Christ Jesus...**
2. Revelation 2:8 **And unto the angel of the church in Smyrna...**
3. Revelation 2:12 **And to the angel of the church in Pergamos...**
4. Revelation 2:18 **And unto the angel of the church in Thyatira...**
5. Revelation 3:1 **And unto the angel of the church in Sardis...**
6. Revelation 3:7 **And to the angel of the church in Philadelphia...**
7. Revelation 3:14 **And unto the angel of the church of the Laodiceans...**

Christ's church is **his body**.

For we are members of <u>his body</u>, of his flesh, and of his bones. Ephesians 5:30 (Mention #14 of "**his body**")

The phrase "**his body**" is mentioned 14 times- 7 times in the O.T. and 7 times in the N.T. Exactly 7 times are about the Lord's body († highlighted).

"**his body**" in the O.T.	"**his body**" in the N.T.
1) **[1]** Deuteronomy 21:23 †	1) **[3]** Luke 23:55 †
2) Judges 8:30	2) **[4]** Luke 24:23 †
3) 1 Samuel 31:10	3) **[5]** John 2:21 †
4) Daniel 4:33	4) Acts 19:12
5) Daniel 5:21	5) 2 Corinthians 5:10
6) Daniel 7:11	6) **[6]** Ephesians 1:23 †
7) **[2]** Daniel 10:6 †	7) **[7]** Ephesians 5:30 †

The first mention of "**His body**" is in Deuteronomy 21, establishing the curse of the cross, where the Lord Jesus Christ would die for our sins.

<u>His body</u> shall not remain all night upon the tree, but thou shalt in any wise bury him that day; (for he that is hanged is accursed of God;) that thy land be not defiled, which the LORD thy God giveth thee for an inheritance. Deuteronomy 21:23

The #6 mention of "**his body**" in the O.T. is talking about the antichrist's body and is the #6666 word/phrase of Daniel. (In contrast, the #8888 word/phrase of Daniel is the only mention in the O.T. of "**the Messiah**")

I beheld then because of the voice of the great words which the horn spake: I beheld even till the beast was slain, and <u>his body</u> destroyed, and given to the burning flame. Daniel 7:11

Those who make up the body of Christ, his church, are "**in Christ**."

So we, being many, are one body <u>in Christ</u>, and every one members one of another. Romans 12:5 (Mention #7 of "**in Christ**")

The phrase "**in Christ**" is mentioned 77 times in the KJB, and is the #777 word/phrase of the #(7×7) book of the Bible, Ephesians.

But now <u>in Christ</u> Jesus ye who sometimes were far off are made nigh by the blood of Christ. Ephesians 2:13

Amen, thank you Lord!

And in the #7 book mentioning "**in Christ**" (Philippians)... in the #49 verse (7×7) where it's mentioned (Philippians 1:13), "**in Christ**" is the #749,777 word/phrase of the Bible.

So that my bonds in Christ are manifest in all the palace, and in all other places; Philippians 1:13

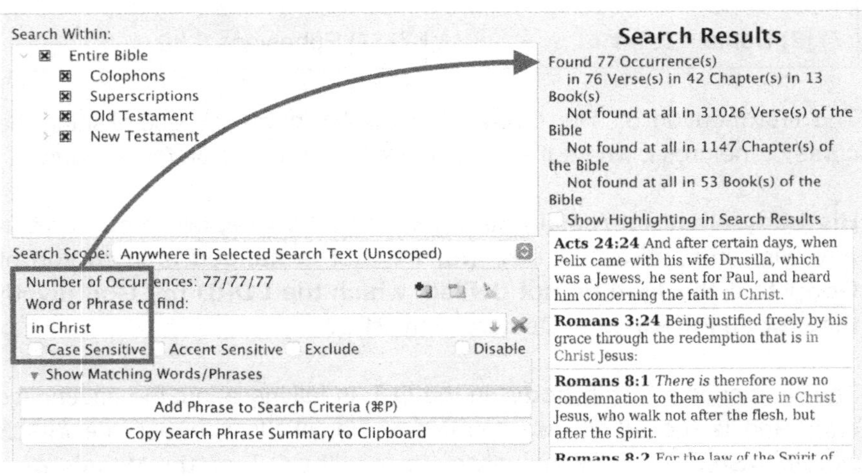

City 777

But ye are come unto mount Sion, and unto the city of the living God, the heavenly Jerusalem, and to an innumerable company of angels, Hebrews 12:22

One of the greatest hopes we have as **the sons of God** (1 John 3:2) is a **city** in which there will be no more tears, pain, death or sorrow. A place where the glory of the Lord, even the Lamb, will give light to all who walk through its everlasting gates of pearl. (Revelation 21)

For here have we no continuing city, but we seek one to come. Hebrews 13:14

This is that same **city** sought by Abraham.

For he looked for a city which hath foundations, whose builder and maker is God. Hebrews 11:10

Even that **city** sought by Abel, Enoch, Noah, Sara, Isaac, Jacob, and the rest of those in God's great chapter of faith (Hebrews 11).

These all died in faith, not having received the promises, but having seen them afar off, and were persuaded of them, and embraced them, and confessed that they were strangers and pilgrims on the earth. Hebrews 11:13

The **city** we seek is that great **holy Jerusalem** that God has promised us. We are strangers on this earth because we have an incorruptible inheritance and a home waiting for us in heaven.

Dearly beloved, I beseech you as strangers and pilgrims…
1 Peter 2:11

I am a stranger in the earth: hide not thy commandments from me. Psalm 119:19

The promise of that great city, as detailed in Revelation 21-22, runs all throughout the Bible. And it brings me pure joy to know that there are exactly **777** verses in the Bible to mention **city**, with the final verse calling it "**the holy city**" in the last chapter of the Bible, Revelation 22:19, warning all to not take away from the perfect word of God.

#777 (and **final**) verse in the KJB to mention **city** Revelation 22:19
And if any man shall take away from the words of the book of this prophecy, God shall take away his part out of the book of life, and out of the holy city, and from the things which are written in this book.

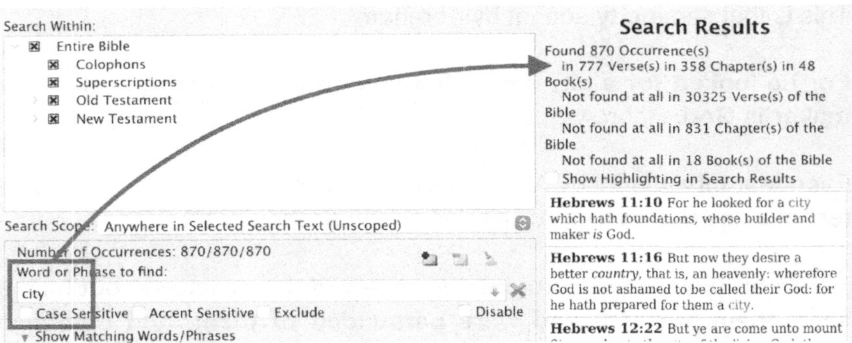

Exactly 7 verses in the New Testament mention both Jerusalem and city in the same verse:

1. Matthew 5:35 **Nor by the earth; for it is his footstool: neither by Jerusalem; for it is the city of the great King.**
2. Matthew 21:10 **And when he was come into Jerusalem, all the city was moved, saying, Who is this?**
3. Luke 24:49 **And, behold, I send the promise of my Father upon you: but tarry ye in the city of Jerusalem, until ye be endued with power from on high.**
4. Hebrews 12:22 **But ye are come unto mount Sion, and unto the city of the living God, the heavenly Jerusalem, and to an innumerable company of angels,**

5. Revelation 3:12 **Him that overcometh will I make a pillar in the temple of my God, and he shall go no more out: and I will write upon him the name of my God, and the name of the city of my God, which is new Jerusalem, which cometh down out of heaven from my God: and I will write upon him my new name.**
6. Revelation 21:2 **And I John saw the holy city, new Jerusalem, coming down from God out of heaven, prepared as a bride adorned for her husband.**
7. Revelation 21:10 **And he carried me away in the spirit to a great and high mountain, and shewed me that great city, the holy Jerusalem, descending out of heaven from God,**

There are exactly 154 mentions of **city** in the New Testament

77+77 mentions

in **144** verses/colophons. *Colophons are inscriptions at the end of Epistles.*

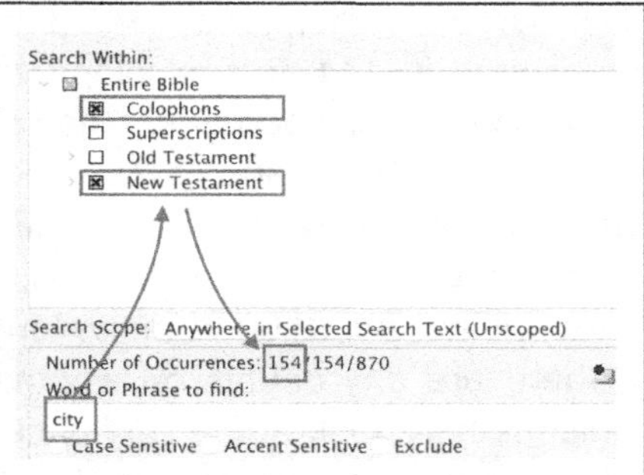

Important note if you are fact-checking with Bible software other than Pure Bible Search: The word **city** is located in a total of 2 Colophons: 2 Corinthians and 1 Timothy. Some Bible software/programs will count these as verses (even though they are not) – which may give you a total count of 779 verses for **city** in the Bible instead of 777. King James Pure Bible Search always counts colophons separately from verses. The proper count is 777 verses + 2 colophons for the entire Bible, and 142 verses + 2 colophons for the N.T.

The #777 mention of **city** in the KJB is when Jesus wept over Jerusalem: **And when he was come near, he beheld the city, and wept over it,** Luke 19:41 (#777 mention of **city**).

When Jesus says "**Swear not at all; neither by heaven; for it is God's throne: Nor by the earth; for it is his footstool: neither by Jerusalem; for it is the city of the great King.**" (Matthew 5:34-35), it's incredible because all mentions of **Jerusalem('s)** + all mentions of "**great king**" = **777** verses. And the context is not to <u>swear</u> by Jerusalem. Swearing is equivalent to "*sevening*" - see p. 232.

First time Jesus says "**Jerusalem**" in the Bible	
Swear not at all; neither by heaven; for it is God's throne: Nor by the earth; for it is his footstool: neither by Jerusalem; for it is the city of the great King. Matthew 5:34-35	
city	**Jerusalem* + great king**
777 verses in the KJB	**777 verses** in the KJB

Jerusalem is mentioned **144** times (12×12) in the N.T. (and **city** is mentioned in **144** verses/colophons in the N.T.), which bears incredible significance because new Jerusalem's wall is 144 cubits long, containing 12 gates with 12 angels and the 12 names of the children of Israel written thereon, with 12 foundations that have the 12 names of the Lamb's apostles written thereon, garnished with 12 precious stones, surrounding the 12,000 furlong-lengthed city (See Revelation 21:12-27). If there are any doubts on whether or not God perfectly numbers that which is holy, look at the very back of your Bible and read Revelation 21. Should we be surprised that the words of God's **holy scriptures** (Rom 1:2, 2 Tim 3:15) are also perfectly numbered? More on the 144 connection is detailed on p. 334.

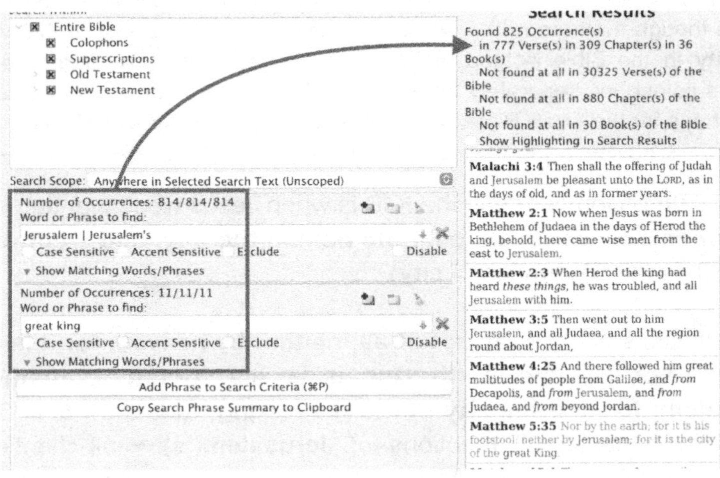

7-Character Book Titles

There are exactly 7 books with 7 characters, including the first and last of the O.T. as well as the first of the N.T. (**Genesis**, **Malachi**, **Matthew**). 5 of the book mentions <u>are words</u> that are found in the Bible itself **(Ezekiel, Obadiah, Malachi, Matthew, Hebrews)**, which are mentioned 49 times; and they produce a total sum of 7×389 verses. 389 is the #77 prime number.

All 7-character Book Titles (Shorthand)			
1	G-e-n-e-s-i-s	1533 verses	*"Genesis" is not mentioned*
2	N-u-m-b-e-r-s	1288 verses	*"Numbers" (Capitalized) is not mentioned*
3	**E-z-e-k-i-e-l**	**1273 verses**	**"Ezekiel"** = 2 mentions in the KJB
4	**O-b-a-d-i-a-h**	**21 verses**	**"Obadiah"** = 20 mentions in the KJB
5	**M-a-l-a-c-h-i**	**55 verses**	**"Malachi"** = 1 mentions in the KJB
6	**M-a-t-t-h-e-w**	**1071 verses**	**"Matthew"** = 5 mentions in the KJB
7	**H-e-b-r-e-w-s**	**303 verses**	**"Hebrews"** = 21 mentions in the KJB
Total: **7 books**		**7×77th Prime verses** (in the 5 books with textual mentions) **77×72 verses** (in all 7 books)	**7×7 textual mentions** (actual mentions as words in the text of the Bible)
All 7-character book names that are words in the text of the Bible **Ezekiel + Obadiah + Malachi + Matthew + Hebrews** **= 7×77th Prime verses, 7×7 mentions**			

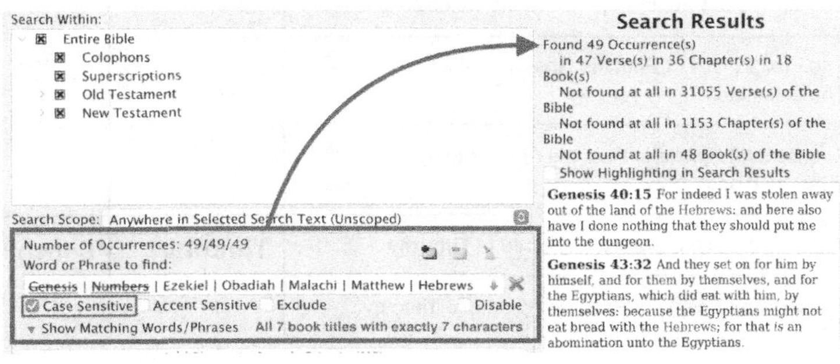

7×77 Names in N.T. Book Titles

Here is a list of all full names of New Testament books, with all the unique names highlighted.

<table>
<tr><th colspan="2">New Testament book titles
with Names of Persons</th><th>Unique Name(s) in Book Title
Possessive ('s) form included if it appears</th><th>Mentions in the New Testament
(Case-sensitive, including Colophons)</th></tr>
<tr><td>1</td><td>The Gospel According to Saint Matthew</td><td>Matthew</td><td>5 mentions</td></tr>
<tr><td>2</td><td>The Gospel According to Saint Mark</td><td>Mark</td><td>5 mentions</td></tr>
<tr><td>3</td><td>The Gospel According to Saint Luke</td><td>Luke</td><td>2 mentions</td></tr>
<tr><td>4</td><td>The Gospel According to Saint John</td><td rowspan="2">John('s)</td><td rowspan="2">133 mentions</td></tr>
<tr><td>5</td><td>The Acts of the Apostles</td></tr>
<tr><td>6</td><td>The Epistle of Paul the Apostle to the Romans</td><td rowspan="9">Paul('s)</td><td rowspan="9">163 mentions</td></tr>
<tr><td>7</td><td>The First Epistle of Paul the Apostle to the Corinthians</td></tr>
<tr><td>8</td><td>The Second Epistle of Paul the Apostle to the Corinthians</td></tr>
<tr><td>9</td><td>The Epistle of Paul the Apostle to the Galatians</td></tr>
<tr><td>10</td><td>The Epistle of Paul the Apostle to the Ephesians</td></tr>
<tr><td>11</td><td>The Epistle of Paul the Apostle to the Philippians</td></tr>
<tr><td>12</td><td>The Epistle of Paul the Apostle to the Colossians</td></tr>
<tr><td>13</td><td>The First Epistle of Paul the Apostle to the Thessalonians</td></tr>
<tr><td>14</td><td>The Second Epistle of Paul the Apostle to the Thessalonians</td></tr>
<tr><td>15</td><td>The First Epistle of Paul the Apostle to Timothy</td><td rowspan="2">Timothy</td><td rowspan="2">9 mentions</td></tr>
<tr><td>16</td><td>The Second Epistle of Paul the Apostle to Timothy</td></tr>
</table>

#	Book Title	Name	Mentions
17	The Epistle of Paul to **Titus**	**Titus**	15 mentions
18	The Epistle of Paul to **Philemon**	**Philemon**	2 mentions
19	The Epistle of Paul the Apostle to the Hebrews		
20	The General Epistle of **James**	**James**	42 mentions
21	The First Epistle General of **Peter**	**Peter('s)**	162 mentions
22	The Second Epistle General of Peter		
23	The First Epistle of John		
24	The Second Epistle of John		
25	The Third Epistle of John		
26	The General Epistle of **Jude**	**Jude**	1 mention
27	The Revelation of Saint John the Divine		
Total Combined Mentions *of* Every man's name found in N.T. book titles **Matthew, Mark, Luke, John('s), Paul('s), Timothy, Titus, Philemon, James, Peter('s), Jude**			539 = **77×7** mentions

The New Testament is sealed with God's number of completion, in a way that nobody could have possibly thought of in an age without computers. Consider Paul's name change from Saul. Consider how Peter is sometimes called Simon, and other times Cephas. Just one of these factors flipped around would throw off the total count of 77×7.

And yet, the verification goes further:

The first five Old Testament books are authored by:
"Moses"
= 77 mentions in the N.T.

The first five New Testament books are authored by:
"Matthew" + "Mark" + "Luke" + "John" *(Not case-sensitive)*
= 77+77 mentions in the N.T.

The gospel was committed to (Galatians 2:7):
"Peter" + "Paul"
= 77+77+77+77+7 mentions in the N.T.

"**King**" (capitalized) + "**James**"
= 77 mentions in the N.T.

Word	Significance	Mentions in the N.T.
Matthew, Mark, Luke, John('s), Paul('s), Timothy, Titus, Philemon, James, Peter('s), Jude (Case-sensitive)	Every man's name found in N.T. book titles	77×7
Moses	Author of the first 5 books of O.T.	77
Matthew, Mark, Luke, John (not case-sensitive)	Authors of the first 5 books of N.T.	77+77
Peter, Paul	Authors of over half of the N.T. books	77+77+77+77+7
King, James (Case-sensitive)	Name of the Bible	77

And if you add the infamous publishing year of 1611 in text form (as it is spoken "**sixteen**" + "**eleven**"), there are exactly…

"King" + "James" + "sixteen" + "eleven" *(Case-sensitive)* in the New Testament		
77+7 mentions	**77 verses**	**7×7 chapters**

7-Sealed

Of the tribe of Simeon were sealed twelve thousand. Of the tribe of Levi were sealed twelve thousand. Of the tribe of Issachar were sealed twelve thousand. Revelation 7:7

Revelation 7 is the #7 and final chapter to mention **sealed** in the N.T.

The #7 mention of **sealed** in the N.T. is in Revelation 7.

1. John 6:27 **...for him hath God the Father sealed.**
2. Romans 15:28 **...and have sealed to them this fruit...**
3. 2 Corinthians 1:22 **Who hath also sealed us, and given...**
4. Ephesians 1:13 **...ye were sealed with that holy Spirit...**
5. Ephesians 4:30 **...holy Spirit of God, whereby ye are sealed...**
6. Revelation 5:1 **...on the backside, sealed with seven seals.**
7. Revelation 7:3 **...sealed the servants of our God...**

Exactly 7 verses in Revelation mention "**sealed.**" The #7 word of Revelation 7:7 is **sealed**, describing the tribe of **Simeon**. **Simeon** is the **7th** tribe of Israel listed. 7×7 mentions of Simeon precede Revelation 7:7.

Exactly 7 verses in Revelation mention "**sealed**"	The #7 word of Revelation 7:7 is "**sealed**"	The tribe of **Simeon** is the 7th tribe of Israel listed in Revelation 7
1. Revelation 5:1 2. Revelation 7:3 3. Revelation 7:4 4. Revelation 7:5 5. Revelation 7:6 6. Revelation 7:7 7. Revelation 7:8	1. Of 2. the 3. tribe 4. of 5. Simeon 6. were **7. sealed**	1. Juda (Rev 7:5) 2. Reuben (Rev 7:5) 3. Gad (Rev 7:5) 4. Aser (Rev 7:6) 5. Nepthalim (Rev 7:6) 6. Manasses (Rev 7:6) 7. **Simeon** (Rev 7:7)

Overall in the New Testament, **sealed** = 7+7+7 mentions / 12 verses.

The #(7+7+7) and final mention of **sealed** in the New Testament is word #(77+77+77+7) of Revelation 7 and word #172,186 of the N.T. (which is perfectly divisible by 7×7×7). 172,186 = 7×7×7 × (70×7+12)

The words **seal / sealed** are mentioned in 7×7 verses of the KJB, with the final (#49) mention in the last chapter: **...Seal not the sayings of the prophecy of this book: for the time is at hand.** Rev (22:10)

Rev 7:7 is the #7 verse from the end of the KJB to mention **seal / sealed**

1. Revelation 22:10 **...Seal not the sayings of the prophecy...**
2. Revelation 20:3 **...and set a seal upon him, that he should...**
3. Revelation 10:4 **...Seal up those things which the seven...**
4. Revelation 9:4 **...the seal of God in their foreheads.**
5. Revelation 8:1 **And when he had opened the seventh seal...**
6. Revelation 7:8 **Of the tribe of Zabulon were sealed...**
7. Revelation 7:7 **Of the tribe of Simeon were sealed...**

And there is a lot we can learn about the way God seals things.

- In Revelation 7:2, we see that God's seal is uniquely His own: **...having the seal of the living God...** Rev 7:2
- In Revelation 7:4-8, we see that God seals thing by patterns of numbers: the 144,000 sealed are divided into 12 groups of 12,000.
- And in Rev 7:3, cross referenced with Rev 22:3,4 shows us that the seal of God contains His name.

God's Seal is His name		
...till we have sealed the servants of our God in their foreheads. Rev 7:3	**...the seal of God in their foreheads...** Rev 9:4	**...his servants shall serve him... his name shall be in their foreheads.** Rev 22:3,4

As seen in these notes, we see nothing short of God's name being uniquely sealed by number patterns in the KJB, using His number of completion and perfection: ***7.***

When a Christian is sealed, instead of using "**Holy Ghost**", the King James Bible uses "**holy Spirit**" which is mentioned 7 times, and consists of 7 Spirits (Rev 5:6). And instead of using "**holy Spirit**" in 2 Cor 1:22, it simply reads "**Spirit**." If it were "**holy Spirit**" instead of **Spirit** in 2 Cor

1:22, the total KJB count would go from 7 to 8. This, once again, indicates intentionality and fine-tuning.

2 Corinthians 1:22 **Who hath also sealed us, and given the earnest of the Spirit in our hearts.**

Ephesians 1:13 **In whom ye also trusted, after that ye heard the word of truth, the gospel of your salvation: in whom also after that ye believed, ye were sealed with that holy Spirit of promise,**

Ephesians 4:30 **And grieve not the holy Spirit of God, whereby ye are sealed unto the day of redemption.**

And, at last, the #7 mention of **seal** / **sealed** in the King James Bible, which I believe speaks for itself without any need of explanation…

The **#7** mention in the KJB of

seal / sealed

(Mentioned in a total of 7×7 verses in the KJB)

Write ye also for the Jews, as it liketh you, in the king's name, and **seal** it with the king's ring: for the writing which is written in the king's name, and sealed with the king's ring, may no man reverse.

Esther 8:8

Part II

The 144 Holy Bible

The KJB has a total of **144** verses with 44 letters, including Genesis 1:1 and Revelation 22:21 (the first and the last).

Genesis 1:1	Revelation 22:21
In the beginning God created the heaven and the earth.	**The grace of our Lord Jesus Christ be with you all. Amen.**
44 letters	**44 letters**

30,958 out of 31,102 verses do not have exactly 44 letters, which means the odds are very slim that both the first and last verses both have 44 letters. That's like putting on a blindfold and spinning this wheel, and only winning if you hit the needle-sized success-area two spins in a row.

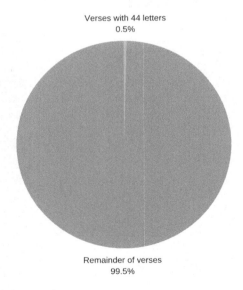

No other verse in the book of Revelation, Jude, 3 John, 2 John, 1 John, 2 Peter, 1 Peter, or James has a verse with 44 letters. But it just so happens that the exact last verse of Revelation has 44 letters. *Really?*

How much lower the odds that there are exactly 144 such verses across the entire Bible?!

144 verses contain 44 letters.

144 is a very good number in the Bible. God elects 144,000 in Rev 7 who are sealed with His name and described in Revelation 14:4, but what really stands out, in this case, is New Jerusalem and her 144-cubit wall.

And he measured the wall thereof, <u>an hundred and forty and four cubits</u>... (Revelation 21:17)

From one end to the other, there are 144 verses with 44 letters. And from one end to the other, New Jerusalem's wall covers a span of 144 cubits. The Bible itself is a type of New Jerusalem in many particular details:

- Perfect / flawlessly preserved
- Where God speaks & dwells
- God lightens it
- Saved people walk in its light
- Its gates can be entered day or night
- Written on it are the 12 Tribes Israel (Old Testament)
- ...and the 12 Apostles (New Testament)
- 144-cubit wall measuring from one end to the other

And in the numerical structure of God's 66-book volume:

- Gen 6:6 is the #144 O.T. verse, Mat 6:6 is the #144 N.T. verse
- 144 *[verses of 44-letters]* from one end to the other
- **Holy** (Capitalized) = **144 mentions**. *(Like the word that is on the side of your Bible.)*
- **Jerusalem** = **144 mentions** (in the New Testament). There are 70 mentions in the Gospels, with the final (#70) in John 12:12.
- **gates** = **144 mentions** in the Bible
- **city** = **144 verses/colophons** (in the N.T.), (142 vrs. + 2 colo.)

Holy, **Jerusalem**, **city**, **gates**...

While I have not verified for certain (it would be difficult), there does not seem to be many other words (if any) with exactly 144 mentions/verses, when searching the entire Bible or by an individual testament. I am not aware of any.

Holy (Capitalized) = 144 mentions in the Bible

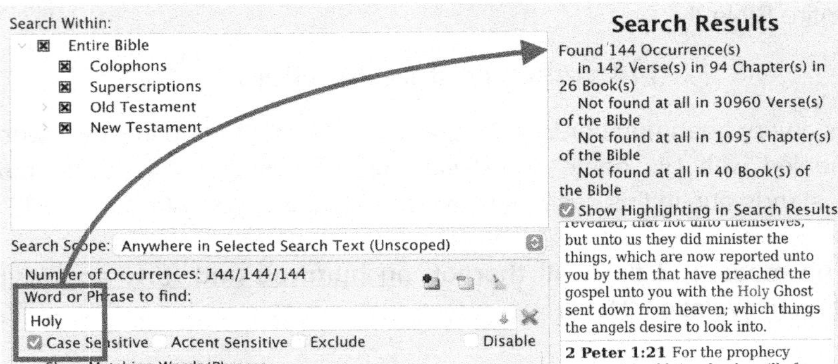

Jerusalem = 144 mentions in the New Testament

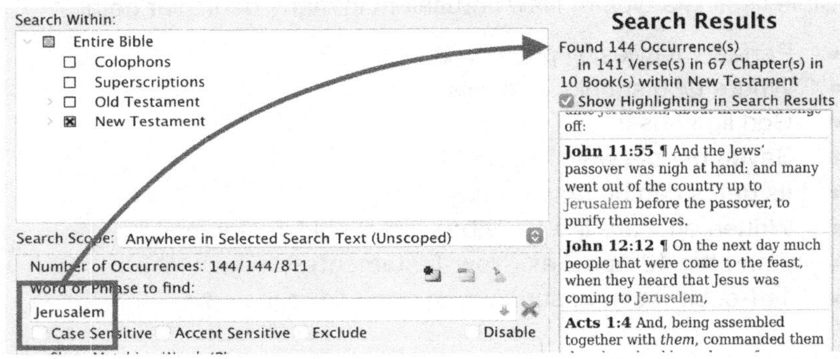

gates = 144 mentions in the Bible

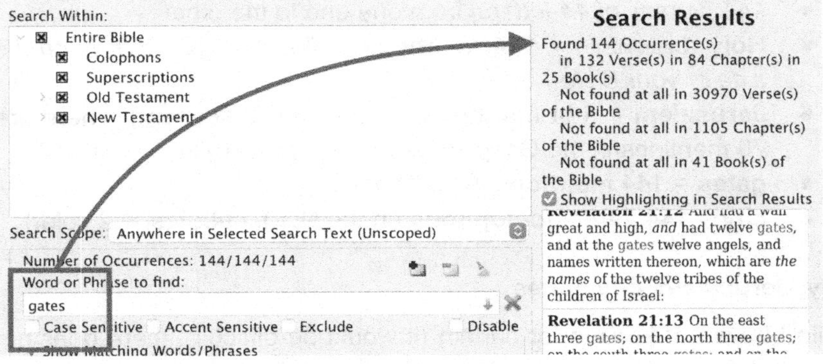

All 144 verses containing 44 letters					
1: Gen 1:1	25: Deu 11:26	49: Ezr 2:34	73: Psa 105:29	97: Lam 3:34	121: Joh 7:13
2: Gen 5:12	26: Jos 12:20	50: Neh 7:14	74: Psa 115:4	98: Lam 3:52	122: Act 12:2
3: Gen 9:8	27: Jos 19:21	51: Neh 7:36	75: Psa 115:15	99: Eze 40:8	123: Act 19:11
4: Gen 10:23	28: Jos 19:46	52: Neh 12:11	76: Psa 119:60	100: Zec 1:2	124: Act 19:41
5: Gen 11:24	29: Jos 21:15	53: Est 4:9	77: Psa 119:70	101: Mal 1:1	125: Rom 4:8
6: Gen 13:2	30: 1Sa 17:29	54: Job 5:16	78: Psa 119:140	102: Mat 5:5	126: Rom 9:12
7: Gen 15:20	31: 2Sa 20:26	55: Job 12:11	79: Psa 134:2	103: Mat 5:7	127: Rom 16:24
8: Gen 24:66	32: 1Ki 1:46	56: Job 36:24	80: Psa 135:8	104: Mat 15:7	128: 1Co 4:18
9: Gen 30:19	33: 1Ch 1:14	57: Job 41:8	81: Psa 136:18	105: Mat 15:16	129: 1Co 7:6
10: Gen 34:18	34: 1Ch 2:40	58: Job 42:6	82: Pro 1:16	106: Mat 25:7	130: 1Co 7:23
11: Gen 36:3	35: 1Ch 6:6	59: Psa 7:10	83: Pro 3:8	107: Mat 25:39	131: 1Co 13:6
12: Gen 43:13	36: 1Ch 6:9	60: Psa 18:31	84: Pro 5:17	108: Mat 27:16	132: 1Co 15:55
13: Gen 48:8	37: 1Ch 6:13	61: Psa 26:2	85: Pro 7:19	109: Mar 6:12	133: 2Co 5:3
14: Exo 6:2	38: 1Ch 6:20	62: Psa 44:4	86: Pro 29:12	110: Mar 8:30	134: 2Co 10:9
15: Exo 19:25	39: 1Ch 6:23	63: Psa 48:7	87: Sol 1:11	111: Mar 10:50	135: Phi 4:23
16: Exo 21:24	40: 1Ch 6:28	64: Psa 55:16	88: Sol 1:17	112: Mar 11:22	136: 2Th 3:18
17: Exo 23:14	41: 1Ch 6:73	65: Psa 71:7	89: Sol 7:3	113: Mar 13:23	137: 1Ti 1:8
18: Exo 39:11	42: 1Ch 6:75	66: Psa 73:21	90: Sol 7:6	114: Mar 15:37	138: 1Ti 3:9
19: Exo 40:28	43: 1Ch 8:27	67: Psa 86:1	91: Isa 8:16	115: Luk 2:28	139: Phm 1:24
20: Lev 11:17	44: 1Ch 12:26	68: Psa 87:3	92: Jer 16:20	116: Luk 3:20	140: Heb 3:11
21: Num 6:8	45: 1Ch 23:12	69: Psa 94:18	93: Jer 33:23	117: Luk 22:9	141: Heb 4:9
22: Num 33:10	46: 2Ch 15:1	70: Psa 95:9	94: Jer 48:22	118: Luk 23:37	142: Heb 7:20
23: Num 33:13	47: Ezr 2:9	71: Psa 105:4	95: Lam 3:6	119: Luk 23:52	143: Heb 10:17
24: Num 33:42	48: Ezr 2:17	72: Psa 105:26	96: Lam 3:23	120: Joh 4:2	144: Rev 22:21
Highlighted verses are noted on the next page.					

Noteworthy 44-letter verses.

[1] Genesis 1:1 - [144] Revelation 22:21

- First and last verses of the Bible
- Same number of consonants and vowels (See p. 340)
- Rev 22:21 is the only last verse of a book to contain 44 letters

[1] Genesis 1:1 - [101] Malachi 1:1

- First verses of the first and last books of the Old Testament. No other book's first verse contains 44 letters
- Malachi 1:1 is the #44 verse from the end of the Bible to have 44 letters

[1] Genesis 1:1 - [62] Psalm 44:4 - [144] Revelation 22:21

- Psalm 44:4 has the same amount of consonants and vowels as Gen 1:1 & Rev 22:21
- Contains the words "**King**" and "**Jacob**" (Jacob = **James**)
- Follows 1611 mentions of "**king**"
- "**King**" is the 12,383 word of Psalms = 1769 × 7

[1] Genesis 1:1 - [134] 2 Corinthians 10:9 - [144] Revelation 22:21

- 2 Cor 10:9 has the same amount of consonants and vowels (without Y-rule) as Gen 1:1 & Rev 22:21
- Contains the phrase "**...terrify you by letters.**"

[18] Exodus 39:11

- Stones on the breastplate, typifying New Jerusalem, "**And the second row, an emerald, a sapphire, and a diamond.**"
- [18] = (14+4)

[1] Genesis 1:1 - [75] Psalm 115:15

- Creation verses

[78] Psalm 119:140 - [91] Isaiah 8:16 - [137] 1 Timothy 1:8

- God's word is very pure, sealed to his disciples, and to be used lawfully

I also noticed that a lot of 44-letter verses have doctrinally significant weight behind them. Just from this little tiny selection of 144 scriptures (on p. 337), you could put together a pretty strong sermon...

An unofficial sermon outline made up of only 44-letter-verses	
Mark 6:12	**And they went out, and preached that men should repent.**
Deut 11:26	**Behold, I set before you this day a blessing and a curse;**
Rom 4:8	**Blessed is the man to whom the Lord will not impute sin.**
Luke 23:37	**And saying, If thou be the king of the Jews, save thyself.**
Mark 15:37	**And Jesus cried with a loud voice, and gave up the ghost.**
Luke 23:52	**This man went unto Pilate, and begged the body of Jesus.**
1 Cor 15:55	**O death, where is thy sting? O grave, where is thy victory?**
1 Cor 7:23	**Ye are bought with a price; be not ye the servants of men.**
Mark 11:22	**And Jesus answering saith unto them, Have faith in God.**
Heb 10:17	**And their sins and iniquities will I remember no more.**
Heb 4:9	**There remaineth therefore a rest to the people of God.**
1 Tim 3:9	**Holding the mystery of the faith in a pure conscience.**
Psa 26:2	**Examine me, O LORD, and prove me; try my reins and my heart.**
Psa 55:16	**As for me, I will call upon God; and the LORD shall save me.**

For who is God save the LORD? or who is a rock save our God? Psalm 18:31

Remember that thou magnify his work, which men behold. Job 36:24

17 Vowels / 27 Consonants in the First and the Last Verses

Genesis 1:1 **In the beginning God created the heaven and the earth.**

Revelation 22:21 **The grace of our Lord Jesus Christ be with you all. Amen.**

The **Alpha and Omega** verses of the Bible. The **first and the last** verses of scripture. The **beginning and the end.**

What else is there to note?

As mentioned in the previous note, both of these verses have exactly 44 letters. But, not only do they have the same amount of letters, they also have the exact same amount of vowels & consonants.

Genesis 1:1	Revelation 22:21
VOWELS: **I e eii o eae e eae a e ea** (Total = **17**)	VOWELS: **e ae o ou o eu i e i ou a Ae** (Total = **17**)
CONSONANTS: **n th bgnnng Gd crtd th hvn nd th rth.** (Total = **27**)	CONSONANTS: **Th grc f r Lrd Jss Chrst b wth y ll. mn.** (Total = **27**)
TOTAL: **17 vow + 27 cons**	TOTAL: **17 vow + 27 cons**

The first and last verses of the KJB are perfectly identical by number of consonants and vowels. Exact matches. This doesn't happen in other Bibles. The Authorized King James stands alone as the pure word of God, down to the last **jot** and **tittle**.

But here is what's incredibly fascinating: both the ***first*** mention of **17** and the ***first*** mention of **27** in the Bible bear textual authority to this first-and-last phenomenon. *How so?* Well, the first mention of 17 marks the very **beginning** of the flood (on the **17th** day of the 2nd month), and the first mention of 27 marks the very **end** of the flood (on the **27th** day of the 2nd month).

First mention of **17** in the Bible **The BEGINNING of the flood**	First mention of **27** in the Bible **The END of the flood**
In the six hundredth year of Noah's life, in the second month, the seventeenth day of the month, the same day were all the fountains of the great deep broken up, and <u>the windows of heaven were opened.</u> Genesis 7:11	**And in the second month, on the seven and twentieth day of the month, <u>was the earth dried.</u>** Genesis 8:14 *(27 verses away from Genesis 7:11)*

Here we have the first mentions of **17** & **27** as the **beginning** and the **ending** verses to the flood, just like we have with Genesis 1:1 and Revelation 22:21 (**17 vow** - **27 cons**). The **beginning** and the **ending** verses of the Bible. It's not just a miracle. It's a Bible miracle.

Need another witness? *Notice the reference:*

They did eat, they drank, they married wives, they were given in marriage, until the day that Noe entered into the ark, and the flood came, and destroyed them all. Luke **17:27**

The flood could also be seen as a type of God's word, which makes it that much more significant. Consider the following characteristics:

- It covered the whole earth and sanctified it (John 17:17)
- It judged all flesh (John 12:48)
- The voice of God sounds like many waters (Revelation 1:15)
- Rain / water are types of God's word (Isaiah 55:10-11)

There is also a close connection to Genesis 1:1 in these verses:

Gen 1:1	**In the beginning God created...**	**...the heaven...**	**...and the earth.**
Gen 7:11, 8:14	*Flood brings a new beginning for mankind*	**...the windows of heaven were opened.** (7:11)	**...the earth dried.** (8:14)

The number 17's last mention is in the #777 chapter of the Bible. (Jeremiah 32:9). The number 27 (when worded as "**seven and twentieth**" like Gen 8:14) only appears two other times in the Bible:

- Once in a **27th** verse. 2 Kings 25:**27**
- Once in a **17th** verse. Ezekiel 29:**17**

And lastly, both Genesis 7:11 and Genesis 8:14 occur "**in the second month**". Those two verses (Gen 7:11, 8:14) are the only two verses in all of Genesis to mention the "**second month**". God deals this way in the Bible in other places, when he begins and ends in the selfsame day / month / etc. (e.g. Exodus 12:40-41).

A quick study of the "**second month**" in the Bible:

- The **second month** is when God first rained manna from heaven (Ex 16:1,4)
- The **second month** is when God commanded Moses to "**take the sum**" of the children of Israel in (Num 1:1)
- The **second month** is when God led Israel away from Mount Sinai (Num 10:11)
- The **second month** is when construction began on the house of the LORD (the first temple) in (1 Kgs 6:1) and (2 Chr 3:2)
- The **second month** is when repair (reconstruction) began on the temple in (Ezra 3:8) after the return of their 70-year captivity
- The **second month** is when Israel has a second chance to celebrate Passover if circumstances prevent them in the first month. This is found in (Num 9:10-11) as well as (2 Chr 30:2-13).

The big question: *Why was the flood account microscopically recorded by day and month- when almost nothing else was in Genesis?* The only persons who could have kept track of this knowledge were Noah or Shem. And each generation after them preserved this knowledge for hundreds of years until Moses finally wrote it down in ink. Or perhaps, nobody knew it, and God just told Moses. Either way, the LORD must have deemed it very important to include in His holy scriptures.

Thus saith the LORD the King of Israel, and his redeemer the LORD of hosts; I am the first, and I am the last; and beside me there is no God. And who, as I, shall call, and shall declare it, and set it in order for me, since I appointed the ancient people? and the things that are coming, and shall come, let them shew unto them. Fear ye not, neither be afraid: have not I told thee from that time, and have declared it? ye are even my witnesses. Is there a God beside me? yea, there is no God; I know not any. Isaiah 44:6-8

	Genesis 1:1			Revelation 22:21		
	Vowels	Cons.	Letters	Vowels	Cons.	Letters
KJB	**17**	**27**	**44**	**17**	**27**	**44**
KJB 1611	**18**	**26**	**44**	**18**	**26**	**44**
NKJV	17	28	45	17	27	44
ESV	17	28	45	13	22	35
NASB 1971	17	28	45	13	22	35
NASB 2020	17	28	45	13	22	35
NIV	17	28	45	16	26	42

Note: the KJB1611 also has a complete pattern, using different numbers. This happens because the **7th word** from the beginning "Heauen" was standardized to "heaven"; and the **7th word** from the end "Iesus" was standardized to "Jesus." No other words were standardized in the first and last verses- only the 7th from the beginning and 7th from the end.

	KJB1611	KJB
Genesis 1:1 *The only standardized word is* **Word #7** *from the beginning:* **Heauen → heaven**	**In the beginning God created the Heauen, and the Earth.**	**In the beginning God created the heaven and the earth.**
Revelation 22:21 *The only standardized word is* **Word #7** *from the end:* **Iesus → Jesus**	**The grace of our Lord Iesus Christ be with you all. Amen.**	**The grace of our Lord Jesus Christ be with you all. Amen.**

1 John 5:7 - The Sum of the First and the Last

Genesis 1:1 **In the beginning God created the heaven and the earth.**

Revelation 22:21 **The grace of our Lord Jesus Christ be with you all. Amen.**

1 John 5:7 **For there are three that bear record in heaven, the Father, the Word, and the Holy Ghost: and these three are one.**

Genesis 1:1 = 17 vowels / 27 consonants / 44 letters / 10 words
Revelation 22:21 = 17 vowels / 27 consonants / 44 letters / 12 words

17 + 17 vowels
27 + 27 consonants
44 + 44 letters
10 + 12 words
= 1 John 5:7

1 John 5:7 = 34 vowels / 54 consonants / 88 letters / 22 words

KJB	Vowels	Cons.	Letters	Words
Genesis 1:1	17	27	44	10
Revelation 22:21	17	27	44	12
Total (Gen 1:1 + Rev 22:21)	**34**	**54**	**88**	**22**
1 John 5:7	**34**	**54**	**88**	**22**

The First Word of the Bible ("In")

In the beginning God created the heaven and the earth. Genesis 1:1

The first word "**In**" is first mentioned in verses 1,6,11. Out of 12,674 mentions of "**in**" in the KJB, this is the only perfect sequence of 1611 that is formed out of verse numbers in the same chapter.

Not only are they located in the same chapter, this is the very first chapter of the Bible, which means these verse numbers stand alone without any need of mentioning the chapter number.

VERSE **1** of the Bible
VERSE **6** of the Bible
VERSE **11** of the Bible

The first word of the Bible forms the pattern: **1-6-11**

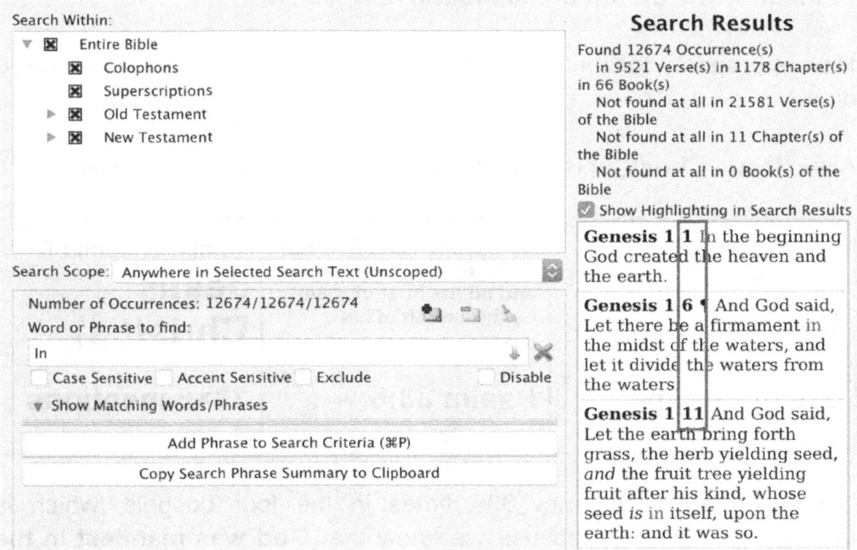

Out of the remaining 9,500+ verses, this phenomenon never happens again in the entire Bible.

If you look at "**In**" when it's *capitalized*, there are 336 mentions.

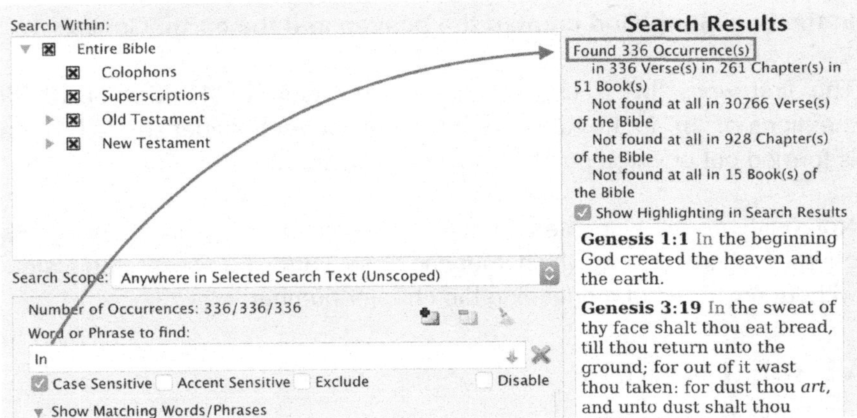

When I first saw that, it immediately reminded me of Psalm 33:6

By the word of the LORD were the heavens made; and all the host of them by the breath of his mouth. Psalm 33:6

How appropriate for the first word of the Bible to match this verse by the digit.

Also, **Jesus Christ('s)** is mentioned 198 = **33×6** times in the Bible.

The **first word** of Genesis 1:1 & John 1:1 **In**	**By the word of the LORD were the heavens made; and all the host of them by the breath of his mouth.**	Total mentions of **Jesus Christ('s)**
336 mentions (capitalized)	**Psalm 33:6**	**33×6 mentions**

"**God**" + "**flesh**" appears 336 times in the four gospels, which is interesting of course because we know that **God was manifest in the flesh…** 1 Timothy 3:16

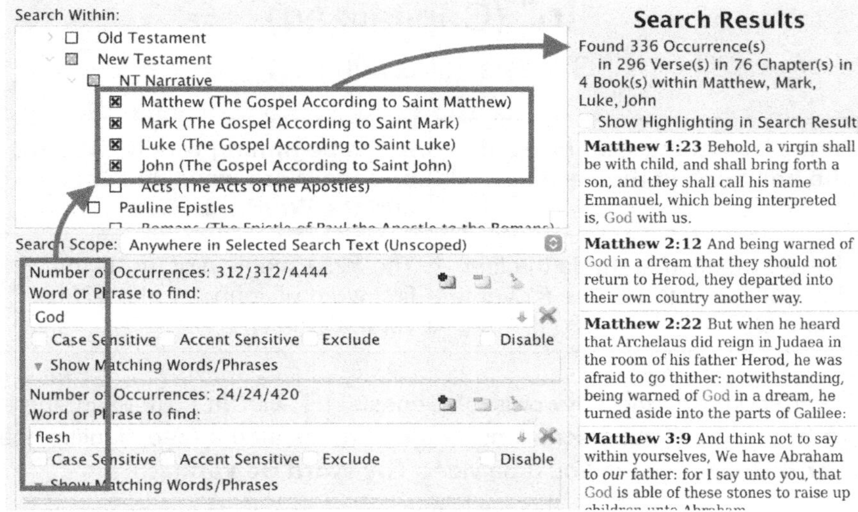

336 is very "connected" with triple sevens.

336 + (7+7+7) × (7+7+7) = 777

336 also has an interesting relationship with the numbers involving the first mentions of **LORD**.

First mention of **LORD** in the O.T. = word #88 of chapter 2 (verse 4)
First mention of **LORD** in the N.T. = word #777 of chapter 22 (verse 44)

$$(8+8)\times(7+7+7) = 336$$
$$7\times(24+24) = 336$$

But most miraculous of all is what happens when you consider both Genesis 1:1 and John 1:1 with the first word "**In**" (Capitalized) in light of the Old and New Testaments…

"**In**" (Capitalized)

Genesis 1:1 & John 1:1

In the beginning God created the heaven and the earth.	**In the beginning was the Word, and the Word was with God, and the Word was God.**
The #1 mention of "**In**" is the first word of Genesis 1:1, the #1 verse of the O.T.	The #291 mention of "**In**" is the first word of John 1:1, the #2901 verse of the N.T.

If you search all the keywords of Genesis 1:1 with **In** (Capitalized), there are **3737** verses/superscriptions in the Old Testament (see significance of **37** & Genesis 1:1 in YouTube video **Thy Word Be Verified**).

In the beginning God created the heaven and the earth.

Genesis 1:1

In (Capitalized) + **beginning** + **God** + **created** + **heaven** + **earth**
= **3737** verses/superscriptions in the Old Testament
(3736 verses + 1 ss)

And if you search the New Testament, all you have to do is replace **God** with **the Word,** because they are one.

...and the Word was God...
All things were made by him...

John 1:1,3

the Word = God

The New Testament revelation of Genesis 1:1

In the beginning was the Word...

John 1:1

Search Filters: **New Testament**		Case Sens	Mentions
Search Phrase 1	**In**	Y	60
Search Phrase 2	**beginning**	-	52
Search Phrase 3	**Word**	-	206
Search Phrase 4	**created**	-	12
Search Phrase 5	**heaven**	-	255
Search Phrase 6	**earth**	-	192
Total Mentions	**In** (Capitalized) **+ beginning + Word + created + heaven + earth** *John 1:1 / Genesis 1:1*		**777**

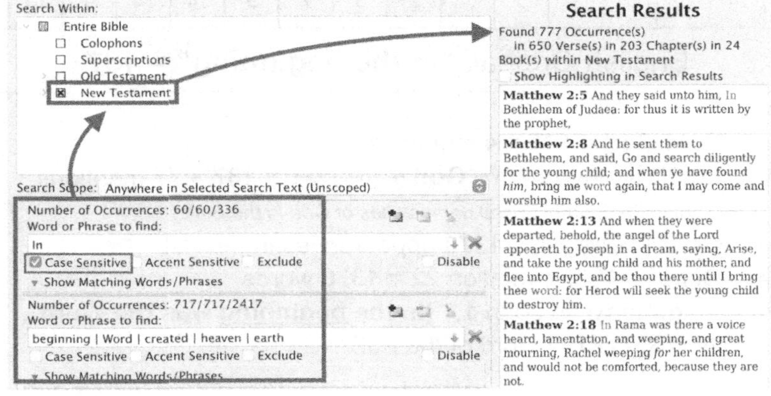

Alpha "α" / "a" - (1/137) Fine-Structure Constant

1/137 is the most glorified number in physics– attributed to the fine tuning of the universe for life to exist. It's also known as the "*Fine-Structure Constant*" or "**Alpha**" or "*the magic number that shaped our universe.*"

American theoretical physicist Richard Feynman is famously quoted, "*It's one of the greatest ... mysteries of physics, you might say the hand of God wrote that number, but we don't know how he pushed his pencil.*"

While the Fine-structure constant is always in slight fluctuation and may have been different "*billions of years ago*" according to physicists, we have no Biblical reason to believe the universe is billions of years old. We will therefore stick to God's revealed scripture along with observational science, not theories and hypotheticals.

If you want to learn more about the Fine-Structure Constant, a simple Google or YouTube search will help you learn more. For the sake of these notes, I'm just going to dive straight in. Remember, this number (1/137) is responsible for the fine-tuning of our universe, making it possible for atoms, chemistry, material, and all life to exist.

"**In the beginning**" = 137 in English Ordinal (A=1, B=2, C=3... Z=26)

I	n		t	h	e		b	e	g	i	n	n	i	n	g
9	14		20	8	5		2	5	7	9	14	14	9	14	7
English Ordinal, "**In the beginning**" = **137**															

- **Lord God** = **137 × 4** mentions
- **LORD** (UPPERCASE) + **God** (Capitalized) = **137 × 77** mentions
  (These are the most-used names/titles of God in the Bible)
- **God*** (Capitalized) = **1370** appearances in the N.T.
- Genesis 1 + Revelation 22 = **1370** words
- "**beginning**" in John 1:1 (**In the beginning was the Word...**) is the **13777×7×7** word of the KJB.

When physicists include the fine-structure constant in their equations, they use the Greek letter alpha (α). Which is translated to the letter "**a**" in English. Jesus, of course, is **Alpha**. **Alpha and Omega**.

"**A**" (Alpha) is a word in the King James Bible. And there is something very interesting that happens with the word "**a**" ... connecting it with (1/137), the alpha of physics (the fine structure constant).

There is only 1 mention of "**a**" in the first 7 verses of the KJB (Gen 1:1-7). Besides that 1 mention of "**a**", there are 137 words. The English Ordinal sum of those 137 words = 5903

5903 is the **#777 Prime Number.**
5903 is Additive Prime #389 *because 5903 is Prime and digit sum is Prime: (5+9+0+3) = 17 and 17 is Prime.*
389 is Prime #77

Which means the first 7 verses of the Bible, except for 1 **Alpha**, contain 137 words with an English Ordinal Value of **Prime #777**

The First 7 verses of the KJB	
Words	English Ordinal Value
1 mention of **Alpha ("a")**	**= 1**
137 other words	= 5903 **(Prime #777)**

The other interesting thing about that single mention of Alpha letter "**a**" (Gen 1:6) is that it's the #373 letter of the Bible.

373 is very important in Bible numerics because it's the value in Greek for [λογος] often transliterated as "Logos" and translated as "**Word**".

In the beginning was the <u>Word</u>... John 1:1

373 is the difference between the Greek and English values of **JESUS.**

Ιησους (Greek Standard)	**JESUS** (English Standard)	**Difference** (888 - 515)
888	515	**= 373**

The #373 mention of **Jesus(')** is in the #37 verse of John. (John 1:37)

1 Corinthians 2 is the only chapter of the N.T. that contains 373 words. Both the #37 and #373 words are "**Christ**" and there are no other mentions of Christ in that chapter.

The #373 word spoken directly by Christ is the only mention of "**jot**" in the Bible. **For verily I say unto you, Till heaven and earth pass, one <u>jot</u> or one tittle shall in no wise pass from the law, till all be fulfilled.** Matthew 5:18

The 7th day, the **sabbath,** marks the completion of creation.
Sabbath = 137 mentions in the Bible (including the Psalm 92 heading)

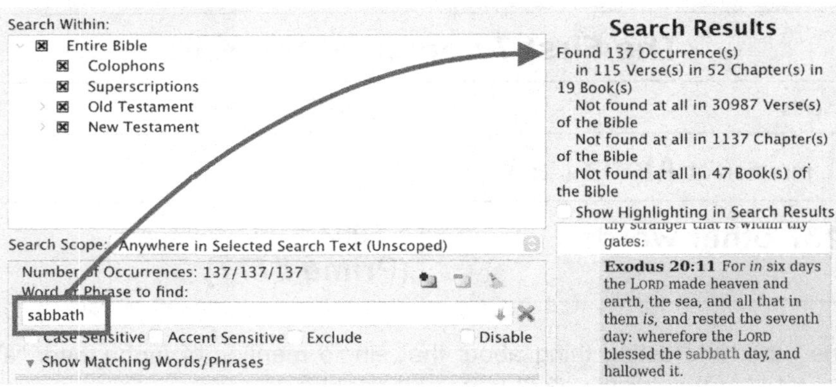

Who created the heaven and the earth, and everything within & without? Physicists didn't know about this number until the early 1900s, when the God of the Bible already had it sealed within the beginning of His book for hundreds of years.

Who do you trust? The words of man or the words of the Creator?

The 153 Fishes: The Signature of the Gospel

Simon Peter saith unto them, I go a fishing... and that night they caught nothing. But when the morning was now come, Jesus stood on the shore: but the disciples knew not that it was Jesus. Then Jesus saith unto them, Children, have ye any meat? They answered him, No. And he said unto them, Cast the net on the right side of the ship, and ye shall find. They cast therefore, and now they were not able to draw it for the multitude of fishes. Therefore that disciple whom Jesus loved saith unto Peter, It is the Lord. Now when Simon Peter heard that it was the Lord, he girt his fisher's coat unto him, (for he was naked,) and did cast himself into the sea. And the other disciples came in a little ship; (for they were not far from land, but as it were two hundred cubits,) dragging the net with fishes. As soon then as they were come to land, they saw a fire of coals there, and fish laid thereon, and bread. Jesus saith unto them, Bring of the fish which ye have now caught. Simon Peter went up, and drew the net to land full of great fishes, an hundred and fifty and three: and for all there were so many, yet was not the net broken. Jesus saith unto them, Come and dine. And none of the disciples durst ask him, Who art thou? knowing that it was the Lord. John 21:3-12

153 is the number of **great fishes** that are caught by Peter and company in the last chapter of the gospels (John 21).

The inevitable question is begged: *why does the Holy Ghost inspire John to record the specific amount of fishes?*

It leaves little to no doubt in the Christian's mind that God has specifically inserted numeric details in the Bible that have some sort of deeper meaning.

And yet the meaning is not revealed in the text.

Despite the wanting interpretation, we need to search nowhere else except the Bible to understand what 153 is pointing to. It's actually quite simple, but the verification behind it is miraculous.

There are only 2 people in the Bible whose names are numerically linked to the number 153.

Those men are **Peter** and **Paul**.

Peter is mentioned in **153** **verses in the KJB**	**Paul** is mentioned in **153** **verses in the KJB**

No other names in the Bible are mentioned in 153 verses, nor is any name in the Bible mentioned 153 times. Only Peter and Paul.

These two men are very important in the Bible. It is **Peter** (who drew the net of 153 fishes) that validates Paul's epistles as scripture.

As also in all his *[Paul's]* **epistles, speaking in them of these things; in which are some things hard to be understood, which they that are unlearned and unstable wrest, as they do also the other scriptures, unto their own destruction.** 2 Peter 3:16

(This is also the 7+7+7 and final mention of **scriptures** in the Bible).

The amount of numeric verifications is unreal. The digits of 153 are found over and over again between **Peter** and **Paul**.

If you look at total mentions (instead of verses), "**Peter**" and "**Paul**" are mentioned a combined 315 times: The digits of 153.

The #315 (and last) mention of **Peter** / **Paul** is in 2 Peter 3:15 which directly precedes the verse verifying Paul's writings as scripture.

Notice the reference: **3:15**, which are the exact digits of 153. Furthermore, the book of 2 Peter, which contains the last mentions of both **Peter** and **Paul**, is exactly **1553 words** in length.

Peter + Paul combined are mentioned **315** **times in the KJB**
Last Mention (#315 of 315) **"Paul" in 2 Peter 3:15**
The book of 2 Peter (which contains the last mention of both **Peter** and **Paul**) has **1553 words**

These digits are even mentioned in the text itself, when directly referring to **Peter** and **Paul**.

In the #(15+3) verse of Galatians, **Paul** talks about meeting **Peter**, and while doing so, mentions "**three**" and "**fifteen**" ...all the digits of 153.

Digits of 315 / 153 in the text (**Paul** meeting **Peter**)
Then after three years I went up to Jerusalem to see Peter, and abode with him fifteen days. Galatians 1:18
3 years / **15** days

But why **Peter** and **Paul**? What do they have to do with each other? How do they relate to the 153 fishes?

The answer is simple: *These are the two men to whom the gospel is committed.*

The 153 fishes are mentioned in the last chapter of the gospels and the allegory of fishing always points back to the gospel... "**Follow me, and I will make you fishers of men.**" Matthew 4:19

And of all people in the Bible, **Peter** and **Paul** (mentioned in 153 verses each, 315 combined mentions, final mention in a 3:15 verse) are specifically the men to whom the gospel was committed.

The gospel of the circumcision (the Jews) was committed unto **Peter** and the gospel of the uncircumcision (the Gentiles) was committed unto **Paul**.

This is clearly stated in Galatians, where **Peter** and **Paul** are mentioned a combined 7 times. (The only book where that happens).

And astonishingly, it is stated in Galatians 2:7, which houses the **#153** mention of **Peter**.

Galatians 2:7 - The signature of the gospel The **#153** mention of **Peter** **reveals the Peter-Paul connection** and **the meaning** of **153**
But contrariwise, when they saw that the gospel of the uncircumcision was committed unto me *[Paul]*, as the gospel of the circumcision was unto Peter; Galatians 2:7
Galatians 2:7 is the #29089 verse of the Bible, which is divisible by 1531

This is 100% MIRACULOUS.

Consider Peter's name... how he is also named **Simon** and **Cephas** throughout the New Testament. If any of those Simon/Cephas mentions were "**Peter**" instead, then this anomaly would not have happened.

Consider Paul's name- that it used to be Saul (mentioned 25 times).

But out of nowhere... in Acts 13- N.T. book #5, chapter 13, (digits of 153), his name changes to **Paul** and never goes back.

Then Saul, (who also is called Paul), filled with the Holy Ghost, set his eyes on him, Acts 13:9 (verse 9 = 1+5+3)

Why didn't his name get switched earlier when he was first converted? There is no explanation in the text. And yet it's perfectly established from that point forward to accommodate exactly 153 verses with **Paul**.

(Side note- if you're fact-checking this with software other than King James Pure Bible Search, and if it tells you **Paul** = 154 verses, then it is counting the colophon of 2 Timothy, which is not a verse. Some programs count colophons as verses because they are not built for specific word counts, and don't know how else to categorize them. The true verse count for **Paul** is 153.)

A second consideration: this pattern works specifically with "**Peter**" and "**Paul**", <u>not</u> including any possessive forms of **Peter<u>'s</u>** (Mat 8:14, John 1:40, 6:8, Acts 12:14) or **Paul<u>'s</u>** (Acts 19:29, 20:37, 21:8, 21:11, 23:16, 25:14).

Just one adjustment to the wording of the scriptures to make any of their mentions possessive (-'s) would throw off the entire counts.

One more sidenote: Some people think it's cherry-picking to exclude **Peter's** and **Paul's** from the counts. No. It would be cherry-picking to use "**Peter**" + "**Paul + Paul's**" but exclude "**Peter's**". It is not cherry-picking to use only standard forms **Peter** + **Paul**. It's consistent- and even more indicative of an intentional pattern. I always look for that consistency when searching for any word or verse counts. Without general consistency across the board, a man could make up whatever patterns he wanted to make up. In the King James Bible, we don't need to cherry-pick to make up patterns. These miraculous things simply exist.

I think I can somewhat relate to Peter in Luke 5:8-9...

When Simon Peter saw it, he fell down at Jesus' knees, saying, Depart from me; for I am a sinful man, O Lord. For he was astonished, and all that were with him, at the draught of the fishes which they had taken: Luke 5:8-9

The middle number of 153 is 77. Again, this points us to "**the gospel**."

The middle of 153 is... **77**	**"the gospel"** is mentioned in **77** **verses in the KJB**
In Galatians... **Paul + Peter** = 7 verses **"the gospel"** = 7 verses (First mention in verse #7 of Gal, Last mention is #(7×7) of the Bible)	
The **#53** mention of **"the gospel"** occurs in the **#53** verse of **Galatians** (Gal 3:8)	
"**the gospel**" in Gal 3:8 is word/phrase **#153** of the chapter	
And the scripture, foreseeing that God would justify the heathen through faith, preached before the gospel unto Abraham, saying, In thee shall all nations be blessed. Galatians 3:8	

Word/phrase #153 of Acts 14: "**they preached the gospel**" in Acts 7+7:7

The #(7×7) mention of "**gospel**" is in the #153 chapter of the N.T. (2 Cor 4) "...**the glorious gospel of Christ...**"
And what verse do we turn to whenever we point to the gospel of Jesus Christ that is for us today?

Surely, you saw this coming!

The gospel of grace begins on…

1 Corinthians 15:3

For I delivered unto you first of all that which I also received, how that Christ died for our sins according to the scriptures; And that he was buried, and that he rose again the third day according to the scriptures:

1 Corinthians 15:3-4

1 Corinthians 15:3 = **153**5 English Reverse Ordinal, and begins on the **#15×3** word of the chapter.

But I certify you, brethren, that the gospel which was preached of me is not after man. For I neither received it of man, neither was I taught it, but by the revelation of Jesus Christ. Galatians 1:11

And how shall they preach, except they be sent? as it is written, How beautiful are the feet of them that preach the gospel of peace, and bring glad tidings of good things! Romans 10:15

And what better confirmation could there be than this…
All appearances of **preach*** = 153 mentions in the KJB

Search Filters: **Entire Bible**		Case Sens	Mentions
Search Phrase 1	**preach**	-	50
Search Phrase 2	**preached**	-	61
Search Phrase 3	**preacher**	-	11
Search Phrase 4	**preachest**	-	1
Search Phrase 5	**preacheth**	-	3
Search Phrase 6	**preaching**	-	27
Total Mentions	**preach*** (in all forms)		**153**

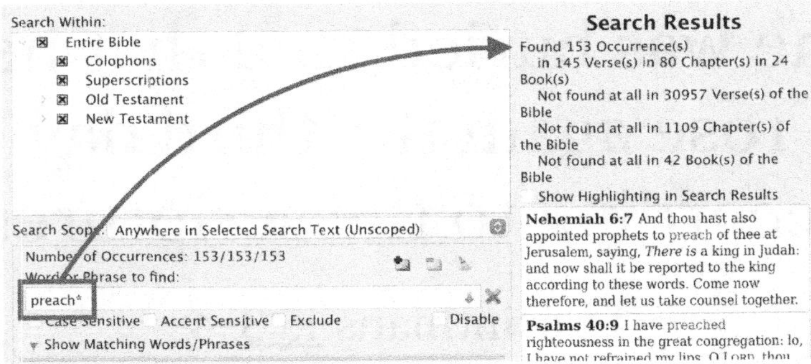

And the scripture, foreseeing that God would justify the heathen through faith, <u>preached</u> before <u>the gospel</u> unto Abraham, saying, In thee shall all nations be blessed. So then they which be of faith are blessed with faithful Abraham.
Galatians 3:8-9

The **SCRIPTURE preached the gospel** unto **Abraham**! What marvelous thing is this?! The book of Genesis did not even exist until Moses penned it nearly half a millennium after Abraham. And yet the scripture preached the gospel unto Abraham!

Christ hath redeemed us from the curse of the law, being made a curse for us: for it is written, Cursed is every one that hangeth on a tree: That the blessing of Abraham might come on the Gentiles through Jesus Christ; that we might receive the promise of the Spirit through faith... Now to Abraham and his seed were the promises made. He saith not, And to seeds, as of many; but as of one, And to thy seed, which is Christ. Galatians 3:13,14,16

The seed of Abraham is Christ, and that seed was directly promised to come from **Abraham**, **Isaac**, **Jacob**, and **Judah**.

The sceptre shall not depart from Judah, nor a lawgiver from between his feet, until Shiloh come; and unto him shall the gathering of the people be. Genesis 49:10

Search Filters: **Entire Bible**		Case Sens	Mentions
Search Phrase 1	**Abraham**	-	231
Search Phrase 2	**Isaac**	-	128
Search Phrase 3	**Jacob**	-	358
Search Phrase 4	**Judah**	-	813
Total Mentions	**Abraham + Isaac + Jacob + Judah**		**1530**

The God of Abraham, and of Isaac, and of Jacob, the God of our fathers, hath glorified his Son Jesus; (Acts 3:13) ... **the Lion of the tribe of Juda** (Rev 5:5)

Abraham begat Isaac; and Isaac begat Jacob; and Jacob begat Judas and his brethren; Matthew 1:2

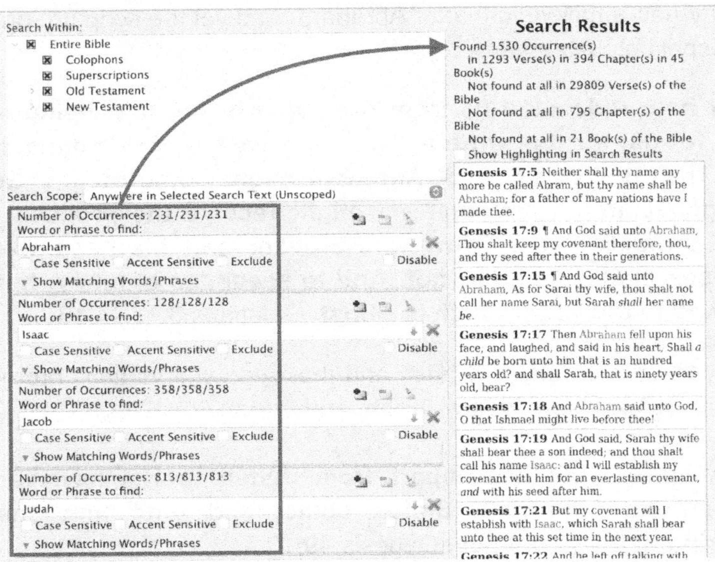

Note: **Judah** is mostly translated as **Judas** & **Juda** in the New Testament, but is translated as **Judah** exactly 1 time (in Hebrews 8:8). Without that single mention of **Judah** in the N.T., the total count would be brought down from 1530 to 1529.

So what do we have… **the gospel** of **Jesus Christ**, **the Son, preached** unto **Abraham,** promised through **Isaac**, **Jacob** and **Judah** in the book of Genesis, and first revealed in the book of Matthew…

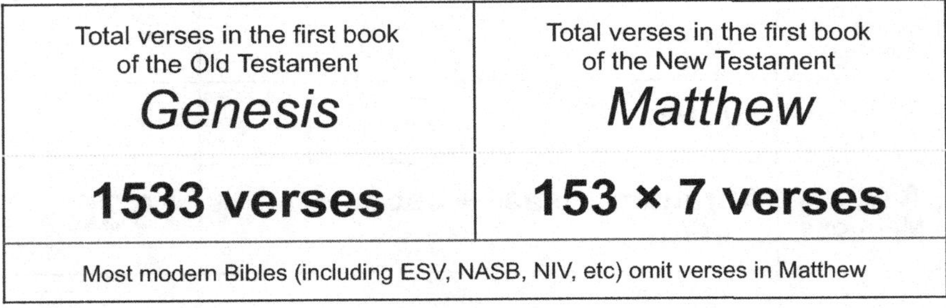

Total verses in the first book of the Old Testament *Genesis*	Total verses in the first book of the New Testament *Matthew*
1533 verses	**153 × 7 verses**
Most modern Bibles (including ESV, NASB, NIV, etc) omit verses in Matthew	

And now, watch, as the chances of randomness drop from practically nothing to almost dead zero.

The very first verse of the gospel of Matthew gives a summarization of all generations of Jesus Christ by claiming genealogy to **David** and **Abraham**. These two are most important of all, because both of them directly received the promise from God that the Christ would come from their seed. And here they are together, in the very first verse of the gospels, the gospel of Matthew.

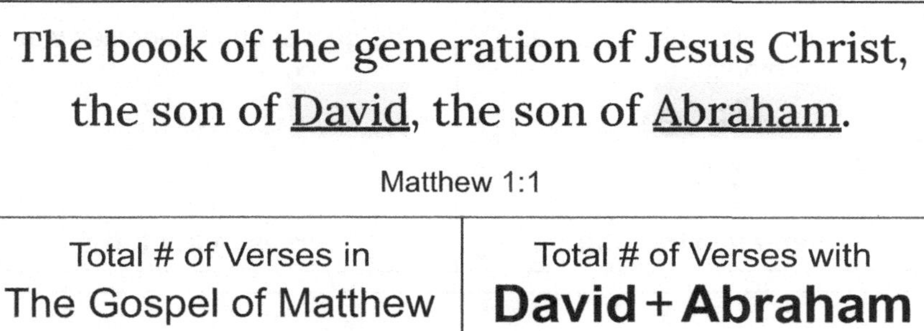
The book of the generation of Jesus Christ, the son of David, the son of Abraham.

Matthew 1:1

Total # of Verses in The Gospel of Matthew	Total # of Verses with **David + Abraham**
153 × 7 verses	**153 × 7 verses**

And let's not forget, Matthew 1 is **777** chapters away from the **#153** chapter of the Bible (Last chapter of *Numbers*)

Lord (Capitalized) + **GOD** (UPPERCASE) are mentioned in **153 × 7 verses**
The Gospel of Matthew contains **153 × 7 verses**
David + **Abraham** (Mat 1:1) are mentioned in **153 × 7 verses**

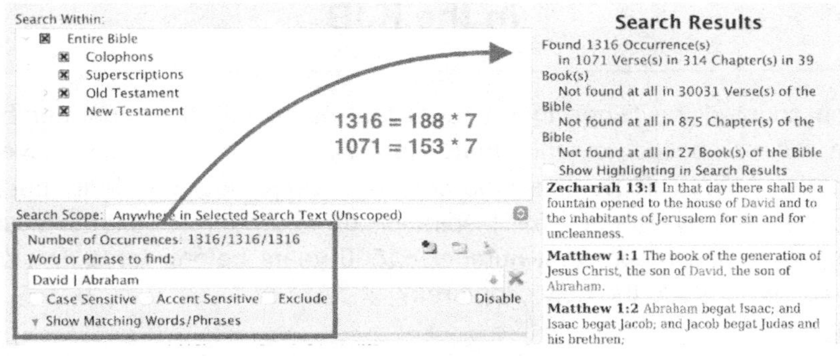

Jesus + **David** + **Abraham** (Mat 1:1) are mentioned in
153 × 13 verses

Jesus is the son of **David** and the son of **Abraham.**
Jesus is **the Son of God.**

The gospel of the Jews was committed to... **Peter** **153** **verses in the KJB**	The gospel of the Gentiles was committed to... **Paul** **153** **verses in the KJB**

The gospel was revealed to Peter and Paul by... **the Son** *(Case-sensitive)*
153 verses **in the KJB**

John counted the fishes they caught that day, memorized that number, and felt compelled to write that exact number in his gospel several decades later. This number was obviously very special to John, but he never says why. Under what inspiration do you think led him to count, memorize, and record that number ~1500 years before verse divisions would be added to the holy scriptures?

He that hath the Son hath life; and he that hath not the Son of God hath not life.

1 John 5:12

After finding these numeric anomalies, I took a deeper look at the context of the 153 fishes passage itself. And it seems beyond any shadow of a doubt to be directly related to **the gospel**. Here is my non-numeric study of the 153 fishes:

Understanding the Context of the 153 fishes

The positional connection. The passage of the 153 fishes takes place in John 21, the last chapter of the gospels.

The chronological connection. The catch of the 153 fishes happens within close proximity of the great commission:

> Mark 16:15
> **Go ye into all the world, and preach the gospel to every creature.**

The fishing connection. The Lord connects fishing with **preaching the gospel**. Right after He begins preaching the gospel at the start of His ministry, He calls Peter and Andrew to become **fishers of men.**

> Mark 1:14-17
> **Now after that John was put in prison, Jesus came into Galilee, preaching the gospel of the kingdom of God, And saying, The time is fulfilled, and the kingdom of God is at hand: repent ye, and believe the gospel. Now as he walked by the sea of Galilee, he saw Simon and Andrew his brother casting a net into the sea: for they were fishers. And Jesus said unto them, Come ye after me, and I will make you to become fishers of men.**

I also noticed how the disciples caught nothing out of their own skill, willpower, or luck. They would try all night, but come up with nothing.

Everything depended *(and continues to depend)* on the word of Christ.

Only at His command do they catch the multitude of the 153 fishes. Just like verse 7 of the #(7×7) chapter of the N.T. (Luke 5:7).

This is an allegory to show us how we are to be "**fishers of men**" - not toiling by our own wisdom and skill, but rather, fully depending on the word of the Lord to tell us when and where to cast the net.

Luke 5:4-8, 10	John 21:3-6
Now when he had left speaking, he said unto Simon, Launch out into the deep, and let down your nets for a draught. And Simon answering said unto him, Master, we have toiled all the night, and have taken nothing: nevertheless at thy word I will let down the net. And when they had this done, they inclosed a great multitude of fishes: and their net brake. And they beckoned unto their partners, which were in the other ship, that they should come and help them. And they came, and filled both the ships, so that they began to sink. When Simon Peter saw it, he fell down at Jesus' knees... And Jesus said unto Simon, Fear not; from henceforth thou shalt catch men.	**Simon Peter saith unto them, I go a fishing. They say unto him, We also go with thee. They went forth, and entered into a ship immediately; and that night they caught nothing. But when the morning was now come, Jesus stood on the shore: but the disciples knew not that it was Jesus. Then Jesus saith unto them, Children, have ye any meat? They answered him, No. And he said unto them, Cast the net on the right side of the ship, and ye shall find. They cast therefore, and now they were not able to draw it for the multitude of fishes.**

The new and better net. Notice how the net breaks the first time. But after Christ's death, blood atonement, and resurrection, the net no longer breaks when the fish (men) are caught.

Luke 5:6	John 21:11
And when they had this done, they inclosed a great multitude of fishes: and their net brake.	**Simon Peter went up, and drew the net to land full of great fishes, an hundred and fifty and three: and for all there were so many, yet was not the net broken.**

The distinction is beautiful and abundantly clear: the net is no longer broken because something has changed from times past: the new testament is now activated and in full effect.

> Ephesians 2:13-17
> **But now in Christ Jesus ye who sometimes were far off are made nigh by the blood of Christ. For he is our peace, who hath made both one, and hath broken down the middle wall of partition between us; Having abolished in his flesh the enmity, even the law of commandments contained in ordinances; for to make in himself of twain one new man, so making peace; And that he might reconcile both unto God in one body by the cross, having slain the enmity thereby: And came and preached peace to you which were afar off, and to them that were nigh.**

The Peter and Paul connection. The gospel is specifically committed unto two men: **Peter** (to the Jews) and **Paul** (to the Gentiles).

> Galatians 2:7-8
> **But contrariwise, when they saw that the gospel of the uncircumcision was committed unto me, as the gospel of the circumcision was unto Peter; (For he that wrought effectually in Peter to the apostleship of the circumcision, the same was mighty in me toward the Gentiles:)**

Peter, who is a fisher by occupation, is the one who initiates the fishing trip in John 21 and is also the one who draws in the net of 153 fishes.

> John 21:3,11
> **Simon Peter saith unto them, I go a fishing... Simon Peter went up, and drew the net to land full of great fishes, an hundred and fifty and three: and for all there were so many, yet was not the net broken.**

Bible Comparison - 153 Fishes

153-Anomaly	KJB	KJB1611	NKJV	ESV	NASB1971	NASB2020	NIV
Verses with **"Peter"**	**153**	153	153	148	152	151	165
Verses with **"Paul"**	**153**	153	152	157	156	169	200
Total Mentions of **Peter + Paul**	**315**	315	314	313	308	331	377
Words in **2 Peter**	**1553**	1554	1510	1549	1561	1572	1547
#mention of **Peter** in Galatians 2:7 (**the gospel** committed unto **Paul / Peter**)	**153**	153	153	149	149	152	168
Verses mentioning **"the gospel"**	77 = **Mid-153**	77 = Mid-153	77 = Mid-153	75	80	78	72
Word/phrase # of Acts 14 "**...they preached the gospel...**"	**153**	153	138	131	147	144	132
N.T. #chapter with the #(7×7) mention of "**gospel**"	**153**	153	157	159	153	157	163
1 Cor 15:3 begins on #word of the chapter	**15×3**	15×3	44	51	46	49	51
All appearances of **preach***	**153**	153	147	95	115	111	107
Total mentions of **Abraham + Isaac + Jacob + Judah**	**1530**	1538	1555	1577	1559	1564	1552
Verses with **David + Abraham**	**153 × 7**	1072	1076	1070	1067	1066	1029
Verses with **David + Abraham + Jesus**	**153 ×13**	1997	1990	1976	1928	2006	2220
Verses with **"the Son"** (case-s)	**153**	7 †	166	150	144	141	138
† In 1611, **the Son** = 7x, **the Sonne** = 110x, **y Sonne** = 2x							

I am the LORD 163

If you have ever read the book of Leviticus, you'll probably recognize this phrase immediately: **I am the LORD.**

Leviticus 19:3 **Ye shall fear every man his mother, and his father, and keep my sabbaths: <u>I am the LORD</u> your God.**

Leviticus 19:4 **Turn ye not unto idols, nor make to yourselves molten gods: <u>I am the LORD</u> your God.**

Leviticus 19:10 **And thou shalt not glean thy vineyard, neither shalt thou gather every grape of thy vineyard; thou shalt leave them for the poor and stranger: <u>I am the LORD</u> your God.**

Leviticus 19:12 **And ye shall not swear by my name falsely, neither shalt thou profane the name of thy God: <u>I am the LORD</u>.**

Leviticus 19:14 **Thou shalt not curse the deaf, nor put a stumblingblock before the blind, but shalt fear thy God: <u>I am the LORD</u>.**

Leviticus 19:16 **Thou shalt not go up and down as a talebearer among thy people: neither shalt thou stand against the blood of thy neighbour: <u>I am the LORD</u>.**

Leviticus 19:18 **Thou shalt not avenge, nor bear any grudge against the children of thy people, but thou shalt love thy neighbour as thyself: <u>I am the LORD</u>.**

Just from these 7 examples, you can see it's a unique phrase, appended onto the end of many of God's commandments. It's almost like a seal or a signature, stamping God's name on the end of a commandment so you remember who exactly gave you this law. A law not from the minds of men, but from Almighty God; JEHOVAH. Because of its unique resemblance to a signature/seal, and its repetitive usage, the total number of mentions could hold some sort of significance.

In total, "**I am the LORD**" is mentioned **163 times** in the KJB.

I am the LORD	**163 mentions** in the Entire Bible
KJB1611 = 163, NKJV = 163, ESV = 187, NASB1971 = 164, NASB2020 = 162 , NIV = 156	

Does 163 have any sort of significance in relation to sealing the Bible? How about the very first 4 words in both English and Hebrew.

Genesis 1:1 English and Hebrew Ordinal A=1, B=2, C=3 ...Z=26				
Word	Ordinal Value	#	Word	Ordinal Value
In	23	1	**בראשית**	76
the	33	2	**ברא**	23
beginning	81	3	**אלהים**	41
God	26	4	**את**	23
Total Value (English Ordinal)	**163**		Total Value (Hebrew Ordinal)	**163**

In the book of Genesis, יְהֹוָה in Hebrew (H3068–Jehovah) is translated **163 times** into the King James.

	**163 mentions** in the book of Genesis **LORD** = 161 mentions **GOD** = 1 mention **Jehovah-jireh** = 1 mention (H3068 + H7200)
H3068 – Jehovah	

Note: GOD is mentioned 2 other times in Genesis (15:2, 15:8), but has a different pronunciation (and Strong's Number) in Hebrew (H3069).

In Revelation, where both the Word (Jesus Christ) as well as the word (God's sayings) are described as **faithful** and **true**.

The Word of God	The word of God
And I saw heaven opened, and behold a white horse; and he that sat upon him was called Faithful and True, and in righteousness he doth judge and make war. Rev 19:11	**And he said unto me, These sayings are faithful and true: and the Lord God of the holy prophets sent his angel to shew unto his servants the things which must shortly be done.** Rev 22:6

faithful + true	**163 mentions** combined in the Entire Bible
KJB1611 = 163, NKJV = 165, ESV = 195, NASB1971 = 163, NASB2020 = 166 , NIV = 234	

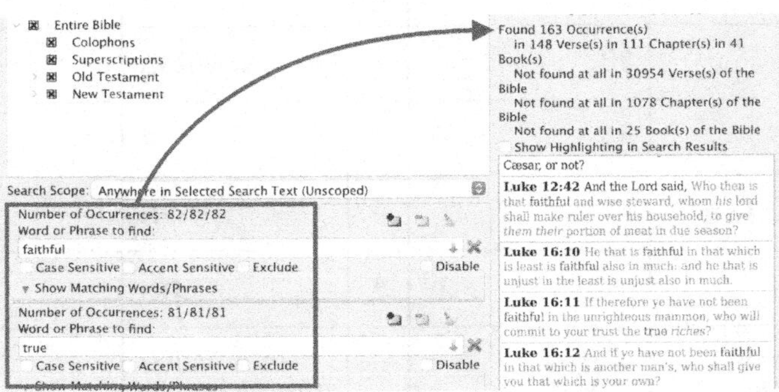

The #66 mention of (**faithful** + **true**) is found in Luke 16:11, and it just so happens that both **faithful** and **true** are both together in that verse.

A total of 7 verses contain **faithful** + **true** in the King James Bible:

1. Jeremiah 42:5 **Then they said to Jeremiah, The LORD be a true and faithful witness between us...**
2. Luke 16:11 **If therefore ye have not been faithful in the unrighteous mammon, who will commit to your trust the true riches?**
3. 1 Peter 5:12 **By Silvanus, a faithful brother unto you, as I suppose, I have written briefly, exhorting, and testifying that this is the true grace of God wherein ye stand.**
4. Revelation 3:14 **...These things saith the Amen, the faithful and true witness, the beginning of the creation of God;**
5. Revelation 19:11 **...and he that sat upon him was called Faithful and True, and in righteousness he doth judge and make war.**
6. Revelation 21:5 **...Write: for these words are true and faithful.**
7. Revelation 22:6 **...These sayings are faithful and true:...**

And a total of (7+7) chapters contain both **faithful** + **true**, starting with the #1611 chapter and ending with the last, Revelation 22.

1. **Nehemiah 9** (The #1611 chapter of the Bible, looped) [v.8,13]
2. **Psalm 119** [v.86,138,160]
3. **Proverbs 14** [v.5,25]
4. **Jeremiah 42** [v.5]
5. **Daniel 6** [v.4,12]
6. **Luke 16** [v.10,11,12]
7. **1 Timothy 3** [v.1,11]
8. **Titus 1** [v.6,9,13]
9. **Hebrews 10** [v.22,23]
10. **1 Peter 5** [v.12]
11. **Revelation 3** [v.7,14]
12. **Revelation 19** [v.2,9,11]
13. **Revelation 21** [v.5]
14. **Revelation 22** [v.6]

The 163 pattern is also verified in Genesis 1:1 in several different ways.

The first 4 words in both Hebrew Ordinal & Hebrew Standard.

Hebrew Ordinal = 163
Hebrew Standard = 1603

Genesis 1:1 Hebrew Ordinal and Standard (If unfamiliar, see Appendix 9)				
Word	Ordinal Value	#	Word	Standard Value
בראשית	76	1	**בראשית**	913
ברא	23	2	**ברא**	203
אלהים	41	3	**אלהים**	86
את	23	4	**את**	401
Total Value (Hebrew Ordinal)	**163**		Total Value (Hebrew Standard)	**1603**

All words up to **God** in English Ordinal, and after **God** in Standard.

Genesis 1:1 English Ordinal and Standard (If unfamiliar, see Appendix 9)				
Word	Ordinal Value	#	Word	Standard Value
In	23	1		
the	33	2		
beginning	81	3		
God	26	4	**God**	71
		5	**created**	308
		6	**the**	213
		7	**heaven**	469
		8	**and**	55
		9	**the**	213
		10	**earth**	304
Total Value (English Ordinal)	**163**		Total Value (English Standard)	**1633**

The mystery of Christ was revealed to Paul (Read Ephesians 3:1-10).

All mentions of **Paul('s)** = **163** mentions in the Bible

the Son (case-sensitive)	**163 mentions** in the Entire Bible
KJB1611 = 7 NKJV = 178 ESV = 161 NASB1971 = 155 NASB2020 = 150 NIV = 147	

Notes on 666

And he causeth all, both small and great, rich and poor, free and bond, to receive a mark in their right hand, or in their foreheads: And that no man might buy or sell, save he that had the mark, or the name of the beast, or the number of his name. Here is wisdom. Let him that hath understanding count the number of the beast: for it is the number of a man; and his number is Six hundred threescore and six. Revelation 13:16-18

When Mr. 666 shows up, every man will have a choice. Either take his mark, or die for the name of Jesus Christ.

The #**666** verse to mention "**Jesus**"
Then Paul answered, What mean ye to weep and to break mine heart? for I am ready not to be bound only, but also to die at Jerusalem for the name of the Lord Jesus. Acts 21:13
This is also the #754 verse of Acts. 754 = [**יהושע המשיח**] **"Jesus Christ"** in Hebrew Standard, and of course, the great tribulation is the time of Jacob's trouble.

The #666 verse is Jesus foretelling the son of perdition's betrayal.

The #**666** verse of the New Testament
Behold, we go up to Jerusalem; and the Son of man shall be betrayed unto the chief priests and unto the scribes, and they shall condemn him to death, Matthew 20:18

The only 666 chapter/verse concatenations of the N.T. are describing those who walk in the same ways as the son of perdition.

Matthew 2**6:66**	John **6:66**
What think ye? They answered and said, He is guilty of death.	**From that time many of his disciples went back, and walked no more with him.**

There is an interesting mathematical phenomenon that occurs in the #666 verse of the Bible. Before you read it, keep this in mind: after Revelation 13:18 (the verse that mentions 666), there are exactly 175 verses left in the scriptures.

Revelation 13:18 + 175 verses = Revelation 22:21

The #**666** verse of the Bible
And these are the days of the years of Abraham's life which he lived, an hundred threescore and fifteen years. Genesis 25:7
175 years = 25×7 Genesis 25:7
Abraham dies, at age 175 in verse #666 Last verse of the Bible minus 175 verses = Revelation 13:18 (666)

This may or may not have prophetic significance. But it's worth looking at. Isaiah 24:5-6 reads, **The earth also is defiled under the inhabitants thereof; because they have transgressed the laws, changed the ordinance, broken the everlasting covenant. Therefore hath the curse devoured the earth, and they that dwell therein are desolate: therefore the inhabitants of the earth are burned, and few men left.**

Read that passage closely. If it's to be taken literally, then the great tribulation will be triggered by the everlasting covenant being broken.

What everlasting covenant is it talking about? I would guess it's the everlasting covenant given to Abraham by God (Genesis 17:7), which would turn out to be permanently established through the blood of Jesus Christ, according to Hebrews 13:20.

Now the God of peace, that brought again from the dead our Lord Jesus, that great shepherd of the sheep, through the blood of the everlasting covenant, Hebrews 13:20

There is no other everlasting covenant mentioned in the New Testament.

If Isaiah 24:5 says the everlasting covenant will be broken, does that mean Christ's blood atonement will be broken to trigger the tribulation?

Now for the hard part.

Here is the #666 verse from Revelation 13:18 (Going backward, since we can only go 175 verses forward)

666 verses away from Revelation 13:18
Now the God of peace, that brought again from the dead our Lord Jesus, that great shepherd of the sheep, <u>through the blood of the everlasting covenant</u>, Hebrews 13:20

This is an hard saying; who can hear it?

If it's true that the antichrist will somehow fulfill Isaiah 24:5 by defiling the blood atonement of Jesus Christ in earth (1 John 5:8), then Revelation 13:18 <u>IS</u> directly correlated with the 175-year-old death of Abraham, since the <u>everlasting covenant</u> was originally given to Abraham.

By the way, these are not just mere speculations based on numeric phenomena. I have a very specific theory about this that I have studied out for several years. I read through the entire Bible and couldn't find anything to stand against it, and I knew nothing about these 666-numeric patterns until over a year after having the theory down on paper.

If you're curious to see how the antichrist <u>might</u> be able to destroy the blood covenant of Jesus Christ in the earth (not in heaven), you can watch the 3.5 hour long Bible Study called "*Abomination of Desolation*" on my YouTube channel *Truth is Christ*. God forbid this theory comes to pass. It's very depressing and disturbing. If you choose to watch, I counsel you to pray to God for wisdom and discernment.

If it does turn out to be true, this mathematical phenomenon in (Genesis 25:7 / Revelation 13:18 / Hebrews 13:20) is perfectly explained by the matching counts. The 666-broken everlasting covenant on earth (Isaiah 24:5-6) would directly correlate with the 175-year-old death of Abraham. It would also explain why "**Holy Ghost**" in Matthew 12:31 (*the blasphemy against the Holy Ghost*) is the #666 word of the chapter. Watch the video for more elaboration.

Do you know what's in Lucifer's heart?

For thou hast said in thine heart, I will ascend into heaven, I will exalt my throne above the stars of God: I will sit also upon the mount of the congregation, in the sides of the north: I will ascend above the heights of the clouds; I will be like the most High. Yet thou shalt be brought down to hell, to the sides of the pit.
Isaiah 14:13-15

What do you think Satan hates most about Jesus Christ?

Is it His death on the cross?
Doubtful.

His blood atonement?
Maybe.

What then? If I were to guess… I would guess Lucifer hates His resurrection from the dead and His ascension to the right hand of the throne of God. This is what Lucifer lusted for himself. ***I will ascend…***

Do you know what modern Bibles do in the gospel of Mark? They cast doubt on its authenticity. Which part? The part where Jesus Christ resurrects and ascends to the right hand of God in heaven.

Here is an ESV:

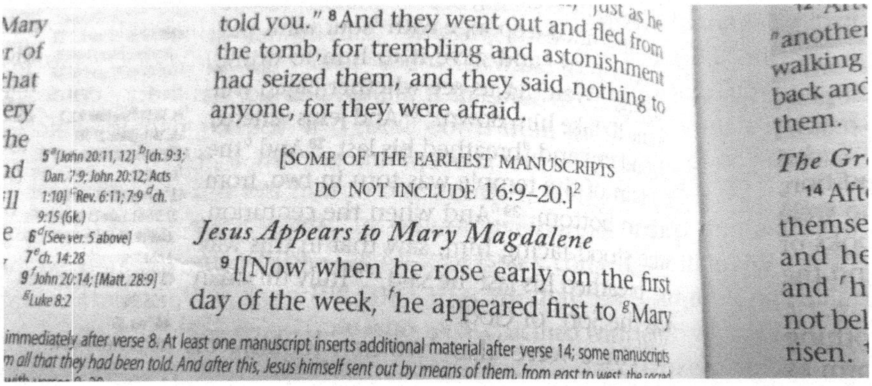

told you." [8]And they went out and fled from
the tomb, for trembling and astonishment
had seized them, and they said nothing to
anyone, for they were afraid.

[SOME OF THE EARLIEST MANUSCRIPTS
DO NOT INCLUDE 16:9–20.][2]

Jesus Appears to Mary Magdalene

[9][[Now when he rose early on the first
day of the week, [f]he appeared first to [g]Mary

5 [a][John 20:11, 12] [b][ch. 9:3; Dan. 7:9; John 20:12; Acts 1:10] [c]Rev. 6:11; 7:9 [d]ch. 9:15 (Gk.)
6 [d][See ver. 5 above]
7 [e]ch. 14:28
9 [f]John 20:14; [Matt. 28:9] [g]Luke 8:2

immediately after verse 8. At least one manuscript inserts additional material after verse 14; some manuscripts
...m all that they had been told. And after this, Jesus himself sent out by means of them, from east to west, the sacred

[a]another
walking
back and
them.

The Gr

[14]Aft
themse
and he
and 'h
not bel
risen.

And here is an NIV:

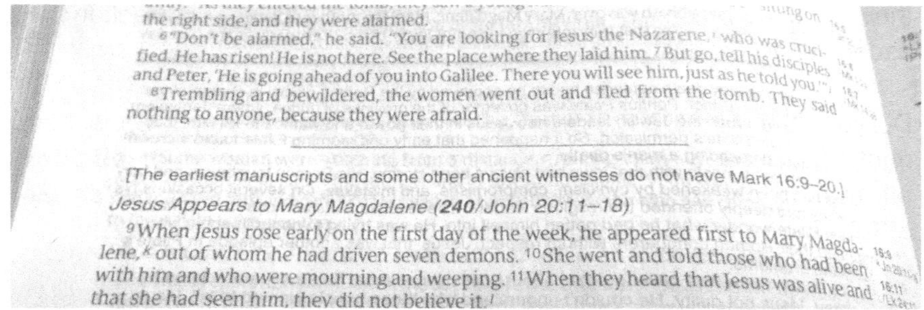

the right side, and they were alarmed.
6 "Don't be alarmed," he said. "You are looking for Jesus the Nazarene, who was crucified. He has risen! He is not here. See the place where they laid him. 7 But go, tell his disciples and Peter, 'He is going ahead of you into Galilee. There you will see him, just as he told you.'"
8 Trembling and bewildered, the women went out and fled from the tomb. They said nothing to anyone, because they were afraid.

[The earliest manuscripts and some other ancient witnesses do not have Mark 16:9–20.]

Jesus Appears to Mary Magdalene (240/John 20:11–18)

9 When Jesus rose early on the first day of the week, he appeared first to Mary Magdalene, out of whom he had driven seven demons. 10 She went and told those who had been with him and who were mourning and weeping. 11 When they heard that Jesus was alive and that she had seen him, they did not believe it.

Let's see how important these verses are, and then take a look at how this all relates to 666.

Mark 16:9-20

9 ¶ Now when Jesus was risen early the first day of the week, he appeared first to Mary Magdalene, out of whom he had cast seven devils.
10 And she went and told them that had been with him, as they mourned and wept.
11 And they, when they had heard that he was alive, and had been seen of her, believed not.
12 ¶ After that he appeared in another form unto two of them, as they walked, and went into the country.
13 And they went and told it unto the residue: neither believed they them.
14 ¶ Afterward he appeared unto the eleven as they sat at meat, and upbraided them with their unbelief and hardness of heart, because they believed not them which had seen him after he was risen.
15 And he said unto them, Go ye into all the world, and preach the gospel to every creature.
16 He that believeth and is baptized shall be saved; but he that believeth not shall be damned.
17 And these signs shall follow them that believe; In my name shall they cast out devils; they shall speak with new tongues;
18 They shall take up serpents; and if they drink any deadly thing, it shall not hurt them; they shall lay hands on the sick, and they shall recover.
19 ¶ So then after the Lord had spoken unto them, he was received up into heaven, and sat on the right hand of God.
20 And they went forth, and preached every where, the Lord working with them, and confirming the word with signs following. Amen.

This is important because the gospel of Mark is the ONLY gospel to specifically state Jesus Christ taking His seat on the right hand of God. Neither Matthew, Luke nor John record this detail.

Without Mark 16:9-20, you have lost the most ancient witness (Mark is the earliest recorded gospel) of Jesus Christ's resurrection and ascension to God's throne.

Do you think Mr. 666 will believe in the ascension of Jesus Christ to the right hand of God as he himself **opposeth and exalteth himself above all that is called God, or that is worshipped; so that he as God sitteth in the temple of God, shewing himself that he is God**...
(2 Thess 2:4)?

I don't think so.

Watch what would happen to the total verse count of Mark when you remove Mark 16:9-20 from the Bible.

If Mark 16:9-20 is not inspired...	
Mark 1	45 verses
Mark 2	28 verses
Mark 3	35 verses
Mark 4	41 verses
Mark 5	43 verses
Mark 6	56 verses
Mark 7	37 verses
Mark 8	38 verses
Mark 9	50 verses
Mark 10	52 verses
Mark 11	33 verses
Mark 12	44 verses
Mark 13	37 verses

Mark 14	72 verses
Mark 15	47 verses
First 15 Chapters of Mark	**658 verses**
Mark 16:1-8	8 verses
Total Verses in Mark if it ends at Mark 16:8 *[Where modern Bibles and scholars suggest it should end]*	**666 verses**
Mark 16:9-20 *[The resurrection and ascension of Jesus Christ to the right hand of God]*	12 verses
Total Verses in Mark	**678 verses**

When your teacher in Bible college tells you the ending of Mark is not inspired, and that no gospel writer was inspired to detail Jesus Christ's ascension to the right hand of God, he is vouching for a 666-verse gospel of Mark *(which will also be taught by somebody else who desires to place his Mark on you)*.

Note: I understand modern Bibles delete other verses in Mark, which makes the count a little bit lower than 666. However, these same modern bibles adhere to the verse numbering standard of the King James Bible. All chapters of Mark, in all modern Bibles, end on the exact # of verses detailed on the table above. While they have empty verses (See Appendix 4), those verse numbers are still counted.

Are you going to ignore this fact and continue using new versions of the Bible that leaven the 16:11 bread? (Mat 6:11, Mat 16:11, John 6:11)

~~If any man have ears to hear, let him hear.~~

Mark 7:16 ESV *(Entire verse is omitted)*

The Word Count in the Text, Jesus 973

The priests: the children of Jedaiah, of the house of Jeshua, nine hundred seventy and three. Nehemiah 7:39

In the KJB, a standard search for **Jesus** (excluding possessive *Jesus'*) is mentioned 973 times.

The word count of the name of **Jesus** with **973** mentions seems to be intentionally included in the text of the Bible itself.

The name **Jedaiah** means "*Jehovah has known*."
The name **Jeshua** is the Hebrew form of **Jesus**. ("*Jehovah's salvation*")

<table>
<tr><td colspan="2">Jesus = 973 mentions in the KJB</td></tr>
<tr><td colspan="2">The priests: the children of <u>Jedaiah</u>, of the house of <u>Jeshua, nine hundred seventy and three</u>.
Nehemiah 7:39</td></tr>
<tr><td>Jedaiah</td><td>Jeshua</td></tr>
<tr><td>Name meaning
Jehovah has known</td><td>Hebrew equivalent of
Jesus</td></tr>
<tr><td colspan="2">KJB1611 = 983 NKJV = 971 ESV = 960 NASB1971 = 911 NASB2020 = 992 NIV = 1264</td></tr>
</table>

Notice how the digits of the verse (Neh 7:39) are the exact digits of 973. If you go 397 verses (digits of 973) backward from Neh 7:39, you'll arrive at Ezra 2:36 **The priests: the children of Jedaiah, of the house of <u>Jeshua, nine hundred seventy and three</u>.**

The conclusion is obvious, isn't it? **The LORD Jehovah has known** how many times the name of **Jesus** would occur in his book thousands of years ahead of schedule.

10,000 - The Last Mention of LORD

And Enoch also, the seventh from Adam, prophesied of these, saying, Behold, the Lord cometh with ten thousands of his saints, To execute judgment upon all, and to convince all that are ungodly among them of all their ungodly deeds which they have ungodly committed, and of all their hard speeches which ungodly sinners have spoken against him. Jude 1:14-15

The last mention of LORD (Uppercase) is found in Revelation as the **Word of God** who returns with 10,000's of his saints.

And he hath on his vesture and on his thigh a name written, KING OF KINGS, AND LORD OF LORDS. Revelation 19:16

And what's significant? This last mention of **LORD** in the King James Bible is the exact #10,000 word of the book of Revelation.

```
 "LORD" is Word/Phrase:
788854 of 790849 of Bible
178573 of 180568 of New Testament
10000 of 11995 of Revelation
438 of 634 of Revelation 19
18 of 20 of Revelation 19:16 [18]
6472 of 6472 of Search Phrase "LORD"
```

And he was clothed with a vesture dipped in blood: and his name is called The Word of God.... And he hath on his vesture and on his thigh a name written, **KING OF KINGS, AND LORD OF LORDS.**

Revelation 19:13,16

The 1109 Code of Matthew 1:1

The book of the generation of Jesus Christ, the son of David, the son of Abraham. Matthew 1:1

This is an expanded version of *The 777 Code of Matthew 1:1* (p. 52), which looked at 5 coinciding keywords of Matthew 1:1 that contain a perfect sum of 777 mentions in the Gospels.

Now we will look at all 7 keywords of Matthew 1:1 in the Gospels.

1. **book**
2. **generation**
3. **Jesus**
4. **Christ**
5. **son**
6. **David**
7. **Abraham**

Search Filters: **Matthew, Mark, Luke, John**		Case Sens	Mentions
Search Phrase 1	**book**	-	8
Search Phrase 2	**generation**	-	32
Search Phrase 3	**Jesus**	-	617
Search Phrase 4	**Christ**	-	60
Search Phrase 5	**son**	-	324
Search Phrase 6	**David**	-	38
Search Phrase 7	**Abraham**	-	30
Total Mentions	**book + generation + Jesus + Christ + son + David + Abraham** *(in the Gospels)*		**1109**
KJB1611 = 1118 NKJV = 1076 ESV = 1057 NASB2020 = 1041 NASB1971 = 1014 NIV = 1345			

1109 is incredibly significant because of its connection with Genesis 1:1 + Matthew 1:1 and "**Lord Jesus Christ**" in English Alphanumerics.

Now then, O LORD God of Israel, let thy word be verified, which thou hast spoken unto thy servant David. 2 Chronicles 6:17

The First Verse of Each Testament English Ordinal (A=1, B=2, C=3... Z=26)	
Genesis 1:1 = **411**	Matthew 1:1 = **698**
In the beginning God created the heaven and the earth.	The book of the generation of Jesus Christ, the son of David, the son of Abraham.
Genesis 1:1 + Matthew 1:1 = 1109	

As a side note, multiplying *English Ordinal* Genesis 1:1 (411) with Matthew 1:1 (698) produces a value that equals 137 × 2094.

411 × 698 = 286,878 = **137 × 2094**

The Significance:

137 = "In the beginning" (see p. 350)
2094 = Genesis 1:1 *English Standard*

Gen 1:1 Ord. (**411**) × **Mat 1:1** Ord. (**698**) =
"**In the beginning**" Ord. (**137**) × **Gen 1:1** Std. (**2094**)

The connection between "**In the beginning**" and the number **2094** (Genesis 1:1 English Standard) is also verified in the KJB. The phrase "**In the beginning**" only shows up 17 times in the Bible, with one of them being word/phrase **#2094** of the book of Ezra. (**...in the beginning of his reign...** Ezra 4:6). That's the only time this phrase shows up in Ezra. Ezra, if you're unaware, is known for preserving the entire Old Testament. I would not doubt this is God's way of verifying to us thousands of years later His inspiration and divine assistance over Ezra's work. God is, and always was sovereign over His perfect and tried word.

So we have **1109** mentions of all 7 of the keywords of Matthew 1:1 in the gospels of Jesus Christ. And we have a perfect sum of 1109 by adding together *English Ordinal* Genesis 1:1 and Matthew 1:1. And we have a verification in Ezra of both *English Ordinal* "**In the beginning**" and Genesis 1:1 *English Standard* (2094) being connected. Now let us look and marvel at the English Standard value of "**Lord Jesus Christ**" which shows up 77+7 times in the KJB.

Lord Jesus Christ *in* English Standard (Same numbering system as Greek and Hebrew numerics used in the Greek T.R. Bible- see appendix 9)																	
L	O	R	D		J	E	S	U	S		C	H	R	I	S	T
30	60	90	4		10	5	100	300	100		3	8	90	9	100	200
Lord = 184					**Jesus** = 515						**Christ** = 410					
Lord Jesus Christ = 1109																

The book of the generation of Jesus Christ, the son of David, the son of Abraham. Matthew 1:1

book + generation + Jesus + Christ + son + David + Abraham
= **1109** mentions in the Gospels.

Genesis 1:1 + Matthew 1:1
= **1109** English Ordinal

"Lord Jesus Christ"
= **1109** English Standard

...he giveth wisdom unto the wise, and knowledge to them that know understanding: He revealeth the deep and secret things...

Daniel 2:21-22

The results in Pure Bible Search:

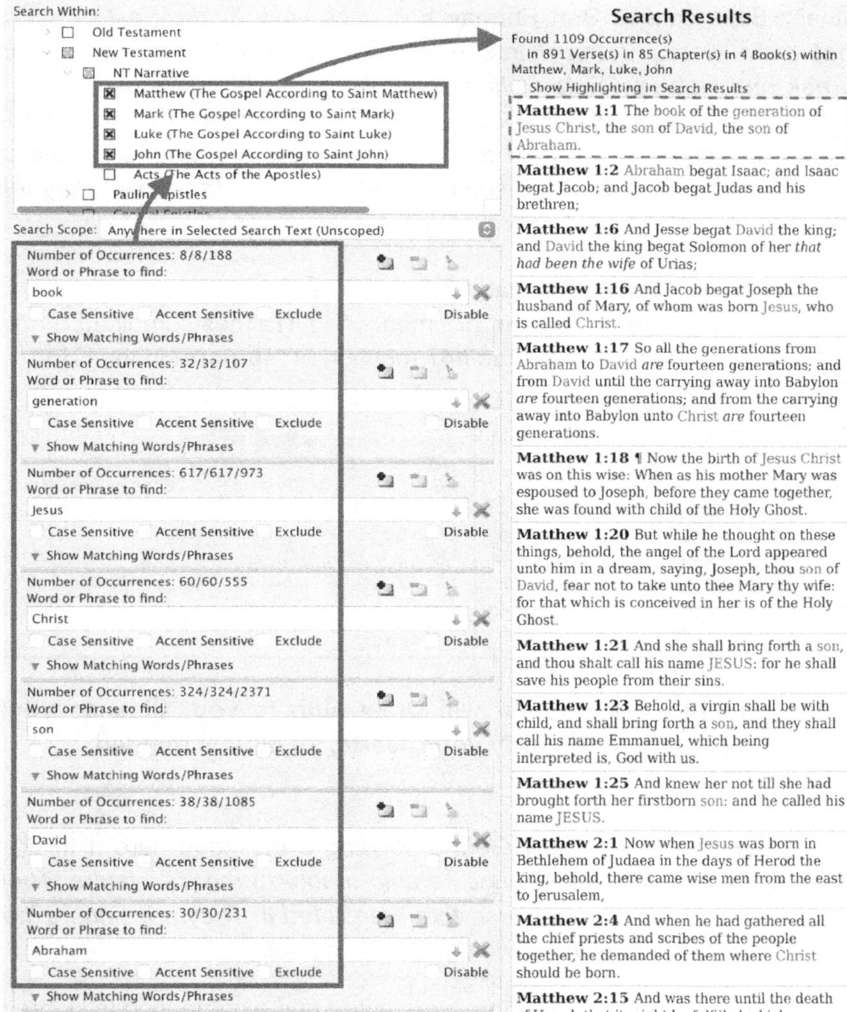

The 47 translators of 1611

Atheist Bible scholar Bart Ehrman has once said, *".. the best guess is that there were 47 translators who were all skilled, highly skilled, in Greek and Hebrew. Today when somebody is highly skilled in Greek... that means we can kind of slosh our way through a Greek text if we have a good dictionary sitting next to us. These guys, including King James, could speak Greek, and did speak Greek to each other when they felt like. And they could read Hebrew like the newspaper..."*

The **1611** King **James** Bible had **47** translators.
The words "**sixteen**" + "**eleven**" are mentioned **47** times combined.
The **#1611** word of **James** is the **#47** mention of "**sinners**" in the KJB.

The **#47** mention of "**sinners**"	"sinners" is Word/Phrase: 770415 of 790849 of Bible 160134 of 180568 of New Testament 1611 of 2304 of James 161 of 369 of James 4 16 of 23 of James 4:8 [16] 47 of 48 of Search Phrase "sinners"
Word **#1611** of the book. (James)	
Word **#161** of the chapter. (James 4)	
Word **#16** of the verse. (James 4:8)	

Draw nigh to God, and he will draw nigh to you. Cleanse your hands, ye sinners; and purify your hearts, ye double minded.
James 4:8

This is just a guess, but if God is sending a message here, I think it would go something like: *Do not worship or idolize the translators. They are not above my word because they translated it. They are sinners that have to be cleansed with My word just like yourself.*

While the King James translators were gifted and experienced in Hebrew and Greek far beyond modern scholarship, God makes it clear who gave them the wisdom, and who gets the glory.

Neither be ye called masters: for one is your Master, even Christ.
Matthew 23:1

The Volume of the Book 390270

The Old Testament is made of 39 books. The New Testament is made of 27 books. There are several patterns in the King James Bible that point directly to this combination of 39/27.

Psalm 40:7 **Then said I, Lo, I come: in the volume of the book it is written of me,**

Who is talking here in this Psalm?

As revealed in Hebrews 10:7-9, **Jesus Christ** is the "**I**" and the "**me**" of Psalm 40:7. **Jesus** comes in "**the volume of the book...**"

And it contains several of His often used phrases:

- **I come**
- **It is written**
- **of me**

Behold, <u>I come</u> quickly: blessed is he that keepeth the sayings of the prophecy of this book.... And, behold, <u>I come</u> quickly; and my reward is with me, to give every man according as his work shall be... He which testifieth these things saith, Surely <u>I come</u> quickly. Amen. Even so, come, Lord Jesus. Revelation 22:7,12,20

But he answered and said, <u>It is written</u>, Man shall not live by bread alone, but by every word that proceedeth out of the mouth of God.... Jesus said unto him, <u>It is written</u> again, Thou shalt not tempt the Lord thy God... Then saith Jesus unto him, Get thee hence, Satan: for <u>it is written</u>, Thou shalt worship the Lord thy God, and him only shalt thou serve. Matthew 4:4,7,10

And the Father himself, which hath sent me, hath borne witness <u>of me</u>. Ye have neither heard his voice at any time, nor seen his shape.... Search the scriptures; for in them ye think ye have eternal life: and they are they which testify <u>of me.</u> ...**For had ye believed Moses, ye would have believed me: for he wrote <u>of me.</u>** John 5:37,39,46

We all know that the New Testament is about **Jesus Christ**. And according to **Jesus**, the Old Testament is all about Him as well. So when Jesus says, "**Lo, I come: in the volume of the book it is written of me**," He is talking about a literal book.

In fact, Webster's 1828 dictionary defines "**volume**" as *A book; a collection of sheets of paper, usually printed or written paper, folded and bound, or covered. A book consisting of sheets once folded, is called a folio, or a folio volume; of sheets twice folded, a quarto; and thus according to the number of leaves in a sheet, it is called an octavo, or a duodecimo. The Scriptures or sacred writings, bound in a single volume, are called the Bible.*

2000 years ago, He came in the volume of the Old Testament. But when He comes again, He comes in the volume of the Old and New Testament. The volume of the book is now the 66-book canon of scripture. Both testaments testify of Jesus Christ.

Now, here is what's interesting (numerically) about Psalm 40:7:

Psalm 40 is the **#66** chapter mentioning "**book**" and the unique phrase in verse 7 "**the volume of the book**" begins on word **#39027**0 of the KJB.

"the volume of the book" is the Bible (39 O.T. / 27 N.T. books)
Then said I, Lo, I come: in the volume of the book it is written of me, Psalm 40:7
#66 chapter of the Bible to mention "**book**"
Word/phrase "**the volume of the book**" begins on word **#39027**0 of the Bible

Furthermore, Psalm 40:7 is **319×27** verses away from Matthew 1:1 where **Jesus Christ** *comes* in the volume of the book. **The book of the generation of Jesus Christ...**

And to top it off, Psalms and Hebrews are exactly 39/27 books apart. (Hebrews 10:7 directly quotes Psalm 40:7).

Psalms **+ 39 books** = Hebrews
Hebrews **+ 27 books** = Psalms (Looping around Revelation to Genesis)

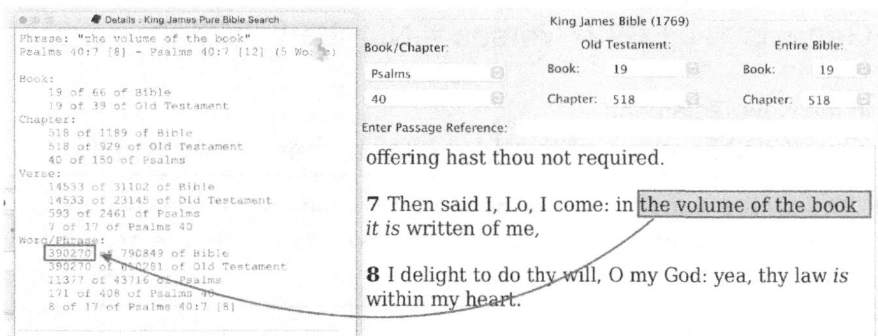

This simple numerical fact could have been found decades ago. It's as easy as counting **one by one** (Ecclesiastes 7:27)… one word at a time throughout the entire King James Bible. And yet it patiently sat dormant, concealed until the age of computers. God chose to wait until His book was the most printed, read, and scrutinized book in world history before unveiling His perfect design within.

Because Christians were persuaded by scholars that *only* the original languages were inspired, they thought it vain to look for any signs of God's hand in the most printed & influential book of all time. If only they stopped putting their trust in the philosophy of men, and would run to God for perfect wisdom.

Heaven and earth shall pass away, but my words shall not pass away. Matthew 24:35

Heaven and earth shall pass away: but my words shall not pass away. Mark 13:31

Heaven and earth shall pass away: but my words shall not pass away. Luke 21:33

O ye of little faith… Matthew 16:8

3927 Holy Bible

In the Old Testament:

Genesis 1:1 + **3927** verses = Numbers 7:77

In the New Testament

The #**3927** verse of the New Testament is Acts 5:12.

And by the hands of the apostles were many signs and wonders wrought among the people; (and they were all with one accord in Solomon's porch. Acts 5:12

Notice who appears in this verse:

Old Testament author **Solomon**	New Testament authors **The apostles**

Consider the details:

- Emphasis is placed on **the hands of the apostles** (The same hands that penned scripture in the New Testament).
- **They were all with one accord** (all in agreement) just like the scriptures; every detail is perfectly placed by the Holy Ghost in unison with the rest of the Bible.
- **In Solomon's porch**, the temple of God, where His presence was in the O.T. This is the #39 and final mention of "**porch**"

But here is what's truly amazing about the #**3927** N.T. verse. What two words are on the cover of 99% of Bibles that have ever been printed?

HOLY	BIBLE
Holy (Capitalized) = **144** mentions	**Bible** ("**book**") = **188** mentions
The **Holy Bible** #(**144 × 188**) verse of the Entire Bible is Acts 5:12 (#**3927** of the New Testament)	

The (**Holy** × **book**) verse of the Bible is the #3927 verse of the N.T.

Holy (Capitalized) = **144** mentions
book ("Bible") = **188** mentions

144 × **188** = 27072

Verse #27072 of the Bible is #3927 of the New Testament

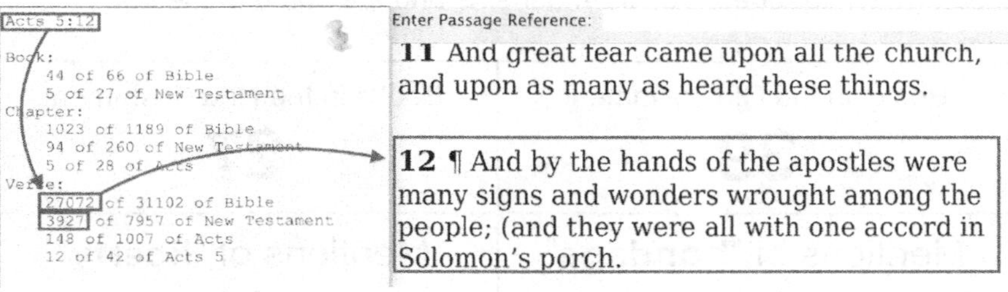

39 Bondage / 27 Liberty

Stand fast therefore in the liberty wherewith Christ hath made us free, and be not entangled again with the yoke of bondage.
Galatians 5:1

In the Bible, the 7-letter words "**liberty**" and "**bondage**" are both representative of the Old and New Testaments. **Bondage** and captivity to sin under the law (O.T.). **Liberty** and freedom in Christ by faith in His blood (N.T.) to redeem us from our sins and the curse of the law.

Books in the Old Testament **39**	Books in the New Testament **27**
Mentions of "**bondage**" **39**	Mentions of "**liberty**" **27**
The word '**bondage**' literally describes the Old Testament Galatians 4:21-25 **Tell me, ye that desire to be under the law, do ye not hear the law? For it is written, that Abraham had two sons, the one by a bondmaid, the other by a freewoman. But he who was of the bondwoman was born after the flesh; but he of the freewoman was by promise. Which things are an allegory: for these are the two covenants; the one from the mount Sinai, which gendereth to bondage, which is Agar. For this Agar is mount Sinai in Arabia, and answereth to Jerusalem which now is, and is in bondage with her children.**	The word '**liberty**' literally describes the New Testament 2 Corinthians 3:6,14-17 **Who also hath made us able ministers of the new testament; not of the letter, but of the spirit: for the letter killeth, but the spirit giveth life... for until this day remaineth the same vail untaken away in the reading of the old testament; which vail is done away in Christ. But even unto this day, when Moses is read, the vail is upon their heart. Nevertheless when it shall turn to the Lord, the vail shall be taken away. Now the Lord is that Spirit: and where the Spirit of the Lord is, there is liberty.**

The whole theme of Galatians is about men trying to bring the church back under the law. If you haven't ever done it, I greatly encourage you to take 30 minutes to read the entire book of Galatians beginning to end.

And that because of false brethren unawares brought in, who came in privily to spy out our <u>liberty</u> which we have in Christ Jesus, that they might bring us into <u>bondage</u>: Galatians 2:4

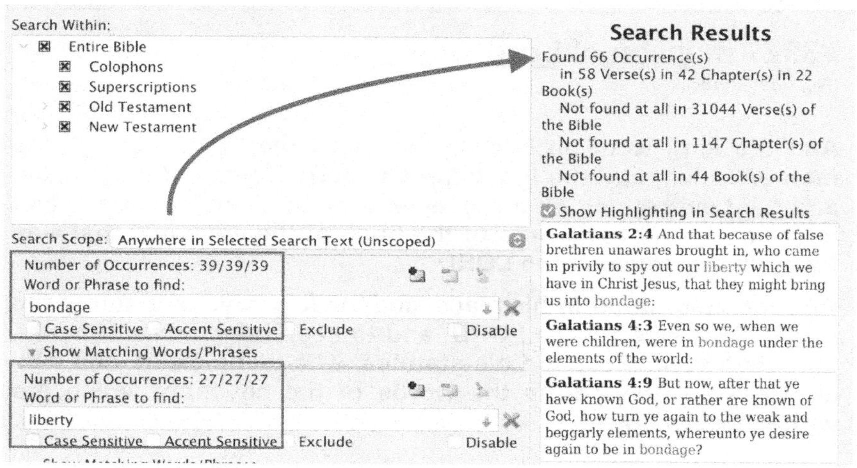

39 mentions of **bondage**

1. Exodus 1:14
2. Exodus 2:23
3. Exodus 2:23 (2x)
4. Exodus 6:5
5. Exodus 6:6
6. Exodus 6:9
7. Exodus 13:3
8. Exodus 13:14
9. Exodus 20:2
10. Deuteronomy 5:6
11. Deuteronomy 6:12
12. Deuteronomy 8:14
13. Deuteronomy 13:5
14. Deuteronomy 13:10
15. Deuteronomy 26:6
16. Joshua 24:17
17. Judges 6:8
18. Ezra 9:8
19. Ezra 9:9
20. Nehemiah 5:5
21. Nehemiah 5:5 (2x)
22. Nehemiah 5:18
23. Nehemiah 9:17
24. Isaiah 14:3
25. John 8:33
26. Acts 7:6
27. Acts 7:7
28. Romans 8:15
29. Romans 8:21
30. 1 Corinthians 7:15
31. 2 Corinthians 11:20
32. Galatians 2:4
33. Galatians 4:3
34. Galatians 4:9
35. Galatians 4:24
36. Galatians 4:25
37. Galatians 5:1
38. Hebrews 2:15
39. 2 Peter 2:19

27 mentions of **liberty**

1. Leviticus 25:10
2. Psalms 119:45
3. Isaiah 61:1
4. Jeremiah 34:8
5. Jeremiah 34:15
6. Jeremiah 34:16
7. Jeremiah 34:17
8. Jeremiah 34:17 (2x)
9. Ezekiel 46:17
10. Luke 4:18
11. Acts 24:23
12. Acts 26:32
13. Acts 27:3
14. Romans 8:21
15. 1 Corinthians 7:39
16. 1 Corinthians 8:9
17. 1 Corinthians 10:29
18. 2 Corinthians 3:17
19. Galatians 2:4
20. Galatians 5:1
21. Galatians 5:13
22. Galatians 5:13 (2x)
23. Hebrews 13:23
24. James 1:25
25. James 2:12
26. 1 Peter 2:16
27. 2 Peter 2:19

3927 mentions of Lord / God

The **#3927** mentions of **Lord**, **God**, and **LORD** all occur within verses that contain powerful descriptions of the Bible. *(There is no #3927 mention of **GOD** (UPPERCASE) because it's only mentioned 310 times)*

#3927 mention of **Lord** *(Not case-sensitive)*
And the king went up into the house of the LORD, and all the men of Judah, and the inhabitants of Jerusalem, and the priests, and the Levites, and all the people, great and small: and he read in their ears all the words of the book of the covenant that was found in the house of the LORD. **And the king stood in his place, and made a covenant before the LORD, to walk after the LORD, and to keep his commandments, and his testimonies, and his statutes, with all his heart, and with all his soul, to perform the words of the covenant which are written in this book.** 2 Chronicles 34:30-31
#3927 mention of **God** *(Not case-sensitive)*
For I through the law am dead to the law, that I might live unto God. Galatians 2:19
#3927 mention of **LORD** *(UPPERCASE)*
The law of the LORD is perfect, converting the soul: the testimony of the LORD is sure, making wise the simple. **The statutes of the LORD are right, rejoicing the heart: the commandment of the LORD is pure, enlightening the eyes.** Psalm 19:7-8

Verses 39 and 27 of the first 66-verse chapter

1 Kings 8 is the first chapter of the Bible to house exactly 66 verses.

The interesting thing is that verse #39 has 39 words and verse #27 has 27 words. And each verse has an OT/NT connection based on the location of Jesus Christ.

1 Kings 8 **66 verses**	
Verse #39	**Verse #27**
39 words	**27 words**
Then hear thou in heaven thy dwelling place, and forgive, and do, and give to every man according to his ways, whose heart thou knowest; (for thou, even thou only, knowest the hearts of all the children of men;) 1 Kings 8:39	**But will God indeed dwell on the earth? behold, the heaven and heaven of heavens cannot contain thee; how much less this house that I have builded?** 1 Kings 8:27
In the Old Testament, God's **dwelling place** was **in heaven**.	In the New Testament, not only was God in heaven, but **God was manifest in the flesh**, to **dwell on the earth** with men, in **the temple of his body**. (1 Tim 3:16, John 2:19-21)

Extra note on the temple of God (which is the context of this passage), it was built in 7 years from the 4th to the 11th year. (1 Kings 6:37-38)

The King James Bible was made in 7 years, from the 4th to 11th year. (1604-1611)

Book and Chapter Equilibrium

There is an amazing mathematical equilibrium formed between the number of chapters and the number of books in the Bible.

The Bible = **1189 chapters** in **39 books** (O.T.) + **27 books** (N.T.)

The number 3927 is 1189 away from 2739, which is the testaments flipped around.

If you were to make a simple excel sheet, you can verify this yourself. Here is an abbreviated version:

1 to **1189** (1189 Chapters)	**3927** to **2739** (39 O.T. / 27 N.T. Books)
1	**3927**
2	3926
3	3925
4	3924
5	3923
6	3922
7	3921
...	...
1183	2745
1184	2744
1185	2743
1186	2742
1187	2741
1188	2740
1189	**2739**

31,102 Verses in the KJB

Are verse divisions inspired by God?

The King James Bible contains 31,102 verses.

Verses were first fully implemented in the Bible in the year **1551** by Robert Estienne (a.k.a. Stephanus).

"In 1551, Robert Estienne (a.k.a. Stephanus) added verse divisions to his fourth edition of the Greek New Testament, while en route between Paris and Lyons, France." [1]

Verse divisions were fully standardized in **1611**.

Many people do not know this, but the King James Bible is the first Bible in existence to use the exact verse system we have today.

The Geneva Bible, which was the first English Bible to use verse divisions, did not use exactly the same verse numbering as the KJB.

This table compares the differences between the Geneva and the KJB.

1602 Geneva Bible vs **1611 King James Bible**	
Luke 15	Geneva = 31 verses
	KJB = 32 verses
Romans 1	Geneva = 31 verses
	KJB = 32 verses
2 Corinthians 13	Geneva = 13 verses
	KJB = 14 verses
Galatians 1	Geneva = 23 verses
	KJB = 24 verses

2 John	Geneva = 12 verses
	KJB = 13 verses
Revelation 12	Geneva = 18 verses
	KJB = 17 verses

The King James Bible became, *and still is*, the final standard when it comes to verse divisions.

That's important to understand.

Even when modern versions delete verses (E.g. Matthew 18:11, Acts 8:37), they keep the verse numbers that were fully established by the King James Bible. They will skip right over the verse: ...8, 9, 10, _, 12, 13... instead of adjusting the verse numbers to fit their corrupted Catholic text. Because they do this, most Christians are still unaware that modern Bibles omit verses of the Bible.

So here's what's incredible about the King James Bible.

The King James Bible contains 31,102 verses.
The middle verses of the Bible are Psalm 103:1-2.

Psalm 103:1-2 contains the exact digits of 31,102.

103:1-2 → 31,102

These two verses are meant to be paired. Both of them start with:

Bless the LORD, O my soul... Psalm 103:1,2

And together, they have T7 words (28) made up of 7 clauses, with the middle clause being:

...bless his holy name. Psalm 103:1

<table>
<tr><th colspan="2">The 7 clauses of the middle verses of the Holy Bible</th></tr>
<tr><td colspan="2">Psalm 103:1-2 (The Middle Verses of the Bible)</td></tr>
<tr><td>1</td><td>Bless the LORD,</td></tr>
<tr><td>2</td><td>O my soul:</td></tr>
<tr><td>3</td><td>and all that is within me,</td></tr>
<tr><td>4</td><td>bless his holy name.</td></tr>
<tr><td>5</td><td>Bless the LORD,</td></tr>
<tr><td>6</td><td>O my soul,</td></tr>
<tr><td>7</td><td>and forget not all his benefits:</td></tr>
<tr><td colspan="2">The first half of the Bible (preceding these verses) contains 7 mentions of “holy name” and 77×7 mentions of “name”
#7 and #8 mentions of “Bless the LORD”
8 is the number of new beginnings. The 2nd half of the Bible begins with the #8 mention of “Bless the LORD” (Ps. 103:2). Which also proceeds the #8 mention of “holy name” in the KJB.</td></tr>
</table>

The first ½ of the Bible concludes with the **#7** mention of **Bless the Lord**
The middle clause of the middle verses is **“bless his holy name.”**
The last ½ of the Bible begins with the **#8** mention of **Bless the Lord**

And here is where it gets very interesting, in relation to verse divisions. Psalm 103:1 is verse #**15551** of the Bible and verse #**1611** of Psalms.

This is the only #1611 verse of any book in the Bible, because Psalms is the longest book. No other book reaches 1611 verses. The next largest book is Genesis with 1533 verses. It just so happens the only #1611 verse of the Bible is the exact halfway verse.

So here we have the halfway verse of the Bible, Psalm 103:1 as verse #15551 of the Bible and #1611 of Psalms, which both point to the years where verse divisions were fully implemented and fully standardized:

1551 → 1611

The Halfway Verse of the Bible Psalm 103:1	
Verse **#15551** of the Bible	Verse **#1611** of Psalms
1551 Verse divisions fully implemented (O.T. & N.T.)	**1611** Verse divisions fully standardized
Bless the LORD, O my soul: and all that is within me, bless his holy name.	
55 letters	**16** words

"...all that is within me..."
#15551 verse of Bible / #1611 verse of Psalms

1. How and when was the Bible divided into chapters and verses? https://bible.org/question/how-and-when-was-bible-divided-chapters-and-verses

At the Name of Jesus

The makeup of the King James Bible.

The King James Bible					
Books		Chapters		Verses	
O.T. 39	N.T. 27	O.T. 929	N.T. 260	O.T. 23,145	N.T. 7957
Total Books **66**		Total Chapters **1189**		Total Verses **31,102**	

The most commonly used name that is equivalent to **Jesus** in the Old Testament is **Joshua**. **Joshua** is also translated as **Jesus** in Acts 7:45 and Hebrews 4:8.

Joshua (Old Testament) = **Jesus** (New Testament)

When you combine both O.T. and N.T. names of **Jesus**, and simply look at His name (not possessive), there is a pattern that gives you the digits of total books, chapters, and verses in the Bible. The entire makeup of the KJB.

Old Testament + New Testament names of **Jesus**			
Joshua + Jesus			
1189 mentions	**1132** verses	**11×23** chapters	**6×6** books
The Bible has **1189** chapters	1132 = digits of 31,102 The Bible has **31,102** verses		The Bible has **66** books

That is astounding and difficult to comprehend. The whole number digits of every single chapter, verse, and book of the Bible, simply with the name of **Jesus** in O.T. + N.T. forms.

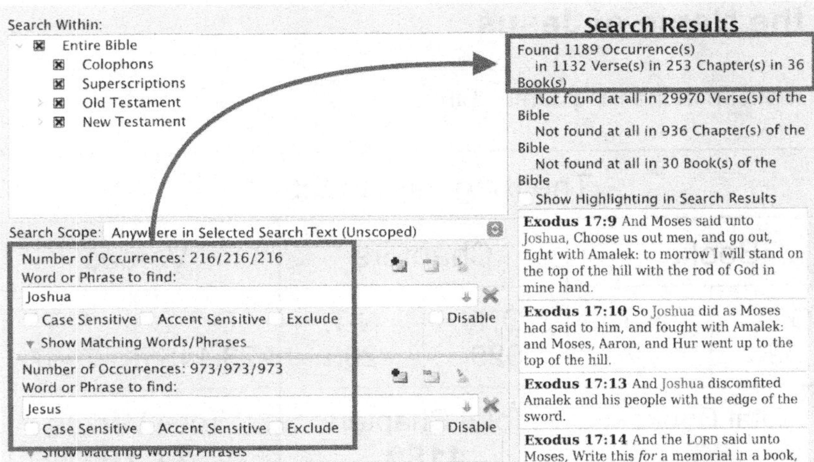

The longest verse of the Bible is Esther 8:9

Curiously, it's about a piece of writing that is sealed by the king's name and translated and distributed to the entire world, and it contains a very unique word: **India**.

There are only two verses in the Bible that contain the word **India**.
Esther **1:1,8:9**

There are **1189** chapters in the Bible.
Bibles are most commonly printed on "**India**" paper.

And who is the one preparing this writing with the king's seal? **Mordecai**.

Mordecai is the (7+7+7) word of the chapter. And this exact mention of **Mordecai** is word #3927 of Esther. (39 OT books / 27 NT books).

On that day did the king Ahasuerus give the house of Haman the Jews' enemy unto Esther the queen. And <u>Mordecai</u> came before the king; for Esther had told what he was unto her. And the king took off his ring, which he had taken from Haman, and gave it unto Mordecai. And Esther set Mordecai over the house of Haman.
Esther 8:1-2

Mordecai is also mentioned in Nehemiah 7:7, which is 7×7 mentions (of "**Mordecai**") away from Esther 8:9, the longest verse of the Bible. His name is sevened in multiple ways, seemingly to verify his significance.

This brings me to one of the most fascinating points in this entire book: The longest verse of the Bible (Esther 8:9) is a type of the Bible. Just like the longest chapter of the Bible (Psalm 119) is entirely about the Bible.

Then were the king's scribes called at that time in the third month, that is, the month Sivan, on the three and twentieth day thereof; and it was written according to all that Mordecai commanded unto the Jews, and to the lieutenants, and the deputies and rulers of the provinces which are from India unto Ethiopia, an hundred twenty and seven provinces, unto every province according to the writing thereof, and unto every people after their language, and to the Jews according to their writing, and according to their language.
Esther 8:9

Why was this not broken up into 2 or 3 smaller verses? I have no idea. But In verses 9-17, several characteristics of the writing match the Bible:

- It is worked on and translated by the king's scribes, (similar to the King James translators) (Esther 8:9)
- It is written for the whole world (Esther 8:9)
- It is published to the whole world (Esther 8:13)
- It brings joy to those serve God (Esther 8:16-17)
- It is feared and converts souls (Esther 8:17)
- It is not written directly by the king but is described as "**the king's commandment**" (Esther 8:17)

All of that is clearly typifying the Holy Bible. And here is the really interesting part as it relates to this book of numeric notes:

- It is sealed with the king's name (Esther 8:8). We have seen over and over and over again in these notes how the King James Bible is sevened/sealed with the name of Jesus Christ.
- It is sealed with the king's ring to prove it is official, uniquely authorized by him, and irreversible. (Esther 8:8)

Here is where it gets interesting.

Longest Chapter of the Bible	**Longest Verse of the Bible**
Psalm **119**	Esther **8:9**
All about God's word	Powerful type of God's word

When we concatenate the digits of the longest chapter and the longest verse, we get **11989.**

Lord + **LORD** + **God** + **GOD** (case sensitive) = **<u>11989</u>** mentions

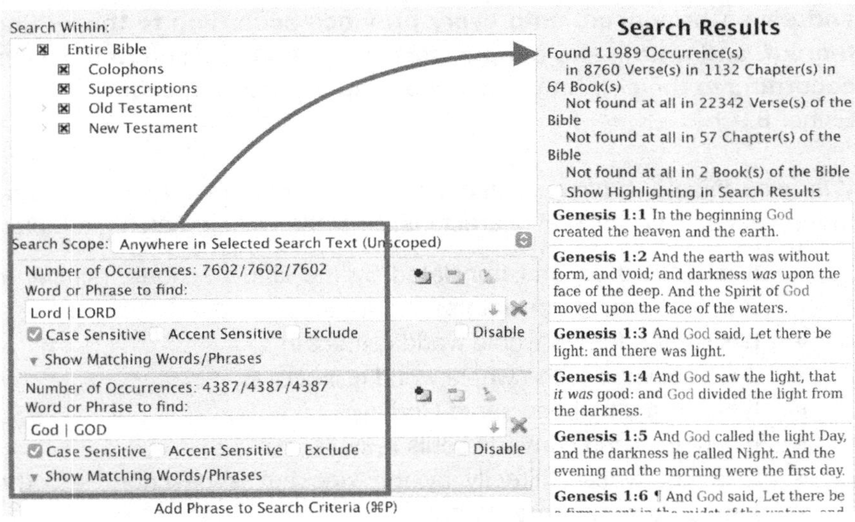

The only 11989 Chapter/Verse concatenation = Psalm 119:89
For ever, O LORD, thy <u>word</u> is settled in heaven.

Psalm 119:89 holds the #218 mention of "**<u>word</u>**" in the Bible
the Father = 218 mentions
the Father + the Word + Holy Ghost (Case-sensitive) = 218 mentions
the Father + the Word + Holy Ghost = 777 mentions

Miraculously, "**word**" in Psalm 119:89 is the #777 mention of a combined search of: **Father + Word + Holy Ghost** *(technically **Father** + **Word** because Holy Ghost does not appear until the N.T.)*

Psalm <u>**119:89**</u> **For ever, O LORD, thy <u>word</u> is settled in heaven.**	"**word**" **#218** mention in the Bible	"**Father**" + "**word**" **#777** mention in the Bible
	the Father + the Word + Holy Ghost (Case-sensitive) = 218 mentions **the Father** (Not case-sensitive) = 218 mentions	**the Father + the Word + Holy Ghost** (Not case-sensitive) = 777 mentions

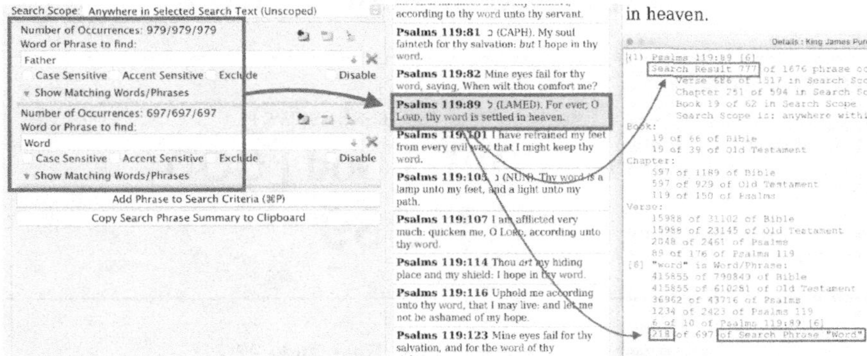

And LAST, but certainly not least… in fact quite the opposite of the least… The LAST MENTION of **Jesus** in the King James Bible is word **#11989** of Revelation.

> That at the name of Jesus every knee should bow, of things in heaven, and things in earth, and things under the earth; And that every tongue should confess that Jesus Christ is Lord, to the glory of God the Father.
>
> Philippians 2:10-11

The KJB Miracle of

11989

Longest Chapter / Longest Verse

Psalm **119** / Esther **8:9**

Both all about God's word

Only **11989** Chapter/Verse Concatenation

Psalm **119:89**

For ever, O LORD, thy word is settled in heaven.

#777 mention of **Father** + **Word**

Total mentions (case-sensitive)

Lord | LORD | God | GOD

= 11989

Last mention of the Bible (Revelation 22:21)

Jesus

= word #

11989

of Revelation

Have not I written to thee excellent things in counsels and knowledge, That I might make thee know the certainty of the words of truth; that thou mightest answer the words of truth to them that send unto thee?

Proverbs 22:20-21

Conclusion

Hundreds of millions of printed King James Bibles around the world, whether Cambridge or Oxford or otherwise, at this very moment, contain most (if not all) of the miracles presented in this little collection of notes. The KJB has long been acknowledged as the most influential book in history, and millions of souls around the world today believe by faith (without knowing any of these miracles) that the King James Bible is God's perfect word without error (which is a sign in itself).

It is simultaneously the most attacked Bible of all time- with scholars and seminaries condemning it (gracefully or harshly) from every direction.

After seeing the level of detail that points to heavenly perfection, how does one reconcile all of these intricate patterns with God's perfect number to random chance? I suppose it will be similar to how the religious leaders of Jesus' day dealt with him; Demonize and attack.

That's okay. Let them say whatever they want! No matter how loud they speak, the patterns in this book will not go away. These miracles EXIST with absolutely no regard to the feelings and feeble opinions of man.

And you are always given a choice: Believe or Don't believe. **But though he had done so many miracles before them, yet they believed not on him:** (John 12:37). **And he marvelled because of their unbelief. And he went round about the villages, teaching.** (Mark 6:6) That's between you and God.

I believe these miracles are brought to us by the Holy Ghost. **Howbeit when he, the Spirit of truth, is come, he will guide you into all truth** (John 16:13)

I believe...

- We can hold in our hands and read the very words of the immortal, eternal, invisible God. The Creator of all things. The King of glory. The Holy One that inhabiteth eternity.
- The entire Bible, from Genesis 1 to Revelation 22, is spiritually alive, faithful and true, and inspired by God.
- The gospel is true. Jesus Christ was crucified and shed his blood without any sin on His record. He died and became a curse for us, but rose again after 3 days, and is alive for evermore.
- Without Jesus Christ, the only begotten Son of God as your personal Saviour, you will die in your sins and face the wrath of God in a literal place of burning and torment.
- There is no other way to the Father. The most humble being in all eternity came down from heaven and perfect glory to be mocked, spit on, and nailed to a tree in your place, to purge you from all your sins, and offer you the free gift of eternal life.

I am the living bread which came down from heaven: if any man eat of this bread, he shall live for ever: and the bread that I will give is my flesh, which I will give for the life of the world.
John 6:51

Jesus Christ, the most influential man in human history, is alive. And He knows your very thoughts as you're reading about Him right now. (John 1:3, 2:25, 16:30)

The word of God, the Holy Bible, knows every secret intention within your heart as you read it. (Heb 4:12)

Now, the man of miracles (Jesus Christ) and the book of miracles (The Holy Bible) have been fully manifest in their due time. (Gal 4:4, Ecc 3:1)

Jesus waited ~4000 years from the time of Adam (when sin first entered this world) to fully reveal Himself as the Word of God. (John 1:14)

The Holy Bible waited roughly ~4000 years from the moment the first word was written (~2000 BC) to be revealed in its final form as we have it today: with every chapter, verse, and word exactly where God foreknew them to be. (Isaiah 28:10-13)

There was once a time when God's word was settled in heaven. And in heaven, indeed, it was, and is, and always will be settled. **For ever, O LORD, thy word is settled in heaven. (**Psalm 119:89)

But now, O natural mind, do you see what the Lord has done? **Thy kingdom come. Thy will be done in earth, as it is in heaven.**
Give us this day our daily bread. (Matthew 6:10-11)

The Word of God, Faithful and True. The **Light.** The **Truth.** (Jesus)
The word of God, faithful and true. The **light.** The **truth.** (God's word)

I am humbled for God to have led me to find all these miraculous things. But this tiny stack of notes has barely touched the surface. We have yet to swim past one foot of the unsearchable ocean of God's wisdom and understanding. May He alone be glorified. **Blessed be the name of God for ever and ever: for wisdom and might are his...** (Daniel 2:20).

Don't glory over these miracles or in any wisdom of mine. Glory that you know He who performed them, and He who gives the wisdom.

Thus saith the LORD, Let not the wise man glory in his wisdom, neither let the mighty man glory in his might, let not the rich man glory in his riches: But let him that glorieth glory in this, that he understandeth and knoweth me, that I am the LORD which exercise lovingkindness, judgment, and righteousness, in the earth: for in these things I delight, saith the LORD. (Jeremiah 9:23-24)

Poor natural mind, I ask one more thing of you: *When Jesus said His words would never pass away, do you think He meant they would still exist in the future, but barely hanging on by a thread? Are God's words in a deteriorated condition today in comparison with the "originals"?*

O ye of little faith...

The Lord Jesus (who performed all those miracles in front of all those people) was rejected, ridiculed, and condemned by those who were supposed to be *the wisest of all.*

But God hath chosen the foolish things of the world to confound the wise; and God hath chosen the weak things of the world to confound the things which are mighty; And base things of the world, and things which are despised, hath God chosen, yea, and things which are not, to bring to nought things that are: That no flesh should glory in his presence. 1 Corinthians 1:27-29

If this Bible is truly displaying miracles of God, shouldn't we expect it to be judged by men of high degree and authority? Shouldn't we expect all of that flesh to cast out the perfect word of God as "imperfect" and "full of error" in comparison to their own privileged understanding of who God is and what God *can* do or *can not* do?

We should absolutely expect, because they absolutely will.

People will spit. People will laugh. People will lord themselves over it.

But that's okay dear brethren, that's okay. My Bible still contains 70×7 + 70×7 mentions of **Jesus**, and 70×7 mentions of **Father** & **Son**, with 7×7×7 of those mentions in the Gospels, and hundreds of other things that defy all logic and probability. Let the scientists, philosophers, and scholars lift their chins and wag their fingers in disbelief. ...**surely the people is grass. The grass withereth, the flower fadeth: but the word of our God shall stand for ever.** Isaiah 40:8

...And this is the word which by the gospel is preached unto you.

1 Peter 1:25

Appendices

Appendix 1 - Timeline of Miracles

The most recognized date/edition of standardization for the King James Bible is the 1769 Blayney Edition.

However, after searching through antique King James Bibles from the 1600s to the 1900s, I've realized the text really wasn't fully settled in 1769. In fact, nobody in modernity uses a 1769 version of the King James Bible. If we did, some of the most incredible patterns in the KJB we find today would not exist. 1769 wasn't a year where many significant miracles appeared either. Most of the important updates in 1769 were already made in 1762. Rather, the 1769 established the 1762 text and made some further modifications and perfections, becoming a gold standard for all future printers.

Am I trying to diminish the 1769? Certainly not. I'm just pointing out facts that I've learned from hard first-hand research as I sorted through all these Bibles (listed on p. 437). The 1769 is still the most recognized landmark in the history of the King James Bible (besides 1611, of course). When somebody says they use the KJB1769, they are simply acknowledging they use the KJB available to us today, knowing there were printing errors and typos in the original 1611. I do not see that as wrong, nor do I see anybody wrong for saying they use the KJB1611. It is all the King James Bible, used by God and steadily tried into its final form that we have today. Don't confuse my words- I believe the King James Bible was always the faithful and true pure word of God since it came out in 1611. On the same token, we can all agree it went through a further, refined purification process to standardize the text until it reached the greatest level of purity as we have it today. This Appendix will visibly demonstrate that process.

As for God, his way is perfect: the word of the LORD is tried: he is a buckler to all those that trust in him. Psalm 18:30

1611 and 1769 are absolutely the most popular years of the KJB recognized by men. There are no other years that are widely recognized as completion dates for the KJB. In fact, they are more like "titles" than "years" of the KJB. Nearly every scholar I've ever read has claimed 1769 as the year of standardization/completion. I even think we can fairly expect God to weave patterns in His word pointing to 1769 because of its title and significance as most people understand it (as seen on pp. 211, 337-338). But when it comes to the actual exact date of completion, the KJB we have today wasn't fully standardized until sometime in the late 19th / early 20th century. And when I say "fully standardized" I am talking about the very fine details such as capitalization and punctuation. Nothing that affects the meaning of the text.

I believe the KJB we have today is just as pure, and even more pure than the KJB of 1611. We have the fully manifested word of God, settled for ~100 years and now available in digital form where every word and every letter has been counted. Any further tampering could be seen as man's attempt of altering word counts with the aid of computers.

And thus, every miracle in the KJB, as it stands with us today, whether it be Oxford or Cambridge (99% of miracles detailed in these notes occur in both modern printings of Oxford and Cambridge and any other printed KJB), can only be accredited to one source: Almighty God.

Here is a timeline/list of the major patterns/anomalies detailed in this book, to see when they first appeared in the text of the KJB. I hope it blesses you to see God's hand moving over the course of decades and centuries to give us something that, I believe, should be the most widely esteemed thing in the entire world. Besides the miracles of Jesus Christ, I can't think of anything more comparable to what we find in the most influential and printed book of human history.

Timeline of Miracles

Years when patterns first appeared and began to be established

Note: Column 1 should not be treated as definitive, but rather as the earliest dates that I was able to verify (I checked most of them firsthand in antique King James Bibles- listed at the end of this appendix on p. 437). Some of the miracles may have appeared in earlier editions that I was not able to verify. Many of the miracles would also settle into place over the course of several years. Column 1 simply represents the earliest year that I could verify when that settling process began to take place (with the exception of the year 1611- in which case the pattern has always existed in the King James Bible).

✷ denotes a miracle that existed originally in the 1611, and then changed, but ended up with the same count as 1611

In KJB since…	Miracle	Causation / Notes	Page #
1611	**7×7** words spoken by **God** in **Matthew 1**	The O.T. counterpart (Genesis 1 = 7×7×7 words) was standardized c. 1762.	45
1611	**Jesus** is the **#7** word from beginning and end of the N.T.		47
1611	**Jesus** appears **77%** through the Bible (by word count)		49
1611	**#(77+70)** mention of **book** in Matthew 1:1		50
1611 ✷	**Amen** (Capitalized) **77** mentions	In 1611, there was actually 1 missed mention of **Amen** in Ephesians 6:24 (printing error), but 1 extra capitalized mention of **Amen** in Numbers 5:22. This kept the total at 77. Then, around 1617, the missing **Amen** was added into Ephesians 6:24 and the second **Amen** of Numbers 5:22 was lowercased to **amen** circa 1637, restoring the total count to 77.	54
1611	**Jesus + heaven** when in the same verse, **7×7** mentions (**#7** words from beginning and end of Bible)		58
1611	Deuteronomy **16:11** contains the **#1611** mention of **LORD** (word **#7** of verse) and the **#(7×7)** mention of **his name**		61
1611	The first verse of Isaiah 49 = **(7×7)** (Jesus speaking) contains the **#(7×7)** mention of **my name**	*No longer detailed in this book.*	-
1611	**777+777** appearances of **Jesus*** + **Christ*** (by person / title)	In 1611, spelling/punctuation was different but the pattern was present *Jesus = Iesus / Iesvs* *Jesus' = Iesus* *Christ's = Christs / Christes*	66
1611	**777+777** mentions of **Jesus(')** + **Christ('s)** (by name / title)	See above ^	67

In KJB since...	Miracle	Causation / Notes	Page #
1611	**7×7×7×7** appearances of **Moses* + Jesus* + Christ*** in verse text	Spelling was standardized in 1619 but word counts were the same **Moyses → Moses** (1 Cor 9:9) **Moyses → Moses** (1 Cor 10:2) circa 1619	70
1611	**(70×7)+(70×7)** mentions of **Jesus(')**	See above ^	73
1611 ✷	**(70×7)+(70×7)** words in Genesis 1 + Malachi 4 (first and last chapters of the O.T.)	Gen 1 KJB1611 = 799 words Mal 4 KJB1611 = 181 words KJB1611 Total = 980 = (70×7)+(70×7) Gen 1 KJB = 797 words Mal 4 KJB = 183 words KJB Total = 980 = (70×7)+(70×7)	73
1611	**(70×7)** mentions of **Jesus(')** in both EVEN and ODD books		75
1611	**7** books mention **Jesus(')** in multiples of **7,** starting with Ephesians (book **#7×7** of the Bible)		76
1611	First sentence spoken by **Jesus** is **7** words, **7+7+7** letters (Luke 2:**49**) (chronologically, age 12)	Remainder of pattern (The 7×7 letter of Jesus' first words- F̲ather) completed circa 1637	100
1611	**I + Come** (Genesis, Revelation) = **777** mentions		103
1611	**7** mentions of **Lord + Jesus** in the last chapter of the Bible		117
1611	Word/phrase "**Alpha and Omega**" begins on word **7×7×7** of Revelation 22		119
1611	**Jesus Christ** = 7 mentions in Revelation		122
1611	**Father + Word + Holy Ghost + God** = **777** mentions in EVEN books of the N.T.		138
1611	**Jesus + Christ + Messias + the Father + the Word + the Holy Ghost** (Case-sensitive) = **777** mentions in the Gospels (Godhead Bodily, Combination B)	Exact capitalization of **Holy Ghost** would first appear circa 1762, but the word count would always remain the same. **holy Ghost → Holy Ghost** (all mentions) circa 1762	150
1611	**Son + God** = **777** chapters in the Old Testament	Spelling standardization of **sonne → son** would appear later, but the pattern (**Sonne + God**) was still present in 1611.	169
1611	**God** = **77+77** mentions in Matthew + Revelation		174

In KJB since...	Miracle	Causation / Notes	Page #
1611	**God + Almighty** = **7×7×7** mentions in Genesis + Revelation	Spelling would be standardized later but the word counts were present in 1611 **Almightie → Almighty** circa 1637-1722	179
1611	**God + Jesus** = **7×7×7** mentions in Genesis + Revelation	Spelling would be standardized in the first King James Bible printed at Cambridge (1629) where the letter "**J**" was first used in a Bible, but the word counts were present in 1611	180
1611	In Revelation only, **God** & **Jesus** = **#7** words from beginning and end of book **God** & **Jesus,** when mentioned in the same chapter = **7** chapters **God** & **Jesus,** when mentioned in the same verse = **7** verses	Spelling would be standardized in the first King James Bible printed at Cambridge (1629) where the letter "**J**" was first used in a Bible, but the same counts were present in 1611	181
1611	All verses mentioning **Godhead** = **77** total words		184
1611	**7** mentions of **the mighty God**, with first mention in the **7×7** chapter (Gen 49) and the last mention in the **777** chapter (Jer 32), with sum of the **7** verse numbers equaling **77**	Spelling would be standardized later but the word counts were present in 1611 **mightie → mighty** circa 1637-1722	185
1611	**#777** mention of **Jesus(')** is in same verse as **#77** mention of **Holy Ghost** (2 Cor 13:14) (excluding antimentions)		187
1611	Exactly **77** appearances of **Jesus Christ* + Christ Jesus*** in the first **7** books of the N.T.- with the last mention in the last verse of book **#7**		190
1611	**(7×7)+(7×7)+(7×7)** chapters contain both **Jesus** and **Christ** (excluding antimentions)		51
1611	Exactly **7** chapters mention **Jesus** in exactly **7** verses, with the sum of chapter numbers equating **7×7**		194
1611	Jesus refers to himself as "**sent**" by God **7×7** times in the Gospels. **Jesus Christ** and **sent** are both mentioned **T7×7** times in the verse text of the N.T.		197-201
1611	**Moses** = **777+70** mentions **Elijah/Elias** = **7×7+7×7** mentions	Spelling was standardized in 1637 but word counts were the same **Moyses → Moses** (1 Cor 9:9) **Moyses → Moses** (1 Cor 10:2) circa 1619 **Eliiah → Elijah** (55 mentions) circa 1629	207

In KJB since…	Miracle	Causation / Notes	Page #
		The letter "j" was used in 14 mentions of **Elijah** in 1611 even though the letter "j" would not enter the BIble entirely until 1629. **Elijah** (with a "j") in 1611 (2 Kings 1:15, 2:1,2,4,6,8,9,11,13,14,15, 9:26, 10:10) All other appearances of "j" in 1611: **Iehouah-ijreh** (Gen 22:14) **Aijalon** (Josh 21:24) **Abijam** (1 Kings 14:31) **Ahijah** (2 Chron 10:15) **Urijah** (Neh 8:4, Jer 26:20,21,23) **Hodijah** (Neh 8:7) **Abijah** (Neh 12:17) **Aijeleth** (Psalm 22 Superscription) **Baijth** (Isaiah 15:2) **Irijah** (Jer 37:13,14) **Tobijah** (Zech 6:10,14)	
1611	Word/phrase **"the LORD"** in Judges 7:20 is word **#777** of the **#7** chapter of the **#7** book (Judges **7**) It's located within the phrase **"The sword of the LORD"** and in the #1769 verse to mention "**the Lord**"		211
1611	**#77** mention of **sabbath** (excl Psalm SS) is the first mention of **sabbath** in the N.T. and in the same passage where Jesus recalls verse **#7777** of the Bible		221
1611	"**G-O-D**" **7-letter** gap-ELS in the very beginning of the Bible (Genesis 1:1)		228
1611 ✷	**7777** sum of words in Genesis and Revelation that start with "**A**" or contain a "**Z**"	Despite multiple updates until the KJB today, the 1611 contained the total sum of 7777 The KJB1611: Words starting with "A" = 7676 words Words containing a "Z" = 101 words The KJB today: Words starting with "A" = 7674 words Words containing a "Z" = 103 words "A" words gained since 1611 Total = **(+5)** **Emorite → Amorite** (Gen 10:16) **thing, → thing <u>also</u>,** (Gen 19:21) **Churches in Asia → churches which <u>are</u> in Asia** (Rev 1:4) **Blessing, honour, glory, → Blessing, <u>and</u> honour, <u>and</u> glory,** (Rev 5:13) "A" words lost since 1611 Total = **(-7)** **Kirtiath arba → Kirjath–arba** (Gen 23:2) **Padan Aram → Padan–aram** (Gen 25:20)	240

In KJB since…	Miracle	Causation / Notes	Page #
		Padan Aram → **Padan–aram** (Gen 28:2) **Padan Aram** → **Padan–aram** (Gen 31:18) **Padan Aram** → **Padan–aram** (Gen 33:18) **Padan Aram** → **Padan–aram** (Gen 35:9) **Padan Aram** → **Padan–aram** (Gen 35:26) "Z" words gained since 1611 Total = **(+2)** **hasel** → **hazel** (Gen 30:37) **Topas** → **topaz** (Rev 21:20) "Z" words lost since 1611 Total = **(0)**	
1611	In the book of Numbers, there are exactly **7×7×7** verses mentioning **"The LORD"**		272
1611	**Jesus Christ** first appears **777** chapters after the book of Numbers		274
1611	**passover* = 77** total mentions with **7×7** in the O.T. and **T7** in the N.T.		276
1611	**passover** + **lamb** = **77** mentions in **70** verses in the first 4 books of the O.T. (shadowing the 4 gospels)	Was spelled "**lambe**" in 1611	278
1611	**7** mentions in the KJB of **"his love"** with the first mention in **Deut 7:7**	Was spelled "**his loue**" in 1611	282
1611	**7×7** mentions of **love** (lowercase) in the Gospels	Was spelled "**loue**" in 1611	282
1611	**777** verses contain **love** and/or **Christ**	Was spelled "**loue**" in 1611	283
1611	**7** verses in the N.T. contain both **begotten** and **Son** (Capitalized)	Was spelled "**Sonne**" in 1611	285
1611	**7** mentions of **"the son of David"** in the New Testament (the first title of Jesus Christ in Matthew 1:1)	Was spelled "**the sonne of Dauid**" in 1611	286
1611	**7** mentions of **"the Son of God"** in Matthew, the first book of the N.T.	Was spelled "**the Sonne of God**" in 1611 (not always capitalized)	287
1611	**7×7** mentions of **word of God**		288
1611	**7** mentions of **the old testament + the new testament**		288
1611	**7+7+7** mentions of **scriptures**		288
1611	**77** mentions of **"it is written"** (excluding antimentions)		291
1611	**7+7+7** mentions of **gospel** in the historical N.T. books (Matthew-Acts) **70** mentions of **gospel** in the signed Pauline Epistles (Romans-Philemon)		292

In KJB since…	Miracle	Causation / Notes	Page #
1611	Only verses to mention the phrase **Holy, holy, holy** (Is 6:3 & Rev 4:8) are verse #17773 and #30777 of the Bible		293
1611	Both #7 mention of **thy work** and #7 mention of **thy works** are in the Sabbath Psalm (Psalm 92)	Was spelled "**thy worke**" / "**thy workes**" in 1611	298
1611	**7+7+7** mentions of **ended** **7+7+7** mentions of **rested** (the exact words describing God on the sabbath day in Gen 2:2)		299, 302
1611	The **7×7×7** verse of the N.T. (Matthew 11:28) contains the first mention of **rest** in the N.T. (proceeding **77+77+77** mentions of **rest** in the O.T.)		303
1611	**7×7** mentions of **most High**	A few times spelled "**most hie**" in 1611	306
1611	**777** mentions of **LORD / Lord** in Psalms (Capitalized / UPPERCASE)		304
1611	**7×7×7** words in **Psalm 7**		307
1611	**7×7** mentions of **Blessed** in Psalms (the first word of Psalms) with **7 Psalms** containing **Blessed** in the first verse.		309
1611	**77** mentions of **church** **7+7+7** mentions in Gospels + Acts **7×7** mentions in the Epistles **7** mentions in Revelation (in verse text, excluding colophons)		317
1611	**144** verses/colophons (N.T.) mentioning **city**		323
1611	**144** mentions of **Jerusalem** (N.T.)	Was spelled "**Hierusalem**" or "**Ierusalem**" in 1611	324, 336
1611	**777** verses mentioning **great king + Jerusalem*** (Significance is in Mat 5:35)		324
1611	**77×7** mentions of all person's names in New Testament book titles: **Matthew, Mark, Luke, John('s), Paul('s), Timothy, Titus, Philemon, James, Peter('s), Jude**		326

In KJB since…	Miracle	Causation / Notes	Page #
1611	First word of the Bible (**In**) is mentioned in a verse-sequence of 1,6,11 (Gen 1)		345
1611	**Peter** is mentioned in **153** verses **Paul** is mentioned in **153** verses (Significance is in John 21/Gal 2:7) **#153** mention of **Peter** is in Gal 2:7 "**The gospel**" is mentioned in **77** (**mid-153**) verses	Was sometimes spelled "**the gospell**" or "**the gopel**" in 1611	354, 356, 358
1611	**39** mentions of **bondage** **27** mentions of **liberty** (Correlating with the 39 O.T. books and 27 N.T. books)	Was mostly spelled "**libertie**" in 1611	394
circa 1612	**777** mentions of **Abraham** + **Isaac** + **Jacob** + **swear** (God's sworn/sevened promise to Abraham is passed from Isaac to Jacob in verse **#777** of the Bible)	A printing error was corrected in 1612 to make the count 777. **Abraham** → **Abrahams** (John 8:33) circa 1612 (**Abraham's** in 1762) Spelling that did not affect word counts was standardized in the following instances: **Isahac** → **Isaac** (Mark 12:26) **Isahac** → **Isaac** (Luke 20:37) circa 1619 **Iaakob** → **Iacob** (Psalm 53:6) circa 1619 (**Jacob** circa 1629) **sweare** → **swear** (all mentions) circa 1637	219
circa 1617	**7** mentions of **Love** (Capitalized)	In 1611, there were 3 extra mentions of **Love** (Capitalized) - all within Song of Solomon **Loue** → **loue** (Song 1:2) circa 1612 **Loue** → **loue** (Song 2:10) **Loue** → **loue** (Song 7:6) circa 1617 (Spelling was different but the count based on capitalization was now correct)	281
circa 1617	**7** mentions of **beloved Son** (Case-Sensitive)	In 1611, there were 2 mentions of **beloved Son** that were lowercase **beloued sonne** → **beloued Sonne** (Luke 3:22) circa 1612 **beloued sonne** → **beloued Sonne** (Mat 17:5) circa 1617 (Spelling was different but the count based on capitalization was now correct)	284
circa 1619	**7** mentions of **Father** + **Son** in Revelation	"**Son of man**" in Revelation 14:14 was lowercase in 1611 **sonne** → **Sonne** (Rev 14:14) circa 1619	94

In KJB since...	Miracle	Causation / Notes	Page #
circa 1619	**7×7+7×7** mentions of **the Father + the Holy Ghost** in the Gospels (Father, Capitalized)	Capitalization of **the Father** was standardized by 1619 **the father → the Father** 2x (Mat 11:27) **the father → the Father** (John 5:20) **the father → the Father** 2x (Luke 10:22) **the father → the Father** 2x (John 14:9) **the father → the Father** 3x (John 14:10) circa 1612 **the father → the Father** 2x (John 10:15) **the father → the Father** (John 10:36) circa 1619 Capitalization of **the Holy Ghost** was standardized in 1762 but the word count was not affected **the holy Ghost → the Holy Ghost** **The holy Ghost → The Holy Ghost** (All mentions) circa 1762	205
circa 1619	**T7** mentions of **Lamb** (Capitalized) and **77** mentions of **lamb** (lowercase)	Capitalization standardization **Lambe → lambe** (2 Sam 12:6) **Lambe → lambe** (Acts 8:32) **Lambe → lambe** (1 Pet 1:19) circa 1619 (Spelling was different but the count based on capitalization was now correct)	276
circa 1628	Letter **"F"** in **Father's** is the **7×7** letter spoken by Jesus in gospels (chronological, age 12) (Luke 2:**49**)	Contained extra letters in 1611 **bee → be** (Luke 2:49) circa 1619 **yee → ye** (Luke 2:49) circa 1628	101
circa 1629	First and last verses (Gen 1:1 & Rev 22:21) contain exactly: 17 vowels 27 consonants *(Matching the first and last days of Noah's flood- Gen 7:11, 8:14)*	In 1611, the #7 words from the beginning/end had different spelling-affecting consonant / vowel counts. This pattern first appeared in the first Bible printed at Cambridge. **Heauen → heaven** (Gen 1:1) **Iesus → Jesus** (Rev 22:21) circa 1629	340
circa 1629	Genesis 1:1 = **777** English Reverse Ordinal	Spelling standardization. **Heauen → heaven** (Gen 1:1) circa 1629 See the note on top of the next page regarding the **"&"** symbol- which was sometimes used in Genesis 1:1	238
circa 1630	Sum of vowels and consonants of Gen 1:1 & Rev 22:21 are equivalent to 1 John 5:7	Spelling standardization. **Heauen → heaven** (Gen 1:1) **Iesus → Jesus** (Rev 22:21) circa 1629 **beare → bear** (1 John 5:7) circa 1630	344

In KJB since…	Miracle	Causation / Notes	Page #
circa 1630	"**S-E-V-E-N**" **70**-letter ELS in Genesis 2 when the **LORD** (first mention in KJB) makes the heavens and the earth	Spelling was standardized in Gen 2:4-6a by 1630. The neighboring pattern (*Genesis 1 77-letter ELS*) would appear ~20 years later. **herbe** → **herb** (Gen 2:5) **raine** → **rain** (Gen 2:5) circa 1630 Note: The use of the "**&**" symbol (in place of the word "**and**") was prevalent and would pop up in different places amongst the years. However this symbol is not a letter, and always represented the three-letter word "**and**"	230
circa 1630	**city** = **777** verses in the Bible	There was 1 less verse with **city** in 1611 because it was pluralized (**cities**). It was corrected to **city** by 1630. **cities** → **city** (2 King 18:8) circa 1630	322
circa 1637	First prophecy fulfilled in N.T. (Isaiah **7:14**) starts on word **7×7×7** of Isaiah **7**	Originally two words are now conjoined (in two places) to change overall word count **high way** → **high-way** (Is 7:3) **faint hearted** → **faint-hearted** (Is 7:4) circa 1637 (dashes removed circa 1769)	108
circa 1637	The word **seven** is mentioned in **77** verses (in Genesis and Revelation)	In 1611, there were 79 verses because **sevenfold** was separated into two words. **seuen fold** → **seven-fold** (Gen 4:15) **seuen fold** → **seven-fold** (Gen 4:24) **seuen folde** → **seven-fold** (Gen 4:24) circa 1637 The compound word counts as one word- thus completing the pattern in 1637. Complete standardization (removal of the dash) would occur in 1769 **seven-fold** → **sevenfold** circa 1769	223
circa 1638	**God + Spirit** = 4949 mentions = **707×7**	In 1611, there were 4445 mentions of **God**, and in the KJB today there are 4444. The updated total count is included after each year: **God** (1611) Total Count = 4445 **God** → **Gad** (Jer 49:1) circa 1616, Total Count = 4444 **good** → **God** (Ps 69:32) circa 1617, Total Count = 4445 **LORD** → **LORD thy God** (Deut 26:1) **Sonne** → **Sonne of God** (1 Jn 5:12) circa 1629, Total Count = 4447 **God** → **the LORD** (2 Chron 8:16) **God** → **the LORD** (2 Chron 28:11) **God** → **the LORD** (Is 49:13) circa 1638, Total Count = 4444	140

In KJB since…	Miracle	Causation / Notes	Page #
circa 1638	**70×7** mentions of "**God the Father**" + all other mentions of **God**/**Father** in the Gospels (Capitalized)	Capitalization was fully standardized by 1619 except 1 mention **father** → **Father** (Mat 6:8) **father** → **Father** (Mat 6:14) **father** → **Father** (Mat 6:15) **father** → **Father** 2x (Mat 6:18) **father** → **Father** (Mat 6:26) **father** → **Father** (Mat 6:32) **father** → **Father** 3x (Mat 11:27) **father** → **Father** (Mat 18:14) **father** → **Father** (Mat 18:19) **father** → **Father** (Mat 20:23) **father** → **Father** (Mat 26:39) **father** → **Father** (Mat 26:42) **father** → **Father** (Mark 14:36) **father** → **Father** 2x (Luke 10:21) **father** → **Father** 2x (Luke 10:22) **father** → **Father** (John 5:18) **father** → **Father** (John 5:20) **father** → **Father** (John 10:30) **father** → **Father** 2x (John 14:9) **father** → **Father** 3x (John 14:10) **father** → **Father** (John 15:24) circa 1612 **father** → **Father** (Mat 5:45) **father** → **Father** (Mat 5:48) **father** → **Father** (Mat 6:1) **father** → **Father** (Mat 6:4) **father** → **Father** (Mat 15:13) **father** → **Father** (Mat 16:27) **father** → **Father** (Mat 26:53) **father** → **Father** 2x (John 10:15) **father** → **Father** (John 10:17) **father** → **Father** (John 10:18) **father** → **Father** (John 10:29) **father** → **Father** (John 10:36) **father** → **Father** (John 12:26) **father** → **Father** (John 18:11) circa 1617 **father** → **Father** (Mat 5:16) **father** → **Father** 2x (Mat 6:6) **father** → **Father** (Mat 6:9) **father** → **Father** (Mat 7:21) **father** → **Father** (Mat 13:43) **father** → **Father** (Mat 18:10) **father** → **Father** (Luke 12:30) circa 1619 **father** → **Father** (Mat 23:9) circa 1638 The mention in Mat 23:9 first appeared in a 1638 edition by Robert Barker (the King's Printer), and would not show up until later in Cambridge editions.	206
circa 1638	**Father('s)** (Capitalized) = **7×7** mentions in Matthew + Revelation	In 1611, 31 mentions of **Father** (God) were lowercase. All except 1 were capitalized by 1637. **fathers** → **Father's** (Mat 26:29) circa 1617 See above for **Father** (non-possessive) ^ circa 1612-1638	173

In KJB since…	Miracle	Causation / Notes	Page #
circa 1653	The first verse made up of **77** letters in the Bible contains the first mention of **seven** in the Bible and is made up of **7×7** consonants and **T7** vowels.	In 1611, Gen 5:7 read as follows: **And Seth liued, after he begate Enos, eight hundred and seuen yeeres, and begate sonnes and daughters.** (KJB1611) However, the first mention of **seven** was in Genesis 4:15 in 1611. This lasted until **seuen fold** was conjoined into **seven-fold** circa 1637. This is when the first mention of **seven** was established in Genesis 5:7 (circa 1637) In 1637, Gen 5:7 read as follows: **And Seth lived after he begat Enos eight hundred and seven yeares, and begat sonnes and daughters.** (KJB1637) Only two words needed updated to complete the pattern: **yeares → yeers** circa 1645 (Spelling was different but the count was now correct) **yeers → years** **sonnes → sons** circa 1653	224
circa 1653	"**G-O-D**" **777-letter** gap-ELS in the beginning of the N.T. (Matthew 1:1)	Spelling standardization to many words that would affect the word count including **begate (begat), bin (been), borne (born), fourteene (fourteen), vntill (until), carying (carrying), shee (she), childe (child), publique (publick), hee (he), dreame (dream), feare (fear), sonne (son)** The final two standardizations to take place were: **untill → until** (Mat 1:17) **sonne → son** (Mat 1:20) 1653	229
circa 1653	"**S-E-V-E-N**" **77**-letter ELS in Genesis 1 when God makes man in His own image	Spelling was standardized in Gen 1:25-28 by 1653. The neighboring pattern (*Genesis 2 70-letter ELS*) was already in place (circa 1630). **foule → fowl** (Gen 1:26) **owne → own** (Gen 1:27) **hee → he** 2x (Gen 1:27) circa 1630 **cattell → cattel** (Gen 1:26) (Letter count) circa 1637 (**cattle** circa 1662) **likenesse → likeness** (Gen 1:26) **aire → air** (Gen 1:26) circa 1653 Note: The use of the "**&**" symbol (in place of the word "**and**") was prevalent and would pop up in different places amongst the years. However this symbol is not a letter, and always represented the three-letter word "**and**"	230

In KJB since…	Miracle	Causation / Notes	Page #
circa 1716	**7** mentions of **word** (lowercase) in Genesis **7** mentions of **word** (lowercase) in Revelation	In 1611, there were 7 mentions of **word** (lowercase) in Genesis and 8 mentions of **word** (lowercase) in Revelation because **The Word of God** (Rev 19:13) was lowercase. **word** → **Word** (Rev 19:13) circa 1716 (was also capitalized in 1638 but didn't yet settle into the text)	288
circa 1716	Last chronological sentence spoken by **Jesus** in gospels is **7+7+7+7** words, **(7×7)+(7×7)+7** letters, and **"F"** in **Father** is **77** letters from the end of Jesus' last chronological words (Luke 24:**49**)	Contained extra letters in 1611 **citie** → **city** (Luke 24:49) circa 1619 **Hierusalem** → **Jerusalem** (Luke 24:49) circa 1637 **untill** → **until** (Luke 24:49) circa 1716	100-101
circa 1716	**God** = **7** mentions in Revelation 22, first mention = **#(7+7+7)** word of chapter / **#77** letter of chapter	In 1611, there were 7 mentions of **God** in Rev 22, and the #(7+7+7) word was **God**, but extra letters prevented the count of **God** beginning on the #77 letter **mee** → **me** (Rev 22:1) circa 1612 **cleere** → **clear** (Rev 22:1) circa 1637 **Chrystall** → **crystal** (Rev 22:1) circa 1716	117-118
circa 1716	**God*** in the New Testament (Capitalized/UPPERCASE) **70×7** mentions in Gospels + Acts **777** mentions in Epistles **99** mentions in Revelation	In 1611, Revelation contained 99 mentions. In the Epistles, a fixed printing error in 1629 and capitalization standardization would lead to 777 mentions circa 1637. The 490 mentions in Gospels + Acts would be finalized by at least 1716. (It may have been earlier.) **Sonne** → **Sonne of God** (1 Jn 5:12) circa 1629 **God** → **god** (Acts 7:43) **God** → **god** (Acts 12:22) **God** → **god** (2 Cor 4:4) **Gods** → **gods** (Gal 4:8) circa 1637 **God** → **god** (Acts 28:6) circa 1716	170
circa 1716	**70×7** mentions of **sent** in the Old Testament **70×7 + 70×7** mentions of **Jesus*** in the New Testament	In 1611, "**scent**" was archaically spelled as **sent**. **sent** → **scent** (Job 14:9) **sent** → **scent** (Jer 48:11) **sent** → **scent** (Hos 14:7) circa 1716	202

In KJB since...	Miracle	Causation / Notes	Page #
circa 1716	**In + Amen** (Genesis, Revelation) **777 mentions**	Originally two words that were separated are now conjoined to update the total word count. **in stead → instead** (Gen 2:21,4:25,44:33) **in deede → indeed** (Gen 17:19) circa 1716	55
circa 1716	Psalm 45 = **7×7×7** words The entire Psalm is the Father speaking to the Son, calling Him God (Ps.45:6, Heb 1:8)	Originally two words that were separated are now conjoined to update the total word count. **needle worke → needle-work** (Ps 45:14) circa 1637 (**needlework** circa 1769) **in stead → instead** (Ps 45:16) circa 1716	182
circa 1762	**7×7×7** words spoken by **God** in **Genesis 1**	Originally two words are now conjoined. **it self → itself** (Gen 1:11) circa 1762	45
circa 1762	**Matthew 1:1**, **777** code: **generation** + **Jesus** + **Christ** + **David** + **Abraham** = **777** mentions (in the Gospels)	In 1611, there was one extra mention of **Abraham** due to a printing oversight, which would be corrected in 1612. The rest of the miracle would lay concealed until 1762 when **Jesus'** (possessive) became a separate word from **Jesus**. **Abraham → Abrahams** (John 8:33) circa 1612 (**Abraham's** in 1762) **Jesus → Jesus'** (Mat 15:30) **Jesus → Jesus'** (Mat 27:57) **Jesus → Jesus'** (Luke 5:8) **Jesus → Jesus'** (Luke 8:41) **Jesus → Jesus'** (Luke 10:39) **Jesus → Jesus'** (John 12:9) **Jesus → Jesus'** (John 13:23) **Jesus → Jesus'** (John 13:25) circa 1762	52
circa 1762	The **#7** words from the beginning and the end of the Bible, **heaven** + **Jesus** = **777+777** mentions (Excluding Justus - Col 4:11, See Appendix 7)	Apostrophes were added to possessive nouns, forming separate words. The total count went from 1564 to 1554 in 1762. **Jesus → Jesus'** (Mat 15:30) **Jesus → Jesus'** (Mat 27:57) **Jesus → Jesus'** (Luke 5:8) **Jesus → Jesus'** (Luke 8:41) **Jesus → Jesus'** (Luke 10:39) **Jesus → Jesus'** (John 12:9) **Jesus → Jesus'** (John 13:23) **Jesus → Jesus'** (John 13:25) **Jesus → Jesus'** (2 Cor 4:5) **Jesus → Jesus'** (2 Cor 4:11) circa 1762	57
circa 1762	**1611** mentions of **our Lord + Jesus + Christ** (Case Sensitive)	Apostrophes were added to possessive nouns, forming separate words. **Jesus → Jesus'** (See previous note) circa 1762	63
circa 1762	**Jesus + JESUS + Christ + the Father + the Word + the Holy Ghost** (Case-sensitive) = **777** mentions in the Gospels (Godhead Bodily, Combination A)	In 1611, **the Father** was lowercase in 12 instances in the gospels. All were updated by 1637- possibly earlier. Possessive forms of **Jesus** were updated in 1762 to fully establish the pattern. The updated total count is included after each year:	149

In KJB since...	Miracle	Causation / Notes	Page #
		Total Count in 1611: 773 **the father → the Father** 2x (Mat 11:27) **the father → the Father** 2x (Luke 10:22) **the father → the Father** (John 5:20) **the father → the Father** 2x (John 10:15) **the father → the Father** (John 10:36) **the father → the Father** 2x (John 14:9) **the father → the Father** 2x (John 14:10) circa 1637, Total count: 785 Apostrophes were added to possessive nouns, forming separate words. **Jesus → Jesus'** (Mat 15:30) **Jesus → Jesus'** (Mat 27:57) **Jesus → Jesus'** (Luke 5:8) **Jesus → Jesus'** (Luke 8:41) **Jesus → Jesus'** (Luke 10:39) **Jesus → Jesus'** (John 12:9) **Jesus → Jesus'** (John 13:23) **Jesus → Jesus'** (John 13:25) circa 1762, Total count: 777 Note: **holy Ghost** (1611) was also established in its final form of capitalized **Holy Ghost** circa 1762, but the total number of mentions (90) was always the same.	
circa 1762	**the Father* + Jesus* + Christ + the Holy Ghost** (Case-sensitive) = **777** mentions in the Gospels (Godhead Bodily, Combination C)	In 1611, **the Father** was lowercase in 12 instances in the gospels. And **JESUS** (UPPERCASE) was **Jesus** (Capitalized) in 4 instances. Total Count in 1611: 769 **the father → the Father** 12x circa 1637, Total count: 781 **Jesus → JESUS** (Mat 1:21) **Jesus → JESUS** (Mat 1:25) **Jesus → JESUS** (Luke 1:31) **Jesus → JESUS** (Luke 2:21) circa 1762, Total count: 777 **holy Ghost → Holy Ghost** (all mentions) circa 1762	150
circa 1762	**the Father + Jesus* + Christ + the Holy Ghost** (Case-sensitive) = **777** mentions in the Gospels (Godhead Bodily, Combination D)	See previous note for details ^ **the Father** (Capitalized circa 1637) **JESUS** (UPPERCASE circa 1762)	150
circa 1762	**JESUS** (UPPERCASE) sum of verse numbers = **77+77** At birth = **7×7+7×7** (circa 1762) At death = **7×7+7** (circa 1611)	In 1611, **JESUS** (UPPERCASE) was **Jesus** (Capitalized) in 4 instances. **Jesus → JESUS** (Mat 1:21) **Jesus → JESUS** (Mat 1:25) **Jesus → JESUS** (Luke 1:31) **Jesus → JESUS** (Luke 2:21) circa 1762	167-168
circa 1762	First mention of **LORD** (UPPERCASE) in N.T. is word **#777** of the chapter	In 1611, there were not any UPPERCASE mentions of **LORD** in the gospels. **LORD** was originally **Lord** Changed to **LORD** circa 1637	105

In KJB since...	Miracle	Causation / Notes	Page #
		Also, two words were conjoined (in three places) to change overall word count **high wayes → highways** (Mat 22:9,10) circa 1637 **thy selfe → thyself** (Mat 22:39) circa 1762	
circa 1762	**God + Jesus + Holy Spirit** = **777+777+777** mentions in the N.T.	In 1611, there was one less mention of **God** due to the printer's oversight, and the rest of the miracle fell into place when **Jesus'** (possessive) became a separate word from **Jesus**. **Sonne → Sonne of God** (1 Jn 5:12) circa 1629 **Jesus → Jesus'** (Mat 15:30) **Jesus → Jesus'** (Mat 27:57) **Jesus → Jesus'** (Luke 5:8) **Jesus → Jesus'** (Luke 8:41) **Jesus → Jesus'** (Luke 10:39) **Jesus → Jesus'** (John 12:9) **Jesus → Jesus'** (John 13:23) **Jesus → Jesus'** (John 13:25) **Jesus → Jesus'** (2 Cor 4:5) **Jesus → Jesus'** (2 Cor 4:11) circa 1762	157
circa 1762	**7×7+77** mentions of **Father + Son** in the Epistles (Capitalized, God/Jesus)	By 1637, capitalization of **son** / **Son** / **father** / **Father** was nearly 100% perfected in the Epistles, except for Hebrews 3:6, which would be standardized in 1762: **sonne → Son** (Rom 5:10) **father → Father** (Rom 8:15) **sonne → Son** (Rom 8:29,32) **sonne → Son** (Gal 1:16) **sonne → Son** (Gal 2:20) **sonne → Son** (1 Thess 1:10) **Sonne → son** (Heb 2:6) **Father → father** (Heb 7:10) circa 1637 **Sonne → son** (Heb 3:6) circa 1762	94
circa 1762	**Jesus Christ** = **T7×7** mentions	In 1611, an extra mention of **Jesus Christ** existed, which would later be standardized to **Christ Jesus** **Jesus Christ → Christ Jesus** (Rom 3:24) circa 1762 Avoid the New Cambridge Paragraph Bible, which was a recent attempt to revise the KJB. The editor, David Norton decided to revert **Christ Jesus** in Romans 3:24 back to **Jesus Christ** and unknowingly deleted this miracle that has been settled in the KJB for 250+ years.	96
circa 1762	**the Lord + Jesus* + Christ + Messias** = **777** mentions in the Gospels (Case-sensitive)	in 1611, there were 7 extra mentions of "**the Lord**" (case sensitive) **the Lord → the lord** (Mat 18:27) **the Lord → the lord** (Luke 14:23) **the Lord → the lord** (John 15:20) circa 1637 **the Lord → The Lord** (Mark 12:29) circa 1728	160

In KJB since…	Miracle	Causation / Notes	Page #
		the Lord → the lord (Mat 21:40) **the Lord → the lord** (Mark 12:9) **the Lord → the lord** (Luke 12:37) circa 1762	
circa 1762	**The Lord + the Lord + the Lord's Jesus + Christ + Messias = 777** mentions in the Gospels (Case-sensitive)	Capitalization and possessive updates affected the total count until it was standard in 1762. **the Lord → the lord** (Mat 18:27) **The Lord → The LORD** (Mat 22:44) **The Lord → The LORD** (Mark 12:36) **The Lord → The lord** (Luke 12:46) **the Lord → the lord** (Luke 14:23) **The Lord → The LORD** (Luke 20:42) **the Lord → the lord** (John 15:20) circa 1637 **the Lord → the lord** (Mat 21:40) **the Lords → the Lord's** (Mat 21:42) **The Lord → The lord** (Mat 24:50) **the Lord → the lord** (Mark 12:9) **the Lords → the Lord's** (Mark 12:11) **the Lords → the Lord's** (Luke 2:26) **the Lord → the lord** (Luke 12:37) **Jesus → Jesus'** (Mat 15:30) **Jesus → Jesus'** (Mat 27:57) **Jesus → Jesus'** (Luke 5:8) **Jesus → Jesus'** (Luke 8:41) **Jesus → Jesus'** (Luke 10:39) **Jesus → Jesus'** (John 12:9) **Jesus → Jesus'** (John 13:23) **Jesus → Jesus'** (John 13:25) circa 1762	161
circa 1762	**The Father + the Word + Holy Ghost = 777** mentions	In 1611, spelling variations were different (E.g. "the worde") but including all those spelling variations still produced a sum of 776, short by 1 mention. The #777 mention first appeared when pluralization of "**the words of Jesus**" was dropped to "**the word of Jesus**" in 1762. Interestingly, this is the #7 verse in the N.T. to mention "**the word**" and the ONLY mention in the entire Bible of "**the word of Jesus**". **the words → the word** (Mat 26:75) circa 1762 Note- This change may have occurred sooner than 1762; John Wesley's *Explanatory Notes Upon The New Testament* from 1757 reads "**the word of Jesus**" in Mat 26:75	130
circa 1762	**Jehovah = 7** mentions **Word** (Capitalized) = **7** mentions **Holy Spirit = 7** mentions	In 1611, **holy Spirit** was misspelled as "**holy Sririt**" in Ephesians 4:30, but the word itself was still there. There was 1 mention of **Word** (Capitalized) that would eventually be lowercase (**word**), and 2 proper mentions of **word** (lowercase) that would eventually be capitalized (**Word**). **holy Sririt → holy Spirit** (Eph 4:30) circa 1612 **Word → word** (1 Thess 1:8) circa 1617	140

In KJB since…	Miracle	Causation / Notes	Page #
		word → Word (Rev 19:13) circa 1716 (was also capitalized in 1638 but didn't yet settle into the text) **word → Word** (1 Jn 1:1) circa 1762	
circa 1762	The **#77** mention of **Jesus** is next to the **#7** mention of **Christ** in Matthew 16:16,17	This would first appear when **Jesus'** became a separate word in 1762 and could be counted as a different word. **Jesus → Jesus'** (Mat 15:30) circa 1762	188
circa 1762	**7×7+7×7** mentions of **the Lord** in the Gospels (Capitalized or UPPERCASE)	Capitalization updates affected the total count until it was standard in 1762. **the Lord → the lord** (Mat 18:27) **The Lord → The lord** (Luke 12:46) **the Lord → the lord** (Luke 14:23) **the Lord → the lord** (John 15:20) circa 1637 **the Lord → the lord** (Mat 21:40) **The Lord → The lord** (Mat 24:50) **the Lord → the lord** (Mark 12:9) **the Lord → the lord** (Luke 12:37) circa 1762	204
circa 1762	**Moses** = **77** mentions in the N.T. with the #1 mention as word #**77** of the chapter (Mat 8) #**777** mention of **Moses** is the summarization of the entire O.T. (in John 1:17)	In 1611, **Moses** (also spelled **Moyses**) was mentioned 80 times in the N.T. because there was no punctuation to separate possessive mentions (**Moses'**). The first mention of Moses in the N.T. (Mat 8:4) was word #78 of the chapter until spelling standardization conjoined two words into one. **Moyses → Moses** (1 Cor 9:9) **Moyses → Moses** (1 Cor 10:2) circa 1619 **thy selfe → thyself** (Mat 8:4) **Moses → Moses'** (Mat 23:2) **Moses → Moses'** (John 9:28) **Moses → Moses'** (Heb 10:28) circa 1762	69, 70
circa 1769	**7×7** mentions of all **7**-letter names that are also book titles **Ezekiel + Obadiah + Malachi + Matthew + Hebrews**	In 1611 there was a possessive mention of Hebrews' that wouldn't contain an apostrophe until 1769 **Hebrewes → Hebrews'** (Ex 2:6) circa 1769	325
circa 1769	**Spirit + the water + the blood** = **770** mentions	Standardization changed the word count for **the water** in 3 places until it was settled in 1769 **the water flood → the water-flood** (Ps 69:15) **the water springs → the water-springs** (Ps 107:33) circa 1762 **the water flood → the waterflood** (Ps 69:15) **the water springs → the watersprings** (Ps 107:33) **the water-gate → the water gate** (Neh 8:16) circa 1769	134

In KJB since…	Miracle	Causation / Notes	Page #
circa 1873	**7×7×7** mentions of **Father** + **Son** in the Gospels (Capitalized, God/Jesus)	In older editions of KJBs, "**Son of David**" was lowercase in several places where it's capitalized today. Even in 1769, there were several mentions of **father** and **son** that should have been capitalized as they were in 1762, but the capitalizations were not carried over to Blayney's 1769 Oxford edition. The last standardizations (**son** capitalized to **Son**) were in Matthew 21:9, 21:15, 22:42 & Mark 10:47 - which would be updated in 1873 in the Cambridge Paragraph Bible, and then sometime afterward in the rest of Bibles in the early 20th century. It's unknown if the 1873 Paragraph Bible inspired the editors of the main line of Cambridge Bibles to make these changes, but it definitely seems to be the first to implement these important capitalizations. Note- Some printers still print the 1873 Cambridge Paragraph KJB, but I do not recommend it to anybody. Many important words are changed. While all printed KJBs today have adopted the **Son** capitalizations from 1873, they (rightfully) discarded the corruptions. Capitalized in Paris 1762, but not capitalized in Blayney 1769. **father → Father** (Mat 6:8) **sonne → Son** (Matt 11:19) **father→ Father** (John 20:17) **father → Father** (Mat 23:9) circa 1762 Capitalized post-1769 **sonne → Son** (Mat 9:27) **sonne → Son** (Mat 15:22) **sonne → Son** (Mark 10:48) **sonne → Son** (Mark 12:35) **sonne → Son** (Luke 18:38,39) circa 1778 **sonne → Son** (Mat 21:9,15) **sonne → Son** (Mat 22:42) **sonne → Son** (Mark 10:47) circa 1873	90
circa 1873	**70×7** mentions of **Father** + **Son** in the Bible	See note above on **Father** and **Son** in the Gospels ^ In the Old Testament, there are 5 mentions of **Father** & **Son** in the KJB. **Son** (Ps 2:7) **Son** (Ps 2:12) **Father** (Is 9:6) **Son** (Dan 3:25) **Son** (Dan 7:13) Standardization circa 1762 Not all of them were capitalized in 1611, and over the years, these mentions bounced back and forth continuously between lowercase and capitalized. They were perfected in 1762 & 1769, but there would be deviations over the next couple decades until it settled in the early 19th century. For example, a 1793 Edinburgh	92

In KJB since…	Miracle	Causation / Notes	Page #
		has them perfect but a 1795 Cambridge lowercases **Son** → **son** in Ps 2:7 & 2:12. There were also two additional mentions of **Sonne** (Capitalized) in 1611 that are not capitalized in KJBs today, (Is 7:14 & 9:6). **Sonne** in Isaiah 7:14 would be standardized (**son**) somewhere around 1700, and **Sonne** in Isaiah 9:6 was standardized (**son**) circa 1630. These capitalized mentions in 1611 (Is 7:14, 9:6) could have easily stuck until today because they are both talking directly about Jesus Christ. But for some mysterious reason, they didn't. It's interesting to note that between 1611 and today, there were 7 mentions of **Father** and **Son** (Capitalized) in the O.T., but only 5 remain- which is exactly what is needed to complete the overall pattern/miracle of **70×7** mentions in the entire Bible. Deuteronomy 29:29. Amen.	
circa 1873	**The Father* + The Son* + The Holy Ghost*** = 389 appearances **(Mid-777** and the **#77 Prime)**	See note above on **Father** and **Son** ^	143
circa 1873	**Holy One + Father + Son + Spirit** (All Capitalized) = **777 mentions**	See note above on **Father** and **Son** ^ Note: This pattern is present in almost all Cambridge and Oxford KJBs today, but does not work in the KJB-PCE (Pure Cambridge Edition), which lowercases **Spirit** → **spirit** in Acts 11:12,28 and 1 John 5:8. It also does not work in the Cambridge Emerald text which lowercases "**Spirit of God**" to "**spirit of God**" in Genesis 1:2	146
circa 1873	**Father + Son + Holy Ghost + Holy Spirit + Jesus Christ** (Fully Capitalized, excluding antimentions) = **777** mentions (in the entire Bible)	See note above on **Father** and **Son** ^ Much like "**holy Spirit**" in modern KJBs, "**Holy Ghost**" started off as "**holy Ghost**" in 1611 and stayed that way until 1762. When **Father** and **Son** capitalizations were fully updated in the late 19th - early 20th century, the pattern was completed. **Jesus Christ** (Fully settled count) circa 1762 **holy Ghost** → **Holy Ghost** (all mentions) circa 1762 **father** → **Father** (Fully settled count) circa 1831 **sonne** → **Son** (Fully settled count) circa 1873	154

In KJB since…	Miracle	Causation / Notes	Page #
circa 1900's *(Estimated)*	UPPERCASE Names/Titles of GOD & Jesus; **LORD + GOD + JEHOVAH + I AM + JAH + BRANCH + KING + JESUS + Jesus + Jesus'** = **7777** mentions (Case-sensitive)	Due to the massive number of mentions, I did not check this manually. It may have been sooner, but I am conservatively guessing that this count was one of the last to fall into place with the current, settled Cambridge text. There were several instances of verses where **Lord** (Capitalized) and **LORD** (UPPERCASE) were see-sawed back and forth over the years. Here are just a few mentions of **LORD / Lord** that differ from the past. (This is not an exhaustive list) 1611 vs. Current **LORD** → **Lord** (Gen 18:27) **LORD** → **Lord** (Gen 20:4) **LORD** → **Lord** (Ex 15:17)(#2) **LORD** → **Lord** (Num 14:17) **LORD** → **Lord** (Jud 13:8)(#2) **LORD** → **Lord** (1 Ki 3:10) **LORD** → **Lord** (1 Ki 22:6) **LORD** → **Lord** (2 Ki 7:6) **LORD** → **Lord** (Neh 1:11) **LORD** → **Lord** (Neh 3:5) **LORD** → **Lord** (Neh 8:10)(#1) **LORD** → **Lord** (Ps 2:4) **LORD** → **Lord** (Ps 135:5)(#2) **LORD** → **Lord** (Mal 3:1)(#1) **Lord** → **LORD** (Mat 22:44) **Lord** → **LORD** (Mark 12:36) **Lord** → **LORD** (Luke 20:42) 1769 vs. Current **LORD** → **Lord** (Gen 18:27,30,31,32) **LORD** → **Lord** (Gen 20:4) **Lord** → **LORD** (Gen 30:30) **LORD** → **Lord** (Ex 34:9) **Lord** → **LORD** (Deut 29:23) **LORD** → **Lord** (Josh 3:11) **LORD** → **Lord** (48 times in Psalms) **LORD** → **Lord** (11 times in Lam.) **LORD** → **Lord** (Mat 16:22)	163

List of Bibles Checked

Year	Printer	Available contents
1611	London, Robert Barker	Entire Bible
1612	London, Robert Barker	Entire Bible
1613	London, Robert Barker	Genesis to Deuteronomy
1617	London, Robert Barker	Entire Bible
1619	London, Bonham Norton & John Bill	Entire Bible
1628	London, Bonham Norton & John Bill	Entire Bible
1629	Cambridge, Thomas & John Buck	A few leaves
1630	Cambridge, Thomas & John Buck	Entire Bible
1634	London, Robert Barker	Entire Bible
1637	Cambridge, Thomas Buck & Roger Daniel	Entire Bible
1638	London, Robert Barker	New Testament
1640	Cambridge, Thomas Buck & Roger Daniel	Entire Bible
1645	Cambridge, Roger Daniel	Entire Bible
1653	London, John Field	Entire Bible
1662	*Unspecified*	Entire Bible
1664	*Unspecified*	Entire Bible
1700	London, Charles Bill	Entire Bible
1716	London, John Baskett	Entire Bible
1716	Edinburgh	Entire Bible
1722	Edinburgh, James Watson	Entire Bible
1728	London, John Baskett	Entire Bible
1747	Edinburgh, Richard Watkins	Entire Bible
1760	Oxford, Thomas Baskett	Genesis to Psalm 51
1762	Cambridge, Joseph Bentham	Entire Bible
1762	Dublin, Boulter Grierson	Entire Bible
1763	London, Mark Baskett	Entire Bible
1769	Oxford, T. Wright and W. Gill	Entire Bible
1773	Cambridge, John Archdeacon	Genesis to Song of Solomon
1778	Oxford, T. Wright and W. Gill	Entire Bible
1782	Dublin, David Hay	Entire Bible
1793	Edinburgh, Mark and Charles Kerr	Entire Bible
1795	Oxford, William Jackson and William Dawson	Entire Bible
1795	Cambridge, John Archdeacon and John Burges	Entire Bible
1820	Edinburgh, Sir D. Hunter Blair and J. Bruce	Entire Bible
1830	Oxford, Samuel Collingwood and Co.	Entire Bible
1857	Glasgow, W. R. M'Phun	Entire Bible
1870	Oxford, Henry Frowde	Entire Bible
1873	Cambridge, C. J. Clay	Entire Bible
1887	Oxford, Henry Frowde	Entire Bible
1909	Cambridge, John Clay	Entire Bible
1937	Cambridge	Entire Bible

Appendix 2 - KJB (Cambridge) Book Stats

Word Counts by Book
King James Bible

#	NT	Book	Chapters	Verses	Words Verse text only	Letters	Words Verse text + Superscriptions / Colophons
1		**Genesis**	50	**1533**	38262	151839	
2		**Exodus**	40	**1213**	32685	131764	
3		**Leviticus**	27	**859**	24541	98919	
4		**Numbers**	36	**1288**	32896	137870	
5		**Deuteronomy**	34	**959**	28352	113983	
6		**Joshua**	24	**658**	18854	78363	
7		**Judges**	21	**618**	18966	76833	
8		**Ruth**	4	**85**	2574	9999	
9		**1 Samuel**	31	**810**	25048	100194	
10		**2 Samuel**	24	**695**	20600	82477	
11		**1 Kings**	22	**816**	24513	98688	
12		**2 Kings**	25	**719**	23517	93612	
13		**1 Chronicles**	29	**942**	20365	86607	
14		**2 Chronicles**	36	**822**	26069	109280	
15		**Ezra**	10	**280**	7440	31701	
16		**Nehemiah**	13	**406**	10480	44697	
17		**Esther**	10	**167**	5633	23736	
18		**Job**	42	**1070**	18098	73238	
19		**Psalms**	150	**2461**	42682	173920	43716
20		**Proverbs**	31	**915**	15038	62668	
21		**Ecclesiastes**	12	**222**	5579	21968	
22		**Song of Solomon**	8	**117**	2658	10540	
23		**Isaiah**	66	**1292**	37036	150959	
24		**Jeremiah**	52	**1364**	42654	174337	

#	NT	Book	Chapters	Verses	Words Verse text only	Letters	Words Verse text + Superscriptions / Colophons
25		**Lamentations**	5	154	3411	14165	
26		**Ezekiel**	48	1273	39401	160026	
27		**Daniel**	12	357	11602	48436	
28		**Hosea**	14	197	5174	21119	
29		**Joel**	3	73	2033	8357	
30		**Amos**	9	146	4216	16985	
31		**Obadiah**	1	21	669	2818	
32		**Jonah**	4	48	1320	5087	
33		**Micah**	7	105	3152	12716	
34		**Nahum**	3	47	1284	5421	
35		**Habakkuk**	3	56	1475	6209	
36		**Zephaniah**	3	53	1616	6640	
37		**Haggai**	2	38	1130	4400	
38		**Zechariah**	14	211	6443	25547	
39		**Malachi**	4	55	1781	7124	
40	**1**	**Matthew**	28	1071	23684	96630	
41	**2**	**Mark**	16	678	15166	61319	
42	**3**	**Luke**	24	1151	25939	104286	
43	**4**	**John**	21	879	19094	75497	
44	**5**	**Acts**	28	1007	24245	101700	
45	**6**	**Romans**	16	433	9422	39285	9438
46	**7**	**1 Corinthians**	16	437	9462	37936	9480
47	**8**	**2 Corinthians**	13	257	6065	24958	6083
48	**9**	**Galatians**	6	149	3084	12646	3090
49	**10**	**Ephesians**	6	155	3022	12822	3030
50	**11**	**Philippians**	4	104	2183	9029	2193
51	**12**	**Colossians**	4	95	1979	8418	1989
52	**13**	**1 Thessalonians**	5	89	1837	7542	1847
53	**14**	**2 Thessalonians**	3	47	1022	4275	1032
54	**15**	**1 Timothy**	6	113	2244	10062	2260

#	NT	Book	Chapters	Verses	Words Verse text only	Letters	Words Verse text + Superscriptions / Colophons
55	**16**	**2 Timothy**	4	83	1666	7246	1694
56	**17**	**Titus**	3	46	896	4067	915
57	**18**	**Philemon**	1	25	430	1817	439
58	**19**	**Hebrews**	13	303	6897	29322	6905
59	**20**	**James**	5	108	2304	9432	
60	**21**	**1 Peter**	5	105	2476	10587	
61	**22**	**2 Peter**	3	61	1553	6937	
62	**23**	**1 John**	5	105	2517	9849	
63	**24**	**2 John**	1	13	298	1204	
64	**25**	**3 John**	1	14	294	1250	
65	**26**	**Jude**	1	25	608	2811	
66	**27**	**Revelation**	22	404	11995	48240	

Old Testament	**New Testament**	**Entire Bible**
39 books	27 books	66 books
929 chapters	260 chapters	1189 chapters
23,145 verses	7957 verses	31,102 verses
116 superscriptions	14 colophons	130 ss / colo
609,247 words (verse text only)	180,382 words (verse text only)	789,629 words (verse text only)
610,281 words (including Psalms headings/superscriptions)	180,568 words (including colophons at the end of epistles)	790,849 words (including O.T. superscriptions & N.T. colophons)
2,483,242 letters (verse text only)	739,167 letters (verse text only)	3,222,409 letters (verse text only)
2,487,380 letters (including Psalms headings/superscriptions)	740,090 letters (including colophons at the end of epistles)	3,227,470 letters (including O.T. superscriptions & N.T. colophons)

Word Counts by Chapter
King James Bible

# Book	# Chapter (#OT/NT)		Book	Chapter	# Verses	# Words
1	1	1	**Genesis**	**1**	31	797
1	2	2	**Genesis**	**2**	25	632
1	3	3	**Genesis**	**3**	24	695
1	4	4	**Genesis**	**4**	26	632
1	5	5	**Genesis**	**5**	32	504
1	6	6	**Genesis**	**6**	22	579
1	7	7	**Genesis**	**7**	24	584
1	8	8	**Genesis**	**8**	22	586
1	9	9	**Genesis**	**9**	29	658
1	10	10	**Genesis**	**10**	32	495
1	11	11	**Genesis**	**11**	32	606
1	12	12	**Genesis**	**12**	20	536
1	13	13	**Genesis**	**13**	18	457
1	14	14	**Genesis**	**14**	24	606
1	15	15	**Genesis**	**15**	21	471
1	16	16	**Genesis**	**16**	16	412
1	17	17	**Genesis**	**17**	27	679
1	18	18	**Genesis**	**18**	33	867
1	19	19	**Genesis**	**19**	38	1,108
1	20	20	**Genesis**	**20**	18	498
1	21	21	**Genesis**	**21**	34	774
1	22	22	**Genesis**	**22**	24	629
1	23	23	**Genesis**	**23**	20	539
1	24	24	**Genesis**	**24**	67	1,816
1	25	25	**Genesis**	**25**	34	706
1	26	26	**Genesis**	**26**	35	889
1	27	27	**Genesis**	**27**	46	1,262
1	28	28	**Genesis**	**28**	22	621
1	29	29	**Genesis**	**29**	35	830
1	30	30	**Genesis**	**30**	43	1,022
1	31	31	**Genesis**	**31**	55	1,417
1	32	32	**Genesis**	**32**	32	794
1	33	33	**Genesis**	**33**	20	508
1	34	34	**Genesis**	**34**	31	790

# Book	# Chapter (#OT/NT)		Book	Chapter	# Verses	# Words
1	35	35	**Genesis**	**35**	29	664
1	36	36	**Genesis**	**36**	43	845
1	37	37	**Genesis**	**37**	36	942
1	38	38	**Genesis**	**38**	30	819
1	39	39	**Genesis**	**39**	23	666
1	40	40	**Genesis**	**40**	23	580
1	41	41	**Genesis**	**41**	57	1,404
1	42	42	**Genesis**	**42**	38	977
1	43	43	**Genesis**	**43**	34	938
1	44	44	**Genesis**	**44**	34	874
1	45	45	**Genesis**	**45**	28	731
1	46	46	**Genesis**	**46**	34	766
1	47	47	**Genesis**	**47**	31	965
1	48	48	**Genesis**	**48**	22	639
1	49	49	**Genesis**	**49**	33	766
1	50	50	**Genesis**	**50**	26	687
1			**GENESIS**		**1,533**	**38,262**
2	51	51	**Exodus**	**1**	22	457
2	52	52	**Exodus**	**2**	25	657
2	53	53	**Exodus**	**3**	22	791
2	54	54	**Exodus**	**4**	31	891
2	55	55	**Exodus**	**5**	23	594
2	56	56	**Exodus**	**6**	30	753
2	57	57	**Exodus**	**7**	25	692
2	58	58	**Exodus**	**8**	32	936
2	59	59	**Exodus**	**9**	35	982
2	60	60	**Exodus**	**10**	29	899
2	61	61	**Exodus**	**11**	10	324
2	62	62	**Exodus**	**12**	51	1,493
2	63	63	**Exodus**	**13**	22	675
2	64	64	**Exodus**	**14**	31	931
2	65	65	**Exodus**	**15**	27	713
2	66	66	**Exodus**	**16**	36	1,062
2	67	67	**Exodus**	**17**	16	465
2	68	68	**Exodus**	**18**	27	760
2	69	69	**Exodus**	**19**	25	702

# Book	# Chapter (#OT/NT)		Book	Chapter	# Verses	# Words
2	70	70	**Exodus**	**20**	26	561
2	71	71	**Exodus**	**21**	36	893
2	72	72	**Exodus**	**22**	31	790
2	73	73	**Exodus**	**23**	33	827
2	74	74	**Exodus**	**24**	18	492
2	75	75	**Exodus**	**25**	40	926
2	76	76	**Exodus**	**26**	37	937
2	77	77	**Exodus**	**27**	21	558
2	78	78	**Exodus**	**28**	43	1,235
2	79	79	**Exodus**	**29**	46	1,341
2	80	80	**Exodus**	**30**	38	970
2	81	81	**Exodus**	**31**	18	438
2	82	82	**Exodus**	**32**	35	1,093
2	83	83	**Exodus**	**33**	23	710
2	84	84	**Exodus**	**34**	35	1,004
2	85	85	**Exodus**	**35**	35	820
2	86	86	**Exodus**	**36**	38	892
2	87	87	**Exodus**	**37**	29	738
2	88	88	**Exodus**	**38**	31	832
2	89	89	**Exodus**	**39**	43	1,030
2	90	90	**Exodus**	**40**	38	821
2			**EXODUS**		**1,213**	**32,685**
3	91	91	**Leviticus**	**1**	17	525
3	92	92	**Leviticus**	**2**	16	486
3	93	93	**Leviticus**	**3**	17	511
3	94	94	**Leviticus**	**4**	35	1,157
3	95	95	**Leviticus**	**5**	19	723
3	96	96	**Leviticus**	**6**	30	892
3	97	97	**Leviticus**	**7**	38	1,056
3	98	98	**Leviticus**	**8**	36	988
3	99	99	**Leviticus**	**9**	24	624
3	100	100	**Leviticus**	**10**	20	628
3	101	101	**Leviticus**	**11**	47	1,115
3	102	102	**Leviticus**	**12**	8	262
3	103	103	**Leviticus**	**13**	59	1,857
3	104	104	**Leviticus**	**14**	57	1,713
3	105	105	**Leviticus**	**15**	33	919

# Book	# Chapter (#OT/NT)		Book	Chapter	# Verses	# Words
3	106	106	**Leviticus**	**16**	34	1,157
3	107	107	**Leviticus**	**17**	16	553
3	108	108	**Leviticus**	**18**	30	667
3	109	109	**Leviticus**	**19**	37	898
3	110	110	**Leviticus**	**20**	27	836
3	111	111	**Leviticus**	**21**	24	587
3	112	112	**Leviticus**	**22**	33	879
3	113	113	**Leviticus**	**23**	44	1,222
3	114	114	**Leviticus**	**24**	23	551
3	115	115	**Leviticus**	**25**	55	1,532
3	116	116	**Leviticus**	**26**	46	1,247
3	117	117	**Leviticus**	**27**	34	956
3			**LEVITICUS**		**859**	**24,541**
4	118	118	**Numbers**	**1**	54	1,333
4	119	119	**Numbers**	**2**	34	828
4	120	120	**Numbers**	**3**	51	1,291
4	121	121	**Numbers**	**4**	49	1,416
4	122	122	**Numbers**	**5**	31	898
4	123	123	**Numbers**	**6**	27	742
4	124	124	**Numbers**	**7**	89	1,939
4	125	125	**Numbers**	**8**	26	687
4	126	126	**Numbers**	**9**	23	722
4	127	127	**Numbers**	**10**	36	891
4	128	128	**Numbers**	**11**	35	1,056
4	129	129	**Numbers**	**12**	16	384
4	130	130	**Numbers**	**13**	33	741
4	131	131	**Numbers**	**14**	45	1,181
4	132	132	**Numbers**	**15**	41	1,068
4	133	133	**Numbers**	**16**	50	1,341
4	134	134	**Numbers**	**17**	13	335
4	135	135	**Numbers**	**18**	32	1,112
4	136	136	**Numbers**	**19**	22	683
4	137	137	**Numbers**	**20**	29	792
4	138	138	**Numbers**	**21**	35	931
4	139	139	**Numbers**	**22**	41	1,201
4	140	140	**Numbers**	**23**	30	743

# Book	# Chapter (#OT/NT)		Book	Chapter	# Verses	# Words
4	141	141	**Numbers**	**24**	25	659
4	142	142	**Numbers**	**25**	18	445
4	143	143	**Numbers**	**26**	65	1,446
4	144	144	**Numbers**	**27**	23	610
4	145	145	**Numbers**	**28**	31	779
4	146	146	**Numbers**	**29**	40	954
4	147	147	**Numbers**	**30**	16	503
4	148	148	**Numbers**	**31**	54	1,208
4	149	149	**Numbers**	**32**	42	1,009
4	150	150	**Numbers**	**33**	56	928
4	151	151	**Numbers**	**34**	29	630
4	152	152	**Numbers**	**35**	34	965
4	153	153	**Numbers**	**36**	13	445
4			**NUMBERS**		**1,288**	**32,896**
5	154	154	**Deuteronomy**	**1**	46	1,262
5	155	155	**Deuteronomy**	**2**	37	1,021
5	156	156	**Deuteronomy**	**3**	29	815
5	157	157	**Deuteronomy**	**4**	49	1,503
5	158	158	**Deuteronomy**	**5**	33	921
5	159	159	**Deuteronomy**	**6**	25	643
5	160	160	**Deuteronomy**	**7**	26	843
5	161	161	**Deuteronomy**	**8**	20	566
5	162	162	**Deuteronomy**	**9**	29	963
5	163	163	**Deuteronomy**	**10**	22	604
5	164	164	**Deuteronomy**	**11**	32	950
5	165	165	**Deuteronomy**	**12**	32	1,055
5	166	166	**Deuteronomy**	**13**	18	627
5	167	167	**Deuteronomy**	**14**	29	708
5	168	168	**Deuteronomy**	**15**	23	707
5	169	169	**Deuteronomy**	**16**	22	710
5	170	170	**Deuteronomy**	**17**	20	707
5	171	171	**Deuteronomy**	**18**	22	611
5	172	172	**Deuteronomy**	**19**	21	608
5	173	173	**Deuteronomy**	**20**	20	646
5	174	174	**Deuteronomy**	**21**	23	731
5	175	175	**Deuteronomy**	**22**	30	894
5	176	176	**Deuteronomy**	**23**	25	685

# Book	# Chapter (#OT/NT)		Book	Chapter	# Verses	# Words
5	177	177	**Deuteronomy**	**24**	22	681
5	178	178	**Deuteronomy**	**25**	19	562
5	179	179	**Deuteronomy**	**26**	19	667
5	180	180	**Deuteronomy**	**27**	26	599
5	181	181	**Deuteronomy**	**28**	68	2,075
5	182	182	**Deuteronomy**	**29**	29	851
5	183	183	**Deuteronomy**	**30**	20	665
5	184	184	**Deuteronomy**	**31**	30	1,041
5	185	185	**Deuteronomy**	**32**	52	1,306
5	186	186	**Deuteronomy**	**33**	29	805
5	187	187	**Deuteronomy**	**34**	12	320
5			**DEUTERONOMY**		**959**	**28,352**
THE LAW (GENESIS - DEUTERONOMY)					**5,852**	**156,736**
6	188	188	**Joshua**	**1**	18	573
6	189	189	**Joshua**	**2**	24	768
6	190	190	**Joshua**	**3**	17	566
6	191	191	**Joshua**	**4**	24	707
6	192	192	**Joshua**	**5**	15	550
6	193	193	**Joshua**	**6**	27	904
6	194	194	**Joshua**	**7**	26	927
6	195	195	**Joshua**	**8**	35	1,221
6	196	196	**Joshua**	**9**	27	800
6	197	197	**Joshua**	**10**	43	1,393
6	198	198	**Joshua**	**11**	23	717
6	199	199	**Joshua**	**12**	24	486
6	200	200	**Joshua**	**13**	33	825
6	201	201	**Joshua**	**14**	15	485
6	202	202	**Joshua**	**15**	63	1,032
6	203	203	**Joshua**	**16**	10	253
6	204	204	**Joshua**	**17**	18	660
6	205	205	**Joshua**	**18**	28	770
6	206	206	**Joshua**	**19**	51	944
6	207	207	**Joshua**	**20**	9	308
6	208	208	**Joshua**	**21**	45	1,026
6	209	209	**Joshua**	**22**	34	1,321
6	210	210	**Joshua**	**23**	16	574

# Book	# Chapter (#OT/NT)		Book	Chapter	# Verses	# Words
6	211	211	**Joshua**	**24**	33	1,044
6			**JOSHUA**		**658**	**18,854**
7	212	212	**Judges**	**1**	36	962
7	213	213	**Judges**	**2**	23	692
7	214	214	**Judges**	**3**	31	842
7	215	215	**Judges**	**4**	24	761
7	216	216	**Judges**	**5**	31	755
7	217	217	**Judges**	**6**	40	1,295
7	218	218	**Judges**	**7**	25	952
7	219	219	**Judges**	**8**	35	987
7	220	220	**Judges**	**9**	57	1,667
7	221	221	**Judges**	**10**	18	473
7	222	222	**Judges**	**11**	40	1,235
7	223	223	**Judges**	**12**	15	399
7	224	224	**Judges**	**13**	25	765
7	225	225	**Judges**	**14**	20	706
7	226	226	**Judges**	**15**	20	648
7	227	227	**Judges**	**16**	31	1,110
7	228	228	**Judges**	**17**	13	385
7	229	229	**Judges**	**18**	31	1,035
7	230	230	**Judges**	**19**	30	1,102
7	231	231	**Judges**	**20**	48	1,455
7	232	232	**Judges**	**21**	25	740
7			**JUDGES**		**618**	**18,966**
8	233	233	**Ruth**	**1**	22	649
8	234	234	**Ruth**	**2**	23	763
8	235	235	**Ruth**	**3**	18	541
8	236	236	**Ruth**	**4**	22	621
8			**RUTH**		**85**	**2,574**
9	237	237	**1 Samuel**	**1**	28	782
9	238	238	**1 Samuel**	**2**	36	1,104
9	239	239	**1 Samuel**	**3**	21	549
9	240	240	**1 Samuel**	**4**	22	733
9	241	241	**1 Samuel**	**5**	12	439
9	242	242	**1 Samuel**	**6**	21	752
9	243	243	**1 Samuel**	**7**	17	510
9	244	244	**1 Samuel**	**8**	22	541
9	245	245	**1 Samuel**	**9**	27	990

# Book	# Chapter (#OT/NT)		Book	Chapter	# Verses	# Words
9	246	246	**1 Samuel**	**10**	27	863
9	247	247	**1 Samuel**	**11**	15	503
9	248	248	**1 Samuel**	**12**	25	771
9	249	249	**1 Samuel**	**13**	23	697
9	250	250	**1 Samuel**	**14**	52	1,606
9	251	251	**1 Samuel**	**15**	35	981
9	252	252	**1 Samuel**	**16**	23	680
9	253	253	**1 Samuel**	**17**	58	1,719
9	254	254	**1 Samuel**	**18**	30	845
9	255	255	**1 Samuel**	**19**	24	696
9	256	256	**1 Samuel**	**20**	42	1,289
9	257	257	**1 Samuel**	**21**	15	499
9	258	258	**1 Samuel**	**22**	23	761
9	259	259	**1 Samuel**	**23**	29	831
9	260	260	**1 Samuel**	**24**	22	661
9	261	261	**1 Samuel**	**25**	44	1,452
9	262	262	**1 Samuel**	**26**	25	849
9	263	263	**1 Samuel**	**27**	12	385
9	264	264	**1 Samuel**	**28**	25	835
9	265	265	**1 Samuel**	**29**	11	421
9	266	266	**1 Samuel**	**30**	31	956
9	267	267	**1 Samuel**	**31**	13	348
9			**1 SAMUEL**		**810**	**25,048**
10	268	268	**2 Samuel**	**1**	27	712
10	269	269	**2 Samuel**	**2**	32	911
10	270	270	**2 Samuel**	**3**	39	1,143
10	271	271	**2 Samuel**	**4**	12	434
10	272	272	**2 Samuel**	**5**	25	624
10	273	273	**2 Samuel**	**6**	23	713
10	274	274	**2 Samuel**	**7**	29	858
10	275	275	**2 Samuel**	**8**	18	447
10	276	276	**2 Samuel**	**9**	13	408
10	277	277	**2 Samuel**	**10**	19	608
10	278	278	**2 Samuel**	**11**	27	814
10	279	279	**2 Samuel**	**12**	31	992
10	280	280	**2 Samuel**	**13**	39	1,149

# Book	# Chapter (#OT/NT)		Book	Chapter	# Verses	# Words
10	281	281	**2 Samuel**	**14**	33	1,117
10	282	282	**2 Samuel**	**15**	37	1,118
10	283	283	**2 Samuel**	**16**	23	738
10	284	284	**2 Samuel**	**17**	29	935
10	285	285	**2 Samuel**	**18**	33	1,096
10	286	286	**2 Samuel**	**19**	43	1,473
10	287	287	**2 Samuel**	**20**	26	848
10	288	288	**2 Samuel**	**21**	22	778
10	289	289	**2 Samuel**	**22**	51	951
10	290	290	**2 Samuel**	**23**	39	878
10	291	291	**2 Samuel**	**24**	25	855
10			**2 SAMUEL**		**695**	**20,600**
11	292	292	**1 Kings**	**1**	53	1,500
11	293	293	**1 Kings**	**2**	46	1,510
11	294	294	**1 Kings**	**3**	28	850
11	295	295	**1 Kings**	**4**	34	706
11	296	296	**1 Kings**	**5**	18	527
11	297	297	**1 Kings**	**6**	38	1,018
11	298	298	**1 Kings**	**7**	51	1,482
11	299	299	**1 Kings**	**8**	66	2,139
11	300	300	**1 Kings**	**9**	28	826
11	301	301	**1 Kings**	**10**	29	839
11	302	302	**1 Kings**	**11**	43	1,253
11	303	303	**1 Kings**	**12**	33	1,038
11	304	304	**1 Kings**	**13**	34	1,138
11	305	305	**1 Kings**	**14**	31	987
11	306	306	**1 Kings**	**15**	34	951
11	307	307	**1 Kings**	**16**	34	1,035
11	308	308	**1 Kings**	**17**	24	680
11	309	309	**1 Kings**	**18**	46	1,397
11	310	310	**1 Kings**	**19**	21	732
11	311	311	**1 Kings**	**20**	43	1,480
11	312	312	**1 Kings**	**21**	29	908
11	313	313	**1 Kings**	**22**	53	1,517
11			**1 KINGS**		**816**	**24,513**
12	314	314	**2 Kings**	**1**	18	669
12	315	315	**2 Kings**	**2**	25	848

# Book	# Chapter (#OT/NT)		Book	Chapter	# Verses	# Words
12	316	316	**2 Kings**	**3**	27	848
12	317	317	**2 Kings**	**4**	44	1,369
12	318	318	**2 Kings**	**5**	27	975
12	319	319	**2 Kings**	**6**	33	1,019
12	320	320	**2 Kings**	**7**	20	824
12	321	321	**2 Kings**	**8**	29	953
12	322	322	**2 Kings**	**9**	37	1,205
12	323	323	**2 Kings**	**10**	36	1,203
12	324	324	**2 Kings**	**11**	21	738
12	325	325	**2 Kings**	**12**	21	688
12	326	326	**2 Kings**	**13**	25	775
12	327	327	**2 Kings**	**14**	29	881
12	328	328	**2 Kings**	**15**	38	1,092
12	329	329	**2 Kings**	**16**	20	656
12	330	330	**2 Kings**	**17**	41	1,245
12	331	331	**2 Kings**	**18**	37	1,220
12	332	332	**2 Kings**	**19**	37	1,147
12	333	333	**2 Kings**	**20**	21	660
12	334	334	**2 Kings**	**21**	26	747
12	335	335	**2 Kings**	**22**	20	712
12	336	336	**2 Kings**	**23**	37	1,477
12	337	337	**2 Kings**	**24**	20	584
12	338	338	**2 Kings**	**25**	30	982
12			**2 KINGS**		**719**	**23,517**
13	339	339	**1 Chronicles**	**1**	54	683
13	340	340	**1 Chronicles**	**2**	55	846
13	341	341	**1 Chronicles**	**3**	24	347
13	342	342	**1 Chronicles**	**4**	43	852
13	343	343	**1 Chronicles**	**5**	26	664
13	344	344	**1 Chronicles**	**6**	81	1,341
13	345	345	**1 Chronicles**	**7**	40	831
13	346	346	**1 Chronicles**	**8**	40	491
13	347	347	**1 Chronicles**	**9**	44	960
13	348	348	**1 Chronicles**	**10**	14	364
13	349	349	**1 Chronicles**	**11**	47	944
13	350	350	**1 Chronicles**	**12**	40	987

# Book	# Chapter (#OT/NT)		Book	Chapter	# Verses	# Words
13	351	351	**1 Chronicles**	**13**	14	386
13	352	352	**1 Chronicles**	**14**	17	357
13	353	353	**1 Chronicles**	**15**	29	714
13	354	354	**1 Chronicles**	**16**	43	850
13	355	355	**1 Chronicles**	**17**	27	779
13	356	356	**1 Chronicles**	**18**	17	399
13	357	357	**1 Chronicles**	**19**	19	630
13	358	358	**1 Chronicles**	**20**	8	289
13	359	359	**1 Chronicles**	**21**	30	914
13	360	360	**1 Chronicles**	**22**	19	605
13	361	361	**1 Chronicles**	**23**	32	681
13	362	362	**1 Chronicles**	**24**	31	541
13	363	363	**1 Chronicles**	**25**	31	543
13	364	364	**1 Chronicles**	**26**	32	710
13	365	365	**1 Chronicles**	**27**	34	805
13	366	366	**1 Chronicles**	**28**	21	864
13	367	367	**1 Chronicles**	**29**	30	988
13			**1 CHRONICLES**		**942**	**20,365**
14	368	368	**2 Chronicles**	**1**	17	530
14	369	369	**2 Chronicles**	**2**	18	645
14	370	370	**2 Chronicles**	**3**	17	481
14	371	371	**2 Chronicles**	**4**	22	595
14	372	372	**2 Chronicles**	**5**	14	497
14	373	373	**2 Chronicles**	**6**	42	1,402
14	374	374	**2 Chronicles**	**7**	22	748
14	375	375	**2 Chronicles**	**8**	18	536
14	376	376	**2 Chronicles**	**9**	31	882
14	377	377	**2 Chronicles**	**10**	19	560
14	378	378	**2 Chronicles**	**11**	23	486
14	379	379	**2 Chronicles**	**12**	16	481
14	380	380	**2 Chronicles**	**13**	22	642
14	381	381	**2 Chronicles**	**14**	15	448
14	382	382	**2 Chronicles**	**15**	19	518
14	383	383	**2 Chronicles**	**16**	14	479
14	384	384	**2 Chronicles**	**17**	19	459
14	385	385	**2 Chronicles**	**18**	34	1,050
14	386	386	**2 Chronicles**	**19**	11	352

# Book	# Chapter (#OT/NT)		Book	Chapter	# Verses	# Words
14	387	387	**2 Chronicles**	**20**	37	1,148
14	388	388	**2 Chronicles**	**21**	20	623
14	389	389	**2 Chronicles**	**22**	12	444
14	390	390	**2 Chronicles**	**23**	21	788
14	391	391	**2 Chronicles**	**24**	27	933
14	392	392	**2 Chronicles**	**25**	28	970
14	393	393	**2 Chronicles**	**26**	23	721
14	394	394	**2 Chronicles**	**27**	9	244
14	395	395	**2 Chronicles**	**28**	27	896
14	396	396	**2 Chronicles**	**29**	36	1,157
14	397	397	**2 Chronicles**	**30**	27	869
14	398	398	**2 Chronicles**	**31**	21	757
14	399	399	**2 Chronicles**	**32**	33	1,084
14	400	400	**2 Chronicles**	**33**	25	780
14	401	401	**2 Chronicles**	**34**	33	1,223
14	402	402	**2 Chronicles**	**35**	27	900
14	403	403	**2 Chronicles**	**36**	23	741
14			**2 CHRONICLES**		**822**	**26,069**
15	404	404	**Ezra**	**1**	11	371
15	405	405	**Ezra**	**2**	70	998
15	406	406	**Ezra**	**3**	13	547
15	407	407	**Ezra**	**4**	24	769
15	408	408	**Ezra**	**5**	17	583
15	409	409	**Ezra**	**6**	22	778
15	410	410	**Ezra**	**7**	28	863
15	411	411	**Ezra**	**8**	36	990
15	412	412	**Ezra**	**9**	15	617
15	413	413	**Ezra**	**10**	44	924
15			**EZRA**		**280**	**7,440**
16	414	414	**Nehemiah**	**1**	11	390
16	415	415	**Nehemiah**	**2**	20	718
16	416	416	**Nehemiah**	**3**	32	896
16	417	417	**Nehemiah**	**4**	23	716
16	418	418	**Nehemiah**	**5**	19	636
16	419	419	**Nehemiah**	**6**	19	602
16	420	420	**Nehemiah**	**7**	73	1,176

# Book	# Chapter (#OT/NT)		Book	Chapter	# Verses	# Words
16	421	421	**Nehemiah**	**8**	18	686
16	422	422	**Nehemiah**	**9**	38	1,328
16	423	423	**Nehemiah**	**10**	39	652
16	424	424	**Nehemiah**	**11**	36	788
16	425	425	**Nehemiah**	**12**	47	930
16	426	426	**Nehemiah**	**13**	31	962
16			**NEHEMIAH**		**406**	**10,480**
17	427	427	**Esther**	**1**	22	716
17	428	428	**Esther**	**2**	23	806
17	429	429	**Esther**	**3**	15	552
17	430	430	**Esther**	**4**	17	517
17	431	431	**Esther**	**5**	14	494
17	432	432	**Esther**	**6**	14	476
17	433	433	**Esther**	**7**	10	345
17	434	434	**Esther**	**8**	17	650
17	435	435	**Esther**	**9**	32	984
17	436	436	**Esther**	**10**	3	93
17			**ESTHER**		**167**	**5,633**
NARRATIVE / HISTORY (JOSHUA - ESTHER)					**7,018**	**204,059**
18	437	437	**Job**	**1**	22	641
18	438	438	**Job**	**2**	13	387
18	439	439	**Job**	**3**	26	434
18	440	440	**Job**	**4**	21	336
18	441	441	**Job**	**5**	27	446
18	442	442	**Job**	**6**	30	482
18	443	443	**Job**	**7**	21	394
18	444	444	**Job**	**8**	22	340
18	445	445	**Job**	**9**	35	544
18	446	446	**Job**	**10**	22	402
18	447	447	**Job**	**11**	20	337
18	448	448	**Job**	**12**	25	399
18	449	449	**Job**	**13**	28	413
18	450	450	**Job**	**14**	22	410
18	451	451	**Job**	**15**	35	549
18	452	452	**Job**	**16**	22	375
18	453	453	**Job**	**17**	16	262
18	454	454	**Job**	**18**	21	342
18	455	455	**Job**	**19**	29	475

# Book	# Chapter (#OT/NT)		Book	Chapter	# Verses	# Words
18	456	456	**Job**	**20**	29	521
18	457	457	**Job**	**21**	34	522
18	458	458	**Job**	**22**	30	482
18	459	459	**Job**	**23**	17	280
18	460	460	**Job**	**24**	25	481
18	461	461	**Job**	**25**	6	90
18	462	462	**Job**	**26**	14	206
18	463	463	**Job**	**27**	23	373
18	464	464	**Job**	**28**	28	455
18	465	465	**Job**	**29**	25	404
18	466	466	**Job**	**30**	31	514
18	467	467	**Job**	**31**	40	691
18	468	468	**Job**	**32**	22	375
18	469	469	**Job**	**33**	33	525
18	470	470	**Job**	**34**	37	615
18	471	471	**Job**	**35**	16	254
18	472	472	**Job**	**36**	33	495
18	473	473	**Job**	**37**	24	402
18	474	474	**Job**	**38**	41	659
18	475	475	**Job**	**39**	30	477
18	476	476	**Job**	**40**	24	361
18	477	477	**Job**	**41**	34	507
18	478	478	**Job**	**42**	17	441
18			**JOB**		**1,070**	**18,098**
19	479	479	**Psalms**	**1**	6	130
19	480	480	**Psalms**	**2**	12	206
19	481	481	**Psalms**	**3**	8	150
19	482	482	**Psalms**	**4**	8	175
19	483	483	**Psalms**	**5**	12	255
19	484	484	**Psalms**	**6**	10	171
19	485	485	**Psalms**	**7**	17	343
19	486	486	**Psalms**	**8**	9	176
19	487	487	**Psalms**	**9**	20	377
19	488	488	**Psalms**	**10**	18	350
19	489	489	**Psalms**	**11**	7	136
19	490	490	**Psalms**	**12**	8	157

# Book	# Chapter (#OT/NT)		Book	Chapter	# Verses	# Words
19	491	491	**Psalms**	**13**	6	115
19	492	492	**Psalms**	**14**	7	157
19	493	493	**Psalms**	**15**	5	103
19	494	494	**Psalms**	**16**	11	209
19	495	495	**Psalms**	**17**	15	315
19	496	496	**Psalms**	**18**	50	965
19	497	497	**Psalms**	**19**	14	280
19	498	498	**Psalms**	**20**	9	152
19	499	499	**Psalms**	**21**	13	254
19	500	500	**Psalms**	**22**	31	591
19	501	501	**Psalms**	**23**	6	122
19	502	502	**Psalms**	**24**	10	182
19	503	503	**Psalms**	**25**	22	346
19	504	504	**Psalms**	**26**	12	187
19	505	505	**Psalms**	**27**	14	344
19	506	506	**Psalms**	**28**	9	205
19	507	507	**Psalms**	**29**	11	183
19	508	508	**Psalms**	**30**	12	243
19	509	509	**Psalms**	**31**	24	506
19	510	510	**Psalms**	**32**	11	246
19	511	511	**Psalms**	**33**	22	350
19	512	512	**Psalms**	**34**	22	365
19	513	513	**Psalms**	**35**	28	568
19	514	514	**Psalms**	**36**	12	236
19	515	515	**Psalms**	**37**	40	706
19	516	516	**Psalms**	**38**	22	369
19	517	517	**Psalms**	**39**	13	281
19	518	518	**Psalms**	**40**	17	408
19	519	519	**Psalms**	**41**	13	248
19	520	520	**Psalms**	**42**	11	290
19	521	521	**Psalms**	**43**	5	130
19	522	522	**Psalms**	**44**	26	461
19	523	523	**Psalms**	**45**	17	343
19	524	524	**Psalms**	**46**	11	217
19	525	525	**Psalms**	**47**	9	154
19	526	526	**Psalms**	**48**	14	238
19	527	527	**Psalms**	**49**	20	348

# Book	# Chapter (#OT/NT)		Book	Chapter	# Verses	# Words
19	528	528	**Psalms**	**50**	23	404
19	529	529	**Psalms**	**51**	19	344
19	530	530	**Psalms**	**52**	9	194
19	531	531	**Psalms**	**53**	6	163
19	532	532	**Psalms**	**54**	7	136
19	533	533	**Psalms**	**55**	23	446
19	534	534	**Psalms**	**56**	13	241
19	535	535	**Psalms**	**57**	11	246
19	536	536	**Psalms**	**58**	11	226
19	537	537	**Psalms**	**59**	17	358
19	538	538	**Psalms**	**60**	12	244
19	539	539	**Psalms**	**61**	8	143
19	540	540	**Psalms**	**62**	12	238
19	541	541	**Psalms**	**63**	11	206
19	542	542	**Psalms**	**64**	10	192
19	543	543	**Psalms**	**65**	13	277
19	544	544	**Psalms**	**66**	20	335
19	545	545	**Psalms**	**67**	7	121
19	546	546	**Psalms**	**68**	35	708
19	547	547	**Psalms**	**69**	36	680
19	548	548	**Psalms**	**70**	5	114
19	549	549	**Psalms**	**71**	24	471
19	550	550	**Psalms**	**72**	20	373
19	551	551	**Psalms**	**73**	28	427
19	552	552	**Psalms**	**74**	23	416
19	553	553	**Psalms**	**75**	10	200
19	554	554	**Psalms**	**76**	12	205
19	555	555	**Psalms**	**77**	20	340
19	556	556	**Psalms**	**78**	72	1,228
19	557	557	**Psalms**	**79**	13	281
19	558	558	**Psalms**	**80**	19	344
19	559	559	**Psalms**	**81**	16	298
19	560	560	**Psalms**	**82**	8	120
19	561	561	**Psalms**	**83**	18	279
19	562	562	**Psalms**	**84**	12	239
19	563	563	**Psalms**	**85**	13	218

# Book	# Chapter (#OT/NT)		Book	Chapter	# Verses	# Words
19	564	564	**Psalms**	**86**	17	316
19	565	565	**Psalms**	**87**	7	122
19	566	566	**Psalms**	**88**	18	317
19	567	567	**Psalms**	**89**	52	884
19	568	568	**Psalms**	**90**	17	328
19	569	569	**Psalms**	**91**	16	288
19	570	570	**Psalms**	**92**	15	266
19	571	571	**Psalms**	**93**	5	92
19	572	572	**Psalms**	**94**	23	356
19	573	573	**Psalms**	**95**	11	199
19	574	574	**Psalms**	**96**	13	226
19	575	575	**Psalms**	**97**	12	189
19	576	576	**Psalms**	**98**	9	172
19	577	577	**Psalms**	**99**	9	157
19	578	578	**Psalms**	**100**	5	90
19	579	579	**Psalms**	**101**	8	177
19	580	580	**Psalms**	**102**	28	472
19	581	581	**Psalms**	**103**	22	346
19	582	582	**Psalms**	**104**	35	598
19	583	583	**Psalms**	**105**	45	632
19	584	584	**Psalms**	**106**	48	762
19	585	585	**Psalms**	**107**	43	685
19	586	586	**Psalms**	**108**	13	212
19	587	587	**Psalms**	**109**	31	542
19	588	588	**Psalms**	**110**	7	146
19	589	589	**Psalms**	**111**	10	177
19	590	590	**Psalms**	**112**	10	172
19	591	591	**Psalms**	**113**	9	142
19	592	592	**Psalms**	**114**	8	106
19	593	593	**Psalms**	**115**	18	274
19	594	594	**Psalms**	**116**	19	287
19	595	595	**Psalms**	**117**	2	33
19	596	596	**Psalms**	**118**	29	465
19	597	597	**Psalms**	**119**	176	2,423
19	598	598	**Psalms**	**120**	7	92
19	599	599	**Psalms**	**121**	8	114
19	600	600	**Psalms**	**122**	9	130

# Book	# Chapter (#OT/NT)		Book	Chapter	# Verses	# Words
19	601	601	**Psalms**	**123**	4	98
19	602	602	**Psalms**	**124**	8	127
19	603	603	**Psalms**	**125**	5	112
19	604	604	**Psalms**	**126**	6	98
19	605	605	**Psalms**	**127**	5	116
19	606	606	**Psalms**	**128**	6	105
19	607	607	**Psalms**	**129**	8	123
19	608	608	**Psalms**	**130**	8	120
19	609	609	**Psalms**	**131**	3	66
19	610	610	**Psalms**	**132**	18	280
19	611	611	**Psalms**	**133**	3	75
19	612	612	**Psalms**	**134**	3	48
19	613	613	**Psalms**	**135**	21	329
19	614	614	**Psalms**	**136**	26	353
19	615	615	**Psalms**	**137**	9	165
19	616	616	**Psalms**	**138**	8	176
19	617	617	**Psalms**	**139**	24	418
19	618	618	**Psalms**	**140**	13	247
19	619	619	**Psalms**	**141**	10	207
19	620	620	**Psalms**	**142**	7	162
19	621	621	**Psalms**	**143**	12	256
19	622	622	**Psalms**	**144**	15	306
19	623	623	**Psalms**	**145**	21	335
19	624	624	**Psalms**	**146**	10	178
19	625	625	**Psalms**	**147**	20	299
19	626	626	**Psalms**	**148**	14	202
19	627	627	**Psalms**	**149**	9	143
19	628	628	**Psalms**	**150**	6	85
19			**PSALMS**		**2,461**	**43,716**
73 PSALMS OF DAVID					**1,064**	**20,486**
20	629	629	**Proverbs**	**1**	33	519
20	630	630	**Proverbs**	**2**	22	309
20	631	631	**Proverbs**	**3**	35	541
20	632	632	**Proverbs**	**4**	27	418
20	633	633	**Proverbs**	**5**	23	354
20	634	634	**Proverbs**	**6**	35	546

# Book	# Chapter (#OT/NT)		Book	Chapter	# Verses	# Words
20	635	635	**Proverbs**	**7**	27	411
20	636	636	**Proverbs**	**8**	36	562
20	637	637	**Proverbs**	**9**	18	288
20	638	638	**Proverbs**	**10**	32	527
20	639	639	**Proverbs**	**11**	31	524
20	640	640	**Proverbs**	**12**	28	476
20	641	641	**Proverbs**	**13**	25	400
20	642	642	**Proverbs**	**14**	35	572
20	643	643	**Proverbs**	**15**	33	544
20	644	644	**Proverbs**	**16**	33	543
20	645	645	**Proverbs**	**17**	28	476
20	646	646	**Proverbs**	**18**	24	381
20	647	647	**Proverbs**	**19**	29	506
20	648	648	**Proverbs**	**20**	30	498
20	649	649	**Proverbs**	**21**	31	501
20	650	650	**Proverbs**	**22**	29	495
20	651	651	**Proverbs**	**23**	35	566
20	652	652	**Proverbs**	**24**	34	580
20	653	653	**Proverbs**	**25**	28	522
20	654	654	**Proverbs**	**26**	28	459
20	655	655	**Proverbs**	**27**	27	460
20	656	656	**Proverbs**	**28**	28	528
20	657	657	**Proverbs**	**29**	27	425
20	658	658	**Proverbs**	**30**	33	640
20	659	659	**Proverbs**	**31**	31	467
20			**PROVERBS**		**915**	**15,038**
21	660	660	**Ecclesiastes**	**1**	18	380
21	661	661	**Ecclesiastes**	**2**	26	734
21	662	662	**Ecclesiastes**	**3**	22	517
21	663	663	**Ecclesiastes**	**4**	16	380
21	664	664	**Ecclesiastes**	**5**	20	533
21	665	665	**Ecclesiastes**	**6**	12	301
21	666	666	**Ecclesiastes**	**7**	29	617
21	667	667	**Ecclesiastes**	**8**	17	515
21	668	668	**Ecclesiastes**	**9**	18	555
21	669	669	**Ecclesiastes**	**10**	20	402
21	670	670	**Ecclesiastes**	**11**	10	273

# Book	# Chapter (#OT/NT)		Book	Chapter	# Verses	# Words
21	671	671	Ecclesiastes	12	14	372
21			ECCLESIASTES		222	5,579
22	672	672	Song of Solomon	1	17	326
22	673	673	Song of Solomon	2	17	351
22	674	674	Song of Solomon	3	11	287
22	675	675	Song of Solomon	4	16	363
22	676	676	Song of Solomon	5	16	397
22	677	677	Song of Solomon	6	13	282
22	678	678	Song of Solomon	7	13	292
22	679	679	Song of Solomon	8	14	360
22			SONG OF SOLOMON		117	2,658
WISDOM (JOB - SONG OF SOLOMON)					4,785	85,089
23	680	680	Isaiah	1	31	758
23	681	681	Isaiah	2	22	567
23	682	682	Isaiah	3	26	587
23	683	683	Isaiah	4	6	209
23	684	684	Isaiah	5	30	863
23	685	685	Isaiah	6	13	366
23	686	686	Isaiah	7	25	693
23	687	687	Isaiah	8	22	558
23	688	688	Isaiah	9	21	599
23	689	689	Isaiah	10	34	928
23	690	690	Isaiah	11	16	519
23	691	691	Isaiah	12	6	134
23	692	692	Isaiah	13	22	576
23	693	693	Isaiah	14	32	856
23	694	694	Isaiah	15	9	266
23	695	695	Isaiah	16	14	415
23	696	696	Isaiah	17	14	428
23	697	697	Isaiah	18	7	255
23	698	698	Isaiah	19	25	730
23	699	699	Isaiah	20	6	169
23	700	700	Isaiah	21	17	417
23	701	701	Isaiah	22	25	676
23	702	702	Isaiah	23	18	469
23	703	703	Isaiah	24	23	592

# Book	# Chapter (#OT/NT)		Book	Chapter	# Verses	# Words
23	704	704	**Isaiah**	**25**	12	381
23	705	705	**Isaiah**	**26**	21	550
23	706	706	**Isaiah**	**27**	13	405
23	707	707	**Isaiah**	**28**	29	814
23	708	708	**Isaiah**	**29**	24	742
23	709	709	**Isaiah**	**30**	33	1,059
23	710	710	**Isaiah**	**31**	9	322
23	711	711	**Isaiah**	**32**	20	436
23	712	712	**Isaiah**	**33**	24	585
23	713	713	**Isaiah**	**34**	17	522
23	714	714	**Isaiah**	**35**	10	277
23	715	715	**Isaiah**	**36**	22	690
23	716	716	**Isaiah**	**37**	38	1,131
23	717	717	**Isaiah**	**38**	22	592
23	718	718	**Isaiah**	**39**	8	268
23	719	719	**Isaiah**	**40**	31	796
23	720	720	**Isaiah**	**41**	29	804
23	721	721	**Isaiah**	**42**	25	676
23	722	722	**Isaiah**	**43**	28	711
23	723	723	**Isaiah**	**44**	28	886
23	724	724	**Isaiah**	**45**	25	774
23	725	725	**Isaiah**	**46**	13	342
23	726	726	**Isaiah**	**47**	15	471
23	727	727	**Isaiah**	**48**	22	627
23	728	728	**Isaiah**	**49**	26	867
23	729	729	**Isaiah**	**50**	11	365
23	730	730	**Isaiah**	**51**	23	771
23	731	731	**Isaiah**	**52**	15	405
23	732	732	**Isaiah**	**53**	12	387
23	733	733	**Isaiah**	**54**	17	493
23	734	734	**Isaiah**	**55**	13	399
23	735	735	**Isaiah**	**56**	12	361
23	736	736	**Isaiah**	**57**	21	569
23	737	737	**Isaiah**	**58**	14	521
23	738	738	**Isaiah**	**59**	21	590
23	739	739	**Isaiah**	**60**	22	665
23	740	740	**Isaiah**	**61**	11	380

# Book	# Chapter (#OT/NT)		Book	Chapter	# Verses	# Words
23	741	741	**Isaiah**	**62**	12	362
23	742	742	**Isaiah**	**63**	19	538
23	743	743	**Isaiah**	**64**	12	308
23	744	744	**Isaiah**	**65**	25	753
23	745	745	**Isaiah**	**66**	24	811
23			**ISAIAH**		**1,292**	**37,036**
24	746	746	**Jeremiah**	**1**	19	528
24	747	747	**Jeremiah**	**2**	37	1,019
24	748	748	**Jeremiah**	**3**	25	802
24	749	749	**Jeremiah**	**4**	31	861
24	750	750	**Jeremiah**	**5**	31	874
24	751	751	**Jeremiah**	**6**	30	827
24	752	752	**Jeremiah**	**7**	34	970
24	753	753	**Jeremiah**	**8**	22	706
24	754	754	**Jeremiah**	**9**	26	772
24	755	755	**Jeremiah**	**10**	25	674
24	756	756	**Jeremiah**	**11**	23	749
24	757	757	**Jeremiah**	**12**	17	544
24	758	758	**Jeremiah**	**13**	27	739
24	759	759	**Jeremiah**	**14**	22	688
24	760	760	**Jeremiah**	**15**	21	702
24	761	761	**Jeremiah**	**16**	21	699
24	762	762	**Jeremiah**	**17**	27	829
24	763	763	**Jeremiah**	**18**	23	659
24	764	764	**Jeremiah**	**19**	15	541
24	765	765	**Jeremiah**	**20**	18	594
24	766	766	**Jeremiah**	**21**	14	498
24	767	767	**Jeremiah**	**22**	30	837
24	768	768	**Jeremiah**	**23**	40	1,186
24	769	769	**Jeremiah**	**24**	10	361
24	770	770	**Jeremiah**	**25**	38	1,138
24	771	771	**Jeremiah**	**26**	24	800
24	772	772	**Jeremiah**	**27**	22	762
24	773	773	**Jeremiah**	**28**	17	540
24	774	774	**Jeremiah**	**29**	32	1,005
24	775	775	**Jeremiah**	**30**	24	717

# Book	# Chapter (#OT/NT)		Book	Chapter	# Verses	# Words
24	776	776	**Jeremiah**	**31**	40	1,294
24	777	777	**Jeremiah**	**32**	44	1,432
24	778	778	**Jeremiah**	**33**	26	842
24	779	779	**Jeremiah**	**34**	22	824
24	780	780	**Jeremiah**	**35**	19	657
24	781	781	**Jeremiah**	**36**	32	1,110
24	782	782	**Jeremiah**	**37**	21	611
24	783	783	**Jeremiah**	**38**	28	984
24	784	784	**Jeremiah**	**39**	18	545
24	785	785	**Jeremiah**	**40**	16	681
24	786	786	**Jeremiah**	**41**	18	664
24	787	787	**Jeremiah**	**42**	22	774
24	788	788	**Jeremiah**	**43**	13	460
24	789	789	**Jeremiah**	**44**	30	1,228
24	790	790	**Jeremiah**	**45**	5	152
24	791	791	**Jeremiah**	**46**	28	821
24	792	792	**Jeremiah**	**47**	7	215
24	793	793	**Jeremiah**	**48**	47	1,172
24	794	794	**Jeremiah**	**49**	39	1,180
24	795	795	**Jeremiah**	**50**	46	1,460
24	796	796	**Jeremiah**	**51**	64	1,853
24	797	797	**Jeremiah**	**52**	34	1,074
24			**JEREMIAH**		**1,364**	**42,654**
25	798	798	**Lamentations**	**1**	22	758
25	799	799	**Lamentations**	**2**	22	883
25	800	800	**Lamentations**	**3**	66	876
25	801	801	**Lamentations**	**4**	22	598
25	802	802	**Lamentations**	**5**	22	296
25			**LAMENTATIONS**		**154**	**3,411**
26	803	803	**Ezekiel**	**1**	28	870
26	804	804	**Ezekiel**	**2**	10	273
26	805	805	**Ezekiel**	**3**	27	809
26	806	806	**Ezekiel**	**4**	17	519
26	807	807	**Ezekiel**	**5**	17	628
26	808	808	**Ezekiel**	**6**	14	470
26	809	809	**Ezekiel**	**7**	27	768
26	810	810	**Ezekiel**	**8**	18	655

# Book	# Chapter (#OT/NT)		Book	Chapter	# Verses	# Words
26	811	811	Ezekiel	9	11	400
26	812	812	Ezekiel	10	22	659
26	813	813	Ezekiel	11	25	721
26	814	814	Ezekiel	12	28	799
26	815	815	Ezekiel	13	23	738
26	816	816	Ezekiel	14	23	746
26	817	817	Ezekiel	15	8	205
26	818	818	Ezekiel	16	63	1,820
26	819	819	Ezekiel	17	24	773
26	820	820	Ezekiel	18	32	919
26	821	821	Ezekiel	19	14	356
26	822	822	Ezekiel	20	49	1,601
26	823	823	Ezekiel	21	32	945
26	824	824	Ezekiel	22	31	840
26	825	825	Ezekiel	23	49	1,322
26	826	826	Ezekiel	24	27	774
26	827	827	Ezekiel	25	17	507
26	828	828	Ezekiel	26	21	727
26	829	829	Ezekiel	27	36	907
26	830	830	Ezekiel	28	26	809
26	831	831	Ezekiel	29	21	714
26	832	832	Ezekiel	30	26	760
26	833	833	Ezekiel	31	18	680
26	834	834	Ezekiel	32	32	1,077
26	835	835	Ezekiel	33	33	1,071
26	836	836	Ezekiel	34	31	958
26	837	837	Ezekiel	35	15	402
26	838	838	Ezekiel	36	38	1,180
26	839	839	Ezekiel	37	28	870
26	840	840	Ezekiel	38	23	776
26	841	841	Ezekiel	39	29	928
26	842	842	Ezekiel	40	49	1,530
26	843	843	Ezekiel	41	26	802
26	844	844	Ezekiel	42	20	568
26	845	845	Ezekiel	43	27	907
26	846	846	Ezekiel	44	31	1,031

# Book	# Chapter (#OT/NT)		Book	Chapter	# Verses	# Words
26	847	847	**Ezekiel**	**45**	25	882
26	848	848	**Ezekiel**	**46**	24	880
26	849	849	**Ezekiel**	**47**	23	780
26	850	850	**Ezekiel**	**48**	35	1,045
26			**EZEKIEL**		**1,273**	**39,401**
27	851	851	**Daniel**	**1**	21	589
27	852	852	**Daniel**	**2**	49	1,500
27	853	853	**Daniel**	**3**	30	992
27	854	854	**Daniel**	**4**	37	1,290
27	855	855	**Daniel**	**5**	31	995
27	856	856	**Daniel**	**6**	28	905
27	857	857	**Daniel**	**7**	28	926
27	858	858	**Daniel**	**8**	27	852
27	859	859	**Daniel**	**9**	27	966
27	860	860	**Daniel**	**10**	21	647
27	861	861	**Daniel**	**11**	45	1,529
27	862	862	**Daniel**	**12**	13	411
27			**DANIEL**		**357**	**11,602**
MAJOR PROPHETS (ISAIAH - DANIEL)					**4,440**	**134,104**
28	863	863	**Hosea**	**1**	11	355
28	864	864	**Hosea**	**2**	23	678
28	865	865	**Hosea**	**3**	5	156
28	866	866	**Hosea**	**4**	19	465
28	867	867	**Hosea**	**5**	15	368
28	868	868	**Hosea**	**6**	11	254
28	869	869	**Hosea**	**7**	16	398
28	870	870	**Hosea**	**8**	14	330
28	871	871	**Hosea**	**9**	17	468
28	872	872	**Hosea**	**10**	15	425
28	873	873	**Hosea**	**11**	12	308
28	874	874	**Hosea**	**12**	14	311
28	875	875	**Hosea**	**13**	16	426
28	876	876	**Hosea**	**14**	9	232
28			**HOSEA**		**197**	**5,174**
29	877	877	**Joel**	**1**	20	508
29	878	878	**Joel**	**2**	32	958
29	879	879	**Joel**	**3**	21	567
29			**JOEL**		**73**	**2,033**

# Book	# Chapter (#OT/NT)		Book	Chapter	# Verses	# Words
30	880	880	**Amos**	**1**	15	455
30	881	881	**Amos**	**2**	16	441
30	882	882	**Amos**	**3**	15	397
30	883	883	**Amos**	**4**	13	432
30	884	884	**Amos**	**5**	27	658
30	885	885	**Amos**	**6**	14	399
30	886	886	**Amos**	**7**	17	471
30	887	887	**Amos**	**8**	14	414
30	888	888	**Amos**	**9**	15	549
30			**AMOS**		**146**	**4,216**
31	889	889	**Obadiah**	**1**	21	669
31			**OBADIAH**		**21**	**669**
32	890	890	**Jonah**	**1**	17	514
32	891	891	**Jonah**	**2**	10	214
32	892	892	**Jonah**	**3**	10	260
32	893	893	**Jonah**	**4**	11	332
32			**JONAH**		**48**	**1,320**
33	894	894	**Micah**	**1**	16	452
33	895	895	**Micah**	**2**	13	400
33	896	896	**Micah**	**3**	12	354
33	897	897	**Micah**	**4**	13	476
33	898	898	**Micah**	**5**	15	447
33	899	899	**Micah**	**6**	16	440
33	900	900	**Micah**	**7**	20	583
33			**MICAH**		**105**	**3,152**
34	901	901	**Nahum**	**1**	15	394
34	902	902	**Nahum**	**2**	13	371
34	903	903	**Nahum**	**3**	19	519
34			**NAHUM**		**47**	**1,284**
35	904	904	**Habakkuk**	**1**	17	423
35	905	905	**Habakkuk**	**2**	20	563
35	906	906	**Habakkuk**	**3**	19	489
35			**HABAKKUK**		**56**	**1,475**
36	907	907	**Zephaniah**	**1**	18	555
36	908	908	**Zephaniah**	**2**	15	463
36	909	909	**Zephaniah**	**3**	20	598

# Book	# Chapter (#OT/NT)		Book	Chapter	# Verses	# Words
36			**ZEPHANIAH**		**53**	**1,616**
37	910	910	**Haggai**	**1**	15	451
37	911	911	**Haggai**	**2**	23	679
37			**HAGGAI**		**38**	**1,130**
38	912	912	**Zechariah**	**1**	21	622
38	913	913	**Zechariah**	**2**	13	317
38	914	914	**Zechariah**	**3**	10	296
38	915	915	**Zechariah**	**4**	14	365
38	916	916	**Zechariah**	**5**	11	338
38	917	917	**Zechariah**	**6**	15	424
38	918	918	**Zechariah**	**7**	14	378
38	919	919	**Zechariah**	**8**	23	703
38	920	920	**Zechariah**	**9**	17	537
38	921	921	**Zechariah**	**10**	12	408
38	922	922	**Zechariah**	**11**	17	502
38	923	923	**Zechariah**	**12**	14	462
38	924	924	**Zechariah**	**13**	9	337
38	925	925	**Zechariah**	**14**	21	754
38			**ZECHARIAH**		**211**	**6,443**
39	926	926	**Malachi**	**1**	14	487
39	927	927	**Malachi**	**2**	17	546
39	928	928	**Malachi**	**3**	18	565
39	929	929	**Malachi**	**4**	6	183
39			**MALACHI**		**55**	**1,781**
MINOR PROPHETS (HOSEA - MALACHI)					**1,050**	**30,293**
ALL PROPHETS (ISAIAH - MALACHI)					**5,490**	**164,397**
OLD TESTAMENT					**23,145**	**610,281**

The New Testament

# Book	# Chapter (#OT/NT)		Book	Chapter	# Verses	# Words
40 (1)	930	1	**Matthew**	**1**	25	473
40 (1)	931	2	**Matthew**	**2**	23	619
40 (1)	932	3	**Matthew**	**3**	17	387
40 (1)	933	4	**Matthew**	**4**	25	557
40 (1)	934	5	**Matthew**	**5**	48	1,081
40 (1)	935	6	**Matthew**	**6**	34	794
40 (1)	936	7	**Matthew**	**7**	29	626
40 (1)	937	8	**Matthew**	**8**	34	773

# Book	# Chapter (#OT/NT)		Book	Chapter	# Verses	# Words
40 (1)	938	9	**Matthew**	**9**	38	837
40 (1)	939	10	**Matthew**	**10**	42	919
40 (1)	940	11	**Matthew**	**11**	30	668
40 (1)	941	12	**Matthew**	**12**	50	1,168
40 (1)	942	13	**Matthew**	**13**	58	1,367
40 (1)	943	14	**Matthew**	**14**	36	721
40 (1)	944	15	**Matthew**	**15**	39	785
40 (1)	945	16	**Matthew**	**16**	28	688
40 (1)	946	17	**Matthew**	**17**	27	620
40 (1)	947	18	**Matthew**	**18**	35	869
40 (1)	948	19	**Matthew**	**19**	30	719
40 (1)	949	20	**Matthew**	**20**	34	779
40 (1)	950	21	**Matthew**	**21**	46	1,126
40 (1)	951	22	**Matthew**	**22**	46	828
40 (1)	952	23	**Matthew**	**23**	39	833
40 (1)	953	24	**Matthew**	**24**	51	1,047
40 (1)	954	25	**Matthew**	**25**	46	995
40 (1)	955	26	**Matthew**	**26**	75	1,625
40 (1)	956	27	**Matthew**	**27**	66	1,359
40 (1)	957	28	**Matthew**	**28**	20	421
40 – 1			**MATTHEW**		**1,071**	**23,684**
41 (2)	958	29	**Mark**	**1**	45	930
41 (2)	959	30	**Mark**	**2**	28	724
41 (2)	960	31	**Mark**	**3**	35	663
41 (2)	961	32	**Mark**	**4**	41	923
41 (2)	962	33	**Mark**	**5**	43	952
41 (2)	963	34	**Mark**	**6**	56	1,323
41 (2)	964	35	**Mark**	**7**	37	806
41 (2)	965	36	**Mark**	**8**	38	842
41 (2)	966	37	**Mark**	**9**	50	1,164
41 (2)	967	38	**Mark**	**10**	52	1,218
41 (2)	968	39	**Mark**	**11**	33	778
41 (2)	969	40	**Mark**	**12**	44	1,058
41 (2)	970	41	**Mark**	**13**	37	828
41 (2)	971	42	**Mark**	**14**	72	1,595
41 (2)	972	43	**Mark**	**15**	47	913

# Book	# Chapter (#OT/NT)		Book	Chapter	# Verses	# Words
41 (2)	973	44	**Mark**	**16**	20	449
41 – 2			**MARK**		**678**	**15,166**
42 (3)	974	45	**Luke**	**1**	80	1,583
42 (3)	975	46	**Luke**	**2**	52	1,094
42 (3)	976	47	**Luke**	**3**	38	1,017
42 (3)	977	48	**Luke**	**4**	44	1,021
42 (3)	978	49	**Luke**	**5**	39	949
42 (3)	979	50	**Luke**	**6**	49	1,229
42 (3)	980	51	**Luke**	**7**	50	1,209
42 (3)	981	52	**Luke**	**8**	56	1,431
42 (3)	982	53	**Luke**	**9**	62	1,457
42 (3)	983	54	**Luke**	**10**	42	992
42 (3)	984	55	**Luke**	**11**	54	1,331
42 (3)	985	56	**Luke**	**12**	59	1,407
42 (3)	986	57	**Luke**	**13**	35	864
42 (3)	987	58	**Luke**	**14**	35	812
42 (3)	988	59	**Luke**	**15**	32	725
42 (3)	989	60	**Luke**	**16**	31	752
42 (3)	990	61	**Luke**	**17**	37	809
42 (3)	991	62	**Luke**	**18**	43	868
42 (3)	992	63	**Luke**	**19**	48	1,047
42 (3)	993	64	**Luke**	**20**	47	954
42 (3)	994	65	**Luke**	**21**	38	820
42 (3)	995	66	**Luke**	**22**	71	1,396
42 (3)	996	67	**Luke**	**23**	56	1,117
42 (3)	997	68	**Luke**	**24**	53	1,055
42 – 3			**LUKE**		**1,151**	**25,939**
43 (4)	998	69	**John**	**1**	51	1,004
43 (4)	999	70	**John**	**2**	25	510
43 (4)	1000	71	**John**	**3**	36	763
43 (4)	1001	72	**John**	**4**	54	1,094
43 (4)	1002	73	**John**	**5**	47	1,001
43 (4)	1003	74	**John**	**6**	71	1,506
43 (4)	1004	75	**John**	**7**	53	1,002
43 (4)	1005	76	**John**	**8**	59	1,307
43 (4)	1006	77	**John**	**9**	41	876
43 (4)	1007	78	**John**	**10**	42	820

# Book	# Chapter (#OT/NT)		Book	Chapter	# Verses	# Words
43 (4)	1008	79	John	11	57	1,157
43 (4)	1009	80	John	12	50	1,060
43 (4)	1010	81	John	13	38	826
43 (4)	1011	82	John	14	31	731
43 (4)	1012	83	John	15	27	613
43 (4)	1013	84	John	16	33	789
43 (4)	1014	85	John	17	26	636
43 (4)	1015	86	John	18	40	947
43 (4)	1016	87	John	19	42	1,010
43 (4)	1017	88	John	20	31	749
43 (4)	1018	89	John	21	25	693
43 – 4			**JOHN**		**879**	**19,094**
GOSPELS (MATTHEW - JOHN)					**3,779**	**83,883**
44 (5)	1019	90	Acts	1	26	661
44 (5)	1020	91	Acts	2	47	1,021
44 (5)	1021	92	Acts	3	26	634
44 (5)	1022	93	Acts	4	37	865
44 (5)	1023	94	Acts	5	42	1,026
44 (5)	1024	95	Acts	6	15	355
44 (5)	1025	96	Acts	7	60	1,430
44 (5)	1026	97	Acts	8	40	883
44 (5)	1027	98	Acts	9	43	1,046
44 (5)	1028	99	Acts	10	48	1,108
44 (5)	1029	100	Acts	11	30	667
44 (5)	1030	101	Acts	12	25	662
44 (5)	1031	102	Acts	13	52	1,272
44 (5)	1032	103	Acts	14	28	627
44 (5)	1033	104	Acts	15	41	925
44 (5)	1034	105	Acts	16	40	943
44 (5)	1035	106	Acts	17	34	855
44 (5)	1036	107	Acts	18	28	664
44 (5)	1037	108	Acts	19	41	975
44 (5)	1038	109	Acts	20	38	882
44 (5)	1039	110	Acts	21	40	1,067
44 (5)	1040	111	Acts	22	30	773
44 (5)	1041	112	Acts	23	35	921

# Book	# Chapter (#OT/NT)		Book	Chapter	# Verses	# Words
44 (5)	1042	113	**Acts**	**24**	27	640
44 (5)	1043	114	**Acts**	**25**	27	711
44 (5)	1044	115	**Acts**	**26**	32	781
44 (5)	1045	116	**Acts**	**27**	44	1,033
44 (5)	1046	117	**Acts**	**28**	31	818
44 – 5			**ACTS**		**1,007**	**24,245**
HISTORICAL (MATTHEW - ACTS)					**4,786**	**108,128**
45 (6)	1047	118	**Romans**	**1**	32	714
45 (6)	1048	119	**Romans**	**2**	29	604
45 (6)	1049	120	**Romans**	**3**	31	562
45 (6)	1050	121	**Romans**	**4**	25	546
45 (6)	1051	122	**Romans**	**5**	21	480
45 (6)	1052	123	**Romans**	**6**	23	484
45 (6)	1053	124	**Romans**	**7**	25	605
45 (6)	1054	125	**Romans**	**8**	39	903
45 (6)	1055	126	**Romans**	**9**	33	719
45 (6)	1056	127	**Romans**	**10**	21	461
45 (6)	1057	128	**Romans**	**11**	36	818
45 (6)	1058	129	**Romans**	**12**	21	397
45 (6)	1059	130	**Romans**	**13**	14	361
45 (6)	1060	131	**Romans**	**14**	23	525
45 (6)	1061	132	**Romans**	**15**	33	742
45 (6)	1062	133	**Romans**	**16**	27	501
			Romans	**Colophon**	0	16
45 – 6			**ROMANS**		**433**	**9,438**
46 (7)	1063	134	**1 Corinthians**	**1**	31	649
46 (7)	1064	135	**1 Corinthians**	**2**	16	373
46 (7)	1065	136	**1 Corinthians**	**3**	23	459
46 (7)	1066	137	**1 Corinthians**	**4**	21	509
46 (7)	1067	138	**1 Corinthians**	**5**	13	321
46 (7)	1068	139	**1 Corinthians**	**6**	20	465
46 (7)	1069	140	**1 Corinthians**	**7**	40	959
46 (7)	1070	141	**1 Corinthians**	**8**	13	309
46 (7)	1071	142	**1 Corinthians**	**9**	27	671
46 (7)	1072	143	**1 Corinthians**	**10**	33	667
46 (7)	1073	144	**1 Corinthians**	**11**	34	718
46 (7)	1074	145	**1 Corinthians**	**12**	31	593

# Book	# Chapter (#OT/NT)		Book	Chapter	# Verses	# Words
46 (7)	1075	146	1 Corinthians	13	13	270
46 (7)	1076	147	1 Corinthians	14	40	887
46 (7)	1077	148	1 Corinthians	15	58	1,166
46 (7)	1078	149	1 Corinthians	16	24	446
			1 Corinthians	Colophon	0	18
46 – 7			**1 CORINTHIANS**		**437**	**9,480**
47 (8)	1079	150	2 Corinthians	1	24	591
47 (8)	1080	151	2 Corinthians	2	17	401
47 (8)	1081	152	2 Corinthians	3	18	389
47 (8)	1082	153	2 Corinthians	4	18	406
47 (8)	1083	154	2 Corinthians	5	21	487
47 (8)	1084	155	2 Corinthians	6	18	357
47 (8)	1085	156	2 Corinthians	7	16	452
47 (8)	1086	157	2 Corinthians	8	24	568
47 (8)	1087	158	2 Corinthians	9	15	355
47 (8)	1088	159	2 Corinthians	10	18	437
47 (8)	1089	160	2 Corinthians	11	33	718
47 (8)	1090	161	2 Corinthians	12	21	589
47 (8)	1091	162	2 Corinthians	13	14	315
			2 Corinthians	Colophon	0	18
47 – 8			**2 CORINTHIANS**		**257**	**6,083**
48 (9)	1092	163	Galatians	1	24	453
48 (9)	1093	164	Galatians	2	21	573
48 (9)	1094	165	Galatians	3	29	648
48 (9)	1095	166	Galatians	4	31	610
48 (9)	1096	167	Galatians	5	26	447
48 (9)	1097	168	Galatians	6	18	353
			Galatians	Colophon	0	6
48 – 9			**GALATIANS**		**149**	**3,090**
49 (10)	1098	169	Ephesians	1	23	508
49 (10)	1099	170	Ephesians	2	22	453
49 (10)	1100	171	Ephesians	3	21	410
49 (10)	1101	172	Ephesians	4	32	617
49 (10)	1102	173	Ephesians	5	33	564
49 (10)	1103	174	Ephesians	6	24	470

# Book	# Chapter (#OT/NT)		Book	Chapter	# Verses	# Words
			Ephesians	Colophon	0	8
49 – 10			**EPHESIANS**		**155**	**3,030**
50 (11)	1104	175	**Philippians**	**1**	30	632
50 (11)	1105	176	**Philippians**	**2**	30	601
50 (11)	1106	177	**Philippians**	**3**	21	483
50 (11)	1107	178	**Philippians**	**4**	23	467
			Philippians	Colophon	0	10
50 – 11			**PHILIPPIANS**		**104**	**2,193**
51 (12)	1108	179	**Colossians**	**1**	29	656
51 (12)	1109	180	**Colossians**	**2**	23	503
51 (12)	1110	181	**Colossians**	**3**	25	457
51 (12)	1111	182	**Colossians**	**4**	18	363
			Colossians	Colophon	0	10
51 – 12			**COLOSSIANS**		**95**	**1,989**
52 (13)	1112	183	**1 Thessalonians**	**1**	10	253
52 (13)	1113	184	**1 Thessalonians**	**2**	20	479
52 (13)	1114	185	**1 Thessalonians**	**3**	13	295
52 (13)	1115	186	**1 Thessalonians**	**4**	18	396
52 (13)	1116	187	**1 Thessalonians**	**5**	28	414
			1 Thessalonians	Colophon	0	10
52 – 13			**1 THESSALONIANS**		**89**	**1,847**
53 (14)	1117	188	**2 Thessalonians**	**1**	12	291
53 (14)	1118	189	**2 Thessalonians**	**2**	17	381
53 (14)	1119	190	**2 Thessalonians**	**3**	18	350
			2 Thessalonians	Colophon	0	10
53 – 14			**2 THESSALONIANS**		**47**	**1,032**
54 (15)	1120	191	**1 Timothy**	**1**	20	432
54 (15)	1121	192	**1 Timothy**	**2**	15	247
54 (15)	1122	193	**1 Timothy**	**3**	16	324
54 (15)	1123	194	**1 Timothy**	**4**	16	310
54 (15)	1124	195	**1 Timothy**	**5**	25	470
54 (15)	1125	196	**1 Timothy**	**6**	21	461
			1 Timothy	Colophon	0	16
54 – 15			**1 TIMOTHY**		**113**	**2,260**
55 (16)	1126	197	**2 Timothy**	**1**	18	438
55 (16)	1127	198	**2 Timothy**	**2**	26	506

# Book	# Chapter (#OT/NT)		Book	Chapter	# Verses	# Words
55 (16)	1128	199	**2 Timothy**	**3**	17	297
55 (16)	1129	200	**2 Timothy**	**4**	22	425
			2 Timothy	**Colophon**	0	28
55 – 16			**2 TIMOTHY**		**83**	**1,694**
56 (17)	1130	201	**Titus**	**1**	16	337
56 (17)	1131	202	**Titus**	**2**	15	265
56 (17)	1132	203	**Titus**	**3**	15	294
			Titus	**Colophon**	0	19
56 – 17			**TITUS**		**46**	**915**
57 (18)	1133	204	**Philemon**	**1**	25	430
			Philemon	**Colophon**	0	9
57 – 18			**PHILEMON**		**25**	**439**
PAULINE EPISTLES (ROMANS - PHILEMON)					**2,033**	**43,490**
58 (19)	1134	205	**Hebrews**	**1**	14	338
58 (19)	1135	206	**Hebrews**	**2**	18	472
58 (19)	1136	207	**Hebrews**	**3**	19	362
58 (19)	1137	208	**Hebrews**	**4**	16	404
58 (19)	1138	209	**Hebrews**	**5**	14	321
58 (19)	1139	210	**Hebrews**	**6**	20	425
58 (19)	1140	211	**Hebrews**	**7**	28	607
58 (19)	1141	212	**Hebrews**	**8**	13	387
58 (19)	1142	213	**Hebrews**	**9**	28	678
58 (19)	1143	214	**Hebrews**	**10**	39	784
58 (19)	1144	215	**Hebrews**	**11**	40	922
58 (19)	1145	216	**Hebrews**	**12**	29	696
58 (19)	1146	217	**Hebrews**	**13**	25	501
			Hebrews	**Colophon**	0	8
58 – 19			**HEBREWS**		**303**	**6,905**
PAULINE EPISTLES *incl. Hebrews* (ROMANS - HEBREWS)					**2,336**	**50,395**
59 (20)	1147	218	**James**	**1**	27	544
59 (20)	1148	219	**James**	**2**	26	528
59 (20)	1149	220	**James**	**3**	18	378
59 (20)	1150	221	**James**	**4**	17	369
59 (20)	1151	222	**James**	**5**	20	485
59 – 20			**JAMES**		**108**	**2,304**

# Book	# Chapter (#OT/NT)		Book	Chapter	# Verses	# Words
60 (21)	1152	223	**1 Peter**	**1**	25	597
60 (21)	1153	224	**1 Peter**	**2**	25	549
60 (21)	1154	225	**1 Peter**	**3**	22	551
60 (21)	1155	226	**1 Peter**	**4**	19	479
60 (21)	1156	227	**1 Peter**	**5**	14	300
60 – 21			**1 PETER**		**105**	**2,476**
61 (22)	1157	228	**2 Peter**	**1**	21	488
61 (22)	1158	229	**2 Peter**	**2**	22	581
61 (22)	1159	230	**2 Peter**	**3**	18	484
61 – 22			**2 PETER**		**61**	**1,553**
62 (23)	1160	231	**1 John**	**1**	10	247
62 (23)	1161	232	**1 John**	**2**	29	736
62 (23)	1162	233	**1 John**	**3**	24	534
62 (23)	1163	234	**1 John**	**4**	21	480
62 (23)	1164	235	**1 John**	**5**	21	520
62 – 23			**1 JOHN**		**105**	**2,517**
63 (24)	1165	236	**2 John**	**1**	13	298
63 – 24			**2 JOHN**		**13**	**298**
64 (25)	1166	237	**3 John**	**1**	14	294
64 – 25			**3 JOHN**		**14**	**294**
65 (26)	1167	238	**Jude**	**1**	25	608
65 – 26			**JUDE**		**25**	**608**
GENERAL EPISTLES (JAMES - JUDE)					**431**	**10,050**
66 (27)	1168	239	**Revelation**	**1**	20	592
66 (27)	1169	240	**Revelation**	**2**	29	802
66 (27)	1170	241	**Revelation**	**3**	22	658
66 (27)	1171	242	**Revelation**	**4**	11	348
66 (27)	1172	243	**Revelation**	**5**	14	435
66 (27)	1173	244	**Revelation**	**6**	17	540
66 (27)	1174	245	**Revelation**	**7**	17	491
66 (27)	1175	246	**Revelation**	**8**	13	397
66 (27)	1176	247	**Revelation**	**9**	21	592
66 (27)	1177	248	**Revelation**	**10**	11	353
66 (27)	1178	249	**Revelation**	**11**	19	580
66 (27)	1179	250	**Revelation**	**12**	17	497
66 (27)	1180	251	**Revelation**	**13**	18	538
66 (27)	1181	252	**Revelation**	**14**	20	651
66 (27)	1182	253	**Revelation**	**15**	8	252

# Book	# Chapter (#OT/NT)		Book	Chapter	# Verses	# Words
66 (27)	1183	254	**Revelation**	**16**	21	567
66 (27)	1184	255	**Revelation**	**17**	18	522
66 (27)	1185	256	**Revelation**	**18**	24	747
66 (27)	1186	257	**Revelation**	**19**	21	634
66 (27)	1187	258	**Revelation**	**20**	15	477
66 (27)	1188	259	**Revelation**	**21**	27	749
66 (27)	1189	260	**Revelation**	**22**	21	573
66 – 27			**REVELATION**		**404**	**11,995**
NEW TESTAMENT					**7,957**	**180,568**
THE KING JAMES BIBLE					**31,102**	**790,849**

Appendix 3 - Bible Numerics vs. "divination"

Several people have accused Bible numerics research as practicing "*numerology*" or "*divination*".

What is divination, exactly?

According to Encyclopedia Britannica, "*divination*" is "*encountered most frequently in contemporary mass society in the form of horoscopes, astrology, crystal gazing, tarot cards, and the Ouija board*."

Divination involves a mystical source, which is used by somebody to interpret a prediction of future events.

In the Bible, **divination** is well defined in Ezekiel 13, having to do with false visions/dreams seen by false prophets that are not sent from God. False prophets prophesying of future events- but not receiving any word from God. Read Ezekiel 13 to see for yourself.

None of that has anything to do with counting or gaining knowledge of book counts, chapter counts, verse counts, word counts, letter counts, etc. that are in the Bible.

On the contrary, God counts and measures things all the time in the Bible, especially things/places that are holy. Does He want us to close our eyes whenever we read those passages?

If any of the notes in this book were to be considered numerology or divination, you would have to also say by that same logic: "It's numerology/divination to count the number of books in the Bible."

Is that right? No, it's just a mathematical fact- and it's an important fact to know. If your Bible has 65 books, you should probably find the one that's missing.

Is it divination to say, "God intended His volume to have 66 books." ...?
No, you simply have faith that God gave you His completed word.

Is it numerology to say, "There are 7 mentions of Jesus Christ in the book of Revelation"? Is it divination to point out mathematical anomalies and patterns that factually exist in the most printed book of human history? Is it wrong to conclude that those concealed patterns are all miraculously pointing to God's inspiration- where He precisely measured things and names that are important to Him in His own book?

Well, either He inspired them, or they are all here by random chance.

If you believe the Bible, where God has specific counts/measurements for Noah's ark, the tabernacle, the things in the tabernacle, feast days, sacrifices, the temple, New Jerusalem, etc... the Bible literally records the number of pomegranates on each pommel of each chapiter of each pillar in the temple (2 Chronicles 4:13). If God provides detailed patterns and measurements for what HE considers to be holy, why wouldn't the HOLY Bible (Romans 1:2, 2 Timothy 3:15) also be measured in exactness by our infinite Creator?

Either there are many patterns that go beyond random chance, or there are just a few anomalies that could be easily found or outperformed in other books, or other Bible versions, if you looked hard enough.

That's fair enough, right?

I challenge anybody who has read through this book of notes to produce a series of patterns of greater magnitude/significance in any other book on the planet.

Appendix 4 - Verse Comparison: KJB vs Modern

Here is a simple Bible comparison chart that shows just how different the modern Bible versions are from the KJB. These changes are very important because God's truth cannot proclaim conflicting messages. God is not the author of confusion. Modern Bibles are destroying the trustworthiness of the Bible, which is the very foundation of the gospel.

Affected versions check include: NKJV (New King James Version), ESV (English Standard Version), NASB1995 & NASB2020 (New American Standard Bible), NIV (New International Version), NLT (New Living Translation), CSB (Christian Standard Bible), HCSB (Holmon Christian Standard Bible), AMP (Amplified Version), NET (New English Translation), NRSV (New Revised Standard Version), MEV (Modern English Version), CEB (Common English Bible), GNT (Good News Translation), ISV (International Standard Version). Other versions were not checked.

Note: this is a partial list. There are literally thousands of changes.

KJB	**Modern**	*Corrupted in*	Notes
Genesis 1:26 KJB **And God said, Let us make man in our image, after our likeness: and let them have dominion over the fish of the sea, and over the fowl of the air, and over the cattle, and over all the earth, and over every creeping thing that creepeth upon the earth.**	Genesis 1:26 NIV **Then God said, "Let us make mankind in our image, in our likeness, so that they may rule over the fish in the sea and the birds in the sky, over the livestock and all the wild animals, and over all the creatures that move along the ground."**	NIV NLT NRSV GNT	
Genesis 1:27 KJB **So God created man in his own image, in the image of God created he him; male and female created he them.**	Genesis 1:27 NIV **So God created mankind in his own image, in the image of God he created them; male and female he created them.**	NIV NLT NET NRSV CEB GNT ISV	Who was made in the image of God? Adam? or *both* Adam and Eve?
Genesis 3:16 KJB **Unto the woman he said, I will greatly multiply thy sorrow and thy conception; in sorrow thou shalt bring forth children; and thy desire shall be to thy husband, and he shall rule over thee.**	Genesis 3:16 ESV **To the woman he said, "I will surely multiply your pain in childbearing; in pain you shall bring forth children. Your desire shall be contrary to your husband, but he shall rule over you."** Genesis 3:16 NET **To the woman he said, "I will greatly increase your labor pains; with pain you will give birth to children. You will want to control your husband, but he will dominate you."**	ESV NLT NET ISV	
Genesis 12:19 KJB **Why saidst thou, She is my sister? so I might have taken her to me to wife: now therefore behold thy wife, take her, and go thy way.**	Genesis 12:19 ESV **Why did you say, 'She is my sister,' so that I took her for my wife? Now then, here is your wife; take her, and go."**	ESV NASB1995 NASB2020 NIV NLT CSB NRSV AMP NET	New Bibles alter the wording to indicate Pharaoh actually took Sarai to be his wife

KJB	Modern	*Corrupted in*	Notes
Genesis 22:17 KJB **That in blessing I will bless thee, and in multiplying I will multiply thy seed as the stars of the heaven, and as the sand which is upon the sea shore; and thy seed shall possess the gate of his enemies;**	Genesis 22:17 NKJV **blessing I will bless you, and multiplying I will multiply your descendants as the stars of the heaven and as the sand which is on the seashore; and your descendants shall possess the gate of their enemies.**	NKJV NASB1995 NASB2020 NIV NLT CSB NRSV AMP NET	Prophecy of Jesus Christ distorted. See Galatians 3:16.
Genesis 27:39 KJB **And Isaac his father answered and said unto him, Behold, thy dwelling shall be the fatness of the earth, and of the dew of heaven from above;**	Genesis 27:39 ESV **Then Isaac his father answered and said to him: "Behold, away from the fatness of the earth shall your dwelling be, and away from the dew of heaven on high.**	ESV NASB1995 NASB2020 NIV NLT CSB HCSB	AMP NRSV MEV CEB GNT ISV
Genesis 30:27 KJB **And Laban said unto him, I pray thee, if I have found favour in thine eyes, tarry: for I have learned by experience that the LORD hath blessed me for thy sake.**	Genesis 30:27 ESV **But Laban said to him, "If I have found favor in your sight, I have learned by divination that the LORD has blessed me because of you.** Genesis 30:27 NLT **"Please listen to me," Laban replied. "I have become wealthy, for the LORD has blessed me because of you.**	ESV NASB1995 NASB2020 NIV NLT CSB HCSB AMP NET NRSV MEV CEB GNT ISV	
Genesis 36:24 KJB **And these are the children of Zibeon; both Ajah, and Anah: this was that Anah that found the mules in the wilderness, as he fed the asses of Zibeon his father.**	Genesis 36:24 NKJV **These were the sons of Zibeon: both Ajah and Anah. This was the Anah who found the water in the wilderness as he pastured the donkeys of his father Zibeon.**	NKJV ESV NASB1995 NASB2020 NIV NLT CSB HCSB	AMP NET NRSV MEV CEB GNT ISV
Genesis 47:21 KJB **And as for the people, he removed them to cities from one end of the borders of Egypt even to the other end thereof.**	Genesis 47:21 ESV **As for the people, he made servants of them from one end of Egypt to the other.** Genesis 47:21 GNT **Joseph made slaves of the people from one end of Egypt to the other.**	ESV NIV NLT CSB NET NRSV GNT	
Genesis 49:6 KJB **O my soul, come not thou into their secret; unto their assembly, mine honour, be not thou united: for in their anger they slew a man, and in their selfwill they digged down a wall.**	Genesis 49:6 NKJV **Let not my soul enter their council; Let not my honor be united to their assembly; For in their anger they slew a man, And in their self-will they hamstrung an ox.**	NKJV ESV NASB1995 NASB2020 NIV NLT CSB HCSB	AMP NET NRSV MEV CEB GNT ISV
Genesis 49:10 KJB **The sceptre shall not depart from Judah, nor a lawgiver from between his feet, until Shiloh come; and unto him shall the gathering of the people be.**	Genesis 49:10 ESV **The scepter shall not depart from Judah, nor the ruler's staff from between his feet, until tribute comes to him; and to him shall be the obedience of the peoples.**	ESV NIV NLT CSB HCSB NET NRSV CEB GNT ISV	

KJB	Modern	*Corrupted in*	Notes
Exodus 6:3 KJB **And I appeared unto Abraham, unto Isaac, and unto Jacob, by the name of God Almighty, but by my name JEHOVAH was I not known to them.**	Exodus 6:3 NKJV **I appeared to Abraham, to Isaac, and to Jacob, as God Almighty, but by My name LORD I was not known to them.** Exodus 6:3 NLT **I appeared to Abraham, to Isaac, and to Jacob as El-Shaddai—'God Almighty'—but I did not reveal my name, Yahweh, to them.**	NKJV ESV NASB1995 NASB2020 NIV NLT CSB HCSB AMP NET NRSV MEV CEB GNT ISV	"**JEHOVAH**" is also omitted from new Bibles in: Genesis 22:14 Exodus 17:15 Judges 6:24 Psalm 83:18 Isaiah 12:2, 26:4
Exodus 29:22 KJB **Also thou shalt take of the ram the fat and the rump, and the fat that covereth the inwards, and the caul above the liver, and the two kidneys, and the fat that is upon them, and the right shoulder; for it is a ram of consecration:**	Exodus 29:22 NKJV **"Also you shall take the fat of the ram, the fat tail, the fat that covers the entrails, the fatty lobe attached to the liver, the two kidneys and the fat on them, the right thigh (for it is a ram of consecration),**	NKJV ESV NASB1995 NASB2020 NIV NLT CSB HCSB AMP NET	NRSV CEB GNT ISV
Exodus 34:14 KJB **For thou shalt worship no other god: for the LORD, whose name is Jealous, is a jealous God:**	Exodus 34:14 HCSB **You are never to bow down to another god because Yahweh, being jealous by nature, is a jealous God.** Exodus 34:14 CEB **You must not bow down to another god, because the LORD is passionate: the LORD'S name means "a passionate God."**	CSB HCSB CEB GNT	
Exodus 34:33 KJB **And till Moses had done speaking with them, he put a vail on his face.**	Exodus 34:33 NJKV **And when Moses had finished speaking with them, he put a veil on his face.**	NKJV ESV NASB1995 NASB2020 NIV NLT CSB HCSB AMP NET NRSV MEV CEB GNT ISV	Most modern versions say the opposite of the KJB- that Moses waited until he was done speaking to put the vail on his face, thus contradicting the apostle Paul in 2 Cor 3:13-14
Leviticus 10:6 KJB **And Moses said unto Aaron, and unto Eleazar and unto Ithamar, his sons, Uncover not your heads, neither rend your clothes; lest ye die, and lest wrath come upon all the people: but let your brethren, the whole house of Israel, bewail the burning which the LORD hath kindled.**	Leviticus 10:6 NLT **Then Moses said to Aaron and his sons Eleazar and Ithamar, "Do not show grief by leaving your hair uncombed or by tearing your clothes. If you do, you will die, and the LORD'S anger will strike the whole community of Israel. However, the rest of the Israelites, your relatives, may mourn because of the LORD'S fiery destruction of Nadab and Abihu.** Leviticus 10:6 MEV **...Do not let your hair be loosely disheveled...**	ESV NIV NLT NLT CSB HCSB AMP NET NRSV MEV CEB GNT ISV	They say new versions are important because the KJB is archaic and hard to understand. Yet, they often introduce tough vocabulary themselves. The "Modern English Version" along with the NET and a few others, uses a term that I have never used or heard in my entire life: "*loosely disheveled*". They have both increased reading difficulty and distorted the word of God at the same time.

KJB	Modern	Corrupted in	Notes
Leviticus 13:47 KJB **The garment also that the plague of leprosy is in, whether it be a woollen garment, or a linen garment;**	Leviticus 13:47 NLT **"Now suppose mildew contaminates some woolen or linen clothing,**	NIV NLT CSB HCSB NET NRSV	CEB GNT ISV
Leviticus 16:10 KJB **But the goat, on which the lot fell to be the scapegoat, shall be presented alive before the LORD, to make an atonement with him, and to let him go for a scapegoat into the wilderness.**	Leviticus 16:10 ESV **but the goat on which the lot fell for Azazel shall be presented alive before the LORD to make atonement over it, that it may be sent away into the wilderness to Azazel.** Leviticus 16:10 GNT **The goat chosen for Azazel shall be presented alive to the LORD and sent off into the desert to Azazel, in order to take away the sins of the people.**	ESV NLT HCSB NET NRSV CEB GNT	Who is Azazel? The book of Enoch (which is not inspired) says Azazel is a rebellious leader of watchers that fell before the flood and taught men war and witchcraft. Other sources say Azazel is a goat-like demon dwelling in the desert. *"The confusion (and the error) of some Bible translators is that they see the Hebrew word # 5799 "gazah-zehl" as being a personal name - Azazel -, whereas others (correctly) see this Hebrew word as being a compound noun made up of two words - Scapegoat. The King James Bible (and even the NASB, NIV and many others) got it right."* - Will Kinney https://brandplucked.webs.com
Numbers 11:25 KJB **And the LORD came down in a cloud, and spake unto him, and took of the spirit that was upon him, and gave it unto the seventy elders: and it came to pass, that, when the spirit rested upon them, they prophesied, and did not cease.**	Numbers 11:25 NKJV **Then the LORD came down in the cloud, and spoke to him, and took of the Spirit that was upon him, and placed the same upon the seventy elders; and it happened, when the Spirit rested upon them, that they prophesied, although they never did so again.**	NKJV ESV NASB1995 NASB2020 NIV NLT CSB HCSB AMP NET NRSV MEV	CEB GNT ISV
Deuteronomy 16:21 KJB **Thou shalt not plant thee a grove of any trees near unto the altar of the LORD thy God, which thou shalt make thee.**	Deuteronomy 16:21 NIV **Do not set up any wooden Asherah pole beside the altar you build to the LORD your God,**	NKJV ESV NASB1995 NASB2020 NIV NLT CSB HCSB	AMP NET NRSV MEV CEB GNT ISV
Deuteronomy 23:17 KJB **There shall be no whore of the daughters of Israel, nor a sodomite of the sons of Israel.**	Deuteronomy 23:17 NKJV **"There shall be no ritual harlot of the daughters of Israel, or a perverted one of the sons of Israel.** Deuteronomy 23:17 ESV **"None of the daughters of Israel shall be a cult prostitute, and none of the sons of Israel shall be a cult prostitute.** Deuteronomy 23:17 NLT **"No Israelite, whether man or**	NKJV ESV NASB1995 NASB2020 NIV NLT CSB HCSB NET NRSV MEV CEB GNT ISV	"**Sodomites**" is also removed from: 1 Kings 14:24 1 Kings 15:12 1 Kings 22:46 2 Kings 23:7

KJB	Modern	Corrupted in	Notes
	woman, may become a temple prostitute. Deuteronomy 23:17 NET **There must never be a sacred prostitute among the young women of Israel nor a sacred male prostitute among the young men of Israel.** Deuteronomy 23:17 NRSV **"None of the daughters of Israel shall serve in an illicit shrine; none of the sons of Israel shall serve in an illicit shrine.** Deuteronomy 23:17 CEB **No Israelite daughter is allowed to be a consecrated worker. Neither is any Israelite son allowed to be a consecrated worker.**		
Deuteronomy 32:5 KJB **They have corrupted themselves, their spot is not the spot of his children: they are a perverse and crooked generation.**	Deuteronomy 32:5 NKJV **"They have corrupted themselves; They are not His children, Because of their blemish: A perverse and crooked generation.** Deuteronomy 32:5 CEB **But children who weren't his own sinned against him with their defects; they are a twisted and perverse generation.**	NKJV ESV NASB1995 NASB2020 NIV NLT CSB HCSB AMP NET NRSV MEV CEB GNT ISV	
Judges 15:19 KJB **But God clave an hollow place that was in the jaw, and there came water thereout; and when he had drunk, his spirit came again, and he revived: wherefore he called the name thereof En–hakkore, which is in Lehi unto this day.**	Judges 15:19 NKJV **So God split the hollow place that is in Lehi, and water came out, and he drank; and his spirit returned, and he revived. Therefore he called its name En Hakkore, which is in Lehi to this day.**	NKJV ESV NASB1995 NASB2020 NIV NLT CSB HCSB AMP NET	NRSV MEV CEB GNT ISV
1 Samuel 13:1 KJB **Saul reigned one year; and when he had reigned two years over Israel,**	1 Samuel 13:1 ESV **Saul lived for one year and then became king, and when he had reigned for two years over Israel,** 1 Samuel 13:1 NASB2020 **Saul was thirty years old when he began to reign, and he reigned for forty-two years over Israel.** 1 Samuel 13:1 NRSV **Saul was ... years old when he began to reign, and he reigned ... and two years over Israel.** 1 Samuel 13:1 GNT *Omitted*	ESV NASB1995 NASB2020 NIV NLT CSB HCSB AMP NET NRSV MEV CEB GNT ISV	The ESV makes a pretty stunning claim- that Saul was a 1 year old baby when he became king over Israel. Can you imagine a 1 year old who **from his shoulders and upward he was higher than any of the people**...? (1 Sam 9:2 KJB) The NASB and many other modern translations have way different numbers and meanings. The NRSV literally has dots instead of words/numbers. The GNT completely omits the verse.

KJB	Modern	*Corrupted in*	Notes
1 Samuel 25:17 KJB **Now therefore know and consider what thou wilt do; for evil is determined against our master, and against all his household: for he is such a son of Belial, that a man cannot speak to him.**	1 Samuel 25:17 NKJV **Now therefore, know and consider what you will do, for harm is determined against our master and against all his household. For he is such a scoundrel that one cannot speak to him."**	NKJV ESV NASB1995 NASB2020 NIV NLT CSB HCSB AMP NET NRSV MEV CEB GNT ISV	Modern versions remove Satan's name Belial, undermining the doctrine of Satan's literal personhood. **Belial** is also removed from: Deuteronomy 13:13 Judges 19:22, 20:13 1 Samuel 1:16, 2:12, 10:27, 25:25, 30:22 2 Samuel 16:7, 20:1, 23:6 1 Kings 21:10,13 2 Chronicles 13:7
2 Samuel 5:21 KJB **And there they left their images, and David and his men burned them.**	2 Samuel 5:21 NKJV **And they left their images there, and David and his men carried them away.**	NKJV ESV NASB1995 NASB2020 NIV NLT CSB	HCSB NET NRSV MEV CEB GNT ISV
2 Samuel 14:14 KJB **For we must needs die, and are as water spilt on the ground, which cannot be gathered up again; neither doth God respect any person: yet doth he devise means, that his banished be not expelled from him.**	2 Samuel 14:14 NKJV **For we will surely die and become like water spilled on the ground, which cannot be gathered up again. Yet God does not take away a life; but He devises means, so that His banished ones are not expelled from Him.** 2 Samuel 14:14 GNT **We will all die; we are like water spilled on the ground, which can't be gathered again. Even God does not bring the dead back to life, but the king can at least find a way to bring a man back from exile.**	NKJV ESV NASB1995 NASB2020 NIV NLT CSB HCSB AMP NET NRSV MEV CEB GNT ISV	Most modern versions are similar to the NKJV.
2 Samuel 15:7 KJB **And it came to pass after forty years, that Absalom said unto the king, I pray thee, let me go and pay my vow, which I have vowed unto the LORD, in Hebron.**	2 Samuel 15:7 ESV **And at the end of four years Absalom said to the king, "Please let me go and pay my vow, which I have vowed to the LORD, in Hebron.**	ESV NASB2020 NIV NLT CSB HCSB AMP NET NRSV CEB GNT	The NASB1995 says "**forty**" and the NASB2020 says "**four**"
2 Samuel 21:19 KJB **And there was again a battle in Gob with the Philistines, where Elhanan the son of Jaare–oregim, a Beth–lehemite, slew the brother of Goliath the Gittite, the staff of whose spear was like a weaver's beam.**	2 Samuel 21:19 NASB2020 **And there was war with the Philistines again at Gob, and Elhanan the son of Jaare-oregim the Bethlehemite killed Goliath the Gittite, the shaft of whose spear was like a weaver's beam.**	ESV NASB1995 NASB2020 CSB HCSB AMP NRSV MEV GNT ISV	Goliath was most likely dead already- seeing that his head was cut off by David in 1 Samuel 17:51 1 Chronicles 20:5 confirms: **...Elhanan the son of Jair slew Lahmi the brother of Goliath the Gittite...**

KJB	Modern	Corrupted in	Notes
2 Kings 23:29 KJB **In his days Pharaoh–nechoh king of Egypt went up against the king of Assyria to the river Euphrates: and king Josiah went against him; and he slew him at Megiddo, when he had seen him.**	2 Kings 23:29 NKJV **In his days Pharaoh Necho king of Egypt went to the aid of the king of Assyria, to the River Euphrates; and King Josiah went against him. And Pharaoh Necho killed him at Megiddo when he confronted him.** 2 Kings 23:29 AMP **In his days Pharaoh Neco (Necho) king of Egypt went up to the king of Assyria to the river Euphrates [to help him fight Nabopolassar the king of Babylon]. King Josiah went out to meet him, but Pharaoh killed Josiah at Megiddo when he saw him.**	NKJV NIV NLT CSB HCSB AMP NET GNT	
2 Kings 25:8-9 KJB **And in the fifth month, on the seventh day of the month, which is the nineteenth year of king Nebuchadnezzar king of Babylon, came Nebuzar–adan, captain of the guard, a servant of the king of Babylon, unto Jerusalem:** **And he burnt the house of the LORD, and the king's house, and all the houses of Jerusalem, and every great *man's* house burnt he with fire.**	2 Kings 25:8-9 NKJV **And in the fifth month, on the seventh day of the month (which was the nineteenth year of King Nebuchadnezzar king of Babylon), Nebuzaradan the captain of the guard, a servant of the king of Babylon, came to Jerusalem. He burned the house of the LORD and the king's house; all the houses of Jerusalem, that is, all the houses of the great, he burned with fire.**	NKJV NASB1995 NASB2020 NIV NLT CSB HCSB AMP NET CEB GNT	This tiny detail using "**to**" instead of "**unto**" creates a contradiction in the NKJV (the other modern Bibles listed to the left also contradict themselves). There is no contradiction in the KJB. Here's why: In 2 Kings 25:8, the date is recorded as the 5th month, 7th day of the month. There is a parallel verse in the Bible to this passage, Jeremiah 52:12, which records the date as the 5th month, 10th day of the month. (which is 3 days after the recorded date in 2 Kings). The important difference is formed by one letter. In 2 Kings 25:8 (KJB), the word "**unto**" is used- meaning the army of the Chaldees came **unto** (up against) Jerusalem on the 7th day of the month to destroy it. Jeremiah 52:8 (KJB) reads "**into**" - meaning the Chaldees actually entered the city on the 10th day of the month to burn everything down. **...in the fifth month, on the seventh day of the month... came Nebuzar–adan... unto Jerusalem** (2 Ki 25:8) **...in the fifth month, in the tenth day of the month... came Nebuzar–adan... into Jerusalem,** (Jer 52:12) Most modern Bibles do not

KJB	Modern	*Corrupted in*	Notes
			make any sort of distinction between these two events. The NKJV reads "**...to Jerusalem**" in both 2 Ki. 25:8 and Jer 52:12. This creates an apparent contradiction with no way of reconciling, since the dates are not the same. The ESV also reads "**...to Jerusalem**" in 2 Ki. 25:8 (Day 7) like the NKJV, but gets it right because its parallel passage reads, "**entered Jerusalem**" in Jer 52:12 ESV (Day 10)
Job 16:20 KJB **My friends scorn me: but mine eye poureth out tears unto God.**	Job 16:20 NIV **My intercessor is my friend as my eyes pour out tears to God;**	NIV NET GNT	
Psalm 4:4 KJB **Stand in awe, and sin not: commune with your own heart upon your bed, and be still. Selah.**	Psalm 4:4 NKJV **Be angry, and do not sin. Meditate within your heart on your bed, and be still. Selah** Psalm 4:4 NIV **Tremble and do not sin; when you are on your beds, search your hearts and be silent.** Psalm 4:4 NLT **Don't sin by letting anger control you. Think about it overnight and remain silent. Interlude** Psalm 4:4 AMP **Tremble [with anger or fear], and do not sin; Meditate in your heart upon your bed and be still [reflect on your sin and repent of your rebellion]. Selah.**	ESV NASB1995 NASB2020 NIV NLT CSB HCSB AMP NET NRSV CEB GNT ISV	
Psalm 9 Superscription KJB *To the chief Musician upon Muthlabben, A Psalm of David.*	Psalm 9 Superscription NKJV *To the Chief Musician. To the tune of "Death of the Son." A Psalm of David.*	NKJV NIV NLT MEV ISV	
Psalm 10:4-5 KJB **The wicked, through the pride of his countenance, will not seek after God: God is not in all his thoughts.** **His ways are always grievous; thy judgments are far above out of his sight: as for all his enemies, he puffeth at them.**	Psalm 10:4-5 NKJV **The wicked in his proud countenance does not seek God; God is in none of his thoughts.** **His ways are always prospering; Your judgments are far above, out of his sight; As for all his enemies, he sneers at them.** Psalm 10:4-5 NASB1995 **The wicked, in the haughtiness of his countenance, does not seek Him. All his thoughts are, "There is no God."** **His ways prosper at all times...**	NKJV ESV NASB1995 NASB2020 NIV NLT CSB HCSB AMP NET NRSV MEV CEB GNT ISV	

KJB	Modern	*Corrupted in*	Notes
Psalm 12:6-7 KJB **The words of the LORD are pure words: as silver tried in a furnace of earth, purified seven times. Thou shalt keep them, O LORD, thou shalt preserve them from this generation for ever.**	Psalm 12:6-7 NASB2020 **The words of the LORD are pure words; Like silver refined in a furnace on the ground, filtered seven times. You, LORD, will keep them; You will protect him from this generation forever.** Psalm 12:7 ESV **...you will guard us from this generation forever.** Psalm 12:7 NLT **Therefore, LORD, we know you will protect the oppressed, preserving them forever from this lying generation,** Psalm 12:6-7 NET **The LORD'S words are absolutely reliable. They are as untainted as silver purified in a furnace on the ground, where it is thoroughly refined. You, LORD, will protect them; you will continually shelter each one from these evil people,**	ESV NASB1995 NASB2020 NIV NLT CSB HCSB AMP NET NRSV CEB GNT	The doctrine of God's forever preserved words, distorted.
Psalm 100:5 KJB **For the LORD is good; his mercy is everlasting; and his truth endureth to all generations.**	Psalm 100:5 NIV **For the LORD is good and his love endures forever; his faithfulness continues through all generations.**	ESV NASB1995 NASB2020 NIV NLT CSB HCSB	AMP NET NRSV MEV CEB GNT ISV
Psalm 119:140 KJB **Thy word is very pure: therefore thy servant loveth it.**	Psalm 119:140 ESV **Your promise is well tried, and your servant loves it.** Psalm 119:140 GNT **How certain your promise is! How I love it!**	ESV NIV NLT NRSV CEB GNT	
Psalm 138:2 KJB **I will worship toward thy holy temple, and praise thy name for thy lovingkindness and for thy truth: for thou hast magnified thy word above all thy name.**	Psalm 138:2 ESV **I bow down toward your holy temple and give thanks to your name for your steadfast love and your faithfulness, for you have exalted above all things your name and your word.** Psalm 138:2 NIV **...for you have so exalted your solemn decree that it surpasses your fame.** Psalm 138:2 NLT **...for your promises are backed by all the honor of your name.** Psalm 138:2 NET **...for you have exalted your promise above the entire sky.**	ESV NASB1995 NASB2020 NIV NLT CSB HCSB AMP NET NRSV CEB GNT ISV	God has magnified His word above all His name. That's severe. God promises to take men's parts out of the book of life for taking away from His words at the end of the Bible. Many modern versions distort the very verse to show just how important God's word is-according to Himself.

KJB	Modern	*Corrupted in*	Notes
Proverbs 8:22 KJB **The LORD possessed me in the beginning of his way, before his works of old.**	Proverbs 8:22 NASB2020 **"The LORD created me at the beginning of His way, Before His works of old.** Proverbs 8:22 CSB **"The LORD acquired me at the beginning of his creation, before his works of long ago.**	ESV NASB2020 NIV NLT CSB HCSB AMP NET NRSV CEB GNT ISV	Who is speaking in this verse? Directly in context, "**wisdom**" is talking (Prov 8:12). Most students of scripture agree it's either the Holy Ghost or Jesus Christ as the preincarnate Word of God. Neither of whom were "**created**" as modern versions declare. Both are from everlasting to everlasting. The CSB says the LORD had to **acquire** (get) **wisdom** (or the Holy Ghost / the Word). This directly implies God needed to go somewhere else to acquire part of Himself- which is downright blasphemous and an open door to gnostic heresies that claim the LORD of the Old Testament is a created demiurge.
Proverbs 18:1 KJB **Through desire a man, having separated himself, seeketh and intermeddleth with all wisdom.**	Proverbs 18:1 NKJV **A man who isolates himself seeks his own desire; He rages against all wise judgment.** Proverbs 18:1 NLT **Unfriendly people care only about themselves; they lash out at common sense.** Proverbs 18:1 GNT **People who do not get along with others are interested only in themselves; they will disagree with what everyone else knows is right.**	NKJV ESV NASB1995 NASB2020 NIV NLT CSB HCSB AMP NET NRSV MEV CEB GNT ISV	
Proverbs 19:18 KJB **Chasten thy son while there is hope, and let not thy soul spare for his crying.**	Proverbs 19:18 NKJV **Chasten your son while there is hope, And do not set your heart on his destruction.** Proverbs 19:18 CEB **Discipline your children while there is hope, but don't plan to kill them.**	NKJV ESV NASB1995 NASB2020 NIV NLT CSB HCSB AMP NET NRSV	CEB GNT ISV
Proverbs 22:12 KJB **The eyes of the LORD preserve knowledge, and he overthroweth the words of the transgressor.**	Proverbs 22:12 NKJV **The eyes of the LORD preserve knowledge, But He overthrows the words of the faithless.** Proverbs 22:12 NLT **The LORD preserves those with knowledge, but he ruins the plans of the treacherous.**	NKJV ESV NASB1995 NASB2020 NIV NLT CSB HCSB AMP NET NRSV MEV	CEB GNT ISV

KJB	Modern	*Corrupted in*	Notes
Proverbs 22:21 KJB **That I might make thee know the certainty of the words of truth; that thou mightest answer the words of truth to them that send unto thee?**	Proverbs 22:21 NIV **teaching you to be honest and to speak the truth, so that you bring back truthful reports to those you serve?** Proverbs 22:21 ISV **to teach you true and reliable advice, so you can give truthful answers to those who sent you?**	NIV NLT CSB HCSB ISV	
Proverbs 25:23 KJB **The north wind driveth away rain: so doth an angry countenance a backbiting tongue.**	Proverbs 25:23 NKJV **The north wind brings forth rain, And a backbiting tongue an angry countenance.**	NKJV ESV NASB1995 NASB2020 NIV NLT CSB HCSB AMP NET NRSV MEV CEB GNT ISV	The only problem with modern versions is that the north wind doesn't bring rain to Israel. The NET footnote self-admittedly reads: *One difficulty here is that it is the west wind that brings rain to Israel (e.g., 1 Kgs 18:41-44)*
Proverbs 26:22 KJB **The words of a talebearer are as wounds, and they go down into the innermost parts of the belly.**	Proverbs 26:22 ESV **The words of a whisperer are like delicious morsels; they go down into the inner parts of the body.**	NKJV ESV NASB1995 NASB2020 NIV NLT CSB	HCSB AMP NET NRSV CEB GNT ISV
Ecclesiastes 2:8 KJB **I gathered me also silver and gold, and the peculiar treasure of kings and of the provinces: I gat me men singers and women singers, and the delights of the sons of men, as musical instruments, and that of all sorts.**	Ecclesiastes 2:8 NASB2020 **I also amassed for myself silver and gold, and the treasure of kings and provinces. I provided for myself male and female singers, and the pleasures of the sons of mankind: many concubines.** Ecclesiastes 2:8 NIV **I amassed silver and gold for myself, and the treasure of kings and provinces. I acquired male and female singers, and a harem as well—the delights of a man's heart.** Ecclesiastes 2:8 NLT **I collected great sums of silver and gold, the treasure of many kings and provinces. I hired wonderful singers, both men and women, and had many beautiful concubines. I had everything a man could desire!**	ESV NASB1995 NASB2020 NIV NLT CSB HCSB AMP NET NRSV MEV CEB GNT ISV	Modern bibles distort Ecclesiastes 2:8 and 2:25 to create a doctrine from hell. The following message is produced when you read the entire chapter in context (in a modern version such as the NASB) 1. Concubines are a pleasure & enjoyment of life that are a result of wisdom and hard work (Ecc 2:8,9,10) 2. Pleasure of life (concubines) comes from God and there is nothing better in life than to enjoy what God has given you (Ecc 2:24,25) Conclusion (from modern Bibles) - *True wisdom is enjoying the concubines that God has rewarded you with for your wisdom and labour.*
Ecclesiastes 2:25 KJB **For who can eat, or who else can hasten hereunto, more than I?**	Ecclesiastes 2:25 NASB2020 **For who can eat and who can have enjoyment without Him?**	NKJV ESV NASB1995 NASB2020 NIV NLT CSB HCSB AMP NET NRSV MEV	CEB GNT ISV

KJB	Modern	Corrupted in	Notes
Ecclesiastes 3:11 KJB **He hath made every thing beautiful in his time: also he hath set the world in their heart, so that no man can find out the work that God maketh from the beginning to the end.**	Ecclesiastes 3:11 NKJV **He has made everything beautiful in its time. Also He has put eternity in their hearts, except that no one can find out the work that God does from beginning to end.** Ecclesiastes 3:11 NET **God has made everything fit beautifully in its appropriate time, but he has also placed ignorance in the human heart so that people cannot discover what God has ordained, from the beginning to the end of their lives.** Ecclesiastes 3:11 NRSV **...he has put a sense of past and future into their minds...** Ecclesiastes 3:11 MEV **...He has also put obscurity in their hearts...**	NKJV ESV NASB1995 NASB2020 NIV NLT CSB HCSB AMP NET NRSV MEV CEB GNT ISV	
Ecclesiastes 8:8 KJB **There is no man that hath power over the spirit to retain the spirit; neither hath he power in the day of death: and there is no discharge in that war; neither shall wickedness deliver those that are given to it.**	Ecclesiastes 8:8 NASB2020 **No one has authority over the wind to restrain the wind, nor authority over the day of death; and there is no military discharge in the time of war, and evil will not save those who practice it.** Ecclesiastes 8:8 ESV **No man has power to retain the spirit, or power over the day of death. There is no discharge from war, nor will wickedness deliver those who are given to it.** Ecclesiastes 8:8 MEV **There is not a man with mastery over the wind to restrain it, nor with power over the day of death. And no one can discharge a battle, nor can wickedness rescue the one possessing it.**	ESV NASB1995 NASB2020 NIV CSB HCSB AMP NET NRSV MEV CEB GNT ISV	
Ecclesiastes 8:10 KJB **And so I saw the wicked buried, who had come and gone from the place of the holy, and they were forgotten in the city where they had so done: this is also vanity.**	Ecclesiastes 8:10 ESV **Then I saw the wicked buried. They used to go in and out of the holy place and were praised in the city where they had done such things. This also is vanity.** Ecclesiastes 8:10 NET **Not only that, but I have seen the wicked approaching and entering the temple, and as they left the holy temple, they boasted in the city that they had done so. This also is an enigma.**	ESV NIV NLT CSB HCSB AMP NET NRSV MEV GNT	

KJB	Modern	Corrupted in	Notes
Ecclesiastes 11:1 KJB **Cast thy bread upon the waters: for thou shalt find it after many days.**	Ecclesiastes 11:1 NIV **Ship your grain across the sea; after many days you may receive a return.** Ecclesiastes 11:1 GNT **Invest your money in foreign trade, and one of these days you will make a profit.**	NIV NLT NET NRSV CEB GNT	
Ecclesiastes 11:5 KJB **As thou knowest not what is the way of the spirit, nor how the bones do grow in the womb of her that is with child: even so thou knowest not the works of God who maketh all.**	Ecclesiastes 11:5 NASB2020 **Just as you do not know the path of the wind, and how bones are formed in the womb of the pregnant woman, so you do not know the activity of God who makes everything.** Ecclesiastes 11:5 NKJV **As you do not know what is the way of the wind, Or how the bones grow in the womb of her who is with child, So you do not know the works of God who makes everything.** Ecclesiastes 11:5 ESV **As you do not know the way the spirit comes to the bones in the womb of a woman with child, so you do not know the work of God who makes everything.**	NKJV ESV NASB1995 NASB2020 NIV NLT CSB HCSB NET NRSV MEV CEB GNT ISV	The NASB replaces "**her that is with child**" with "**pregnant woman**" Meditate over this. The medical term is not "*killing a child*" but rather "*ending a pregnancy*" Modern versions (ESV, NASB, NIV, etc) use this pro-abortion-friendly terminology quite often. **with child → pregnant** Genesis 16:11, 19:36, 38:24,25 Exodus 21:22 1 Samuel 4:19 2 Samuel 11:5 2 Kings 8:12, 15:16 Ecclesiastes 11:5 Isaiah 26:17,18 Jeremiah 31:8 Hosea 13:16 Amos 1:13 Matthew 1:18,23, 24:19 Mark 3:17 Luke 2:5, 21:23 1 Thessalonians 5:3 Revelation 12:2
Eclessiastes 12:5 KJB **Also when they shall be afraid of that which is high, and fears shall be in the way, and the almond tree shall flourish, and the grasshopper shall be a burden, and desire shall fail: because man goeth to his long home, and the mourners go about the streets:**	Ecclesiastes 12:5 NASB2020 **Furthermore, people are afraid of a high place and of terrors on the road; the almond tree blossoms, the grasshopper drags itself along, and the caper berry is ineffective. For man goes to his eternal home while the mourners move around in the street.** Ecclesiastes 12:5 NLT **Remember him before you become fearful of falling and worry about danger in the streets; before your hair turns white like an almond tree in bloom, and you drag along without energy like a dying grasshopper, and the caperberry no longer inspires sexual desire. Remember him before you near the grave, your everlasting home, when the mourners will weep at your funeral.**	NKJV ESV NASB1995 NASB2020 NIV NLT CSB HCSB AMP NET NRSV MEV CEB GNT ISV	

KJB	Modern	*Corrupted in*	Notes
Isaiah 7:14 KJB **Therefore the Lord himself shall give you a sign; Behold, a virgin shall conceive, and bear a son, and shall call his name Immanuel.**	Isaiah 7:14 NKJV **Therefore the Lord Himself will give you a sign: Behold, the virgin shall conceive and bear a Son, and shall call His name Immanuel.** Isaiah 7:14 NRSV **Therefore the Lord himself will give you a sign. Look, the young woman is with child and shall bear a son and shall name him Immanuel.**	NKJV ESV NASB2020 NIV NLT CSB HCSB AMP NET NRSV MEV CEB GNT ISV	Just about all modern Bibles have 1 of 2 issues: Issue #1 **a virgin** vs **the virgin** This is a subtle but massive difference. Using "**the**" instead of "**a**" indicates heavy significance toward the individual - even deification. The Roman Catholic church, in particular, venerates "*the blessed virgin Mary*" to such a degree. Modern Bibles also read "**the virgin**" in Matthew 1:23 where the King James reads, "**a virgin**" Or, Issue #2 **a virgin** vs **the young woman** This is self-explanatory. How many millions of babies were born of young women? And how would that be a sign from the Lord? Such a distortion robs the Bible of its only prophecy predicting Christ's miraculous virgin birth.
Isaiah 9:1 KJB **Nevertheless the dimness shall not be such as was in her vexation, when at the first he lightly afflicted the land of Zebulun and the land of Naphtali, and afterward did more grievously afflict her by the way of the sea, beyond Jordan, in Galilee of the nations.**	Isaiah 9:1 NASB2020 **But there will be no more gloom for her who was in anguish. In earlier times He treated the land of Zebulun and the land of Naphtali with contempt, but later on He will make it glorious, by the way of the sea, on the other side of the Jordan, Galilee of the Gentiles.**	ESV NASB1995 NASB2020 NIV NLT CSB HCSB AMP NET NRSV MEV CEB GNT ISV	
Isaiah 9:3 KJB **Thou hast multiplied the nation, and not increased the joy: they joy before thee according to the joy in harvest, and as men rejoice when they divide the spoil.**	Isaiah 9:3 NKJV **You have multiplied the nation And increased its joy; They rejoice before You According to the joy of harvest, As men rejoice when they divide the spoil.**	NKJV ESV NASB1885 NASB2020 NIV NLT CSB HCSB AMP NET NRSV MEV CEB GNT ISV	

KJB	Modern	Corrupted in	Notes
Isaiah 14:12 KJB **How art thou fallen from heaven, O Lucifer, son of the morning! how art thou cut down to the ground, which didst weaken the nations!**	Isaiah 14:12 NASB2020 **How you have fallen from heaven, You star of the morning, son of the dawn! You have been cut down to the earth, You who defeated the nations!** Isaiah 14:12 ESV **"How you are fallen from heaven, O Day Star, son of Dawn! How you are cut down to the ground, you who laid the nations low!** Isaiah 14:12 NIV **How you have fallen from heaven, morning star, son of the dawn! You have been cast down to the earth, you who once laid low the nations!**	ESV NASB1995 NASB2020 NIV NLT CSB HCSB AMP NET NRSV CEB GNT ISV	The name of Satan, "**Lucifer**" is removed from modern versions and replaced with "**morning star**" or "**star of the morning**" or "**Day Star**" This confusion mixes up the identities of Satan and the Lord Jesus Christ. **I Jesus have sent mine angel to testify unto you these things in the churches. I am the root and the offspring of David, and the bright and morning star.** Revelation 22:16 **We have also a more sure word of prophecy; whereunto ye do well that ye take heed, as unto a light that shineth in a dark place, until the day dawn, and the day star arise in your hearts:** 2 Peter 1:19 Also in Isaiah 14:12, the ESV has **son of Dawn**, which establishes grounds for an entirely new doctrine- where some sort of higher being (who is not God) is the creator or father of Satan.
Isaiah 32:1-2 KJB **Behold, a king shall reign in righteousness, and princes shall rule in judgment. And a man shall be as an hiding place from the wind, and a covert from the tempest; as rivers of water in a dry place, as the shadow of a great rock in a weary land.**	Isaiah 32:1-2 NIV **See, a king will reign in righteousness and rulers will rule with justice. Each one will be like a shelter from the wind and a refuge from the storm, like streams of water in the desert and the shadow of a great rock in a thirsty land.**	ESV NASB1995 NASB2020 NIV NLT CSB HCSB AMP NET NRSV CEB GNT ISV	The **man** is the **king**, Jesus Christ. Modern versions distort this prophecy by taking His glory and giving it to His princes.
Isaiah 53:10 KJB **Yet it pleased the LORD to bruise him; he hath put him to grief: when thou shalt make his soul an offering for sin, he shall see his seed, he shall prolong his days, and the pleasure of the LORD shall prosper in his hand.**	Isaiah 53:10 NASB2020 **But the LORD desired To crush Him, causing Him grief; If He renders Himself as a guilt offering, He will see His offspring, He will prolong His days, And the good pleasure of the LORD will prosper in His hand.** Isaiah 53:10 HCSB **Yet the LORD was pleased to crush Him severely. When You make Him a restitution offering...** Isaiah 53:10 NET **Though the LORD desired to crush him and make him ill, once restitution is made, he will see descendants...**	ESV NASB1995 NASB2020 NIV NLT CSB HCSB AMP NET NRSV MEV CEB GNT ISV	

KJB	Modern	*Corrupted in*	Notes
Isaiah 54:1 KJB **Sing, O barren, thou that didst not bear; break forth into singing, and cry aloud, thou that didst not travail with child: for more are the children of the desolate than the children of the married wife, saith the LORD.**	Isaiah 54:1 ESV **"Sing, O barren one, who did not bear; break forth into singing and cry aloud, you who have not been in labor! For the children of the desolate one will be more than the children of her who is married," says the LORD.**	ESV NASB1995 NASB2020 NIV NLT CSB HCSB NET NRSV CEB GNT ISV	As discussed in the note on Ecclesiastes 11:5, the word "**with child**" is often changed to "**pregnant**" Even when the term "**pregnant**" is not used, "**child**" is still removed from the text. Why do these versions go to such lengths to remove the fact that there is a **child** in the mother's womb? See also Jeremiah 31:8
Jeremiah 31:8 KJB **Behold, I will bring them from the north country, and gather them from the coasts of the earth, and with them the blind and the lame, the woman with child and her that travaileth with child together: a great company shall return thither.**	Jeremiah 31:8 ESV **Behold, I will bring them from the north country and gather them from the farthest parts of the earth, among them the blind and the lame, the pregnant woman and she who is in labor, together; a great company, they shall return here.**	ESV NASB2020 NIV NLT CSB HCSB NET CEB GNT ISV	See notes on Ecclesiastes 11:5 and Isaiah 54:1
Daniel 3:25 KJB **He answered and said, Lo, I see four men loose, walking in the midst of the fire, and they have no hurt; and the form of the fourth is like the Son of God.**	Daniel 3:25 AMP **He answered, "Look! I see four men untied, walking around in the midst of the fire, and they are not hurt! And the appearance of the fourth is like a son of the gods!"**	ESV NASB1995 NASB2020 NIV NLT CSB HCSB AMP NET NRSV CEB GNT ISV	The AMP footnotes for Daniel 3:25 directly attack the capitalization in the King James Bible, stating: "*The KJV has "the Son of God" here, referring to the pre-incarnate Christ, because the usual term for God is Elohim, a plural form. Even if it was the pre-incarnate Christ, however, the pagan king would not have had Him in mind but a "son" of the Babylonian gods, perhaps a minor deity or an angel.*" Perhaps the pagan king did not have Jesus Christ in mind, but the Holy Ghost did. Scripture is not just a collection of ancient writings, it is a holy volume of God's living words which came into this world through men who spake as they were moved by the Holy Ghost. Why do you think the Holy Ghost couldn't prophesy through Nebuchadnezzar's mouth when He just sent prophetic thoughts into his mind one chapter ago? (Daniel 2:29-30)

KJB	Modern	Corrupted in	Notes
Daniel 9:25 KJB **Know therefore and understand, that from the going forth of the commandment to restore and to build Jerusalem unto the Messiah the Prince shall be seven weeks, and threescore and two weeks: the street shall be built again, and the wall, even in troublous times.**	Daniel 9:25 ESV **Know therefore and understand that from the going out of the word to restore and build Jerusalem to the coming of an anointed one, a prince, there shall be seven weeks. Then for sixty-two weeks it shall be built again with squares and moat, but in a troubled time.**	ESV NIV NLT CSB NET NRSV CEB GNT ISV	There are several anointed ones in the Bible (for example, Satan- see Ezek 28:14) and indeed many princes, but only one **Messiah the Prince**.
Daniel 9:26 KJB **And after threescore and two weeks shall Messiah be cut off, but not for himself: and the people of the prince that shall come shall destroy the city and the sanctuary; and the end thereof shall be with a flood, and unto the end of the war desolations are determined.**	Daniel 9:26 NASB2020 **Then after the sixty-two weeks, the Messiah will be cut off and have nothing, and the people of the prince who is to come will destroy the city and the sanctuary. And its end will come with a flood; even to the end there will be war; desolations are determined.** Daniel 9:26 ESV **And after the sixty-two weeks, an anointed one shall be cut off and shall have nothing...**	ESV NASB1995 NASB2020 NIV NLT CSB HCSB AMP NET NRSV MEV CEB GNT ISV	Prophecy of Jesus Christ's sacrifice, desolated. Did Jesus "have nothing" when he was cut off? ...even though He was reconciling the world unto Himself? The ESV strikes out. **Messiah** is only mentioned these two times in the Old Testament, and the ESV blotted it out both times (Dan 9:25,26).
Hosea 10:1 KJB **Israel is an empty vine, he bringeth forth fruit unto himself: according to the multitude of his fruit he hath increased the altars; according to the goodness of his land they have made goodly images.**	Hosea 10:1 NASB2020 **Israel is a luxuriant vine; He produces fruit for himself. The more his fruit, The more altars he made; The richer his land, The better he made the memorial stones.** Hosea 10:1 CSB **Israel is a lush vine; it yields fruit for itself. The more his fruit increased, the more he increased the altars. The better his land produced, the better they made the sacred pillars.** Hosea 10:1 NET **Israel was a fertile vine that yielded fruit. As his fruit multiplied, he multiplied altars to Baal. As his land prospered, they adorned the fertility pillars.**	NKJV ESV NASB1995 NASB2020 NIV NLT CSB HCSB AMP NET NRSV MEV CEB GNT ISV	
Hosea 11:12 KJB **...but Judah yet ruleth with God, and is faithful with the saints.**	Hosea 11:12 NKJV **...But Judah still walks with God, Even with the Holy One who is faithful.** Hosea 11:12 NASB2020 **...Judah is still unruly against God, Even against the Holy One who is faithful.** Hosea 11:12 CSB **...Judah still wanders with God and is faithful to the holy ones.**	NKJV ESV NASB1995 NASB2020 NIV NLT CSB HCSB AMP NET NRSV MEV CEB GNT	

KJB	Modern	Corrupted in	Notes
Hosea 13:14 KJB **I will ransom them from the power of the grave; I will redeem them from death: O death, I will be thy plagues; O grave, I will be thy destruction: repentance shall be hid from mine eyes.**	Hosea 13:14 ESV **I shall ransom them from the power of Sheol; I shall redeem them from Death. O Death, where are your plagues? O Sheol, where is your sting? Compassion is hidden from my eyes.** Hosea 13:14 NET **Will I deliver them from the power of Sheol? No, I will not! Will I redeem them from death? No, I will not! O Death, bring on your plagues! O Sheol, bring on your destruction! My eyes will not show any compassion!**	NKJV ESV NASB1995 NASB2020 NIV NLT CSB HCSB AMP NET NRSV MEV CEB GNT ISV	
Amos 4:4 KJB **Come to Beth–el, and transgress; at Gilgal multiply transgression; and bring your sacrifices every morning, and your tithes after three years:**	Amos 4:4 NKJV **"Come to Bethel and transgress, At Gilgal multiply transgression; Bring your sacrifices every morning, Your tithes every three days.** Amos 4:4 ISV **"Come to Bethel and sin, to Gilgal and sin even more! Bring along your morning sacrifices, and pay your tithes every other day**	NKJV ESV NASB1995 NASB2020 NLT CSB HCSB AMP NET NRSV MEV CEB GNT ISV	
Micah 5:2 KJB **But thou, Beth–lehem Ephratah, though thou be little among the thousands of Judah, yet out of thee shall he come forth unto me that is to be ruler in Israel; whose goings forth have been from of old, from everlasting.**	Micah 5:2 NIV **"But you, Bethlehem Ephrathah, though you are small among the clans of Judah, out of you will come for me one who will be ruler over Israel, whose origins are from of old, from ancient times."**	ESV NIV NLT CSB HCSB AMP NET NRSV MEV CEB GNT	A very important prophecy blasphemously distorted, where the NIV and others declare that Jesus Christ has "**origins**" - created in ancient times.
Zechariah 13:6 KJB **And one shall say unto him, What are these wounds in thine hands? Then he shall answer, Those with which I was wounded in the house of my friends.**	Zechariah 13:6 NKJV **And one will say to him, 'What are these wounds between your arms?' Then he will answer, 'Those with which I was wounded in the house of my friends.'** Zechariah 13:6 ESV **And if one asks him, 'What are these wounds on your back?'...** Zechariah 13:6 NIV **If someone asks, 'What are these wounds on your body?'...** Zechariah 13:6 NLT **And if someone asks, 'Then what about those wounds on your chest?'...** Zechariah 13:6 MEV **If someone asks, "What are these wounds on your arms?"...**	NKJV ESV NASB1995 NASB2020 NIV NLT CSB HCSB AMP NET NRSV MEV GNT	Between your arms? On your back? On your body? On your chest? On your arms? Another prophecy of Jesus Christ distorted. **Then saith he to Thomas, Reach hither thy finger, and behold my hands...** John 20:27

KJB	Modern	*Corrupted in*	Notes
Matthew 1:25 KJB **And knew her not till she had brought forth her firstborn son: and he called his name JESUS.**	Matthew 1:25 ESV **but knew her not until she had given birth to a son. And he called his name Jesus.**	ESV NASB1995 NASB2020 NIV NLT CSB	HCSB NET NRSV CEB GNT ISV
Matthew 5:22 KJB **But I say unto you, That whosoever is angry with his brother without a cause shall be in danger of the judgment: and whosoever shall say to his brother, Raca, shall be in danger of the council: but whosoever shall say, Thou fool, shall be in danger of hell fire.**	Matthew 5:22 NASB2020 **But I say to you that everyone who is angry with his brother shall be answerable to the court; and whoever says to his brother, 'You good-for-nothing,' shall be answerable to the supreme court; and whoever says, 'You fool,' shall be guilty enough to go into the fiery hell.**	ESV NASB1995 NASB2020 NIV NLT CSB HCSB AMP NET NRSV CEB GNT	Jesus Christ's words. "**without a cause**" is taken away.
Matthew 5:44 KJB **But I say unto you, Love your enemies, bless them that curse you, do good to them that hate you, and pray for them which despitefully use you, and persecute you;**	Matthew 5:44 NIV **But I tell you, love your enemies and pray for those who persecute you,**	ESV NASB1995 NASB2020 NIV NLT CSB HCSB AMP NET NRSV CEB GNT ISV	Jesus Christ's words. Several phrases taken away.
Matthew 6:13 KJB **And lead us not into temptation, but deliver us from evil: For thine is the kingdom, and the power, and the glory, for ever. Amen.**	Matthew 6:13 NASB2020 **And do not lead us into temptation, but deliver us from evil.**	ESV NASB1995 NASB2020 NIV NLT CSB NET NRSV CEB GNT ISV	Jesus Christ's words. Several phrases taken away.
Matthew 7:14 KJB **Because strait is the gate, and narrow is the way, which leadeth unto life, and few there be that find it.**	Matthew 7:14 NKJV **Because narrow is the gate and difficult is the way which leads to life, and there are few who find it.**	NKJV ESV NLT CSB HCSB AMP NET NRSV CEB GNT	The way is not difficult. The way is Jesus Christ. **I am the way, the truth, and the life: no man cometh unto the Father, but by me.** John 14:6
Matthew 17:21 KJB **Howbeit this kind goeth not out but by prayer and fasting.**	Matthew 17:21 ESV *Omitted*	ESV NASB2020 NIV NLT CSB NET NRSV CEB GNT	Jesus Christ's words. Entire verse taken away.
Matthew 18:11 KJB **For the Son of man is come to save that which was lost.**	Matthew 18:11 NIV *Omitted*	Same versions as Mat 17:21 ^	Jesus Christ's words. Entire verse taken away.
Matthew 18:22 KJB **Jesus saith unto him, I say not unto thee, Until seven times: but, Until seventy times seven.**	Matthew 18:22 NRSV **Jesus said to him, "Not seven times, but, I tell you, seventy-seven times.**	ESV NASB2020 NIV NET NRSV CEB ISV	The most incredible numeric patterns in the King James Bible are demonstrated by the perfect number of 70×7. See pp. 75,92,170,206.

KJB	Modern	*Corrupted in*	Notes
Matthew 23:14 KJB **Woe unto you, scribes and Pharisees, hypocrites! for ye devour widows' houses, and for a pretence make long prayer: therefore ye shall receive the greater damnation.**	Matthew 23:14 NASB2020 *Omitted*	ESV NASB2020 NIV NLT CSB NET NRSV CEB GNT	Jesus Christ's words. Entire verse taken away.
Matthew 25:13 KJB **Watch therefore, for ye know neither the day nor the hour wherein the Son of man cometh.**	Matthew 25:13 ESV **Watch therefore, for you know neither the day nor the hour.**	ESV NASB1995 NASB2020 NIV CSB HCSB NET NRSV CEB GNT ISV	Jesus Christ's words. "**wherein the Son of man cometh**" is taken away.
Matthew 27:4 KJB **Saying, I have sinned in that I have betrayed the innocent blood. And they said, What is that to us? see thou to that.**	Matthew 27:4 NKJV **saying, "I have sinned by betraying innocent blood." And they said, "What is that to us? You see to it!"** Matthew 27:4 NLT **...I have betrayed an innocent man."...**	NKJV ESV NASB1995 NASB2020 NIV NLT CSB HCSB AMP NET NRSV MEV CEB GNT ISV	A very important "**the**" is taken away. Modern Bibles say "**the virgin**" instead of "**a virgin**" when referencing Mary (Is 7:14, Mat 1:23) but won't include "**the**" in front of the Lamb's atoning blood.
Mark 1:2-3 KJB **As it is written in the prophets, Behold, I send my messenger before thy face, which shall prepare thy way before thee.** **The voice of one crying in the wilderness, Prepare ye the way of the Lord, make his paths straight.**	Mark 1:2-3 NIV **as it is written in Isaiah the prophet: "I will send my messenger ahead of you, who will prepare your way"—"a voice of one calling in the wilderness, 'Prepare the way for the Lord, make straight paths for him.'"** Mark 1:2-3 AMP **As it is written and forever remains in the [writings of the] prophet Isaiah: "Behold, I send My messenger ahead of You, Who will prepare Your way—A voice of one shouting in the wilderness,'Prepare the way of the Lord, Make His paths straight!'"**	ESV NASB1995 NASB2020 NIV NLT CSB HCSB AMP NET NRSV CEB GNT ISV	The King James says "**prophets**" (plural) because there is more than one prophet being quoted. The second quote was written by Isaiah, but the first was by Malachi. **Behold, I will send my messenger, and he shall prepare the way before me...** (Malachi 3:1) **The voice of him that crieth in the wilderness, Prepare ye the way of the LORD, make straight in the desert a highway for our God.** (Isaiah 40:3)
Mark 1:41 KJB **And Jesus, moved with compassion, put forth his hand, and touched him, and saith unto him, I will; be thou clean.**	Mark 1:41 NIV **Jesus was indignant. He reached out his hand and touched the man. "I am willing," he said. "Be clean!"**	NIV NET CEB	
Mark 2:26 KJB **How he went into the house of God in the days of Abiathar the high priest, and did eat the shewbread, which is not lawful to eat but for the priests, and gave also to them which were with him?**	Mark 2:26 NLT **He went into the house of God (during the days when Abiathar was high priest) and broke the law by eating the sacred loaves of bread that only the priests are allowed to eat. He also gave some to his companions."**	NLT NET NRSV MEV CEB GNT	The KJB is correct in saying "**in the days of Abiathar**" which is in the time when Abiathar was alive. Some modern Bibles erroneously state that Abiathar was the high priest when David ate the shewbread, which is false.

KJB	Modern	Corrupted in	Notes
			Ahimelech (the father of Abiathar) was high priest at this point in time, and was soon after slaughtered by Saul. Only his son Abiathar survived and would become high priest under the reign of David. His priesthood was very important in the history of Israel, which is why Jesus mentions him.
Mark 7:16 KJB **If any man have ears to hear, let him hear.**	Mark 7:16 ESV *Omitted*	ESV NASB2020 NIV NLT CSB NET NRSV CEB GNT	Jesus Christ's words. Entire verse taken away.
Mark 9:29 KJB **And he said unto them, This kind can come forth by nothing, but by prayer and fasting.**	Mark 9:29 NASB2020 **And He said to them, "This kind cannot come out by anything except prayer."**	ESV NASB1995 NASB2020 NIV NLT CSB AMP NET NRSV CEB GNT	Jesus Christ's words. "**and fasting**" is taken away.
Mark 9:44,46 KJB **Where their worm dieth not, and the fire is not quenched.**	Mark 9:44,46 CSB *Omitted*	ESV NASB2020 NIV NLT CSB NET NRSV CEB GNT	Jesus Christ's words. Entire verses taken away. Both verses (Mark 9:44 and 9:46 are the same)
Mark 10:24 KJB **And the disciples were astonished at his words. But Jesus answereth again, and saith unto them, Children, how hard is it for them that trust in riches to enter into the kingdom of God!**	Mark 10:24 ESV **And the disciples were amazed at his words. But Jesus said to them again, "Children, how difficult it is to enter the kingdom of God!**	ESV NASB1995 NASB2020 NIV NLT CSB HCSB NET NRSV CEB GNT	Jesus Christ's words. "**for them that trust in riches**" is taken away.
Mark 11:26 KJB **But if ye do not forgive, neither will your Father which is in heaven forgive your trespasses.**	Mark 11:26 NLT *Omitted*	ESV NIV NLT CSB NET NRSV CEB GNT	Jesus Christ's words. Entire verse taken away.
Mark 15:28 KJB **And the scripture was fulfilled, which saith, And he was numbered with the transgressors.**	Mark 15:28 NRSV *Omitted*	ESV NASB2020 NIV NLT CSB NET NRSV CEB GNT ISV	Fulfilled prophecy from Isaiah 53:12. Entire verse taken away.

KJB	Modern	*Corrupted in*	Notes
Luke 2:14 KJB **Glory to God in the highest, and on earth peace, good will toward men.**	Luke 2:14 ESV **"Glory to God in the highest, and on earth peace among those with whom he is pleased!**	ESV NASB1995 NASB2020 NIV	This adulterated text is sending a very different message from God to man at the birth of Christ.
Luke 2:33 KJB **And Joseph and his mother marvelled at those things which were spoken of him.**	Luke 2:33 NASB2020 **And His father and mother were amazed at the things which were being said about Him.**	ESV NASB1995 NASB2020 NIV NLT CSB HCSB NET NRSV CEB GNT ISV	In Luke 2:48, Mary says, "**behold, thy father and I have sought thee sorrowing.**" which accurately records the words spoken by Mary to Jesus. Luke 2:33, however is written by Luke under inspiration of the Holy Ghost- where it is properly recorded in the KJB as "**Joseph**" because he was not Jesus' biological father.
Luke 4:4 KJB **And Jesus answered him, saying, It is written, That man shall not live by bread alone, but by every word of God.**	Luke 4:4 NIV **Jesus answered, "It is written: 'Man shall not live on bread alone.'"**	ESV NASB1995 NASB2020 NIV NLT CSB HCSB AMP NET NRSV CEB GNT	Jesus Christ's words. "**but by every word of God**" is taken away. This vile corruption in modern versions appears to be the devil literally taking revenge on his defeat in the wilderness, where he was forever disgraced by the Lord Jesus Christ and the written word of God.
Luke 4:8 KJB **And Jesus answered and said unto him, Get thee behind me, Satan: for it is written, Thou shalt worship the Lord thy God, and him only shalt thou serve.**	Luke 4:8 ESV **And Jesus answered him, "It is written, "'You shall worship the Lord your God, and him only shall you serve.'"**	ESV NASB1995 NASB2020 NIV NLT CSB HCSB AMP NET NRSV CEB GNT ISV	Jesus Christ's words. "**Get thee behind me, Satan**" is taken away.
Luke 9:55-56 KJB **But he turned, and rebuked them, and said, Ye know not what manner of spirit ye are of. For the Son of man is not come to destroy men's lives, but to save them. And they went to another village.**	Luke 9:55-56 HCSB **But He turned and rebuked them, and they went to another village.**	ESV NASB2020 NIV NLT CSB HCSB NET NRSV CEB GNT ISV	Jesus Christ's words. The entire sentence "**Ye know not what manner of spirit ye are of. For the Son of man is not come to destroy men's lives, but to save them.**" is taken away.
Luke 17:36 KJB **Two men shall be in the field; the one shall be taken, and the other left.**	Luke 17:36 NIV *Omitted*	ESV NIV NLT CSB NET NRSV CEB GNT ISV	Jesus Christ's words. Entire verse taken away.

KJB	Modern	*Corrupted in*	Notes
Luke 23:42 KJB **And he said unto Jesus, Lord, remember me when thou comest into thy kingdom.**	Luke 23:42 NASB2020 **And he was saying, "Jesus, remember me when You come into Your kingdom!"**	ESV NASB1995 NASB2020 NIV NLT CSB HCSB AMP NET NRSV CEB GNT ISV	The dying thief's confession to Jesus Christ as "**Lord**" is taken away from modern versions. **For whosoever shall call upon the name of the Lord shall be saved.** Romans 10:13
John 1:3 KJB **All things were made by him; and without him was not any thing made that was made.**	John 1:3 NKJV **All things were made through Him, and without Him nothing was made that was made.**	NKJV ESV NASB1995 NASB2020 NIV NLT CSB HCSB AMP NRSV MEV CEB GNT ISV	It is true that all things were made through Jesus Christ, but it is also true that all things were made **by** Him. There is a subtle loss of meaning with the word "**through**" in this very important text about Jesus Christ as the Word. The word "**through**" limits the meaning- making it seem as if Jesus was just a channel in which God used to make everything. The word "**by**" gives the correct impression that the Father and the Word **are one** (John 10:30, 1 Jn 5:7), Jesus Christ is not just the means by which all things were created. He is the Creator Himself (John 1:1).
John 1:12 KJB **But as many as received him, to them gave he power to become the sons of God, even to them that believe on his name:**	John 1:12 NKJV **But as many as received Him, to them He gave the right to become children of God, to those who believe in His name:**	NKJV ESV NASB1995 NASB2020 NIV NLT CSB HCSB AMP NET CEB GNT ISV	The word "**power**" involves not only authorization, but spiritual virtue going out from God to literally make a new creature, born of the Spirit. The phrase "**the right**" simply implies legal permission.
John 1:14 KJB **And the Word was made flesh, and dwelt among us, (and we beheld his glory, the glory as of the only begotten of the Father,) full of grace and truth.**	John 1:14 NIV **The Word became flesh and made his dwelling among us. We have seen his glory, the glory of the one and only Son, who came from the Father, full of grace and truth.**	ESV NASB2020 NIV NLT CSB HCSB NET NRSV MEV CEB GNT ISV	The word "**begotten**" literally means to be paternally progenerated by your father and to share a unique, personal, genetic relationship with him. Jesus Christ is the **only begotten** Son of God, not ***the one and only*** Son. Adam was **the son of God** (Luke 3:38). There were **sons of God** who begat giants in the days of Noa. (Gen 6:4). The beings in Psalm 82:6 are **children of the most HIgh** (also referenced by Christ in John 10:35). But none of those angels, gods, nor Adam, were of God's **seed.** They were not **begotten**. They were simply made by Him.

KJB	Modern	Corrupted in	Notes
John 1:18 KJB **No man hath seen God at any time; the only begotten Son, which is in the bosom of the Father, he hath declared him.**	John 1:18 NASB1995 **No one has seen God at any time; the only begotten God who is in the bosom of the Father, He has explained Him.** John 1:18 NASB2020 **No one has seen God at any time; God the only Son, who is in the arms of the Father, He has explained Him.** John 1:18 ESV **No one has ever seen God; the only God, who is at the Father's side, he has made him known.** John 1:18 ISV **No one has ever seen God. The uniquely existing God, who is close to the Father's side, has revealed him.**	ESV NASB1995 NASB2020 NIV NLT CSB HCSB AMP NET NRSV MEV CEB GNT ISV	There is a big difference between God the Father calling Jesus "**God**" in Hebrews 1:8 / Psalm 45:6 vs. the scriptures declaring that there is a **uniquely existing God** standing next to God the Father. **Hear, O Israel: The LORD our God is one LORD:** Deuteronomy 6:4 **For there are three that bear record in heaven, the Father, the Word, and the Holy Ghost: and these three are one.** 1 John 5:7
John 3:13 KJB **And no man hath ascended up to heaven, but he that came down from heaven, even the Son of man which is in heaven.**	John 3:13 ESV **No one has ascended into heaven except he who descended from heaven, the Son of Man.**	ESV NASB1995 NASB2020 NIV NLT CSB HCSB AMP NET NRSV CEB GNT	Jesus Christ's words. "**which is in heaven**" is taken away. This is the greatest verse in the Bible revealing Christ's omnipresence. Modern versions completely destroyed it. The word "**up**" is also missing in most modern versions, which is important because it concretely affirms the third heaven to be physically above us.
John 3:15 KJB **That whosoever believeth in him should not perish, but have eternal life.**	John 3:15 CSB **so that everyone who believes in him may have eternal life.**	ESV NASB1995 NASB2020 NIV NLT CSB HCSB AMP NET NRSV CEB GNT ISV	Jesus Christ's words. "**should not perish, but**" is taken away.

KJB	**Modern**	*Corrupted in*	Notes
John 3:16 KJB **For God so loved the world, that he gave his only begotten Son, that whosoever believeth in him should not perish, but have everlasting life.**	John 3:16 ESV **"For God so loved the world, that he gave his only Son, that whoever believes in him should not perish but have eternal life.**	ESV NASB2020 NIV NLT CSB HCSB NET NRSV CEB GNT ISV	Jesus Christ's words. "**begotten**" is taken away. To remove "**begotten**" is to attack the deity of Christ and His relationship with the Father. See notes for **begotten** on previous page: John 1:14
John 3:18 KJB **He that believeth on him is not condemned: but he that believeth not is condemned already, because he hath not believed in the name of the only begotten Son of God.**	John 3:18 NASB2020 **The one who believes in Him is not judged; the one who does not believe has been judged already, because he has not believed in the name of the only Son of God.**	ESV NASB2020 NIV NLT CSB HCSB NET NRSV CEB GNT ISV	Jesus Christ's words. "**begotten**" is taken away.
John 4:24 KJB **God is a Spirit: and they that worship him must worship him in spirit and in truth.**	John 4:24 NKJV **God is Spirit, and those who worship Him must worship in spirit and truth."** John 4:24 NIV **God is spirit, and his worshipers must worship in the Spirit and in truth."**	NKJV ESV NASB1995 NASB2020 NIV NLT CSB HCSB AMP NET NRSV	MEV CEB GNT ISV
John 5:4 KJB **For an angel went down at a certain season into the pool, and troubled the water: whosoever then first after the troubling of the water stepped in was made whole of whatsoever disease he had.**	John 5:4 NRSV *Omitted*	ESV NASB2020 NIV NLT CSB NET NRSV CEB GNT	Entire verse taken away.
John 5:39 KJB **Search the scriptures; for in them ye think ye have eternal life: and they are they which testify of me.**	John 5:39 NKJV **You search the Scriptures, for in them you think you have eternal life; and these are they which testify of Me.**	NKJV ESV NASB1995 NASB2020 NIV NLT CSB HCSB AMP NET NRSV MEV CEB GNT ISV	The active command to "**Search the scriptures**" (which is not only a challenge to all hearers in the time of Christ, but also to all readers of the Bible today) is changed into a passive fact about the audience listening to Jesus in that time. The command/ challenge to search the scriptures is taken away.
John 6:47 KJB **Verily, verily, I say unto you, He that believeth on me hath everlasting life.**	John 6:47 ESV **Truly, truly, I say to you, whoever believes has eternal life.**	ESV NASB1995 NASB2020 NIV NLT CSB HCSB NET NRSV CEB GNT	Jesus Christ's words. "**on me**" is taken away.

KJB	Modern	*Corrupted in*	Notes
John 7:8 KJB **Go ye up unto this feast: I go not up yet unto this feast; for my time is not yet full come.**	John 7:8 NIV **You go to the festival. I am not going up to this festival, because my time has not yet fully come."**	ESV NASB1995 NASB2020 NIV NLT CSB AMP NET NRSV CEB GNT	Jesus Christ's words. "**yet**" is taken away. This is one of the most severe omissions from modern Bibles, because it makes out Jesus Christ to be a liar and/or a deceiver. In modern versions, Jesus says he won't go up to the feast. Then he goes against his own words and secretly goes to the feast 2 verses later. The KJB accurately records Jesus as saying he will not **YET** go up to the feast because he knows perfectly well that he will go to the feast in secret. Here is the full passage for context: **Go ye up unto this feast: I go not up yet unto this feast; for my time is not yet full come.** **When he had said these words unto them, he abode still in Galilee.** **But when his brethren were gone up, then went he also up unto the feast, not openly, but as it were in secret.** John 7:9-10 KJB
John 8:35 KJB **And the servant abideth not in the house for ever: but the Son abideth ever.**	John 8:35 NKJV **And a slave does not abide in the house forever, but a son abides forever.**	NKJV ESV NASB1995 NASB2020 NIV NLT CSB HCSB AMP NET NRSV MEV CEB GNT ISV	Modern Bibles, in complete unison, believe Jesus was just using an idiom here and not directly referencing Himself. The King James Bible says otherwise, which directly contributes to the miraculous pattern of **Father + Son** in the KJB, as detailed on p. 94, as well as Appendix 11.
John 9:35 KJB **Jesus heard that they had cast him out; and when he had found him, he said unto him, Dost thou believe on the Son of God?**	John 9:35 NASB2020 **Jesus heard that they had put him out, and upon finding him, He said, "Do you believe in the Son of Man?"** John 9:35 CEB **Jesus heard they had expelled the man born blind. Finding him, Jesus said, "Do you believe in the Human One?"**	ESV NASB1995 NASB2020 NIV NLT CSB HCSB AMP NET NRSV CEB GNT ISV	Jesus declares himself to be the Son of God and proceeds to allow this man to worship him. Modern versions remove his deity.

KJB	Modern	*Corrupted in*	Notes
John 11:33 KJB **When Jesus therefore saw her weeping, and the Jews also weeping which came with her, he groaned in the spirit, and was troubled,**	John 11:33 NLT **When Jesus saw her weeping and saw the other people wailing with her, a deep anger welled up within him, and he was deeply troubled.**	NLT HCSB	(In context, this is when Jesus comes to raise Lazarus from the dead.) Was Jesus angry and then weeping moments after? **Jesus wept.** (John 11:35)
John 12:4 KJB **Then saith one of his disciples, Judas Iscariot, Simon's son, which should betray him,**	John 12:4 ESV **But Judas Iscariot, one of his disciples (he who was about to betray him), said,**	ESV NASB1995 NASB2020 NIV NLT CSB HCSB AMP NET NRSV CEB GNT ISV	Identity of Judas Iscariot is removed (**Simon's son**)
John 17:12 KJB **While I was with them in the world, I kept them in thy name: those that thou gavest me I have kept, and none of them is lost, but the son of perdition; that the scripture might be fulfilled.**	John 17:12 NIV **While I was with them, I protected them and kept them safe by that name you gave me. None has been lost except the one doomed to destruction so that Scripture would be fulfilled.**	ESV NASB2020 NIV NLT CSB HCSB AMP NET NRSV CEB GNT ISV	Jesus Christ's words. "**in the world**" is taken away. Several other words and phrases are added/ missing/skewed with altered shades of meaning.
Acts 2:30 KJB **Therefore being a prophet, and knowing that God had sworn with an oath to him, that of the fruit of his loins, according to the flesh, he would raise up Christ to sit on his throne;**	Acts 2:30 NIV **But he was a prophet and knew that God had promised him on oath that he would place one of his descendants on his throne.**	ESV NASB1995 NASB2020 NIV NLT CSB HCSB AMP NET NRSV CEB GNT ISV	Prophecy of Christ is not only skewed in the Old Testament of modern versions, but also the New. For skewed O.T. prophecy of Jesus, see: Genesis 22:17 Daniel 9:26 Micah 5:2 Zechariah 13:6
Acts 7:20 KJB **In which time Moses was born, and was exceeding fair, and nourished up in his father's house three months:**	Acts 7:20 NKJV **At this time Moses was born, and was well pleasing to God; and he was brought up in his father's house for three months.** Acts 7:20 ESV **At this time Moses was born; and he was beautiful in God's sight...**	NKJV ESV NASB1995 NASB2020 NIV NLT CSB HCSB AMP NET NRSV MEV CEB ISV	Exodus 2:2 "**...he was a goodly child...**" confirms the reading of the KJB. The NKJV suggests Moses was well pleasing to God as a 3-month old baby who could do nothing but eat, sleep, cry and poop.
Acts 8:9 KJB **But there was a certain man, called Simon, which beforetime in the same city used sorcery, and bewitched the people of Samaria, giving out that himself was some great one:**	Acts 8:9 NKJV **But there was a certain man called Simon, who previously practiced sorcery in the city and astonished the people of Samaria, claiming that he was someone great,**	NKJV ESV NASB1995 NASB2020 NIV NLT CSB HCSB AMP	NET NRSV MEV CEB GNT ISV
Acts 8:37 KJB **And Philip said, If thou believest with all thine heart, thou mayest. And he answered and said, I believe that Jesus Christ is the Son of God.**	Acts 8:37 NASB2020 *Omitted*	ESV NASB2020 NIV NLT CSB NET NRSV CEB GNT ISV	Entire verse taken away. The only verse in the Bible that shows the clear order of baptism- believing in Christ (salvation) precedes baptism.

KJB	Modern	*Corrupted in*	Notes
Acts 10:30 KJB **And Cornelius said, Four days ago I was fasting until this hour; and at the ninth hour I prayed in my house, and, behold, a man stood before me in bright clothing,**	Acts 10:30 ESV **And Cornelius said, "Four days ago, about this hour, I was praying in my house at the ninth hour, and behold, a man stood before me in bright clothing**	ESV NASB1995 NASB2020 NIV NLT CSB HCSB AMP	NET NRSV CEB GNT ISV
Acts 15:24 KJB **Forasmuch as we have heard, that certain which went out from us have troubled you with words, subverting your souls, saying, Ye must be circumcised, and keep the law: to whom we gave no such commandment:**	Acts 15:24 ESV **Since we have heard that some persons have gone out from us and troubled you with words, unsettling your minds, although we gave them no instructions,** Acts 15:24 NKJV **Since we have heard that some who went out from us have troubled you with words, unsettling your souls, saying, "You must be circumcised and keep the law"—to whom we gave no such commandment—**	ESV NASB1995 NASB2020 NIV NLT CSB HCSB AMP NET NRSV CEB GNT ISV - NKJV MEV	The entire phrase "**saying, Ye must be circumcised, and keep the law**" is taken away in most new bibles. I first learned of this mutilation when a brother in Christ was trying to prevent another brother from falling prey to the Hebrew Roots / Torah Observance movement, but was unable to convince his brother that the KJB reading of this verse was inspired, since it wasn't in the CSB that he was using. The words "**unsettling**" or "**upsetting**" are used instead of "**subverting**" - which properly relays the severity of the issue.
Acts 15:34 KJB **Notwithstanding it pleased Silas to abide there still.**	Acts 15:34 NIV *Omitted*	ESV NASB2020 NIV NLT CSB HCSB NET NRSV CEB GNT ISV	Entire verse taken away.
Acts 24:7 KJB **But the chief captain Lysias came upon us, and with great violence took him away out of our hands,**	Acts 24:7 CSB *Omitted*	ESV NASB2020 NIV NLT CSB NET NRSV CEB GNT ISV	Entire verses taken away.
Acts 28:29 KJB **And when he had said these words, the Jews departed, and had great reasoning among themselves.**	Acts 28:29 NASB2020 *Omitted*		
Romans 8:1 KJB **There is therefore now no condemnation to them which are in Christ Jesus, who walk not after the flesh, but after the Spirit.**	Romans 8:1 ESV **There is therefore now no condemnation for those who are in Christ Jesus.**	ESV NASB1995 NASB2020 NIV NLT CSB HCSB AMP NET NRSV CEB GNT ISV	The entire phrase "**who walk not after the flesh, but after the Spirit**" is taken away.

KJB	Modern	*Corrupted in*	Notes
1 Corinthians 1:18 KJB **For the preaching of the cross is to them that perish foolishness; but unto us which are saved it is the power of God.**	1 Corinthians 1:18 NKJV **For the message of the cross is foolishness to those who are perishing, but to us who are being saved it is the power of God.**	NKJV ESV NASB1995 NASB2020 NIV NLT CSB HCSB AMP NET NRSV MEV CEB GNT ISV	Are you **saved** or are you **being saved**?
1 Corinthians 7:5 KJB **Defraud ye not one the other, except it be with consent for a time, that ye may give yourselves to fasting and prayer; and come together again, that Satan tempt you not for your incontinency.**	1 Corinthians 7:5 NIV **Do not deprive each other except perhaps by mutual consent and for a time, so that you may devote yourselves to prayer. Then come together again so that Satan will not tempt you because of your lack of self-control.**	ESV NASB1995 NASB2020 NIV NLT CSB HCSB AMP NET NRSV CEB GNT ISV	
1 Corinthians 11:24 KJB **And when he had given thanks, he brake it, and said, Take, eat: this is my body, which is broken for you: this do in remembrance of me.**	1 Corinthians 11:24 NIV **and when he had given thanks, he broke it and said, "This is my body, which is for you; do this in remembrance of me."**	ESV NASB1995 NASB2020 NIV NLT CSB HCSB AMP NET NRSV CEB GNT ISV	The word "**broken**" is removed. This takes away from remembering Christ's suffering which He endured at the cross for us.
1 Corinthians 15:47 KJB **The first man is of the earth, earthy: the second man is the Lord from heaven.**	1 Corinthians 15:47 ESV **The first man was from the earth, a man of dust; the second man is from heaven.**	ESV NASB1995 NASB2020 NIV CSB HCSB	NET NRSV CEB GNT ISV
2 Corinthians 2:15 KJB **For we are unto God a sweet savour of Christ, in them that are saved, and in them that perish:**	2 Corinthians 2:15 NKJV **For we are to God the fragrance of Christ among those who are being saved and among those who are perishing.**	NKJV ESV NASB1995 NASB2020 NIV NLT CSB	HCSB AMP NET NRSV CEB GNT ISV
2 Corinthians 2:17 KJB **For we are not as many, which corrupt the word of God: but as of sincerity, but as of God, in the sight of God speak we in Christ.**	2 Corinthians 2:17 NKJV **For we are not, as so many, peddling the word of God; but as of sincerity, but as from God, we speak in the sight of God in Christ.**	NKJV ESV NASB1995 NASB2020 NIV NLT CSB HCSB	AMP NET NRSV MEV CEB GNT ISV
2 Corinthians 6:5 KJB **In stripes, in imprisonments, in tumults, in labours, in watchings, in fastings;**	2 Corinthians 6:5 NASB2020 **in beatings, in imprisonments, in mob attacks, in labors, in sleeplessness, in hunger,**	ESV NASB1995 NASB2020 NIV NLT	CSB MEV HCSB CEB AMP GNT NET ISV NRSV

KJB	Modern	*Corrupted in*	Notes
2 Corinthians 11:27 KJB **In weariness and painfulness, in watchings often, in hunger and thirst, in fastings often, in cold and nakedness.**	2 Corinthians 11:27 ESV **in toil and hardship, through many a sleepless night, in hunger and thirst, often without food, in cold and exposure.** 2 Corinthians 11:27 NKJV **in weariness and toil, in sleeplessness often, in hunger and thirst, in fastings often, in cold and nakedness—**	NKJV NASB1995 NASB2020 NIV NLT CSB HCSB NET NRSV CEB GNT ISV	
Galatians 3:17 KJB **And this I say, that the covenant, that was confirmed before of God in Christ, the law, which was four hundred and thirty years after, cannot disannul, that it should make the promise of none effect.**	Galatians 3:17 ESV **This is what I mean: the law, which came 430 years afterward, does not annul a covenant previously ratified by God, so as to make the promise void.**	ESV NASB1995 NASB2020 NIV NLT CSB HCSB AMP NET	NRSV CEB GNT ISV
Galatians 3:24-25 KJB **Wherefore the law was our schoolmaster to bring us unto Christ, that we might be justified by faith.** **But after that faith is come, we are no longer under a schoolmaster.**	Galatians 3:24-25 NASB2020 **Therefore the Law has become our guardian to lead us to Christ, so that we may be justified by faith.** **But now that faith has come, we are no longer under a guardian.**	ESV NASB2020 NIV NLT CSB HCSB NET CEB GNT ISV	A **schoolmaster** teaches. A **guardian** protects. The **law** guards over nobody, but is rather **the law of sin and death** (Romans 8:2) that will make all the whole world **guilty before God.** (Romans 3:19). Through the law we learn that we are sinners against the Most High, in desperate need of a Saviour.
Galatians 4:7 KJB **Wherefore thou art no more a servant, but a son; and if a son, then an heir of God through Christ.**	Galatians 4:7 NLT **So you are no longer a slave, but a son, and if a son, then an heir through God.**	ESV NASB1995 NASB2020 NIV NLT CSB HCSB NET NRSV CEB GNT ISV	**...no man cometh unto the Father, but by me.** John 14:6
Galatians 5:12 KJB **I would they were even cut off which trouble you.**	Galatians 5:12 NKJV **I could wish that those who trouble you would even cut themselves off!** Galatians 5:12 ESV **I wish those who unsettle you would emasculate themselves!** Galatians 5:12 NASB1995 **I wish that those who are troubling you would even mutilate themselves.** Galatians 5:12 HCSB **I wish those who are disturbing you might also get themselves castrated!**	NKJV ESV NASB1995 NASB2020 NIV NLT CSB HCSB AMP NET NRSV MEV CEB GNT ISV	To be **cut off** is a very common saying in the Bible, used well over a hundred times in the O.T. and even by Paul elsewhere in scripture. It has nothing to do with chopping off a man's privates, but rather cutting fellowship from those who pervert the word of God. **...if thou continue in his goodness: otherwise thou also shalt be cut off.** Romans 11:22

KJB	Modern	Corrupted in	Notes
Galatians 6:15 KJB **For in Christ Jesus neither circumcision availeth any thing, nor uncircumcision, but a new creature.**	Galatians 6:15 NKJV **For in Christ Jesus neither circumcision nor uncircumcision avails anything, but a new creation.**	NKJV ESV NASB1995 NASB2020 NIV NLT CSB	HCSB AMP NET NRSV MEV CEB ISV
Ephesians 1:14 KJB **Which is the earnest of our inheritance until the redemption of the purchased possession, unto the praise of his glory.**	Ephesians 1:14 ESV **who is the guarantee of our inheritance until we acquire possession of it, to the praise of his glory.** Ephesians 1:14 NASB1995 **who is given as a pledge of our inheritance, with a view to the redemption of God's own possession, to the praise of His glory.** Ephesians 1:14 NASB2020 **who is a first installment of our inheritance, in regard to the redemption of God's own possession, to the praise of His glory.** Ephesians 1:14 NLT **The Spirit is God's guarantee that he will give us the inheritance he promised and that he has purchased us to be his own people. He did this so we would praise and glorify him.**	ESV NASB1995 NASB2020 NIV NLT CSB HCSB NET NRSV MEV CEB ISV	The word "**purchased**" is removed. But it wouldn't matter too much even if it was included- the middle of this verse is distorted in vastly different ways depending on the translation.
Ephesians 3:9 KJB **And to make all men see what is the fellowship of the mystery, which from the beginning of the world hath been hid in God, who created all things by Jesus Christ:**	Ephesians 3:9 ESV **and to bring to light for everyone what is the plan of the mystery hidden for ages in God, who created all things,**	ESV NASB1995 NASB2020 NIV NLT CSB HCSB AMP NET NRSV CEB GNT ISV	The phrase "**by Jesus Christ**" is taken away.
Ephesians 4:6 KJB **One God and Father of all, who is above all, and through all, and in you all.**	Ephesians 4:6 NIV **one God and Father of all, who is over all and through all and in all.**	ESV NASB1995 NASB2020 NIV NLT CSB HCSB AMP NET NRSV CEB GNT ISV	The word "**you**" is taken away.
Ephesians 5:1 KJB **Be ye therefore followers of God, as dear children;**	Ephesians 5:1 NKJV **Therefore be imitators of God as dear children.**	NKJV ESV NASB1995 NASB2020 NLT CSB HCSB AMP NET NRSV MEV CEB GNT ISV	Are we to make our own commandments? Should you declare yourself as the **I AM**? How foolish! Leave that stuff to the son of perdition. (2 Thess 2:4) **...he as God sitteth in the temple of God, shewing himself that he is God.**

KJB	**Modern**	*Corrupted in*	Notes
Philippians 2:6 KJB **Who, being in the form of God, thought it not robbery to be equal with God:**	Philippians 2:6 ESV **who, though he was in the form of God, did not count equality with God a thing to be grasped,** Philippians 2:6 NIV **Who, being in very nature God, did not consider equality with God something to be used to his own advantage;**	ESV NASB1995 NASB2020 NIV NLT CSB HCSB AMP NET NRSV MEV CEB GNT ISV	This distortion conveys the opposite meaning (of a very important scripture).
Philippians 4:13 KJB **I can do all things through Christ which strengtheneth me.**	Philippians 4:13 NASB2020 **I can do all things through Him who strengthens me.** Philippians 4:13 NET **I am able to do all things through the one who strengthens me.**	ESV NASB1995 NASB2020 NIV CSB HCSB NET NRSV CEB ISV	
Colossians 1:14 KJB **In whom we have redemption through his blood, even the forgiveness of sins:**	Colossians 1:14 NASB2020 **in whom we have redemption, the forgiveness of sins.**	ESV NASB1995 NASB2020 NIV NLT CSB HCSB AMP NET NRSV CEB GNT ISV	The phrase "**through his blood**" is removed.
Colossians 2:11 KJB **In whom also ye are circumcised with the circumcision made without hands, in putting off the body of the sins of the flesh by the circumcision of Christ:**	Colossians 2:11 ESV **In him also you were circumcised with a circumcision made without hands, by putting off the body of the flesh, by the circumcision of Christ,**	ESV NASB1995 NASB2020 NIV NLT CSB HCSB AMP NET NRSV CEB ISV	The phrase "**of the sins**" is removed in most modern versions. Other versions such as the NLT, CEB, GNT & ISV remove "**of the flesh**"
Colossians 2:18 KJB **Let no man beguile you of your reward in a voluntary humility and worshipping of angels, intruding into those things which he hath not seen, vainly puffed up by his fleshly mind,**	Colossians 2:18 NASB2020 **Take care that no one keeps defrauding you of your prize by delighting in humility and the worship of the angels, taking his stand on visions he has seen, inflated without cause by his fleshly mind,** Colossians 2:18 NIV **Do not let anyone who delights in false humility and the worship of angels disqualify you. Such a person also goes into great detail about what they have seen; they are puffed up with idle notions by their unspiritual mind.**	ESV NASB1995 NASB2020 NIV NLT CSB HCSB AMP NET NRSV MEV GNT ISV	

KJB	Modern	Corrupted in	Notes
Colossians 3:6 KJB **For which things' sake the wrath of God cometh on the children of disobedience:**	Colossians 3:6 NIV **Because of these, the wrath of God is coming.** Colossians 3:6 CSB **Because of these, God's wrath is coming upon the disobedient,**	ESV NIV NLT CSB HCSB NRSV CEB GNT ISV	The phrase "**on the children of disobedience**" is removed in many modern versions. Other versions will take replace "**children of disobedience**" with"**the disobedient**"
2 Thessalonians 2:3 KJB **Let no man deceive you by any means: for that day shall not come, except there come a falling away first, and that man of sin be revealed, the son of perdition;**	2 Thessalonians 2:3 NIV **Don't let anyone deceive you in any way, for that day will not come until the rebellion occurs and the man of lawlessness is revealed, the man doomed to destruction.**	ESV NASB1995 NASB2020 NIV NLT CSB HCSB AMP NET NRSV MEV CEB GNT ISV	
1 Timothy 3:16 KJB **And without controversy great is the mystery of godliness: God was manifest in the flesh, justified in the Spirit...**	1 Timothy 3:16 CSB **And most certainly, the mystery of godliness is great: He was manifested in the flesh, vindicated in the Spirit...** 1 Timothy 3:16 AMP **...He (Jesus Christ) who was revealed in human flesh...**	ESV NASB1995 NASB2020 NIV NLT CSB HCSB AMP NET NRSV CEB GNT ISV	One of the greatest verses in the Bible on the incarnation / deity / person of Christ is obliterated in modern versions.
1 Timothy 6:10 KJB **For the love of money is the root of all evil: which while some coveted after, they have erred from the faith, and pierced themselves through with many sorrows.**	1 Timothy 6:10 NKJV **For the love of money is a root of all kinds of evil, for which some have strayed from the faith in their greediness, and pierced themselves through with many sorrows.**	NKJV ESV NASB1995 NASB2020 NIV NLT CSB HCSB	AMP NRSV CEB GNT ISV
2 Timothy 2:15 KJB **Study to shew thyself approved unto God, a workman that needeth not to be ashamed, rightly dividing the word of truth.**	2 Timothy 2:15 NIV **Do your best to present yourself to God as one approved, a worker who does not need to be ashamed and who correctly handles the word of truth.** 2 Timothy 2:15 NKJV **Be diligent to present yourself approved to God, a worker who does not need to be ashamed, rightly dividing the word of truth.** 2 Timothy 2:15 NLT **Work hard so you can present yourself to God and receive his approval. Be a good worker, one who does not need to be ashamed and who correctly explains the word of truth.**	NKJV ESV NASB1995 NASB2020 NIV NLT CSB HCSB AMP NET NRSV CEB GNT ISV	

KJB	**Modern**	*Corrupted in*	Notes
Titus 2:4 KJB **That they may teach the young women to be sober, to love their husbands, to love their children,**	Titus 2:4 NKJV **that they admonish the young women to love their husbands, to love their children,** Titus 2:4 ESV **and so train the young women to love...** Titus 2:4 NASB1995 **so that they may encourage the young women to love...** Titus 2:4 NIV **Then they can urge the younger women to love...**	NKJV ESV NASB1995 NASB2020 NIV NLT CSB HCSB AMP NET NRSV MEV CEB GNT ISV	The phrase "**to be sober**" is removed, and the word "**teach**" is changed to various words with different shades of meaning.
Hebrews 1:3 KJB **Who being the brightness of his glory, and the express image of his person, and upholding all things by the word of his power, when he had by himself purged our sins, sat down on the right hand of the Majesty on high;**	Hebrews 1:3 ESV **He is the radiance of the glory of God and the exact imprint of his nature, and he upholds the universe by the word of his power. After making purification for sins, he sat down at the right hand of the Majesty on high,**	ESV NASB1995 NASB2020 NIV NLT CSB HCSB NET NRSV CEB GNT ISV	The phrase "**by himself**" is taken away.
Hebrews 4:12 KJB **For the word of God is quick, and powerful, and sharper than any twoedged sword...**	Hebrews 4:12 NIV **For the word of God is alive and active. Sharper than any double-edged sword...** Hebrews 4:12 CSB **For the word of God is living and effective and sharper than any double-edged sword...**	ESV NASB1995 NASB2020 NIV CSB HCSB NET NRSV MEV	CEB GNT ISV
1 Peter 1:23 KJB **Being born again, not of corruptible seed, but of incorruptible, by the word of God, which liveth and abideth for ever.**	1 Peter 1:23 NRSV **You have been born anew, not of perishable but of imperishable seed, through the living and enduring word of God.**	ESV NASB1995 NASB2020 NIV NLT CSB	NET NRSV CEB
1 Peter 2:2 KJB **As newborn babes, desire the sincere milk of the word, that ye may grow thereby:**	1 Peter 2:2 HCSB **Like newborn infants, desire the pure spiritual milk, so that you may grow by it for your salvation,** 1 Peter 2:2 NLT **Like newborn babies, you must crave pure spiritual milk so that you will grow into a full experience of salvation. Cry out for this nourishment,** 1 Peter 2:2 AMP **like newborn babies [you should] long for the pure milk of the word, so that by it you may be nurtured and grow in respect to salvation [its ultimate fulfillment],**	ESV NASB1995 NASB2020 NIV NLT CSB HCSB AMP NET NRSV CEB GNT ISV	The phrase "**for your salvation**" is added to the end of the verse- distorting the doctrine of salvation. Other versions have "**[to / into / in / up to / in respect to] your salvation**" The phrase "**milk of the word**" is also changed to "**spiritual milk**" in many versions.

KJB	Modern	Corrupted in	Notes
1 John 3:16 KJB **Hereby perceive we the love of God, because he laid down his life for us: and we ought to lay down our lives for the brethren.**	1 John 3:16 NKJV **By this we know love, because He laid down His life for us. And we also ought to lay down our lives for the brethren.**	NKJV ESV NASB1995 NASB2020 NIV NLT CSB HCSB AMP NET NRSV CEB GNT ISV	The second part of the verse says "...**he laid down his life for us...**" In the KJB, the "**he**" is talking about "**God**" - God laid down his life for us. Modern versions, however, do not have the phrase "**the love of God**" and once again, the deity of Christ is removed (as in other 3:16 verses).
1 John 4:3 KJB **And every spirit that confesseth not that Jesus Christ is come in the flesh is not of God: and this is that spirit of antichrist, whereof ye have heard that it should come; and even now already is it in the world.**	1 John 4:3 ESV **and every spirit that does not confess Jesus is not from God. This is the spirit of the antichrist, which you heard was coming and now is in the world already.**	ESV NASB1995 NASB2020 NIV NLT CSB HCSB NET NRSV CEB GNT ISV	The words "**Christ is come in the flesh**" are taken away.
1 John 5:7-8 KJB **For there are three that bear record in heaven, the Father, the Word, and the Holy Ghost: and these three are one.** **And there are three that bear witness in earth, the Spirit, and the water, and the blood: and these three agree in one.**	1 John 5:7-8 ESV **For there are three that testify: the Spirit and the water and the blood; and these three agree.**	ESV NASB1995 NASB2020 NIV NLT CSB HCSB NET NRSV	The words "**For there are three that bear record in heaven, the Father, the Word, and the Holy Ghost: and these three are one.**" and "**in earth**" and "**in one**" are taken away. The most important passage of the Bible regarding the Godhead and the great atonement between heaven and earth.
Revelation 1:11 KJB **Saying, I am Alpha and Omega, the first and the last: and, What thou seest, write in a book, and send it unto the seven churches which are in Asia; unto Ephesus, and unto Smyrna, and unto Pergamos, and unto Thyatira, and unto Sardis, and unto Philadelphia, and unto Laodicea.**	Revelation 1:11 NIV **which said: "Write on a scroll what you see and send it to the seven churches: to Ephesus, Smyrna, Pergamum, Thyatira, Sardis, Philadelphia and Laodicea."**	ESV NASB1995 NASB2020 NIV NLT CSB HCSB AMP NET NRSV CEB GNT ISV	The words "**I am Alpha and Omega, the first and the last:**" are taken away. In the KJB, God declares Himself the first and the last 7 times. In modern versions, 6 times. See p. 120.
Revelation 1:18 KJB **I am he that liveth, and was dead; and, behold, I am alive for evermore, Amen; and have the keys of hell and of death.**	Revelation 1:18 NKJV **I am He who lives, and was dead, and behold, I am alive forevermore. Amen. And I have the keys of Hades and of Death.** Revelation 1:18 NLT **...And I hold the keys of death and the grave.** Revelation 1:18 GNT **...I have authority over death and the world of the dead.** Revelation 1:18 AMP **...and I have the keys of... death and of Hades (the realm of the dead).**	NKJV ESV NASB1995 NASB2020 NIV NLT CSB HCSB AMP NET NRSV MEV CEB GNT ISV	The doctrine of **hell** distorted.

KJB	Modern	Corrupted in	Notes
Revelation 5:9-10 KJB **And they sung a new song, saying, Thou art worthy to take the book, and to open the seals thereof: for thou wast slain, and hast redeemed us to God by thy blood out of every kindred, and tongue, and people, and nation; And hast made us unto our God kings and priests: and we shall reign on the earth.**	Revelation 5:9-10 ESV **And they sang a new song, saying, "Worthy are you to take the scroll and to open its seals, for you were slain, and by your blood you ransomed people for God from every tribe and language and people and nation, and you have made them a kingdom and priests to our God, and they shall reign on the earth."**	ESV NASB1995 NASB2020 NIV NLT CSB HCSB AMP NET NRSV CEB GNT ISV	The identity of the 24 elders obscured. The KJB clearly depicts the 24 elders as men who are from earth that needed redemption by the blood of the Lamb, whereas modern versions make them out to be heavenly beings that needed no redemption.
Revelation 13:1 KJB **And I stood upon the sand of the sea, and saw a beast rise up out of the sea, having seven heads and ten horns, and upon his horns ten crowns, and upon his heads the name of blasphemy.**	Revelation 13:1 NIV **The dragon stood on the shore of the sea. And I saw a beast coming out of the sea. It had ten horns and seven heads, with ten crowns on its horns, and on each head a blasphemous name.** Revelation 13:1 ESV **And I saw a beast rising out of the sea, with ten horns and seven heads, with ten diadems on its horns and blasphemous names on its heads.**	NKJV ESV NASB1995 NASB2020 NIV NLT CSB HCSB AMP NET NRSV MEV CEB GNT ISV	Some versions change "**I**" (John) to "**the dragon**" and some versions like the ESV take away the entire phrase "**And I stood upon the sand of the sea**" Most versions do not have "**the name of blasphemy**" as the KJB declares- which is pointing to one specific name, but rather "**blasphemous names**" (plural) or "**a blasphemous name**" (a non-specific name).
Revelation 22:19 KJB **And if any man shall take away from the words of the book of this prophecy, God shall take away his part out of the book of life, and out of the holy city, and from the things which are written in this book.**	Revelation 22:19 NIV **And if anyone takes words away from this scroll of prophecy, God will take away from that person any share in the tree of life and in the Holy City, which are described in this scroll.**	ESV NASB1995 NASB2020 NIV NLT CSB HCSB AMP NET	NRSV CEB GNT ISV

Appendix 5 - List of Issues in Modern Bibles

Besides the many miracles of numeric perfection that occur in the KJB, there are several strong reasons to avoid modern translations. Many Christians who are searching for a comparison of Bible translations online will run into a chart that compares "Word for word" vs "Thought for thought." This type of chart is highly misleading and evading the real issues that should affect whether or not Christians should read from modern Bibles.

1. Modern Bibles say and mean different things, sometimes total opposite things (See Appendix 4) in thousands of verses. God, however, is not the author of confusion. His word is very pure.
2. Massive confusion and distortion to the text has led to much less trust in the overall accuracy and authority of God's word.
3. Important doctrines are affected.
    a. the blood of Christ (Mat 27:4, Col 1:14)
    b. Christ's deity (1 Tim 3:16, Mic 5:2, Phil 2:6)
    c. begotten Sonship of Christ (Ps 2:7, John 1:14,3:16)
    d. the omnipresence of Christ (John 3:13)
    e. the mission of Christ (Mat 18:11, Luke 9:56)
    f. prophecy of Christ (Dan 9:26, Zech 13:6)
    g. the word of God (Ps 12:7,100:5,138:2, Luke 4:4, 2 Cor 2:17)
    h. studying God's word (John 5:39, 2 Tim 2:15)
    i. fasting (Mat 17:21, Mark 9:29, Act 10:30, 1 Cor 7:5, 2 Cor 6:5,11:27)
    j. salvation (Matthew 7:14, 1 Corinthians 1:18)
    k. baptism after salvation (Acts 8:37)
    l. the Godhead (1 John 5:7)
    m. hell (Luke 16:23, Revelation 1:18)
4. Obvious errors are included.
    a. Saul's becoming king at 1 year old (1 Samuel 13:1 ESV)
    b. Goliath getting killed twice (2 Samuel 21:19 NASB2020)
    c. God performing abortion (Numbers 5:11-31 NIV2011)
    d. Satan is the son of a being called Dawn (Isaiah 14:12 ESV)
    e. Isaiah misquotation (quote is from Malachi) (Mark 1:2)
    f. Jesus lying (John 7:8)
    g. Jesus wrongly identifying the high priest (Mark 2:26 NLT)
    h. Salvation is difficult (Matthew 7:14 NKJV)
5. People are reading the Bible less and less (because it's no longer believed to be absolutely true).

6. People are memorizing the Bible less and less (because it's always changing).
7. People tremble at God's word less and less (because it's considered an ancient writing written to ancient people).
8. A massive amount of time is allocated to trying to understand what words are supposed to mean in the original languages (languages which are completely unfamiliar to us), instead of believing what God has already given in our own language. God gives His word with certainty. (Proverbs 22:21)
9. Modern Bibles use a completely different Greek text (Nestle-Aland) than the KJB (Received Text).
10. Their Greek text was first introduced by two men (Westcott and Hort) who held heretical beliefs, and were members of occult secret societies.
11. Their Greek text is supervised by the Vatican.[1]
12. Their Greek text is not definitive, and always updating.[1]
13. Modern Bibles have a very short life-span- quickly going out of date or out of print.
14. They remove Satan's name: Lucifer. (Isaiah 14:12)
15. They remove God's name: JEHOVAH. (Exodus 6:3)

---

1. Nestle Aland 27, page 45 of Introduction
2. Is the World's Oldest Bible a Fake? David W. Daniels

Appendix 6 - 100,000 changes from the KJB1611

One of the often regurgitated arguments of original-onlyist Bible users who attack King James onlyists, is that there were 100,000 changes from 1611 to the KJB we use today. This was popularized by scholars such as Dan Wallace, who I directly quote from his own writing:

...we must remember that the King James Bible of today is not the King James of 1611. It has undergone three revisions, incorporating more than 100,000 changes! [1]

First of all (and most obviously), we did not have a 100% perfect Bible in 1611. All KJB believers must accept this fact. If we did, there would be no need for subsequent editions. Which begs the question: *If God is truly behind the KJB, why did He allow that?* My answer: I don't know exactly- but maybe you can ask the Lord when we meet Him in the air. Be sure to also ask why Jesus didn't perform miracles from the moment of His birth. Surely that would have been an even greater sign and proof of His deity, right?

Here is the hard truth of the matter: even if it would have been more impressive, God didn't do it like that. Christ did not begin His ministry at 12 years of age, nor 18, nor 21, nor 28 which all would have been adequate ages. He began to be about 30 years old before starting to do the work which God sent Him to do, as recorded in the gospels.

God has His timing and will and reasons for the way He does things. He decides when the time is right. And when He decides the time is right, *the time is right*. And we can either seek Him and have faith and follow where He leads us, or we can ignore/reject the light that He has given. Just because the King James Bible existed in 1611, didn't mean God had yet perfected it according to His own definition of perfection.

Dear brethren, I hope you agree that God can do whatever He wants, for nothing is impossible with Him. But He doesn't always do things the way that we imagine He would. His ways are much higher than ours.

I believe one of the reasons He waited to perfect the King James Bible is that He does not want the translators of the King James Bible to receive the attention and the glory and praise for all of these wonders that have been recently discovered. All praise and glory belongs to GOD alone, who (I believe) took the 1611 text and intertwined all these miracles into it until it was finalized in the settled form we have today.

So, were there printing errors in 1611? Yes, of course! Printing more than half a million words on a printing press was not an easy thing to do. Nevertheless, this "*100,000 changes from 1611 to today*" argument is a grossly misleading attack on the King James Bible. Printing error corrections do not mean the translation or the meaning of the translation was changed at any given point.

Now then, why do scholars claim the KJB had 100,000 changes in the text from the 1611 to today? Well, the reasons seem to be two-fold.

- Firstly, they want to cast doubt on the King James Bible, so that you will no longer trust it with the same authority as you did once before, *now knowing* that it has been changed 100,000 times. The scholars want that authority for themselves, so they can give you their own readings of what they believe is the faithful and true text.
- Secondly, it seems as if they are trying to justify themselves revising the Bible (Dan Wallace, who helped to popularize this argument, released his own version of the Bible called the NET). Since the King James Bible was revised over and over again, hundreds of thousands of times, he thinks, *the Bible is a working text. With my great knowledge, I can produce a better one.*

Here's the problem: As you are about to see, these changes do not affect the meaning of the text whatsoever in the KJB. Capitalization and spelling consists of almost all of the changes. Other changes were printing errors that were mostly corrected within the first 30 years of the 1611 edition, by two of the original translators (Samuel Ward and John Bois). The KJB is now settled and has been for hundreds of years.

Modern Bibles, on the other hand, are ALWAYS changing and NEVER settled. The very Greek text they are based upon states that the text is a working text and not to be considered as definitive. Here is a true saying: *If you have a "settled" modern Bible, it's because it's out of print!*

So instead of just talking about it, let's actually look at the differences between the 1611 and the KJB we read today. And just for fun, let's also include the highly esteemed NASB1995 vs the NASB2020.

Let's see if these 100,000 changes over 400+ years prove the argument of "*the King James Bible of today is not the King James of 1611.*" And let's see how they compare to 1 revision in the NASB after just 25 years.

Spelling/stylistic changes highlighted yellow. Word/phrase changes highlighted red.

Isaiah 53				
	KJB 1611 - KJB (present) 400+ years apart		**NASB 1995-2020** 25 years apart	
V.	KJB1611	KJB	NASB1995	NASB2020
1	**Who hath beleeued our report? and to whom is the arme of the LORD reuealed?**	**Who hath believed our report? and to whom is the arm of the LORD revealed?**	**Who has believed our message? And to whom has the arm of the LORD been revealed?**	**Who has believed our report? And to whom has the arm of the LORD been revealed?**
2	**For he ſhall grow vp before him as a tender plant, and as a root out of a drie ground: hee hath no forme nor comelineſſe: and when wee ſhall see him, there is no beautie that we ſhould deſire him.**	**For he shall grow up before him as a tender plant, and as a root out of a dry ground: he hath no form nor comeliness; and when we shall see him, there is no beauty that we should desire him.**	**For He grew up before Him like a tender shoot, And like a root out of parched ground; He has no stately form or majesty That we should look upon Him, Nor appearance that we should be attracted to Him.**	**For He grew up before Him like a tender shoot, And like a root out of dry ground; He has no stately form or majesty That we would look at Him, Nor an appearance that we would take pleasure in Him.**
3	**He is deſpiſed and reiected of men, a man of ſorrows, and acquainted with griefe: and we hid as it were our faces from him; hee was deſpiſed, and wee eſteemed him not.**	**He is despised and rejected of men; a man of sorrows, and acquainted with grief: and we hid as it were our faces from him; he was despised, and we esteemed him not.**	**He was despised and forsaken of men, A man of sorrows and acquainted with grief; And like one from whom men hide their face He was despised, and we did not esteem Him.**	**He was despised and abandoned by men, A man of great pain and familiar with sickness; And like one from whom people hide their faces, He was despised, and we had no regard for Him.**

V.	KJB1611	KJB	NASB1995	NASB2020
4	Surely he hath borne our griefes, and caried our ſorrowes: yet we did eſteeme him ſtriken, ſmitten of God, and afflicted.	Surely he hath borne our griefs, and carried our sorrows: yet we did esteem him stricken, smitten of God, and afflicted.	Surely our griefs He Himself bore, And our sorrows He carried; Yet we ourselves esteemed Him stricken, Smitten of God, and afflicted.	However, it was our sicknesses that He Himself bore, And our pains that He carried; Yet we ourselves assumed that He had been afflicted, Struck down by God, and humiliated.
5	But he was wounded for our tranſgreſſions, he was bruiſed for our iniquities: the chaſtiſement of our peace was vpon him, and with his ſtripes we are healed.	But he was wounded for our transgressions, he was bruised for our iniquities: the chastisement of our peace was upon him; and with his stripes we are healed.	But He was pierced through for our transgressions, He was crushed for our iniquities; The chastening for our well-being fell upon Him, And by His scourging we are healed.	But He was pierced for our offenses, He was crushed for our wrongdoings; The punishment for our well-being was laid upon Him, And by His wounds we are healed.
6	All we like ſheepe haue gone aſtray: we haue turned euery one to his owne way, and the LORD hath layd on him the iniquitie of vs all.	All we like sheep have gone astray; we have turned every one to his own way; and the LORD hath laid on him the iniquity of us all.	All of us like sheep have gone astray, Each of us has turned to his own way; But the LORD has caused the iniquity of us all To fall on Him.	All of us, like sheep, have gone astray, Each of us has turned to his own way; But the LORD has caused the wrongdoing of us all To fall on Him.
7	He was oppreſſed, and he was afflicted, yet he opened not his mouth: he is brought as a lambe to the ſlaughter, and as a ſheepe before her ſhearers is dumme, ſo he openeth not his mouth.	He was oppressed, and he was afflicted, yet he opened not his mouth: he is brought as a lamb to the slaughter, and as a sheep before her shearers is dumb, so he openeth not his mouth.	He was oppressed and He was afflicted, Yet He did not open His mouth; Like a lamb that is led to slaughter, And like a sheep that is silent before its shearers, So He did not open His mouth.	He was oppressed and afflicted, Yet He did not open His mouth; Like a lamb that is led to slaughter, And like a sheep that is silent before its shearers, So He did not open His mouth.

V.	KJB1611	KJB	NASB1995	NASB2020
8	He was taken from priſon, and from iudgement: and who ſhall declare his generation? for he was cut off out of the land of the liuing, for the tranſgreſſion of my people was he ſtricken.	He was taken from prison and from judgment: and who shall declare his generation? for he was cut off out of the land of the living: for the transgression of my people was he stricken.	By oppression and judgment He was taken away; And as for His generation, who considered That He was cut off out of the land of the living For the transgression of my people, to whom the stroke was due?	By oppression and judgment He was taken away; And as for His generation, who considered That He was cut off from the land of the living For the wrongdoing of my people, to whom the blow was due?
9	And he made his graue with the wicked, and with the rich in his death, becauſe he had done no violence, neither was any deceit in his mouth.	And he made his grave with the wicked, and with the rich in his death; because he had done no violence, neither was any deceit in his mouth.	His grave was assigned with wicked men, Yet He was with a rich man in His death, Because He had done no violence, Nor was there any deceit in His mouth.	And His grave was assigned with wicked men, Yet He was with a rich man in His death, Because He had done no violence, Nor was there any deceit in His mouth.
10	Yet it pleased the LORD to bruiſe him, he hath put him to griefe: when thou ſhalt make his ſoule an offring for ſinne, he ſhall ſee his ſeede, hee ſhall prolong his daies, and the pleaſure of the LORD ſhall proſper in his hand.	Yet it pleased the LORD to bruise him; he hath put him to grief: when thou shalt make his soul an offering for sin, he shall see his seed, he shall prolong his days, and the pleasure of the LORD shall prosper in his hand.	But the LORD was pleased To crush Him, putting Him to grief; If He would render Himself as a guilt offering, He will see His offspring, He will prolong His days, And the good pleasure of the LORD will prosper in His hand.	But the LORD desired To crush Him, causing Him grief; If He renders Himself as a guilt offering, He will see His offspring, He will prolong His days, And the good pleasure of the LORD will prosper in His hand.
11	He ſhall ſee of the trauell of his ſoule, and ſhalbe ſatiſfied: by his knowledge ſhall my righteous ſeruant iuſtifie many: for hee ſhall beare their iniquities.	He shall see of the travail of his soul, and shall be satisfied: by his knowledge shall my righteous servant justify many; for he shall bear their iniquities.	As a result of the anguish of His soul, He will see it and be satisfied; By His knowledge the Righteous One, My Servant, will justify the many, As He will bear their iniquities.	As a result of the anguish of His soul, He will see it and be satisfied; By His knowledge the Righteous One, My Servant, will justify the many, For He will bear their wrongdoings.

V.	KJB1611	KJB	NASB1995	NASB2020
12	**Therefore will I diuide him a portion with the great, and he ſhall diuide the ſpoile with the ſtrong: becauſe hee hath powred out his ſoule vnto death: and he was numbred with the tranſgreſſours, and he bare the ſinne of many, and made interceſſion for the tranſgreſſours.**	**Therefore will I divide him a portion with the great, and he shall divide the spoil with the strong; because he hath poured out his soul unto death: and he was numbered with the transgressors; and he bare the sin of many, and made intercession for the transgressors.**	**Therefore, I will allot Him a portion with the great, And He will divide the booty with the strong; Because He poured out Himself to death, And was numbered with the transgressors; Yet He Himself bore the sin of many, And interceded for the transgressors.**	**Therefore, I will allot Him a portion with the great, And He will divide the plunder with the strong, Because He poured out His life unto death, And was counted with wrongdoers; Yet He Himself bore the sin of many, And interceded for the wrongdoers.**
	KJB 1611 to KJB (present) 400+ years apart *Several revisions, hundreds of editions*		**NASB 1995-2020** 25 years apart *Just 1 revision*	
	Spelling/Punctuation/Stylistic changes: **110** Word/Phrase changes: **0** **0 of the 110** changes alter the meaning of the text in Isaiah 53		Spelling/Punctuation/Stylistic changes: **5** Word/Phrase changes: **47** **20 of the 52** changes alter the meaning of the text in Isaiah 53	

These are 110 of the *100,000 changes* in the King James Bible. This is what 400 years of "*revisions and updates*" (as the scholars proclaim) has done to the KJB… in comparison to just 1 revision in 25 years of their heralded NASB.

While many will claim the NASB didn't change anything important, I would say otherwise. **Every word of God is pure…** Proverbs 30:5

When have you ever substituted the word "**grief**" for "**sickness**" in your daily life? Have you ever heard somebody use those two words interchangeably?

A "**wrongdoing**" (doing wrong) is a much less descriptive word than **iniquity** (wickedness) or **transgression** (transgressing the law).

God was **pleased** to receive the atonement made by Jesus Christ. Or do you believe ***the LORD desired to crush Him***?

Here is a list of changes that affect meaning in one chapter (Isaiah 53) in one revision of the NASB - some of them may require the reader to look back and check them in context to understand why they affect meaning:

Isaiah 53 (NASB1995 → NASB2020)

1. (53:1) **message → report**
2. (53:2) **be attracted to → take pleasure in**
3. (53:3) **sorrows → great pain**
4. (53:3) **grief → sickness**
5. (53:4) **Surely → However**
6. (53:4) **our griefs → our sicknesses**
7. (53:4) **sorrows → pains**
8. (53:4) **esteemed → assumed**
9. (53:4) **afflicted → humiliated**
10. (53:5) **pierced through → pierced**
11. (53:5) **iniquities → wrongdoings**
12. (53:5) **fell** *(by chance)* → **was laid** *(by higher authority)*
13. (53:5) **scourging → wounds**
14. (53:6) **iniquity → wrongdoing**
15. (53:8) **transgression → wrongdoing**
16. (53:10) **was pleased To crush Him → desired To crush Him**
17. (53:10) **putting Him to grief → causing Him grief**
18. (53:11) **iniquities → wrongdoings**
19. (53:12) **the transgressors → wrongdoers**
20. (53:12) **transgressors → wrongdoers**

---

1. Why So Many Versions? Daniel B. Wallace https://bible.org/article/why-so-many-versions

Appendix 7 - Jesus, Joshua, Justus

One of the interesting things about the word count of **Jesus** in the KJB (that you'll see often throughout these notes) is that there are multiple instances where **Jesus** in the KJB is *not* directly referring to **Jesus Christ.**

Here are all the *antimentions* of **Jesus** in the King James Bible:

- **Bar-jesus**. 1 instance. The sorcerer / false prophet mentioned in Acts 13:6. He does not appear in any default searches for **Jesus** in the software that I use to verify these counts (King James Pure Bible Search.) Therefore, I do not reference him very often. He is always excluded by default.
- **Joshua**. 2 instances. The successor of Moses, called **Jesus** in Acts 7:45 and Hebrews 4:8.
- **Justus.** 1 instance. One of Paul's fellowworkers, called **Jesus** in Colossians 4:11.

I believe the two instances of Joshua-**Jesus** are much more significant (scripture-wise) than "**Justus.**" In fact, I've heard some argue that the two instances of Joshua-**Jesus** in Acts 7:45 & Hebrews 4:8 are actually referring to Jesus Christ Himself as the Angel who led Israel into the promised land. I won't argue against this, because Exodus 23:20-23 makes a strong case for it. Nevertheless, I personally believe from the context of the verses that Stephen was referring to Joshua when he actually spoke these words historically to the council of the high priest (Acts 7:45), and the writer of Hebrews was talking about Joshua who brought the children of Israel into the promised land but did not achieve to give them true rest (Hebrews 4:8). It is, however, a fact that both **Joshua** and **Jesus** are the same name (*meaning "Jehovah is salvation"*), and it's a fact that Joshua is a powerful type of Jesus Christ, especially foreshadowing His second advent.

Joshua was also directly led by **Jesus** (pre-incarnate) as the Angel with the LORD'S name **in him** (Exodus 23:20-21). This is established by the fact that Joshua worships the "**captain of the LORD'S host**" without any rebuke or redirection to worship God instead (Revelation 22:8-9).

Every word of God is pure, yea every jot and tittle. I believe in faith that there are deep reasons why God has arranged for these particular "antimentions" of **Jesus** to appear in His Bible. And I also believe we are to judge spiritual things spiritually (1 Corinthians 2:14-15). My judgment is that "Joshua-**Jesus**" has much more weight and significance than "Justus-**Jesus**," which should, in theory, lead to more significant patterns occurring by *including* the mentions of "Joshua-**Jesus**" and *excluding* the mention of "Justus-**Jesus**." There are also very significant patterns where you include both Justus and Joshua, because after all, God allowed them to be in His book, and the name of **Jesus** is still higher than all other names, chosen from the foundation of the world.

"**Jesus**" in 2 Corinthians 11:4 is tricky, and I believe it is referring to another *version* of Jesus Christ- but it must be at least referencing **Jesus Christ**, similar to how people would say, "*He is just another Steve Irwin*." I would therefore judge that it's not an antimention, but very close to one. The same applies to "**I am Christ**" in Mat 24:5, Mark 13:6, Luke 21:8.

Word count variations of **Jesus** In the King James Bible

Search	Count		Notes / Description	Examples (Page #)
	Jesus + Jesus'	**Jesus**		
Jesus *Excluding Joshua & Justus (Acts 7:45, Col 4:11, Heb 4:8)*	980	970	The true number of mentions of **Jesus** in the Bible when referring to Jesus Christ, the Son of God. 980 = 490 + 490 = 70×7 + 70×7 See Matthew 18:22	66, 70, 72, 75, 114, 163, 187, 188, 192, 227
Jesus *Excluding Justus (Col 4:11)*	982	972	All mentions of the name of **Jesus** including **Joshua** (Acts 7:45, Heb 4:8)	57
Jesus	983	973	All mentions of the name of **Jesus** including **Joshua** and **Justus** (Acts 7:45, Col 4:11, Heb 4:8)	157, 382
JESUS *UPPERCASE mentions only*	6 (7)		All mentions of **JESUS** when it's UPPERCASE. All other searches in this table include it as well; I only added it here to show how many mentions exist separately. By itself, these 6 mentions point to His humanity (All references occur at His birth/circumcision or death on the cross). 6 is the number of man. There is a concealed 7th mention found in most paper Bibles- pointing to His deity, but it's not UPPERCASE in the text itself. It's UPPERCASE because most Bible printers will UPPERCASE the first word of each chapter for stylistic purposes. That 7th mention of UPPERCASE **JESUS** is the first word of John 8, which is the chapter where Jesus declares, **Before Abraham was, I am.** John 8:58	

Appendix 8 - Standardization of Jesus'

In the KJB1611, **Jesus'** (possessive) did not include an apostrophe.

Here is a comparison that shows the standardization. This separation between the words **Jesus** and **Jesus'** created several miraculous phenomena in the KJB we read today. For example, **heaven + Jesus(')** = 1564 mentions, but **heaven + Jesus** = 777+777 mentions. (The first #7 and last #7 words of the Bible) - see p. 57.

Standardization (from **Jesus** to **Jesus'**) occurred circa 1762	
KJB1611 - **Iesus** Luke 5:8	KJB1762 - **Jesus'** Luke 5:8
And they came, & filled both ſo that they began to ſinke. 8 When Simon Peter ſaw downe at Ieſus knees, ſaying from me, for I am a ſinfull Lord. 9 For he was aſtoniſhed, a	came, and filled both the began to ſink. 8 When Simon Peter ſ e 2 Sam. 6. 9. 1 Kings 17. 18. at Jeſus' knees, ſaying, for I am a ſinful man, (9 For he was aſtoni were with him, at the d

The 10 mentions of **Jesus'** (possessive) are found in:

1. Matthew 15:30
2. Matthew 27:57
3. Luke 5:8
4. Luke 8:41
5. Luke 10:39
6. John 12:9
7. John 13:23
8. John 13:25
9. 2 Corinthians 4:5
10. 2 Corinthians 4:11

Appendix 9 - Alphanumeric Values

Alphanumerics is a type of code found in the Bible where each letter is equal to a number depending on its alphabetical position. For example, A=1, B=2, C=3... Z=26.

While many try to associate it with the occult, this is simply an ancient method of counting that has been in existence for thousands of years, in both Hebrew and Greek. It is directly used in the Greek text that underlies the KJB, and clear evidence suggests that God not only knew about it, He wrote the Bible with it in mind to prove His sovereign authorship of not just the Bible, but language itself.

There are two primary ways of calculating numeric values: Ordinal vs Standard. There are other methods as well, but these are the primary.

Ordinal values are simply the numerical order of each letter in its respective alphabetical position. The primary purpose of Ordinal is not to count large numbers, but rather to look at the overall order in which something appears.

Standard alphanumerics, also known as gematria or isopsephy is used in the Greek text itself to calculate the number of 666 in Revelation 13:18, as well as 144 in Revelation 7:4

The following charts show how to find the value for each letter depending on the language. To get a value of a word, all you have to do is add up all the values of the individual letters that make up that word.

Examples:

In English **Ordinal**, the value of "**God**" is (**G**=7) + (**O**=15) + (**D**=4) = **26**
The value of "**Lord**" is (**L**=12) + (**O**=15) + (**R**=18) + (**D**=4) = **49**

In English **Standard**, the value of "**God**" is (**G**=7) + (**O**=60) + (**D**=4) = **71**
The value of "**Lord**" is (**L**=30) + (**O**=60) + (**R**=90) + (**D**=4) = **184**

Alphanumeric Values:

Ordinal Alphanumerics				Standard Alphanumerics			
Hebrew	Greek	English	**Ordinal**	Hebrew	Greek	English	**Standard**
א	Α α	A a	**1**	א	Α α	A a	**1**
ב	Β β	B b	**2**	ב	Β β	B b	**2**
ג	Γ γ	C c	**3**	ג	Γ γ	C c	**3**
ד	Δ δ	D d	**4**	ד	Δ δ	D d	**4**
ה	Ε ε	E e	**5**	ה	Ε ε	E e	**5**
ו	Ζ ζ	F f	**6**	ו	Ϛ ϛ*	F f	**6**
ז	Η η	G g	**7**	ז	Ζ ζ	G g	**7**
ח	Θ θ	H h	**8**	ח	Η η	H h	**8**
ט	Ι ι	I i	**9**	ט	Θ θ	I i	**9**
י	Κ κ	J j	**10**	י	Ι ι	J j	**10**
כך	Λ λ	K k	**11**	כך	Κ κ	K k	**20**
ל	Μ μ	L l	**12**	ל	Λ λ	L l	**30**
מם	Ν ν	M m	**13**	מם	Μ μ	M m	**40**
נן	Ξ ξ	N n	**14**	נן	Ν ν	N n	**50**
ס	Ο ο	O o	**15**	ס	Ξ ξ	O o	**60**
ע	Π π	P p	**16**	ע	Ο ο	P p	**70**
פף	Ρ ρ	Q q	**17**	פף	Π π	Q q	**80**
צץ	Σ σ ς	R r	**18**	צץ	Ϙ ϙ *	R r	**90**
ק	Τ τ	S s	**19**	ק	Ρ ρ	S s	**100**
ר	Υ υ	T t	**20**	ר	Σ σ ς	T t	**200**
ש	Φ φ	U u	**21**	ש	Τ τ	U u	**300**
ת	Χ χ	V v	**22**	ת	Υ υ	V v	**400**
	Ψ ψ	W w	**23**		Φ φ	W w	**500**
	Ω ω	X x	**24**		Χ χ	X x	**600**
		Y y	**25**		Ψ ψ	Y y	**700**
		Z z	**26**		Ω ω	Z z	**800**

*Greek letters [Ϛ ϛ] and [Ϙ ϙ] are ancient obsolete letters that are were removed from the Greek alphabet long before the New Testament was written. While they are still included in Standard numerics due to their numerical values, they are not included in Ordinal.

Examples: (English alphanumeric values of **LORD** and **GOD**)

Ordinal	**L**	**O**	**R**	**D**		**G**	**O**	**D**
	12	15	18	4		7	15	4
	LORD = 49 (Ordinal)					**GOD** = 26 (Ordinal)		
Standard	**L**	**O**	**R**	**D**		**G**	**O**	**D**
	30	60	90	4		7	60	4
	LORD = 184 (Standard)					**GOD** = 71 (Standard)		

Appendix 10 - Mention vs Appearance

The difference between a "mention" and an "appearance" is simple to grasp: A mention is a mention. An appearance is very similar to a mention, but could also be seen within another word. See examples below:

"seven" (Example of Mentions vs Appearances)	
Mentions	Appearances
seven (463x in 391 verses)	**seven** (463x in 391 verses)
	sevens (2x in 2 verses)
	seventh (120x in 115 verses)
	sevenfold (6x in 5 verses)
	seventy (61x in 60 verses)
	seventeen (10x in 10 verses)
	seventeenth (6x in 6 verses)
Total Mentions **seven =** 463x in 391 verses	Total Appearances **seven* =** 668x in 562 verses

To search for appearances in King James Pure Bible Search, add an asterisk (*) after the word. For example: **seven***

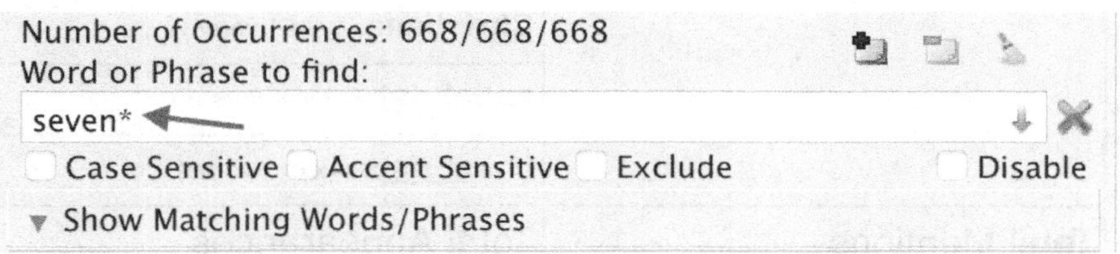

Oftentimes, when searching for appearances, you will want to exclude certain results. For example, you may want to exclude "seventy" and "seventeen(th)" from a search for appearances of seven*

To do that, you simply need to enter those words into separate search phrase boxes and click the "Exclude" toggle.

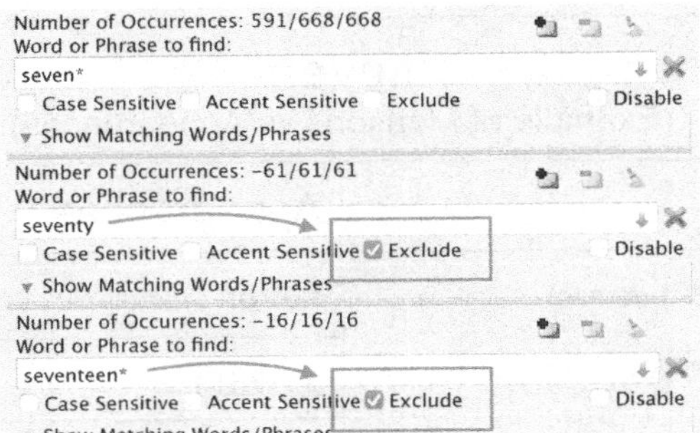

Here is one more example, just to show you how appearances can also have prefixes, not just suffixes (endings).

"Christ" (Example of Mentions vs Appearances)	
Mentions	Appearances
Christ (555x in 552 verses)	**Christ** (555x in 552 verses)
	Christ's (16x in 14 verses)
	Christs (2x in 2 verses)
	Christian (2x in 2 verses)
	Christians (1x in 1 verse)
	antichrist (4x in 4 verses)
	antichrists (1x in 1 verse)
Total Mentions **Christ =** (555x in 552 verses)	Total Appearances ***Christ* =** (581x in 538 verses)

To search for appearances in King James Pure Bible Search where you are also considering prefixes (E.g. **anti<u>christ</u>**), add an asterisk (*) both before and after the word. For example: ***Christ***

As a side note, I always exclude **Christs** (both mentions in context are **false Christs**), **antichrist**, and **antichrists** from my counts when searching for patterns related to **Jesus Christ.**

Appendix 11 - All mentions of Father + Son

List of mentions from the note on **70×7 Father & Son**. See pp. 92-94.

Father + Son Capitalized, standard mentions (non-possessive), *when referring to* **God** or **Jesus**		
Order in Category	Order in Bible	Verse
	1	**Psalms 2:7 I will declare the decree: the LORD hath said unto me, Thou art my Son; this day have I begotten thee.**
	2	**Psalms 2:12 Kiss the Son, lest he be angry, and ye perish from the way, when his wrath is kindled but a little. Blessed are all they that put their trust in him.**
	3	**Isaiah 9:6 For unto us a child is born, unto us a son is given: and the government shall be upon his shoulder: and his name shall be called Wonderful, Counsellor, The mighty God, The everlasting Father, The Prince of Peace.**
	4	**Daniel 3:25 He answered and said, Lo, I see four men loose, walking in the midst of the fire, and they have no hurt; and the form of the fourth is like the Son of God.**
	5	**Daniel 7:13 I saw in the night visions, and, behold, one like the Son of man came with the clouds of heaven, and came to the Ancient of days, and they brought him near before him.**
Order in Gospels		**Father** + **Son** in the Gospels
1	6	**Matthew 3:17 And lo a voice from heaven, saying, This is my beloved Son, in whom I am well pleased.**
2	7	**Matthew 4:3 And when the tempter came to him, he said, If thou be the Son of God, command that these stones be made bread.**
3	8	**Matthew 4:6 And saith unto him, If thou be the Son of God, cast thyself down: for it is written, He shall give his angels charge concerning thee: and in their hands they shall bear thee up, lest at any time thou dash thy foot against a stone.**
4	9	**Matthew 5:16 Let your light so shine before men, that they may see your good works, and glorify your Father which is in heaven.**
5	10	**Matthew 5:45 That ye may be the children of your Father which is in heaven: for he maketh his sun to rise on the evil and on the good, and sendeth rain on the just and on the unjust.**
6	11	**Matthew 5:48 Be ye therefore perfect, even as your Father which is in heaven is perfect.**
7	12	**Matthew 6:1 Take heed that ye do not your alms before men, to be seen of them: otherwise ye have no reward of your Father which is in heaven.**
8	13	**Matthew 6:4 That thine alms may be in secret: and thy Father which seeth in secret himself shall reward thee openly.**

# in Gospels	# in Bible	All mentions of **Father** + **Son** *(Capitalized, standard (non-possessive), God / Jesus)*
9	14	**Matthew 6:6 (1 of 2) But thou, when thou prayest, enter into thy closet, and when thou hast shut thy door, pray to thy Father which is in secret; and thy Father which seeth in secret shall reward thee openly.**
10	15	**Matthew 6:6 (2 of 2) But thou, when thou prayest, enter into thy closet, and when thou hast shut thy door, pray to thy Father which is in secret; and thy Father which seeth in secret shall reward thee openly.**
11	16	**Matthew 6:8 Be not ye therefore like unto them: for your Father knoweth what things ye have need of, before ye ask him.**
12	17	**Matthew 6:9 After this manner therefore pray ye: Our Father which art in heaven, Hallowed be thy name.**
13	18	**Matthew 6:14 For if ye forgive men their trespasses, your heavenly Father will also forgive you:**
14	19	**Matthew 6:15 But if ye forgive not men their trespasses, neither will your Father forgive your trespasses.**
15	20	**Matthew 6:18 (1 of 2) That thou appear not unto men to fast, but unto thy Father which is in secret: and thy Father, which seeth in secret, shall reward thee openly.**
16	21	**Matthew 6:18 (2 of 2) That thou appear not unto men to fast, but unto thy Father which is in secret: and thy Father, which seeth in secret, shall reward thee openly.**
17	22	**Matthew 6:26 Behold the fowls of the air: for they sow not, neither do they reap, nor gather into barns; yet your heavenly Father feedeth them. Are ye not much better than they?**
18	23	**Matthew 6:32 (For after all these things do the Gentiles seek:) for your heavenly Father knoweth that ye have need of all these things.**
19	24	**Matthew 7:11 If ye then, being evil, know how to give good gifts unto your children, how much more shall your Father which is in heaven give good things to them that ask him?**
20	25	**Matthew 7:21 Not every one that saith unto me, Lord, Lord, shall enter into the kingdom of heaven; but he that doeth the will of my Father which is in heaven.**
21	26	**Matthew 8:20 And Jesus saith unto him, The foxes have holes, and the birds of the air have nests; but the Son of man hath not where to lay his head.**
22	27	**Matthew 8:29 And, behold, they cried out, saying, What have we to do with thee, Jesus, thou Son of God? art thou come hither to torment us before the time?**
23	28	**Matthew 9:6 But that ye may know that the Son of man hath power on earth to forgive sins, (then saith he to the sick of the palsy,) Arise, take up thy bed, and go unto thine house.**
24	29	**Matthew 9:27 And when Jesus departed thence, two blind men followed him, crying, and saying, Thou Son of David, have mercy on us.**
25	30	**Matthew 10:20 For it is not ye that speak, but the Spirit of your Father which speaketh in you.**
26	31	**Matthew 10:23 But when they persecute you in this city, flee ye into another: for verily I say unto you, Ye shall not have gone over the cities of Israel, till the Son of man be come.**
27	32	**Matthew 10:29 Are not two sparrows sold for a farthing? and one of them shall not fall on the ground without your Father.**
28	33	**Matthew 10:32 Whosoever therefore shall confess me before men, him will I confess also before my Father which is in heaven.**

# in Gospels	# in Bible	All mentions of **Father + Son** *(Capitalized, standard (non-possessive), God / Jesus)*
29	34	**Matthew 10:33 But whosoever shall deny me before men, him will I also deny before my Father which is in heaven.**
30	35	**Matthew 11:19 The Son of man came eating and drinking, and they say, Behold a man gluttonous, and a winebibber, a friend of publicans and sinners. But wisdom is justified of her children.**
31	36	**Matthew 11:25 At that time Jesus answered and said, I thank thee, O Father, Lord of heaven and earth, because thou hast hid these things from the wise and prudent, and hast revealed them unto babes.**
32	37	**Matthew 11:26 Even so, Father: for so it seemed good in thy sight.**
33	38	**Matthew 11:27 (1 of 6) All things are delivered unto me of my Father: and no man knoweth the Son, but the Father; neither knoweth any man the Father, save the Son, and he to whomsoever the Son will reveal him.**
34	39	**Matthew 11:27 (2 of 6) All things are delivered unto me of my Father: and no man knoweth the Son, but the Father; neither knoweth any man the Father, save the Son, and he to whomsoever the Son will reveal him.**
35	40	**Matthew 11:27 (3 of 6) All things are delivered unto me of my Father: and no man knoweth the Son, but the Father; neither knoweth any man the Father, save the Son, and he to whomsoever the Son will reveal him.**
36	41	**Matthew 11:27 (4 of 6) All things are delivered unto me of my Father: and no man knoweth the Son, but the Father; neither knoweth any man the Father, save the Son, and he to whomsoever the Son will reveal him.**
37	42	**Matthew 11:27 (5 of 6) All things are delivered unto me of my Father: and no man knoweth the Son, but the Father; neither knoweth any man the Father, save the Son, and he to whomsoever the Son will reveal him.**
38	43	**Matthew 11:27 (6 of 6) All things are delivered unto me of my Father: and no man knoweth the Son, but the Father; neither knoweth any man the Father, save the Son, and he to whomsoever the Son will reveal him.**
39	44	**Matthew 12:8 For the Son of man is Lord even of the sabbath day.**
40	45	**Matthew 12:32 And whosoever speaketh a word against the Son of man, it shall be forgiven him: but whosoever speaketh against the Holy Ghost, it shall not be forgiven him, neither in this world, neither in the world to come.**
41	46	**Matthew 12:40 For as Jonas was three days and three nights in the whale's belly; so shall the Son of man be three days and three nights in the heart of the earth.**
42	47	**Matthew 12:50 For whosoever shall do the will of my Father which is in heaven, the same is my brother, and sister, and mother.**
43	48	**Matthew 13:37 He answered and said unto them, He that soweth the good seed is the Son of man;**
44	49	**Matthew 13:41 The Son of man shall send forth his angels, and they shall gather out of his kingdom all things that offend, and them which do iniquity;**
45	50	**Matthew 13:43 Then shall the righteous shine forth as the sun in the kingdom of their Father. Who hath ears to hear, let him hear.**
46	51	**Matthew 14:33 Then they that were in the ship came and worshipped him, saying, Of a truth thou art the Son of God.**
47	52	**Matthew 15:13 But he answered and said, Every plant, which my heavenly Father hath not planted, shall be rooted up.**

# in Gospels	# in Bible	All mentions of **Father** + **Son** *(Capitalized, standard (non-possessive), God / Jesus)*
48	53	**Matthew 15:22 And, behold, a woman of Canaan came out of the same coasts, and cried unto him, saying, Have mercy on me, O Lord, thou Son of David; my daughter is grievously vexed with a devil.**
49	54	**Matthew 16:13 When Jesus came into the coasts of Caesarea Philippi, he asked his disciples, saying, Whom do men say that I the Son of man am?**
50	55	**Matthew 16:16 And Simon Peter answered and said, Thou art the Christ, the Son of the living God.**
51	56	**Matthew 16:17 And Jesus answered and said unto him, Blessed art thou, Simon Bar-jona: for flesh and blood hath not revealed it unto thee, but my Father which is in heaven.**
52	57	**Matthew 16:27 (1 of 2) For the Son of man shall come in the glory of his Father with his angels; and then he shall reward every man according to his works.**
53	58	**Matthew 16:27 (2 of 2) For the Son of man shall come in the glory of his Father with his angels; and then he shall reward every man according to his works.**
54	59	**Matthew 16:28 Verily I say unto you, There be some standing here, which shall not taste of death, till they see the Son of man coming in his kingdom.**
55	60	**Matthew 17:5 While he yet spake, behold, a bright cloud overshadowed them: and behold a voice out of the cloud, which said, This is my beloved Son, in whom I am well pleased; hear ye him.**
56	61	**Matthew 17:9 And as they came down from the mountain, Jesus charged them, saying, Tell the vision to no man, until the Son of man be risen again from the dead.**
57	62	**Matthew 17:12 But I say unto you, That Elias is come already, and they knew him not, but have done unto him whatsoever they listed. Likewise shall also the Son of man suffer of them.**
58	63	**Matthew 17:22 And while they abode in Galilee, Jesus said unto them, The Son of man shall be betrayed into the hands of men:**
59	64	**Matthew 18:10 Take heed that ye despise not one of these little ones; for I say unto you, That in heaven their angels do always behold the face of my Father which is in heaven.**
60	65	**Matthew 18:11 For the Son of man is come to save that which was lost.**
61	66	**Matthew 18:14 Even so it is not the will of your Father which is in heaven, that one of these little ones should perish.**
62	67	**Matthew 18:19 Again I say unto you, That if two of you shall agree on earth as touching any thing that they shall ask, it shall be done for them of my Father which is in heaven.**
63	68	**Matthew 18:35 So likewise shall my heavenly Father do also unto you, if ye from your hearts forgive not every one his brother their trespasses.**
64	69	**Matthew 19:28 And Jesus said unto them, Verily I say unto you, That ye which have followed me, in the regeneration when the Son of man shall sit in the throne of his glory, ye also shall sit upon twelve thrones, judging the twelve tribes of Israel.**
65	70	**Matthew 20:18 Behold, we go up to Jerusalem; and the Son of man shall be betrayed unto the chief priests and unto the scribes, and they shall condemn him to death,**
66	71	**Matthew 20:23 And he saith unto them, Ye shall drink indeed of my cup, and be baptized with the baptism that I am baptized with: but to sit on my right hand, and on my left, is not mine to give, but it shall be given to them for whom it is prepared of my Father.**
67	72	**Matthew 20:28 Even as the Son of man came not to be ministered unto, but to minister, and to give his life a ransom for many.**

# in Gospels	# in Bible	All mentions of **Father** + **Son** *(Capitalized, standard (non-possessive), God / Jesus)*
68	73	**Matthew 20:30 And, behold, two blind men sitting by the way side, when they heard that Jesus passed by, cried out, saying, Have mercy on us, O Lord, thou Son of David.**
69	74	**Matthew 20:31 And the multitude rebuked them, because they should hold their peace: but they cried the more, saying, Have mercy on us, O Lord, thou Son of David.**
70	75	**Matthew 21:9 And the multitudes that went before, and that followed, cried, saying, Hosanna to the Son of David: Blessed is he that cometh in the name of the Lord; Hosanna in the highest.**
71	76	**Matthew 21:15 And when the chief priests and scribes saw the wonderful things that he did, and the children crying in the temple, and saying, Hosanna to the Son of David; they were sore displeased,**
72	77	**Matthew 22:42 Saying, What think ye of Christ? whose son is he? They say unto him, The Son of David.**
73	78	**Matthew 23:9 And call no man your father upon the earth: for one is your Father, which is in heaven.**
74	79	**Matthew 24:27 For as the lightning cometh out of the east, and shineth even unto the west; so shall also the coming of the Son of man be.**
75	80	**Matthew 24:30 (1 of 2) And then shall appear the sign of the Son of man in heaven: and then shall all the tribes of the earth mourn, and they shall see the Son of man coming in the clouds of heaven with power and great glory.**
76	81	**Matthew 24:30 (2 of 2) And then shall appear the sign of the Son of man in heaven: and then shall all the tribes of the earth mourn, and they shall see the Son of man coming in the clouds of heaven with power and great glory.**
77	82	**Matthew 24:36 But of that day and hour knoweth no man, no, not the angels of heaven, but my Father only.**
78	83	**Matthew 24:37 But as the days of Noe were, so shall also the coming of the Son of man be.**
79	84	**Matthew 24:39 And knew not until the flood came, and took them all away; so shall also the coming of the Son of man be.**
80	85	**Matthew 24:44 Therefore be ye also ready: for in such an hour as ye think not the Son of man cometh.**
81	86	**Matthew 25:13 Watch therefore, for ye know neither the day nor the hour wherein the Son of man cometh.**
82	87	**Matthew 25:31 When the Son of man shall come in his glory, and all the holy angels with him, then shall he sit upon the throne of his glory:**
83	88	**Matthew 25:34 Then shall the King say unto them on his right hand, Come, ye blessed of my Father, inherit the kingdom prepared for you from the foundation of the world:**
84	89	**Matthew 26:2 Ye know that after two days is the feast of the passover, and the Son of man is betrayed to be crucified.**
85	90	**Matthew 26:24 (1 of 2) The Son of man goeth as it is written of him: but woe unto that man by whom the Son of man is betrayed! it had been good for that man if he had not been born.**
86	91	**Matthew 26:24 (2 of 2) The Son of man goeth as it is written of him: but woe unto that man by whom the Son of man is betrayed! it had been good for that man if he had not been born.**

# in Gospels	# in Bible	All mentions of **Father** + **Son** *(Capitalized, standard (non-possessive), God / Jesus)*
87	92	**Matthew 26:39 And he went a little further, and fell on his face, and prayed, saying, O my Father, if it be possible, let this cup pass from me: nevertheless not as I will, but as thou wilt.**
88	93	**Matthew 26:42 He went away again the second time, and prayed, saying, O my Father, if this cup may not pass away from me, except I drink it, thy will be done.**
89	94	**Matthew 26:45 Then cometh he to his disciples, and saith unto them, Sleep on now, and take your rest: behold, the hour is at hand, and the Son of man is betrayed into the hands of sinners.**
90	95	**Matthew 26:53 Thinkest thou that I cannot now pray to my Father, and he shall presently give me more than twelve legions of angels?**
91	96	**Matthew 26:63 But Jesus held his peace. And the high priest answered and said unto him, I adjure thee by the living God, that thou tell us whether thou be the Christ, the Son of God.**
92	97	**Matthew 26:64 Jesus saith unto him, Thou hast said: nevertheless I say unto you, Hereafter shall ye see the Son of man sitting on the right hand of power, and coming in the clouds of heaven.**
93	98	**Matthew 27:40 And saying, Thou that destroyest the temple, and buildest it in three days, save thyself. If thou be the Son of God, come down from the cross.**
94	99	**Matthew 27:43 He trusted in God; let him deliver him now, if he will have him: for he said, I am the Son of God.**
95	100	**Matthew 27:54 Now when the centurion, and they that were with him, watching Jesus, saw the earthquake, and those things that were done, they feared greatly, saying, Truly this was the Son of God.**
96	101	**Matthew 28:19 (1 of 2) Go ye therefore, and teach all nations, baptizing them in the name of the Father, and of the Son, and of the Holy Ghost:**
97	102	**Matthew 28:19 (1 of 2) Go ye therefore, and teach all nations, baptizing them in the name of the Father, and of the Son, and of the Holy Ghost:**
98	103	**Mark 1:1 The beginning of the gospel of Jesus Christ, the Son of God;**
99	104	**Mark 1:11 And there came a voice from heaven, saying, Thou art my beloved Son, in whom I am well pleased.**
100	105	**Mark 2:10 But that ye may know that the Son of man hath power on earth to forgive sins, (he saith to the sick of the palsy,)**
101	106	**Mark 2:28 Therefore the Son of man is Lord also of the sabbath.**
102	107	**Mark 3:11 And unclean spirits, when they saw him, fell down before him, and cried, saying, Thou art the Son of God.**
103	108	**Mark 5:7 And cried with a loud voice, and said, What have I to do with thee, Jesus, thou Son of the most high God? I adjure thee by God, that thou torment me not.**
104	109	**Mark 8:31 And he began to teach them, that the Son of man must suffer many things, and be rejected of the elders, and of the chief priests, and scribes, and be killed, and after three days rise again.**
105	110	**Mark 8:38 (1 of 2) Whosoever therefore shall be ashamed of me and of my words in this adulterous and sinful generation; of him also shall the Son of man be ashamed, when he cometh in the glory of his Father with the holy angels.**
106	111	**Mark 8:38 (2 of 2) Whosoever therefore shall be ashamed of me and of my words in this adulterous and sinful generation; of him also shall the Son of man be ashamed, when he cometh in the glory of his Father with the holy angels.**
107	112	**Mark 9:7 And there was a cloud that overshadowed them: and a voice came out of the cloud, saying, This is my beloved Son: hear him.**

# in Gospels	# in Bible	All mentions of **Father + Son** *(Capitalized, standard (non-possessive), God / Jesus)*
108	113	**Mark 9:9 And as they came down from the mountain, he charged them that they should tell no man what things they had seen, till the Son of man were risen from the dead.**
109	114	**Mark 9:12 And he answered and told them, Elias verily cometh first, and restoreth all things; and how it is written of the Son of man, that he must suffer many things, and be set at nought.**
110	115	**Mark 9:31 For he taught his disciples, and said unto them, The Son of man is delivered into the hands of men, and they shall kill him; and after that he is killed, he shall rise the third day.**
111	116	**Mark 10:33 Saying, Behold, we go up to Jerusalem; and the Son of man shall be delivered unto the chief priests, and unto the scribes; and they shall condemn him to death, and shall deliver him to the Gentiles:**
112	117	**Mark 10:45 For even the Son of man came not to be ministered unto, but to minister, and to give his life a ransom for many.**
113	118	**Mark 10:47 And when he heard that it was Jesus of Nazareth, he began to cry out, and say, Jesus, thou Son of David, have mercy on me.**
114	119	**Mark 10:48 And many charged him that he should hold his peace: but he cried the more a great deal, Thou Son of David, have mercy on me.**
115	120	**Mark 11:25 And when ye stand praying, forgive, if ye have ought against any: that your Father also which is in heaven may forgive you your trespasses.**
116	121	**Mark 11:26 But if ye do not forgive, neither will your Father which is in heaven forgive your trespasses.**
117	122	**Mark 12:35 And Jesus answered and said, while he taught in the temple, How say the scribes that Christ is the Son of David?**
118	123	**Mark 13:26 And then shall they see the Son of man coming in the clouds with great power and glory.**
119	124	**Mark 13:32 (1 of 2) But of that day and that hour knoweth no man, no, not the angels which are in heaven, neither the Son, but the Father.**
120	125	**Mark 13:32 (2 of 2) But of that day and that hour knoweth no man, no, not the angels which are in heaven, neither the Son, but the Father.**
121	126	**Mark 13:34 For the Son of man is as a man taking a far journey, who left his house, and gave authority to his servants, and to every man his work, and commanded the porter to watch.**
122	127	**Mark 14:21 (1 of 2) The Son of man indeed goeth, as it is written of him: but woe to that man by whom the Son of man is betrayed! good were it for that man if he had never been born.**
123	128	**Mark 14:21 (2 of 2) The Son of man indeed goeth, as it is written of him: but woe to that man by whom the Son of man is betrayed! good were it for that man if he had never been born.**
124	129	**Mark 14:36 And he said, Abba, Father, all things are possible unto thee; take away this cup from me: nevertheless not what I will, but what thou wilt.**
125	130	**Mark 14:41 And he cometh the third time, and saith unto them, Sleep on now, and take your rest: it is enough, the hour is come; behold, the Son of man is betrayed into the hands of sinners.**
126	131	**Mark 14:61 But he held his peace, and answered nothing. Again the high priest asked him, and said unto him, Art thou the Christ, the Son of the Blessed?**

# in Gospels	# in Bible	All mentions of **Father** + **Son** *(Capitalized, standard (non-possessive), God / Jesus)*
127	132	**Mark 14:62 And Jesus said, I am: and ye shall see the Son of man sitting on the right hand of power, and coming in the clouds of heaven.**
128	133	**Mark 15:39 And when the centurion, which stood over against him, saw that he so cried out, and gave up the ghost, he said, Truly this man was the Son of God.**
129	134	**Luke 1:32 He shall be great, and shall be called the Son of the Highest: and the Lord God shall give unto him the throne of his father David:**
130	135	**Luke 1:35 And the angel answered and said unto her, The Holy Ghost shall come upon thee, and the power of the Highest shall overshadow thee: therefore also that holy thing which shall be born of thee shall be called the Son of God.**
131	136	**Luke 2:48 And when they saw him, they were amazed: and his mother said unto him, Son, why hast thou thus dealt with us? behold, thy father and I have sought thee sorrowing.**
132	137	**Luke 3:22 And the Holy Ghost descended in a bodily shape like a dove upon him, and a voice came from heaven, which said, Thou art my beloved Son; in thee I am well pleased.**
133	138	**Luke 4:3 And the devil said unto him, If thou be the Son of God, command this stone that it be made bread.**
134	139	**Luke 4:9 And he brought him to Jerusalem, and set him on a pinnacle of the temple, and said unto him, If thou be the Son of God, cast thyself down from hence:**
135	140	**Luke 4:41 And devils also came out of many, crying out, and saying, Thou art Christ the Son of God. And he rebuking them suffered them not to speak: for they knew that he was Christ.**
136	141	**Luke 5:24 But that ye may know that the Son of man hath power upon earth to forgive sins, (he said unto the sick of the palsy,) I say unto thee, Arise, and take up thy couch, and go into thine house.**
137	142	**Luke 6:5 And he said unto them, That the Son of man is Lord also of the sabbath.**
138	143	**Luke 6:22 Blessed are ye, when men shall hate you, and when they shall separate you from their company, and shall reproach you, and cast out your name as evil, for the Son of man's sake.**
139	144	**Luke 6:36 Be ye therefore merciful, as your Father also is merciful.**
140	145	**Luke 7:34 The Son of man is come eating and drinking; and ye say, Behold a gluttonous man, and a winebibber, a friend of publicans and sinners!**
141	146	**Luke 8:28 When he saw Jesus, he cried out, and fell down before him, and with a loud voice said, What have I to do with thee, Jesus, thou Son of God most high? I beseech thee, torment me not.**
142	147	**Luke 9:22 Saying, The Son of man must suffer many things, and be rejected of the elders and chief priests and scribes, and be slain, and be raised the third day.**
143	148	**Luke 9:26 For whosoever shall be ashamed of me and of my words, of him shall the Son of man be ashamed, when he shall come in his own glory, and in his Father's, and of the holy angels.**
144	149	**Luke 9:35 And there came a voice out of the cloud, saying, This is my beloved Son: hear him.**
145	150	**Luke 9:44 Let these sayings sink down into your ears: for the Son of man shall be delivered into the hands of men.**
146	151	**Luke 9:56 For the Son of man is not come to destroy men's lives, but to save them. And they went to another village.**
147	152	**Luke 9:58 And Jesus said unto him, Foxes have holes, and birds of the air have nests; but the Son of man hath not where to lay his head.**

# in Gospels	# in Bible	All mentions of **Father** + **Son** *(Capitalized, standard (non-possessive), God / Jesus)*
148	153	**Luke 10:21 (1 of 2) In that hour Jesus rejoiced in spirit, and said, I thank thee, O Father, Lord of heaven and earth, that thou hast hid these things from the wise and prudent, and hast revealed them unto babes: even so, Father; for so it seemed good in thy sight.**
149	154	**Luke 10:21 (2 of 2) In that hour Jesus rejoiced in spirit, and said, I thank thee, O Father, Lord of heaven and earth, that thou hast hid these things from the wise and prudent, and hast revealed them unto babes: even so, Father; for so it seemed good in thy sight.**
150	155	**Luke 10:22 (1 of 6) All things are delivered to me of my Father: and no man knoweth who the Son is, but the Father; and who the Father is, but the Son, and he to whom the Son will reveal him.**
151	156	**Luke 10:22 (2 of 6) All things are delivered to me of my Father: and no man knoweth who the Son is, but the Father; and who the Father is, but the Son, and he to whom the Son will reveal him.**
152	157	**Luke 10:22 (3 of 6) All things are delivered to me of my Father: and no man knoweth who the Son is, but the Father; and who the Father is, but the Son, and he to whom the Son will reveal him.**
153	158	**Luke 10:22 (4 of 6) All things are delivered to me of my Father: and no man knoweth who the Son is, but the Father; and who the Father is, but the Son, and he to whom the Son will reveal him.**
154	159	**Luke 10:22 (5 of 6) All things are delivered to me of my Father: and no man knoweth who the Son is, but the Father; and who the Father is, but the Son, and he to whom the Son will reveal him.**
155	160	**Luke 10:22 (6 of 6) All things are delivered to me of my Father: and no man knoweth who the Son is, but the Father; and who the Father is, but the Son, and he to whom the Son will reveal him.**
156	161	**Luke 11:2 And he said unto them, When ye pray, say, Our Father which art in heaven, Hallowed be thy name. Thy kingdom come. Thy will be done, as in heaven, so in earth.**
157	162	**Luke 11:13 If ye then, being evil, know how to give good gifts unto your children: how much more shall your heavenly Father give the Holy Spirit to them that ask him?**
158	163	**Luke 11:30 For as Jonas was a sign unto the Ninevites, so shall also the Son of man be to this generation.**
159	164	**Luke 12:8 Also I say unto you, Whosoever shall confess me before men, him shall the Son of man also confess before the angels of God:**
160	165	**Luke 12:10 And whosoever shall speak a word against the Son of man, it shall be forgiven him: but unto him that blasphemeth against the Holy Ghost it shall not be forgiven.**
161	166	**Luke 12:30 For all these things do the nations of the world seek after: and your Father knoweth that ye have need of these things.**
162	167	**Luke 12:40 Be ye therefore ready also: for the Son of man cometh at an hour when ye think not.**
163	168	**Luke 15:12 And the younger of them said to his father, Father, give me the portion of goods that falleth to me. And he divided unto them his living.**
164	169	**Luke 15:18 I will arise and go to my father, and will say unto him, Father, I have sinned against heaven, and before thee,**
165	170	**Luke 15:21 And the son said unto him, Father, I have sinned against heaven, and in thy sight, and am no more worthy to be called thy son.**

# in Gospels	# in Bible	All mentions of **Father** + **Son** *(Capitalized, standard (non-possessive), God / Jesus)*
166	171	**Luke 17:22 And he said unto the disciples, The days will come, when ye shall desire to see one of the days of the Son of man, and ye shall not see it.**
167	172	**Luke 17:24 For as the lightning, that lighteneth out of the one part under heaven, shineth unto the other part under heaven; so shall also the Son of man be in his day.**
168	173	**Luke 17:26 And as it was in the days of Noe, so shall it be also in the days of the Son of man.**
169	174	**Luke 17:30 Even thus shall it be in the day when the Son of man is revealed.**
170	175	**Luke 18:8 I tell you that he will avenge them speedily. Nevertheless when the Son of man cometh, shall he find faith on the earth?**
171	176	**Luke 18:31 Then he took unto him the twelve, and said unto them, Behold, we go up to Jerusalem, and all things that are written by the prophets concerning the Son of man shall be accomplished.**
172	177	**Luke 18:38 And he cried, saying, Jesus, thou Son of David, have mercy on me.**
173	178	**Luke 18:39 And they which went before rebuked him, that he should hold his peace: but he cried so much the more, Thou Son of David, have mercy on me.**
174	179	**Luke 19:10 For the Son of man is come to seek and to save that which was lost.**
175	180	**Luke 21:27 And then shall they see the Son of man coming in a cloud with power and great glory.**
176	181	**Luke 21:36 Watch ye therefore, and pray always, that ye may be accounted worthy to escape all these things that shall come to pass, and to stand before the Son of man.**
177	182	**Luke 22:22 And truly the Son of man goeth, as it was determined: but woe unto that man by whom he is betrayed!**
178	183	**Luke 22:29 And I appoint unto you a kingdom, as my Father hath appointed unto me;**
179	184	**Luke 22:42 Saying, Father, if thou be willing, remove this cup from me: nevertheless not my will, but thine, be done.**
180	185	**Luke 22:48 But Jesus said unto him, Judas, betrayest thou the Son of man with a kiss?**
181	186	**Luke 22:69 Hereafter shall the Son of man sit on the right hand of the power of God.**
182	187	**Luke 22:70 Then said they all, Art thou then the Son of God? And he said unto them, Ye say that I am.**
183	188	**Luke 23:34 Then said Jesus, Father, forgive them; for they know not what they do. And they parted his raiment, and cast lots.**
184	189	**Luke 23:46 And when Jesus had cried with a loud voice, he said, Father, into thy hands I commend my spirit: and having said thus, he gave up the ghost.**
185	190	**Luke 24:7 Saying, The Son of man must be delivered into the hands of sinful men, and be crucified, and the third day rise again.**
186	191	**Luke 24:49 And, behold, I send the promise of my Father upon you: but tarry ye in the city of Jerusalem, until ye be endued with power from on high.**
187	192	**John 1:14 And the Word was made flesh, and dwelt among us, (and we beheld his glory, the glory as of the only begotten of the Father,) full of grace and truth.**
188	193	**John 1:18 (1 of 2) No man hath seen God at any time; the only begotten Son, which is in the bosom of the Father, he hath declared him.**
189	194	**John 1:18 (2 of 2) No man hath seen God at any time; the only begotten Son, which is in the bosom of the Father, he hath declared him.**
190	195	**John 1:34 And I saw, and bare record that this is the Son of God.**

# in Gospels	# in Bible	All mentions of **Father** + **Son** *(Capitalized, standard (non-possessive), God / Jesus)*
191	196	**John 1:49 Nathanael answered and saith unto him, Rabbi, thou art the Son of God; thou art the King of Israel.**
192	197	**John 1:51 And he saith unto him, Verily, verily, I say unto you, Hereafter ye shall see heaven open, and the angels of God ascending and descending upon the Son of man.**
193	198	**John 3:13 And no man hath ascended up to heaven, but he that came down from heaven, even the Son of man which is in heaven.**
194	199	**John 3:14 And as Moses lifted up the serpent in the wilderness, even so must the Son of man be lifted up:**
195	200	**John 3:16 For God so loved the world, that he gave his only begotten Son, that whosoever believeth in him should not perish, but have everlasting life.**
196	201	**John 3:17 For God sent not his Son into the world to condemn the world; but that the world through him might be saved.**
197	202	**John 3:18 He that believeth on him is not condemned: but he that believeth not is condemned already, because he hath not believed in the name of the only begotten Son of Son.**
198	203	**John 3:35 (1 of 2) The Father loveth the Son, and hath given all things into his hand.**
199	204	**John 3:35 (2 of 2) The Father loveth the Son, and hath given all things into his hand.**
200	205	**John 3:36 (1 of 2) He that believeth on the Son hath everlasting life: and he that believeth not the Son shall not see life; but the wrath of God abideth on him.**
201	206	**John 3:36 (2 of 2) He that believeth on the Son hath everlasting life: and he that believeth not the Son shall not see life; but the wrath of God abideth on him.**
202	207	**John 4:21 Jesus saith unto her, Woman, believe me, the hour cometh, when ye shall neither in this mountain, nor yet at Jerusalem, worship the Father.**
203	208	**John 4:23 (1 of 2) But the hour cometh, and now is, when the true worshippers shall worship the Father in spirit and in truth: for the Father seeketh such to worship him.**
204	209	**John 4:23 (2 of 2) But the hour cometh, and now is, when the true worshippers shall worship the Father in spirit and in truth: for the Father seeketh such to worship him.**
205	210	**John 5:17 But Jesus answered them, My Father worketh hitherto, and I work.**
206	211	**John 5:18 Therefore the Jews sought the more to kill him, because he not only had broken the sabbath, but said also that God was his Father, making himself equal with God.**
207	212	**John 5:19 (1 of 3) Then answered Jesus and said unto them, Verily, verily, I say unto you, The Son can do nothing of himself, but what he seeth the Father do: for what things soever he doeth, these also doeth the Son likewise.**
208	213	**John 5:19 (2 of 3) Then answered Jesus and said unto them, Verily, verily, I say unto you, The Son can do nothing of himself, but what he seeth the Father do: for what things soever he doeth, these also doeth the Son likewise.**
209	214	**John 5:19 (3 of 3) Then answered Jesus and said unto them, Verily, verily, I say unto you, The Son can do nothing of himself, but what he seeth the Father do: for what things soever he doeth, these also doeth the Son likewise.**
210	215	**John 5:20 (1 of 2) For the Father loveth the Son, and sheweth him all things that himself doeth: and he will shew him greater works than these, that ye may marvel.**
211	216	**John 5:20 (2 of 2) For the Father loveth the Son, and sheweth him all things that himself doeth: and he will shew him greater works than these, that ye may marvel.**

# in Gospels	# in Bible	All mentions of **Father** + **Son** *(Capitalized, standard (non-possessive), God / Jesus)*
212	217	**John 5:21 (1 of 2) For as the Father raiseth up the dead, and quickeneth them; even so the Son quickeneth whom he will.**
213	218	**John 5:21 (2 of 2) For as the Father raiseth up the dead, and quickeneth them; even so the Son quickeneth whom he will.**
214	219	**John 5:22 (1 of 2) For the Father judgeth no man, but hath committed all judgment unto the Son:**
215	220	**John 5:22 (2 of 2) For the Father judgeth no man, but hath committed all judgment unto the Son:**
216	221	**John 5:23 (1 of 4) That all men should honour the Son, even as they honour the Father. He that honoureth not the Son honoureth not the Father which hath sent him.**
217	222	**John 5:23 (2 of 4) That all men should honour the Son, even as they honour the Father. He that honoureth not the Son honoureth not the Father which hath sent him.**
218	223	**John 5:23 (3 of 4) That all men should honour the Son, even as they honour the Father. He that honoureth not the Son honoureth not the Father which hath sent him.**
219	224	**John 5:23 (4 of 4) That all men should honour the Son, even as they honour the Father. He that honoureth not the Son honoureth not the Father which hath sent him.**
220	225	**John 5:25 Verily, verily, I say unto you, The hour is coming, and now is, when the dead shall hear the voice of the Son of God: and they that hear shall live.**
221	226	**John 5:26 (1 of 2) For as the Father hath life in himself; so hath he given to the Son to have life in himself;**
222	227	**John 5:26 (2 of 2) For as the Father hath life in himself; so hath he given to the Son to have life in himself;**
223	228	**John 5:27 And hath given him authority to execute judgment also, because he is the Son of man.**
224	229	**John 5:30 I can of mine own self do nothing: as I hear, I judge: and my judgment is just; because I seek not mine own will, but the will of the Father which hath sent me.**
225	230	**John 5:36 (1 of 2) But I have greater witness than that of John: for the works which the Father hath given me to finish, the same works that I do, bear witness of me, that the Father hath sent me.**
226	231	**John 5:36 (2 of 2) But I have greater witness than that of John: for the works which the Father hath given me to finish, the same works that I do, bear witness of me, that the Father hath sent me.**
227	232	**John 5:37 And the Father himself, which hath sent me, hath borne witness of me. Ye have neither heard his voice at any time, nor seen his shape.**
228	233	**John 5:45 Do not think that I will accuse you to the Father: there is one that accuseth you, even Moses, in whom ye trust.**
229	234	**John 6:27 (1 of 2) Labour not for the meat which perisheth, but for that meat which endureth unto everlasting life, which the Son of man shall give unto you: for him hath God the Father sealed.**
230	235	**John 6:27 (2 of 2) Labour not for the meat which perisheth, but for that meat which endureth unto everlasting life, which the Son of man shall give unto you: for him hath God the Father sealed.**
231	236	**John 6:32 Then Jesus said unto them, Verily, verily, I say unto you, Moses gave you not that bread from heaven; but my Father giveth you the true bread from heaven.**
232	237	**John 6:37 All that the Father giveth me shall come to me; and him that cometh to me I will in no wise cast out.**
233	238	**John 6:40 And this is the will of him that sent me, that every one which seeth the Son, and believeth on him, may have everlasting life: and I will raise him up at the last day.**

# in Gospels	# in Bible	All mentions of Father + Son *(Capitalized, standard (non-possessive), God / Jesus)*
234	239	**John 6:44 No man can come to me, except the Father which hath sent me draw him: and I will raise him up at the last day.**
235	240	**John 6:45 It is written in the prophets, And they shall be all taught of God. Every man therefore that hath heard, and hath learned of the Father, cometh unto me.**
236	241	**John 6:46 (1 of 2) Not that any man hath seen the Father, save he which is of God, he hath seen the Father.**
237	242	**John 6:46 (2 of 2) Not that any man hath seen the Father, save he which is of God, he hath seen the Father.**
238	243	**John 6:53 Then Jesus said unto them, Verily, verily, I say unto you, Except ye eat the flesh of the Son of man, and drink his blood, ye have no life in you.**
239	244	**John 6:57 (1 of 2) As the living Father hath sent me, and I live by the Father: so he that eateth me, even he shall live by me.**
240	245	**John 6:57 (2 of 2) As the living Father hath sent me, and I live by the Father: so he that eateth me, even he shall live by me.**
241	246	**John 6:62 What and if ye shall see the Son of man ascend up where he was before?**
242	247	**John 6:65 And he said, Therefore said I unto you, that no man can come unto me, except it were given unto him of my Father.**
243	248	**John 6:69 And we believe and are sure that thou art that Christ, the Son of the living God.**
244	249	**John 8:16 And yet if I judge, my judgment is true: for I am not alone, but I and the Father that sent me.**
245	250	**John 8:18 I am one that bear witness of myself, and the Father that sent me beareth witness of me.**
246	251	**John 8:19 (1 of 3) Then said they unto him, Where is thy Father? Jesus answered, Ye neither know me, nor my Father: if ye had known me, ye should have known my Father also.**
247	252	**John 8:19 (2 of 3) Then said they unto him, Where is thy Father? Jesus answered, Ye neither know me, nor my Father: if ye had known me, ye should have known my Father also.**
248	253	**John 8:19 (3 of 3) Then said they unto him, Where is thy Father? Jesus answered, Ye neither know me, nor my Father: if ye had known me, ye should have known my Father also.**
249	254	**John 8:27 They understood not that he spake to them of the Father.**
250	255	**John 8:28 (1 of 2) Then said Jesus unto them, When ye have lifted up the Son of man, then shall ye know that I am he, and that I do nothing of myself; but as my Father hath taught me, I speak these things.**
251	256	**John 8:28 (2 of 2) Then said Jesus unto them, When ye have lifted up the Son of man, then shall ye know that I am he, and that I do nothing of myself; but as my Father hath taught me, I speak these things.**
252	257	**John 8:29 And he that sent me is with me: the Father hath not left me alone; for I do always those things that please him.**
253	258	**John 8:35 And the servant abideth not in the house for ever: but the Son abideth ever.**
254	259	**John 8:36 If the Son therefore shall make you free, ye shall be free indeed.**

# in Gospels	# in Bible	All mentions of **Father** + **Son** *(Capitalized, standard (non-possessive), God / Jesus)*
255	260	**John 8:38 I speak that which I have seen with my Father: and ye do that which ye have seen with your father.**
256	261	**John 8:41 Ye do the deeds of your father. Then said they to him, We be not born of fornication; we have one Father, even God.**
257	262	**John 8:42 Jesus said unto them, If God were your Father, ye would love me: for I proceeded forth and came from God; neither came I of myself, but he sent me.**
258	263	**John 8:49 Jesus answered, I have not a devil; but I honour my Father, and ye do dishonour me.**
259	264	**John 8:54 Jesus answered, If I honour myself, my honour is nothing: it is my Father that honoureth me; of whom ye say, that he is your God:**
260	265	**John 9:35 Jesus heard that they had cast him out; and when he had found him, he said unto him, Dost thou believe on the Son of God?**
261	266	**John 10:15 (1 of 2) As the Father knoweth me, even so know I the Father: and I lay down my life for the sheep.**
262	267	**John 10:15 (2 of 2) As the Father knoweth me, even so know I the Father: and I lay down my life for the sheep.**
263	268	**John 10:17 Therefore doth my Father love me, because I lay down my life, that I might take it again.**
264	269	**John 10:18 No man taketh it from me, but I lay it down of myself. I have power to lay it down, and I have power to take it again. This commandment have I received of my Father.**
265	270	**John 10:29 My Father, which gave them me, is greater than all; and no man is able to pluck them out of my Father's hand.**
266	271	**John 10:30 I and my Father are one.**
267	272	**John 10:32 Jesus answered them, Many good works have I shewed you from my Father; for which of those works do ye stone me?**
268	273	**John 10:36 (1 of 2) Say ye of him, whom the Father hath sanctified, and sent into the world, Thou blasphemest; because I said, I am the Son of God?**
269	274	**John 10:36 (2 of 2) Say ye of him, whom the Father hath sanctified, and sent into the world, Thou blasphemest; because I said, I am the Son of God?**
270	275	**John 10:37 If I do not the works of my Father, believe me not.**
271	276	**John 10:38 But if I do, though ye believe not me, believe the works: that ye may know, and believe, that the Father is in me, and I in him.**
272	277	**John 11:4 When Jesus heard that, he said, This sickness is not unto death, but for the glory of God, that the Son of God might be glorified thereby.**
273	278	**John 11:27 She saith unto him, Yea, Lord: I believe that thou art the Christ, the Son of God, which should come into the world.**
274	279	**John 11:41 Then they took away the stone from the place where the dead was laid. And Jesus lifted up his eyes, and said, Father, I thank thee that thou hast heard me.**
275	280	**John 12:23 And Jesus answered them, saying, The hour is come, that the Son of man should be glorified.**
276	281	**John 12:26 If any man serve me, let him follow me; and where I am, there shall also my servant be: if any man serve me, him will my Father honour.**
277	282	**John 12:27 Now is my soul troubled; and what shall I say? Father, save me from this hour: but for this cause came I unto this hour.**
278	283	**John 12:28 Father, glorify thy name. Then came there a voice from heaven, saying, I have both glorified it, and will glorify it again.**

# in Gospels	# in Bible	All mentions of **Father** + **Son** *(Capitalized, standard (non-possessive), God / Jesus)*
279	284	**John 12:34 (1 of 2) The people answered him, We have heard out of the law that Christ abideth for ever: and how sayest thou, The Son of man must be lifted up? who is this Son of man?**
280	285	**John 12:34 (2 of 2) The people answered him, We have heard out of the law that Christ abideth for ever: and how sayest thou, The Son of man must be lifted up? who is this Son of man?**
281	286	**John 12:49 For I have not spoken of myself; but the Father which sent me, he gave me a commandment, what I should say, and what I should speak.**
282	287	**John 12:50 And I know that his commandment is life everlasting: whatsoever I speak therefore, even as the Father said unto me, so I speak.**
283	288	**John 13:1 Now before the feast of the passover, when Jesus knew that his hour was come that he should depart out of this world unto the Father, having loved his own which were in the world, he loved them unto the end.**
284	289	**John 13:3 Jesus knowing that the Father had given all things into his hands, and that he was come from God, and went to God;**
285	290	**John 13:31 Therefore, when he was gone out, Jesus said, Now is the Son of man glorified, and God is glorified in him.**
286	291	**John 14:6 Jesus saith unto him, I am the way, the truth, and the life: no man cometh unto the Father, but by me.**
287	292	**John 14:7 If ye had known me, ye should have known my Father also: and from henceforth ye know him, and have seen him.**
288	293	**John 14:8 Philip saith unto him, Lord, shew us the Father, and it sufficeth us.**
289	294	**John 14:9 (1 of 2) Jesus saith unto him, Have I been so long time with you, and yet hast thou not known me, Philip? he that hath seen me hath seen the Father; and how sayest thou then, Shew us the Father?**
290	295	**John 14:9 (2 of 2) Jesus saith unto him, Have I been so long time with you, and yet hast thou not known me, Philip? he that hath seen me hath seen the Father; and how sayest thou then, Shew us the Father?**
291	296	**John 14:10 (1 of 3) Believest thou not that I am in the Father, and the Father in me? the words that I speak unto you I speak not of myself: but the Father that dwelleth in me, he doeth the works.**
292	297	**John 14:10 (2 of 3) Believest thou not that I am in the Father, and the Father in me? the words that I speak unto you I speak not of myself: but the Father that dwelleth in me, he doeth the works.**
293	298	**John 14:10 (3 of 3) Believest thou not that I am in the Father, and the Father in me? the words that I speak unto you I speak not of myself: but the Father that dwelleth in me, he doeth the works.**
294	299	**John 14:11 (1 of 2) Believe me that I am in the Father, and the Father in me: or else believe me for the very works' sake.**
295	300	**John 14:11 (2 of 2) Believe me that I am in the Father, and the Father in me: or else believe me for the very works' sake.**
296	301	**John 14:12 Verily, verily, I say unto you, He that believeth on me, the works that I do shall he do also; and greater works than these shall he do; because I go unto my Father.**
297	302	**John 14:13 (1 of 2) And whatsoever ye shall ask in my name, that will I do, that the Father may be glorified in the Son.**
298	303	**John 14:13 (2 of 2) And whatsoever ye shall ask in my name, that will I do, that the Father may be glorified in the Son.**

# in Gospels	# in Bible	All mentions of **Father** + **Son** *(Capitalized, standard (non-possessive), God / Jesus)*
299	304	**John 14:16 And I will pray the Father, and he shall give you another Comforter, that he may abide with you for ever;**
300	305	**John 14:20 At that day ye shall know that I am in my Father, and ye in me, and I in you.**
301	306	**John 14:21 He that hath my commandments, and keepeth them, he it is that loveth me: and he that loveth me shall be loved of my Father, and I will love him, and will manifest myself to him.**
302	307	**John 14:23 Jesus answered and said unto him, If a man love me, he will keep my words: and my Father will love him, and we will come unto him, and make our abode with him.**
303	308	**John 14:26 But the Comforter, which is the Holy Ghost, whom the Father will send in my name, he shall teach you all things, and bring all things to your remembrance, whatsoever I have said unto you.**
304	309	**John 14:28 (1 of 2) Ye have heard how I said unto you, I go away, and come again unto you. If ye loved me, ye would rejoice, because I said, I go unto the Father: for my Father is greater than I.**
305	310	**John 14:28 (2 of 2) Ye have heard how I said unto you, I go away, and come again unto you. If ye loved me, ye would rejoice, because I said, I go unto the Father: for my Father is greater than I.**
306	311	**John 14:31 (1 of 2) But that the world may know that I love the Father; and as the Father gave me commandment, even so I do. Arise, let us go hence.**
307	312	**John 14:31 (2 of 2) But that the world may know that I love the Father; and as the Father gave me commandment, even so I do. Arise, let us go hence.**
308	313	**John 15:1 I am the true vine, and my Father is the husbandman.**
309	314	**John 15:8 Herein is my Father glorified, that ye bear much fruit; so shall ye be my disciples.**
310	315	**John 15:9 As the Father hath loved me, so have I loved you: continue ye in my love.**
311	316	**John 15:15 Henceforth I call you not servants; for the servant knoweth not what his lord doeth: but I have called you friends; for all things that I have heard of my Father I have made known unto you.**
312	317	**John 15:16 Ye have not chosen me, but I have chosen you, and ordained you, that ye should go and bring forth fruit, and that your fruit should remain: that whatsoever ye shall ask of the Father in my name, he may give it you.**
313	318	**John 15:23 He that hateth me hateth my Father also.**
314	319	**John 15:24 If I had not done among them the works which none other man did, they had not had sin: but now have they both seen and hated both me and my Father.**
315	320	**John 15:26 (1 of 2) But when the Comforter is come, whom I will send unto you from the Father, even the Spirit of truth, which proceedeth from the Father, he shall testify of me:**
316	321	**John 15:26 (2 of 2) But when the Comforter is come, whom I will send unto you from the Father, even the Spirit of truth, which proceedeth from the Father, he shall testify of me:**
317	322	**John 16:3 And these things will they do unto you, because they have not known the Father, nor me.**
318	323	**John 16:10 Of righteousness, because I go to my Father, and ye see me no more;**
319	324	**John 16:15 All things that the Father hath are mine: therefore said I, that he shall take of mine, and shall shew it unto you.**

# in Gospels	# in Bible	All mentions of **Father + Son** *(Capitalized, standard (non-possessive), God / Jesus)*
320	325	**John 16:16 A little while, and ye shall not see me: and again, a little while, and ye shall see me, because I go to the Father.**
321	326	**John 16:17 Then said some of his disciples among themselves, What is this that he saith unto us, A little while, and ye shall not see me: and again, a little while, and ye shall see me: and, Because I go to the Father?**
322	327	**John 16:23 And in that day ye shall ask me nothing. Verily, verily, I say unto you, Whatsoever ye shall ask the Father in my name, he will give it you.**
323	328	**John 16:25 These things have I spoken unto you in proverbs: but the time cometh, when I shall no more speak unto you in proverbs, but I shall shew you plainly of the Father.**
324	329	**John 16:26 At that day ye shall ask in my name: and I say not unto you, that I will pray the Father for you:**
325	330	**John 16:27 For the Father himself loveth you, because ye have loved me, and have believed that I came out from God.**
326	331	**John 16:28 (1 of 2) I came forth from the Father, and am come into the world: again, I leave the world, and go to the Father.**
327	332	**John 16:28 (2 of 2) I came forth from the Father, and am come into the world: again, I leave the world, and go to the Father.**
328	333	**John 16:32 Behold, the hour cometh, yea, is now come, that ye shall be scattered, every man to his own, and shall leave me alone: and yet I am not alone, because the Father is with me.**
329	334	**John 17:1 (1 of 3) These words spake Jesus, and lifted up his eyes to heaven, and said, Father, the hour is come; glorify thy Son, that thy Son also may glorify thee:**
330	335	**John 17:1 (2 of 3) These words spake Jesus, and lifted up his eyes to heaven, and said, Father, the hour is come; glorify thy Son, that thy Son also may glorify thee:**
331	336	**John 17:1 (3 of 3) These words spake Jesus, and lifted up his eyes to heaven, and said, Father, the hour is come; glorify thy Son, that thy Son also may glorify thee:**
332	337	**John 17:5 And now, O Father, glorify thou me with thine own self with the glory which I had with thee before the world was.**
333	338	**John 17:11 And now I am no more in the world, but these are in the world, and I come to thee. Holy Father, keep through thine own name those whom thou hast given me, that they may be one, as we are.**
334	339	**John 17:21 That they all may be one; as thou, Father, art in me, and I in thee, that they also may be one in us: that the world may believe that thou hast sent me.**
335	340	**John 17:24 Father, I will that they also, whom thou hast given me, be with me where I am; that they may behold my glory, which thou hast given me: for thou lovedst me before the foundation of the world.**
336	341	**John 17:25 O righteous Father, the world hath not known thee: but I have known thee, and these have known that thou hast sent me.**
337	342	**John 18:11 Then said Jesus unto Peter, Put up thy sword into the sheath: the cup which my Father hath given me, shall I not drink it?**
338	343	**John 19:7 The Jews answered him, We have a law, and by our law he ought to die, because he made himself the Son of God.**
339	344	**John 20:17 (1 of 3) Jesus saith unto her, Touch me not; for I am not yet ascended to my Father: but go to my brethren, and say unto them, I ascend unto my Father, and your Father; and to my God, and your God.**

# in Gospels	# in Bible	All mentions of **Father** + **Son** *(Capitalized, standard (non-possessive), God / Jesus)*
340	345	**John 20:17 (2 of 3) Jesus saith unto her, Touch me not; for I am not yet ascended to my Father: but go to my brethren, and say unto them, I ascend unto my Father, and your Father; and to my God, and your God.**
341	346	**John 20:17 (3 of 3) Jesus saith unto her, Touch me not; for I am not yet ascended to my Father: but go to my brethren, and say unto them, I ascend unto my Father, and your Father; and to my God, and your God.**
342	347	**John 20:21 Then said Jesus to them again, Peace be unto you: as my Father hath sent me, even so send I you.**
343 = 7×7×7 Mentions in the Gospels	348	**John 20:31 But these are written, that ye might believe that Jesus is the Christ, the Son of God; and that believing ye might have life through his name.**
	349	**Acts 1:4 And, being assembled together with them, commanded them that they should not depart from Jerusalem, but wait for the promise of the Father, which, saith he, ye have heard of me.**
	350	**Acts 1:7 And he said unto them, It is not for you to know the times or the seasons, which the Father hath put in his own power.**
	351	**Acts 2:33 Therefore being by the right hand of God exalted, and having received of the Father the promise of the Holy Ghost, he hath shed forth this, which ye now see and hear.**
	352	**Acts 3:13 The God of Abraham, and of Isaac, and of Jacob, the God of our fathers, hath glorified his Son Jesus; whom ye delivered up, and denied him in the presence of Pilate, when he was determined to let him go.**
	353	**Acts 3:26 Unto you first God, having raised up his Son Jesus, sent him to bless you, in turning away every one of you from his iniquities.**
	354	**Acts 7:56 And said, Behold, I see the heavens opened, and the Son of man standing on the right hand of God.**
	355	**Acts 8:37 And Philip said, If thou believest with all thine heart, thou mayest. And he answered and said, I believe that Jesus Christ is the Son of God.**
	356	**Acts 9:20 And straightway he preached Christ in the synagogues, that he is the Son of God.**
	357	**Acts 13:33 God hath fulfilled the same unto us their children, in that he hath raised up Jesus again; as it is also written in the second psalm, Thou art my Son, this day have I begotten thee.**
Order in Epistles		**Father + Son** in the Epistles
1	358	**Romans 1:3 Concerning his Son Jesus Christ our Lord, which was made of the seed of David according to the flesh;**
2	359	**Romans 1:4 And declared to be the Son of God with power, according to the spirit of holiness, by the resurrection from the dead:**
3	360	**Romans 1:7 To all that be in Rome, beloved of God, called to be saints: Grace to you and peace from God our Father, and the Lord Jesus Christ.**

# in Epistles	# in Bible	All mentions of **Father + Son** *(Capitalized, standard (non-possessive), God / Jesus)*
4	361	**Romans 1:9 For God is my witness, whom I serve with my spirit in the gospel of his Son, that without ceasing I make mention of you always in my prayers;**
5	362	**Romans 5:10 For if, when we were enemies, we were reconciled to God by the death of his Son, much more, being reconciled, we shall be saved by his life.**
6	363	**Romans 6:4 Therefore we are buried with him by baptism into death: that like as Christ was raised up from the dead by the glory of the Father, even so we also should walk in newness of life.**
7	364	**Romans 8:3 For what the law could not do, in that it was weak through the flesh, God sending his own Son in the likeness of sinful flesh, and for sin, condemned sin in the flesh:**
8	365	**Romans 8:15 For ye have not received the spirit of bondage again to fear; but ye have received the Spirit of adoption, whereby we cry, Abba, Father.**
9	366	**Romans 8:29 For whom he did foreknow, he also did predestinate to be conformed to the image of his Son, that he might be the firstborn among many brethren.**
10	367	**Romans 8:32 He that spared not his own Son, but delivered him up for us all, how shall he not with him also freely give us all things?**
11	368	**Romans 15:6 That ye may with one mind and one mouth glorify God, even the Father of our Lord Jesus Christ.**
12	369	**1 Corinthians 1:3 Grace be unto you, and peace, from God our Father, and from the Lord Jesus Christ.**
13	370	**1 Corinthians 1:9 God is faithful, by whom ye were called unto the fellowship of his Son Jesus Christ our Lord.**
14	371	**1 Corinthians 8:6 But to us there is but one God, the Father, of whom are all things, and we in him; and one Lord Jesus Christ, by whom are all things, and we by him.**
15	372	**1 Corinthians 15:24 Then cometh the end, when he shall have delivered up the kingdom to God, even the Father; when he shall have put down all rule and all authority and power.**
16	373	**1 Corinthians 15:28 And when all things shall be subdued unto him, then shall the Son also himself be subject unto him that put all things under him, that God may be all in all.**
17	374	**2 Corinthians 1:2 Grace be to you and peace from God our Father, and from the Lord Jesus Christ.**
18	375	**2 Corinthians 1:3 (1 of 2) Blessed be God, even the Father of our Lord Jesus Christ, the Father of mercies, and the God of all comfort;**
19	376	**2 Corinthians 1:3 (2 of 2) Blessed be God, even the Father of our Lord Jesus Christ, the Father of mercies, and the God of all comfort;**
20	377	**2 Corinthians 1:19 For the Son of God, Jesus Christ, who was preached among you by us, even by me and Silvanus and Timotheus, was not yea and nay, but in him was yea.**
21	378	**2 Corinthians 6:18 And will be a Father unto you, and ye shall be my sons and daughters, saith the Lord Almighty.**
22	379	**2 Corinthians 11:31 The God and Father of our Lord Jesus Christ, which is blessed for evermore, knoweth that I lie not.**
23	380	**Galatians 1:1 Paul, an apostle, (not of men, neither by man, but by Jesus Christ, and God the Father, who raised him from the dead;)**

# in Epistles	# in Bible	All mentions of **Father** + **Son** *(Capitalized, standard (non-possessive), God / Jesus)*
24	381	**Galatians 1:3 Grace be to you and peace from God the Father, and from our Lord Jesus Christ,**
25	382	**Galatians 1:4 Who gave himself for our sins, that he might deliver us from this present evil world, according to the will of God and our Father:**
26	383	**Galatians 1:16 To reveal his Son in me, that I might preach him among the heathen; immediately I conferred not with flesh and blood:**
27	384	**Galatians 2:20 I am crucified with Christ: nevertheless I live; yet not I, but Christ liveth in me: and the life which I now live in the flesh I live by the faith of the Son of God, who loved me, and gave himself for me.**
28	385	**Galatians 4:4 But when the fulness of the time was come, God sent forth his Son, made of a woman, made under the law,**
29	386	**Galatians 4:6 (1 of 2) And because ye are sons, God hath sent forth the Spirit of his Son into your hearts, crying, Abba, Father.**
30	387	**Galatians 4:6 (2 of 2) And because ye are sons, God hath sent forth the Spirit of his Son into your hearts, crying, Abba, Father.**
31	388	**Ephesians 1:2 Grace be to you, and peace, from God our Father, and from the Lord Jesus Christ.**
32	389	**Ephesians 1:3 Blessed be the God and Father of our Lord Jesus Christ, who hath blessed us with all spiritual blessings in heavenly places in Christ:**
33	390	**Ephesians 1:17 That the God of our Lord Jesus Christ, the Father of glory, may give unto you the spirit of wisdom and revelation in the knowledge of him:**
34	391	**Ephesians 2:18 For through him we both have access by one Spirit unto the Father.**
35	392	**Ephesians 3:14 For this cause I bow my knees unto the Father of our Lord Jesus Christ,**
36	393	**Ephesians 4:6 One God and Father of all, who is above all, and through all, and in you all.**
37	394	**Ephesians 4:13 Till we all come in the unity of the faith, and of the knowledge of the Son of God, unto a perfect man, unto the measure of the stature of the fulness of Christ:**
38	395	**Ephesians 5:20 Giving thanks always for all things unto God and the Father in the name of our Lord Jesus Christ;**
39	396	**Ephesians 6:23 Peace be to the brethren, and love with faith, from God the Father and the Lord Jesus Christ.**
40	397	**Philippians 1:2 Grace be unto you, and peace, from God our Father, and from the Lord Jesus Christ.**
41	398	**Philippians 2:11 And that every tongue should confess that Jesus Christ is Lord, to the glory of God the Father.**
42	399	**Philippians 4:20 Now unto God and our Father be glory for ever and ever. Amen.**
43	400	**Colossians 1:2 To the saints and faithful brethren in Christ which are at Colosse: Grace be unto you, and peace, from God our Father and the Lord Jesus Christ.**
44	401	**Colossians 1:3 We give thanks to God and the Father of our Lord Jesus Christ, praying always for you,**
45	402	**Colossians 1:12 Giving thanks unto the Father, which hath made us meet to be partakers of the inheritance of the saints in light:**
46	403	**Colossians 1:13 Who hath delivered us from the power of darkness, and hath translated us into the kingdom of his dear Son:**

# in Epistles	# in Bible	All mentions of **Father** + **Son** *(Capitalized, standard (non-possessive), God / Jesus)*
47	404	**Colossians 1:19 For it pleased the Father that in him should all fulness dwell;**
48	405	**Colossians 2:2 That their hearts might be comforted, being knit together in love, and unto all riches of the full assurance of understanding, to the acknowledgement of the mystery of God, and of the Father, and of Christ;**
49	406	**Colossians 3:17 And whatsoever ye do in word or deed, do all in the name of the Lord Jesus, giving thanks to God and the Father by him.**
50	407	**1 Thessalonians 1:1 (1 of 2) Paul, and Silvanus, and Timotheus, unto the church of the Thessalonians which is in God the Father and in the Lord Jesus Christ: Grace be unto you, and peace, from God our Father, and the Lord Jesus Christ.**
51	408	**1 Thessalonians 1:1 (2 of 2) Paul, and Silvanus, and Timotheus, unto the church of the Thessalonians which is in God the Father and in the Lord Jesus Christ: Grace be unto you, and peace, from God our Father, and the Lord Jesus Christ.**
52	409	**1 Thessalonians 1:3 Remembering without ceasing your work of faith, and labour of love, and patience of hope in our Lord Jesus Christ, in the sight of God and our Father;**
53	410	**1 Thessalonians 1:10 And to wait for his Son from heaven, whom he raised from the dead, even Jesus, which delivered us from the wrath to come.**
54	411	**1 Thessalonians 3:11 Now God himself and our Father, and our Lord Jesus Christ, direct our way unto you.**
55	412	**1 Thessalonians 3:13 To the end he may stablish your hearts unblameable in holiness before God, even our Father, at the coming of our Lord Jesus Christ with all his saints.**
56	413	**2 Thessalonians 1:1 Paul, and Silvanus, and Timotheus, unto the church of the Thessalonians in God our Father and the Lord Jesus Christ:**
57	414	**2 Thessalonians 1:2 Grace unto you, and peace, from God our Father and the Lord Jesus Christ.**
58	415	**2 Thessalonians 2:16 Now our Lord Jesus Christ himself, and God, even our Father, which hath loved us, and hath given us everlasting consolation and good hope through grace,**
59	416	**1 Timothy 1:2 Unto Timothy, my own son in the faith: Grace, mercy, and peace, from God our Father and Jesus Christ our Lord.**
60	417	**2 Timothy 1:2 To Timothy, my dearly beloved son: Grace, mercy, and peace, from God the Father and Christ Jesus our Lord.**
61	418	**Titus 1:4 To Titus, mine own son after the common faith: Grace, mercy, and peace, from God the Father and the Lord Jesus Christ our Saviour.**
62	419	**Philemon 1:3 Grace to you, and peace, from God our Father and the Lord Jesus Christ.**
63	420	**Hebrews 1:2 Hath in these last days spoken unto us by his Son, whom he hath appointed heir of all things, by whom also he made the worlds;**
64	421	**Hebrews 1:5 (1 of 3) For unto which of the angels said he at any time, Thou art my Son, this day have I begotten thee? And again, I will be to him a Father, and he shall be to me a Son?**
65	422	**Hebrews 1:5 (2 of 3) For unto which of the angels said he at any time, Thou art my Son, this day have I begotten thee? And again, I will be to him a Father, and he shall be to me a Son?**
66	423	**Hebrews 1:5 (3 of 3) For unto which of the angels said he at any time, Thou art my Son, this day have I begotten thee? And again, I will be to him a Father, and he shall be to me a Son?**

# in Epistles	# in Bible	All mentions of **Father** + **Son** *(Capitalized, standard (non-possessive), God / Jesus)*
67	424	**Hebrews 1:8 But unto the Son he saith, Thy throne, O God, is for ever and ever: a sceptre of righteousness is the sceptre of thy kingdom.**
68	425	**Hebrews 4:14 Seeing then that we have a great high priest, that is passed into the heavens, Jesus the Son of God, let us hold fast our profession.**
69	426	**Hebrews 5:5 So also Christ glorified not himself to be made an high priest; but he that said unto him, Thou art my Son, to day have I begotten thee.**
70	427	**Hebrews 5:8 Though he were a Son, yet learned he obedience by the things which he suffered;**
71	428	**Hebrews 6:6 If they shall fall away, to renew them again unto repentance; seeing they crucify to themselves the Son of God afresh, and put him to an open shame.**
72	429	**Hebrews 7:3 Without father, without mother, without descent, having neither beginning of days, nor end of life; but made like unto the Son of God; abideth a priest continually.**
73	430	**Hebrews 7:28 For the law maketh men high priests which have infirmity; but the word of the oath, which was since the law, maketh the Son, who is consecrated for evermore.**
74	431	**Hebrews 10:29 Of how much sorer punishment, suppose ye, shall he be thought worthy, who hath trodden under foot the Son of God, and hath counted the blood of the covenant, wherewith he was sanctified, an unholy thing, and hath done despite unto the Spirit of grace?**
75	432	**Hebrews 12:9 Furthermore we have had fathers of our flesh which corrected us, and we gave them reverence: shall we not much rather be in subjection unto the Father of spirits, and live?**
76	433	**James 1:17 Every good gift and every perfect gift is from above, and cometh down from the Father of lights, with whom is no variableness, neither shadow of turning.**
77	434	**James 1:27 Pure religion and undefiled before God and the Father is this, To visit the fatherless and widows in their affliction, and to keep himself unspotted from the world.**
78	435	**James 3:9 Therewith bless we God, even the Father; and therewith curse we men, which are made after the similitude of God.**
79	436	**1 Peter 1:2 Elect according to the foreknowledge of God the Father, through sanctification of the Spirit, unto obedience and sprinkling of the blood of Jesus Christ: Grace unto you, and peace, be multiplied.**
80	437	**1 Peter 1:3 Blessed be the God and Father of our Lord Jesus Christ, which according to his abundant mercy hath begotten us again unto a lively hope by the resurrection of Jesus Christ from the dead,**
81	438	**1 Peter 1:17 And if ye call on the Father, who without respect of persons judgeth according to every man's work, pass the time of your sojourning here in fear:**
82	439	**2 Peter 1:17 (1 of 2) For he received from God the Father honour and glory, when there came such a voice to him from the excellent glory, This is my beloved Son, in whom I am well pleased.**
83	440	**2 Peter 1:17 (2 of 2) For he received from God the Father honour and glory, when there came such a voice to him from the excellent glory, This is my beloved Son, in whom I am well pleased.**
84	441	**1 John 1:2 (For the life was manifested, and we have seen it, and bear witness, and shew unto you that eternal life, which was with the Father, and was manifested unto us;)**
85	442	**1 John 1:3 (1 of 2) That which we have seen and heard declare we unto you, that ye also may have fellowship with us: and truly our fellowship is with the Father, and with his Son Jesus Christ.**

# in Epistles	# in Bible	All mentions of **Father + Son** *(Capitalized, standard (non-possessive), God / Jesus)*
86	443	**1 John 1:3 (2 of 2) That which we have seen and heard declare we unto you, that ye also may have fellowship with us: and truly our fellowship is with the Father, and with his Son Jesus Christ.**
87	444	**1 John 1:7 But if we walk in the light, as he is in the light, we have fellowship one with another, and the blood of Jesus Christ his Son cleanseth us from all sin.**
88	445	**1 John 2:1 My little children, these things write I unto you, that ye sin not. And if any man sin, we have an advocate with the Father, Jesus Christ the righteous:**
89	446	**1 John 2:13 I write unto you, fathers, because ye have known him that is from the beginning. I write unto you, young men, because ye have overcome the wicked one. I write unto you, little children, because ye have known the Father.**
90	447	**1 John 2:15 Love not the world, neither the things that are in the world. If any man love the world, the love of the Father is not in him.**
91	448	**1 John 2:16 For all that is in the world, the lust of the flesh, and the lust of the eyes, and the pride of life, is not of the Father, but is of the world.**
92	449	**1 John 2:22 (1 of 2) Who is a liar but he that denieth that Jesus is the Christ? He is antichrist, that denieth the Father and the Son.**
93	450	**1 John 2:22 (1 of 2) Who is a liar but he that denieth that Jesus is the Christ? He is antichrist, that denieth the Father and the Son.**
94	451	**1 John 2:23 (1 of 4) Whosoever denieth the Son, the same hath not the Father: (but) he that acknowledgeth the Son hath the Father also.**
95	452	**1 John 2:23 (2 of 4) Whosoever denieth the Son, the same hath not the Father: (but) he that acknowledgeth the Son hath the Father also.**
96	453	**1 John 2:23 (3 of 4) Whosoever denieth the Son, the same hath not the Father: (but) he that acknowledgeth the Son hath the Father also.**
97	454	**1 John 2:23 (4 of 4) Whosoever denieth the Son, the same hath not the Father: (but) he that acknowledgeth the Son hath the Father also.**
98	455	**1 John 2:24 (1 of 2) Let that therefore abide in you, which ye have heard from the beginning. If that which ye have heard from the beginning shall remain in you, ye also shall continue in the Son, and in the Father.**
99	456	**1 John 2:24 (2 of 2) Let that therefore abide in you, which ye have heard from the beginning. If that which ye have heard from the beginning shall remain in you, ye also shall continue in the Son, and in the Father.**
100	457	**1 John 3:1 Behold, what manner of love the Father hath bestowed upon us, that we should be called the sons of God: therefore the world knoweth us not, because it knew him not.**
101	458	**1 John 3:8 He that committeth sin is of the devil; for the devil sinneth from the beginning. For this purpose the Son of God was manifested, that he might destroy the works of the devil.**
102	459	**1 John 3:23 And this is his commandment, That we should believe on the name of his Son Jesus Christ, and love one another, as he gave us commandment.**
103	460	**1 John 4:9 In this was manifested the love of God toward us, because that God sent his only begotten Son into the world, that we might live through him.**
104	461	**1 John 4:10 Herein is love, not that we loved God, but that he loved us, and sent his Son to be the propitiation for our sins.**
105	462	**1 John 4:14 (1 of 2) And we have seen and do testify that the Father sent the Son to be the Saviour of the world.**
106	463	**1 John 4:14 (2 of 2) And we have seen and do testify that the Father sent the Son to be the Saviour of the world.**

# in Epistles	# in Bible	All mentions of **Father** + **Son** *(Capitalized, standard (non-possessive), God / Jesus)*
107	464	**1 John 4:15 Whosoever shall confess that Jesus is the Son of God, God dwelleth in him, and he in God.**
108	465	**1 John 5:5 Who is he that overcometh the world, but he that believeth that Jesus is the Son of God?**
109	466	**1 John 5:7 For there are three that bear record in heaven, the Father, the Word, and the Holy Ghost: and these three are one.**
110	467	**1 John 5:9 If we receive the witness of men, the witness of God is greater: for this is the witness of God which he hath testified of his Son.**
111	468	**1 John 5:10 (1 of 2) He that believeth on the Son of God hath the witness in himself: he that believeth not God hath made him a liar; because he believeth not the record that God gave of his Son.**
112	469	**1 John 5:10 (2 of 2) He that believeth on the Son of God hath the witness in himself: he that believeth not God hath made him a liar; because he believeth not the record that God gave of his Son.**
113	470	**1 John 5:11 And this is the record, that God hath given to us eternal life, and this life is in his Son.**
114	471	**1 John 5:12 (1 of 2) He that hath the Son hath life; and he that hath not the Son of God hath not life.**
115	472	**1 John 5:12 (2 of 2) He that hath the Son hath life; and he that hath not the Son of God hath not life.**
116	473	**1 John 5:13 (1 of 2) These things have I written unto you that believe on the name of the Son of God; that ye may know that ye have eternal life, and that ye may believe on the name of the Son of God.**
117	474	**1 John 5:13 (2 of 2) These things have I written unto you that believe on the name of the Son of God; that ye may know that ye have eternal life, and that ye may believe on the name of the Son of God.**
118	475	**1 John 5:20 (1 of 2) And we know that the Son of God is come, and hath given us an understanding, that we may know him that is true, and we are in him that is true, even in his Son Jesus Christ. This is the true God, and eternal life.**
119	476	**1 John 5:20 (2 of 2) And we know that the Son of God is come, and hath given us an understanding, that we may know him that is true, and we are in him that is true, even in his Son Jesus Christ. This is the true God, and eternal life.**
120	477	**2 John 1:3 (1 of 3) Grace be with you, mercy, and peace, from God the Father, and from the Lord Jesus Christ, the Son of the Father, in truth and love.**
121	478	**2 John 1:3 (2 of 3) Grace be with you, mercy, and peace, from God the Father, and from the Lord Jesus Christ, the Son of the Father, in truth and love.**
122	479	**2 John 1:3 (3 of 3) Grace be with you, mercy, and peace, from God the Father, and from the Lord Jesus Christ, the Son of the Father, in truth and love.**
123	480	**2 John 1:4 I rejoiced greatly that I found of thy children walking in truth, as we have received a commandment from the Father.**
124	481	**2 John 1:9 (1 of 2) Whosoever transgresseth, and abideth not in the doctrine of Christ, hath not God. He that abideth in the doctrine of Christ, he hath both the Father and the Son.**
125	482	**2 John 1:9 (2 of 2) Whosoever transgresseth, and abideth not in the doctrine of Christ, hath not God. He that abideth in the doctrine of Christ, he hath both the Father and the Son.**
126 = **7×7+77** **Mentions in the Epistles**	483	**Jude 1:1 Jude, the servant of Jesus Christ, and brother of James, to them that are sanctified by God the Father, and preserved in Jesus Christ, and called:**

Order in Revelation		**Father + Son** in Revelation
1	484	**Revelation 1:6 And hath made us kings and priests unto God and his Father; to him be glory and dominion for ever and ever. Amen.**
2	485	**Revelation 1:13 And in the midst of the seven candlesticks one like unto the Son of man, clothed with a garment down to the foot, and girt about the paps with a golden girdle.**
3	486	**Revelation 2:18 And unto the angel of the church in Thyatira write; These things saith the Son of God, who hath his eyes like unto a flame of fire, and his feet are like fine brass;**
4	487	**Revelation 2:27 And he shall rule them with a rod of iron; as the vessels of a potter shall they be broken to shivers: even as I received of my Father.**
5	488	**Revelation 3:5 He that overcometh, the same shall be clothed in white raiment; and I will not blot out his name out of the book of life, but I will confess his name before my Father, and before his angels.**
6	489	**Revelation 3:21 To him that overcometh will I grant to sit with me in my throne, even as I also overcame, and am set down with my Father in his throne.**
7 **Mentions in Revelation**	490 = **70 × 7** **Mentions in the Bible**	**Revelation 14:14 And I looked, and behold a white cloud, and upon the cloud one sat like unto the Son of man, having on his head a golden crown, and in his hand a sharp sickle.**

Father + **Son** = **7×7×7** mentions in the Gospels
Father + **Son** = **7×7 + 77** mentions in the Epistles
Father + **Son** = **7** mentions in Revelation
Father + **Son** = **70×7** mentions in the Bible

(Capitalized, standard (non-possessive), God / Jesus)

See pp. 88-94 for detailed notes.

Index

Sorted by Word

Index

Index

Index

Index

Index

Index

Index

Index

Index

Index

Index

Index

Index

Index

Index

Index

Sorted by Category

Index

Index

Index

In that hour Jesus rejoiced in spirit, and said, I thank thee, O Father, Lord of heaven and earth, that thou hast hid these things from the wise and prudent, and hast revealed them unto babes: even so, Father; for so it seemed good in thy sight.

All things are delivered to me of my Father: and no man knoweth who the Son is, but the Father; and who the Father is, but the Son, and he to whom the Son will reveal him.

And he turned him unto his disciples, and said privately, Blessed are the eyes which see the things that ye see:

For I tell you, that many prophets and kings have desired to see those things which ye see, and have not seen them; and to hear those things which ye hear, and have not heard them.

Luke 10:21-24

Salvation

He that hath the Son hath life; and he that hath not the Son of God hath not life.

1 John 5:12

WITHOUT JESUS CHRIST, you will die in your sins. And after you die and stand before God, who is holy and no respecter of persons, you will be judged by God's holy word and cast into the lake of fire to burn for all eternity.

But that doesn't have to happen to you. And that's because of one man. Just one. **Because strait is the gate, and narrow is the way, which leadeth unto life, and few there be that find it.** (Matthew 7:14)

~2000 years ago, Jesus accomplished the greatest feat in history. He lived a perfect sinless life.

He loved God the Father with all his heart, soul, strength and mind every single day without fail, while also loving his neighbor as himself. There was no reason at all for him to die, because he was the only man in history to earn eternal life by God's standard (Luke 10:25-28).

And yet, there was not a drop of pride in his bones. He is the good shepherd. And he chose to lay down his life for his sheep, despite their sin and ungodliness.

When he suffered, bled & died on the cross as a perfect sacrifice, his blood bought you from all your sins. Death had no power or claim on him. And on the third day, God raised him from the dead.

Today He is seated on the right hand of the throne of God.

Do you believe this? Have you trusted Him from your heart? Repent. Believe. Call upon him for salvation. He will hear your cry, and by the power & grace of God, you will pass from death unto life.

There is nothing you can do to pay for your sins.

Jesus Christ already did that for you on the cross at Calvary.

To be born again, all you have to do is come before Him as a sinner, and ask Him to save you. Call upon Him with singleness of heart, when nobody except God is watching you.

He will hear you and He will accept you. **And whosoever will, let him take the water of life freely.** Revelation 22:17

For all have sinned, and come short of the glory of God; Romans 3:23

But God commendeth his love toward us, in that, while we were yet sinners, Christ died for us. Romans 5:8

That if thou shalt confess with thy mouth the Lord Jesus, and shalt believe in thine heart that God hath raised him from the dead, thou shalt be saved. For with the heart man believeth unto righteousness; and with the mouth confession is made unto salvation. Romans 10:9-10

For whosoever shall call upon the name of the Lord shall be saved.
Romans 10:13

For by grace are ye saved through faith; and that not of yourselves: it is the gift of God: Ephesians 2:8

All things are delivered unto me of my Father: and no man knoweth the Son, but the Father; neither knoweth any man the Father, save the Son, and he to whomsoever the Son will reveal him.
Come unto me, all ye that labour and are heavy laden, and I will give you rest. Take my yoke upon you, and learn of me; for I am meek and lowly in heart: and ye shall find rest unto your souls.
Matthew 11:27-29

What you might not realize about Heaven and Hell...

Heaven will be filled with people who murdered, stole, lied, practiced homosexuality, abused their children, blasphemed Jesus, cheated on their spouses... **but** in humility came to God as sinners and put their faith in Jesus Christ and His blood to wash away all their sins past, present and future.

Hell will be filled with people who helped the poor, went to church, got baptized, fed the homeless, doctored the sick, donated to children's hospitals, helped their neighbors, and loved their families with all their hearts... but proudly rejected Jesus Christ and his perfect loving sacrifice that would have cleansed them from all their sins.

Where will you be?

And whosoever was not found written in the book of life was cast into the lake of fire.
Revelation 20:15

Jesus answered and said unto him, Verily, verily, I say unto thee, Except a man be born again, he cannot see the kingdom of God.

John 3:3

I have sworn by myself, the word is gone out of my mouth in righteousness, and shall not return, That unto me every knee shall bow, every tongue shall swear.

That at the name of Jesus every knee should bow, of things in heaven, and things in earth, and things under the earth;

And that every tongue should confess that Jesus Christ is Lord, to the glory of God the Father.

Isaiah 45:23; Philippians 2:10-11

The Last Mention *of* our Lord Jesus Christ
in Revelation 22:21

Word	Within	Mention / Appearance #
our	Genesis, Revelation	**77**
our	Revelation	**7+7**
Lord	Matthew, Revelation	**7×7+7×7**
Lord *Case-sensitive*	Matthew, Revelation	**77**
Lord *Case-sensitive*	Genesis, Matthew–Acts, Revelation (7 books total)	**7×7×7**
Lord *Case-sensitive*	Revelation	**7+7+7**
Jesus	Revelation	**7+7**
Jesus Christ	Revelation	**7**
Christ	Matthew, Revelation	**T7** *1 + 2 + 3 + 4 + 5 + 6 + 7 = T7*
God, Jesus *Total mentions combined*	Genesis, Revelation	**7×7×7** *See page 180*
Jesus, David *Total mentions combined*	Entire Bible	**7×7×7×6** *See page 52-53*
Jesus(') *Excluding Justus & Joshua named Jesus. See appendix 7*	Entire Bible	**70×7+70×7** *See page 72*
Lord, Jesus	Revelation 22	**7** *See page 117*
Lord Jesus	Entire Bible	**7×7th Prime** *17 = #7 Prime*
our Lord Jesus	Entire Bible	**7×7+7**
Jesus Christ	Entire Bible	**T7×7** *See page 96*
Lord Jesus Christ	Entire Bible	**77+7**
our, Lord, Jesus, Christ *Case-sensitive. Total mentions combined*	New Testament	**7×7×52** *There are 52 weeks in a year*
heaven, Jesus *(The #7 words from beginning and end) Total mentions combined, excluding Justus. See appendix 7*	Entire Bible	**777+777** *See page 57*
Jesus('), Christ('s) *Total mentions combined*	Entire Bible	**777+777** *See page 67*
Jesus*, Christ* *Total appearances combined, excluding Justus & Joshua named Jesus & false Christs (Mat 24:24, Mark 13:22)*	Entire Bible	**777+777** *See page 66*
Moses*, Jesus*, Christ* *Total appearances combined, excluding antimentions, Excluding Superscriptions*	Entire Bible	**7×7×7×7** *See page 70*
LORD, Jesus *Case-sensitive*	Genesis, Revelation	**16×11**
King, Jesus, Christ *excluding Justus & Joshua. See appendix 7*	New Testament	**1611** *See page 62*
our Lord, Jesus, Christ *Case-sensitive, excluding Justus & Joshua. See appendix 7*	Entire Bible	**1611** *See page 63*
Father, Son, Holy Ghost, Holy Spirit, Jesus Christ *Case-sensitive, Excluding all antimentions*	Entire Bible	**777** *See page 153-155*
God, Jesus, Holy Spirit	New Testament	**777+777+777** *See page 157*
LORD, GOD, JEHOVAH, I AM, JAH, BRANCH, KING, JESUS, Jesus(') *Case-sensitive (All UPPERCASE names/titles of God + Jesus)*	Entire Bible	**7777** *See page 163-166*

To learn more about salvation, go to:
truthischrist.com/grace

Or reach me directly:
peterson6x@gmail.com

Thank you for reading.

May the Lord Jesus Christ bless you with
all his riches of wisdom and grace.

Downloadable search files:

sealedbytheking.com

To learn more about salvation, go to:
truthischrist.com/grace

Or reach me directly:
peterson6x@gmail.com

Thank you for reading.

May the Lord Jesus Christ bless you with
all his riches of wisdom and grace.

The 7 Sayings of Jesus Christ on the Cross

1

Eli, Eli, lama sabachthani?
Matthew 27:46, Mark 15:34

2

Father, forgive them; for they know not what they do.
Luke 23:34

3

Verily I say unto thee, To day shalt thou be with me in paradise.
Luke 23:43

4

Father, into thy hands I commend my spirit
Luke 23:46

5

Woman, behold thy son! . . . Behold thy mother!
John 19:26-27

6

I thirst.
John 19:28

7

It is finished
John 19:30

Complimentary Search Files
w/ Instructions:

www.sealedbytheking.com

Subscribe on YouTube:

Truth is Christ

https://www.youtube.com/@TruthisChrist

IN THE BEGINNING GOD CREATED THE HEAVEN AND THE EARTH
777
THE GRACE OF OUR LORD JESUS CHRIST BE WITH YOU ALL AMEN

Made in the USA
Las Vegas, NV
14 September 2023